THE
WHOLESALE-
BY-MAIL
CATALOG®
1991

THE WHOLESALE-BY-MAIL® Catalog 1991

BY THE PRINT PROJECT

Lowell Miller, Executive Producer

Prudence McCullough, Editor

HarperPerennial
A Division of HarperCollins*Publishers*

The Wholesale-by-Mail Catalog® is a resource for use by the general public. Companies in this catalog are listed at the sole discretion of the editors, and no advertising fees are solicited or accepted.

THE WHOLESALE-BY-MAIL CATALOG®1991. Copyright 1989, 1990 by Lowell Miller and Prudence McCullough. All rights reserved. Printed in the United States of America. No part of this book may be used or reproduced in any manner whatsoever without written permission except in the case of brief quotations embodied in critical articles and reviews. For information address HarperCollins Publishers, 10 East 53rd Street, New York, N.Y. 10022.

First HarperPerennial edition published 1991

Designed by Cassandra Pappas

LIBRARY OF CONGRESS CATALOG CARD NUMBER 89-45135

ISSN 1049-0116
ISBN 0-06-096545-2

BOMC offers recordings and compact discs, cassettes and records. For information and catalog write to BOMR, Camp Hill, PA 17012.

CONTENTS

INTRODUCTION

We're pleased to bring you *The Wholesale-by-Mail Catalog® 1991,* the consumer's guide to mail-order values. This newly revised edition includes firms selling at 30% below list or comparable retail—the traditional definition of "wholesale." You can buy just about anything by mail at a savings: greenhouses, burglar alarms, Mexican spices, deerskin gloves, French crystal, squash racquets, antique jewelry, TV scripts, software, nurses' shoes—the list is almost endless. Using *The Wholesale-by-Mail Catalog® 1991,* you can save considerable sums on all kinds of purchases—and you won't have to wait for a sale.

Before sending for a catalog or placing an order, be sure to read the explanations of the Listing Code beginning on page viii—you'll find it easier to understand and use this book. For a primer on mail order, see "The Complete Guide to Buying by Mail," beginning on page 538.

Enjoy your shopping, and please let us know about your experiences with the firms listed here. Turn to "Feedback," page 587, if you'd like to contact us.

THE PRINT PROJECT
Lowell Miller, Executive Producer
Prudence McCullough, Editor

THE LISTING CODE

To save space and avoid repetition, we've presented some of the information in the listings in a simple coded form at the head of each entry. All of the "hard" factual information is listed and abbreviated as follows:

1. Company name, mailing address, and phone number
2. Literature form: catalog, brochure, flyer, leaflet, price list, etc.; the price, followed by "refundable" or "deductible" if the cost is refundable or otherwise redeemable through ordering; *SASE:* send self-addressed, stamped, business-sized envelope (#10) with request; "Information": price quote or information given by phone and/or letter (no catalog)
3. Save: the percentage of savings you may expect on the suggested list or comparable retail prices of the goods and/or services. *Do not deduct this percentage from the order total* unless so instructed in the listing text or catalog
4. Pay: methods of payment accepted for orders (assume that catalog fees must be paid by check or money order unless listing states otherwise):
   (a)   personal check
   (b)   MO: bank or postal money order
   (c)   IMO: bank or postal international money order
   (d)   certified check: includes certified check, teller's check, cashier's check, or bank draft
   (e)   Access: Access credit card
   (f)   AE: American Express credit card
   (g)   CB: Carte Blanche credit card
   (h)   CHOICE: CHOICE credit card
   (i)   DC: Diners Club credit card

    (j)   Discover: Discover credit card
    (k)   EC: Eurocard credit card
    (l)   MC: MasterCard credit card
    (m) Optima: Optima credit card
    (n)   V: VISA credit card
5. Sells: type of goods sold
6. Store: address and hours of the firm's retail location or other outlets, if applicable

$ THE DOLLAR CODE

The dollar-code symbol represents our opinion of the overall worth of the firm to the average bargain hunter. We take into account the quality of the goods, quantity of the offerings, depth of the discount, and, when information is available, the quality of the service. The final judgment is somewhat subjective, but when you've analyzed as many firms as we have, certain ones simply stand out and others fade away.

$$$$ is a top rating; $ is the lowest. A low rating, however, may reflect a limited number of products and does not indicate that the company is a poor source for those products. There has to be some way of separating the thrilling buys from the merely good. Whenever possible, the ratings reflect our opinion of that firm as it compares to others within the same product category. The omission of a dollar-sign rating should not be considered a "poor" rating of a business. All it means is that we did not feel, for whatever reason, qualified to make a judgment. Companies to which we would have had to give a "poor" rating were simply not listed.

✉ THE ENVELOPE SYMBOL

This shows that the firm accepts mail orders.

☎ THE PHONE SYMBOL

This shows that the firm accepts orders over the phone. Many of the firms listed here have toll-free order lines, and virtually all require use of a credit card to pay for goods ordered by phone. Toll-free order lines (800 numbers) are included in some of the listings, but they should not be used to request information or catalogs unless the listing states that this is permitted, or no other phone line is given.

🍁 THE MAPLE LEAF

This shows that the firm will ship goods to Canada. Canadian shoppers should check current import restrictions and duty rates before ordering, and request shipping charges or an estimate before finalizing the order. *Please note:* U.S. firms generally wish to receive payment for goods and catalogs in U.S. funds.

▬ THE FLAG SYMBOL

This shows that the firm will ship goods to APO and FPO (U.S. military) addresses. For more information, see "Shipments Abroad," page 547.

✔ THE DISCOUNT SYMBOL

This shows that the firm offers a special discount or other type of offer to readers of *The Wholesale-by-Mail Catalog® 1990*. For more information, see "WBMC Reader Offers," page 550.

THE COMPLETE GUIDE TO BUYING BY MAIL

In the back of this book, you'll find our comprehensive guide to buying by mail. We've tried to anticipate and answer your questions about ordering, shipping, payment, delivery, warranties, and other mail-order concerns. Should a problem arise with a mail-order transaction, this information should help you resolve it. *Please note:* Additional consumer information can be found in the chapter introductions.

USING THIS BOOK

_____

The Wholesale-by-Mail Catalog® 1991 has been written to be used by novice mail-order shoppers, as well as veterans. But in either case, the following hints should prove helpful in getting the most from the book:

"SEE ALSO"

To maintain brevity and minimize confusion, each firm is listed in the chapter that best reflects its principal category of goods or services. Companies are *cross-referenced*, as appropriate, in the "See Also" sections at the end of other chapters. These references appear on the last page of every chapter of listings, headed "See Also." For example, the *See Also* page at the end of the "Animal Supplies" chapter shows that Gohn Bros. stocks horse blankets. The firm's main listing is in the "Clothing" chapter, which is where you will find the complete description of the company and its services. Since this feature can often direct you to many sources you might otherwise overlook, please be sure to read the *See Also*'s when shopping for a particular product!

PATIENCE

Since companies are constantly revising their catalogs and printing new ones, we ask you to be patient while waiting for literature to arrive. Specifically, please allow *six to eight weeks* for delivery, unless the firm's listing indicates a longer possible delay. If the catalog doesn't arrive within the designated period, consult the "Catalogs" section of "The Complete Guide to Buying by Mail" at the back of this book for information on the steps you should take to get it. Please remember that some products, such as flower bulbs and highly perishable foods, can be ordered only at certain times of the year.

PRICE QUOTES

Some firms do not issue catalogs at all. Most of these operate under a price-quote system: You tell them the exact make and model number of the item you want and they give you the price and shipping cost. Price quotes are given by mail and phone. Businesses that operate this way are clearly indicated in the listings. (Be sure to check the "Special Factors" notes at the end of each listing as well as the core information.) Price-quote firms often have the lowest prices on such goods as appliances, audio and TV components, and furniture; they usually sell well below both the standard manufacturers' suggested list prices and the less formal minimum prices that some manufacturers try to enforce. Before writing or calling for a price quote or making a purchase in this way, remember to read the "Price Quotes" section of "The Complete Guide to Buying by Mail." In addition, see "The Grey Market" in the introduction to the "Cameras" chapter for information on several types of goods that are often sold on a price-quote basis.

MINIMUM ORDERS

In a few cases, the very best buys are available from firms that require a minimum order in dollars or goods (although most of the companies in this book impose no such restriction). Don't be put off by a minimum requirement. Minimum requirements are usually not ironclad: Most firms will accept orders below the minimum, although an extra "handling fee" is often imposed for the privilege. Be sure to check the catalog, though, for the last word on this. If you want something that's a real bargain, chances are you have friends or work associates who'll want it as well. Even if you can't find a buying partner, remember that a great bargain can also be a great gift. If appropriate, stock up on a special product—doing so may also keep you one small step ahead of inflation.

A CAVEAT

The Wholesale-by-Mail Catalog® 1991 is compiled as a resource for consumers, to help you to find the bargains available by mail. *Never* order goods directly from this book, even if prices are given in the listing. *Always* contact the company first to get a catalog or a current price quote, and be sure to follow specific ordering and payment instructions. *Please do not request extra discounts or wholesale prices, unless the listing states that these are available.* All of the information in this book is based on our research and fact-checking as of press time, and is subject to change.

ANIMAL SUPPLIES

Livestock and pet supplies and equipment, veterinary instruments and biologicals, live-animal referrals, and services

According to one industry source, Americans spent $5.9 billion on pet food *alone* in 1988. The most obvious pleasure afforded by a pet is companionship, but there are other benefits commending Puff and Spot. For example, some doctors "prescribe" pets for hypertensive patients, since the simple act of stroking an animal seems to lower blood pressure. Some believe that pets are an antidote to garden-variety depression, and they're now widely used in therapy programs for nursing-home patients, hospitalized children, and psychiatric patients. (For further reading on this topic, see *Pet Therapy: A Study and Resource Guide for the Use of Companion Animals in Selected Therapies*. Request the current price of the publication and ordering information from Humane Society, Pikes Peak Region, P.O. Box 187, Colorado Springs, CO 80901.)

Most of us adopt pets for less pragmatic reasons, and we're seldom aware of the long-term costs of ownership: The average cat or dog can cost upward of $10,000 over a typical pet's lifetime. The companies listed here can help you to realize significant savings on everything from toys and collars to cages, carriers, and even food and medications.

If you're planning to adopt a pet, see *Getting More for Your Money*, by the Better Business Bureau. It includes a section on selecting cats, dogs, fish, and birds. (Send a self-addressed, stamped envelope and request for the publications list to the Council of Better Business Bureaus, Inc., 1515 Wilson Blvd., Arlington, VA 22209, Attn.: Publications Dept.) Dog fanciers undecided on breed can turn to *The Perfect Puppy—How to Select Your Dog by Its Behavior,* by Ben and Lyn Hart (W.H. Freeman,

1

1988). The authors assess popular breeds on the basis of such criteria as playfulness, tendency to bark, ease of obedience training, congeniality with other dogs, and patience with children.

If you already have a pet, increasing your animal's well-being and longevity, and saving money in the process, is simple: Become an informed owner. Attention to routine care pays off in many ways. For example, if you learn the actual nutritional needs of your animal, you can judge pet food by its nutrient listing—and not by the ads. Iams and Science Diet are often cited as nutritionally balanced, and are offered in canine and feline formulations. For product information and the name of the nearest distributor, write to Iams Customer Service, 7250 Poe Ave., Dayton, OH 45414, or call 800-525-4267. Write to Hill's Pet Products, P.O. Box 148, Topeka, KS 66601, Attn.: Customer Services, for information on Science Diet, or call 800-445-5777. (The Kennel Vet Corp., listed in this chapter, sells Science Diet dog food by mail.)

By mastering basic grooming techniques, you can spare your pet the unpleasantness of overwashing and improper clipping, and save considerable sums in salon costs. And using simple training methods developed by professionals should work as effectively at home as it does at obedience school—and all it costs is some time and patience. Ask your vet for guidelines and recommended publications, and look at what's available at your local bookstore or library. *The Common Sense Book of Kitten and Cat Care* and *The Common Sense Book of Puppy and Dog Care* (Bantam Books), by Harry Miller, are excellent reference tools. The advice of the late Barbara Woodhouse is especially valuable to owners of recalcitrant or problematical canines, and can be found in *Encyclopedia of Dogs and Puppies* and *Dog Training My Way* (Berkley Books), as well as *No Bad Dogs* (Summit Books, 1982). *The Complete Dog Book,* by the American Kennel Club, Inc., is a highly praised general reference that dog owners may want to add to their own libraries. Scores of guides to the care of fish, birds, reptiles, and more exotic creatures are also available; the Simon & Schuster Guides (Fireside), on cats, fish, dogs, birds, horses, and other animals, are especially helpful and easy to use. Consult your local library or bookstore for available titles.

Knowledgeable pet owners can also avoid taking their pets to the vet at every temporary change in habit or body function, and can evaluate early symptoms of real illnesses more accurately and seek prompt medical attention. Nipping a potentially serious condition in the bud is almost always cheaper than a course of treatment for a fully developed disease. More important, of course, is the fact that appropriate care is less traumatic to the beloved pet.

You may wish to consider having your pet insured against injury and illness. The Animal Health Insurance Agency, 24 Delay St., Danbury, CT 06810, insures cats and dogs under ten years old against illness and injury. Veterinary Pet Insurance, 400 N. Tustin Ave., Santa Ana, CA 92705, imposes an age limit on new applications (the animal must be 11 or younger). Write for details, rates, and restrictions.

Several of the firms listed here retain veterinarians who can answer questions on products and use, but they're not permitted to give specific medical advice. Consult your own vet for that, and be sure to seek his or her assistance if you plan to administer any vaccines or medications yourself. Keep the number of a local 24-hour service that handles medical emergencies posted near the phone, and become familiar with symptoms and the first-aid measures you may have to take in order to transport the animal to the clinic. Every pet owner should have such information at hand, and one of the best booklets around that covers such basics is the "Angell Memorial Guide to Animal First Aid," published by the American Humane Education Society and MSPCA. The 22-page guide tells you how to restrain and handle an injured animal, bind a wound, and deal with burns, drowning, heat stroke, problem deliveries, choking, shock, poisoning, and many other problems. Rosters of toxic household substances and plants are included, as well as a list of tips to help prevent accidents and injuries. The booklet costs $1; request it by title from the American Humane Education Society, 350 South Huntingdon Avenue, Boston, MA 02130.

If you're among the owners of this country's 50 million pet birds, tell your vet about the Avian Referral Service, which helps vets get advice on bird problems. Your vet should write to AAHA, Avian Referral Service, P.O. Box 15899, Denver, CO 80215, for more information. You can add *The Basic Bird Book,* by Elizabeth Randolph with Douglas G. Aspros, D.V.M. as consultant (Ballantine Books, 1989), for a comprehensive guide to choosing and caring for a bird. If *wild* birds are your pleasure, you may enjoy membership in the National Bird-Feeding Society, which entitles you to a newsletter on the care and feeding of wild birds. Membership costs $15 a year; for more information, send a self-addressed, stamped envelope to National Bird-Feeding Society, 1163 Shermer Rd., Northbrook, IL 60062.

One caution when buying medical supplies for animals: The FDA requires that you swear to the fact that your purchases of hypodermic syringes, needles, and antibiotics are for animal use only, and that you submit your vet's prescription with your order. Be sure to do this whether the catalog states this regulation or not—it's the law. Check with your local health department before ordering to see whether local ordinances permit receipt of such materials. Be sure to keep drugs, treatments, and medical instruments out of the reach of both pets and small children.

DAIRY ASSOCIATION CO., INC.

DEPT. BI
LYNDONVILLE, VT
05851-0145
802/626-3610

Brochure: free
Save: up to 35%
Pay: check or MO
Sells: livestock treatments and leather balm
Store: mail order only

$$$$ ✉ ☎ 🍁 (see text) 🇺🇸

The Dairy Association Co., Inc., established in 1890, is known to generations of herd farmers for its Bag Balm ointment. The firm also sells Hoof Softener and Tackmaster leather conditioner—all at excellent savings.

Bag Balm, formulated to soothe the chapped, scraped, sunburned udders of cows, is also recommended by horse trainers for cracked heels, galls, cuts, hobble burns, and other ailments. It can be used on sheep, goats, dogs, and cats as well, and is super for weatherbeaten, chapped hands. A ten-ounce can, over $5 elsewhere, costs $3.95 here; a 4-1/2-pound pail costs $26.00. Dilators and milking tubes for injured udders are also available. Green Mt. Horse Products, a division of Dairy Association, produces Hoof Softener—made of pine oil, lanolin, and vegetable oils, it helps to keep hoofs pliable and sound ($4.15 per pint). The firm's Tackmaster is TLC for leather—a one-step, all-around conditioner, cleaner, and preservative cheaper than similar products at $1.85 for four ounces.

Canadian readers, please note: Contact Dr. A.D. Daniels Co. Ltd., N. Rock Island, Quebec, for prices and ordering information.

Special Factors: Price quote by phone or letter with SASE; shipping is included; phone orders are accepted for C.O.D. payment.

DALECO MASTER BREEDER PRODUCTS

3340 LAND DRIVE
FORT WAYNE, IN 46809
219/747-7376

Catalog: $4
Save: up to 40%
Pay: check, MO, MC, V
Sells: tropical fish supplies and aquarium specialties
Store: mail order only

$$$ ✉ ☎ 🍁 (see text)

Daleco publishes a catalog/reference book entitled "The Aquarists Supply

Manual," which is packed with useful information for the owner of fresh and saltwater fish. The catalog costs $4 if mailed bulk rate, $6 by first-class mail (to U.S. addresses only). Daleco has been in business since 1966.

Daleco sells tank filters, aquarium heaters, lights, tank stands, air and water pumps, foods, water test kits, UV water sterilizers, water conditioners, reef trickle filter systems, and related goods. Over 40 brands are represented, including Aquanetics, Dupla, Hagen, Hawaiian Marine, Jungle Laboratories, Perfecto, Tetra, Vortex, and many others. The products are selected for serious hobbyists and breeders, for whom the catalog's "Fish Problem Solver" and "Fish Disease" charts should prove useful. The Manual is worth the $4 for the information alone, but the prices are good—savings run up to 40%. Shipping and handling are free on orders over $25 shipped in the contiguous U.S. The catalog comes with a voucher entitling you to $4 off your first order over $50—don't overlook it when you order.

Canadian readers, please note: The Manual costs $6 (in U.S. funds) via surface mail, $9 via airmail.

Special Factors: Price quote by phone or letter with SASE; shipping included on orders over $25; authorized returns are accepted.

THE DOG'S OUTFITTER

P.O. BOX 2010
HAZLETON, PA 18201
717/384-5555

Catalog: free
Save: up to 50%
Pay: check, MO, MC, V
Sells: vet, kennel, groomer, and pet supplies
Store: mail order only

Despite the fact that the catalog from this firm is geared to professionals, it has one of the best selections of products for pet *owners* that we've seen. The Dog's Outfitter has been in business since 1969, and is exclusive in name only: The catalog is full of products for cats, and there's even a page devoted to the needs of ferrets.

If you can meet the $75 minimum order requirement, you can realize savings on a full range of pet products sold here—grooming tools, shampoo, flea and tick collars and insecticides, cages, gates and doors, training aids, feeding and watering equipment, nutritional supplements, collars and leads, pet beds, carriers, toys and bones, and even books and gifts. The brands include A&W, Bio-Groom, Dubl Duck, General Cage, Havahart, Lambert Kay,

Oster, PetAg, Resco, Ring 5, Safari (fiberglass cages), Speedy, André Tisserand (shears), Twinco, and Zodiac.

We saw several items pet owners might appreciate: molting combs for dogs and cats, no-tears pet shampoo, herbal flea collars, pet doors to fit *screen* doors, a variety of yard scoops, all types of feeding bowls and crocks, "small animal" nurser kits, reflective collars and leads, dog parkas, bulk rawhide bones, and toys in boxes of 50. There are gifts, pet jewelry (for owners), note cards, and books (Arco, Howell, T.F.H.), and grooming videos from Oster and Animal Academy training tapes.

Unlike many animal-supply discounters, The Dog's Outfitter has its own warehouse in Pennsylvania, and does not drop ship (have the manufacturer or distributor send the goods)—which should improve chances of getting prompt delivery.

Special Factors: Satisfaction is guaranteed; price quote by phone or letter with SASE; shipping is included on most items; authorized returns of new and unused goods are accepted within 10 days for exchange, refund, or credit; minimum order is $75; C.O.D. orders are accepted.

KANSAS CITY VACCINE COMPANY

P.O. BOX 5713
KANSAS CITY, MO
64102-5713
816/842-5966

Price List: free
Save: up to 35%
Pay: check, MO, certified check
Sells: vet supplies and biologicals
Store: 1611 Genesee St., Kansas City, MO; Monday through Friday 8:30–4

$$$

Dairy farmers, herders, and veterinarians have relied on KCV for its comprehensive stock of supplies and equipment since 1912. The price list, geared to medical/commercial needs, is published twice yearly.

You'll find products for cattle, horses, sheep, hogs, poultry, dogs, and cats here—vaccines, antitoxins, flea and tick treatments, grooming tools, wormers, stethoscopes, soaps, tattoo markers, nutritional supplements, and other related items. The brands include Chaparral, Franklin, Happy Jack, Havoc, Kopertox, Lindane, Norden, Oster, Red-Kote, Resco, Ritchey, Sunbeam, Trax-M, and Tylosin, among others. Kansas City Vaccine is ideal for the vet or animal handler, since most of the products are for professionals.

Special Factors: Price quote by phone or letter with SASE; vaccines and biologicals are sent where ordinances permit; quantity discounts are available; minimum order is $10.

THE KENNEL VET CORP.

DEPT. WBMC
P.O. BOX 835
BELLMORE, NY 11710
516/783-5400
FAX: 516/783-7516

Catalog: free
Save: up to 70%
Pay: check, MO, MC, V, AE, Discover
Sells: vet, kennel, and pet supplies
Store: 1811 Newbridge Rd., Bellmore,
   NY; Monday through Friday 9–5,
   Saturday 10–4

If you own or raise dogs, you'll find the compact, 84-page catalog from Kennel Vet great reading. This firm, in business since 1971, beats the discounted prices of many firms—savings of up to 70% are possible. Supplies for cats and horses are also stocked.

Kennel Vet offers vaccines and biologicals, remedies for common health problems, vitamins and nutritional supplements, repellents and deodorizers, droppings composters, shampoos and grooming products, flea and tick control products, cages, kennels, pet doors, grooming tables, dryers, leashes, leads, feeding devices, rawhide bones and rubber toys, and other goods. The brands represented include Adams, Gem-Line, General, Holiday, Johnson, Lambert Kay, Lawrence (brushes), Mid-West, Mycodex, Natra-Pet, Norden, Oster, Redi, Ring 5, St. Aubrey, Sulfodene, Vet-Kem, and others. This firm also sells Iams and Science Diet dog food, by mail as well as in the store. Kennel Vet's book department is superb—veterinary manuals, scores of books on dog breeds, and selected books on cats, birds, and horses are sold. The publishers include Alpine, Arco, Denlinger, Howell, Macmillan, and T.F.H., and prices are all discounted.

Special Factors: Authorized returns are accepted; shipping is included on orders of $60 or more (with some exceptions—see the catalog); vaccines and biologicals are sent where ordinances permit; orders are shipped worldwide.

MASTER ANIMAL CARE

411 SEVENTH AVE.
TWO HARBORS, MN
55616
218/834-3200
FAX: 218/834-5538

Catalog: free
Save: up to 40%
Pay: check, MO, MC, V, Discover
Sells: dog and cat supplies and biologicals
Store: mail order only

$$ ✉ ☎ 🍁 ▆

Master Animal Care specializes in dog and cat health supplies, selling them at highly competitive prices. The "Master Animal Care" catalog, which includes helpful information on health care and vaccinating procedures, includes products for both cats and dogs. Master's "Cat Care," a 32-page color catalog, features an extensive line of exclusively feline products, and a holiday catalog of pet-related goods is also published yearly.

Grooming tools, a range of cages, feeding devices, training aids, leashes and leads, and related goods are featured in the 56-page Animal Care catalog, at prices up to 40% below list. You'll find the latest pet products at Master—airline approved cages in designer colors, timer-operated feeding dishes that keep two meals fresh; natural and biodegradable cleaners and disinfectants, electronic training devices, bulk packages of rawhide bones and dog biscuits, hot-oil skin treatments for dogs and cats, and much more.

Special Factors: Satisfaction is guaranteed; returns are accepted for exchange, refund, or credit.

NORTHERN WHOLESALE VETERINARY SUPPLY, INC.

P.O. BOX 2256
ROCKFORD, IL 61131
800-356-5852

Catalog: free
Save: up to 50%
Pay: check, MO, MC, V
Sells: vet, kennel, and pet supplies
Store: mail order only

$$$ ✉ ☎ 🍁

Vets, breeders, and livestock farmers can save up to 50% on hundreds of products from Northern Wholesale, which has been in business since 1970. The catalog is geared for the animal-care professional, but offers goods for pet owners as well.

The 112-page catalog offers vaccines and biologicals, nutritional supplements, grooming tools and preparations, surgical instruments, carriers and cages, leashes and leads, horse tack, flea and tick treatments, feeding devices, books, and many other items. The brands include Absorbine, Carnation, Groom-Rite, Lambert Kay, Orvus, Oster, Pfizer, Rubbermaid, Squibb, Stewart, Sunbeam, and Theralin. Heavy-duty footwear from LaCrosse and Red Ball is also available. Please note that the catalog focuses on veterinary care products for cattle, sheep, rabbits, horses, and swine, and the pet products that are available are principally medicinal.

Special Factors: Quantity discounts are available on some items; veterinarian is on staff; C.O.D. orders are accepted.

OMAHA VACCINE COMPANY, INC.

**3030 L ST.
OMAHA, NE 68107
402/731-9600**

Catalog: free
Save: up to 50%
Pay: check, MO, MC, V
Sells: vet, kennel, and pet supplies
Store: same address; Monday through Friday 8–5, Saturday 8–12 noon

$$$ ✉ 🍁

Omaha's 104-page "Master Catalog," published several times a year, features products for livestock, horses, and pets. Established in 1967, OVC does most of its business with livestock producers and veterinarians.

The Master Catalog features vaccines and biologicals, medications, surgical implements, grooming tools, wormers, nutritional supplements, flea and tick products, cages and carriers, leads and leashes, horse tack, Wells Lamont work gloves, and Red Ball boots, among other goods.

Omaha also publishes two specialty catalogs: the 52-page "Best Care" edition, "a catalog about dogs and cats," and "First Place," a 48-page catalog for "horse and rider." The horse catalog should be especially useful to the noncommercial owner, since it features a solid selection of tack, saddles, manuals, and a number of videotapes that run from "Emergency First Aid" to special-interest tapes on dressage, cross-country riding, and calf roping. Pet owners should request "Best Care," since it's devoted to the needs of dogs and cats, as well as the whims of those who keep them.

Special Factors: Some pharmaceutical products are available by prescription only (shipment is subject to local ordinances); shipping is included on many items; C.O.D. orders are accepted; minimum order is $10.

PBS LIVESTOCK DRUGS

P.O. BOX 9101
CANTON, OH 44711-9101
800-321-0235
IN OH 800-362-9838

Catalog: $2, refundable
Save: up to 50%
Pay: check, MO, MC, V
Sells: vet and livestock supplies
Store: Canton, Wooster, Circleville, and
Wilmington, OH; Monday through Friday
9–5, Saturday 9–12, all locations

$$$

PBS, established in 1941, publishes an 80-page catalog that offers commercial dairy, beef, swine, and sheep producers a complete selection of biologicals and veterinary products at 20% to 50% below list prices.

The stock includes biologicals, nutritional supplements, surgical instruments, ointments, treatments, tags, and many other name-brand goods for all livestock varieties. PBS also publishes a separate catalog, "Horse Health U.S.A.,"featuring products for horses. A number of items are of general interest: isopropyl alcohol, Bag Balm, unrefined wheat germ oil, mineral oil, K-Y jelly, disposable plastic boots and gloves, etc. Excellent values can be found in PBS's clothing selection; in addition to Tingley work boots and rain suits, there are vests, bandannas, chambray shirts, dungarees, coveralls, and overalls—from size 3 months to 60" waist—by OshKosh B'Gosh. The catalog is written for livestock farmers and also has a small selection of goods that are of interest to pet owners.

Special Factors: Satisfaction is guaranteed; price quotes by phone; shipping is included on most items; vaccines and biologicals are sent where ordinances permit.

R.C. STEELE CO.

BOX 910-WC
1989 TRANSIT WAY
BROCKPORT, NY 14420
800-872-3773

Catalog: free
Save: up to 50%
Pay: check, MO, MC, V
Sells: vet, kennel, groomer, and pet supplies
Store: 1989 Transit Way, Brockport, NY

$$$

R.C. Steele Co., which was founded in 1959, is the wholesale division of

Sporting Dog Specialties. The prices are excellent—some as much as 50% less than comparable retail—and the only drawback is the $50 minimum order.

Like its parent company, R.C. Steele sells a full range of goods for active dogs: carriers and cages, pet doors, insecticides, feeding equipment, droppings composters, training dummies and other devices, training jumps, leashes and leads, grooming supplies and tools, and similar goods. There are great buys on rawhide bones, which are sold in case lots at a fraction of full retail, and all types of pet beds, at about half the going rate. The 68-page color catalog includes books from Arco, Denlinger, Howell, T.F.H., and other publishers, as well as American Kennel Club videotapes of breed shows.

R.C. Steele offers a small selection of products for cats, and gifts for pet and pet owner alike: gourmet dog cookies, dog breed switchplates, bone-shaped cookie cutters, and needlepoint dog breed portrait. If you travel with your pet, consider getting the pet life preserver and safety harness (for car travel), and for camping and hiking, the dog backpacks—so Rover can tote his kibbles on the trail!

Special Factors: Authorized returns are accepted; minimum order is $50.

THAT FISH PLACE

237 CENTERVILLE RD.
LANCASTER, PA 17603
800-233-3829
IN CANADA, 800-334-7338
IN PA 800-222-FISH
717/299-5691

Catalog: $2
Save: up to 50%
Pay: check, MO, MC, V
Sells: aquarium and fish supplies
Store: same address; Monday through Thursday 10–8, Friday and Saturday 10–9, Sunday 12–5

"They have excellent discounts, are always pleasant on the phone, and have a good selection of merchandise for aquarium hobbyists. They also offer a small selection of merchandise for other small animals. I cannot tell you much about their return policy—I haven't had to return anything."

That's a verbatim quote from a reader's letter, recommending That Fish Place for a listing. This firm has been selling supplies for the aquarium hobbyist since 1973, and stocks the works: aquariums, air pumps, cleaners, feeders, filters, lighting, heaters, fish food, medication, plants, ornaments, water conditioners, and much more. The catalog features several pages of goods for ponds—filters, plants, fountains, etc.—and supplies for birds and dogs as well. Scores of books on fish species and care are available, and the catalog includes diagnostic charts that can help you determine what might be ailing your fish or aquarium. As our reader said, the discounts are excellent—up to 50% on list—and quarterly sales brochures can save you even more.

Special Factors: Authorized, unused returns are accepted (a 15% restocking fee may be charged); minimum order is $15; orders are shipped worldwide.

TOMAHAWK LIVE TRAP COMPANY

**P.O. BOX 323-WBM
TOMAHAWK, WI 54487
715/453-3550**

Catalog: $1.95 (see text)
Save: up to 50%
Pay: check, MO, MC, V
Sells: proprietary humane animal traps
Store: Tomahawk, WI; Monday through
    Friday 8–5; also Jung Seed, 335 S. High
    St., Randolph (and Coburn) Whitewater,
    WI; and Plow & Hearth, Orange, VA

The U.S. Army Medical Corps, state and federal conservation departments, dog wardens, universities, and others who want to catch a critter without endangering its pelt or life use Tomahawk's box traps. It seems almost ironical that the founders of this firm originally operated a fur farm and developed the traps to cope with their own runaways. The success of the traps put an end to the farm, a conclusion that should gladden the hearts of all animal-rights activists.

Tomahawk, which was established in 1930, has traps for 58 different animals, everything from mice (about $11) to large dogs (about $142), as well as traps designed for fish and turtles, birds, and beavers. Models include rigid and collapsible styles, transfer cages, station wagon and carrying cages, and several with sliding doors (for shipping animals). Special sizes can be made to order. The comprehensive, 56-page catalog ($1.95) includes valuable information on trapping animals, and a list of common foods that can be used to lure over 20 animals. Trap dimensions and specifications are listed for each cage, as well as the discount prices. A brochure and price lists are also available free upon request (include a self-addressed, stamped envelope).

If you identify yourself as a WBMC reader, you may deduct 10% from your goods total (not including shipping) on your *first order only.* This WBMC reader discount expires February 1, 1992.

Special Factors: Price quote by phone or letter with SASE; quantity discounts of 50% are available on orders of six or more of the same trap; C.O.D. orders are accepted.

UNITED PHARMACAL COMPANY, INC.

**P.O. BOX 969, DEPT. WBM
ST. JOSEPH, MO 64502
816/233-8800**

Catalog: free
Save: up to 50%
Pay: check, MO, MC, V, AE, Discover
Sells: vet, kennel, and pet supplies
Store: 3705 Pear St., St. Joseph, MO;
Monday through Friday 7:30–6, Saturday 7:30–5

UPCO, established in 1952, publishes a 144-page catalog of thousands of name-brand products for dogs, cats, birds, and horses—a valuable source for pet owners and professionals.

UPCO offers an extensive inventory of antibiotics, wormers, medical instruments, nutritional supplements, skin treatments, insecticides, grooming aids, and other goods for the professional. The equine department includes medications and supplements, farrier supplies, and tack. UPCO also has a selection of bird cages and supplies and some products for hamsters, gerbils, guinea pigs, ferrets, and rabbits. Owners of dogs and cats will appreciate the savings on leashes and leads, collars, feeders, books, toys, feeding dishes and stations, pet doors, and other goods. The manufacturers represented include Absorbine, Borden, Dubl Duck, Farnam, Happy Jack, Lambert Kay, Nylabone, Oster, St. Aubrey, and Zema, to note a few. Professional groomers should note the selection of grooming products for show dogs. And there are hundreds of books and manuals that cover the care and breeding of a variety of animals.

Canadian readers, please note: Vaccines are not shipped to Canada.

Special Factors: Quantity discounts are available; C.O.D. orders are accepted; returns are accepted within 20 days; minimum order is $10.

WESTERN SUPPLIERS

P.O. BOX 428
AUBREY, TX 76227
817/365-3133

Catalog: free
Save: up to 40%
Pay: check, MO, MC, V
Sells: saddles and tack
Store: mail order only

$$$ ✉ ☎ ♦

Western Suppliers has been selling saddles, tack, grooming tools and products, and equine-related goods since 1972. Request the "wholesale" price list for the discount prices.

The catalog lists page after page of Western saddles, from those built for years of daily use to beautiful show saddles of hand-tooled, oiled leather. Prices start at under $100 for youth and pony models, and go up to several hundred for show saddles. There are tie straps, harnesses, bits, spurs, saddlebags, feed buckets, lariats, whips, bridles, stirrups, breast collars, reins, headstalls, and even tack decorations of German silver. Western also sells grooming tools—clippers, curry combs, sweat scrapers, mane combs, nippers, and hoof picks, among others. If you're looking for horse blankets, saddle pads, shipping boots, quilted leg wraps, skid boots, splint boots, chaps, or Absorbine products, Western stocks them all.

Special Factor: Price quote by phone or letter with SASE.

WHOLESALE VETERINARY SUPPLY, INC.

P.O. BOX 2256
ROCKFORD, IL 61131
800-435-6940

Catalog: free
Save: up to 50%
Pay: check, MO, MC, V
Sells: vet, livestock, and pet supplies
Store: 4801 Shepherd Trail, Rockford, Il;
Monday through Friday 8–6, Saturday 8–4

$$$ ✉ ☎ ♦ ▬

Wholesale Veterinary Supply offers over 8,000 products for cats, dogs, rabbits, cattle, and horses in its 112-page catalog. This firm was established in 1971, and it keeps abreast of new developments in research and preventive medicine.

WVS's professional products include vaccines and biologicals, nutritional supplements, surgical instruments, and grooming tools and preparations. In addition, the catalog offers cages and carriers, leashes and leads, flea and tick treatments, and a wide range of other products for pets and livestock (cattle, swine, sheep, and poultry). There are reference works on veterinary care, plus a collection of videotapes on equestrian topics. You'll also find leather-care products, flashlights, knives, disinfectants and cleaning products, Georgia and Cedar Crest work shoes, Laredo Western boots, and related goods. Well-known manufacturers—Absorbine, Andis, Farnam, Fortex, Holiday, Lambert Kay, Oster, Roche, Sergeant's, Shaw's, WAHL—are represented, as well as hard-to-find labels and imports. Prices we spot-checked were good—35% and 40% below full retail.

Special Factors: Price quote by phone or letter with SASE; C.O.D. orders are accepted; authorized returns are accepted within 30 days; vaccines and biologicals are sent where ordinances permit; minimum order is $30.

SEE ALSO

Cabela's Inc. • dog beds; hunting dog training equipment • SPORTS
Central Tractor Farm & Family Center • livestock handling equipment; vet products • FARM
Defender Industries, Inc. • pet life preservers • AUTO
Gander Mountain, Inc. • hunting and fishing gear • SPORTS
Glorybee Bee Box, Inc. • apiary equipment and supplies • FARM
Gohn Bros. • horse blankets • CLOTHING
Mellinger's Inc. • live pest controls, fly traps, bird feeders, etc. • FARM
Star Pharmaceutical, Inc. • pet vitamins • HEALTH
Weston Bowl Mill • bird feeders and bird calls • GENERAL

APPLIANCES, AUDIO, TV, AND VIDEO

Major, small, and personal-care appliances;

sewing machines and vacuum cleaners;

audio components and personal stereo;

TV and video equipment; tapes, discs, and

services

In 1988, consumers in the U.S. spent over $40 billion on electronics — CD players, microwave ovens, VCRs, etc. One market analyst reckoned that over 50% of the homes in the U.S. have a VCR, TV, microwave oven, and audio system. Prices of such desirable goods as camcorders, computers, and VCRs have come down over the past few years, while the selection of models and features has increased. The trade-off may be reduced product life spans, as consumers become accustomed to replacing rather than repairing electronics and appliances that seem programmed to expire with the warranty.

The firms listed here offer every conceivable electronic or battery-run device: White goods (washers, dryers, refrigerators, and ranges), brown goods (TVs, air conditioners, etc.), small kitchen and personal-care appliances, pocket calculators, phone equipment, sewing machines, vacuum cleaners, and floor machines are featured. Some of the firms also sell blank audiotapes and videotapes, luggage, cameras, typewriters, computers, pens, and video games.

Discounts of up to 40% are routine, but consider more than price when you're shopping. The Better Business Bureau publishes a number of "Booklets on Wise Buying" that can help you improve your decisions. Tracts on appliance service contracts, air conditioning, home computers, microwave ovens, phones, and video equipment are all available. Contact your local BBB to obtain them, or send a SASE for the complete listing of pamphlets and an order form to: Council of Better Business Bureaus, Inc., 1515 Wilson Blvd., Arlington, VA 22209, Attn.: Publications Dept.

Consumer Reports reviews name-brand products monthly and publishes summaries of these in its yearly *Buying Guide*. Use the magazine and annual as *adjuncts* to shopping, and note that suggested list and "benchmark" retail selling prices stated with model information may be out of date (this is stated by Consumers Union in its guide). *Consumer Reports* also reports on product recalls, deceptive selling practices, health issues, money management, and related topics of concern to us all. For subscription information, see the current issue or write to Consumers Union, 256 Washington St., Mount Vernon, NY 10553.

Although *The Durability Factor* (Rodale Press, 1982), edited by Roger B. Yepsen Jr., deals extensively with appliances and electronics, it's really an all-around "guide to finding long-lasting cars, housing, clothing, appliances, tools, and toys." The book includes brief histories of these industries, and clear-eyed examinations of what lasts, and why. The information has been gleaned from research among consumers, repair centers, manufacturers, and the editors of consumer publications. Although there's a useful appendix with a geographically organized list of appliance parts distributors, you'll probably find this book contributes more to your appreciation of what constitutes quality than to how to find the refrigerator of your dreams.

Appliance and electronics manufacturers are often willing to send literature on specific models upon request. The consumer contacts and addresses of hundreds of major corporations are listed in *Consumer's Resource Handbook*, available from the Consumer Information Center (see the listing in "Books").

The Association of Home Appliance Manufacturers (AHAM) publishes yearly guides to features and specifications of refrigerators in *Consumer Selection Guide for Refrigerators and Freezers*. Air conditioners are examined as well in *Consumer Selection Guide for Room Air Conditioners*, which includes the "Cooling Load Estimate Form." Complete this worksheet *before* you decide on the model you want, since it will help you determine how many BTUs your home or room requires. Send a check or money order for $1.50 for each title requested to AHAM, Public and Consumer Relations Dept., 20 N. Wacker Dr., Chicago, IL 60606.

The electronics boom of the mid-1980s has helped to popularize the sale of service contracts (erroneously termed "extended warranties"), often pushed on big-ticket items at the point of sale on in-store purchases. Are they worth the money? According to one analyst who examined the warranties, service contracts, and repair records of color TVs, air conditioners, refrigerators, washers, and ranges in a National Science Foundation/MIT study, the answer is no. The bottom line is price: In many cases, the *probable* repair bill is lower than the cost of the service contract. But if you've had a post-warranty appliance breakdown, you may feel that a contract is worthwhile insurance. If you decide to buy one, get answers to these questions:

- Does the service contract duplicate the manufacturer's warranty coverage?
- Does the service contract cover parts and labor?
- Is the company selling the contract stable, and is its service department well-regarded? (National merchandisers like Sears, Roebuck and Co. rate well here; cut-rate electronics chains inspire less confidence.)
- Could you troubleshoot or repair the appliance yourself? Several major manufacturers provide 800 lines for such purposes, and can even give you advice on making repairs.
- What's your *own* history of appliance and electronics breakdowns? If machines seem to enjoy long and healthy lives in your care, you may not need the insurance.

If the product in question is a VCR, however, the odds may favor the service contract. Even expensive machines seem to be susceptible to failure, and repair costs are usually high. You can reduce wear and tear by using a rewinder, having the tape heads cleaned professionally at least once a year (more often if you view rental tapes frequently), and following the manufacturers' use and care instructions explicitly. The same advice applies to your audio components. It's especially important to keep your CDs and LPs as clean as possible to enhance fidelity and preserve your equipment. The Audio Advisor, Lyle Cartridges, and several other firms in this chapter offer a variety of cleaning solutions and devices for both LPs and CDs.

If you run into trouble with a *major appliance* and can't get it resolved, you may be able to get help from the Major Appliance Consumer Action Panel (MACAP). MACAP, which is sponsored by AHAM (see above), can request action from a manufacturer and make recommendations for resolution of the complaint. (The Panel's advice is not binding, but it resolves over 80% of the cases it handles.) You can turn to MACAP with problems about dishwashers, ranges, microwave ovens, washers, dryers, refrigerators, freezers, garbage disposals, trash compactors, air conditioners, water heaters, and dehumidifiers. If your complaint concerns one of these appliances, and your attempts to get the problem resolved with the seller and the manufacturer have been futile, write to Major Appliance Consumer Action Panel, 20 N. Wacker Dr., Chicago, IL 60606. Your letter should state the manufacturer's name, model number of the appliance, and date purchased, and should include *copies* of relevant receipts and correspondence. You can also call 800-621-0477 for information.

Grey-market (parallel-import) products are sometimes sold by appliance discounters. We have made every effort to list only those firms that *do not* sell these goods. (For a complete discussion of the issue, see the chapter introduction of "Cameras.")

For listings of additional firms selling appliances and electronics, see "General," "Office" (including the "Computing" subchapter), and "Tools."

AAA-ALL FACTORY, INC.

**241 CEDAR
ABILENE, TX 79601
915/677-1311**

Flyer: $2, refundable

Save: up to 75%

Pay: check, MO, MC, V, Discover

Sells: vacuum cleaners, floor shampooers and polishers

Store: same address; Monday through Friday 8:30–5

Clean up and save with AAA-All Factory—the top names in vacuum cleaners are sold here at up to 75% below list. AAA has been in business since 1975, and sells supplies and accessories as well as floor machines.

The latest models in canister, upright, convertible, and mini-vacuums are offered here, by Eureka, Filter Queen, Hoover, Kirby, Oreck, Panasonic, Regina, Rexair (the Rainbow), and Royal. Both home and commercial lines of vacuum cleaners, floor buffers, and rug shampooers are stocked. Bags and belts for machines by these makers are also available.

Canadian readers, please note: Only U.S. funds are accepted.

Special Factors: Satisfaction is guaranteed; price quote by phone or letter with SASE; layaway plan is available; C.O.D. orders are accepted; returns are accepted within 10 days.

ABC VACUUM CLEANER WAREHOUSE

6720 BURNET RD., WM91
AUSTIN, TX 78757
512/459-7643

Price List: free

Save: up to 50%

Pay: check, MO, MC, V, AE, Discover

Sells: vacuum cleaners

Store: same address; Monday through
Friday 9–6, Saturday 9–5

$$$ ✉ ☎ ▬

ABC purchases from overstocked distributors and passes the savings—up to 50% on top names in vacuum cleaners—on to you. ABC has been in business since 1977 and says "If we can't save you money, we don't deserve your business."

Don't buy a vacuum cleaner before pricing it here. ABC sells machines by Filter Queen, Kirby, Oreck, Panasonic, Riccar, Royal, Thermax, and Tri-Star, all at substantial savings. The popular Rainbow, by Rexair, is sold at a discount, as well as accessories and parts. Top-of-the-line models by Eureka and Hoover are also available. See the price list for bags and filters, as well as accessories and attachments for selected models. And ABC offers repair services by mail—call for information if you're having trouble getting your machine repaired locally.

Special Factors: Price quote by phone or letter; no seconds or rebuilt models are sold; C.O.D. orders are accepted.

THE AUDIO ADVISOR, INC.

225 OAKES S.W.
GRAND RAPIDS, MI
49503
800-669-4434
616/451-3868
FAX: 616/451-0709

Catalog: $1

Save: up to 50%

Pay: MO, MC, V, AE, Discover

Sells: high-end audio components

Store: mail order only

$$ ✉ ☎ 🍁 ▬

The Audio Advisor sells high-end audio components and can locate hard-to-find items for your system. Terms of the sales policy are spelled out clearly in the brochure, and the staff welcomes any questions you may have. The Audio Advisor was founded in 1979 and offers savings of up to 50% (10% to 20% discounts prevail). *No grey-market goods are sold here.*

The Audio Advisor sells state-of-the-art equipment, including players for records, CDs, cassettes, and digital discs, as well as turntables, tuners, receivers, radios, amps, preamps, equalizers, speakers, headphones, and the cables and connectors needed to create a system from it all.

Maintenance is critical with more sensitive, high-end equipment, and the Advisor can provide a full range of care products, including Tweek, LAST cleaners, tape head demagnetizers, stylus cleaners, and Nitty Gritty record cleaning machines. A selection of recordings (LP, direct disc, and CD) from such labels as Chesky Records, Proprius Records, Reference Recordings, Sheffield Labs, and Wilson Audiophile is offered as well. Collectors should note the sets of LP recordings of Frank Sinatra, the Beatles, Miles Davis, and other greats, which have been remastered by Mobile Fidelity Sound Labs from the original stereo master tapes.

Special Factor: Price quote by phone or letter with SASE.

BERNIE'S DISCOUNT CENTER, INC.

821 SIXTH AVE., D-4
NEW YORK, NY 10001
212/564-8758

Information: price quote
Save: up to 50%
Pay: check, MO, MC, V, AE (see text)
Sells: appliances and TV and audio components
Store: same address; Monday through Friday 9–5:30, Saturday (except July and August) 11–3:30

$$$ ✉   ☎

Bernie's was founded in 1948 and sells products at 10% to 15% above dealers' cost—averaging out to discounts of 20% to 40%. One of the city's best sources for discounted electronics and appliances, Bernie's tries to carry at least three top buys in each product category. *Bernie's does not handle grey-market goods.*

Bernie's offers electronics (audio, TV, and video equipment) by Aiwa, Fisher, Hitachi, JVC, Mitsubishi, Panasonic, RCA, SCM, Sony, Sylvania, and Toshiba; white and brown goods (shipped in the New York City area only) by Airtemp, Amana, Caloric, Emerson, Friedrich, G.E., Gibson, Hotpoint, Jenn-Air, KitchenAid, Magic Chef, Maytag, Sanyo, Tappan, Welbilt, Whirlpool, and White-Westinghouse; and microwave ovens and small and personal-care appliances (shipped nationwide) by Bionaire, Black & Decker, Braun, Bunn, Clairol, Eureka, Farberware, Hamilton Beach, Hitachi, Hoover, Interplak, KitchenAid, Krups, Mr. Coffee, Norelco, Oster, Panasonic, Presto, Remington, Russell Hobbs, Simac, Sunbeam, Teledyne (Water Pik), Toastmaster, Wearever, West Bend, and other manufacturers.

Please note: Purchases charged to American Express cards are shipped to billing addresses only, and MasterCard and VISA are accepted for *in-store* purchases only.

Special Factors: Price quote by phone or letter with SASE; store is closed Saturdays in July and August.

COLE'S APPLIANCE & FURNITURE CO.

4026 LINCOLN AVE.
CHICAGO, IL 60618
312/525-1797

Information: price quote
Save: up to 40%
Pay: check, MO, MC, V, Discover
Sells: appliances and home furnishings
Store: same address; Monday and Thursday 9:30–9, Tuesday, Friday, and Saturday 9:30–5:30 (closed Wednesday and Sunday)

Cole's, founded in 1946, sells electronics (TV and video), appliances, and home furnishings at discounts of up to 40%. We weren't given a list of manufacturers represented by the firm, but were told that Cole's carries "all major brands," making it a source worth calling—especially if you live in the mid-West and are trying to save on shipping costs.

Special Factor: Price quote by phone or letter with SASE.

CRUTCHFIELD CORPORATION

I CRUTCHFIELD PARK, DEPT. WH
CHARLOTTESVILLE, VA
22906-6020
800-336-5566

Catalog: free (see text)

Save: up to 40%

Pay: check, MO, MC, V, AE, CB, DC, Discover, Optima

Sells: car and home stereo components, video products, and phone equipment

Store: same address; also 153 South Main St., Harrisonburg, VA; Monday to Saturday 10–6, Friday 10–8, both locations

Crutchfield's informative, 120-page catalog of home and car audio components and video equipment is loaded with buying tips and product specifications on featured goods, which are sold at up to 40% below list price. Crutchfield was established in 1974, is a factory-authorized repair station for most brands, and *does not sell grey-market goods.*

Crutchfield carries car audio components (including equipment for pickup trucks and hatchbacks) by Alphasonik, AR, Cerwin Vega, Clarion, Infinity, Jensen, JVC, Panasonic, Pioneer, Proton, Pyle, Sherwood, and Sony. The catalog we reviewed also offered radar detectors, CB radios, and scanners by BEL, Cobra, Uniden, and Whistler, dozens of types of car antennas, and Crimestopper alarm systems to protect it all.

The home audio portion of the catalog includes pages of features comparisons of current models of receivers, CD players, cassette decks, and speakers, and shows amps, tuners, turntables, cartridges, equalizers, portable and personal audio, headphones, remote controls, speaker stands, cassette cabinets, and Discwasher and LAST maintenance products. The brands represented include Advent, Akai, AR, Audio-Technica, Bose, Celestion, Cerwin Vega, Dual, Infinity, JVC, Kenwood, NHT, Ortofon, Pioneer, Proton, Shure, and Sony. You'll also find camcorders and video components from Akai, Canon, JVC, and Sony, as well as Keepsafer home security systems.

Crutchfield publishes a separate catalog, "Personal Office," which offers PCs and peripherals, fax machines, word processors, transcribers, personal copiers, phone machines, and related office equipment and supplies—all at a discount. The brands include ALPS, ATI, Casio, Cobra, Epson, Everex, Franklin, Hewlett-Packard, Murata, Panasonic, Proton, Record a Call, Ricoh, and Tatung. Popular business software for MS-DOS and Macintosh systems is also available at savings of up to 40% on list prices.

Please note: The Crutchfield catalogs are free to readers of this book. Be sure to identify yourself as a WBMC reader when you request your copy, and specify the "Personal Office" catalog if you wish to receive that edition.

Special Factors: Satisfaction is guaranteed; phone staff can advise on component and equipment selection; shipping is included; returns are accepted within 30 days.

DERRY'S SEWING CENTER

**430 ST. FERDINAND
FLORISSANT, MO 63031
314/837-6103**

Brochure: $1 and a self-addressed, stamped envelope
Save: up to 35%
Pay: MO, MC, V, Discover
Sells: sewing machines and vacuum cleaners
Store: same address; Monday through Friday 10–7

Replacing an outmoded sewing machine will cost less at Derry's, which carries models by Necchi, Simplicity, Singer, and Viking. Savings run up to 35%, and parts for new and older machines are available as well. The brochures show the current Singer and Simplicity lines of standard sewing machines and overlock machines, but you can call or write for a price quote if you know which model you want. This firm also sells Panasonic vacuum cleaners and bags to fit most models.

Derry's has been in business since 1979, and provides in-warranty service on the Simplicity and Singer sewing machines. *No grey-market goods are sold here.*

Special Factors: Price quote by phone or letter with SASE and $1; minimum order is $5.

DIAL-A-BRAND, INC.

57 S. MAIN ST.
FREEPORT, NY 11520
800-628-8260
IN NY 800-237-3220

Information: price quote
Save: up to 40%
Pay: check, MO, MC, V
Sells: appliances, TVs, and video
  equipment
Store: same address; Monday through
  Saturday 9–5

$$$ ✉   ☎

Dial-a-Brand, founded in 1967, has earned the kudos of institutions and individuals with its wide range of appliances and popular electronics, sold at up to 40% below list prices. *Dial-a-Brand sells no grey-market goods.*

  Name-brand air conditioners, TVs, video equipment, microwave ovens, and large appliances are available from this firm. Dial-a-Brand ships chiefly within the New York/New Jersey/Connecticut area, but deliveries are made nationwide. (Note that freight charges may offset savings on outsized or heavy items shipped long distances.)

Special Factors: Price quote by phone or letter with SASE; returns are accepted for exchange if goods are defective or damaged in transit; minimum order is $100.

DISCOUNT APPLIANCE CENTERS

2908 HAMILTON ST.
HYATTSVILLE, MD 20782
301/559-6801

Information: price quote
Save: up to 60%
Pay: check, MO, MC, V, AE, CHOICE,
  DC, Optima
Sells: vacuum cleaners and sewing
  machines
Store: same address

$$ ✉   ☎   🍁   ▬

Discount Appliance Centers offers name-brand sewing machines, vacuum cleaners, and accessories and supplies for both at good discounts. Savvy shoppers will write for prices and availability information—price quotes are given by phone as staff time permits and no catalog is available. The parent firm was established in 1965.

The latest models in vacuum cleaners by Airway, Electrolux, Eureka, Filter Queen, Hoover, Kirby, Mastercraft, Oreck, Panasonic, Rainbow, Royal, Sanitaire, and Tri-Star are sold here at up to 60% below list. Bags, belts, and attachments are available as well. Sewing machines by Bernina, Consew, Elna, Juki, Necchi, New Home, Pfaff, Riccar, Singer, and Viking are also offered. Orders are shipped to Alaska, Hawaii, and the Virgin Islands, as well as to Canada.

Discount Appliance Centers is offering readers of this book a 10% discount on all orders (deducted from the goods total only). Identify yourself as a WBMC reader when you order. This WBMC reader discount expires February 1, 1992.

Special Factors: Price quote by letter with SASE; minimum order is $50.

FOTO ELECTRIC SUPPLY CO., INC.

31 ESSEX ST.
NEW YORK, NY 10002
212/673-5222

Information: price quote
Save: 30% plus
Pay: check, MO, MC, V, Optima
Sells: large appliances, TVs, video equipment, and cameras
Store: same address; Sunday through Thursday 9–7, Friday 9–2

$$$ ✉ ☎ 🍁 🇺🇸

Foto tells us that it's done very little advertising in the 28 years the firm has been in business because the customers do it all, gratis. Foto has been written up in almost every New York City shopping guide, and ships to Europe, Israel, South America, and Canada, as well as all over the U.S.A.

Foto sells audio and video equipment by Aiwa, JVC, Panasonic, Philips, Sony, and other firms, as well as blank videotape. White goods by Amana, G.E., Magic Chef, Maytag, Sub-Zero (refrigerators), Thermador (ranges), White-Westinghouse, and Whirlpool are available. Foto also stocks many other name-brand goods—phone machines, cameras by all of the major manufacturers, and film by Kodak and Polaroid. The firm's audio department, at 29 Essex Street, features mid- to high-end equipment, all of which is sold by mail.

Special Factors: Price quote *by letter only* with SASE; orders are shipped worldwide.

HARRY'S DISCOUNTS & APPLIANCES CORP.

**8701 18TH AVE.
BROOKLYN, NY 11214
718/236-5150**

Information: price quote
Save: up to 30%
Pay: check, MO, MC, V
Sells: electronics and appliances
Store: same address; Monday through
Friday 9–5:30

$$ ✉

Harry's, founded in 1959, stocks a wide range of appliances and electronics at respectable savings. *No grey-market goods are sold here.*

Harry's can deliver every Hitachi line, Sony TVs, and small appliances and air conditioners by Black & Decker, Emerson, G.E., Hitachi, Oster, Sunbeam, Toastmaster, and other manufacturers. Fisher audio components, Eureka vacuum cleaners, and many other appliances and electronics lines are stocked as well.

Special Factors: Price quote by phone or letter with SASE; outsized items are shipped by truck only within the five boroughs of New York City, Long Island, and parts of New Jersey.

ILLINOIS AUDIO, INC.

**12 E. DELAWARE PL.
CHICAGO, IL 60611
800-621-8042
IN IL 312/664-0020**

Price List: free
Save: up to 40%
Pay: check, MO, MC, V
Sells: audio and video equipment and
components
Store: mail order only

$$$ ✉ ☎

Illinois Audio has been selling top-of-the-line audio components since 1971. This firm's competitive position is summed up on the price list: "If You See a Better Price, Call Us!" Illinois Audio *does not sell grey-market goods.*

The company's price list itemizes a fraction of the available goods. They include components by ADC, Aiwa, AKG, Audio Source, Audio-Technica, BASF, Discwasher, Dual, Fuji, Jensen (auto audio), JVC, Kenwood, Koss, Maxell, Monster Cable, Panasonic, Recoton, Sansui, Scotch, Sennheiser, Sharp, Sherwood, Shure, Sony, TDK, Teac, Technics, and other firms.

Special Factors: Price quote by phone or letter; all goods are new, shipped in factory-sealed cartons with U.S. manufacturers' warranties; authorized returns are accepted (a restocking fee may be charged).

INTERNATIONAL ELECTRONIC WORLD

**MORAVIA CENTER
 INDUSTRIAL PARK
BALTIMORE, MD 21206
301/488-9600**

Catalog: free (see text)
Save: 30% average
Pay: check, MO, MC, V, CHOICE, Discover
Sells: audio and video components
Store: 6330 Frankford Ave., Baltimore, MD; Monday through Friday 9–9, Saturday 10–5

The catalog from International Electronic World presents the latest in audio and video components from well-known names. The order form is designed to be used to request price quotes, and additional data on selected product categories will be sent on request. IEW, which opened its doors in 1950, *sells no grey-market goods.*

The stock here includes audio and video components, auto audio, audiotape, CDs, cables and connectors, maintenance products, and related goods. Among the manufacturers represented are Advent, AKG, Audio-Technica, Bose, Denon, Dual, Fisher, Hitachi, Infinity, JVC, Koss, Magnavox, Mitsubishi, Monster Cable, NEC, Onkyo, Panasonic, Philips, Proton, Scott, Sony, Stanton, Teac, Technics, and Zenith. Bush furniture, studio and professional products, fax machines, and telephones are also available. If you're interested in setting up a satellite dish or improving your system, you can call for information.

IEW also publishes a 50-page catalog of compact disks, which is available for $2. In addition to classical, jazz, R&B, rock, new age, country, and movie soundtrack recordings, the CD catalog offers CD players, blank audiotapes, headphones, storage accessories, and maintenance products.

Please note: International Electronic World is offering readers of this book a 5% discount on selected items. Please mention WBMC when calling or writing for a price quote to take advantage of this offer.

Special Factors: Price quote by phone or letter authorized returns are accepted; C.O.D. orders are accepted.

LVT PRICE QUOTE HOTLINE, INC.

BOX 444-W91
COMMACK, NY
11725-0444
516/234-8884

Brochure: free
Save: up to 30%
Pay: check, MO, certified check
Sells: appliances, electronics, and office
machines
Store: mail order only

$$ ✉   ☎

LVT, established in 1976, gives you instant access to over 4,000 products from over 75 manufacturers, at savings of up to 30% on suggested list or full retail prices. The brochure includes a roster of available brands, and price quotes are given on individual items. *LVT does not sell grey-market goods.*

First read LVT's brochure for details on ordering and shipping policies, then call with the manufacturer's name and exact model number for a price quote on major appliances, bread-making machines, microwave ovens, air conditioners, vacuum cleaners, washers and dryers, TVs, video equipment, phones and phone machines, calculators, typewriters, scanners, radar detectors, copiers, fax machines, and word processors.

The brands available include Admiral, Airtemp, Amana, AT&T, Bearcat, Bel-Tronics, Bionaire, Broan, Brother, Caloric, Canon, Carrier, Casio, Cobra, Code-A-Phone, Creda, Cuisinart, Dacor, Emerson, Eureka, Excellence, Fedders, Franke, Freedom Phone, Friedrich, Frigidaire, G.E., Hewlett-Packard, Hitachi, Hoover, Insinkerator, Jenn-Air, JVC, KitchenAid, KWC, Magic Chef, Maxon, Maytag, Miami Carey, Miele, Modern Maid, Mont Blanc, Murata, Panasonic, Phone-Mate, Quasar, Rangaire, RCA, Record a Call, Regency, Ricoh, Roper, Samsung, Sanyo, Scotsman, Sharp, Simplicity, Smith Corona, Sony, Southwestern Bell, Speed Queen, Sub-Zero, Sylvania, Tappan, Texas Instruments, Thermador, Toshiba, Uniden, Victor, Viking, Welbilt, Whirlpool, Whistler, White-Westinghouse, Wolf, and Zenith.

Special Factors: Price quote by phone or letter with SASE; UPS shipping, handling, and insurance are included in quotes; all sales are final; all goods are sold with manufacturers' warranties; phone order lines are open Monday through Saturday 9–6, EST.

LYLE CARTRIDGES

**115 SO. CORONA AVE.
VALLEY STREAM, NY
 11582
800-221-0906
INQUIRIES AND NY
 ORDERS 516/599-1112
FAX: 516/561-7793**

Catalog: free with self-addressed, stamped envelope
Save: up to 60%
Pay: check, MO, MC, V, AE, Discover, Optima
Sells: phono cartridges, replacement styli, and accessories
Store: same address; Monday through Friday 9–5

$$$$ ✉ ☎ 🍁 ▤

Lyle Cartridges has been in business since 1952 and is one of the best sources we've found for the cartridges and replacement styli (factory original) that bring your music to life. If you're sticking by your LPs despite CDs, you'll really appreciate this reliable, well-informed source.

Lyle stocks phono cartridges and replacement styli by Audio Quest, Audio-Technica, Bang & Olufsen, Dynavector, Grado/Signature, Monster Cable, Ortofon, Pickering, Shure, Signet, Stanton, and Sumiko. Record-care products by Discwasher, LAST, and Ortofon are stocked, as well as Tweek's contact enhancer. Monster Cable's line of cables and connectors is also available. Lyle is the first source to consult if you have to replace arm parts, since you may be able to save on both labor and material costs. Prices of these parts are up to 60% less than list or comparable retail, and orders are shipped worldwide.

Special Factors: Price quote by phone or letter with self-addressed, stamped envelope; authorized returns are accepted; defective goods are replaced; minimum order is $15, $25 with credit cards.

MIDAMERICA VACUUM CLEANER SUPPLY CO.

666 UNIVERSITY AVE.
ST. PAUL, MN 55104-4896
612/222-0763

Catalog: $5
Save: 25% plus
Pay: check, MO, MC, V, AE, Discover
Sells: vacuum cleaners, floor machines, and appliance parts
Store: same address; Monday through Friday 9–5:30, Saturday 9–3

Midamerica's bible of parts and supplies is a valuable source for the do-it-yourself appliance owner. Vacuum cleaners and floor machines are also sold by this firm—at up to 50% below list. Midamerica was established in 1952.

See the catalog for parts and accessories for vacuum cleaners, floor machines, blenders, coffee makers, irons, shavers, mixers, pressure cookers, and toasters. Brand-new vacuum cleaners by Eureka, Hoover, MagNuM, Oreck, Panasonic, Progress (Mercedes), Rexair (Rainbow), Royal, Sanitaire, and Shop-Vac are also shown, and central vacuum systems, bags, belts, lights, and related products are listed as well.

Special Factors: Price quote by phone or letter with SASE; quantity discounts are available; consult your appliance manual before attempting repairs; minimum order is $15.

ORECK CORPORATION

100 PLANTATION RD.
NEW ORLEANS, LA
70123-9989
504/733-8761

Catalog: free
Save: up to 25%
Pay: check, MO, MC, V, AE, DC, Discover
Sells: vacuum cleaners, rug shampooers, and supplies
Store: mail order only

This is the home of Oreck vacuum cleaners, floor machines, air purifiers, and accessories. Oreck, established in 1963, offers excellent machines that are used extensively by hotels and institutions.

The XL988, Oreck's best-seller, is a powerful, eight-pound upright with an effective edge-cleaning device and a 25-foot cord. The "top-fill" mechanism keeps the vacuum operating at optimum suction until the bag is completely full, and it's designed to be repaired by the user—replacement parts are available. Also sold: a compact canister style with disposable dust bags, a stick/tank convertible vacuum, nonelectric carpet sweepers, heavy-duty canister models for commercial and institutional use, rug shampooers, floor buffers and polishers, power-failure lights, powerful beam flashlights, and bags to fit many vacuum cleaner models other than Oreck (sold in case lots only).

Oreck is listed here because the price of its most popular vacuum cleaner is often discounted about 25%, and bonuses are usually offered with purchases.

Special Factors: Satisfaction is guaranteed; returns are accepted within 30 days.

PERCY'S INC.

19 GLENNIE ST.
WORCESTER, MA 01605
508/755-5334
FAX: 508/797-5578

Information: price quote
Save: up to 40%
Pay: MO, certified check, MC, V, Discover
Sells: large appliances, audio and TV components, office machines, etc.
Store: same address; Monday through Friday 9–9, Saturday 9–5

Percy's has more than 50 years of experience backing its motto, "The difficult we do immediately. The impossible takes a few minutes longer." There's no delay for the discounts—prices are 3% above wholesale cost, or up to 40% below list. *Percy's sells no grey-market goods.*

Percy's stocks washers, dryers, dishwashers, refrigerators, freezers, ranges, standard and microwave ovens, TVs, video equipment and tapes, audio components, copiers, fax machines, radar detectors, dehumidifiers, disposals, and other appliances by Bose, Caloric, Fisher, Frigidaire, G.E., Hitachi, Hotpoint, Jenn-Air, Litton, Magic Chef, Magnavox, Maytag, Mitsubishi, Panasonic, Quasar, RCA, Sharp, Sub-Zero, Thermador, Toshiba, Whirlpool, White-Westinghouse, Zenith, and other manufacturers. Please note that Percy's *does not sell small appliances,* and *does not publish a catalog.*

Special Factor: Price quote by phone or letter with SASE.

S & S SOUND CITY

58 W. 45TH ST.
NEW YORK, NY
  10036-4280
212/575-0210
FAX: 212/221-7907

Brochure: free (see text)
Save: up to 50%
Pay: check, MO, MC, V, Discover
Sells: small appliances and audio, TV, and
  video components
Store: same address; Monday through
  Friday 9–7, Saturday 9–6

S & S, in business since 1975, sells TVs and video equipment, audio components, radios, telephones, microwave ovens, and air conditioners. The owners aim to be "the nicest people in town," and will do their best to get what you need if it's not in stock.

The inventory includes goods from AT&T, Fisher, G.E., Harman Kardon, Hitachi, JVC, Magnavox, NEC, Panasonic, Quasar, RCA, Record a Call, Samsung, Sharp, Sony, Southwestern Bell, Teac, Toshiba, and Yamaha. S & S sent us a holiday brochure that showcased popular gift selections; call or write for a price quote if you're shopping out of season or you don't see the item you want in the brochure.

Special Factors: Price quote by phone or letter with SASE; returns are accepted within 7 days; special orders are accepted.

SEWIN' IN VERMONT

84 CONCORD AVE.
ST. JOHNSBURY, VT
  05819
800-451-5124
IN VT 802/748-3803

Brochure and Price List: free
Save: up to 40%
Pay: check, MO, MC, V
Sells: sewing machines and accessories
Store: same address; Monday through
  Friday 9–5, Saturday 9–1

If you're shopping for a name-brand sewing machine or serger but don't want to pay top-of-the-line prices, Sewin' in Vermont has the answer. It carries several of the best American and European brands at prices 15% to 40% below list.

Sewin' in Vermont stocks the latest models of Bernina, Elna, New Home,

Riccar, Singer, and Viking sewing machines, and sergers from various manufacturers. These machines have professional features and can be bought here for less than half the suggested retail, but savings average around 35%. Professional irons and presses are also available. The knowledgeable sales staff can help you choose the right equipment for your needs; you can call the 800 number for information and price quotes.

Special Factor: Price quote by phone or letter with SASE.

SINGER SEWING CENTER OF COLLEGE STATION

**1669 TEXAS AVE.
COLLEGE STATION, TX
77840
800-338-5672**

Information: price quote
Save: 40% average
Pay: check, MO, MC, V, AE, Discover
Sells: sewing machines, sergers, and vacuum cleaners
Store: same address; Monday through Friday 10–8, Saturday 10–5; also Pittsburgh Sewing Center, 511 N. Broadway, Pittsburgh, KS; Monday through Friday 9–5, Saturday 9–5

$$ ⌖ ☎ ♣ ▬

Singer Sewing Center, in business since 1976, sells sewing machines, sergers, and vacuum cleaners. You can call or write for a price quote on models by Bernina, Elna, Necchi, Singer, Pfaff, and other well-known manufacturers. All of the machines sold here are new, and layaways are accepted—inquire for information.

Special Factors: Price quote by phone or letter with SASE; layaway plan is available; C.O.D. orders are accepted; minimum parts order is $25.

SUBURBAN SEW 'N SWEEP, INC.

8814 OGDEN AVE.
BROOKFIELD, IL 60513
800-642-4056
708/485-2834

Brochure: free
Save: up to 50%
Pay: check, MO, MC, V, AE, Discover
Sells: sewing machines
Store: same address; Monday through Saturday 9–5

$$

Suburban Sew 'N Sweep, Inc., also known as The Sewing Machine Outlet, has been selling sewing machines since 1975. You can send for the brochure, or call or write for a price quote on sewing and overlock machines by New Home, Singer, White, and other top brands. Discounts vary from model to model, but run up to 50%. Suburban Sew 'N Sweep is an authorized dealer for several major brands.

Special Factors: Price quote by phone or letter with SASE; C.O.D. orders are accepted.

WHOLESALE TAPE AND SUPPLY COMPANY

P.O. BOX 8277
CHATTANOOGA, TN
37411
800-251-7228
IN TN 615/894-9427
FAX: 615/894-7281

Catalog: free
Save: up to 50%
Pay: check, MO, MC, V, AE, Discover
Sells: audio and video tapes, duplication services, machines
Store: 2255 Center St., Suite 102, Chattanooga, TN

$$$

Wholesale Tape has been selling audio/visual supplies and services worldwide since 1977, and publishes a catalog featuring blank audio and video cassettes, reel-to-reel tapes in all configurations, duplicating machines, and accessories. *No grey-market goods are sold here.*

Wholesale Tape manufactures audiotapes for professional duplication. Six types of tape are available, sold in clear, white, and black shells (housing), in standard tape lengths (12 to 122 minutes). Custom tape lengths are available, and quantity discounts are offered. Wholesale Tape also sells professional-quality audio and video recording tape from Agfa, Ampex, Maxell, Memorex, and TDK. (We saw a TDK endless-loop tape with sensing foil listed for $3.81; it costs $9.98 in a New York City "discount" store.) Tape duplication equipment is offered, including models by Pentagon and Telex.

If you need an audiotape or videotape copied but don't have the necessary equipment, you may be interested in Wholesale Tape's duplicating services. You can have just one copy made, but the best prices are on orders of 50 or more copies. Custom labels can be produced, and cassette boxes, albums, shipping envelopes, and storage units are also sold.

Special Factors: Satisfaction is guaranteed; price quote by phone or letter with SASE; quantity discounts are offered; C.O.D. orders are accepted; minimum order is $20; orders are shipped worldwide.

WISCONSIN DISCOUNT STEREO

2417 W. BADGER RD.
MADISON, WI 53713
800-356-9514
IN WI 608/271-6889

Information: price quote
Save: up to 70%
Pay: MO, MC, V
Sells: audio and video components
Store: same address; Monday through Friday 8–8, Saturday 9–5; also six other locations (see text)

WDS, which began doing business by mail in 1977, carries "most major brands of electronics—the largest selection in the United States, possibly the world." There is no catalog, and you must call for prices. *WDS sells no grey-market goods.*

WDS offers audio components, portable stereo, auto audio, and video equipment by ADC, Aiwa, Bose, Clarion, Design Acoustics, Discwasher, Dual, G.E., Hitachi, JBL, Jensen, JVC, Kenwood, Marantz, NEC, Panasonic, Proton, RCA, Sansui, Sharp, Sherwood, Sony, Sylvania, Teac, Toshiba, Zenith, and many other manufacturers. The savings can run as high as 70%, but generally range from 30% to 40%. WDS guarantees "a lower delivered price than any other factory-authorized dealer" on most items.

Special Factors: Price quote by phone preferred; C.O.D. orders are accepted; returns are accepted within 10 days (a restocking fee may be charged).

IRV WOLFSON COMPANY

**3221 W. IRVING PARK RD.
CHICAGO, IL 60618
312/267-7828
FAX: 312/267-7154**

Information: price quote

Save: up to 40%

Pay: check, MO, certified check

Sells: domestic- and foreign-current appliances, TVs, etc.

Store: same address; Monday and Thursday 9–9, Tuesday, Wednesday, Friday, Saturday 9–5, Sunday 12–4

Irv Wolfson Company has been selling 220-volt/50-cycle appliances and electronics since 1952, at prices 7% over cost (up to 40% below retail prices). Domestic-current goods, as well as some name-brand furnishings, built-in appliances, Franke sinks, and KWC faucets are also offered. *No grey-market goods are sold here.*

Irv Wolfson Company offers foreign-current TVs and video equipment, white goods, microwave ovens, air conditioners, kitchen appliances, vacuum cleaners, personal-care appliances, electric blankets, and other goods for the home. The brands include Amana, Caloric, Carrier, Eureka, Friedrich, Gaggenau, G.E., Jenn-Air, JVC, KitchenAid, Magic Chef, Maytag, Modern Maid, Oster, Panasonic, Roper, Sharp, Singer, Speed Queen, Sub-Zero, Tappan, Thermador, Whirlpool, White-Westinghouse, and other manufacturers. "Stepdown" autotransformers, current converters, and plug adapters are also stocked. The customer service department can help you if you're ordering goods to be used abroad.

Special Factor: Price quote by phone or letter with SASE.

SEE ALSO

A Cook's Wares • food processors and other appliances • *HOME: KITCHEN*

Crystal Sonics • auto audio • *AUTO*

Defender Industries, Inc. • marine electronics • *AUTO*

E & B Marine Supply, Inc. • marine electronics • *AUTO*

Fivenson Food Equipment, Inc. • commercial restaurant equipment • *HOME: KITCHEN*

H and M Commercial Services ● commercial ice machines ● *HOME: KITCHEN*

Kaplan Bros. Blue Flame Corp. ● Garland commercial stoves ● *HOME: KITCHEN*

Lamp Warehouse ● name-brand lamps and ceiling fans ● *HOME: DECOR*

MAK, Inc. ● Cuisinart food processors ● *HOME: KITCHEN*

Skipper Marine Electronics, Inc. ● marine electronics ● *AUTO*

Solo Slide Fasteners, Inc. ● professional irons, steamers, industrial sewing and overlock machines, etc. ● *CRAFTS*

Staples, Inc. ● office machines, small refrigerators ● *OFFICE*

Thread Discount Sales ● sergers, overlock machines, and related equipment ● *CRAFTS*

Yachtmail Co. Ltd. ● marine electronics ● *AUTO*

ART, ANTIQUES, AND COLLECTIBLES

Fine art, limited editions, antiques, and collectibles

Since antiques and collectibles can be investments as well as objects of pleasure, it makes sense to buy at dealer prices so you can maximize your profits if you resell. Buying expressly for resale is not wise, however, unless you're an expert. There are too many variables contributing to the real market worth of works of art and collectibles to make the field safe for neophytes and wishful thinkers. For example, an ivory Hall pitcher in perfect condition may cost $30, while the same pitcher in delphinium blue might be $60. The hopeful who seizes upon a $15 ivory pitcher in a junk shop as a "find" may find no dealer willing to purchase the item, or may be offered $15 at most. Even professional repairs and restoration can devalue an otherwise pristine object, especially in high-end collecting. You'll proceed much more happily in assembling a collection if you remember that you can rarely outsmart a dealer and if you buy only what you like and would enjoy keeping.

It's best to know what you want when buying by mail, for you're not likely to get more than a photo of the items available. And remember that one-of-a-kind items are subject to prior sale, so order promptly upon receipt of the mailing and give second and third choices if possible. Purchase from firms that accept returns so you can send the piece back if it's not to your liking.

Getting to know the market is one of the pleasures of "antiquing" and collecting, and there are hundreds of reference books and guides available to give you the necessary grounding. The indefatigable Kovels compile *Kovels' Antiques & Collectibles Price List* on a regular basis. It will give you an idea of the price spread among items of similar type and vintage. It doesn't include much beyond the one-line descriptions, but it can tell you the going rate for thousands of antiques and collectibles in the U.S. market. Whether you're a seasoned connoisseur or a novice, you'll find *The Kovels' Collectors' Source Book* (Crown Publishers, 1983) a great help in finding sources for specific types of antiques and collectibles, locating restoration and repair services, assembling a bookshelf of magazines and reference texts on your area of interest, learning about related clubs and societies, and much more.

Prints and lithographs are very easily forged, which is why you should buy from a legitimate dealer only. For a reference and more information, write to the International Fine Print Dealers Association, 485 Madison Ave., New York, NY 10022, or call 212/759-4469.

Once you're somewhat familiar with your field, you'll find that you can learn volumes by seeing the objects firsthand. Visit flea markets, antique shops, art galleries, and museums as often as possible; attend the viewings held before auctions of "your" collectible. And don't just look—*ask questions.* Dealers are usually proud of both their knowledge and their wares, and by demonstrating an appreciation of the latter you should elicit a good deal of the former. Dealers will often point out special attributes of a piece and draw your attention to critical details you might have overlooked. The people who run "junk" shops that carry everything from old postcards to furniture can sometimes spot new collecting trends—what's "walking out of here"—as well as the has-beens that they "just can't move at all, at any price." Avoid the latter unless you love them or don't care a whit about appreciation.

A collection worthy of investment usually merits the protection of archival quality materials. University Products, Inc., is an excellent source for display binders, albums, boxes, and restoration materials for art works, books, manuscripts, photographs, textiles, posters, and postcards. The firm's archival products catalog includes goods for mounting, display, and storage. See the firm's listing in "General" for more information.

ANTIQUE IMPORTS UNLIMITED

P.O. BOX 2978-WBMC
COVINGTON, LA
70434-2978
504/892-0014

Price List: see text
Save: up to 60%
Pay: check, MO, MC, V
Sells: antiques and collectibles
Store: mail order only

Antique Imports markets a range of antiques and ephemera through several series of price lists. You can get "dealer" prices here—up to 60%

less than those charged for comparable goods in antique shops. Don't miss the jewelry listings—the value of the gemstones alone often exceeds the

Antique Imports' "Antique and Collectible Jewelry" catalog (10 to 12 issues of about 22 pages, $30) features old jewelry, charms, and watches, and usually includes exceptional values. The "Antiques and Collectibles" catalog (3 to 5 issues, $20) offers glassware, china, metalware, coins, stamps, and related miscellany. A recent catalog listed brass house hardware, an Irish branding iron, and a Victorian cigar holder of amber and sterling silver. A single issue of either catalog costs $3. Placing an order entitles you to two free issues of the catalog from which you ordered, and if your orders total $1,000 in one year you will receive your choice of catalogs free of charge.

Special Factors: Price lists include detailed descriptions but no illustrations; all goods are one-of-a-kind items, subject to prior sale; listing second choices is recommended; minimum order is $75 in each category.

GALLERY GRAPHICS, INC.

227 MAIN ST.
P.O. BOX 502
NOEL, MO 64854
417/475-6116

Catalog: $5, refundable
Save: 50% plus
Pay: check or MO
Sells: art prints and stationery
Store: mail order only

Gallery Graphics' most popular lines are its reproduction antique prints, note cards, and Christmas cards, which feature nostalgic themes. Gallery Graphics, formerly known as Decor Prints, was established in 1979.

Copies of sentimental turn-of-the-century lithographs, advertising posters, and magazine illustrations, priced at $2 and $3.25, are featured in "The Antique Classic Collection." Nostalgic themes also appear on Gallery Graphics' line of blank note cards, and the firm also sells memo and tack boards, and flue hole covers. The prints may be ordered in shrink wrapping at an additional charge, and many are available matted and framed. This source is geared to the resale buyer; please note that the minimum order is $100 (on first orders).

Special Factors: Deduct the cost of the catalog from your first order; authorized returns are accepted; minimum first order is $100 ($75 on reorders).

MISCELLANEOUS MAN

Catalog: $3; $5 for two issues
Save: up to 75%
Pay: check, MO, MC, V
Sells: rare and vintage posters and labels
Store: mail order only

P.O. BOX 1776-W91
NEW FREEDOM, PA 17349
717/235-4766
FAX: 717/235-2853

$$$$ ✉ ☎ 🍁 🇺🇸

George Theofiles, ephemerologist extraordinaire, is the moving force behind Miscellaneous Man. He trades in vintage posters, handbills, graphics, labels, brochures, and other memorabilia, all of which are original—no reproductions or reprints are sold. Miscellaneous Man was founded in 1970.

Each black-and-white catalog offers an average of 1,600 to 1,800 items, including theater and movie publicity materials, collections of colorful product labels, broadsides, and posters. The poster categories run from "aviation" to "weaponry," and include such popular themes as World Wars I and II, sports of all sorts, wines and spirits, food advertising, labor, publishing, fashion, Black Americana, the opera, and travel, among others. Collections of unused broom handle labels, antique seed packets, luggage stickers, cigar box labels, and other such detritus have appeared in previous catalogs. Size and condition are noted in the catalog entries, and photos of individual items may be purchased for $2.

Everything is sold here at prices 30% or more below the going rate. In fact, vintage seed packets and fruit and vegetable labels that cost $25 to $50 in metropolitan galleries may be found here for as little as $1 in the yearly sale collections. If you're about to purchase a vintage poster, give Miscellaneous Man a call first. We've found that although the prices are sometimes comparable (especially on scarce or rare posters), Miscellaneous Man routinely charges 30% to 75% less than New York City sources—and the selection is much better.

Special Factors: Price quote by phone or letter with SASE; stock moves quickly—order promptly and list second choices; layaways are accepted; returns are accepted within 3 days; minimum order is $50 with credit cards.

MUSEUM EDITIONS NEW YORK LTD.

12 HARRISON ST., 3RD FLOOR
NEW YORK, NY 10013
212/431-1913

Catalog: $5, refundable
Save: up to 50%
Pay: check, MO, MC, V
Sells: fine contemporary art reprints
Store: same address; Monday through Friday 9–5 (by appointment only)

$$$

Museum Editions, established in 1982, produces a stunning 32-page color catalog of reproductions of the posters used to announce exhibits in museums and art galleries. If your taste runs to modern and contemporary art, you'll have a field day deciding what to choose for your walls.

Modern masterpieces by Klee, Pissarro, O'Keeffe, Rothko, Hopper, Hockney, Hiroshige, Glaser, Katz, and Randy Green are among those shown in a current catalog. There are examples of photography (including Avery's serial shots of James Dean), photorealism, scores of posters of flora and fauna (from Georgia O'Keeffe's paintings of flowers of the Southwest to Monet's "Water Lilies"), and other posters depicting asparagus, Tiffany windows, the seaside at Nice, Mickey Mouse, the Brooklyn Bridge, and scores of varied subjects. Prices average $15 to $25. Custom framing is available; inquire for information.

Special Factors: Catalog is free to corporate buyers (send request on letterhead); cost of catalog is redeemable with retail orders.

ORIGINAL PAPER COLLECTIBLES

700-W CLIPPER GAP RD.
AUBURN, CA 95603

Brochure and Sample Label: free with *long,* self-addressed, stamped envelope
Save: up to 75%
Pay: check or MO
Sells: original, vintage labels
Store: mail order only

$$$

William Wauters began his business in 1970, when fruit crate labels were among the hot collectibles in antique and curio shops nationwide. The fact that Original Paper Collectibles has thrived over the years attests to the enduring appeal of the label designs.

At this writing, Mr. Wauters offers labels originally intended for brooms, cigar boxes, flour sacks, soda pop, canned fruits and vegetables, and produce—apples, pears, lettuce, oranges, asparagus, lemons, and other fruits and vegetables. Old used stock certificates, all of which have illustrations, are also sold.

The collections offer the best per-label prices, and Mr. Wauters tells us that dealers routinely double his prices when they resell. The price list we received described the most popular collection of fruit crate labels that included orange, apple, asparagus, lemon, pear, lettuce, cherry, grape, and carrot varieties—150 for $25. (A vintage poster gallery in New York City charges that much for a *single* label.) Collectors of Black Americana will find labels depicting black characters, and there are even Australian labels.

Sliding discounts are given on orders of $100, $250, $500, and $1,000. If you're searching for a specific label, you may find it among the listings of individual labels, which are grouped by size and type. And if you're looking for something to cover the walls, ask here—decorators are invited to inquire about damaged labels, which can be used as wall treatments!

Special Factors: Satisfaction is guaranteed; price quote by letter with SASE; quantity discounts are available; orders are shipped worldwide.

QUILTS UNLIMITED

P.O. BOX 1479, DEPT. WBM
WILLIAMSBURG, VA
23187
804/253-8700

Catalog and Photographs: $5; $25, year's subscription (see text)

Save: up to 30%

Pay: check, MO, MC, V

Sells: new, old, and antique quilts

Store: Merchants Square, Williamsburg, VA; Monday through Sunday 10–6; 203 E. Washington St., Lewisburg, WV; Monday through Saturday 10–5; Cottage Row at The Homestead Resort, Hot Springs, VA; Monday through Sunday 10–5; and The Greenbrier, White Sulphur Springs, WV; Monday through Saturday 10–5, Sunday 10–3 (April–November only)

     (see text)

Quilts Unlimited, established in 1981 and run by two avid collectors, brings you great buys on vintage quilts through monthly mailings of booklets and color photos.

Previous mailings have shown quilts of every sort, including patchwork, appliqué, stuffed work, tops, crib quilts, and Amish quilts. Many are priced in the $400 to $800 range, up to 30% less than prices charged by dealers for quilts of similar age, size, detail, and condition. The descriptions in the literature include information on material used, number of stitches per inch, whether the work was done by hand or machine, whether signatures or dates are present, estimated age and provenance, presence of any damage or wear, size, and pattern name.

Quilts Unlimited also offers a lovely selection of crib quilts and wall hangings, which are hand-quilted by Appalachian, Amish, and Mennonite women. Patchwork classics are featured: Double Wedding Ring, Bear Paw, Diamond in the Square, and Schoolhouse are a few of the designs. Many of the quilts are available in two sizes (for cribs and hangings), and prices run from $95 to $145 at this writing—extremely reasonable. These would make lovely housewarming or shower gifts. Quilts Unlimited also offers special services, including quilts in larger sizes and custom color combinations.

The regular price for a year's subscription of photograph mailings is $35, but you pay $25 if you mention WBMC when you order.

Special Factors: Stock moves quickly—order promptly; returns are accepted within 5 days (see the catalog for details); orders are shipped worldwide.

RICK'S MOVIE GRAPHICS, INC.

P.O. BOX 23709-WM
GAINESVILLE, FL
32602-3709
904/373-7202

Catalog: $3, refundable
Save: up to 65%
Pay: check, MO, MC, V
Sells: current and vintage movie posters
Store: mail order only

Today's collectibles become tomorrow's investments—sometimes. The possibilities of appreciation no doubt attract some of the people who buy movie posters, but most of us just want mementos of favorite flicks.

Rick's Movie Graphics has been serving both kinds of customers since

1985, and publishes an 80-page, illustrated catalog packed with current releases and "vintage" posters dating back to the 1950s. The listings are coded to indicate whether the posters have been rolled or folded. At an average price of $15, the new releases deliver a lot of visual bang for the buck—and a price that's 10% to 30% below the going rate. (The prices on vintage posters are higher, but other dealers are charging so much more that the savings through Rick's can reach 30% to 65% in this category.)

Among the offerings in the catalog we reviewed were British posters of *Quadrophenia, No Nukes,* and *The Last Temptation of Christ.* We found *Cat People, Body Heat,* and *Blade Runner* among hundreds of titles under the "most requested" banner, and whole pages devoted to Rocky, Indiana Jones, Star Trek, James Bond, Disney, Batman, Friday the 13th, and other series. The catalog shows a fraction of the inventory, and new titles and collections are constantly added to stock. If you don't see the poster you're looking for, write to Rick's and include a a self-addressed, stamped envelope for a reply.

Please note: Only U.S. funds are accepted.

Special Factors: Price quote by phone or letter with SASE; returns are accepted within 5 days for exchange, refund, or credit; orders are shipped worldwide.

COMPANIES OUTSIDE THE U.S.A.

The following firms are experienced in dealing with customers in the U.S. and Canada. We've included them because they offer goods not widely available at a discount in the U.S., because they have a better selection, or because they may offer the same goods at great savings.

Before ordering from a non-U.S. firm, please read through the applicable sections of "The Complete Guide to Buying by Mail" at the back of this book. We recommend paying for your catalog with a camouflaged enclosure of cash. (Sending cash saves the company the bank charge of converting your check to different currency.) We further advise you to pay for your merchandise by credit card whenever possible, so that your transaction will be protected by the part of the Fair Credit Billing Act that allows you to dispute charges for goods not received. See page 545 for a complete discussion of the Act. Please note that only this portion of the Act applies, and the FTC's Mail Order Rule governing delivery time *does not.*

ATLANTIC BRIDGE COLLECTION CORP. LTD.

DEPT. WBM
BALLYBANE
GALWAY, IRELAND
011-353-91-53657
FAX: 011-353-91-53443

Catalog: $2
Save: up to 40%
Pay: check, IMO, MC, V, AE, Access
Sells: porcelain collectibles, tableware, crystal, and handcrafts
Store: same address (call for directions)

$$$

Some of the most popular porcelain figurines and collectibles can be found at Atlantic Bridge Collection, which offers new issues for collectors of Anri, Belleek, Beswick, Coalport, Goebel, Irish Dresden, Lladró, Royal Doulton, Spode, and Wedgwood. Royal Crown Derby paperweights and miniature cottages, Beatrix Potter nursery figures, pewter giftware, collectors' tea pots, Caithness paperweights, and Peter Rabbit nurseryware are often shown in the catalog. Place settings of selected dinnerware patterns are available, and crystal giftware and suites by Galway, Tipperary, and Waterford are offered. We found especially good values on crystal vases and candlesticks. The Irish specialties and handcrafts include Claddagh jewelry, gifts engraved with coats of arms, double-damask linen and Nottingham lace tablecloths, and Aran handknits for men and women. Prices are given in U.S. dollars, and bonuses and special discounts are often available.

Special Factors: Satisfaction is guaranteed; minimum order is $25 with credit cards; orders are shipped worldwide.

THE FRIAR'S HOUSE

BENE'T ST.
CAMBRIDGE CB2 2QN
ENGLAND
011-44-223-60275
FAX: 011-44-223-264110

Catalog: free
Save: 25% average
Pay: check, IMO, MC, V, AE, DC, Access
Sells: porcelain collectibles, tableware, and handcrafts
Store: same address; Monday through Saturday 9–5:30, Sunday (in summer only) 11–4

The Friar's House publishes a 16-page color catalog that shows highlights of its stock: fine china and crystal place settings and gifts, and a wide range of fine British handcrafts. This family-run firm has been in business since 1976.

The Friar's House offers some of the lines most favored by collectors, including Coalport, Lladró, Royal Crown Derby, and Royal Doulton; porcelain figurines, the appealing naturalistic animal statuettes from Albany of England, Border Fine Arts, Heredities, and North Light; enameled boxes and gifts by Crummles; rustic dwellings in miniature from Brambley Hedge, David Winter Cottages, and Lilliput Lane; Swarovski crystal whimsies; and lovely vases and paperweights from Caithness Glass. The Friar's House also offers the Enchantica line of fantasy figures from Holland Studio Craft—wizards, elves, dragons, and goblins.

Fine china and stemware are stocked as well. Lines from Aynsley, Edinburgh, Portmeirion, Royal Brierley, Royal Crown Derby, Royal Doulton, Royal Worcester, Waterford, and Wedgwood are all available. The best in nursery china—Bunnykins and Beatrix Potter goods from several firms—is also offered. The catalog gives prices in British pounds, but ours included a price list in U.S. dollars.

Special Factor: Price quote by phone or letter.

SAXKJAERS

**53 KØBMAGERGADE
1150 COPENHAGEN K
DENMARK
011-45-331-10777
FAX # 011-45-333-27210**

Catalog: $2 (by air), refundable
Save: 40% plus
Pay: check, IMO, MC, V, AE
Sells: collectible porcelain editions and gifts
Store: same address; also Krystalgade 3, 1172, Copenhagen

$$$

Saxkjaers, a family business founded in 1904, is the definitive source for collectors' plates issued by Bing & Grøndahl, Hummel, and Royal Copenhagen. The yearly issues of Christmas plates will stir even the tamest acquisitive instincts. But don't worry; unless you choose to buy the plates from earlier years, the habit is quite affordable. The catalog shows the current Royal Copenhagen Christmas plate (and lists editions as early as 1908) and shows the complementing cup-and-saucer set and Christmas ornament. Bing & Grøndahl plates are available from 1895 to the current year, as are Mother's Day plates from both firms, and china bells, thimbles, and other special issues at savings of at least 40% on the U.S. prices. Although prices indicate that appreciation is possible—the 1895 B&G plate now sells for $4,300—common sense cautions against treating limited editions as investments.

In addition to the plates, the color catalog shows figurines and vases, including many Bing & Grøndahl pieces. The collections of porcelain animals, children depicted in scores of poses, romantic and character figures, and vases decorated with scenes should help to solve many gift dilemmas. The catalog also offers the exquisite Mats Jonasson crystal "portraits," beautifully detailed, realistic images of animals carved and etched by hand into irregular blocks of 32% lead crystal. (A well-known Fifth Avenue crystal firm sells similar pieces for hundreds to thousands of dollars; the Jonasson sculptures cost from $35 to $224 at Saxkjaers, including shipping.) Also shown are Royal Copenhagen figurines, vases, and dinnerware, Bing & Grøndahl dinnerware, Hummel figurines, George Jensen silverware and gifts, Danish dolls and elves, jewelry, and even down comforters. Prices at Saxkjaers include surface postage and insurance against all problems; airmail shipping is available at a surcharge.

The Saxkjaers family runs the entire company. Mr. Saxkjaers tells us that barely a day goes by when a U.S. visitor doesn't drop in, The coffee pot is always on for a customer, so stop by if you find yourself in Copenhagen (downtown, "opposite the old round Tower—impossible to miss"). Saxk-jaers is efficient as well as hospitable—letters and inquiries are answered the day they're received, and all efforts are made to ensure your happiness with your order.

Special Factors: Satisfaction is guaranteed; shipping (surface mail) and insurance are included; orders are shipped worldwide.

SEE ALSO

Beverly Bremer Silver Shop • heirloom and estate silver pieces • HOME: TABLE SETTINGS

Caprilands Herb Farm • collectors' dolls • FARM

Editions • first editions and rare books • BOOKS

The Emerald Collection • figurines and collectibles • HOME: TABLE SETTINGS

Forty-Fives • original 45's from 1950 to the current year • BOOKS

Front Row Photos • photos and photo buttons of rock stars • BOOKS

Guitar Trader • vintage fretted instruments • MUSIC

Mandolin Brothers, Ltd. • vintage fretted instruments • MUSIC

Pages/Booktraders Ltd. • rare and out-of-print books • BOOKS

Plexi-Craft Quality Products Corp. • acrylic display pedestals • HOME: FURNISHINGS

Rainbow Music • vintage guitars and amps • MUSIC

The Renovator's Supply, Inc. • reproduction period hardware, lighting fixtures, etc. • HOME: MAINTENANCE

Rogers & Rosenthal • figurines and collectibles • HOME: TABLE SETTINGS

The Scholar's Bookshelf • remaindered university-press art books • BOOKS

Script City • movie posters, entertainment collectibles • BOOKS

Shannon Duty Free Mail Order • collectible porcelain figurines • HOME: TABLE SETTINGS

Skandinavisk Glas • collectible porcelain and crystal objets d'art • HOME: TABLE SETTINGS

University Products, Inc. • archival-quality collection storage, mounting, and display materials • GENERAL MERCHANDISE

ART MATERIALS

Materials, tools, equipment, and supplies
for the fine and applied arts

Name-brand art materials are seldom discounted more than 10% in retail shops unless they're purchased in quantity. But mail-order firms usually offer savings of twice that, and they also sell "proprietary" products. These may be manufactured by lesser-known firms, and are much less expensive than their branded equivalents—in fact, many working artists buy nothing but. Private-label goods actually may be the products of the same firms that manufacture top brands, but because they're identified as the "house brand," they're usually cheaper.

The firms listed here offer pigments, paper, brushes, canvas, frames, stretchers, pads, studio furniture, vehicles and solvents, silk-screening supplies, carving tools, and many other goods. If you don't know the market and the range of available goods, you'll find the general art-supplies catalog offered by many distributors to be quite helpful. You can obtain a copy for $2 from New York Central Art Supply, listed in this chapter. For detailed information on the properties and uses of almost every medium available today, see *The Artists' Handbook of Materials and Techniques* (Viking Press, 1981). It can usually be found in good bookstores and public libraries, and it's available from Jerry's Artarama (listed in this chapter) at 20% off. The *Handbook* is considered indispensable by many artists, and it can introduce you to old techniques that may broaden your artistic horizons.

In the previous edition of this book, we noted with pleasure that 35 art-materials manufacturers, representing 90% of the industry, were participating in a voluntary program to include hazard warnings on the labels of their products. In the fall of 1988, Congress passed the Art Materials Labeling Act, making mandatory the standards used in the voluntary program. Congress also directed the Consumer Products Safety Commission to create standards for the industry, and banned the use of hazardous materials by children in the sixth grade or younger. This is important legislation, since the list of substances found in widely used materials includes toluene, asbestos, chloroform, xylene, n-hexane, carbolic acid, trichlorethylene, and benzene, to note just a few. Many of us do not use adequate precautions when handling these materials, and it's believed that exposure levels in schools, workshops, and studios often exceed the limits set for industrial workers using the same substances. Some of the hazardous materials are linked to nervous disorders and higher rates of miscarriage and fetal damage, respiratory disease, heart attacks, liver and kidney disease, leukemia, and cancer of the bladder, colon, rectum, kidneys, and brain. But there should be no need to suspend your creative activities if you learn how to protect your health and that of those around you:

- Choose the least toxic and hazardous products available.
- If your work creates dust or fumes, use a quality, OSHA-approved respirator suitable to the task. There are masks to filter organic vapors, ammonia, asbestos, toxic dusts, mists and fumes, and paint spray.
- Remember that protective gloves reduce the absorption of chemicals through the skin, earplugs give you protection against hearing damage from loud machinery, and safety goggles help to prevent blinding accidents.
- A good window-exhaust system is vital to reducing inhaled vapors. You need to have a real airflow when working with fume-producing materials — not just an open window. (One source cites the definition of "adequate ventilation" as *16 complete air changes per hour.*)
- Keep children and animals out of the work place, since chemicals reach higher levels of concentration in their systems.
- Don't eat, drink, or smoke in your work area.
- Keep safety equipment on hand to deal with emergencies: an eyewash station if you're using caustic materials, a first-aid kit, a fire extinguisher if you use combustible materials. (Direct Safety Company, listed in "Tools," sells all of these and a wide range of respirators, gloves, and earplugs.)
- Ask your school board to have the current stock of classroom art products replaced by materials that reflect the new labeling requirements.

For further reading, consult the excellent work by Michael McCann,

Artist Beware: The Hazards and Precautions in Working with Art and Craft Materials (Watson-Guptill Publications, 1979). *Health Hazards Manual for Artists* (Nick Lyons Books, 1985), a smaller book by the Mr. McCann, includes specifics on materials commonly used by children. Both are sold by Ceramic Supply of New York & New Jersey (listed in this chapter). Mr. McCann is a chemist and industrial hygienist who founded the Center for Safety in the Arts (CSA), which deals with current art-safety issues in *Art Hazards News,* a four-page newsletter published ten times a year. For current subscription rates and more information, write to Center for Safety in the Arts at 5 Beekman St., Suite 1030, New York, NY 10038, or call 212/227-6220.

For information on firms selling related products, see "Crafts and Hobbies" and "General," and don't overlook the listings in "Surplus."

AMERICAN FRAME CORPORATION

1340 TOMAHAWK DR.
MAUMEE, OH 43537
800-537-0944
FAX: 419/893-3553

Catalog: free
Save: up to 50%
Pay: check, MO, MC, V, AE, Optima
Sells: sectional frames, mat board, acrylic picture glass, etc.
Store: same address; Monday through Friday 9–5

$$$ ✉   ☎

American Frame, in business since 1973, offers *wood* sectional frames—new to us, and a great idea—as well as metal sectional frames in a huge range of colors. Prices are substantially lower than those charged by several New York City art-supply stores we checked, averaging 35% to 50% less.

The basswood, mahogany, oak, and cherry frame sections are finished in a variety of stains, some are gilded and further embellished, and one style features a fabric inset that simulates the appearance of a linen liner next to the picture. The profile and dimensions of the sections are shown in detail, and each wood frame (two pairs of sections) is sent with corner insets for assembling each section, spring clips to hold the mounted art work securely in place, and wall protectors, which keep the frame from lying directly against the wall. (Assembly requires attaching one end of the spring clips to the frame with screws, which are provided, and gluing the joints. Clamping is not necessary.)

The metal frames are offered in a choice of six profiles, to accommodate ordinary flat work, standard canvases, and extra-deep canvases. There are ten colors in the metallics line and 18 shades in the enameled colors, including pewter, satin black, pale yellow, wine, salmon, jade, and taupe, to name a few. The metal frames also come with complete assembly hardware.

Crescent board—acid-free mat, mounting, and foam core—is sold in groups of ten or more sheets, depending on the item. The mat board is offered in over 100 colors in the 32" by 40" size, and no cutting is done. Acid-free acrylic picture "glass" is cut to order in dimensions up to 22" by 28".

Special Factor: Shipping is included on orders over $500.

ART SUPPLY WAREHOUSE, INC.

360 MAIN AVE.
NORWALK, CT 06851
800-243-5038
IN CT 203/846-2279

Catalog: free
Save: up to 60%
Pay: check, MO, MC, V
Sells: art supplies
Store: same address; Monday through Saturday 9:30–5:30; also 95 Chestnut St., Providence, RI

$$$ ✉   ☎   🍁   (see text)   🇺🇸

The fine arts are well-supplied here, with a 76-page catalog of name-brand materials and equipment at up to 60% below list prices. Art Supply Warehouse, founded in 1979, even pays shipping on orders sent within the continental U.S.

The stock includes oil and acrylic paints, pigments, and fixatives and solvents by Bellini, Blockx, Bocour, Deka, Grumbacher, Holbein, Liquitex, Paasche, Pelikan, Rembrandt, Shiva, Robert Simmons, Weber, Winsor & Newton, and other firms. There are oil pastels, chalks, colored pencils, markers, inks, pens, brushes, palette knives, and other tools. You'll find paper and board by Bainbridge, D'Arches, Strathmore, Westport, Whatman, Winsor & Newton, and other firms, for watercolors, illustrating, pen and ink work, drawing, calligraphy, and general use. Stretched and roll canvas by Berge, V.A. Claessens, and Fredrix is available, as well as stretchers, easels, art boxes, and related studio gear. Equipment and materials for airbrushing, drafting, sumi-e, silkscreening, textile arts, and other creative pursuits are also shown, as well as the Northlight Books series of manuals.

Canadian readers, please note: Payment must be made in U.S. dollars.

Special Factors: Satisfaction is guaranteed; returns are accepted; quantity discounts are available; shipping is included on orders sent within the continental U.S.

DICK BLICK CO.

P.O. BOX 1267-WM
GALESBURG, IL 61401
309/343-6181

Catalog: $3
Save: up to 30%
Pay: check, MO, MC, V
Sells: name-brand and proprietary art supplies
Store: Plainville, CT; Roswell, GA; Decatur, Galesburg, Moline, Peoria, Springfield, and Wheaton, IL; Iowa City, IA; Dearborn, MI; Emmaus and Wilkesbarre, PA; and Henderson, NV

Dick Blick, established in 1911, lists over 20,000 items in its 464-page compendium of art supplies and equipment, which is geared to schools but of interest to all. Store locations are listed in the catalog.

Blick has everything in general art and craft supplies: Liquitex paints, Shiva pigments, Crayola crayons and finger paints, drawing tables and other art furniture, paint brushes, Alfac transfer letters, kraft paper, canvas, scissors, and adhesives. There is a complete selection of silk-screening materials, display lighting, printmaking equipment, wood-carving tools, molding materials, kilns, glazes, copper enamels, decoupage supplies, lapidary equipment, leather-working kits, dyes, macrame materials, Leclerc and other looms, blackboards, and much more. The catalog has over 20 pages of films, slides, videotapes, manuals, and books on arts and crafts. The quality house-label goods offer real savings, and the selection is unbeatable.

Special Factors: Price quote by phone or letter with SASE on quantity orders; quantity discounts are available; minimum order is $10 with credit cards.

CERAMIC SUPPLY OF NEW YORK & NEW JERSEY, INC.

**534 LA GUARDIA PL.
NEW YORK, NY 10012
212/475-7236
OR
10 DELL GLEN AVE.
LODI, NJ 07644
201/340-3005**

Catalog: $4
Save: up to 40%
Pay: check, MO, MC, V
Sells: sculpture, pottery, glazing, and crafts supplies
Store: same addresses; Monday through Friday 9–5, Saturday 10–5, both locations

$$

This firm serves parts of both of its name states with free delivery on orders of $100 or more, by UPS and common carrier. If you live in California, you may be better off finding another source for clay, but there are good values on glazes, brushes, and any number of lightweight supplies that can be shipped worldwide at nominal expense.

Ceramic Supply stocks gas and electric kilns, raku and fiber kilns, glazes, resists, mediums, brushes, airbrushing tools, slip-casting equipment, potters' wheels, armatures, grinders, and other ceramic and sculpting equipment and supplies. The catalog also lists music box movements, clock parts, lamp parts, and studio furniture. Don't overlook the reference section, which includes a number of books on art-related hazards.

Special Factors: Returns are accepted within 10 days (a restocking fee may be charged); minimum order is $35; orders are shipped worldwide.

CO-OP ARTISTS' MATERIALS

**P.O. BOX 53097, DEPT.
H.R.
ATLANTA, GA 30355**

Catalog: $2, refundable
Save: 30% average
Pay: check, MO, MC, V, AE
Sells: fine-arts materials
Store: mail order only

$$$

Co-Op Artists' Materials publishes a 144-page catalog with a comprehensive selection of products for fine and graphic arts. The prices average 30% below list or full retail, and the firm is committed to customer satisfaction.

Tools, materials, and equipment for painting, drafting, airbrush work, the graphic arts, and design are sold here. The brands represented include Badger, D'Arches, Fabriano, Grumbacher, Koh-I-Noor, Langnickel, Letraset, Liquitex, Mont Blanc, Neolt, Paasche, Pentel, Raphaël, Strathmore, and Winsor & Newton. Sales catalogs are published periodically that offer even greater savings than the annual catalog.

Special Factors: Satisfaction is guaranteed; price quote by phone or letter with SASE; authorized returns are accepted within 30 days for exchange, refund, or credit; minimum order is $25 on C.O.D. and credit card orders; C.O.D. orders are accepted.

CROWN ART PRODUCTS CO., INC.

**90 DAYTON AVE.
PASSAIC, NJ 07055
201/777-6010**

Catalog: free
Save: up to 50%
Pay: check, MO, MC, V, AE
Sells: sectional frames and crafts supplies
Store: same address; Monday through Friday 9–4:30, Saturday 11:30–6

Crown Art, founded in 1974, is well-known as a source for silk-screening supplies and equipment; its owner is a proficient silk-screen artist who has developed several unique products for the craft. Silk-screening workshops and lessons are also offered, to novices and professionals.

Crown is known best for its lines of silk-screening supplies, including screens, tools, and inks of all types: Crown Aqua water-based, Crown Opaque, Crown Puff (to create raised designs), metallic, and oil and water-based poster inks, among others. Ready-to-print customized silk screens, screen printing stretcher strips, and a portable screen-printing exposure unit are available. Crown Art also sells a number of items of interest to craftspersons generally: paints and airbrush inks for fabrics, including an "air cure, no heat" fabric dye; needlework stretcher strips; glass stains and liquid leading; "puzzle preserve" for protecting jigsaw puzzles; "fantastic fabric mount" adhesive, a tacky mounting surface that does not affect the fabric; Thick Gloss, a 3-D raised shiny fabric paint in a squeeze bottle; and Glitter Gloss, a glittery version of Thick Gloss.

The catalog includes a guide to the characteristics and appropriate applications of the inks and paints. If you're an art teacher, printer, or dealer, contact Crown for information on its special discount program.

Special Factor: Price quote by phone or letter with SASE on special sizes and volume orders.

FLAX ARTIST'S MATERIALS

1699 MARKET ST., DEPT.
   1FRW
P.O. BOX 7216
SAN FRANCISCO, CA
   94120
415/468-7530
FAX: 415/468-1940

Catalog: $5 (see text)
Save: up to 30%
Pay: check, MO, MC, V, AE
Sells: art and graphic design materials
Store: same address; Monday through Friday 9–6:30, Saturday 10–6; also 510 East El Camino Real, Sunnyvale, CA; Monday through Saturday 10–6

First things first: Flax Artist's Materials is *not* Sam Flax (well known on the East Coast), but was founded by members of the same family in 1939. Though both firms sells supplies and equipment for the fine arts, drafting, and graphic design, Flax Artist's Materials discounts *everything* in its two California stores.

Flax's big catalog ($5) shows goods at list prices, but the free quarterly sales catalogs offer savings of up to 30%. Art professionals should find the $5 investment a worthy expense, since there are all sorts of uncommon tools and supplies listed in the big book, in addition to the usual roundup of paper, canvas, pigments, vehicles, brushes, and the like. The firm's strength is in graphic design and commercial art products, and this is where you'll find the newest colors from Pantone, realistic fake edibles for food shots, airbrushing supplies and equipment, the sleekest studio furniture and storage units, layout tools and supplies, markers in every possible color, professional templates, portfolios and presentation binders, sumi supplies, brushes for decorative paint finishes (graining, mottling, stippling, etc.), frames, and even a small selection of conservation supplies. Choice goods show up in the sale catalogs, though not everything is sold at a discount.

Please note: There is a $25 minimum on orders from the big catalog only.

Special Factors: Price quote by phone or letter with SASE; minimum order is $25 from the big catalog.

JERRY'S ARTARAMA, INC.

**P.O. BOX 1105-WMC
NEW HYDE PARK, NY
11040
516/328-6633**

Catalog: $2.50
Save: up to 50%
Pay: check, MO, MC, V, Discover
Sells: name-brand and generic art supplies
Store: 248-12 Union Tpk., Bellerose, NY;
Monday through Saturday 9:30–6,
Sunday 11–5

$$$ ✉   ☎   🍁   🇺🇸

Jerry's Artarama publishes a 102-page compendium of materials, tools, and equipment for commercial and fine arts that is inspiration itself—imported goods seldom discounted elsewhere are featured at real savings. The company was established in 1968, and it stocks over 10,000 different items.

The catalog offers pigments, brushes, vehicles and solvents, studio furniture, lighting, visual equipment, canvas and framing supplies, papers, film products, books, videotapes, and other products, with an extensive section of oil, watercolor, and acrylic painting supplies. There are supplies for drawing, graphic arts, drafting, calligraphy, printmaking, sumi-e, air-brushing, and professional framing. Bill Alexander, Alvin, Blockx, Conte, Deka, D'Arches, Fabriano, Fredrix, Grumbacher, Holbein, Isabey, Iwata, Koh-I-Noor, Langnickel, Neolt, Bob Ross, Robert Simmons, Stabilo, Stacor, Strathmore, Winsor & Newton, X-Acto, and many other brands are available.

Special Factors: Satisfaction is unconditionally guaranteed; price quote by letter with SASE; color charts and product specifications are available on request; quantity discounts are available; minimum order is $20, $50 with phone orders.

NEW YORK CENTRAL ART SUPPLY CO.

**62 THIRD AVE.
NEW YORK, NY 10003
800-950-6111
212/477-0400
FAX: 212/475-2513**

Catalog: $3 (see text)
Save: up to 40%
Pay: check, MO, MC, V, AE, DC, Discover
Sells: art supplies and equipment
Store: same address; Monday through
Saturday 8:30–6:15; also 102 Third Ave.,
New York, NY; Monday through
Saturday 9:30–6:15

New York Central has been supplying metropolitan artists since 1905, and is well-known for its stock of fine papers. The store at 102 Third Avenue specializes in studio furniture and custom framing. Four catalogs are available: the "General" catalog ($3), listing over 10,000 items for the fine and applied arts; the 96-page "Fine Art" catalog (free) of pigments, mediums, brushes, and canvas; "Fine Papers" ($2), which describes the firm's selection of over 2,000 papers and related goods; and "Printmaking and Drawing" ($2), which includes supplies and materials for silkscreening, batik, drawing, textile painting, calligraphy, and other crafts.

The 220-page general catalog describes itself as "a complete resource of materials for artists, designers, architects, draftsmen, engineers, graphic arts, students, teachers, sculptors, hobbyists and photographers." You can order mat board, paper and pads, canvas, stretchers, graphic arts tools and design aids, paints and mediums, markers, brushes, easels, airbrush equipment, frames, and books, among other goods. The brands are among the best and most popular: Alvin (drafting furniture), Bainbridge, Berol, Chartpak, Conte, D'Arches, Deka, Fredrix, Grumbacher, Hyplar, Keuffel & Esser, Koh-I-Noor, Letraset, Luxo, Mars-Staedtler, Osmiroid, Pantone, Stabilo, Strathmore, and Winsor & Newton, among others. The general catalog includes a number of color charts that show the available range for several pens and markers, making it a good reference tool.

Special Factors: Price quote by phone or letter with SASE; specify the catalog desired; institutional accounts are available; minimum order is $25; orders are shipped worldwide.

PEARL PAINT CO.

**308 CANAL ST.
NEW YORK, NY 10013
800-221-6845
INQUIRIES AND NY
    ORDERS 212/431-7932**

Catalog: free

Save: up to 70%

Pay: MO, certified check, MC, V

Sells: name-brand and proprietary art supplies

Store: same address and 42 Lispenard St., New York, NY (architectural furniture showroom); Monday to Saturday 9–5:30, Thursday 9–7, Sunday (except July and August) 11–4:45, both locations; also Tampa, North Miami, Miami, and Ft. Lauderdale, FL; Atlanta, GA; Cherry Hill, Woodbridge, and Paramus, NJ; East Meadow, NY; and Alexandria, VA

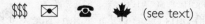 $$$ ✉ ☎ 🍁 (see text)

Pearl Paint is known throughout New York City as an excellent source for art and craft supplies at a discount. The firm, established in 1933, has stores in four other states as well (locations are listed in the catalog). Since the 60-page catalog represents just 2% of available stock, inquiries are invited on goods that are not listed.

Pearl offers fine-arts materials, tools, equipment, and materials for every possible craft: pigments, brushes, vehicles and solvents, stretchers, papers of all kinds, canvas, manuals, studio furniture, and much more. The brands stocked include Alvin, Aquatec, Bainbridge, Bellini, Deka, Fabriano, Grumbacher, Holbein, Iwata, Lascaux, Letraset, Liquitex, Paasche, Pantone, Pelikan, Pentel, Sculpture House, Sennelier, Robert Simmons, Staedtler, and Winsor & Newton, to name a few. Pearl also stocks fine writing instruments, house paint, tints, and finishes, including gilding and "faux" finishing supplies.

Canadian readers, please note: Orders are shipped by UPS only.

Special Factors: Quantity discounts are available; specials are run on selected items; minimum order is $50.

DANIEL SMITH

**4130 FIRST AVE. SOUTH
SEATTLE, WA 98134
800-426-6740 (U.S. AND
 CANADA)
206/223-9599**

Catalog: $5 (see text)
Save: 25% to 30% average
Pay: check, MO, MC, V
Sells: fine-arts supplies and equipment
Store: same address; Monday through
 Saturday 9–6, Sunday 12–5

What a pleasure it is to thumb through the Daniel Smith "A Catalog of Artists' Materials"—a catalog by artists, for artists. One edition we reviewed began with a handsomely illustrated discourse on cobalt blue, and included book reviews, a valuable chart comparing properties of scores of types of paper, and explanatory notes on related topics. Daniel Smith was recommended to us by an artist, who pointed out that the discounts (25% to 30% on average) were not rock bottom, but that she believed you could not find better service.

The 200-plus-page color Reference Catalog presents one of the most extensive paper collections we've seen, including paper from Arches, Canson, Fabriano, Magnani, Pentalic, Rising, Strathmore, Waterford, and other manufacturers, for watercolors, printmaking, drawing, etching, bookmaking, and other applications. There are specialty papers we've not seen in other catalogs, including banana paper from the Philippines, Mexican bark paper, genuine papyrus, and Japanese "fantasy" paper embedded with ginkgo leaves and butterfly wings. Catalogs with selected items are issued six times a year.

Watercolor painters should see the Daniel Smith Metallic Watercolors, as well as dry and moist colors from Grumbacher, Holbein, Maimeri, Schmincke, Sennelier, and Winsor & Newton. Daniel Smith sells acrylic, oil, gouache, tempera, and casein paints by several of these firms, as well as its own oil paints. A full line of sumi materials and tools is available; there are brushes by Daniel Smith and Grumbacher, Isabey, Robert Simmons, Strathmore, and Winsor & Newton for all painting media. Canvas, Nielsen frames, airbrush equipment, fabric paints and solvents, pastels, colored pencils, calligraphy pens, printmaking and etching materials, and other tools and supplies are also stocked. You'll find a fine collection of studio furniture, portfolios, easels, and reference books as well.

Canadian readers, please note: Only U.S. funds are accepted.

Special Factors: Satisfaction is guaranteed; authorized returns are accepted for exchange, refund, or credit; minimum order of paper is $25.

STU-ART SUPPLIES, INC.

2045 GRAND AVE., DEPT. WBM
BALDWIN, NY 11510-2999
516/546-5151

Catalog and Samples: free
Save: up to 50%
Pay: check, MO, MC, V
Sells: name-brand sectional frames and supplies
Store: same address; Monday through Saturday 9–5

This framing source nonpareil provides everything you'll need to do a professional job. Stu-Art has supplied galleries and institutions since 1970, and it offers the best materials, a wide range of sizes, and savings of up to 50% on list prices.

Stu-Art features Nielsen metal frames in nine profiles for flat-stretched canvas and dimensional art (deep) mounting in a stunning array of metallic finishes, soft pastels, and deep decorator colors. Single and double mats are available in rectangles and ovals, and all mats are acid-free. The catalog includes exact specifications of the frames, and samples of the mats. If you see this catalog before going to the framing shop, you may decide you can do the job yourself.

Stu-Art also sells nonglare and clear plastic (which can be used in place of picture glass), unfinished ash and tenite sectional frames, and shrink film and dispensers.

Special Factors: Shipping is included on UPS-delivered orders over $300 net; authorized returns are accepted (a restocking fee may be charged); minimum orders is $15 on sectional frames, $25 on other goods.

UTRECHT ART AND DRAFTING SUPPLY

33 35TH ST.
BROOKLYN, NY 11232
718/768-2525

Catalog: free
Save: up to 50%
Pay: check, MO, MC, V
Sells: name-brand and proprietary art supplies
Store: 111 Fourth Ave, New York, NY; Monday through Saturday 9:30–6; also 1250 "I" St., N.W., Washington, DC; 332 S. Michigan Ave., Chicago, IL; 333 Massachusetts Ave., Boston, MA; and Utrecht at P.C.A., Spruce St. off S. Broad, Philadelphia, PA

$$$ ✉ ☎ 🍁

Utrecht has been selling professional art, sculpture, and printmaking supplies and equipment since 1949, and manufactures some of the best-priced oil and acrylic paints on the market.

This firm offers canvas, stretchers, frames, pads, paper, brushes, tools of all kinds, books, easels, tables, pigments, palettes, and much more. In addition to Utrecht's own line, materials by Chartpak, Eberhard Faber, Grumbacher, Niji, Pentel, Strathmore, and other manufacturers are featured in the catalog, which also includes product specifications and useful information.

Special Factors: Additional quantity discounts of 5% to 20% are available on selected Utrecht goods; minimum order is $40.

SEE ALSO

A to Z Luggage Co., Inc. • artists' portfolios • *LEATHER*
Craftsman Wood Service Co. • art and craft materials • *CRAFTS*
Dharma Trading Co. • tools and materials for fabric painting and dyeing • *CRAFTS*
Great Northern Weaving • rug-weaving supplies • *CRAFTS*
Innovation Luggage • artists' portfolios • *LEATHER*
Jerryco, Inc. • various surplus tools and materials for art and craft projects • *SURPLUS*

The Potters Shop Inc. • books on pottery and ceramics • *BOOKS*
Suncoast Discount Arts & Crafts • artists' canvas, brushes, paints, etc.
   • *CRAFTS*
Thai Silks • silk fabrics suitable for fabric painting • *CRAFTS*
Utex Trading Enterprises • silk fabrics suitable for fabric painting •
   CRAFTS

AUTO, MARINE, AND AVIATION EQUIPMENT

Parts, supplies, maintenance products, and services

The firms listed in this chapter sell virtually anything you may need for your auto, motorcycle, RV, truck, or van (with a few exceptions), including mufflers, shocks, tires, batteries, and much more. Some also stock products for vintage cars, and one offers products for the "general pilot." Look here for one of the best values around on parts: salvaged goods. Expect savings of up to 70% (compared to the price of new parts), and note the guarantees of satisfaction offered by most of these firms.

You can also buy cars, trucks, and vans through American Auto Brokers and Nationwide Auto Brokers, which are listed here. Here are some good sources of information to assist you in making the best selection:

- *The Car Book*, by Jack Gillis (Harper & Row), is an annual guide that rates current domestic and imported models on their performance in crash tests, fuel economy, preventive maintenance costs, repair costs, and insurance rates. The edition we reviewed included vital information on evaluating warranties, service contracts, insurance, tires, children's car seats, and used cars. The comprehensive, easy-to-understand "Complaint" chapter is invaluable, as is the "Check-list" at the back of the book, a workbook section that helps you ask the right questions. You can purchase the current edition from The Center for Auto Safety, 2001 S St., N.W., Suite 410, Washington, DC 20009. Please send a long, self-addressed, stamped envelope for the publications list and ordering information.
- *Consumer Reports* publishes reliable vehicle ratings yearly, and offers the Consumer Reports Auto Price Service to help you get the best buy on the model you choose. The Auto Price Service provides

a computer printout that shows the list price and dealer's cost for the model you specify, and the same data for each factory-installed option. If the CR Auto Test Division recommends any optional equipment for that particular model, these options are also listed. And the Auto Price Service provides guidelines on negotiating the lowest possible price. At this writing, one report costs $11; two are $20; three, $27; and each additional report thereafter, $7. See the current *Consumer Reports* for information, or write to Consumer Reports Auto Price Service, Box 8005, Novi, MI 48050.

- The Better Business Bureau publishes "Tips on Buying a New Car" and "Tips on Tires." Send a self-addressed, stamped envelope to the Council of Better Business Bureaus, Inc., 1515 Wilson Blvd., Arlington, VA 22209, Attn.: Publications Dept., and request the list of available brochures and ordering information.

- *How to Buy a Car: The Essential Guide for Buying a New or Used Car* (St. Martin's Press, 1986) details the process from a car salesman's point of view. Author James R. Ross lays bare the strategies for negotiating the best deal, evaluating financing, getting service, and surviving.

Service and survival are the reasons many people join auto clubs, but most of them provide far more than emergency towing. The best-known club, the American Automobile Association (AAA), boasts nearly 30 million members among its affiliates, and offers a wide range of incentives to join. The AAA of New York, for example, provides travel-planning services, lodging and car rental discounts, no-fee American Express Travelers Cheques, a variety of services related to travel abroad, personal accident insurance, assistance in solving license problems, and other benefits. Services may vary from affiliate to affiliate; to find the AAA club nearest you, call 800-336-4357. Other clubs worth contacting for rates and services are Amoco Motor Club (800-782-7887), and Exxon Travel Club (713/680-5723).

Marine suppliers are also listed in this chapter. If you've spent anywhere from a few hundred to tens of thousands of dollars on a canoe, sailboat, or yacht, you'll want to minimize the upkeep expenses. You can save 30% *routinely* on the cost of maintenance products and equipment by buying from these suppliers, who sell every type of coating, tool, and device to keep your vessel afloat. Exhaustive selections of electronics, hardware, instruments, and other goods are offered, as well as galley accoutrements and foul-weather clothing. Even landlubbers should take a look at these catalogs for the well-designed slickers and oiled sweaters—and the handsome teak bath and kitchen fixtures designed for yacht installations are equally useful on terra firma.

And for private pilots who'd like to save on some of the gear and electronics they need while flying high, we've included an aviation discounter, Marv Golden. Like the marine suppliers, this firm also sells goods of interest to nonspecialists.

AMERICAN AUTOMOBILE BROKERS, INC.

24001 SOUTHFIELD RD., SUITE 110
SOUTHFIELD, MI 48075
313/569-5900
FAX: 313/569-2022

Information: price quote
Save: see text
Pay: check or MO (see text)
Sells: cars, trucks, vans, and jeeps
Store: mail order only

$$$ ✉ ☎

Two of the major unpleasantries in buying a car are paying all that money and knowing that you shelled out more than you had to. One way to avoid the latter is to make sure you get a quote from American Automobile Brokers.

This brokerage has been selling cars, trucks, and vans since 1972. The domestic manufacturers represented include General Motors, Ford/Lincoln-Mercury, and Chrysler Corp. (AMC). The foreign makes run from Alfa Romeo to Toyota, and include BMW, Honda, Isuzu, Mercedes, Mitsubishi, Porsche, Saab, and more. (AAB does not sell Hyundai, Peugeot, or Yugo.) AAB's procedure is simple: You can call or write with complete details about the vehicle and options desired, or send a self-addressed, stamped envelope for the company's price-quote form. You get *one free quote;* additional quotes cost $3 each. You must send a self-addressed, stamped envelope both when requesting the form and when sending it back for the quote.

How much can you save? It depends on the prices in your area. Remember that AAB's price includes dealer prep and delivery from the factory to a dealership near you by train or truck (for domestic vehicles). Shop your local dealers, then get a quote from AAB.

Special Factors: Price quote by phone, letter, or American Automobile Brokers form with SASE; checks and money orders are accepted for deposit only, with balance payable by certified check, cashier's check, or wire transfer.

BELLE TIRE DISTRIBUTORS, INC.

PERFORMANCE DIV.
3500 ENTERPRISE DR.
ALLEN PARK, MI 48101
313/271-9400

Catalog: free
Save: up to 35%
Pay: check or MO
Sells: radial tires
Store: same address; also Detroit, Farmington, Madison Heights, Plymouth, Port Huron, Roseville, Sterling Heights, Taylor, Troy, West Bloomfield, and Woodhaven, MI; Monday and Thursday 8–8, Tuesday, Wednesday, and Friday 8–6, Saturday 8–3

$$

If you're in the market for tires, Belle can save you up to 35% on list prices. Belle stocks radial tires by Bridgestone, Firestone, B.F. Goodrich, Goodyear, Kelly Springfield, Michelin, Pirelli, Uniroyal, and Yokohama. Orders are shipped promptly, and the surcharge is $5 to $20 per tire, depending on the destination.

Special Factors: Price quote by phone or letter with SASE; only new tires are sold, no retreads; orders are shipped worldwide.

CAPITAL CYCLE CORPORATION

P.O. BOX 528
STERLING, VA 22170
704/444-2500
FAX: 704/444-9546

Catalog: free
Save: up to 50%
Pay: check, MO, MC, V, AE
Sells: BMW motorcycle parts and accessories
Store: 1508 Moran Rd., Sterling, VA; Monday through Friday 8:30–6, Saturday 9–5

$$$

Capital Cycle is the nation's definitive source for BMW motorcycle spare parts—over 8,000 genuine, original parts are available, at up to 50% less than dealer prices. Capital Cycle was established 1972.

Capital offers genuine BMW motorcycle parts manufactured from 1955 through the current year, and a fraction of the enormous inventory is listed in the well-organized, 48-page catalog. You'll find engine parts and electronics, carburetors, fuel tanks, mufflers, pipes, clutches, gears, steering bearings, shocks, springs, handlebars, mirrors, brakes, tires, rims, forks, fenders, fairings, locks and keys, paint, seats, switches and relays, tachometers, voltmeters, lights, tools, and much more. Parts books and factory repair manuals for BMW cycles are offered, and a selection of BMW car parts is stocked as well. Capital Cycle knows its customers as well as its stock: Only a catalog for BMW owners would close with listings of goose-down quilts (at excellent prices) and a rental villa in Jamaica.

Canadian readers, please note: Only U.S. funds are accepted.

Special Factors: Price quote by phone or letter with SASE; quantity discounts are available; UPS ground shipping is included; repair services are available by mail; authorized returns are accepted within 30 days (a 15% restocking fee may be charged); minimum order is $20.

CAR/PUTER INTERNATIONAL CORP.

**499 SHERIDAN ST., SUITE 400
DANIA, FL 33004
800-722-4440
IN FL 305-921-2400**

Brochure: free
Save: see text
Pay: check, MO, MC, V, AE, DC
Sells: dealer referrals
Store: mail order only

$$$

To get the best deal on a new car, you'll have to know the dealers' cost, and then you'll have to find the lowest dealer markup on it. Car/Puter can do both—for most cars, vans, and pickups (including some imports).

Car/Puter, in business since 1964, brings in prices at 5% above cost, routinely saving customers $1,000 or more. For $20 and a nominal handling fee, the firm will send you a computer printout for the make, model, and body type of the specified vehicle that lists the dealers' costs, including those for factory-installed options. When available, the printout lists the name of the recommended dealer in your area; otherwise, in most instances, you can contact the firm's Referral Division for more information. The firm's brochure answers commonly asked questions, and provides the "Pricing Request Form" on which you can order the printout.

Special Factor: "Lowest prices" are guaranteed (see the brochure for details).

CENTRAL MICHIGAN TRACTOR & PARTS

**2713 N. U.S. HWY. 2
ST. JOHNS, MI 48879
517/224-6802**

Information: price quote
Save: up to 50%
Pay: check, MO, MC, V
Sells: used and salvaged tractor parts
Store: mail order only

$$$ ✉ 🍁

This firm, also known as Tractor Salvage, can save you up to 50% on parts for tractors and combines. It stocks used, reconditioned, and rebuilt parts, all of which are backed by a 30-day guarantee.

Central stocks everything from starters to cylinder blocks for machines made by almost every major manufacturer. Some of the goods are reconditioned, some are rebuilt; a rebuilt part is overhauled completely and you can expect it to function as well and for as long as a new one. Central maintains want lists for parts not in stock. Call between 8 and 5:30, Monday through Friday, or 8 and 4:30 on Saturdays.

Special Factor: Price quote by phone or letter.

CHERRY AUTO PARTS

**5650 N. DETROIT AVE.
TOLEDO, OH 43612
800-537-8677
IN OH 800-472-8639
419/476-7222
FAX: 419/470-6338**

Brochure: free
Save: up to 70%
Pay: MO, MC, V
Sells: used and rebuilt foreign-car parts
Store: same address; Monday through Friday 8:30–5, Saturday 8:30–12; also 17770 Telegraph Rd., Romulus, MI (Detroit area); Monday through Friday 8:30–5, Saturday 9–12

 $$$ ✉ ☎ 🍁

Why pay top dollar for new car parts if you can get perfectly good ones, used, for up to 70% less? Cherry Auto Parts, "The Midwest's Leading Foreign Car Dismantler," can supply you with used and rebuilt foreign-car components at up to 70% less than the cost of new parts. Cherry Auto has been in business since 1947.

Cherry stocks rebuilt cylinder heads, engines, starters, alternators, calipers, drive axles, and other vital parts. If you drive an Alfa Romeo, Audi, Austin, BMW, Chrysler Imports car (Arrow, Challenger, Champ, Colt, Conquest, Sapporo), Datsun (Nissan), Fiat, Ford Imports car (Courier, Fiesta), Honda, Isuzu, Jaguar, Lancia, Luv, Mazda, Mercedes, Merkur, MG, Mitsubishi, Opel, Peugeot, Porsche, Renault, Rover, Saab, Spectrum, Sprint, Subaru, Toyota, Triumph, Volkswagen, Volvo, etc., you may save up to 70% on your parts bills by getting them here. Cherry can access two nationwide computerized parts-locating networks to trace hard-to-find parts promptly.

Special Factors: Price quote by phone (preferred) or letter with SASE; "all parts are guaranteed in stock at the time of quotation, guaranteed to be the correct part, and in good condition as described"; minimum order is $15.

CLARK'S CORVAIR PARTS, INC.

RTE. 2
SHELBURNE FALLS, MA
  01370
413/625-9776

Catalog: $4
Save: up to 40%
Pay: check, MO, MC, V
Sells: Corvair parts
Store: mail order only

$$$

Clark's lists its inventory of over 4,500 Corvair parts in an indexed, 400-page catalog that's published every even-numbered year. (Small supplements are also released to update the big book.) Many parts offered here are available nowhere else, and savings run up to 40%. This indispensable source for the Corvair owner has been in business since 1973.

Clark's stocks original and replacement General Motors parts, reproductions, and goods by Champion, Chevrolet, Clevite, Delco, Gabriel, Gates, General Motors, Loctite, Michigan Bearings, Moog, Permatex, Sealed Powers, TRW, and hundreds of other suppliers. Brakes, cables, lights, air filters, body parts and panels, carburetor and engine parts, gauges, gas tanks, manuals, pistons, points, seals, rims, specialty tools, paint, reproduction upholstery, trim, carpets, and many other parts and supplies are available.

Special Factors: Price quote by phone or letter with SASE; returns are accepted; C.O.D. orders are accepted; minimum order is $10.

CLINTON CYCLE & SALVAGE, INC.

6709 OLD BRANCH AVE.
CAMP SPRINGS, MD
20748
800-332-8264
IN MD 301/449-3550

Price List: free

Save: up to 75%

Pay: check, MO, MC, V, AE, CHOICE, Discover

Sells: used motorcycle parts

Store: mail order only

$$

Clinton's salvage operations are a boon to anyone who owns a road bike that's 250cc or larger. Reclaimed parts of every type turn up here, at prices up to 75% less than those of new parts. The firm was founded in 1971.

Clinton specializes in Honda, Kawasaki, Suzuki, and Yamaha parts and assemblies, including large parts and engines for "400" and "UP" bikes. Write or call if you're looking for fenders, tail pieces, wheels, brakes, shocks, lights, carburetors, radiators, or any other part or accessory. Want lists are also maintained.

Special Factors: Satisfaction is guaranteed; price quote by phone or letter with SASE; returns (with receipts) are accepted within 14 days for replacement or refund; minimum order is $15 with credit cards.

CRYSTAL SONICS

1638 SOUTH CENTRAL
AVE., #C4
GLENDALE, CA 91204
818/240-7310

Catalog: $2

Save: up to 60%

Pay: check, MO, MC, V, AE

Sells: auto audio

Store: same address; Monday through Friday 9–6, Saturday 10–3

$$$

Crystal Sonics, in business since 1977, publishes an informative directory of discount auto audio components. In addition to savings of up to 60%, past catalogs have featured guides to audio terminology and extensive product specifications.

Crystal Sonics sells car stereo systems, amps, speakers, baffles, security devices and alarms, antennas, wires and cables, hardware, installation kits, and related paraphernalia. The manufacturers represented include Allsop, Alphasonik, Art Audio, Audio Control, BEL, Boston Acoustics, Clarion, Discwasher, Fujitsu Ten, Harada, Hirschmann, Hot Wires, Infinity, JBL, Jensen, Klasse, Phoenix Gold, Pioneer, Sanyo, Sony, Streetwires, TDK, Triad, and XTC. Crystal Sonics has a large facility at which installations of audio systems are made, and the catalog includes a guide to figuring out which systems will fit your car.

Special Factors: Authorized returns of new, unaltered, unused goods are accepted within 14 days; minimum order is $50 with credit cards; orders are shipped worldwide.

DEFENDER INDUSTRIES, INC.

**255 MAIN ST.
P.O. BOX 820
NEW ROCHELLE, NY
 10801
914/632-3001
FAX: 914/632-6544**

Catalog: $3, refundable
Save: up to 60%
Pay: check, MO, MC, V
Sells: marine supplies, gear, equipment, and clothing
Store: The Marine Discount Supermarket, 321 Main St., New Rochelle, NY; Monday to Friday 9–5:45, Thursday 9–8:45, Saturday 9–4:45 (9–2:45 November-January)

Defender backs its claim to have "the largest selection in the USA at the very lowest prices" with a 244-page catalog that may prove it. Defender, established in 1938, has earned a reputation for good service and reliability and is known as one of the best marine suppliers in the business.

The catalog shows page after page of boat maintenance supplies, resins and coatings, winches, windlasses, cordage, communications devices, foulweather gear, books, tools and hardware, optics, galley fittings, navigation equipment, and electronics. A recent edition offered Harken, Profurl, and Schafer sailboat hardware, Barient and Lewmar winches, Evinrude outboard engines, the full electronics lines from Apelco, Datamarine, Humminbird, Impulse, King, Lowrance and Signet; Shakespeare antenna, Babb and Maxxima radios, optics from Fujinon, Minolta, and Steiner, Avon and Achilles inflatable boats and life rafts; NYNEX mobile phones, Henri Lloyd and Musto vests and boating wear, Sebago and Timberland shoes, Force 10 cookers, and Taylor Made boat tops and covers—and that's a tiny sample of what's available. Defender is also a national leader in boat-building supplies: fiberglass, xynole, epoxy and polyester resins, and other boat construction and maintenance materials are stocked in depth.

Many of the items have other applications—the cookstoves and coolers for camping, the teak and oak racks and trays for the home, the caulks and wood finishes for general maintenance, hardware and tools for the workshop—and there are deck shoes, sunglasses, first-aid kits, foul-weather jackets, lamps and lanterns, watches and clocks, folding chairs, tarps, deck coverings, sailboards, and much more. The inventory is impressive: The firm currently offers 34 lines of foul-weather gear alone and keeps hundreds of Evinrude engines and thousands of anchors in stock. Defender also offers a range of custom services—life raft repacking and repair, rigging services, and canvas goods to order (seat covers, pool covers, car covers, etc.). Many goods are available that are not listed in the catalog, and the firm will special order any marine product.

Defender's wholesale division, Atlantic Main Corp., specializes in "arcane marine hardware." Among other items, this firm sells the "Horseshoe Harness," an alternative to the Lifesling that costs about half as much. Atlantic Main is also the U.S. agent for Holt Allen sailboat hardware. For details, contact Atlantic Main at 319 Main St., New Rochelle, NY 10801.

Special Factors: Price quote by phone or letter with SASE; returns are accepted within 20 days (a restocking fee may be charged); minimum order is $25; orders are shipped worldwide.

E & B MARINE SUPPLY, INC.

201 MEADOW RD.
EDISON, NJ 08818
800-533-5007
FAX: 201/819-9222

Catalog: free
Save: up to 60%
Pay: check, MO, MC, V, AE, Discover
Sells: marine supplies, gear, and equipment
Store: 50 outlets in AL, CT, FL, GA, MA, MD, MI, MS, NJ, NY, PA, RI, and VA
(locations are listed in the catalog)

$$$

E & B Marine, founded in 1946, "consistently maintains the boating industry's lowest discount prices," which has helped to establish the firm as "the nation's leading retailer of quality marine supplies."

E & B offers a full range of products for power boating and sailing, boat maintenance and repair, safety, communications, and navigation, all at a discount. The brand names include Apelco, Aqua Meter, Boatlife, Bow t' Stern, Chelsea, Eagle, Humminbird, Icom, Igloo, Impulse, Interlux, Intermatic, Kidde, Micrologic, Pettit, Polaris, Ray Jeff, Raytheon, SeaFit, Sea-Ranger, and Stearns, among others. Water skis and Achilles inflatables are stocked, as well as boating apparel and sportswear. New products are featured in every catalog, and many items are useful on land as well—clothing, safety equipment, and hardware. Savings vary, but are typically 10% to 25%, and up to 60% on sale items and specials.

Special Factors: Authorized returns are accepted within 90 days; minimum order is $15, $25 on phone orders.

EASTERN CYCLE SALVAGE, INC.

87 PARK ST.
BEVERLY, MA 01915
508/922-3707

Information: price quote
Save: up to 50% (see text)
Pay: MO, MC, V, Discover
Sells: used and reconditioned motorcycle parts
Store: same address; Tuesday through Saturday 9–5

Eastern Cycle sells used and reconditioned motorcycle parts "at savings of up to 50% retail," or half the price of the same parts if new. Engines, fenders, handlebars, kickstands, mufflers, pipes, lights, mirrors, clutches, gears, carburetors, and other cycle parts are available.

Eastern was established in 1971, and over time the firm has built up an enormous inventory of parts, including a section devoted to British and older Japanese models. Customers who visit the store will find used bikes and Cagiva motorcycles.

Please note: The savings are based on the cost of the same parts *if new*. Do not expect or request a discount on the *new* parts Eastern sells.

Special Factors: Price quote by phone or letter with SASE; C.O.D. orders are accepted.

EDGEWOOD NATIONAL, INC.

623 MERIDIAN EAST,
DEPT. WBM
PUYALLUP, WA 98371
206/927-3388

Information: price quote by phone or letter with SASE
Save: up to 40%
Pay: check, MO, MC, V
Sells: parts for 4WD vehicles
Store: same address

$$$ ✉ ☎

Edgewood National discontinued its catalog several years ago, but it does a brisk mail business on an inquiry (price quote) basis. Edgewood was established in 1964.

The specialty here is four-wheel-drive vehicles, for which Edgewood stocks "after-market accessories"—both hard parts and what the manager calls "tinsel," or extras. This is the source to call if you need drive train components, an engine or parts, a suspension, and the like. These are brand-new parts (not reconditioned), comparable to those by the original manufacturer, and savings can reach 40% on some items. The staff is helpful and informed, so it's worth a toll call to discuss your needs and get prices.

Special Factors: Price quote by phone or letter with SASE; authorized returns are accepted (a restocking fee may be charged).

EURO-TIRE, INC.

567 RTE. 46 WEST
FAIRFIELD, NJ 07004
800-631-0080
IN NJ 201/575-0080

Catalog: free
Save: up to 50%
Pay: check, MO, MC, V, AE
Sells: auto tires, wheels, and shocks
Store: same address; Monday, Wednesday, and Thursday 8:30–5, Tuesday and Friday, 8:30–7, Saturday 8:30–3:30; Rte. 4 E., Paramus, NJ; Tuesday, Wednesday, and Friday 8:30–5, Monday and Thursday 8:30–7, Saturday 8:30–3:30; also 393 West Ave., Stamford, CT

$$ ✉ ☎

Euro-Tire's specialty is European tires and auto components, which are sold at up to 50% off list prices. Domestic car tires and products are also available. This firm, which began doing business in 1974, has an informed and helpful staff.

Save on tires by Bridgestone, Continental, Dunlop, Fulda, Goodyear, Kléber, Michelin, Pirelli, Semperit, Vredestein, and Yokohama through Euro-Tire. Cibie halogen headlamps, and shock absorbers by Bilstein, Boge, and Koni are offered, as well as light alloy wheels by BBS, Centra, MSW, Rial, and Ronal. Euro-Tire's concise 24-page catalog gives complete details on its sales and warranty policies.

Special Factors: Price quote by phone; no seconds or retreads are sold; returns are accepted within 60 days; minimum order is $25; orders are shipped worldwide.

GOLDBERGS' MARINE DISTRIBUTORS

201 MEADOW RD., DEPT. WBM-91
EDISON, NJ 08818
800-BOATING

Catalog: free
Save: up to 60%
Pay: check, MO, MC, V, AE, Discover
Sells: marine supplies, gear, and equipment
Store: 12 W. 37th St., New York, NY;
also Whitman Plaza Shopping Center,
3rd and Oregon Aves., Philadelphia, PA

$$$$ ✉   ☎   🍁   ▀

Goldbergs', "where thousands of boaters save millions of dollars," publishes a hefty color catalog yearly with regular updates. New items are added constantly, and discounts run up to 60%—even more in the sales catalog. Goldbergs' Marine has been doing business since 1946.

Goldbergs' sells everything from anchors to zinc collars—rope, bilge pumps, fishing tackle, rigging, knives, lifeboats, life preservers, navigation equipment, boat covers, winches, and even kitchen (galley) sinks. Among the goods we found in a recent catalog were SeaRanger electronics, Taylor Made buoys, PowerWinch windlasses and winches, motors, Norlantic and Winslow dinghies, Stearns life preservers, and Bass boating shoes.

The emphasis is on pleasure-boat equipment, but much of the sailing apparel—French fishermen's and oiled-wool sweaters, sunglasses, boots, caps, slickers—would appeal to landlubbers. A selection of stylish galley gear, teak bulkhead racks, and other yacht accessories rounds out the substantial catalog.

Special Factors: Price quote by phone or letter with SASE; authorized returns are accepted within 10 days (policy is stated in the catalog); minimum order is $10.

MARV GOLDEN DISCOUNT SALES, INC.

8690 AERO DR., SUITE 102
SAN DIEGO, CA 92123
619/569-5220
FAX: 619/569-4508

Flyer: free
Save: up to 35%
Pay: check, MO, MC, V, AE, Discover, Optima
Sells: equipment for the "general aviation" pilot
Store: same address; Monday through Friday 7–6, Saturday 8–3, PST

Marv Golden Discount Sales has been in business since 1983, and offers the general-aviation pilot savings of up to 35% on headsets, electronics, and accessories.

You can write for the current flyer of specials, or call for quotes on such items as David Clark and Peltor headsets, Astrotech digital clocks, Long Ranger lorans, Jeppesen charts and binders, Aerox oxygen systems, and flight bags and other accessories. Intercoms by Flightcom, Sigtronics, Soft Comm, Telex, and other manufacturers are available, as well as computers from Jeppesen and Navtronic, and 720-channel transceivers from Icom, King, Narco, and Terra. If you don't see what you're looking for in the flyer, call—it might be available.

Special Factors: Satisfaction is guaranteed; price quote by phone or letter with SASE; shipping is included on prepaid orders; quantity discounts are available; authorized, unused returns in original packaging are accepted within 30 days for credit; C.O.D. orders are accepted; orders are shipped worldwide.

IMPCO, INC.

909 THOMPSON ST.
HOUSTON, TX 77077
800/243-1220
713/868-1638
FAX: 713/869-0186

Catalog: free
Save: 30% average
Pay: check, MO, MC, V
Sells: OEM Mercedes-Benz diesel parts (see text)
Store: same address; Monday through Friday 9–6

$$ ✉ ☎ 🍁 ▤

If you own a diesel Mercedes-Benz car made between 1977 and 1985, you can get "original equipment manufacturer" (OEM) parts for it here, at savings that average 30%. IMPCO, in business since 1984, sells only first-quality parts.

The 48-page catalog lists a full range of body parts, from front fender moldings to trunk seals, as well as electrical parts and supplies, bulbs, cooling and heating system components, upholstery materials, filters, brake parts, suspension and drive-line parts, window switches, accessories, tools, and even Owner's Workshop manuals. IMPCO also sells Meguiar's car-care products, Lexol leather cleaner and conditioner, and maintenance products for diesel engines. If you're looking for a part not listed or have any questions, call and ask.

Special Factors: Satisfaction is guaranteed; price quote by phone or letter with SASE; minimum order is $20 on phone orders; C.O.D. orders are accepted.

IRON WORKS CYCLE

731 PITTSBURGH ST.
SCOTTDALE, PA 15683
412/887-8010
FAX: 412/887-0639

Information: price quote
Save: 30% average
Pay: check, MO, MC, V
Sells: motocross and street bike accessories
Store: same address; Monday, Wednesday, Friday 9–6, Tuesday and Thursday 9–8, Saturday 9–3

Iron Works Cycle has been selling motocross and street bike equipment and accessories since 1987, at savings averaging 30%. The firm has no catalog, but you can call, write, or fax for prices on goods by Arai, Axo, Belray, Bieffe, Boyesen, Bridgestone, Continental, Dunlop, EBC, J.T. Racing, Kenda, Kerker, Maxima, Metzeler, Oakley, O'Neal USA, PBI, Renthal, RK, Scott, Shoei, Thor, and Twin Air. Tires, helmets, motorcycle chain, brakes, exhausts, jet kits, gloves, and related goods are available.

Special Factors: Price quote by phone or letter with SASE; minimum order is $25; C.O.D. orders are accepted; orders are shipped worldwide.

NATIONWIDE AUTO BROKERS, INC.

17517 WEST 10 MILE RD.
SOUTHFIELD, MI 48075
313/559-6661
FAX: 313/559-4782

Brochure: free (see text)
Save: up to 18% (see text)
Pay: check, MO, MC, V
Sells: price quotes and vehicles (see text)
Store: mail order only

$$$

Part of the ordeal of buying a new car is the unpleasant feeling that the dealerships are taking *you* for a ride, to the tune of thousands of dollars. Nationwide Auto Brokers can sell you a computer printout detailing the dealer and retail prices, which should enable you to negotiate those markups down to hundreds. Nationwide can also sell you almost any car, truck, or van at dealer cost plus $50 to $125, which represents potential savings of hundreds of dollars. In addition to domestic models, Nationwide will give quotes on most foreign cars, but availability is limited.

Nationwide Auto has been brokering cars since 1966, and works with some of the largest buying groups in the country. For $10.95, Nationwide will send you a printout on the make and model of your choice, listing basics and all options—engines, packages, power features, radios, exterior goodies, tires, wheels, and the like. (The sample Buick Regal quote we received ran to seven pages.) You can go from here to your local car dealer and negotiate with these figures, but it may be easier, and cheaper, to have Nationwide broker the car for you. You can use the same printout as a purchase order and have Nationwide deliver the vehicle to you by a bonded driver or have it delivered to a local dealership, at a surcharge. You can also pick up the vehicle at the firm's headquarters in Southfield, MI. Financing is available through GMAC or Ford Motor Credit, manufacturers' incentives and rebates are honored, and the factory warranties are good at authorized dealerships throughout the U.S. and Canada. You can write to Nationwide Auto for a brochure, or call to order a printout and charge it to your credit card.

Special Factor: Financing is available (but vehicles must be picked up at Nationwide's facility).

RACER WHOLESALE

████████

**10390 ALPHARETTA ST.,
SUITE 620
ROSWELL, GA 30075
404/998-7777
FAX: 404/993-4417**

Catalog: free
Save: up to 70%
Pay: check, MO, MC, V
Sells: auto racing safety equipment
Store: mail order only

$$$ ✉ ☎ 🍁 ▬

Racer Wholesale has been serving the professional and serious amateur auto racing market since 1985, with safety equipment and accessories at savings of up to 70% on list prices.

The 32-page catalog shows a selection of professional driving and crew suits, from AutoPro, Bell, Pyrotect, Racequip, and other manufacturers, as well as gloves, boots, helmets, belts and harnesses, window nets, arm restraints, fire extinguishers, and other safety goods. Auto equipment is also available: K & N filters and accessories, Flowmaster mufflers, Oberg filters and heavy-duty oil coolers, Aeroquip hoses and connections, fueling accessories, towing equipment, Wink wide-view mirrors, battery cutoff switches, and related products are all available. List and discounted prices are both given in the separate price list, and Racer Wholesale has a policy of "guaranteed lowest prices"—details are given in the catalog.

Special Factors: Price quote by phone or letter with SASE; authorized, unused returns (except special orders) are accepted within 15 days for exchange, refund, or credit (a restocking fee may be charged); C.O.D. orders are accepted.

SKIPPER MARINE ELECTRONICS, INC.

**3170 COMMERCIAL AVE.
NORTHBROOK, IL 60062
800-621-2378**

Catalog: free (see text)
Save: up to 30%
Pay: check, MO, MC, V
Sells: marine electronics
Store: same address; also 20307 South
  Western Ave., Torrance, CA; and 5053
  N.W. 10th Terrace, Ft. Lauderdale, FL

$$$ ✉ ☎ 🍁

Skipper Marine Electronics is a factory-authorized dealer and service center for all of the electronics it sells. Consequently, Skipper can adjust and calibrate the electronics it sells, prior to delivery, without impairing the warranties. Several technicians are on staff who can discuss equipment needs and answer questions on installation.

Skipper Marine's catalogs are published in the form of buying guides, each of which is devoted to a different category: VHF marine radios, fishing and powerboat instruments, sailboat instruments, navigation instruments, and miscellaneous electronics. The guides are helpful, describing the product's functions, noting valuable features, and explaining why you should buy said equipment from Skipper. Among the manufacturers represented here are Apelco, Cybernet, Datamarine, Eagle, Echotec, Furuno, Humminbird, Impulse, Interphase, King Marine, Lowrance, Micronar, Raytheon, Si-Tex, Signet, Uniden, Unimetrics, and Wesmar.

Skipper also offers boat owners an electronic maintenance service, which will tune, calibrate, align, and clean (as applicable) marine radios, navigators, autopilots, chart recorders, lorans, and other marine electronics. Equipment need not have been purchased at Skipper to be serviced, and the schedule of charges is listed in the "Electronics Maintenance Program" brochure.

Skipper has been doing business since 1963, and its sales policy is clearly stated in the buyers' guides. When you request information, remember to state your area of interest.

Special Factors: Price quote by phone or letter; authorized returns are accepted; shipping is included; C.O.D. orders are accepted.

TELETIRE

**17642 ARMSTRONG AVE.
IRVINE, CA 92714
800-835-8473
IN CA 714/250-9141**

Brochure: free
Save: 30% average
Pay: check, MO, MC, V, Discover
Sells: tires and wheels
Store: mail order only

$$$ ✉ ☎

How often should you rotate your car's tires? What is UTQG? What do speed ratings actually mean? Teletire answers these and many other questions you may have about tires in its free brochure, which also showcases a great selection of tires and wheels.

This company maintains a multi-million-dollar inventory of tires for passenger cars, trucks, vans, and RVs, and also stocks road wheels. You'll find different models by American Racing, BBS, Bridgestone, Centerline, Continental, Dunlop, Enkei, Fittpaldi, Michelin, Pirelli, Quantum, and Yokohama in the brochure. If the tires or wheels you're looking for aren't listed, call or write for a price quote. Teletire, which began doing business in 1969, is affiliated with Telepro (see the listing in "Sports").

Special Factors: Price quote by phone or letter; unused, undamaged returns are accepted within 30 days (a restocking fee may be charged).

TITAN RUBBER INTERNATIONAL

**ONE BRYAN DR.
WHEELING, WV
26003-0137
800-443-8473**

Information: price quote
Save: up to 50%
Pay: check, MO, MC, V, Discover
Sells: performance tires and wheels
Store: same address; Monday through Friday 8–5; also 75 locations nationwide

$$$ ✉ ☎ 🍁

Titan Rubber, also known as Tire America, does not publish a catalog but can provide technical assistance by phone to help you make the best selection of tires for your vehicle and driving style. The firm has been in business since 1959, and sells at prices up to 50% below the going rate.

Titan features high-performance and RV tires and performance wheels by American Racing, BBS, Cartech, Dunlop, Falken, Fittpaldi, Fulda, Gislaved,

B.F. Goodrich, Goodyear, Hayashi, Michelin, MSW, Pirelli, Ronal, RW, Sentry, and Weds. Tire and wheel packages for a number of vehicles may be available—inquire for information. These are first-quality goods—no seconds or retreads—and they're all sold with the manufacturers' warranties.

Special Factors: Price quote by phone or letter with SASE; no catalog is available.

WEST MARINE PRODUCTS

500 WESTRIDGE DR.
WATSONVILLE, CA 95076
800-538-0775

Catalog: free
Save: up to 50%
Pay: check, MO, MC, V
Sells: marine supplies and equipment
Store: 15 outlets on the West Coast
(locations are listed in the catalog)

West Marine Products publishes a 136-page catalog that features no-nonsense lines of electronics, hardware, and maintenance products for sailboats and powerboats.

West Marine carries a comprehensive selection of gear and materials: epoxies and finishes, cordage, anchors, windlasses, buoys, horns, seacocks, winches, electronics, communications devices, navigation instruments, safety equipment, lumber, hardware, kerosene lamps, boating clothing, marine optics, inflatable boats, and a complete line of galley gear. The manufacturers include Apelco, Barient, Cannon, Datamarine, Harken, Interphase, Lewmar, Magellan, Marinco, Navico, Patagonia, Ritchie, Schaefer, Stearns, Steiner, Taylor Made, and Weems & Plath, among others. Savings run up to 50%, and many top brands are available. Over 5,000 items are in stock but not shown in the catalog, so if you don't see what you're looking for, give West Marine a call.

Special Factor: Satisfaction is guaranteed.

COMPANIES OUTSIDE THE U.S.A.

Yachtmail, a well-known yacht chandler, is experienced in dealing with customers in the U.S. and Canada. We've included the firm because it offers goods not widely available at a discount in the U.S. and because it has a better selection of certain goods.

Before ordering from a non-U.S. firm, please read through the applicable sections of "The Complete Guide to Buying by Mail" at the back of this book. We recommend paying for your catalog with a camouflaged enclosure of cash. (Sending cash saves the company the bank charge of converting your check to a different currency.) We further advise you to pay for your merchandise by credit card whenever possible, so that your transaction will be protected by the part of the Fair Credit Billing Act that allows you to dispute charges for goods not received. See page 000–000 for a complete discussion of the Act. Please note that only this portion of the Act applies, and the FTC's Mail Order Rule governing delivery time *does not*.

YACHTMAIL CO. LTD.

ADMIRAL'S COURT, THE QUAY
LYMINGTON, HANTS
SO41 9ET
011-44-590-672784
FAX: 011-44-590-670089

Price List: free
Save: up to 50%
Pay: check, IMO, MC, V, Access
Sells: yachting equipment and electronics
Store: same address; Hamble Point Marina, School Lane, Hamble, Hants; and Point Hamble Marina, Satchelliane, Hamble, Hants; Monday through Sunday 9–5, all locations

$$$ ✉   🍁

Yachtmail, founded in 1966, specializes in cruiser-yacht gear and inflatables but also sells navigation instruments, winches, pumps, lights, clocks, barometers, and other goods. English brands, considered by many to be equal or superior to American makes, are often hard to find in the U.S. and are usually expensive. At Yachtmail, prices on goods by these firms are usually 30% below U.S. rates, and sometimes even lower. Smaller items can be shipped at nominal rates, so you don't impair your savings.

Yachtmail tells us that the most popular items with U.S. buyers are Autohelm and Navico autopilots, Avon life rafts, satellite navigators, echo sounders, log speedometers, and sextants. The company is often cited for its prices on Avon dinghies, which are usually 30% less than U.S. discount prices. The price list we received also itemized Lewmar winches and fixtures, EPIRBs, flares, binoculars, life jackets, foul-weather clothing by Douglass Gill, Henri Lloyd, Musto, and Splashdown, and other useful goods. If you're planning to outfit your yacht or boat, be sure to contact Yachtmail for prices. Goods are generally shipped by airmail or air freight. The price list is a guide to the *range* of products available, but if you're looking for a British-made article that's not mentioned, write and inquire—it may be available.

Special Factors: Price quote by phone or letter with SASE; certain items are unsuitable for mailing; orders are shipped worldwide.

SEE ALSO

Allyn Air Seat Co. • air-filled seat liners for motorcycles, cars, and trucks • *SPORTS*

Audio Unlimited • mid-end auto audio • *APPLIANCES*

Bart's Water Ski Center, Inc. • boat mounts and hardware for water-skiing equipment • *SPORTS*

Bass Pro Shops • boating gear and electronics • *SPORTS*

Bennett Brothers, Inc. • infants' car seats • *GENERAL MERCHANDISE*

BRE Lumber • lumber and flooring for marine use • *HOME: MAINTENANCE*

Cabela's Inc. • boat seats, covers, electronics, etc. • *SPORTS*

Cambridge Wools, Ltd. • sheepskin car covers • *CRAFTS*

Campmor • inflatable boats • *SPORTS*

Central Tractor Farm & Family Center • replacement tractor and engine parts; shop manuals • *FARM*

Crutchfield Corporation • auto audio • *APPLIANCES*

Danley's • name-brand marine binoculars • *CAMERAS*

Direct Safety Company • wheel chocks, traffic control equipment, auto emergency kits, etc. • *TOOLS*

E.T. Supply • aircraft replacement parts • *SURPLUS*

Fish'n Shack • boating equipment, Coleman dinghies, and Lake Raider boats • *SPORTS*

Gander Mountain, Inc. • boat seats, covers, electronics, motors, etc. • *SPORTS*

International Electronic World • auto audio • *APPLIANCES*

Leather Unlimited • Harley-Davidson personal accessories • *CRAFTS*

LVT Price Quote Hotline, Inc. • radar detectors, scanners, CBs, etc. • *APPLIANCES*

Manufacturer's Supply • parts for motorcycles, snowmobiles, 3WDs, etc. • *TOOLS*

Mardiron Optics • name-brand marine optics • *CAMERAS*

Northern Hydraulics, Inc. • wheels and parts for ATVs, minibikes, etc.
• *TOOLS*

Overton's Sports Center, Inc. • marine equipment and electronics •
SPORTS

Pagano Gloves, Inc. • deerskin motorcycle jackets • *CLOTHING*

Sailboard Warehouse, Inc. • sailboard car racks • *SPORTS*

R.C. Steele Co. • life preservers and auto safety harnesses for pets •
ANIMAL

The Surplus Store • inflatable dinghies • *SURPLUS*

WearGuard Corp. • mechanics' overalls, shoes, safety vests, etc. •
CLOTHING

Wisconsin Discount Stereo • auto audio • *APPLIANCES*

BOOKS, MAGAZINES, RECORDS, AND TAPES

Publications of every sort, cards and stationery, prerecorded films and videotapes, and services

There's just no point in paying the cover price for any book or full rates for magazine subscriptions when you can get many by mail at discounts of 30% to 80%. If you buy just one book a month, you could be saving over $100 per year from these sources. And if you're currently buying your favorite magazines from the newsstand, you can cut your costs in half by ordering subscriptions through the brokers listed here.

Make the most of these sources by keeping a file of book reviews, recommendations, and similar notes. Refer to it whenever you receive a new catalog, and you won't miss that elusive volume. (*The New York Times Book Review,* an excellent weekly, is available by mail in the U.S. and Canada for under $32 per year at this writing; contact The New York Times Book Review, Subscription Sales, P.O. Box 492, Hackensack, NJ 07602, for current rates and foreign subscription information.) If you're searching for a rare or out-of-print publication, check with a firm that deals in such material. (Consult *Books in Print,* in any library, to see whether the book is still being published or has been reprinted.) Strand Book Store (listed here) will maintain want lists, and although you can't expect "discount" prices on such books, Strand usually prices them competitively.

Most collectors know that protecting the investment value of rare volumes and albums requires proper storage and display. University Products, Inc., offers an excellent selection of conservation supplies, including acid-free book-jacket covers, manuscript cases and folders, rare-book boxes, record sleeves, interleaving sheets, and archival-quality repair materials, among other products. See the firm's listing in "General" for more information.

In addition to books and magazines, you'll find firms listed in this chapter that sell stationery, cards, gift wrapping and ribbon, records and tapes, library embossers, and photos of rock stars.

Don't overlook the "See Also's" at the end of this chapter. Many of the firms listed in this book also offer well-chosen reference books and videotapes on topics related to their specialties, usually at discount prices. And please note that firms selling computer software and programs can be found in the "Computing" section of the "Office" chapter.

AMERICAN FAMILY PUBLISHERS

P.O. BOX 62000
TAMPA, FL 33662-2000
800-237-2400

Information: inquire
Save: up to 70%
Pay: check or MO
Sells: magazine subscriptions
Store: mail order only

$$$ ✉

American Family Publishers is one of several magazine clearinghouses that offer subscriptions to dozens of popular periodicals at rates that are usually much better than those offered by the publishers themselves.

Subscriptions to *Architectural Digest, Popular Science, The Atlantic, TV Guide, Money, Bowling Digest, Time, Savvy, Jet,* and *The Family Handyman* have been offered in past mailings. AFP recently introduced books—*The Columbia University Complete Home Medical Guide,* Rodale's home-improvement series, cookbooks, and other popular reference books. Bonuses, premiums, and sweepstakes are usually featured in the offers.

Special Factors: Satisfaction is guaranteed; inquire for information; installment plan is available.

THE AMERICAN STATIONERY CO., INC.

100 PARK AVE., DEPT. 3
PERU, IN 46970
800-822-2577
FAX: 317/473-5901

Catalog: free
Save: up to 35%
Pay: check, MO, MC, V, Discover
Sells: custom-printed stationery
Store: mail order only

$$$ ✉ ☎ 🇺🇸

American Stationery, founded in 1919, offers a good assortment of tasteful personalized stationery at prices up to 35% less than those charged by other firms for comparable goods and printing.

American Stationery's correspondence selections include embossed sheets and notes in four colors, deckle-edged and plain sheets and envelopes in white, ivory, pink, grey, and pale blue, and heavyweight Monarch sheets, erasable sheets, business envelopes, and "executive" stationery of heavy, chain-laid paper. (We found some excellent buys in the most recent catalog, including the "typewriter box" of 100 printed sheets and the same number of printed envelopes for $13.50; a box of the same size and quality cost $28.50 through another mail-order source.) Stationery for children, personalized memo pads, bill-paying envelopes, bordered postcards, stationery sets, gummed and self-sticking return-address labels, and similar products are shown in the color catalog. This firm also produces "The American Wedding Album," a 32-page color catalog with actual samples of wedding invitations and accessories—at savings similar to those offered on the stationery line.

Special Factors: Satisfaction is guaranteed; returns are accepted for replacement or refund.

ASTRONOMICAL SOCIETY OF THE PACIFIC

**390 ASHTON AVE.
SAN FRANCISCO, CA
94112
415/337-1100**

Catalog: two first-class stamps
Save: up to 50%
Pay: check, MO, MC, V
Sells: books, posters, slides, and videotapes on astronomy topics
Store: mail order only

$$$

The Astronomical Society of the Pacific, a not-for-profit organization, was founded in 1889 to support astronomical research and improve the public's appreciation of science, especially astronomy. In service of this goal, ASP publishes a variety of materials—videotapes, books, charts and maps of the heavens, slides, and audiotapes. The 32-page catalog shows an intriguing collection: *Universe,* an award-winning video commissioned by NASA and narrated by William Shatner; *Voyager: Missions to Jupiter and Saturn;* a four-tape audio recording of Stephen W. Hawking's *A Brief History of Time;* the Royal Observatory of Canada's *Observer's Handbook;*

breathtaking posters of the planets; an intriguing "moon phase calendar" for the whole year; computer programs that can simulate travel through the galaxy; and several slide sets covering nebulas and galaxies, the moon, Mars, the solar system, Supernova 1987A, and even the universe of radio waves.

ASP's prices seem reasonable but not particularly low ($29.95 for videotapes and $8.95 for posters), until you check the catalogs of supplies for *educators,* to which ASP's publications can be fairly compared. Some school sources charge a stellar $300-plus for a single videotape. So even if you're not in the market for ASP's publications yourself, let your school board or PTA know that this source exists.

Special Factors: Institutional accounts are available; orders are shipped worldwide.

BARNES & NOBLE BOOKSTORES, INC.

**126 FIFTH AVE.
NEW YORK, NY 10011
201/767-7079 EXT. 839X**

Catalog: free
Save: up to 94%
Pay: check, MO, MC, V, AE, CB, DC
Sells: books, records, audiotapes, and videotapes
Store: same address; Monday through Friday 9:45–6:15, Saturday 9:45–6, Sunday 10–5; other locations nationwide

 $$$ ✉ 🍁 ▆ (see text)

Barnes & Noble, founded in 1873, is "committed to a policy of offering you hundreds of new and exciting books at inflation-fighting prices." In addition, the catalog mailings feature hundreds of records, audiotapes, and videotapes at discounts of up to 50%—and even more during sales and specials.

The regularly published catalogs from Barnes & Noble are packed with best-sellers, paperbacks, reprints, and publishers' overstock. The areas of interest include history, mystery, chemistry, literature, film, medicine, satire, juvenilia, current fiction, linguistics, religion, reference, crafts, and photography. Recordings of classical music, jazz, and old radio programs are offered frequently, as well as vintage movies, from *The Thirty-Nine Steps* to *Pumping Iron*. Past catalogs have offered such related goods as collapsible beechwood bookshelves, book embossers, atlases, calendars, book ends, cassette cases and cabinets, and book lights.

Canadian and APO/FPO readers, please note: Inquire for shipping charges, and allow extra time for order processing.

Special Factors: Satisfaction is guaranteed; institutional accounts are available; returns are accepted; minimum order is $15 with credit cards.

BERKSHIRE RECORD OUTLET, INC.

RR 1, RTE 102,
PLEASANT ST.
LEE, MA 01238
413/243-4080

Catalog: free
Save: 33% plus
Pay: check, MO, MC, V, Access, Discover
Sells: classical recordings
Store: same address; Monday through
Saturday 11:30–5:30

 $$$

Thousands of recordings, most of classical music, are listed in Berkshire's 122-page, quarterly catalog. This is a treasury of overstocked and remaindered recordings that are offered at savings of 33%-plus on published prices.

The catalog is organized alphabetically by label name (from Abbey to Xtra), and within that, by price groups. Each entry is also coded to indicate whether the recording is in stereo, mono, quadraphonic, or reprocessed stereo (or digital or analog in CD entries), and the country of origin is noted if the recording is an import. This source is a gold mine for the classical music lover, although ethnic music and poetry readings do show up in the catalog.

If you're just looking for a good recording of a favorite concerto or movement, you may be overwhelmed by the selection. We'd advise you to share the catalog with a knowledgeable friend who can help you choose. Berkshire has wisely advised customers that orders can't be changed after they're placed—so be sure of what you want *before* you order.

Special Factors: Price quote by phone or letter with SASE; order promptly, since quantities may be limited.

BOSE EXPRESS MUSIC

**50 W. 17TH ST.
NEW YORK, NY 10011
800-233-6357**

Catalog: $6, refundable
Save: up to 35%
Pay: check, MO, MC, V, AE
Sells: records, audiotapes, CDs, laser discs,
  and videotapes
Store: mail order only

Bose Express Music, established in 1985, provides an easy way to buy backlisted and current music and video releases at a discount. This source is ideal for audiophiles who don't have access to the large record emporiums in metropolitan areas. The 224-page catalog includes discount coupons worth about $50. The catalog, featuring over 45,000 titles, costs $6; the price includes a year's subscription to monthly updates, and is refundable with your first order.

The big catalog and monthly updates list hundreds of new record, tape, CD, and video releases. List prices are given for all of the titles, but a large selection of best-sellers is featured at a discount in the updates. You'll find rock, pop, R&B, gospel, sound tracks, opera, classical, and Broadway show tunes here, plus rock videos, workout tapes, and new and old movies. On just one page of the LP and tape section of the catalog, we found Melanie and Bette Midler sharing space with George Michaels, Sergio Mendes, and Ethel Merman.

Since shipping, handling, and insurance cost $3.65 per order, splurging on gifts and your own audio/video library seems almost justified. The discount coupons in the large catalog reward orders of several items with freebies and extra savings, so don't overlook them. And if you don't see what you're looking for in the catalog or updates, call—Bose Express Music will get any available title in print.

Special Factors: Price quote by phone or letter with SASE; returns of defective goods are accepted within 10 days for exchange, credit, or refund; orders are shipped worldwide.

CONSUMER INFORMATION CENTER

**P.O. BOX 100
PUEBLO, CO 81002**

Catalog: free
Save: see text
Pay: check or MO
Sells: consumer publications
Store: mail order only

$$$$ ✉

The Consumer Information Center was established in 1970 "to help federal agencies promote and distribute useful consumer information." The Center publishes a 16-page quarterly catalog of pamphlets and manuals, many of which are free.

The information categories include careers and education, child care, guides to federal benefits and laws, food handling and nutrition, health topics, home building and buying, energy conservation, appliances and electronics, home improvement and safety, travel, hobbies, and money management. You can subscribe to FDA Consumer through the catalog, and order pamphlets that help you to learn about ultrasound, find out about Social Security, get tips on buying a mobile home, and obtain records under the Freedom of Information Act, among other things. Among the catalog offerings is another catalog—a listing of dozens of federal consumer guides that are available in Spanish. Among the most helpful publications we know is the "Consumer's Resource Handbook," a guide to effective complaint procedures, which lists the best sources of help: contacts, addresses, and phone numbers of the customer relations departments of hundreds of major corporations, Better Business Bureau offices worldwide, trade associations, consumer protection offices, and federal agencies. There are over 90 pages of valuable information here, at the best possible price—free. Please note: Order the Handbook through the Consumer Information Center catalog.

Special Factor: A $1 handling fee is charged on all orders.

CURRENT, INC.

**THE CURRENT BUILDING
COLORADO SPRINGS, CO 80941**
303/593-5990

Catalog: free
Save: up to 45%
Pay: check or MO
Sells: stationery, cards, and gifts
Store: Citadel Shopping Center, Colorado Springs, CO; Monday through Friday 10–9, Saturday 10–6, Sunday 12–5; also 3550 S. Inca St., Denver, CO; Monday through Friday 10–7, Saturday 9–5, Sunday 12–5

$$$ ✉

Current, a family-owned business founded in 1950, publishes an 88-page color catalog of stationery and cards that feature appealing designs, ranging from animal and nature scenes to quilt motifs and other Americana. All-occasion and holiday cards are available, as well as notes, stationery, gift wrapping, ribbon, recipe cards and files, toys, games, home organizers, calendars, memo boards, note pads, canning labels, and gifts. Prices are reasonable and discounts are given based on the number of items ordered.

Special Factors: Satisfaction is guaranteed; sliding discounts of 20% and more are offered on orders of 8 or more items; returns are accepted.

DAEDALUS BOOKS, INC.

**P.O. BOX 9132 (WBM)
HYATTSVILLE, MD 20781-0932**
301/779-4224

Catalog: free
Save: up to 90%
Pay: check, MO, MC, V, AE, Optima
Sells: remaindered literary publications
Store: mail order only

$$$$ ✉   ☎   🍁   ▆

Daedalus, founded in 1980, offers fine books from trade publishers and university presses at 50% to 90% off the publishers' prices. These remainders, culled from thousands, will appeal to the literary reader looking for culture on the cheap.

Randy Shilts' *And the Band Played On* ($4.98, from $24.98), selected novels of Philip Roth, T. Coraghessen Boyle's *World's End* ($4.98, from $19.95), and works by Walt Whitman, John Kenneth Galbraith, Joan Didion, Edna O'Brien, and Leon Edel are among past offerings. The categories include literature and general interest, visual and performing arts, philosophy, history, feminism, politics, and the social sciences. A gift certificate from Daedalus presented with the latest edition of the catalog should delight any serious reader.

Canadian readers, please note: Payment must be made by credit card, money order drawn in U.S. funds, or a check drawn on a U.S. bank.

Special Factors: Order promptly, since stock moves quickly; institutional accounts are available; returns are accepted within 30 days; minimum order is $10 with credit cards; orders are shipped worldwide.

DIRECT BOOK SERVICE

P.O. BOX 15357-WM
SEATTLE, WA 98115
800-776-BOOK

Information: price quote (see text)
Save: up to 30% (see text)
Pay: check, MO, MC, V
Sells: books
Store: mail order only

In the course of researching this edition of WBMC, we found ourselves running down an old lead we had on file for a discount bookseller in Seattle. We'd learned that the firm had changed its name and focus, and was now a specialty bookseller—and no longer discounted. But the owner of Direct Book Service was familiar with WBMC, and mentioned an idea to us that she'd had for some time: selling multiple copies of the same book title to individuals, at savings averaging 20%. We found the idea very appealing, for its money-saving potential for children's and adults' reading groups, writing groups, and study programs. And since a number of the titles on typical college book lists are not textbooks, an industrious student could organize purchases—and savings—for an entire class. We've even known individuals who've given copies of their favorite novels to all their friends, and could have saved $50 or more overall on each title had they been able to buy from Direct Book Service.

This program for individuals (not institutions) applies to *any book in print* from any publisher, with a minimum order of ten copies of each title. (Textbooks and reference and technical books are *not* included.) For more information, send Direct Book Service your book list, and specify the number of copies needed of each book. Remember: You can buy just one *title*, but you must buy a minimum of *ten copies of that title* to qualify for the discount. And please note: Direct Book Service does not have a catalog, so please don't request one! Call or write for prices of specific titles.

Special Factors: Price quote by phone or letter with SASE; quantity discounts are available; minimum order is 10 copies of the same title; orders are shipped worldwide.

DISCOUNT BOOKS & VIDEO, INC.

P.O. BOX 928
VINELAND, NJ 08360-0928
800/448-2019
609/691-1620

Catalog: free
Save: up to 90%
Pay: check, MO, MC, V
Sells: remaindered books, CDs, audiotapes, and videotapes
Store: mail order only

$$$ ✉ ☎ 🇺🇸

Discount Books & Videos sells publishers' overstock and remaindered publications at savings of up to 90% on the original prices. The firm was established in 1984 and discounts books, audiotapes, and videotapes.

The 64-page catalog we reviewed offered bargains on books about American history and politics, music, Judaica, health and nutrition, philosophy, law, crafts, cooking, computers, social sciences, medicine, and other areas of interest, including scores of titles on African history. Fiction, literature, criticism, and scholarly texts are featured, and Discount Books & Videos carries what few other overstock sellers seem to get: technical books and textbooks. The catalog includes several pages of audio cassettes—classical music, jazz, rock, opera, and motivational—and CDs. Hundreds of videotapes are also available, including comedy classics, old favorites from the 40s and 50s, sports highlights, instructional, and educational "video learning kits." Quantities of many of the books are limited, so order promptly.

Special Factors: Satisfaction is guaranteed; returns are accepted within 30 days for refund or credit; institutional accounts are available; minimum order is $15 with credit cards.

DOVER PUBLICATIONS, INC.

**31 EAST 2ND ST.
MINEOLA, NY 11501
516/294-7000**

Catalog: free

Save: up to 50% (see text)

Pay: check, MO, certified check

Sells: Dover publications

Store: same address; Monday through Friday 8:30–3:45; also 180 Varick St., 9th Floor, New York, NY; Monday through Friday 9–4:30

$$$$ ✉ 🍁 ▃

Many of the firms listed in this book sell a selection of Dover books, but if you deal with the publisher directly you can buy *any* Dover publication now in print. Dover has been publishing for over 40 years, and its books are noted for the quality of their paper and bindings, as well as their content. The catalog we reviewed offered paperbacks on crafts and hobbies of all types, Americana, mathematics and physics, American Indian arts, fiction (including reprints of Trollope and whodunits), architecture, cooking, games, travel, music, and many other topics. Dover is known for its Pictorial Archives (designs and graphics of a culture or an era, typography, banners and scrolls, borders, etc.), the Clip-Art Series (copyright-free art that can be used in newsletters, ads, menus, etc.), postcard sets (from NASA shots to Tiffany windows), stickers and seals, and coloring books and posters.

Dover's facsimiles and reprints of rare and valuable texts deserve special mention. Dover has produced a facsimile of William Blake's *Songs of Innocence,* a reprint of an 1864 illustrated catalog of Civil War military goods, and the earliest known cookbook, *Cookery and Dining in Imperial Rome,* by Apicius, to cite a few. The publisher's reprint of Gustav Stickley's catalog of Mission furniture designs can be found on the bookshelves of half of New York City's antiques dealers, and is probably more widely read now than it was when originally published.

In addition, Dover publishes "Listen & Learn" language tapes (most of which are available on LP), as well as bird song tapes and musical scores by Scriabin, Liszt, Scott Joplin, Couperin, Ravel, Bizet, Brahms, and other greats.

The prices are easily up to 50% less than those charged for comparable publications, and the books themselves are made for long use: We have a 15-year-old Dover text on silk-screening and block printing that's in very good shape; some of its shelf mates have yellowed, but Dover's pages are still bright. And because it was made in sewn signatures, its binding has held up despite rough handling during various art projects. Dover doesn't *have* to discount its books because they're well-priced to begin with!

Canadian readers, please note: The shipping surcharge on orders sent to Canada is 20%.

Special Factors: Satisfaction is guaranteed; returns are accepted within 10 days for refund.

EDITIONS

DESK WM
BOICEVILLE, NY 12412
914/657-7000

Catalog: $2
Save: up to 50%
Pay: check, MO, MC, V
Sells: old, used, and rare books
Store: 153 Rte. 28, Shokan, NY; Saturday, Sunday, and Monday 10–5

$$$$ ✉ ☎ 🍁 🇺🇸

Editions is one of our favorite sources for old and out-of-print books, which it sells at prices routinely 30% to 50% less than similar sources. Beyond price, the service is terrific: prompt delivery and attention to any problems that arise. Editions has been selling by mail since 1948, and also runs a separate store in Shokan, New York, on weekends.

The 64-page Editions catalogs are published approximately every four weeks, and include *partial* listings from a range of categories. (For example, one catalog may list poetry titles from Eliot to Neruda, and the next issue will run from Powys to Wyse.) Each catalog lists about 10,000 titles from categories that include fiction, literature, history, the social sciences, natural history, travel, women, soldiers and war, the Irish, Americana, the British, theater, philosophy and religion, food, labor, espionage, sports, antiques, gardening, animals, publishing, and Judaica.

We've found books at Editions priced far below what specialty book-sellers were charging. For example, a volume of Weegee's photographs priced at $58 in a recent Editions catalog was offered by a local book dealer for nearly $100, *sans* dust jacket. (Most of the books at Editions cost under $20.) While assembling a collection of food history and cookery books, we found an excellent selection among Editions' books, at prices that would shame several of our other sources. We've also found a number of original hardcover titles, in fine condition, at prices lower than those of their paperback editions.

Collectors and researchers may wish to see the catalogs for the first editions and books from the Heritage Press and Lakeside Press, as well as the occasional listings of regimental histories, genealogies, and books on local history.

Special Factors: Returns are accepted within 3 days; minimum order is $25 with credit cards.

FORTY-FIVES

**P.O. BOX 358
LEMOYNE, PA 17043-0358**

Catalog: $2 (see text)
Save: up to 50%
Pay: check or MO
Sells: original-label 45rpm records
Store: mail order only

$$ ✉ 🍁 🇺🇸

Forty-Fives has been selling vintage and current 45's since 1979, and its closely typed 18-page price list will summon memories you might have thought lost to time.

The catalog lists records released from 1950 through the current year, and entries include title and artist, the condition rating, and, in many cases, the label name. The records are grouped by price, which is the only reason you will find Gladys Knight and the Pips back-to-back with the Lennon Sisters, as you do here. Most of the choices are Top 40, AM hits of their day, and prices are very low—80% cost $1 each, and the remainder cost up to $20 or so, as of this writing. A small selection of LPs is available as well. These are chiefly pop and rock oldies, but a separate country & western price list is available—send a long, stamped, self-addressed envelope.

Please note that Forty-Fives asks you to order without enclosing payment; the firm will bill you for the records that are still available when your order is received. Orders of $15 or more qualify for a bonus 45—selected by Forty-Fives. (This is limited to one bonus per order, and three bonuses per customer.)

If you're putting together a party tape of your own favorites, check the current issue of the catalog for songs you may be missing. Any place that offers "Chewy Chewy," "Blue Money," "Judy in Disguise," "Aquarius," and "Ruby, Don't Take Your Love to Town"—simultaneously—rules nothing out.

Special Factors: Note ordering instructions and pay only when billed for records; minimum order is $5; orders are shipped worldwide.

FRONT ROW PHOTOS

**BOX 484-W91
NESCONSET, NY 11767**

Catalog: $1
Save: up to 50%
Pay: check or MO
Sells: rock star and celebrity photos
Store: mail order only

Front Row offers serious rock fans and photo collectors an easy way to get the shots they missed at the concert—without hazarding camera confiscation. Front Row, founded in 1978, offers thousands of photos at up to 50% less than prices charged elsewhere for similar goods. The catalog includes a sample photo—Front Row's choice.

The exhaustive inventory of concert photos of top rock, new wave, and heavy-metal groups runs from the 60s through today, from AC/DC to ZZ Top. The catalog lists thousands of photos of individual performers, groups, and pop celebrities, including the Beatles, Kim Basinger, Elvis, Guns & Roses, Heart, Jimi Hendrix, Led Zeppelin, Stevie Nicks, the Rolling Stones, and the Who, among others. The photos cost $1.60 for the 3-1/2″ by 5-1/4″ size, and $5.75 for the 8″ by 10″ size, and are offered in sets at extra savings.

Special Factors: Satisfaction is guaranteed; undamaged returns are accepted within 10 days; orders are shipped worldwide.

EDWARD R. HAMILTON, BOOKSELLER

**FALLS VILLAGE, CT
06031-5000**

Catalog: free
Save: up to 90%
Pay: check or MO
Sells: closeout and remaindered books
Store: mail order only

Mr. Hamilton's 48-page tabloid catalog, published monthly, lists *thousands* of bargain books in every conceivable category. Savings run an average of 50% to 70% on the publishers' prices. This firm is an old favorite among bargain-hunting bookworms.

You'll find texts of every sort, including art, humor, poetry, fiction, literature, photography, self-help, reference, business, crafts, psychology, history, film, science, cooking, sports, and biography. Past best-sellers show up here frequently, as well as books no other remainder source seems to have. Our experiences with Hamilton have been first-rate: prompt shipments of orders and refund checks for any books that had already sold out.

Special Factors: Satisfaction is guaranteed; returns are accepted; prepaid institutional orders are accepted.

JESSICA'S BISCUIT

**THE COOKBOOK
  PEOPLE**
BOX 301
**NEWTONVILLE, MA
  02160**
617/965-0530
FAX: 617/527-0113

Catalog: $2, refundable
Save: up to 80% (see text)
Pay: check, MO, MC, V
Sells: cookbooks
Store: mail order only

Jessica's Biscuit peppers its beautifully designed catalog so discreetly with sale books that you might overlook them at first. But they're here—scores in the regular catalog, and 40 pages of savings in the sale issues.

The boom in gourmet cooking and home entertaining has fostered a parallel rash of specialty cookbooks, and Jessica's Biscuit seems to offer them all. In addition to national cuisines, a recent catalog offered books with vegetarian, macrobiotic, microwave, diabetic, low-salt, sugar-free, low-cholesterol, wheat-free, fiber-rich, kosher, and low-cost recipes. The regional books run from American to Transylvanian cookery, and volumes devoted to such specialties as muffins, pizza, biscuits, meringue, mushrooms, barbecuing, cheesecake, chili, garlic, and squid have all appeared. Related topics, including canning and preserving, outfitting a working kitchen, buffets, wines, cake decorating, and entertaining in style are covered as well.

Jessica's Biscuit would be a valuable source even without the discounts, but the savings (on the sale titles) average 45% and run as high as 80%, and the catalog makes great reading while you're waiting for the pizza to be delivered.

Special Factors: Satisfaction is guaranteed; returns are accepted.

KICKING MULE RECORDS, INC.

P.O. BOX 158
ALDERPOINT, CA 95411
707/926-5312

Catalog: free
Save: up to 70% (see text)
Pay: check, MO, MC, V, Discover
Sells: recordings under Kicking Mule and other labels
Store: mail order only

$$ ✉ ☎ 🍁 ▰

Kicking Mule was recommended to us by a reader for "mostly blues, folk albums with good acoustic guitar, banjo, mandolin, and dulcimer." Kicking Mule was established in 1972, and it sells recordings under its own label and those of other music publishers.

Kicking Mule records, tapes, books, and teaching tapes are featured in the catalog, but you'll also find "Lark in the Morning" video music lessons, and recordings of guitar, banjo, and dulcimer from Flying Fish, Rounder, Schanachie, and Sugar Hill. Prices average 25% to 40% below list, but specials and volume pricing deepen the discounts to as much as 70% on selected items.

Special Factors: Price quote by phone or letter with SASE; quantity discounts are available.

LASER SOUND DISCOUNTERS

P.O. BOX 7151, DEPT. WBMC
ROCHESTER, MN 55903

Brochure: free
Save: up to 40%
Pay: check, MO, MC, V
Sells: CDs, videotapes, laser discs, etc.
Store: mail order only

$$

Laser Sound Discounters is a small company offering big savings on "most CDs that are currently in production." The firm's brochure describes the sales policy and lists the single disc prices for dozens of labels, from A&M to Windham Hill. Note that disc *titles* are not listed, but you can buy the Schwann Spectrum Compact Disc Catalog from Laser Sound for $4 (it's free with a purchase of ten or more discs), to see what's currently available.

Savings average 25% to 40%, and CD singles, DAT recordings, music videos, laser discs, and carrying cases are also available. If you want to know the price of a title whose label isn't listed in the brochure, write for a price quote..

Special Factors: Price quote by letter with SASE; quantity discounts are available; C.O.D. orders are accepted; orders are shipped worldwide.

METACOM, INC.

ADVENTURES IN CASSETTES
DEPT. C119
5353 NATHAN LANE
PLYMOUTH, MN 55442
800-328-0108
FAX: 612/588-2913

Catalog: free (see text)
Save: up to 30%
Pay: check, MO, MC, V, AE, Discover
Sells: audiotapes, CDs, and videotapes
Store: Mail order only

$$

Metacom, better known as Adventures in Cassettes, has captured the comedy classics of Abbott and Costello, Fanny Brice, Burns and Allen, Fibber McGee and Molly, Jack Benny, Will Rogers, and other radio luminaries on audio cassette, along with mysteries and dramas of the era. Selections from the Gielgud/Richardson Sherlock Holmes series are available, as well as Arch Oboler's "Lights Out, Everybody," "War of the Worlds," recordings of the Damon Runyon Theater, the Lone Ranger, the Green Hornet, Hopalong Cassidy, and other favorites. And you can invoke the mood of bygone Saturday mornings at will with the videotapes of cartoon greats, including the finest moments of Casper the Friendly Ghost and Felix the Cat, among others. The "You Rang" phone answering machine tapes featuring Bugs Bunny and his Looney Tunes pals are available as well.

Music is represented by a wide selection of top-of-the-charts rock and country hits from past years. Adventures in Cassettes also sells language and motivational tapes, which may help you to learn German or French, stop smoking, improve your memory, lose weight, or achieve other goals. Prices of the tapes are comparable to those charged by other discount houses, running from $3.98 to $9.98 each. A coupon for $2 off your first order is enclosed with the catalog. Quantity discounts and bonuses may be offered.

Special Factors: Satisfaction is guaranteed; returns are accepted within 30 days for exchange, refund, or credit; minimum order is $15 with credit cards.

PAGES/BOOKTRADERS LTD.

**801 SOUTH IRWIN AVE.
GREEN BAY, WI 54301
414/437-9566**

Catalog: free
Save: up to 50%
Pay: check, MO, MC, V, AE, Discover, Optima
Sells: new, used, and out-of-print books
Store: same address; Monday through Saturday 10–5

Pages/Booktraders Ltd. has run a run up to 93%.
Green Bay since 1982, and offers selections from its stock of new, used, and rare books through a ten-page catalog. While some new titles are sold at or near publishers' prices, out-of-print and rare book titles may be priced as much as 50% less than what other book dealers are charging.

The catalog we received listed books on art, world history, transportation, mythology, horror, literature, hunting, and a range of other topics. There were many illustrated books and British and first editions among the offerings, and the descriptions included notes on the condition of the books. Pages/Booktraders also offers a book search service for $3 a title, and says that "we can't guarantee finding a book although we do find about half." If you've had no luck with the free search services, you might try again for this nominal fee.

Special Factors: Price quote by phone or letter with SASE; authorized returns are accepted within 7 days for exchange, refund, or credit; orders are shipped worldwide.

THE POTTERS SHOP INC.

31 THORPE RD.
NEEDHAM, MA 02194
617/449-7687

Catalog: free
Save: 30% average
Pay: check or MO
Sells: books on ceramics and pottery
Store: same address; Monday through
　　Thursday 9:30–5:30, Friday 9:30–2

$$　✉　🍁　▆

The Potters Shop, established in 1977, sells books on ceramics and pottery at discounts of at least 15%, and as much as 75% on sale titles. Hard-to-find and imported books are available here, and The Potters Shop searches for books, maintains want lists, and buys used books on the subject. If you find yourself in Needham, stop in at the shop; the books are there, as well as the pottery of local artisans.

The Potters Shop is offering readers of this book an additional 5% discount on their first order. Identify yourself as a WBMC reader when you order. This WBMC reader discount expires February 1, 1992.

Special Factors: Price quote by phone or letter with SASE; shipping is included; orders are shipped worldwide.

PUBLISHERS CENTRAL BUREAU

ONE CHAMPION AVE.,
　DEPT. WBMC-91
AVENEL, NJ 07001-2301
201/382-7960

Catalog: free
Save: up to 93%
Pay: check, MO, MC, V, AE, Optima
Sells: videotapes, books, records, and
　audiotapes
Store: mail order only

$$$　✉　🍁

Publishers Central Bureau is one of the nation's largest clearinghouses for publishers and producers of videotapes and records. Everything seems to turn up here, and first-rate bargains abound—savings run up to 93%.

PCB carries hundreds of videotapes—movie classics, cult hits, hard-to-find shorts, documentaries, workout tapes, and music videos are all available. The monthly catalogs still offer books on every topic—Americana, art and architecture, boating, computers, boxing, trivia, occult and magic, animals, film, humor, crafts, erotica, gardening, diet and beauty, cuisine, etc. Pop-up books for children, trivia games, posters, library embossers, self-inking stampers, and similar goods have appeared in past mailings. Also carried are records and tapes—classical, golden oldies, old radio shows, and opera. Bonuses and sweepstakes are featured frequently.

Special Factors: Satisfaction is guaranteed; returns are accepted within 14 days; minimum order is $10 with credit cards.

PUBLISHERS CLEARING HOUSE

**101 WINNERS CIRCLE
PORT WASHINGTON,
NY 11050**
516/883-5432

Information: inquire
Save: up to 50%
Pay: check or MO
Sells: magazine subscriptions
Store: mail order only

$$$$ ✉ 🍁

Publishers Clearing House acts as an agent for magazine publishers, offering *scores* of subscriptions to popular and special-interest magazines at savings of up to 50% on regular rates. PCH guarantees lowest to-the-public prices.

Subscriptions to *Reader's Digest, Consumer Reports, Organic Gardening, Cook's, Working Mother, TV Guide, Discover, Time,* and *Audio* were among the "99 unbeatable magazine values" offered in a recent mailing. Bonuses, premiums, and sweepstakes are featured.

Our own experiences with PCH have been faultless. We've placed scores of orders over the years, and the one time a problem occurred, PCH responded quickly and resolved it.

Special Factors: Satisfaction is guaranteed; inquire for information; installment plan is available.

THE SCHOLAR'S BOOKSHELF

**51 EVERETT DR.
PRINCETON JUNCTION,
NJ 08550**

Catalog: free
Save: up to 75%
Pay: check, MO, MC, V
Sells: scholarly and university press books
Store: mail order only

$$$ ✉ ☎ 🍁 🇺🇸

University presses still produce highbrow texts for scholars, but a surprising number are of interest—and accessible—to nonprofessionals as well. Such books are not immune to the fate that befalls many of their commercial counterparts, though—remaindering.

The Scholar's Bookshelf turns publishing misfortune into intellectual excitement 14 times a year, offering a wide variety of university press and scholarly imprint remainders at up to 75% off published prices. The 64-page catalog is packed with concise descriptions of volumes on architecture and urban planning, archaeology, art (ancient to modern), photography, history and politics, psychology, philosophy, religion, Judaica, and the sciences. The offerings include facsimiles, illuminated manuscripts (reproductions), and other special editions.

Special Factors: All sales are final, so consider selections carefully; order promptly, since stock may be limited; minimum order is $10, $15 with credit cards; orders are shipped worldwide.

SCRIPT CITY

**8033 SUNSET BLVD.,
SUITE 1500-HR
HOLLYWOOD, CA 90046
213/871-0707
FAX: 213/871-9260**

Catalog: $2, refundable
Save: up to 50% (see text)
Pay: check, MO, MC, V, AE, Discover, CB, DC
Sells: TV and movie scripts, theme gifts, etc.
Store: mail order only

$$ ✉ ☎ 🍁 🇺🇸

Scripts are the featured players here—over 10,000 screenplays used on movie sets, early drafts (that may include lost scenes), and scripts from TV shows, movies, and mini-series. Script City sells copies for under $20 and up, while at least one competitor charges $40 to $50 for the same titles.

The movie categories include Academy Award winners and nominees, late releases, drama/mystery, horror/sci-fi, comedy, action/adventure, and "assorted favorites." The early drafts should be of interest to students of the cinema; what was Woody Allen's vision of *Play It Again, Sam* in the first draft? A short list of treatments (synopses of 30 to 40 pages preceding the screenplay) and storyboards (drawings or photos showing shot sequences) is given, and there are hundreds of scripts for TV shows, pilots, series, and movies.

Much of the catalog is devoted to books, software, audiotapes, and videotapes for the aspiring screenwriter, including vital directories and insiders' guides. Lobby cards, movie posters, publicity photos, and a line of logo-emblazoned T-shirts are all offered. Many of these items are *not* discounted, but it's nice to know where you can buy a "Wiseguy" hat or "thirtysomething" nightshirt if you want one.

Please note: Instructors in the field are entitled to a 10% educators' discount; inquire on your institution's letterhead for details.

Special Factors: Quantity discounts are available; authorized returns are accepted within 7 days for exchange, refund, or credit; institutional accounts are available; orders are shipped worldwide.

STRAND BOOK STORE, INC.

828 BROADWAY
NEW YORK, NY 10003
212/473-1452
FAX: 212/473-2591

Catalog: free
Save: up to 80%
Pay: check, MO, MC, V, AE, Discover
Sells: new and used books
Store: same address; Monday through Friday 9:30–9:30, Saturday 9:30–6:30, Sunday 11–6; also 159 John St., New York, NY; Monday through Sunday 10–9

Manhattan's legendary Strand Book Store boasts eight miles of books—more than two million volumes—and is the largest dealer of used and out-of-print books in the U.S.A. The catalog lists a fraction of the inventory of this firm, which was established in 1929.

The catalog of "Specials," published eight times yearly, lists thousands of titles of works of every sort, from B.A. Botkin's *A Treasury of American Folklore* to the 16-volume, first edition of the *Oxford English Dictionary*

($995 from $1,500). This catalog includes critique and commentary, biographies, books on art, architecture, philosophy, crafts, politics, food, drama, and other fields of interest. The "Review" catalog, available to institutional accounts, lists new releases at 50% off publishers' prices. Send your request for this catalog on your institution's letterhead. Strand has recently introduced several pages of classical and jazz recordings (tape and CD) to the general catalog; they're sold at under $10 each, at this writing.

You must visit to do justice to Strand's staggering inventory, and to find the pricing "accidents"—books ticketed at a few dollars that are worth many times that. (Most New York City book collectors can pluck more than one such volume from their shelves.) Strand does have a Rare Book room, where you'll find first, limited, and scarce editions as well as fine bindings and signed and inscribed books.

Special Factors: Price quote by phone or letter; specify catalog desired and request by postcard or letter; want lists are maintained; book collections are purchased; institutional accounts are available; returns are accepted; minimum order is $15 with credit cards; orders are shipped worldwide.

TARTAN BOOK SALES

500 ARCH ST., DEPT. N14
WILLIAMSPORT, PA 17705
800-233-8467, EXT. 507
INQUIRIES AND PA
ORDERS 717/326-2461,
EXT. 507
FAX: 717/326-6769

Catalog and Brochure: free
Save: up to 74%
Pay: check, MO, MC, V
Sells: used books
Store: same address (Brodart Outlet Bookstore); Thursday and Friday 10–6, Saturday 10–4

$$$$

Tartan, a direct-mail division of Brodart Co., sells hardbound books that have had short-term library circulation. Only undamaged, unsoiled, popular adult fiction and nonfiction books are offered—no paperbacks, juvenile titles, or reference texts. Tartan was established in 1960.

Tom Clancy's *Clear and Present Danger* published at $21.95, sold here for $5.98; Danielle Steele's *Daddy*, published at $19.95, was offered here for $5.49. They were among hundreds of titles in past catalogs, which feature general fiction, nonfiction, mystery, romance, science fiction, and

Westerns. This is a great way to get hardbound books at prices little more than those charged for the paperback editions.

Tartan also does business with other businesses—libraries and bookstores—and publishes separate catalogs for each. To receive the latest listing of over 3,000 titles with a discount schedule, send a request on the letterhead of your institution or company.

Special Factors: Returns are accepted if an error was made in filling the order; orders are shipped worldwide.

SEE ALSO

America's Hobby Center, Inc. ● manuals on model assembly, radio control, etc. ● CRAFTS

Art Supply Warehouse, Inc. ● art books and manuals ● ART MATERIALS

Sam Ash Music Corp. ● sheet music ● MUSIC

Astronomics/Christophers, Ltd. ● star charts and manuals on astronomy ● CAMERAS

Bailey's, Inc. ● books on logging, chain saw use and maintenance, etc. ● TOOLS

Baron Bridge Supplies ● books, cards, and teaching aids for bridge ● TOYS

Bass Pro Shops ● boating and fishing books and videotapes ● SPORTS

Bike Nashbar ● manuals on bicycle repair ● SPORTS

Dick Blick Co. ● films, slides, videotapes, and manuals on arts and crafts ● ART MATERIALS

Bruce Medical Supply ● books on vitamins, health care, and medical topics ● MEDICINE

Butterbrooke Farm Seed Co-Op ● booklets on gardening topics ● FARM

Campmor ● field guides, survival and outdoor guides ● SPORTS

The Caning Shop ● books on seat weaving, upholstery, basketry ● CRAFTS

Capital Cycle Corporation ● factory-repair manuals for BMW cycles ● AUTO

Caprilands Herb Farm ● books on herbs and gardening, making wreaths, and cooking ● FARM

Central Tractor Farm & Family Center ● shop manuals for farm equipment, books on the history of farm implements and equipment ● FARM

Ceramic Supply of New York & New Jersey, Inc. • artists' manuals and books on crafts • *ART MATERIALS*

Cheap Shot Inc. • reloading manuals • *SPORTS*

Cherry Tree Toys, Inc. • manuals on wood projects and toy making • *TOYS*

Circle Craft Supply • books and manuals on arts and crafts • *CRAFTS*

Co-Op Artists' Materials • manuals for the graphic arts, design, decoy carving, painting instruction, etc. • *ART MATERIALS*

Craft King, Inc. • craft project books • *CRAFTS*

Craftsman Wood Service Co. • books on woodworking and crafts • *CRAFTS*

The Cuisinart Cooking Club • cooking newsletter, videotapes, and cookbooks • *HOME: KITCHEN*

Custom Golf Clubs, Inc. • texts on golf club making and repair, golfing, etc. • *SPORTS*

Cycle Goods Corp. • texts on bicycling, repair, and maintenance • *SPORTS*

Daleco Master Breeder Products • books on fish and saltwater fish care and breeding • *ANIMAL*

Defender Industries, Inc. • manuals and videotapes on boating, seamanship, racing, etc. • *AUTO*

Dharma Trading Co. • books on textile dyeing, painting, batiking, etc. • *CRAFTS*

The Dog's Outfitter • books and videotapes on dogs, cats, horses, etc. • *ANIMAL*

Walter Drake & Sons, Inc. • stationery, address labels, etc. • *GENERAL MERCHANDISE*

Eastcoast Software • educational, business, and entertainment programs • *OFFICE: COMPUTING*

Economy Enterprises • plans for building toys, furniture, tools, etc. • *TOOLS*

EduCALC Corporation • computer books and programs • *OFFICE: COMPUTING*

Elderly Instruments • folk, rock, and esoteric recordings, songbooks, history, and manuals • *MUSIC*

The Fiber Studio • books on knitting, spinning, dyeing, and weaving • *CRAFTS*

Fish'n Shack • selection of books and videotapes on hunting and fishing • *SPORTS*

Gallery Graphics, Inc. • nostalgic-theme notes and cards • *ART, ANTIQUES*

Gander Mountain, Inc. • videotapes on hunting and fishing topics • *SPORTS*

Giardinelli Band Instrument Co., Inc. • records and books on music • *MUSIC*

Glorybee Natural Sweeteners, Inc. ● cookbooks featuring honey ●
FOOD

Gohn Bros. ● Amish and country cookbooks, quilting books ● CLOTHING

Marv Golden Discount Sales, Inc. ● aviation flight guides and binders ●
AUTO

Great Northern Weaving ● books on shirret, rug weaving, and rug
braiding ● CRAFTS

H & R Corporation ● reference books on computing and technical topics
● SURPLUS

Hobby Surplus Sales ● model manuals, reproduction train model
catalogs ● CRAFTS

IMPCO, Inc. ● Mercedes-Benz car maintenance manuals ● AUTO

Jerry's Artarama, Inc. ● books and videotapes on fine arts and crafts ●
ART MATERIALS

The Kennel Vet Corp. ● large selection of books on breeds of dogs,
cats, and horses, vet manuals ● ANIMAL

E.C. Kraus Wine & Beermaking Supplies ● books on wine- and beer-
making ● FOOD

Lone Star Percussion ● books on drumming and percussion recordings
● MUSIC

Mandolin Brothers, Ltd. ● music books, audiotapes, videotapes, and
sheet music ● MUSIC

Mass. Army & Navy Store ● survival manuals and outdoor guides ●
SURPLUS

Master Animal Care ● veterinary handbooks ● ANIMAL

Mellinger's Inc. ● reference books on gardening, farming, landscaping, and
food preservation ● FARM

Metropolitan Music Co. ● manuals and plans for making and repairing
stringed instruments ● MUSIC

Bob Morgan Woodworking Supplies ● books on woodworking,
furniture making, cabinetry, toy making, etc. ● CRAFTS

National Educational Music Co., Ltd. ● music software ● MUSIC

New England Cheesemaking Supply Co. ● publications on making
cheese ● HOME: KITCHEN

Newark Dressmaker Supply, Inc. ● patterns, books, and guides on
needlework and other crafts ● CRAFTS

Northern Wholesale Veterinary Supply, Inc. ● books on care and
breeding of livestock, dogs, and cats ● ANIMAL

Omaha Vaccine Co., Inc. ● books on care and breeding of horses,
livestock, dogs, and cats ● ANIMAL

Orion Telescope Center ● star charts and manuals on astronomy ●
CAMERAS

Overton's Sports Center, Inc. ● windsurfing books and videotapes ●
SPORTS

Patti Music Corp. ● sheet music ● MUSIC

Pueblo to People ● books and tapes on Central and South America and Third World issues ● *GENERAL MERCHANDISE*

Porter's Camera Store, Inc. ● books and videos on photography ● *CAMERAS*

Retired Persons Services Inc. ● health-care manuals ● *MEDICINE*

Rocky Mountain Stationery ● handmade cards and notes ● *GENERAL MERCHANDISE*

Romni Wools and Fibres Ltd. ● books on textile arts ● *CRAFTS*

Sailboard Warehouse, Inc. ● windsurfing books and videotapes ● *SPORTS*

Scope City ● star charts, books, manuals ● *CAMERAS*

Shar Products Company ● sheet music, classical music videotapes, and audio cassettes ● *MUSIC*

R.C. Steele Co. ● AKC videotapes of dog shows, manuals for pet professionals ● *ANIMAL*

Straw Into Gold, Inc. ● Folkwear patterns and books on fiber crafts ● *CRAFTS*

Sultan's Delight, Inc. ● cookbooks featuring Middle Eastern and Greek cuisine ● *FOOD*

The Surplus Store ● survival manuals ● *SURPLUS*

That Fish Place ● books on aquariums, fish, and related topics ● *ANIMAL*

Turnbaugh Printers Supply Co. ● texts on printing ● *OFFICE*

Turner Greenhouses ● books on gardening ● *FARM*

United Pharmacal Company, Inc. ● books and manuals on the care and breeding of a variety of animals ● *ANIMAL*

University Products, Inc. ● preservation supplies for book collections, references (books and videos) on archival conservation ● *GENERAL MERCHANDISE*

Veteran Leather Company, Inc. ● guides to leatherworking ● *CRAFTS*

Walnut Acres ● natural foods and vegetarian cookbooks ● *FOOD*

Weinkrantz Musical Supply Co., Inc. ● student music books and cassettes ● *MUSIC*

West Manor Music ● small selection of music manuals ● *MUSIC*

Wholesale Veterinary Supply, Inc. ● veterinary texts and Farnam videos ● *ANIMAL*

Wholesale Tape and Supply Company ● blank audiotapes and videotapes, cases, accessories, etc. ● *APPLIANCES*

The Wine Enthusiast ● books and videotapes on wine ● *FOOD*

CAMERAS, PHOTOGRAPHIC AND DARKROOM EQUIPMENT, OPTICS, FILM, AND SERVICES

Equipment, supplies, and services

Prices of cameras and photographic equipment are, for the most part, quite competitive. Even major electronics outlets with small camera departments can probably offer discounts of up to 40% on list prices. The large camera houses carry much more than cameras, bulbs, and film. The specialized goods available include lighting equipment, screens, film editors, splicers, batteries, projection tables, lenses, filters, adapters, cases, darkroom outfits, and chemicals—and they're all available at good discounts. Even if you don't need custom work done, you can have your film processed, enlargements made, slides duplicated, and other services performed by a discount mail-order lab at about half the price a drugstore or retail outlet would charge.

Unfortunately, the mail-order camera business has been plagued by questionable selling practices. One is the "strip-and-requip" gambit, in which a camera seller takes the outfit as supplied by the manufacturer and *removes* the extra lenses, case, lens covers, flash attachment, and other accessories in the original package. The seller then replaces the lenses with inferior models (usually termed "famous make" in the ad), and offers the stripped outfit at a very low price. The lens covers, case, and attachments are sold separately and the original lenses are also offered at a surcharge. The price of the original package winds up much closer to list when the shopper is through with the "extras" and "improvements." We've seen far fewer examples of this practice in the last few years since it's been given wide publicity, and many firms now make a point of stating that they sell cameras "as outfitted by the manufacturers." The repackaging maneuver and several other less-than-ethical business practices are detailed in the Better Business Bureau booklet "Buying Photographic Equipment by Mail." If your local BBB office doesn't have copies, you can order one through the Council's headquarters in Virginia. See the chapter introduction of "Appliances" for the address.

One of the biggest photographic demons is the "magnetic" photo album, widely sold in department and specialty stores. Seemingly innocuous, its polyvinyl-film sheets give off vinyl chloride gas, and the cardboard pages exude peroxide vapors. Both cause slides and prints to deteriorate. The old albums with black paper pages also cast harmful, destructive gases. Some conservationists believe that an entire generation of family photographs is being destroyed in this way, and by storage in garages, attics, and basements. (Keep photographs in temperate, relatively dry areas, out of light as much as possible.) Archival-quality materials—acid-free albums and storage boxes, Mylar sheet protectors, "safe" slide sheets, etc.—will preserve your pictures. These and other conservation materials are available from University Products, Inc., listed in "General."

THE GREY MARKET

Grey-market goods, also known as "parallel" or "direct" imports, are usually defined as products that are intended for sale in other countries. They are imported outside the approved distribution channels, without authorization of the U.S. trademark owner. Parallel imports may make up as much as 30% of the high-end camera market, and up to $7 billion a year in retail sales.

Parallel imports sell well because they're usually cheaper than their "authorized" counterparts. In previous editions of this book, we have cautioned readers that grey-market goods may not bear warranties that are valid in the U.S. We also know that products might be manufactured under different quality-control standards, and we have urged readers to ask whether a prospective purchase was U.S.-made and whether the warranty would be honored in this country.

But asking questions may not ensure a safe purchase, especially if the seller is not truthful. (For example, some will claim that a product has an "international warranty." There is no such thing.) And you simply won't be told of critically important facts: The importer who uses broomsticks to "reinforce" the door of a luxury car, in order to appear to meet U.S. safety standards, is not going to volunteer this information. The grey-market batteries you buy won't tell you that they were left in a hot warehouse for a month, have little power left, and may leak. Reading the labels will not inform you that the bargain beauty products you bought are adulterated—the perfume spray is propelled by Freon, and the night cream contains an outlawed dye. (The labels, slapped on the packages at the port of entry to meet import regulations, may represent the contents of the *U.S.* product only.)

Champions of parallel imports claim that they promote competition, thereby keeping prices down. When a product's specifications and after-purchase support are identical to those of the "authorized" item, this is a fair assertion. But it is difficult, if not impossible, for a consumer to make this determination. Because of the problems that have occurred, we do not feel that parallel imports, as a group, represent good values. Therefore, we have not *knowingly* listed grey-marketers in this edition of WBMC. We cannot, of course, make any guarantees, and the firms may change their policies in the future. If you wish to be completely sure of a source, contact the *manufacturer* of the product you wish to purchase and ask whether the mail-order company is an authorized distributor of that product. Don't forget to ask the mail-order company whether the warranty is honored by the service centers of the *U.S. manufacturer.* And, as a final precaution, make your purchase by credit card. If all else fails, you may be able to use provisions of the Fair Credit Billing Act to get a "chargeback." (See "Complaints" in "The Complete Guide to Buying by Mail" for more information.)

ABC PHOTO SERVICE

9016 PRINCE WILLIAM ST., DEPT. CS-91 MANASSAS, VA 22110 703/369-2566

Catalog: free
Save: up to 30%
Pay: check, MO, MC, V, AE
Sells: film developing
Store: same address; Monday through Saturday 9–5

ABC Photo Service, established in 1945, offers its services as a professional and commercial photography lab by mail. Specials on standard processing and enlargements are run frequently.

ABC's services include film processing, and automated and custom printing in color and black and white; the print and enlargement sizes range from 3-1/2" by 5" to 48" by 144". The standard print finish is semimatte, although pebble and canvas photo surfaces are available. Photos may also be mounted on canvas panels or canvas stretchers. Duplication services are available for slides, copy negatives, and "internegatives," and ABC also offers wedding album packages. Request the catalog to see the full range of what's available.

Readers outside the continental U.S., please note: Only credit card payments are accepted.

Special Factors: Price quote by phone or letter with SASE; liability for damaged or lost film is limited to replacement with unexposed film; orders are shipped worldwide.

ASTRONOMICS/ CHRISTOPHERS, LTD.

2401 TEE CIRCLE, SUITE 106-W
NORMAN, OK 73069
800-422-7876

Catalogs: free (see text)
Save: up to 50%
Pay: check, MO, MC, V, AE, Discover
Sells: telescopes and optics
Store: same address; Monday through Friday 9:30–5:30, Saturday by appointment

This firm sells telescopes and birding equipment made by the best firms in the business at up to 50% below list, and its stock includes complete lines for astronomical photography. The information-packed birding and astronomical catalogs are free if you send a self-addressed, business-sized envelope with 85¢ in stamps; if you want both catalogs as well as other brochures, send $1.85 and request the "full, 80-page" catalog. Astronomics/Christophers, formerly known as Ad-Libs Astronomics, was established in 1970, and *sells no grey-market goods*.

Optics and accessories by Astromedia, Bausch & Lomb, Bushnell, Celestron, DayStar, Dover, Edmund, aus Jena, Kowa, Leica (Leitz), Lumicon, Meade, MotoFocus, Nikon, Optolyth, Questar, Sky Publishing, Swarovski, Swift, TeleVue, Vernonscope, and Zeiss are available. Astronomics/Christophers stocks catadioptric, refractor, and reflector telescopes, lenses, mirrors, eyepieces, tripods, photo adapters, visual and photographic filters, equatorial mounts and wedges, spotting scopes for bird watching, and many other items. Astronomical and bird-watching binoculars are also offered.

If you're new to astronomy, be sure to see the selection of books and star charts; manuals, slides, maps, atlases, and other reference tools are also available. The catalogs include valuable guides to buying the appropriate binoculars or telescope for your needs, choosing eyepieces and photographic accessories, and complete lists of specifications.

Special Factors: Price quote by phone or letter; shipping is included on prepaid orders delivered within the continental U.S.; minimum order is $25; orders are shipped worldwide.

COLORCHROME

P.O. BOX 330318
SEATTLE, WA 98133
206/364-2485

Brochure: free
Save: up to 40%
Pay: check, MO, MC, V
Sells: 35mm film services
Store: mail order only

$$$ ✉   🍁

Colorchrome, founded in 1975, is the mail-order division of a large lab that processes film for professional photographers and offers you the same quality services at up to 40% below list or comparable retail.

Colorchrome can provide 35mm color film and slide processing, and full-frame enlargements from 3″ by 5″ to 20″ by 30″ in matte, silk, and canvas textures. Flush (borderless) mounting is done on acid-free board; flush-framed, unmounted prints can be set in gold, silver, black, oak, and walnut "floater" frames. Photo calendars and photo jigsaw puzzles are also available. Postpaid mailers are included with the brochure.

Special Factors: Quarterly specials flyers are sent to customers; monthly specials are listed in *Popular Photography;* liability is limited to replacement of lost or damaged film with a like quantity of unexposed film.

DANLEY'S

P.O. BOX 4401-WM
HALFMOON, NY 12065
518/664-2014

Catalog and Price List: free
Save: up to 50%
Pay: check or MO
Sells: optics and accessories
Store: mail order only

$$$ ✉   ☎   🍁   ▀

Danley's carries one of the best selections of top-of-the-line optics for sports, marine use, and other specialized functions at up to 50% off list prices. This source, established in 1960, is a real find for the stargazer, spectator, bird watcher, and hunter.

Danley's stocks binoculars and spotting scopes and such accessories as carrying cases, auto window adapters, camera adapters, and rain guards. The brands include Bausch & Lomb, Bushnell, aus Jena, Kowa, Leica (Leitz), Mirador, Nikon, Steiner, Swift, and Zeiss. Danley's offers every type of binocular and scope made by these firms, including standard and compact models, sports binoculars, armored models for field work, astronomical models, waterproof styles for marine use, zoom lenses, theater glasses, and telescopes. Bausch & Lomb, Stitz, Tiltall, and Velbon tripods are stocked as well.

Canadian readers, please note: Only U.S. funds are accepted.

Special Factors: Price quote by phone or letter with SASE; layaway plan is available; authorized returns are accepted.

MARDIRON OPTICS

THE BINOCULAR PLACE
4 SPARTAN CIRCLE,
DEPT. WBMC
STONEHAM, MA 02180
617/938-8339

Brochure and Price List: two first-class stamps
Save: 33% average
Pay: check or MO
Sells: optics, binoculars, and telescopes
Store: mail order only

 $$$ ✉ 🇺🇸

Mardiron sells binoculars, telescopes, and opera glasses from a select group of manufacturers at savings of up to 45% on list prices. Mardiron has been in business since 1983.

Mardiron features the full line of Steiner binoculars (marine, aeronautical, etc.), which are used extensively by 41 military forces. Binoculars, spotting scopes, and astronomical telescopes by Swift are offered. Also available is Varo's "Nite-Eye," which facilitates night vision (but is not a shooting scope). The largest user of the Nite-Eye is said to be the U.S. Border Patrol. There's a reason these haven't shown up in the electronics novelty catalogs—even at a discount, they cost over $4,000.

The price lists and brochures include Mardiron's recommendations of different models for specific purposes. Telescope accessories are also available. Send two first-class stamps for the literature, and specify whether you're interested in binoculars, spotting scopes, or astronomical telescopes.

Mardiron is offering a special discount to WBMC readers. Buy two or more binoculars or telescopes, and you may deduct 10% from the price of the less expensive item(s). This WBMC reader discount expires February 1, 1992.

Special Factors: Price quote by phone or letter with SASE; shipping is included.

ORION TELESCOPE CENTER

DEPT. WBM
P.O. BOX 1158
SANTA CRUZ, CA 95061
800-447-1001
IN CA 800-443-1001
408/464-0466
FAX: 408/464-0466

Catalog: free
Save: up to 40%
Pay: check, MO, MC, V
Sells: telescopes, binoculars, and accessories
Store: 2450 17th Ave., Santa Cruz, CA; Monday through Saturday 10–5:30; also 10555 S. DeAnza Blvd., Cupertino, CA; Monday to Saturday 10–5:30, Thursday 10–8, Sunday 12–5

 (see text)

Orion can give you the moon at stellar savings on top-quality telescopes and accessories. The handsome, 48-page catalog includes articles on telescope selection and sky watching, as well as complete product descriptions.

Established in 1975, Orion stocks astronomical and terrestrial telescopes, including spotting, reflector, refractor, guide, finder, "deep sky," and other scopes by Celestron, Edmund, Meade, Orion, and TeleVue. Camera adapters, filters, lenses, optical tubes, tripods, eyepieces, star charts, books, and other accessories are available as well. Orion also carries binoculars of several types, including deep-sky, sport, folding, waterproof, and armored models.

Please note: Orion ships only to the U.S. and Canada.

Special Factors: Satisfaction is guaranteed; price quote by phone or letter for institutional orders.

PORTER'S CAMERA STORE, INC.

P.O. BOX 628
CEDAR FALLS, IA 50613
319/268-0104
FAX: 800-779-5524

Catalog: free (see text)
Save: 35% average
Pay: check, MO, MC, V
Sells: cameras and darkroom equipment
Store: 323 Viking Rd., Cedar Falls, IA;
   Monday through Saturday 9:30–5:30

Porter's has been selling cameras and darkroom equipment since 1914, and publishes a 112-page tabloid catalog packed with an enormous range of goods, at prices up to 67% below list. *Porter's sells no grey-market goods.*

Both amateurs and professionals will appreciate the buys here, on cameras and lenses, filters, darkroom equipment, film, bags and cases, batteries, studio equipment, chemicals, paper, and much more. The brands run from Agfa to Vivitar, the sales policy is clearly detailed in the catalog, and Porter's has even deputized one of its staff to answer your questions about equipment. And if you're in Cedar Falls, you can drop by the warehouse outlet store, where you'll find everything tagged at catalog prices—a welcome departure from the two-tier policies prevailing at most discount stores.

Canadian readers, please note: The catalog costs $3 in *Canadian funds,* but orders must be paid in U.S. funds. The catalog describes particulars and includes a shipping rate chart.

Please note: The catalog costs $10 in U.S. funds if sent to an address without a U.S. or Canadian postal code.

Special Factors: Price quote by phone or letter with SASE; authorized returns are accepted; institutional accounts are available; orders are shipped worldwide ($100 minimum order).

PRO PHOTO LABS

**P.O. BOX 3151
S. HACKENSACK, NJ
07606**

Price List: free
Save: up to 50%
Pay: check, MO, MC, V
Sells: film-processing services
Store: mail order only

$$$ ✉ 🍁 ▤

Pro Photo, which says that "over 78% of our orders come from repeat customers," offers film developing and enlargements at excellent prices. Pro Photo will develop your 35mm, 110, 126, and disc film and make prints from your 35mm slides and negatives. Enlargements, color and black-and-white proof sheets, and other custom services are available.

Special Factors: Film mailers are sent on request; liability is limited to the cost of the unexposed film; minimum order is $8 with credit cards; orders are shipped worldwide.

SCOPE CITY

**679 EASY ST.
SIMI VALLEY, CA 93065
805/522-6646**

Catalog: free
Save: up to 35%
Pay: check, MO, MC, V, AE, Discover, Optima
Sells: telescopes, binoculars, and other optics
Store: same address; Monday through Friday 9–6, Saturday 10–6; also 3132 Pacific Coast Hwy., Torrance, 3033 S. Bristol, Costa Mesa, 4766 Clairemont Mesa Blvd., San Diego, and 14324 Ventura Blvd, Sherman Oaks, CA; and 2216 Paradise Rd., Las Vegas, NV

$$ ✉ ☎ 🍁

Scope City has been selling telescopes, binoculars, spotting scopes, and other optics since 1976. The catalog shows telescopes and accessories by Celestron, Edmund, Meade, Parks, Questar, Simmons, and TeleVue. Both field and specialty binoculars by Kronehof, Leica (Leitz), Meade, Optolyth, Parks, and other manufacturers are sold. Scope City also offers lenses, eyepieces, adapters, mirrors, celestial charts, slides, manuals, and other reference tools. Not all of the prices are discounted, but we calculated savings of up to 35% on selected telescope components.

Special Factors: Satisfaction is guaranteed; returns are accepted within 30 days for exchange, refund, or credit.

SOLAR CINE PRODUCTS, INC.

**4247 SOUTH KEDZIE AVE.
CHICAGO, IL 60632
312/254-8310**

Catalog: free
Save: up to 40%
Pay: check, MO, MC, V, DC, Discover
Sells: photo equipment, supplies, and services
Store: same address; Monday through Friday 8:30–5, Saturday 9–1

$$$ ✉   ☎   ▥

Solar Cine's 24-page catalog gives a sample of the thousands of items it carries—all kinds of photographic equipment and accessories from a large number of manufacturers. This firm has been supplying professionals and serious amateurs since 1937.

Solar Cine stocks a full range of still and movie equipment, including videotapes and video batteries. Cameras, lenses, studio lights, light meters, tripods, and darkroom materials are available; the brands include Canon, Elmo, Fuji, Kiwi, Kodak, Minolta, Pentax, Polaroid, Smith-Victor, and Yashica, among others. Scores of books on photography for beginners and professionals are available, as well as electronics and processing services (movies, slides, reprints, and prints). The services are described in the catalog; for more information on cameras and equipment, call or write for a price quote.

Special Factor: Price quote by phone or letter with SASE.

WESTSIDE CAMERA INC.

**2400 BROADWAY
NEW YORK, NY 10024
212/877-8760**

Information: inquire
Save: up to 50%
Pay: check, MO, MC, V, AE
Sells: photo equipment and supplies
Store: same address; Monday through
    Saturday 8–6:45, Saturday 10–6

Westside has been selling photography goods since 1972 and features a comprehensive line of darkroom equipment and supplies that should satisfy both hobbyists and pros. *Westside sells no grey-market goods.*

    Westside carries cameras and photo equipment (including video), darkroom supplies, frames, straps, carrying bags, and film by Agfa, Beseler, Bogen, Canon, Cokin, Dax, Fuji, Gitzo, Hasselblad, Holson, Ilford, Kodak, Leica, Minolta, Nikon, Olympus, Pentax, Polaroid, Ricoh, Sprint Chemistry, Tamrac, Tiltall, Vivitar, Yashica, and other firms.

Special Factors: Price quote by phone or letter with SASE; minimum order is $25.

SEE ALSO

Berry Scuba Co. • underwater cameras • *SPORTS*
Cabela's Inc. • binoculars, spotting scopes, and sunglasses • *SPORTS*
Central Skindivers • underwater cameras • *SPORTS*
Foto Electric Supply Co., Inc. • cameras, film, and videotapes •
    APPLIANCES
Harry's Discounts & Appliances Corp. • blank videotapes •
    APPLIANCES
Jerryco, Inc. • lenses and optics • *SURPLUS*
S & S Sound City • blank videotapes • *APPLIANCES*
20th Century Plastics, Inc. • vinyl slide protectors • *OFFICE*
University Products, Inc. • archival-quality storage materials for
    photographs, slides, film, negatives, microfiche, etc. • *GENERAL
    MERCHANDISE*
Wiley Outdoor Sports, Inc. • binoculars, spotting scopes, etc. •
    MERCHANDISE

CIGARS, PIPES, TOBACCO, AND OTHER SMOKING NEEDS

Cigars, chewing tobacco, cigarette tobacco, snuff, pipes, and smoking accessories

It's not easy being a smoker today, but if you're going to light up, you might as well do it at a discount. The companies listed here sell cigars, pipe tobacco, chewing tobacco, shredded tobacco for cigarette rolling, pipes, and other smoking accessories at savings of up to 75%. If your current smoke is a name-brand cigar, look here for off-brand versions sold at a fraction of the prices of the originals, as well as the famous labels themselves, which are often available at a discount.

The right to smoke in public places is being challenged on several levels. The Surgeon General's objective of a "smoke-free society by the year 2000" probably won't be realized, but local ordinances are being passed all over the country to limit smoking in public places. While debates on such actions rage on, one fact can't be argued: Smoking poses serious hazards to your long-term health.

QUITTING

Millions have quit smoking, aided by everything from hypnosis to nicotine-impregnated gum, but most have done it with something that doesn't cost a cent: sheer willpower. If you want to overcome nicotine addiction, help is available from many sources.

Clinics: The American Cancer Society's local chapters run "Quit Smoking Clinics." Some chapters charge a small fee for the program, but most offer it free of cost. Contact your chapter or write to the American Cancer Society, 261 Madison Ave., New York, NY 10016, for information.

Literature: The American Lung Association publishes two booklets, "Freedom from Smoking in 20 Days" and "A Lifetime of Freedom from Smoking," which are available from local chapters or by writing to the American Lung Association, 1740 Broadway, New York, NY 10019.

Self-hypnosis: If you're committed to quitting, you may find that the behavior-modification message in self-help audiotapes gives your resolve a boost. A range of self-improvement tapes is available from Metacom (Adventures in Cassettes), which is listed in "Books."

Nicotine gum: Nicotine-impregnated chewing gum was introduced to the U.S. market several years ago. It helps to ease cigarette cravings by supplying a dose of nicotine, released by chewing. But the gum doesn't quit *for* you—it just helps you get through the first weeks and months. And there are drawbacks: it may affect your oral health, it can upset your stomach, and it's not cheap. Moreover, medical findings have shown that the presence of nicotine in the body—even without tar—may enhance the development of cancer. If you decide to try the gum, you'll have to contact your physician, since it's sold by prescription only. (Ask your doctor for help in working out an effective program of quitting, since this enhances your chances for success.) You can have your prescription filled by one of the mail-order pharmacies listed in "Medicine."

There's another health risk posed by smoking, and that's fire. Deaths in the home that are caused by smoking exceed those resulting from arson, electrical or heating malfunctions, and kitchen accidents. It's obvious that the possibility of this tragedy is averted if no one in your home smokes.

As a final note, please remember that tobacco is highly toxic and the residue left in cigarette filters and cigar stubs is potent. Children have been known to eat the contents of ashtrays—with disastrous results. Keep tobacco products away from children and omnivorous pets, and make sure they can't reach ashtrays.

FAMOUS SMOKE SHOP, INC.

55 W. 39TH ST., DEPT. WB91
NEW YORK, NY 10018
800-672-5544
IN NY 212/221-1408
FAX: 212/921-5458

Catalog: free
Save: 40% average
Pay: check, MO, MC, V
Sells: cigars, tobacco, and pens
Store: same address; Monday through Friday 7–6, Saturday 8–2

$$$$ ✉ ☎ 🍁 ▤

The draw here is a super selection of name-brand and generic cigars and tobacco. Famous has served finicky New Yorkers since 1939 and can offer you the same privilege the firm's faithful enjoy: a private charge account.

The most prominent cigar makers in the world are represented at Famous Smoke Shop, which has a vast stock of fine, hand-rolled cigars of every taste, length, size, and shape. The firm imports and distributes dozens of brands, including Arturo Fuente, Canaria D'Oro, Cuesta-Rey, Dom Domingo, Don Diego, Flor Palmera, Hoya de Monterrey, Macanudo, Montecruz, Partagas, Primo del Rey, Punch, Royal Jamaica, Temple Hall, Troya, H. Upmann, and Zino Davidoff, among others. Unbranded house cigars, described as equivalent in quality to their famous counterparts, are sold at savings of up to 50% (compared to the brand-name versions), and Dunhill, MacBarens, James Russell, and other pipe tobaccos are also available. Specials are featured regularly, and the bimonthly, 32-page catalog includes helpful tips on choosing cigars.

Famous Smoke Shop is diversifying: For Wall Street wizards and rocket scientists, there are savings on financial and scientific Hewlett-Packard calculators, and Mont Blanc writing utensils are offered at 40% off list prices.

Special Factors: Satisfaction is guaranteed; returns are accepted; minimum order is one box; C.O.D. orders are accepted; orders are shipped worldwide.

WALLY FRANK LTD.

63-25 69TH ST.
MIDDLE VILLAGE, NY
 11379
718/326-2233

Catalog: free
Save: up to 50%
Pay: check, MO, MC, V, AE, CB, DC
Sells: cigars, pipes, and tobacco
Store: mail order only

$$$ ✉ ☎ ▤

Wally Frank has been delighting cigar and pipe smokers since 1930 with savings of up to 50% on famous-label cigars, tobacco, and privately produced smoke-alikes.

The 48-page color catalog shows cigars by Don Diego, Dunhill, Lancer, Martinez, Montecruz, Partagas, Te-Amo, H. Upmann, and other firms, plus Frank's generic equivalents, "irregulars," and closeout specials. In addition, there are briar pipes from under $5 in a large selection of bowl shapes and stem styles, as well as corn cob and meerschaum pipes, pipe-cleaning tools, pouches, racks, cigar and tobacco humidors, cigar cutters, and name-brand pipe tobaccos and generic blends, including a variety of loose chewing tobaccos.

Special Factors: Satisfaction is guaranteed (see the catalog for details); returns are accepted; pipe service and repairs are available; shipping is included on orders over $50.

MAGNUM

500 INDEPENDENCE
 AVE. S.E.
WASHINGTON, D.C.
 20003
202/544-6858

Brochure and Price List: free with
 SASE
Save: up to 50%
Pay: check or MO
Sells: cigar cutter
Store: mail order only

$ ✉ ☎ 🍁 ▤

The cigar smoker who appreciates controversy will love the product sold by this firm: a cigar cutter set into in a .44 magnum shell casing. This conversation starter has a blade of surgical steel that "makes a smooth cut, eliminating damaged wrappers, shredded ends, and loose tobacco." The "44 Magnum" comes in a drawstring pouch, and the firm will be happy to ship it directly to your gift recipients with your card enclosed. The price charged for this cutter is up to 50% below those asked for other cutters of similar caliber. Send a stamped, self-addressed envelope for the brochure or call for more information.

Canadian readers, please note: Only U.S. funds are accepted.

Special Factor: Satisfaction is guaranteed.

MARKS CIGARS

**8TH AND CENTRAL
OCEAN CITY, NJ 08226
800-257-8645
609/399-0935**

Catalog: free
Save: 25% average
Pay: check, MO, MC, V, AE
Sells: cigars
Store: same address; Monday through
    Sunday 7 A.M.–9 P.M.

Marks Cigars was recommended to us by a reader, who praised the firm's prices and service. Marks has been doing business since 1947, and sells hundreds of types of cigars at discounts averaging 25%.

The price list we received listed over 40 manufacturers, including Arturo Fuente, Canaria D'Oro, Don Diego, F.D. Grave, Henri Wintermans, Hoyo de Monterrey, Macanudo, Montecruz, Partagas, Primo del Rey, Punch, Royal Jamaica, Te-Amo, Tesoro, and H. Upmann, among others. The listings note the country of origin, ring size, length, and wrapper color of each cigar. There were no illustrations in the price list we reviewed, but a "cigar picture shape chart" was available. Prices run a good 25% below suggested retail, and if you're looking for a cigar not listed, call or write—it may be in stock.

Special Factor: Price quote by phone or letter with SASE.

FRED STOKER & SONS, INC.

P.O. BOX 707
DRESDEN, TN 38225-0707
901/364-5419

Price List: free
Save: up to 50%
Pay: check or MO
Sells: tobacco products and sweet potato plants
Shop (bonded warehouse): Rte. 1, Dresden, TN; Monday through Friday 8–5

Mr. Fred "Famous Since 1940" Stoker sells homegrown at down-home prices. His chewing, smoking, and snuffing tobaccos are priced up to 50% less than comparable products sold elsewhere.

The Stoker brochure lists flake and chewing tobacco in peach, bourbon, cherry-apple, butternut, wild cherry, coffee, pineapple, wintergreen, mint, cigar, and other flavors in 1-1/2- to 20-pound containers. "Honey" plug tobacco in twists and other sweet chews are listed, and requisite cuspidors and spittoons (including travel models) are available. You can buy long shredded tobacco for roll-your-own cigarettes, and a rolling device and cigarette papers, as well as clipping cigar tobacco. Cigars are offered here—boxes of smokes from the Caribbean—and there are sampler assortments at low prices. Domestic and imported pipe tobacco blends are sold, as well as tobacco pouches, humidors, and other pipe accessories. Snuff is available in plain, sweet, and flavored versions.

Mr. Stoker also runs "Fred's Plant Farm," which sells tobacco seeds ($2 per teaspoonful) and 9 varieties of sweet potato plants. These plant slips are well-priced—from under $4 for a dozen to under $85 for 2,000. (Serious farmers should note that sweet potato seed is sold by the *bushel* in early spring.) And to round out the offerings, Mr. Stoker sells old-fashioned sorghum-flavored table syrup, popping corn, tobacco leaf jewelry, and caps.

Special Factors: Inquire for information on quantity discounts; shipping is included on local deliveries and all plant orders; plants are shipped April 15 to July 1; C.O.D. orders are accepted.

THOMPSON CIGAR COMPANY

5401 HANGAR CT., DEPT. 7836
TAMPA, FL 33634
813/884-6344

Catalog: free
Save: up to 30%
Pay: check, MO, MC, V, AE, DC
Sells: cigars and tobacco
Store: mail order only

$$ ✉ ☎

Thompson Cigar has been selling cigars since 1915, and the firm's 48-page catalog is packed with both national-brand and private-label cigars, at prices up to 30% below comparable retail.

Thompson has a large selection of cigars—Cuesta Rey, Hoya de Monterrey, Macanudo, Montecruz, Partagas, Royal Jamaica, H. Upmann, and many of other makers—both Thompson's own line and the national-brand smokes. The catalog descriptions note the country of import, ring size, length, and relative strength (very mild to heavy). Pipe tobacco blends are stocked, and you'll also find a tempting selection of smoking accessories and gifts: handsome humidors, handmade pipes, cigar cutters, smokers' candles, and ashtrays. The catalog we reviewed showed a number of gifts, including a replica of a Civil War Cavalry saber, U.S. Marine tin soldiers, a Mercedes-Benz 300SL model, British bar towels and coasters, beer steins, and even a hunting and fishing trivia game.

Special Factor: Satisfaction is guaranteed.

SEE ALSO

Sultan's Delight, Inc. ● Middle Eastern tobacco, brass waterpipes ● FOOD

CLOTHING, FURS, AND ACCESSORIES

Clothing, furs, and accessories for men, women, and children

You can buy just about anything to wear by mail today, from just about any part of the country—Amish clothing from Indiana, stock underthings and silk lingerie from New York City's Lower East Side, swimsuits that have qualified for the Olympics, T-shirts printed with your own sentiments, extra-large sizes, executive suiting for both sexes, kids' clothing and infants' basics, army surplus, custom-made deerskin coats and jackets, and much more—at savings of up to 90%.

Learning what goes into quality construction and a well-made garment is vital if you're going to shop by mail. Do your homework while store shopping, so you'll be able to identify the hallmarks of good materials and workmanship *as well as* the look and feel of an inferior garment. At least two books can be recommended for the person who wants to get more out of less: *Dress Better for Less,* by Vicki Audette (Meadowbrook Press, 1981), and *Good Garb,* by William Dasheff and Laura Dearborn (Delta Publishing Company, 1980). *Good Garb* is "a practical guide to practical clothing," and includes valuable tips on identifying quality construction and materials. *Dress Better for Less* focuses on all aspects of shopping, from discount outlets for designer clothes and mail-order catalogs to thrift and resale shops.

Clothing manufactured in the U.S.A. must bear labels that provide specific information on washing, dry cleaning, ironing, drying, and other care. The FTC has prepared a booklet that defines all of the terms used in the labeling and answers a number of typical consumer questions. For a copy, request "What's New About Care Labels" from the Federal Trade Commission, Public Reference Office, Washington, DC 20580.

You can also get it from the horse's mouth: The Neighborhood Cleaners' Association (NCA) publishes the "Consumer Guide to Clothing Care," a brochure of tips on the care and cleaning of different fabrics and trims. Send a long, self-addressed, stamped envelope to NCA, 116 E. 27th St., New York, NY 10016, for the pamphlet.

If you're contemplating the purchase of a fur, take a look at *How to Buy and Maintain a Fur Coat* (Harmony Books, 1986), by Leslie Goldin and Kalea Lulow. It includes information about quality construction characteristics of different furs, and their suitability for different types of wear. Another recommended guide is *How to Buy a Fur That Makes You Look Like a Million,* by Viola Sybert (Villard Books), which also has helpful tips on fur selection.

And if you want to make the best of what you already own, you'll appreciate *Taking Care of Clothes,* by Mablen Jones (St. Martin's Press, 1982). This book deals with evaluating clothing prior to purchase, as well as stain removal, laundering, dry cleaning, ironing and pressing, storage, and caring for leather, fur, and other special materials.

Our favorite clothes-savers include Simple Green, a biodegradable, all-purpose cleaner, for general stain removal; Fels Naptha laundry soap, for ground-in dirt and spots; and green soap tincture, or medicinal soft soap, which seems to work wonders on coffee stains (test before using and rinse it out after half an hour or it might color the garment). Simple Green is sold in hardware stores and is available in economy sizes from Colonial Garden Kitchens (listed in the "Kitchen" section of "Home"); Fels Naptha is sold in supermarkets for under 75¢ a bar; and green soap tincture may be found in drugstores and pharmacies, or ordered from Masuen First Aid & Safety, listed in "Medicine and Science."

ARCTIC SHEEPSKIN OUTLET

**565 CO. RD. T, DEPT. W
HAMMOND, WI 54105
800-657-4656**

Brochure: free
Save: up to 60%
Pay: check, MO, MC, V, AE, Discover
Sells: sheepskin clothing and accessories
Store: I-94 at Co. Rd. T, Hammond, WI; Monday through Saturday 9–5

Arctic Sheepskin Outlet was founded in 1987 by the energetic Joseph Bacon, whose venture into mail-order skylights and insulated glass panels has proven a great success. (See the listing of Arctic Glass & Window Outlet in the "Maintenance" chapter of "Home.")

He's beginning with sheepskin favorites—slippers, mittens, car seat covers, and rugs—from the largest sheepskin tannery in the world. Savings vary from item to item; we found rubber-soled sheepskin moccasins in other catalogs selling for just a few dollars more than Arctic's price of $34.95, but the car seat covers are real buys at $49.95, as are mittens for $14.95, kids' slippers for $8.95, and a "Marlboro Man" coat for just $129. There are also hats with earflaps, sheepskin headbands, rugs ($39.95), and bicycle seat covers. All purchases are covered by Arctic's "money-back guarantee."

Special Factors: Satisfaction is guaranteed; price quote by phone or letter; returns are accepted for exchange, refund, or credit; orders are shipped worldwide.

JOS. A. BANK CLOTHIERS, INC.

25 CROSSROADS DR.
OWINGS MILLS, MD
21117-5499
800-284-3225
FAX: 301/356-5741

Catalog: $1
Save: up to 30%
Pay: check, MO, MC, V, AE
Sells: men's and women's career clothing and sportswear
Store: 40 stores in AL, CO, CT, GA, IL, IN, KY, MA, MD, MI, MN, MO, NC, NJ, NY, OH, PA, TN, TX, and VA (locations are listed in the catalog)

$ ✉ ☎

Traditional clothing with fine tailoring details is Bank's stock-in-trade. This company, in business for over 75 years, makes careeer clothing for men and women and sells it by mail and through its 40 stores nationwide.

Bank's 84-page catalog is devoted to menswear: suits, jackets, pants, accessories, weekend separates, and underwear. The suits are handsomely executed in fine wool worsteds, among them pin and hairline stripes, glen plaids, and herringbones. Chesterfield and cashmere topcoats, tuxedos and formal wear, blazers, tweed jackets, and complementing pants and shirts are sold. Among the good buys we found were a lizard belt for $50 and button-down shirts from $22.50; the suits represented good values at under $300. Braces, silk ties, shoes, pajamas, and underwear are sold as well.

The offerings in the women's catalog are similar in spirit, including fine business ensembles in the "relaxed traditional" style—belted suits, lace-trimmed print dresses, and challis skirts paired with knit jackets, to cite a few examples from the catalog we reviewed. Scarves, belts, jewelry, bow ties, bags, and coordinated weekend separates are also available.

Bank's prices are not cheap, but we compared like garments from other catalogs and found much better prices here on certain items. For example, while another executive-wear direct marketer charges $60 for a pinpoint cotton shirt, we found a similar style in the Bank catalog for $34. Challis and foulard dresses were available at prices about half those being charged in other catalogs. Such savings qualify Jos. A. Bank Clothiers for a listing here, but we believe that the firm is more noteworthy for its selection of fine apparel than for its prices. *Please do not ask for discounts.*

Special Factors: Satisfaction is guaranteed; returns are accepted for exchange, refund, or credit.

CAHALL'S DEPARTMENT STORE

*CAHALL'S BROWN
  DUCK CATALOG*
**P.O. BOX 450-WM
MOUNT ORAB, OH 45154
513/444-2121**

Catalog: $1, refundable
Save: up to 40%
Pay: check, MO, MC, V, Discover
Sells: working clothing and footwear
Store: 108 S. High St., Mount Orab, OH;
  Monday through Saturday 9–6

$$$

The Cahall family opened its department store on April 20, 1946, and took the leap into mail order in 1987, with the "Brown Duck Catalog" of heavy-duty apparel and footwear. You'll find your favorites here at savings of up to 40% on suggested list or retail prices.

Cahall's sells popular lines of work clothing—jeans, shirts, jackets, and overalls—from Carhartt, Five Brothers, Key, Jerzees, Levi, and other well-known manufacturers. The catalog we reviewed had an excellent selection of work shoes and boots for men and women from LaCrosse and Red Wing, in hard-to-find sizes. If you don't see the style you're looking for in the catalog, call—it may be available.

Special Factors: Satisfaction is guaranteed; price quote by phone or letter with SASE; returns are accepted for exchange, refund, or credit.

CHADWICK'S OF BOSTON, LTD.

ONE CHADWICK PLACE
BOX 1600
BROCKTON, MA 02403
508/583-6600

Catalog: free
Save: up to 50%
Pay: check, MO, MC, V, AE, Discover
Sells: women's clothing
Store: mail order only

$$$ ✉ ☎

Chadwick's publishes "The Original Women's Off-Price Catalog," full of "pretty/professional" outfits for office, smashing cocktail dresses for evening, and weekend separates and activewear.

The brands featured in past catalogs have included Abernathy Sport, Averroe, CWTC, David N, FADS, No Excuses, Reed Hunter, and Segue. Typical offerings are stonewashed jeans, intarsia-knit sweaters, yoked corduroy skirts, and preppy classics, as well as challis dirndls, suede jackets, leather skirts, boiled-wool jackets, and reefer coats. The clothing is offered in a range of current colors, and sizes run from 4 to 14. Most of the separates cost between $25 and $40, and the accessories are also well-priced.

Special Factors: Satisfaction is guaranteed; returns are accepted for exchange, refund, or credit.

CHOCK CATALOG CORP.

74 ORCHARD ST., DEPT.
WBMC
NEW YORK, NY
10002-4594
212/473-1929

Catalog: $1
Save: up to 35%
Pay: check, MO, MC, V
Sells: hosiery, underwear, sleepwear, and infants' clothing
Store: same address; Sunday through Thursday 9:30–5:30

$$$ ✉ ☎ 🍁 🇺🇸

Chock is a family operation, established in 1921, which has supplied generations of New Yorkers with unmentionables. The 64-page catalog is packed with good values on name-brand underthings for men, women, children, and infants.

Chock carries duofold thermal underwear for the whole family, women's stockings and panty hose by Berkshire, Hanes, and Mayer; underpants by Carter's, Calvin Klein, Lollipop, and Vanity Fair; and Louis Chock sleepwear for women. The men's underwear includes lines by BVD, Hanes, Jockey, Calvin Klein, Manshape, Munsingwear, and other firms. Pajamas and robes from Botany, Cannon, Knothe, Martex, and Oscar de la Renta are stocked, as well as socks by Burlington, Christian Dior, Interwoven, and Supp-hose. Men's sizes run up to XXXX (58 to 60).

Chock has a separate department for infants and children, which stocks Carter's layette items and nursery needs, cloth diapers and crib linen, Hanes underwear for boys, Carter's underwear and sleepwear for boys and girls, and Trimfit socks for both.

Special Factors: Satisfaction is guaranteed; price quote by phone or letter with SASE; unopened returns with manufacturer's packaging intact are accepted within 30 days; orders are shipped worldwide.

CUSTOM COAT COMPANY, INC.

**P.O. BOX 69
BERLIN, WI 54923
414/361-0900**

Catalog: free
Save: up to 35%
Pay: check, MO, MC, V
Sells: deerskin clothing and tanning services
Store: 227 N. Washington St., Berlin, WI; Monday through Friday 8–5, Saturday 8–3 (8–12 noon May through August)

Custom Coat, established in 1939, offers a service of special interest to hunters: The company will tan your green hides, color them, and create custom clothing and accessories from the leather. The same items can be made up in stock deerskin, and the prices for the services and finished goods are exceptionally reasonable.

The 30-page color catalog shows deerskin vests, town-and-country jackets and coats, classic wrap coats, safari and bush jackets, fringed and Western models, and sports coats, as well as riding, motorcycle, and bomber jackets. There are bags and driving, shooting, hunting, and dress gloves for men and women, plus a selection of mittens for children. Change purses, keycases, billfolds, cigarette cases, golf-club covers, and smooth-soled moccasins are also offered. Custom sizes, lengths, details, and linings can be provided as well. Green deer, elk, and moose hides are accepted for curing and coloring, but no fur work is done.

Special Factor: Tanning rates, guides to shipment of skins, number of hides needed per garment, and other information is listed in the catalog.

D & A MERCHANDISE CO., INC.

**22 ORCHARD ST.
NEW YORK, NY 10002
212/925-4766**

Catalog: $1.50
Save: up to 35%
Pay: check, MO, MC, V
Sells: underwear and hosiery
Store: same address; Sunday through Thursday 9–5, Friday 9–3

D & A, home of "The Underwear King," has been selling name-brand lingerie, socks, hosiery, and underwear for men, women, and boys since 1947.

You'll find solid discounts on first-quality goods here: men's underwear by BVD, Camp, duofold, Jockey, and Munsingwear, and socks by Burlington, Camp, Christian Dior, Interwoven, and Supp-hose. Botany and State of Maine robes and pajamas, Career Club shirts, and Totes rain boots are also available, and boys' underwear by BVD and Hanes is stocked. The women's underwear department offers lines by Bali, Carnival, Chicas, Christian Dior, Do-All, Exquisite Form, Formfit Rogers, Jockey for Her, Lilyette, Lily of France, Lollipop, Lorraine, Maidenform, Olga, Playtex, Poirette, Smoothie, Strouse Adler, Vassarette, Warner's, and other manufacturers. The hosiery brands include Berkshire, Burlington, Camp, Danskin, Hanes, Trimfit, and Wigwam.

Special Factors: Satisfaction is guaranteed; price quote by phone or letter with SASE; returns in original packaging are accepted within 30 days for refund or credit; C.O.D. orders are accepted.

THE DEERSKIN PLACE

**283 AKRON RD.
EPHRATA, PA 17522
717/733-7624**

Brochure and Price List: $1, refundable

Save: up to 50%

Pay: check, MO, MC, V

Sells: deerskin clothing and accessories

Store: same address; Monday through Saturday 9–9, Sunday (September through December) 12–5

The brochure from this firm describes clothing and accessories of deerskin, cowhide, and sheepskin at prices up to 50% less than those charged elsewhere for comparable goods. The Deerskin Place has been in business since 1969.

Among the offerings here are fingertip-length shearling jackets with full collar and patch pockets, $275; fringed buckskin-suede jackets, $169; and sporty deerskin handbags for about $70. The Deerskin Place offers moccasins and casual shoes, knee-high suede boots, and crepe-soled slip-ons for men and women (about $16 to $50); deerskin wallets, clutches, coin purses, and keycases (from about $5 to $25); mittens and gloves for the whole family, beaded belts (under $6), and many other accessories.

The Deerskin Place is offering readers of this book a 10% discount on orders of $250 or more. Be sure to identify yourself as a reader when you order, and deduct the discount from the goods total only. This WBMC reader discount expires February 1, 1992.

Special Factors: Satisfaction is guaranteed; inquire before ordering if unsure of color, size, etc.; returns are accepted; C.O.D. orders are accepted; orders are shipped worldwide.

EXCEPTIONALLY YOURS, INC.

**P.O. BOX 3246, DEPT.
  WBM
FRAMINGHAM, MA 01701
508/877-9757**

Brochure: free with self-addressed,
business-sized, stamped envelope
Save: up to 30%
Pay: check, MO, MC, V
Sells: easy-access clothing
Store: mail order only

$$$

Even a brief experience caring for a person who is confined to bed or wheelchair or who has limited mobility can be frustrating and needlessly difficult—for both parties—if the patient is wearing conventional garments. Judy McKie, a nurse and the mother of a disabled child, understood the problem fully. Exceptionally Yours is her solution.

This firm produces sweatshirts and pants, overalls, skirts, cardigans, jumpers for children, and other separates for children and adults. The materials are soft, comfortable 50/50 polyester and cotton interlock knit or fleece, and a mostly cotton corduroy. All of the clothes are machine washable and dryable. The designs are simple—crewneck tops, cuffed pull-on pants, A-line skirts, full-cut shorts, and a classic cardigan style with pockets, among others. Exceptionally Yours has recently introduced a varsity-style winter jacket, designed for those with limited upper-body mobility. The styles for children include corduroy overalls with trapunto knees and an easy-fitting jumper. The garments are designed for easy accessibility, with Velcro or ring-zipper closures. Maximum motion is permitted with elastic waists, necks, and cuffs; the reinforced stitching and trapunto-padded knees help ensure comfort and long garment life. Great color combinations are offered, with vibrant juxtapositions of pink, red, olive, blue, and other colors on white.

The prices are surprisingly good—most of the separates cost under $25 each, and many are priced below standard, unmodified sweats sold in activewear clothing departments.

Canadian readers, please note: Only U.S. funds are accepted.

Special Factors: Satisfaction is guaranteed; returns are accepted within 30 days for exchange, refund, or credit.

FALL RIVER KNITTING MILLS, INC.

**P.O. BOX 4360, FLINT STATION
FALL RIVER, MA 02723
800-446-1089
IN MA 508/679-5227**

Catalog: free
Save: up to 60%
Pay: check, MO, MC, V, Discover
Sells: sweaters and knitwear
Store: 69 Alden St., Fall River, MA; also ME, NH, RI, and VT (locations are listed in the catalog)

$$$

Fall River Knitting Mills was founded in 1911, when Fall River was a thriving textile center. Buy through the color catalog or from one of the factory outlets, and you can save up to 60% on the prices charged in department stores for the same goods.

The catalog shows turtlenecks, crews, V-necks, cardigans, rugby styles, and vests for men, women, and children. There are brightly colored cottons, including Shaker knits, cable-front crews, and stripes and intarsia designs. Sweater-dresses, knitted skirts and pants, and even a cotton afghan are available. In addition to fashion clothing, Fall River usually offers such wardrobe staples as polo shirts and turtlenecks, at competitive prices. While you're filling your sweater closet, think of your friends—they can always use more sweaters, too.

Special Factors: Satisfaction is guaranteed; returns are accepted.

THE FINALS, LTD.

**21 MINISINK AVE., DEPT. WB
PORT JERVIS, NY 12771
914/856-4456**

Catalog: free
Save: up to 60%
Pay: check, MO, MC, V, AE
Sells: swimwear and athletic apparel
Store: 487 Broadway, New York, NY; also 3314 M St., N.W., Washington, DC

$$

The Finals outfits many U.S. swim teams, and once you've seen its catalog, you'll know why: It offers an unbeatable combination of style, comfort, practicality, and price. The Finals was established in 1976.

The swimsuit fabric, a blend of Antron nylon and Lycra, is ideal for the demands of competition-level use. Sleek, form-fitting tank suits for women ($21.95 and up) and men's briefs ($13.95 and up) are offered in a variety of colors and styles, as well as shirts and suits for lifeguards and surfers. The catalog shows "Second Skin" separates for bicycling and working out, as well as running and track wear, and standard shirts, shorts, warm-ups, and sweats. Singlets and shorts in unisex sizes, tote bags and duffels, Accusplit timepieces, swimming goggles, caps, fins, buoys, tubes, kickboards, and related gear are also shown in the color catalog.

Special Factor: Satisfaction is guaranteed.

PAUL FREDRICK SHIRT COMPANY

140 W. MAIN ST., DEPT. WM
FLEETWOOD, PA 19522
215/944-0909

Catalog: $1
Save: up to 50%
Pay: check, MO, MC, V, AE, DC, Optima
Sells: men's dress shirts
Store: mail order only

$$$

Selling under private labels has emerged as a successful marketing technique in the clothing business. The way it works is simple: Specialty and department stores purchase better-quality garments from different manufacturers and sew the store's label inside. If the goods are well-chosen, customers will develop positive identification with the label. Stores like private labels because the markups are hefty, and the consumer won't go elsewhere for a better price—there's no way to identify which other stores might have the garment under their private labels. The only way around the price is buying directly from the manufacturer. If you're in the market for fine-quality men's shirts, this is the place.

Paul Fredrick is the mail-order division of a shirt manufacturer that's been selling to designers and better stores since 1952. We compared the specifications of Fredrick's $31 men's dress shirt to one selling for $60 in another catalog, and found them identical: both were made of two-ply pima cotton pinpoint, both featured single-needle tailoring, and both had handmade, button-through sleeve plackets and extra-long shirttails. Paul Fredrick offers more options: French or barrel (business) cuffs, and straight, Windsor, English tab, and buttondown collar styles. Fabric choices include pinpoint cotton, and Egyptian cotton broadcloth, in solids and stripes. Sizes run from 14-1/2" to 18-1/2" neck, 32" to 37" sleeve. Three-letter monograms (on the left sleeve cuff) cost $5. This staple of the businessman's wardrobe is Paul Fredrick's only offering at this writing, but other fabrics and garments may be made available in the future.

Special Factors: Satisfaction is guaranteed; returns are accepted.

GOHN BROS.

P.O. BOX 111
105 S. MAIN
MIDDLEBURY, IN 46540
219/825-2400

Catalog: 50¢
Save: up to 60%
Pay: check or MO
Sells: general merchandise and Amish
  specialties
Store: same address; Monday through
  Saturday 8–5:30

$$$$ ✉ 🍁 ▬

Reading the Gohn Bros. catalog takes you back into a world where bonnet board and frock coats were stock items in the general store. Prices—up to 60% below comparable retail—recall earlier eras. Gohn Bros., founded in 1904, publishes its stock list several times a year.

Among the many staples in the yard goods and notions department are all-cotton Sanforized blue denim ($4.89), muslin ($1.98), chambray shirting ($2.59), quilting thread (98¢), cotton percale and quilting prints, pillow tubing, all-cotton sheeting, tailor's canvas, haircloth, mosquito netting, embroidery floss (25¢ per skein), and wool overcoating (at under $12 per yard).

Work-tailored, sturdy Amish clothing is featured, including men's cotton chambray work shirts ($14.98), cotton denim broadfall pants ($14.98), men's underwear, cotton dress socks (89¢), Carolina shoes, rubber galoshes and footwear by LaCrosse and Tingley, work gloves, felt hats, and handkerchiefs. Much of the clothing is stocked in large sizes, and many of the items in the men's department are offered in boys' sizes.

If you're assembling a layette, see the catalog for good buys on the basics—diapers, receiving blankets, sleepers, pacifiers, baby pants, and other goods by Curity and Gerber. Nursing bras are available, and women's underwear and hosiery are offered at low prices.

Special Factors: Satisfaction is guaranteed; C.O.D. orders are accepted.

GOLDMAN & COHEN INC.

55 ORCHARD ST.
NEW YORK, NY 10002
212/966-0737

Information: price quote
Save: up to 60%
Pay: check, MO, MC, V, AE, Discover
Sells: women's underwear
Store: same address; Monday through
Thursday 9–5, Friday 9–3, Sunday 8–
5:30

Goldman & Cohen has been in business since 1954 and doesn't publish a catalog, but that hasn't diminished its reputation among its store and mail customers. Top lingerie and hosiery lines are offered here at sizable savings.

Goldman stocks women's intimate apparel by Bali, Barbizon, Carnival, Christian Dior, Exquisite Form, Lilyette, Maidenform, Olga, Playtex, Vanity Fair, Warner's, and other well-known manufacturers and designers. Loungewear by these firms and hard-to-find sizes are also available, as well as Hanes panty hose. Goldman also carries a full line of nursing and maternity foundations and sleepwear. The experienced saleswomen can assist you in selecting the garments appropriate for your particular needs and in getting the proper fit.

Special Factors: Price quote by phone or letter with SASE; no phone orders or inquiries are accepted on Sunday; orders are shipped world-wide.

HUNTINGTON CLOTHIERS

1285 ALUM CREEK DR.
COLUMBUS, OH 43209
800-848-6203
FAX: 614/252-3855

Catalog: free
Save: up to 50% (see text)
Pay: check, MO, MC, V, AE, DC
Sells: conservative menswear
Store: same address; Monday through Fri-
day 10–6, Saturday 10–5, Sunday 12–5

The 76-page catalog from Huntington Clothiers illustrates all the basics of a conservative wardrobe, from pinstriped suits to pima cotton boxer shorts.

Prices are very competitive with those of old-line haberdashers; some items cost as much as 50% less here than their equivalents in other catalogs.

Huntington manufactures its own shirts in a variety of fabrics, including Oxford cloth (with buttondown and plain collars), pima cotton solids, pima hairline stripes and checks, Sea Island cotton, and Egyptian cotton broadcloth. (Many are also offered in 60% cotton/40% polyester blends.) An Oxford cloth buttondown selling elsewhere for $30 compares to one here costing under $20, and Huntington's pinpoint Oxford cloth costs $33, compared to $46 for a comparable style in another catalog. Monogramming is available.

Huntington also manufactures neckwear—foulards, silk rep stripes, and linen solids and paisley ties—at similar savings. The suits run the gamut from grey chalk stripes and gabardines to poplin and seersucker summer suits to tuxedos. Jackets and blazers in hopsacking, silk, Madras, Belgian linen, and other fabrics are shown, and a wide selection of trousers is offered as well. Sportswear separates, walking shorts, lisle cotton polo shirts, rugby shirts, cotton and wool sweaters, belts, suspenders, underwear, and even shoes are shown in the catalog. Handsome hand-sewn loafers with fringe detail cost $119 here, $50 to $70 less than shoes of comparable workmanship.

Canadian readers, please note: Orders are not shipped to all locations in Canada.

Special Factors: Satisfaction is guaranteed; returns (except monogrammed goods) are accepted.

I DO I DO BRIDAL SALON

1963 86TH ST.
BROOKLYN, NY 11214
718/946-0011

Information: price quote (see text)
Save: up to 50%
Pay: check, MO, MC, V
Sells: gowns for the bridal party
Store: same address

$$$ ✉ ☎ 🍁 ▇

The prospective bride who's set the date and begun shopping for her gown soon learns the real meaning of "the big day," when simply dressing herself, her mother, and attendants can cost in the neighborhood of $10,000.

We have help in the form of I Do I Do, a Brooklyn bridal salon that sells gowns for the entire bridal party at 30% to 50% below list prices. Taking advantage of the savings is simple: Make your gown selection from the ads and editorial pages of *Bride's* or *Modern Bride.* Send I Do I Do the pages with photos of what you want, or call, for a price quote. A 50% deposit is required, as well as the complete measurements of each person being outfitted. Just as this is standard procedure among many bridal salons, you'll also wait about three months for delivery of the gowns. Please note that you must handle alterations yourself—through a local salon or an experienced tailor. Brides who live in the metropolitan area can visit the shop for the same savings, *and* personal attention.

Special Factor: Price quote by phone or letter with SASE.

LANDS' END, INC.

**LANDS' END LANE
DODGEVILLE, WI
 53595-0001
800-356-4444**

Catalog: free
Save: up to 40%
Pay: check, MO, MC, V, AE
Sells: clothing for men, women, and children
Store: 4320 New York St., Aurora, IL; 2241 and 2317 N. Elston Ave., Chicago, IL; 6131 Dempster, Morton Grove, IL; 15782 La Grange Rd., Orland Park, IL; 251 W. Golf, Schaumburg, IL; and #20 Yorktown Convenience Center, Lombard, IL; 6743 Odana Rd. and 411 S. State, Madison, WI

Lands' End began life in 1963, in the basement of a building on Chicago's waterfront. You can find the original store there still (as "Lands' End Outlet"), but the Lands' End of the well-priced buttondown lies among the farmlands of Wisconsin. Past catalogs have included profiles of the firm's staff, and an insider's look into the workings of the shipping room, marketing department, and luggage workshops.

Lands' End sells good-quality, traditional and casual clothing for men, women, and children at prices up to 40% below those charged elsewhere for similar apparel. For example, the current edition of the catalog shows a finely tailored cotton pinpoint shirt for $33.50, Oxford buttondowns for $19.50, men's hopsacking jackets for $165, pleated wool skirts for under $75, and men's penny loafers for under $80. Lands' End is the perfect source for the traditional working wardrobe, and hard to better for casual clothing and weekend wear. This is the source for canvas portfolios and well-fitted attachés, as well as duffels and lightweight luggage.

The seasonal catalogs usually include "Lands' End Outlet," several pages of items featuring markdowns of up to 55%. We have ordered quite happily from this section, and urge you to call if you're mailing your order to make sure stock is available. (This is done automatically when you order by phone.) In our case, the colors of the skirt desired were sold out, but two nicer ones were available. Color selection is a strong feature here, as well as sizing—most women's wear runs to size 16, and many of the men's shirts are stocked in regular and long.

Special Factors: Satisfaction is guaranteed; returns are accepted.

LEE-MCCLAIN CO., INC.

RR 6, BOX 381A
SHELBYVILLE, KY
  40065-9017
502/633-3823

Brochure: free
Save: up to 40%
Pay: check, MO, MC, V
Sells: business apparel
Store: U.S. 60 W., Shelbyville, KY; Monday
  through Saturday 8–4:30

Lee-McClain, which has been manufacturing fine suits and separates since 1933, offers you the same apparel that is marketed in better stores, at up to 40% less than suggested retail prices. The clothing is sold under the "Strathmore" house label.

Suits, jackets, coats, and blazers for men are offered here. The conservative, classic styling features slightly fitted, two-button jackets with center vent and straight-leg pants. Suits begin at $195, and fabric choices include cashmere and blends, camel's hair, wool worsted, flannel, gabardine, pinstripes, herringbones, glen plaids, hopsacking, and other weaves. Seams are matched, and alterations are free. It's hard to beat $225 for a fine camel's hair sports coat, or $59 for slacks in wool worsted.

Special Factors: Swatches are available upon request; list all measurements when ordering; shipping is included.

L'EGGS SHOWCASE OF SAVINGS

L'EGGS BRANDS, INC.
P.O. BOX 1010
RURAL HALL, NC 27098
919/744-1790

Catalog: free
Save: up to 50%
Pay: check, MO, MC, V
Sells: first-quality and irregular women's hosiery and underwear
Store: mail order only

$$$ ✉   ☎

You can save up to 50% on your favorite L'eggs styles and colors, and more on irregulars, through the Showcase. Specialty catalogs featuring nurses' hosiery, stockings, and other products are available. A good selection of styles in larger sizes is offered, which seems quite fitting given the fact that L'eggs is owned by Sara Lee.

Sheer Energy, Active Support, Sheer Elegance, Summer L'eggs, knee highs, Winter L'eggs, L'eggs Regular, and a selection of Hanes and Isotoner panty hose have been shown in past catalogs, in control-top styles, queen sizes, and a wide range of colors. Bali bras and L'eggs slips, half-slips, camisoles, pettipants, bras, panties, socks, and leotards and tights are usually available, as well as maternity panty hose, nursing bras, slips, and briefs. Hanes Activewear, socks, and underwear for men and kids are also available.

Special Factors: Satisfaction is guaranteed; imperfect (irregular) goods are clearly identified; quantity discounts are available; returns are accepted; minimum order is $15 with credit cards.

NATIONAL WHOLESALE CO., INC.

**400 NATIONAL BLVD.,
DEPT. WBM
LEXINGTON, NC 27292**
704/249-0211

Catalog: free
Save: up to 50%
Pay: check, MO, MC, V, AE
Sells: women's hosiery, loungewear, and underwear
Store: Lexington and Wilmington, NC; Monday through Saturday 9–9, Sunday 1–5:30

National Wholesale offers virtually every woman, regardless of height (from 5') or girth (to 60" hips), savings of up to 50% on National's brand of panty hose (compared to similar name-brand products). This firm was established in 1952, and is endorsed by the Lexington Chamber of Commerce.

The 48-page catalog, which is published several times a year, shows control-top, support, sheer mesh, cotton-soled, and other panty hose styles, as well as stockings (support, sheer, and garterless) and knee highs. The "all-sheer" panty hose are offered in a good selection of beiges and browns, pastels, and deep fall and winter shades. There are bras, girdles, and body shapers by Exquisite Form, Glamorise, Kayser, and Playtex; cotton-knit vests, briefs, long-leg underpants, thermal underwear, and pants liners; slips by Figurefit and Pinehurst, and dusters by Swirl. Larger sizes are available. Hosiery is sold by the box (three to six pairs). National also offers an incontinence panty and a half-slip with a waterproof panel.

Special Factors: Satisfaction is guaranteed; only first-quality merchandise is sold; returns are accepted; orders are shipped worldwide.

THOS. OAK & SONS

901 MAIN ST., DEPT. 807
SALEM, VA 24156
800-898-2929

Catalog: free
Save: 25% average
Pay: check, MO, MC, V, AE, Discover
Sells: women's clothing and accessories
Store: mail order only
$$ ✉ ☎

Thos. Oak & Sons, established in 1987, is one of the family of catalogs from the Home Shopping Network. It features moderately priced women's apparel and accessories chosen for comfort and easy care.

The 32-page, color catalog we reviewed showed comfortable dresses and activewear, including town-and-country dresses, around-the-house chemises, overshirts and loose jackets, pull-on pants and skirts, and robes, nightgowns, and foundation garments. Shoes and slippers from Beacon, ComfortSteps, Daniel Green, Hush Puppies, Keds (including Grasshoppers), and Oldmaine Trotters were available, as well as a potpourri of household helpers and accessories.

Thos. Oak & Sons is offering readers of this book a one-time discount of $10 on orders of $29.95 (goods total only) or more. Identify yourself as a reader when you order. This WBMC reader discount expires February 1, 1992.

Special Factors: Satisfaction is guaranteed; returns are accepted for exchange, refund, or credit.

PAGANO GLOVES, INC.

3-5 CHURCH ST.
JOHNSTOWN, NY
12095-2196
518/762-8425

Catalog: $3, refundable
Save: up to 50%
Pay: MO, MC, V
Sells: deerskin clothing and accessories
Store: same address; Monday through
Friday 8–5, Saturday 9:30–3

$$$ ✉ ☎ 🍁

Pagano Gloves has been selling its deerskin clothing, gloves, and footwear since 1946, and offers a large part of its inventory through the 32-page color catalog. Great buys and custom services make this a top source.

The catalog shows fashionable, streamlined coats and jackets, tailored and fringed Western models, motorcycle jackets, and other styles for men and women. There are fleece-lined slippers, slip-ons, and moccasins for men and women, as well as billfolds, keycases, tobacco pouches, and handbags. Several pages of gloves are shown, including lined and unlined dress gloves, mittens, and specialty gloves for driving and shooting. Custom sizes, lengths, and linings are also available at reasonable surcharges. The catalog includes instructions on how to care for deerskin garments and accessories.

Pagano Gloves is offering readers of this book a 10% discount on all orders of $150 or more. Please identify yourself as a reader when you order. This WBMC reader discount expires February 1, 1992.

Special Factors: Include measurements when ordering; guide included in the catalog.

THE PETTICOAT EXPRESS

318 W. 39TH ST.
NEW YORK, NY
  10018-1407
212/594-1276

Flyer: free
Save: 40% plus
Pay: check, MO, certified check
Sells: taffeta slips
Store: mail order only

Petticoat Express offers savvy brides an easy way to cut 40% off the cost of one unseen necessity—the net and taffeta slips that create the charming silhouette of a full-skirted bridal or attendant's gown. The firm was started in 1983.

Petticoat Express sells white, full-length half-slips: an A-line style for dresses of moderate flare ($18); a flounced, bouffant style for full skirts ($20); a double-ruffle bouffant ($25) for maximum fullness; and a style for tea-length (31") skirts for $17. Sizes run from 3/4 to 19/20. The slips are made of taffeta and net, and are also ideal for full-skirted evening dresses.

Special Factor: C.O.D. orders are accepted.

QUINN'S SHIRT SHOP

RTE. 12, P.O. BOX 131
NORTH
GROSVENORDALE, CT
06255
508/943-7183

Price List: $1 with self-addressed, stamped envelope
Save: up to 60%
Pay: check or MO
Sells: Arrow shirts
Store: 245 W. Main St., Dudley, MA; Monday through Saturday 10–5

$$$ ✉ ☎

Quinn's is a factory outlet for the Arrow Shirt company, and offers slightly irregular shirts at up to 60% below the price of first-quality goods. Quinn's has been around since 1955.

You can call or write Quinn's for a price on your favorite shirt style, or send $1 and a stamped, self-addressed envelope for the price list. In addition to Arrow label shirts, Quinn's carries styles by Washington Mills. Quinn's specializes in regular, big, and tall sizes, 14-1/2" to 20" neck, 31" to 38" sleeve. You can order without sending for the price list if you provide the style number or name and size, and specify whether you want short sleeves or long (include the length if long). The shirts may be exchanged if the flaws are too apparent. Burlington socks are also available at savings of 50% on list prices.

Special Factors: Satisfaction is guaranteed; price quote by phone or letter with SASE; returns are accepted for exchange; minimum order is 4 shirts per order; only C.O.D. orders are accepted.

ARTHUR M. REIN

32 NEW YORK AVE.,
DEPT. WC-91
FREEPORT, NY
11520-2017
516/379-6421

Information: see text
Save: up to 50% (see text)
Pay: cashier's check, MO, certified check
Sells: custom-made furs
Store: New York City showroom (no Freeport store); hours by appointment

$$$ ✉ 🍁

First things first: *This firm has no catalog.* What it *does* have are two furriers with a combined 70 years of experience in manufacturing fur garments. Mr.

Rein and his associate make all of their fur coats to order, and sell them at prices up to 50% below those of designer furriers.

After you've shopped for furs locally and familiarized yourself with quality points and prices, call Mr. Rein. He can send you a sample pelt (for a refundable deposit) and discuss the garment you have in mind. Or you can write, describing the garment you have in mind (provide a picture, if possible), and stating your measurements, height, and weight. Mr. Rein can help you choose a fur to complement your life-style, tell you about the longevity of different furs, and advise you on care. He can also define terms of the trade, and explain why manufacturing techniques and pelt quality can mean the difference of thousands of dollars in seemingly similar garments.

Mr. Rein can make garments and accessories from Russian sable, lynx, fisher, marten, fox (red, Norwegian blue, silver, etc.), chinchilla, beaver, muskrat, opossum, raccoon, nutria, otter, ermine, coyote, Blackglama, Emba, and other ranch mink. Any item may be made to order, including duplicates of designer furs, coats, jackets, capes, flings, throws, wall hangings, rugs, boas, capes, muffs, scarves, hats, and other accessories. Fur remodeling, lengthening, color darkening, relining, and other services are offered, and used furs are sometimes available. Fur trim, pelts, tails, and mink Teddy bears are available as well.

Special Factors: Satisfaction is guaranteed; price quote by phone (not collect) or letter with a self-addressed, stamped envelope; all goods are warrantied against defects in workmanship and materials for 1 year; returns (except custom-made articles) are accepted within 3 days for refund; minimum order is $50.

ANTHONY RICHARDS

6836 ENGLE RD.
P.O. BOX 94503
CLEVELAND, OH
44101-4503
800-359-5933

Catalog: free
Save: up to 60%
Pay: check, MO, MC, V
Sells: moderately priced women's clothing
Store: mail order only

$$ ✉ ☎ 🍁 🇺🇸

New York City has dozens of stores that sell women's dresses for $19.98 and two-piece outfits for $24.98. They're located in business districts and are usually mobbed at lunchtime, as office workers snare new ensembles at very affordable prices.

The 56-page Anthony Richards catalog offers the same kinds of clothing in the same price range—ideal for those of us on very tight budgets who need a number of outfits for the office or just an alternative to pants and sweaters for shopping and running errands. Most of the dresses are machine washable, are offered in missy and half-sizes, and are stylish without being trendy. A small selection of nightwear and lingerie is offered, and several shoe styles were shown in the catalog we reviewed.

Special Factors: Satisfaction is guaranteed; minimum order is $10 with credit cards.

ROBY'S INTIMATES

"BRAS-BY-MAIL"
1905 SANSOM ST.
PHILADELPHIA, PA 19103
800-8788-BRA
IN PA 215/751-1730

Catalog: $1, refundable
Save: up to 50%
Pay: check, MO, MC, V
Sells: women's underwear
Store: same address; Monday through Thursday 10–6, Friday 10–4

$$$

Roby's Intimates, also known as "Bras-by-Mail," is run by the second generation of a lingerie-discounting family, transplanted from New York City. Roby's, founded in 1985, can save you up to 50% on women's intimate apparel, including basics, post-surgery garments, and more exotic items.

The firm's stock includes bras, girdles, panties, slips, panty hose, and other goods. The brands include Bali, Berkshire (hosiery), Cannon (terry robes), Carnival, Chantelle, Danskin, Christian Dior, Do-All, Exquisite Form, Formfit Rogers, Gossard, Jezebel, Kayser, Lady Marlene, Lejaby, Lilyette, Lily of France, Maidenform, Olga, Pastunette, Playtex, Poirette, Rago, Smoothie, Vassarette, and Warner's. (If you're looking for something on the risqué side, you may want to send for the "Sexy Lingerie Catalog," which costs $3.) Roby's also carries Camp surgical garments and prosthetics for mastectomy patients. If you don't see what you're looking for in the catalog, call or write for a price quote.

Special Factors: Satisfaction is guaranteed; price quote by phone or letter with SASE; unworn returns with tags and labels attached are accepted within 30 days; minimum order is $20 with credit cards.

ROYAL SILK, LTD.

ROYAL SILK PLAZA
CLIFTON, NJ 07011
800-321-SILK

Catalog: $2, year's subscription
Save: up to 40%
Pay: check, MO, MC, V, AE, DC
Sells: silk clothing and accessories
Store: same address; 14 other stores in
CO, DC, FL, HI, KS, MO, NJ, NY, and
VA (locations are listed in the catalog)

Royal Silk, established in 1978, offers good-quality silk and silk-blend clothing and accessories for men and women at competitive prices. Tips on caring for silk apparel are given in the seasonal catalogs—a year of silk for $2.

The 48-page catalog features a wide range of silk and silk-blend apparel: shirts, jackets, sweaters, dresses, lingerie, and accessories for women, including work-into-evening dresses in crepe de chine, twill, corduroy, batiste, and blends of silk with other fibers. Men's shirts and sweaters, underwear, swimwear, safari shirts, bikinis, robes, scarves, sashes, and blazers are among the items that have been featured in past catalogs.

Royal Silk is an excellent source for the working woman who wants to expand her wardrobe on a limited budget. Even the firm's signature scent, "Royal Silk Parfum," is affordably priced. Women's sizes run from 4 to 16, and some garments are offered in petite sizes. All of the designs are by Royal Silk, and the styles include classics as well as the latest looks. Caring for the garments is easy; most are washable, and Royal Silk makes the chore more pleasant with a solution, "Silk 'n Wash," formulated to remove odors and brighten colors.

Canadian readers, please note: Only U.S. funds are accepted.

Special Factors: Satisfaction is guaranteed; returns are accepted within 10 days.

SAINT LAURIE LTD.

**897 BROADWAY, DEPT.
WBM
NEW YORK, NY 10003
800-221-8660
IN NY 212/473-0100**

Style Sheets and Swatch
  Subscription: $10 (see text)
Save: 33% average
Pay: check, MO, MC, V, AE
Sells: business apparel for men and
  women
Store: same address; Monday to Saturday
  9:30–6, Thursday 9:30–7:30, Sunday
  12–5

Saint Laurie has been manufacturing better suits since 1913 and made its mail-order debut in 1979. Ten dollars brings you the spring and fall swatch collections, beautifully produced brochures of actual fabric samples. The accompanying information brochure has clear line drawings of each garment, notes on tailoring details, and lists the suit separates—trousers or skirts—that may be made up in designated fabrics. Membership in the "Saint Laurie Swatch Club" is automatically extended one year when you order.

The Saint Laurie look is expressed in conservatively styled suits, jackets, skirts, and trousers in fine fabrics: all-wool worsted, Italian and Moygashel linen, handwoven silks, gabardine, sharkskin, pinstripes, cotton seer-sucker, and glen plaids, for example. Men's suits are available in short, regular, long, and extra-long lengths, to size 48; women's apparel is offered in petite, regular, and tall models, in sizes 2 to 18. Tailoring details (belt loop and trouser leg width, shoulder style, vents, pockets, lapels, etc.) are all described in the brochure; and pants are sent unhemmed.

Store visitors will find clothing for all seasons in stock, and may take advantage of Saint Laurie's made-to-measure services and have suits custom-fitted. (If you have your alterations made elsewhere, Saint Laurie will reimburse you up to a pre-established dollar amount.) Everything is made on the premises, where you'll discover further evidence of the firm's concern with fine finishing: a museum dedicated to the tailoring arts.

Canadian readers, please note: Shipping charges on orders sent to Canada are twice the U.S. rate.

Special Factors: Returns of unworn, unaltered garments are accepted within 14 days; showroom is closed Sundays in July and August.

SARA GLOVE COMPANY, INC.

117 BENEDICT ST.
P.O. BOX 1940
WATERBURY, CT
06722-1940
203/574-4090

Catalog: $1
Save: up to 30%
Pay: check, MO, MC, V
Sells: work clothing and gloves
Store: same address; Monday to Friday
8:30–4:30, Thursday 8:30–7

$

Work clothing and safety gear comprise the best part of Sara Glove's business, and are showcased in the new "Worldwide Outfitters" catalog at savings of up to 30%.

Seven of the 40 catalog pages are devoted to gloves, gauntlets, and finger cots (tip protectors). Brown jersey and canvas chore gloves, warm fleece gloves, leather-and-canvas work gloves, and heat-resistant gloves of fabric and leather are among the choices for "dry" work. The waterproof gloves, designed to resist abrasion, solvents, caustics, oil, acids, grease, and chemicals, include a range of vinyl, neoprene, nitrile, and latex models. Several of the gloves are USDA-approved for food handling, food processing, and related commercial uses. A comparable range of safety glasses and goggles is available, as well as ear plugs and muffs, respirators and other breathing filters, fire extinguishers, first-aid kits, and other safety equipment.

Clothing dominates the catalog; there are work shirts in sizes to 5XL, pants, leather jackets and motorcycle apparel, Woolrich shirts, Carhartt work jackets and overalls, Dickies work clothing, lab coats, boots and shoes by Carolina Boots, Double-H, Herman Survivors, Kaufman, and Timberland. Belts and Ray-Ban sunglasses are also sold. Sara Glove's custom department can personalize your work shirts, T-shirts, baseball jackets, and baseball caps with names and corporate logos, at a surcharge.

Special Factors: Satisfaction is guaranteed; quantity discounts are available; C.O.D. orders are accepted; institutional accounts are available.

THE SMART SAVER

P.O. BOX 209
WASCO, IL 60183

Catalog: free
Save: up to 30%
Pay: check or MO
Sells: bras and girdles
Store: mail order only

$$ ✉

The Smart Saver is a family-owned business that has specialized in women's intimate apparel since 1982, and sells Playtex foundations and styles by Exquisite Form, Lollipop, and Vanity Fair.

Bras, girdles, panties, and all-in-ones are shown in the 20-page catalog, which lists both the suggested retail and discount prices. Current offerings include a range of Playtex bras and girdles, Exquisite Form bras, and Lollipop panties. Bra and girdle size guides are given in the catalog. Smart Saver also offers its own line of girdles, at reasonable prices.

Special Factor: Only first-quality merchandise is sold, no seconds or irregulars.

THE SOCK SHOP

SWEETWATER HOSIERY
MILLS
P.O. BOX 390
SWEETWATER, TN 37874
615/337-9203

Price List: free
Save: up to 50%
Pay: check or MO
Sells: hosiery and underwear
Store: 818 N. Main St., Sweetwater, TN;
Monday through Friday 8–5, Saturday
9–2

$$ ✉

The Sock Shop is the factory outlet for Sweetwater Hosiery Mills, which has been in operation since 1896. Prices on first-quality goods are up to 50% less than those charged for comparable items elsewhere.

The wide range of hosiery basics for men, women, and children includes sheer and support stockings, knee-high nylons, and support, queen-sized, control-top, and other panty hose styles, as well as booties, knee highs, footlets, and anklets for women. Men can choose from tube, crew, and dress socks in cotton, acrylic, nylon, and wool blends, and there are dress, crew, and tube socks plus anklets, booties, and knee highs for girls and boys. The underwear offerings include cotton and nylon panties for girls (sizes 2 to 14) and women (4 to 10), and Fruit of the Loom briefs and T-shirts for boys (2 to 20) and men's briefs, boxer shorts, T-shirts, and athletic shirts.

Special Factor: Irregulars are clearly marked.

SOCKS GALORE & MORE

220 SECOND AVE. SOUTH FRANKLIN, TN 37064
800-626-SOCK
IN TN 615/790-SOCK

Catalog: free
Save: up to 80%
Pay: check, MO, MC, V
Sells: socks
Store: outlets in AL, AZ, CA, CO, CT, DE, FL, GA, IN, KY, LA, MA, MD, ME, MI, MN, MO, NC, NH, NJ, NY, OH, OR, PA, SC, TN, TX, VA, WA, WI, and WV (locations are listed in the catalog)

Socks Galore was inspired by a man who was seen doing a brisk business selling socks from the trunk of his car. The future cofounder of Socks Galore, who was watching, suddenly realized that America needed a serious sock store.

Since that day in 1981, the firm has opened over 50 shops across the country and launched a mail-order catalog. Over 2,000 styles are offered in each store, from Camp, Classic Toe, Dri-Sox, E.J. Plum, Giggles, Green Tee, Hue, Humpty-Dumpty, T.A. Cherry, T.G.I.F, and World's Softest Sock and numerous other designer lines. The catalog showcases the most popular styles. There are sizes for men, women, youths, and children; support dress and sport styles, thermal weights, tube socks, all-cotton and blend socks, thick wool socks for outdoor sports, argyles, and even tube socks with pockets are offered.

Because of its arrangements with manufacturers, Socks Galore can offer unlabeled socks that come from the same workrooms that produce expensive branded footwear at savings that can reach 80%. Bonuses of free socks and credits for future purchases are offered when you buy minimum amounts. Considering socks as a gift? Order a "Sock Certificate," a gift voucher made out in the amount you specify, which is sent to the recipient with a copy of the current catalog.

Special Factors: Satisfaction is guaranteed; returns are accepted.

SPORTSWEAR
CLEARINGHOUSE

**P.O. BOX 317746-CI
CINCINNATI, OH
45231-7746
513/522-3511**

Brochure: free
Save: up to 70%
Pay: check, MO, MC, V
Sells: printed sportswear overruns, hats, athletic socks, etc.
Store: mail order only

$$ ✉ ☎ 🍁 ▤

You won't find last season's Sergio Tacchini and Ellesse separates at Sportswear Clearinghouse. The fare here is far more basic—T-shirts, sweats, shorts, socks, and hats, many of which are printed with corporate or institutional logos. The Clearinghouse was established in 1976.

Judging from the brochure we received, it's possible to assemble an outfit, however eclectic, consisting of a Coors logo hat, a T-shirt printed for the American Embassy in Beirut, Penn State athletic shorts, and socks once destined for the promotion department at Marlboro. The Clearinghouse has had T-shirts commemorating different events, sweatshirts, golf shirts (printed for the "staff" of different institutions), and T-shirts bearing the names of universities, corporations, and rock groups like Quiet Riot and Van Halen. Prices are hard to beat; T-shirts and shorts cost a few dollars, and hats and visors are priced under $2. Most of these items are sold in lots of three, six, or a dozen, and the selection of individual slogans is up to the Clearinghouse. Plain, first-quality athletic socks and baseball hats embroidered with the logos of major league teams are also available, as well as baseball/golf hats in neon colors, and two styles of fanny/belly packs.

Special Factors: Satisfaction is guaranteed; unused returns are accepted within 30 days for exchange, refund, or credit; orders are shipped worldwide.

SUSSEX CLOTHES, LTD.

**302 FIFTH AVE.
NEW YORK, NY 10001
212/279-4610**

Swatch and Style Brochure: $5
Save: up to 40%
Pay: MO, MC, V, AE
Sells: men's business apparel
Store: same address; Monday to Saturday
9:30–6, Thursday 9:30–7:30, Sunday 11–
4; also 116 Nassau St., New York, NY;
Monday through Friday 9:30–6, Saturday
10–3

$$$ ✉

Sussex has been manufacturing suits for prominent retailers since 1929, and now offers the same suits directly to consumers through a swatch/style booklet at savings of up to 40%.

The style booklet shows The Sussex Suit, a conservatively tailored men's suit with two-button jacket, natural shoulders, centered vent, flap pockets, moderate lapels, horn buttons, and straight-leg trousers with quarter-top pockets. The Sussex Sportcoat/Blazer is styled like the jacket. The suit is available in wool worsteds, pinstripes, glen plaids, and tick weaves, priced from $265. Sussex offers a choice of two dozen seasonal fabrics, in four sizes (to fit 5′4″ to 6′6″), and fine tailoring details.

Special Factor: Returns of unaltered, unworn garments sent with hang-tags attached are accepted within 14 days.

TAI, INC.

**90 DAYTON AVE.
PASSAIC, NJ 07055
201/777-0905**

Catalog: free
Save: quantity discounts (see text)
Pay: check, MO, MC, V, AE
Sells: silk-screened apparel and accessories
Store: same address; Monday through
Friday 9–4:30, Saturday 11–4:30

$ ✉   ☎   🍁

TAI was founded by Crown Art Products (see the firm's listing in "Art Materials"), which manufactures silk-screening supplies and equipment. Established in 1983, TAI offers a line of clothing and accessories that are hand-screened with military insignias.

The catalog offers a range of items embellished with the motifs of military forces, including aprons, scarves, beach towels, laundry and duffel bags, T-shirts, pennants, decals, and bumper stickers. Choose from insignias of the Airborne divisions, Special Forces groups, the Marines, Rangers, the Foreign Legion, U.S.M.C. Recon, and other forces and divisions.

Special Factors: Price quote by phone or letter with SASE; quantity discounts are available; monthly specials are featured; minimum order is $25 with credit cards.

TODD WORK APPAREL

████████████

**12970 MAURER
 INDUSTRIAL DR.
ST. LOUIS, MO 63127
800-458-3402
FAX: 314/525-0640**

Catalog: free
Save: up to 30%
Pay: check, MO, MC, V, AE, Discover, Optima
Sells: work clothing and uniforms
Store: Ripley, TN; Monday through Saturday 9–5:30

Todd has been selling uniforms and work apparel since 1881, and brings you factory-direct savings through the 52-page, color catalog. Prices are reasonable—up to 30% below the competition—and quantity discounts of 5% to 30% (on orders of 15 to 500 items of any combination) enhance the savings.

The clothing runs from the ubiquitous work shirt for men and women, which is offered in a range of colors, to pants and jeans, sweaters, lab and food-industry coats, jumpsuits, jackets, T-shirts, polo shirts, aprons, rainwear, and baseball hats. Todd can embroider or print your logo or business message on the garments, or on emblems, and the order form is designed to make specifying even complicated orders easy. There are varying minimums for the custom work, but quantity discounts apply.

Special Factors: Satisfaction is guaranteed; price quote by phone or letter with SASE; quantity discounts are available; institutional accounts are available.

WEARGUARD CORP.

BOX 400
HINGHAM, MA 02043
800-343-4406
800-635-3553

Catalog: free
Save: up to 30%
Pay: check, MO, MC, V, AE
Sells: work clothing, rugged casual wear, and accessories
Store: outlets in CT, DE, MA, ME, MI, NH, NJ, NY, PA, and RI

$$$ ✉ ☎ 🍁

WearGuard, founded in 1951, supplies more than a million U.S. companies and consumers with work clothing at 10% to 30% below regular and comparable retail prices.

WearGuard has what may be the best selection of work shirts in the country—21 colors and patterns, in long or short sleeves, sized XS to XXXXXL, from about $16 to $21. In addition, there are T-shirts, polo shirts, chambray shirts, turtlenecks, Western and flannel shirts, jeans, Western boots, Durango Wellingtons, Timberland and Kodiak boots, work shoes, gloves, thermal underwear and union suits, jumpsuits, coveralls, gabardine jackets, boat moccasins, varsity-style jackets, and windbreakers. A similar range of apparel for women is offered, and there are specialty items for truckers and enforcement personnel. The custom department can provide designs on patches, emblems, T-shirts, and work shirts; there are also stock logos and lettering. The screen printing and direct embroidery are done "in house," so service is faster.

Special Factors: Satisfaction is guaranteed; returns are accepted; quantity discounts are available; C.O.D. orders are accepted.

WORKMEN'S GARMENT CO.

15205 WYOMING AVE.
DETROIT, MI 48238
313/834-7236

Catalog: $2, refundable
Save: up to 75%
Pay: check, MO, MC, V
Sells: new and reconditioned work clothing
Store: same address; Monday through Friday 8:30–4:30, Saturday 8:30–1

$$$ ✉ ☎

Workmen's Garment, in business since 1954, can save you up to 75% on the cost of work clothing, much of which is suitable for outdoor wear as well.

New and reconditioned goods are available.

Workmen's declares that "Big or Small, We Fit 'Em All," and really tries: The selection includes new blue denim jeans to size 66 waist, shop coats (to size 60), coveralls (to size 66 chest), work jackets, shirts to size 10XL, pants to size 76 waist, tube socks, and shop aprons. Work clothing in brown duck and blue denim, painters' pants, and similar basics are featured, as well as other work clothing and shoes by well- known manufacturers. The "Wear-Again" reconditioned clothing (washed, pressed, and sterilized) includes coveralls from $5, pants and shirts from $3, work jackets, lab coats, and many other items. If you don't see what you're looking for, call— it may be available.

Special Factors: Satisfaction is guaranteed on new and "Wear-Again" clothing; shipping is included; returns are accepted within 10 days; minimum order is $15.

COMPANIES OUTSIDE THE U.S.A.

The following firms are experienced in dealing with customers in the U.S. and Canada. We've included them because they offer goods not widely available at a discount in the U.S., because they have a better selection, or because they may offer the same goods at great savings.

Before ordering from a non-U.S. firm, please read through the applicable sections of "The Complete Guide to Buying by Mail" at the back of this book. We recommend paying for your catalog with a camouflaged enclosure of cash. (Sending cash saves the company the bank charge of converting your check to different currency.) We further advise you to pay for your merchandise by credit card whenever possible, so that your transaction will be protected by the part of the Fair Credit Billing Act that allows you to dispute charges for goods not received. See page 000–000 for a complete discussion of the Act. Please note that only this portion of the Act applies, and the FTC's Mail Order Rule governing delivery time *does not*.

CLEO (IRELAND) LTD.

18 KILDARE ST.
DUBLIN 2
IRELAND
011-353-1-761421
FAX: 011-353-1-797587

Catalog and Samples: $3.50
Save: up to 30%
Pay: check, IMO, bank draft, MC, V, Access
Sells: Irish fabric and clothing
Store: same address; also 2 Shelbourne St., Kenmare, Co. Kerry; Monday through Saturday 9–5:30 (Kenmare location April to October only)

Cleo's refreshing paintbox of rich country colors is a welcome change from the muddy shadings and anemic pastels often offered in the name of tweed. At this writing, Cleo is offering a deep violet fabric flecked with cerise and aquamarine and varied fabrics in teal, coppery red blended with steel blue, soft lichen green, and creamy natural.

Cleo sells a variety of clothing for men and women, made from the same fabrics and yarns. Among the current styles shown are a Munster cloak for women and an evening cape for men, a handsome Chesterfield for women, and very special "Cleo Wraps," self-fringed oblongs of fabric, woven in a subtle block pattern in four different color ranges. Aran handknits in traditional patterns and a variety of heathery hues are also sold. There are no "bargains" here, but some of these goods cost about as much as mass-produced garments of the same type sold in the U.S. (The Chesterfield, for example, costs less than $300.) The Cleo Wraps are very reasonably priced, ranging from about $35 for the 48″ by 52″ size, to about $75 for the 90″ by 52″ size (matching skirts are available). The Cleo Wraps may be used as shawls, throws, table covers, and even as wall hangings.

Special Factor: Give second color choices when ordering.

MOFFAT WOOLLENS LTD.

**BENMAR, MOFFAT
DUMFRIESSHIRE DG10
9EP
SCOTLAND
011-44-387-683-20799**

Catalog: free
Save: up to 50%
Pay: check, IMO, MC, V, AE, Access, EC
Sells: Scottish knits and woven apparel
Store: same address; Monday through
Friday 9–5:30

$$$

Moffat's 16-page color catalog shows dozens of coordinated skirt and sweater ensembles, in pleasing heathery pastels, tartans, and deep reds and blues. These are the traditionally styled pleated and straight skirts, turtle-neck sweaters, and pullovers, cardigans, and blouses that are staples of a businesswoman's wardrobe.

Kilts, tams, scarves, ties, and stoles are offered in selected tartans, as are delightful separates for children: kilts (in sizes 2 to 12), boys' trousers, and ponchos, among others. There are also lovely sweaters for men and women in lambswool, Shetland wool, Aran and Fair Isle designs, and even animal and thistle motifs. Catalog prices are listed in pounds sterling, excluding postage, and the catalog is shipped by airmail. Goods may be sent by surface mail or airmail, the latter at a surcharge.

Special Factors: Satisfaction is guaranteed; returns are accepted within 14 days for exchange, refund, or credit.

W.S. ROBERTSON (OUTFITTERS) LTD.

**40/41 BANK ST.
GALASHIELS
SCOTLAND
011-44-1-896-2152**

Brochures and Price Lists: $5
Save: up to 30%
Pay: check, IMO, MC, V, Access
Sells: Scottish knitwear
Store: same address; Monday through
Friday 9–5:30

$$

There are cashmere sweaters, and then there are Pringles. Pringle of Scotland has been making fine knitwear since 1815, using such natural fibers as cashmere, camel's hair, "lamaine" (a Merino wool), lambswool, and Shetland wool. W.S. Robertson sells Pringle's pullovers, cardigans, and vests, at savings of up to 30% on U.S. prices. Robertson also carries the stylish Lyle & Scott sweaters. Considered as fine as Pringles by many, they're made in cashmere, lambswool, and Botany wool, and are somewhat less expensive than comparable Pringle models. The highly regarded knits by Ballantyne and Braemar, in cashmere, lambswool, and Shetland wool, are offered as well.

As long as you're having your order delivered to a non-U.K. address, you should deduct 15% (the Value Added Tax, not charged on exported goods). The final figure is your cost. The prices are listed in pounds sterling, and the savings increase when the dollar is strong. If you're not paying in pounds, obtain the rate of exchange from your local bank on the day you order and use that figure to convert the pounds to dollars. Remember to add shipping costs after you compute the export discount.

Special Factor: Price quote by phone or letter on styles not shown in the brochures.

THE WOOL SHOP

HIGH ST.
KILLARNEY, CO. KERRY
IRELAND

Catalog: free
Save: up to 35%
Pay: check, IMO, bank draft
Sells: Aran sweaters
Store: same address; Monday through
Saturday 9:30–6

$$ ✉ 🍁 ▰

The catalog from The Wool Shop shows a variety of Aran-knit pullovers, cardigans, and vests for men, women, and children. All of the garments are knit by hand in Killarney. Prices run from about $65 to $125 for pullovers, and $67 and up for cardigans. Instead of pricing the sweaters individually, the catalog gives the price *range* for each type of garment. Send in the order form with the size, style, neck type, measurements, and color (white, cream, or natural black) specified, and The Wool Shop will send you a price quote. This may seem a cumbersome way to do business, but it's ideal if you want a certain stitch worked into your sweater, need a very large size, or would like something unusual—three quarter sleeves, pockets, or a belt, for example.

The Wool Shop is offering readers of this book a 5% discount on all orders. Identify yourself as a WBMC reader when you order. This WBMC reader discount expires March 31, 1992.

Special Factors: Price quote by letter; orders are shipped worldwide.

SEE ALSO

Ace Leather Products, Inc. ● handbags, attaché cases, and small leather goods ● *LEATHER*

Atlantic Bridge Collection Corp. Ltd. ● Aran handknits ● *ART, ANTIQUES*

Austad's ● golf apparel and shoes ● *SPORTS*

Bailey's, Inc. ● wide range of outdoor apparel clothing for men ● *TOOLS*

Bart's Water Ski Center, Inc. ● water-skiing vests, T-shirts, swim trunks, and wet suits ● *SPORTS*

Bass Pro Shops ● boating and outdoor wear ● *SPORTS*

Beauty Boutique ● small selection of moderately priced women's apparel ● *HEALTH*

Beauty by Spector, Inc. ● wigs and hairpieces for men and women ● *HEALTH*

Better Health Fitness ● Danskin and Everlast sportswear ● *SPORTS*

Bike Nashbar ● bicycling and sports apparel, and sunglasses ● *SPORTS*

Bowhunters Warehouse, Inc. ● camouflage clothing ● *SPORTS*

Bruce Medical Supply ● dressing aids for the disabled, stoma scarves, incontinence products ● *MEDICINE*

The Button Shop ● replacement zippers for jeans, garment shoulder pads ● *CRAFTS*

Cabela's Inc. ● hunting and fishing wear, rugged outdoor clothing and footwear ● *SPORTS*

Cambridge Wools, Ltd. ● Aran-style sweaters ● *CRAFTS*

Campmor ● outdoor clothing and accessories for men, women, and children ● *SPORTS*

Clothcrafters, Inc. ● aprons, garment bags, and tote bags ● *GENERAL MERCHANDISE*

The Company Store, Inc. ● down-filled outerwear, cotton nightwear, and separates ● *HOME: LINEN*

Custom Golf Clubs, Inc. ● golf clothing and footwear ● *SPORTS*

Cycle Goods Corp. ● bicycling apparel and footwear ● *SPORTS*

Defender Industries, Inc. ● foul-weather wear and boating shoes ● *AUTO*

Direct Safety Company ● protective and disposable industrial clothing, hats, and gloves ● *TOOLS*

E & B Marine Supply, Inc. ● foul-weather wear ● *AUTO*

The Eye Solution, Inc. ● Bausch & Lomb, Ray-Ban, and Vuarnet sunglasses ● *MEDICINE*

Fashion Touches ● custom-covered buttons, belts, cuff links, buckles, etc. ● *CRAFTS*

A. Feibusch Corporation ● zippers of all types ● *CRAFTS*

Fish'n Shack ● camouflage clothing, waders, Sperry shoes, etc. ● *SPORTS*

Gander Mountain, Inc. • hunting and fishing clothing, outdoor wear • SPORTS

Gettinger Feather Corp. • feather marabous and boas, loose feathers • CRAFTS

Goldbergs' Marine Distributors • foul-weather wear, boating shoes, etc. • AUTO

Innovation Luggage • handbags and small leather goods • LEATHER

Las Vegas Discount Golf & Tennis • tennis and other sports apparel, tennis and golf shoes • SPORTS

Leather Unlimited Corp. • sheepskin mittens, hats, and bags • CRAFTS

Lingerie for Less • Spenco breast forms • MEDICINE

D. MacGillivray & Coy. • Scottish knitwear, stock and custom-made kilts, etc. • CRAFTS

Mass. Army & Navy Store • government surplus clothing and gear, casual wear • SURPLUS

Mother Hart's Natural Products, Inc. • natural-fiber women's underwear, leotards, leg warmers, etc. • HOME: LINEN

New England Leather Accessories, Inc. • leather handbags and accessories • LEATHER

Omaha Vaccine Company, Inc. • Wells Lamont work gloves, Red Ball boots • ANIMAL

PBS Livestock Drugs • Tingley work boots and rain suits, chambray shirts, OshKosh overalls, etc. • ANIMAL

Overton's Sports Center, Inc. • boating and windsurfing apparel • SPORTS

Performance Bicycle Shop • cycling clothing, footwear, and helmets • SPORTS

Professional Golf & Tennis Suppliers, Inc. • golf, tennis, and running shoes and apparel • SPORTS

Pueblo to People • handwoven clothing and accessories from Central and South America • GENERAL MERCHANDISE

Racer Wholesale • auto racing suits and accessories • AUTO

Rammagerdin • Icelandic clothing • CRAFTS

Retired Persons Services, Inc. • support hosiery, slippers, socks, etc. • MEDICINE

Road Runner Sports • sports apparel and shoes • SPORTS

Ruvel & Co., Inc. • government surplus clothing and outdoor wear • SURPLUS

Sailboard Warehouse, Inc. • windsurfing apparel • SPORTS

Samuels Tennisport • court clothing, sport bags, and accessories • SPORTS

Script City • T-shirts and casual clothing with TV-theme logos, etc. • BOOKS

Shannon Duty Free Mail Order • Irish handknits • HOME: TABLE SETTINGS

Spiegel, Inc. • clothing and footwear for men, women, and children • GENERAL

Sport Shop • camouflage clothing • SPORTS

Stuyvesant Bicycle, Inc. • bicycling clothing, helmets, etc. • SPORTS

Sultan's Delight, Inc. • belly-dancing outfits, Arab headdresses and agals • FOOD

Surgical Products, Inc. • support hosiery, Enna Jettick shoes, therapeutic apparel • MEDICINE

Thai Silks • silk ties, scarves, handkerchiefs, lingerie, and blouses • CRAFTS

Utex Trading Enterprises • silk scarves and ties • CRAFTS

West Marine Products • foul-weather wear • AUTO

Wiley Outdoor Sports, Inc. • hunting (camouflage) clothing and accessories • SPORTS

FOOTWEAR

Shoes, boots, and slippers for men, women, and children

The firms listed in this section specialize in footwear, from arctic boots to moccasins to bridal shoes, at savings of up to 40%. Buying footwear by mail can be a great timesaver if the shoes fit, but something of a hassle if they don't. Given the relatively high rate of returns in the footwear segment of mail-order apparel, this happens with some frequency. There are several ways to enhance your chances of buying the right shoes and make returns as easy as possible when necessary:

- Have your feet measured yearly, so you're sure to order your true size.
- Buy from firms with liberal return policies, preferably an unconditional guarantee of satisfaction and 30-day return period.
- Buy styles and shapes that have fit in the past.
- If the shoes you're buying are also available in a local store, be sure to try on a pair before sending your order.
- When the shoes arrive, unwrap them carefully and save the packaging.
- Try on the shoes in the late afternoon, when your feet have swollen.
- Walk around in a carpeted area to avoid scratching the soles of the shoes.
- Leave the shoes on for at least half an hour, checking for rubbing and pinching after 20 minutes.
- If the shoes fit, consider ordering a second pair *now,* while they're still in stock.
- If the shoes don't fit, return them according to the firm's instructions, indicating whether you want another size or a refund/credit.

Good maintenance is critical in preserving the looks and longevity of your shoes and boots. For helpful tips on caring for all types of footwear, see *The Butler's Guide* (Fireside/Simon & Schuster, 1980), by Stanley Ager and Fiona St. Aubyn, and *Taking Care of Clothes* (St. Martin's Press, 1982), by Mablen Jones. Some of the firms listed in "Leather" sell leather care products, as do a number of companies listed in the "See Also's" of that chapter. If your shoes and boots need professional help and you don't have a good repair service nearby, contact the Houston Shoe Hospital, at 5215 Kirby Dr., Houston, TX 77098, or 713/528-6268. This firm overhauls worn footwear at prices much lower than those charged by New York City shoes repair shops, and does business by mail.

CLOVER NURSING SHOE COMPANY

1948 EAST WHIPP RD., DEPT. WBM KETTERING, OH 45440-2921
513/435-0025

Brochure: free
Save: up to 40%
Pay: check, MO, MC, V
Sells: Nurse Mates and Soft Spots shoes
Store: mail order only

$$$

Nurses look for comfort and good fit in their professional shoes, and many find both in Nurse Mates, a line of shoes manufactured by the Soft Spots company. Clover Nursing Shoe specializes in Nurse Mates, which it sells at the best discounts around—up to 40% off regular retail, every day.

The Nurse Mates line includes over a dozen styles, from streamlined T-straps to sturdy blucher models. The shoes are made of soft leather and built up on lightweight wedge soles that sport a little blue heart. (Some of the Nurse Mates styles are available in colored leather in the regular Soft Spots line.) Clover's prices are great on the Nurse Mates, and the full range of sizes—from 5 to 12, slim (AA) to double-wide (EE)—is carried.

Special Factors: Satisfaction is guaranteed; only first-quality goods are sold.

THE HANOVER SHOE CO.

118 CARLISLE ST., DEPT. 90036 HANOVER, PA 17331
800-426-3708

Catalog: $1
Save: 25% average
Pay: check, MO, MC, V, AE, CB, DC
Sells: footwear for men and women
Store: over 300 stores nationwide

$$$

The Hanover Shoe Company has been making shoes since 1899 and sells through a 32-page color catalog and at over 300 stores across the country. The workmanship and quality of Hanover shoes—which are mainly styles for men—make them comparable to similar styles from other firms that charge much more—often an additional $30 to $75 per pair.

Hanover's top line of Shell Cordovan leather shoes includes classic wing tips, Oxfords, tasseled slip-ons, and penny loafers, and all cost under $175. Properly maintained, Hanover believes you can expect up to 15 years of wear from these shoes (not counting resoling). Hanover's "Master Flex" shoes employ a flexible leather sole and special comfort features, and they're offered in several styles (including a handsome European model and a buckled half-boot) for under $125. Well-made calfskin brogues, wing tips, and Oxfords are offered, as well as a full line of handsewn loafers, patent leather and lizard slip-ons, and other styles. The catalog we reviewed also showed athletic and walking footwear by Clarks, Converse, K-Swiss, New Balance, and Rocky Boots.

Many of Hanover's own shoes are offered in sizes from 6 to 15, in widths from AA to EEE. Hosiery, belts, wallets, and shoe-care products are also featured. The catalog includes an introductory discount offer of $5 off each pair of shoes, and all purchases are backed by the Hanover guarantee of satisfaction. Please note: do *not* request discounts.

Special Factor: Satisfaction is guaranteed.

JUSTIN DISCOUNT BOOTS & COWBOY OUTFITTERS

P.O. BOX 67-JWM
JUSTIN, TX 76247
800-677-BOOT
FAX: 817/648-3282

Catalog: free
Save: 35% average
Pay: check, MO, MC, V
Sells: Western boots and clothing
Store: 101 W. Hwy. 156, Justin, TX;
　　　　Monday through Saturday 9–6

$$$　

This company, although not owned by the Justin Boot Co., sells a number of the Justin boot lines in men's and women's styles. The 52-page color catalog includes a "compare at" price as well as the selling price for most items. We cross-checked several items, and found that the reference prices weren't inflated, and the JDB prices were 20% to 40% less.

The footwear choices run from "ropers," comparatively plain, thick-soled boots with Western vamps that rise to mid-calf (about $90), to artful creations in exotic skins—ostrich, lizard, bull hide, elk, and snakeskin. There are several pages of women's styles, including lizard Western boots, "fashion" ropers in Atlantis blue, pink, "mellow yellow," and pearl grey, as well as traditional colors. Children can get their ropers in red, pink, navy, brown, and other colors, for $44.95 a pair. Coordinating belts are available for many of the boots, and the custom embroidery department will embellish your boots with two initials for $6.50 per letter.

Real cowboys don't wear ostrich dress boots while mending fences, though—they wear work boots. JDB offers sturdy Justin styles with oil-tanned leather uppers and Vibram soles, and a number of specialty boots: insulated and all-weather models, snakeproof and steel-toed boots, and "engineer" boots (for oil field workers and motorcyclists). Justin Discount Boots also sells its own line of straw hats, German silver buckles and belt tips, Indian Main moccasins, leather-care products, and Wrangler shirts, Carhartt jackets, and Wrangler jeans for men, women, and boys.

Special Factors: Satisfaction is guaranteed; unworn, unscuffed, unaltered returns are accepted for exchange, refund, or credit; C.O.D. orders are accepted; orders are shipped worldwide.

MINNETONKA-BY-MAIL

P.O. BOX 444
BRONX, NY 10458

Catalog: $1
Save: 20% plus
Pay: check or MO
Sells: Minnetonka moccasins and casual footwear
Store: mail order only

The moccasin, like loafers and chukka boots, has survived fad and fashion to become a classic in casual footwear. Among Indian-style moccasins, Minnetonka's are probably the most popular.

The firm produces several interpretations of the fringed and tied moccasin with a beaded "Thunderbird" design, including a choice of soles—crepe, boat, soft, and polyurethane, among others. The 16-page color catalog shows mocs with "nubbed" soles for driving, plain styles in moose hide and deerskin, and pile-lined mocs and booties for winter wear. There are laced suede boots, ankle-high booties with fringed tops or large silver side buttons, and a group for children and infants as well. List prices run from about $16 to about $60—sometimes lower than the prices charged for the Minnetonka knockoffs we see each summer in local stores.

Minnetonka-by-Mail has been selling these moccasins since 1981, and is offering a 20% goods discount to new customers who identify themselves as readers of this book when they order. This WBMC reader discount expires February 1, 1992.

Special Factors: Price quote by letter with SASE; shipping is included on orders of 6 or more pairs.

OKUN BROS. SHOES

**356 E. SOUTH ST.-WBM
KALAMAZOO, MI 49007
800-433-6344**

Catalog: free
Save: 18% average (see text)
Pay: check, MO, MC, V, Discover
Sells: dress, casual, and work shoes
Store: same address; Monday through
    Friday 8:30 A.M.–9 P.M., Saturday 8:30–7

Okun Bros., serving the footwear needs of Kalamazoo since 1920, has opened its shoe store to the world through a 48-page catalog of casual and outdoor styles.

We've found casual shoes, plain pumps, athletic shoes for several sports, men's dress shoes, sandals, loafers and moccasins, deck shoes, nurses' shoes, bikers' boots, and work shoes and boots in previous catalogs. The brands and lines available here number over 200, including some of the most popular: Acme, Avia, Bates Floaters, Carolina Shoe Co., Clarks, Coleman, Converse, Cuddlers, Dexter, Dingo, Double H, Easy Spirit, Allen Edmonds, Etonic, Extra Depth, Florsheim, Foot-Joy, Freeman, French Shriner, Frye, Grasshoppers, Daniel Green, Harley-Davidson (motorcycle boots), Johnston & Murphy, L.A. Gear, LaCrosse, Minnetonka, New Balance, Nike, Nunn Bush, Nurse Mates, Pony, Red Wing, Reeboks, Rockport, Rocky, Sebago, Soft Spots, Sorel, Sperry Top-Sider, Stacy Adams, Timberland, Tingley, Wolverine, and Wright (Arch Preserver Shoes). This is a partial list. Thor-Lo "padded" specialty sport socks are also available.

Okun maintains that it can fit nearly any foot, and it has the largest stock of men's work and safety shoes available in Michigan. Some of the brands are rarely found sold at less than full retail. The typical discount is 18%, but heavy boots for sub-zero conditions have been sold here at up to 44% off, and specials in the sales flyers further the savings to 50%. Because only a fraction of the stock can be shown in the catalog, you should inquire about brands and styles not shown—they may be available.

Canadian readers, please note: The shipping surcharge on orders sent to Canada is $10.

Special Factors: Satisfaction is guaranteed; price quote by phone or letter with SASE; unworn returns are accepted.

COMPANIES OUTSIDE THE U.S.A.

The following firm, A.W.G. Otten and Son, is experienced in dealing with customers in the U.S. and Canada. We've included Otten because the Dutch clogs it sells are not widely available at great savings in the U.S. and because the firm offers a wide selection of styles and sizes.

Before ordering from a non-U.S. firm, please read through the applicable sections of "The Complete Guide to Buying by Mail" at the back of this book. We recommend paying for your catalog with a camouflaged enclosure of cash. (Sending cash saves the company the bank charge of converting your check to different currency.) We further advise you to pay for your merchandise by credit card whenever possible, so that your transaction will be protected by the part of the Fair Credit Billing Act that allows you to dispute charges for goods not received. See page 545 for a complete discussion of the Act. Please note that only this portion of the Act applies, and the FTC's Mail Order Rule governing delivery time *does not.*

A.W.G. OTTEN AND SON

P.O. BOX 55655
1007 ND AMSTERDAM
THE NETHERLANDS

Catalog: $1, cash
Save: up to 30%
Pay: IMO, MC, V, AE, DC, Access
Sells: wooden shoes and clogs
Store: 33 1st v.d. Helststraat, 1073 AC Amsterdam; Monday through Friday 9–5:30

Wooden shoes, or *klompen,* are still worn in Holland by gardeners, fishermen, butchers, and dairy workers. Otten and Son's charming brochure details the history and manufacture of wooden shoes. We learned in reading it that in one part of Holland a boy courting a girl would give her carved wooden shoes decorated with her initials. The *klompen* have even affected the language—there are several Dutch words that are derived from the sounds made by walking in wooden shoes.

Otten makes seven models, including souvenir shoes with windmills carved on the toes. Most of the shoes are painted in lively colors, and there is a low-cut model that is easier to walk in than the traditional style. Otten also sells wooden clogs with leather uppers, much like those made by Olof Daughters of Sweden. Prices for the shoes are easily 30% below those charged in import and gift shops in the U.S. Sizes run from a child's size 4 to a man's size 14.

Don't overlook the uses for these shoes—the large sizes can be used as doll beds, letter holders, planters, lamp bases, or even pencil holders. They make wonderful gifts, too.

Special Factor: Quantity discounts are available.

SEE ALSO

Austad's ● golf apparel and shoes ● *SPORTS*
Jos. A. Bank Clothiers, Inc. ● fine quality, traditional men's shoes ● *CLOTHING*
Bike Nashbar ● bicycling footwear ● *SPORTS*
Cabela's Inc. ● hunting and fishing wear, rugged outdoor clothing and footwear ● *SPORTS*
Cahall's Department Store ● rugged footwear for men and women ● *CLOTHING*
Campmor ● rugged footwear for men, women, and children ● *SPORTS*
Custom Coat Company, Inc. ● deerskin moccasins ● *CLOTHING*
Custom Golf Clubs, Inc. ● golf clothing and footwear ● *SPORTS*
Cycle Goods Corp. ● bicycling apparel and footwear ● *SPORTS*
D & A Merchandise Co., Inc. ● Totes footwear ● *CLOTHING*
The Deerskin Place ● suede boots, moccasins, etc. ● *CLOTHING*
Fish'n Shack ● camouflage clothing, waders, Sperry shoes, etc. ● *SPORTS*
Gander Mountain, Inc. ● rugged boots and footwear ● *SPORTS*
Gohn Bros. ● sturdy work shoes and boots for men and women ● *CLOTHING*
Goldbergs' Marine Distributors ● foul-weather wear, boating shoes, etc. ● *AUTO*

Golf Haus ● golf shoes ● *SPORTS*

Holabird Sports Discounters ● shoes for sports activities ● *SPORTS*

Huntington Clothiers ● small selection of men's shoes ● *CLOTHING*

Lands' End, Inc. ● casual and sporty footwear for men and women ● *CLOTHING*

Las Vegas Discount Golf & Tennis ● tennis and other sports apparel; tennis and golf shoes ● *SPORTS*

Northern Hydraulics, Inc. ● Northlake boots ● *TOOLS*

Northern Wholesale Veterinary Supply, Inc. ● heavy-duty boots ● *ANIMAL*

Thos. Oak & Sons ● moderately priced footwear for women ● *CLOTHING*

Omaha Vaccine Company, Inc. ● Wells Lamont work gloves, Red Ball boots ● *ANIMAL*

Pagano Gloves, Inc. ● moccasins ● *CLOTHING*

PBS Livestock Drugs ● Tingley work boots and rain suits, chambray shirts, OshKosh overalls, etc. ● *ANIMAL*

Performance Bicycle Shop ● cycling clothing, footwear, and helmets ● *SPORTS*

Professional Golf & Tennis Suppliers, Inc. ● golf, tennis, and running shoes and apparel ● *SPORTS*

Anthony Richards ● small selection of moderately priced women's shoes ● *CLOTHING*

Road Runner Sports ● sports apparel and shoes ● *SPORTS*

Sara Glove Company, Inc. ● work shoes and boots ● *CLOTHING*

Socks Galore & More ● socks for the whole family ● *CLOTHING*

Spiegel, Inc. ● clothing and footwear for men, women, and children ● *GENERAL MERCHANDISE*

Squash Services, Inc. ● racquet sports footwear ● *SPORTS*

Surgical Products, Inc. ● support hosiery, Enna Jettick shoes, therapeutic apparel ● *MEDICINE*

WearGuard Corp. ● work shoes and boots ● *CLOTHING*

Wholesale Veterinary Supply, Inc. ● work shoes and boots ● *ANIMAL*

Wide World of Sporting Goods ● running shoes ● *SPORTS*

Wiley Outdoor Sports, Inc. ● hunting and outdoor footwear ● *SPORTS*

MOTHER AND CHILD

━━━━

Clothing and accessories for the expectant and nursing mother, and infants and children; baby furniture, strollers, and related goods

Getting more from your budget when buying baby's clothing and gear can generate benefits over a long period of time. For example, if you've allotted $10 for three name-brand undershirts but buy six unbranded shirts for the same amount of money instead, you've bought twice as much *time* between future washloads. Alternatively, you can buy three of the unbranded shirts and put the remainder into the babysitting fund. Or you might invest the surplus in larger clothes as you find them on sale, as a hedge against both your child's growth spurts and inflation.

Clothing criteria may be determined by taste, but choosing equipment is another matter. Before deciding which of the many models of bassinets, cribs, high chairs, playpens, car seats, and other furnishings are best for your needs and budget, confer with other parents, examine the models displayed in stores, and consult experts. We found *The Baby Gear Guide* (Addison-Wesley Publishing Co., 1985), by Taree Bollinger and Patricia Cramer, to be an immensely helpful guide to product features, pros and cons of different model styles, and safety points. Products in more than 35 categories are analyzed, and lists of safety organizations, publications for parents, and manufacturers' addresses are included as well. A more upscale look at what's being marketed for baby is offered by *Babyworks* (Viking, 1985), a lush color book by Jean Mills that features products chosen for their aesthetic appeal as well as their durability and quality.

The firms in this section offer maternity wear and clothing and accessories for infants and children at savings of up to 60%. In addition to these companies, a number of the firms listed throughout this book sell goods for mother and baby. *Bennett Brothers* ("General") offers a large selection of sterling keepsakes for baby, Hedstrom nursery furnishings, car seats, playpens, high chairs, strollers, and toys. *Sears, Roebuck and Co.* ("General") publishes an "Infants 'n Toddlers Specialog" packed with good buys on nursery furniture, strollers, car seats, nursing sets, baby clothing from layette through toddler sizes, and maternity wear. *Spiegel, Inc.* ("General") also offers maternity wear and toys. *Chock Catalog Corp.* ("Clothing") features Carter's receiving blankets and crib sets, Curity diapers, and underwear and nightwear for newborn through toddler sizes. *Gohn Bros.* ("Clothing") sells Curity diapers and Gerber bibs, baby sleepers, waterproof pants, and shirts. And *Campmor* ("Sports") offers baby buntings, Snuglis, and a diaper-changer backpack for the truly intrepid parent. And the *Consumer Information Center* ("Books") usually offers a number of pamphlets with baby-care tips and related information.

BABY BUNZ & CO.

P.O. BOX 1717-WB91
SEBASTOPOL, CA 95473
707/829-5347

Catalog: $1
Save: up to 30%
Pay: check, MO, MC, V
Sells: diapering supplies and layette items
Store: mail order only

If you've decided to use cloth diapers instead of disposables, you'll appreciate all of the prefolded diapers and diaper "systems" on the market. One of the most popular diapering methods among the cloth set is the use of a standard or fitted diaper with a natural-fiber cover.

Baby Bunz & Co. carries the best-known covers, Nikkys, in soft lambswool, waterproof cotton, and poly-lined cotton. Sizes run from newborn to super-large (up to 32 pounds), and training pants are also offered. Prices on the Nikkys are up to 30% below retail. The beautiful, color Baby Bunz brochure also shows the firm's own line of diapers in three styles (contour, prefolded, and flat), which are sold at up to 22% below regular retail. (Guides to folding diapers and diapering with Nikkys are given in the brochure.) Dovetails biodegradable diapers are available, as are Rubber Duckies nylon diaper and pants covers, adorable layettewear from WeeWear and Fix of Sweden, lambskin and wool booties, and bedding—

pima cotton thermal blankets, Merino wool blankets, and a crib-sized lambskin for $55 (regularly $72). Weleda baby-care products are available, as well as bath sponges, natural bristle baby brushes, wooden rattles, a well-designed potty, and the ideal lovey, "First Doll."

Canadian readers, please note: Only U.S. funds are accepted.

Special Factors: Satisfaction is guaranteed; unused returns are accepted within 30 days for replacement, refund, or credit; minimum order is $15 with credit cards.

BEN'S BABYLAND

81 AVENUE A
NEW YORK, NY 10009
212/674-1353

Information: price quote
Save: 20% to 30% average
Pay: check, MO, MC, V
Sells: baby furniture, wheeled goods, etc.
Store: same address; daily 10–5

Ben's Babyland has been in business for about 75 years, selling furniture, strollers, walkers, and other goods for baby at Lower East Side prices—an average 20% to 30% off list.

Stylish metropolitan parents wheel their offspring about in Aprica strollers. Ben's sells them at a discount, as well as Simmons cribs and juvenile furniture, and cheery crib quilts, bumpers, bath sets, and pillows from several manufacturers. If you're looking for car seats, high chairs, strollers, playpens, walkers, or other goods from Strolee and other top names, Ben's can help. Other brands and lines are carried, so call or write (with specific model names, if possible) to check prices and availability.

Special Factor: Price quote by phone or letter with SASE.

BOSOM BUDDIES

P.O. BOX 6138, DEPT.
WBM
KINGSTON, NY 12401
914/338-2038

Catalog: free
Save: up to 50% (see text)
Pay: check or MO
Sells: nursing bras and clothing
Store: mail order only

$$ ✉ 🍁 ▇

Bosom Buddies was founded in 1983 by a nursing mother who saw a market for "breastfeeding fashions." The eight-page catalog includes a guide to taking your measurements so you're sure to order the right bra size.

Bosom Buddies features nursing bras by Decent Exposures, Leading Lady, Mary Jane, and Practical Elegance, including many all-cotton styles. This is a great source for hard-to-find sizes—the Decent Exposures bras run up to size 42H, and other lines go up to 46K. Nightgowns and other clothing designed to make nursing easy are sold as well. Bosom Buddies also carries nursing pads and a full line of equipment for expressing and storing breast milk, and a number of helpful books. Not everything is discounted, but prices are reasonable and savings run up to 50% on sale items.

Special Factor: Order sale merchandise promptly, since quantities may be limited.

HAPPY ENDINGS

12391 S.E. INDIAN RIVER
DR.
HOBE SOUND, FL 33455
407/546-1278
407/283-1042

Brochure: free with self-addressed, stamped envelope
Save: up to 30%
Pay: check or MO
Sells: diapers
Store: mail order only

$ ✉ 🍁 ▇

Here's a unique approach to creating *one* diaper that adapts to growing babies: Design the diaper so that, by folding in both ends, the parent creates a newborn's diaper; by folding in one end, a "medium" diaper; and with a third fold, it becomes a toddler's diaper. Happy Endings sells this style of cloth diapers, in white with colored trim around the edge of the gathered leg. You can choose from a number of trim shades (or all white) for under $30 per dozen, which is up to 30% less than prices charged elsewhere for similar styles. A guide to folding and tips on care are given in the brochure.

Canadian readers, please note: There is a surcharge of $1 per dozen on diapers shipped to Canada.

Special Factor: Minimum order is 1 dozen diapers.

MOTHER'S PLACE

**P.O. BOX 94512
CLEVELAND, OH
44101-4512
800-829-0080**

Catalog: free
Save: up to 60%
Pay: check, MO, MC, V
Sells: maternity clothing
Store: mail order only

$$$

At just 16 pages, the Mother's Place catalog may seem small, but it's big on answers to the problems of dressing attractively through pregnancy without going broke.

The selection includes dresses, jumpers, blouses and shirts, sweaters, jackets, activewear, and lingerie and nightwear. The dresses are cut full enough to see you through all stages of pregnancy, and most feature an attractive contrasting collar and bow that focus attention on the face. The styles range from a tailored linen-look pleated jumper with blouse to a deep rose floral tea dress with lace collar and Empire waist. There are overblouses, "big shirts," and turtlenecks to combine with the very inexpensive slacks (available in five colors) for a wardrobe of options, and most of what we saw was machine washable. If you're holding the line with expenses, Mother's Place will help you get through your pregnancy attractively and inexpensively.

Special Factors: Satisfaction is guaranteed; minimum order is $10 with credit cards.

MOTHERS WORK

DEPT. WB91
1309 NOBLE ST., 5TH FL.
PHILADELPHIA, PA 19123
215/625-9259
FAX: 215/440-9845

Catalog and Swatches: $3, deductible
Save: up to 30%
Pay: check, MO, MC, V
Sells: maternity clothing
Store: 37 stores in CA, CO, CT, DC, FL,
  GA, IL, LA, MA, MD, MN, MO, NC, NJ,
  NY, OH, PA, TN, TX, and VA (locations
  are listed in the catalog)

$$ ✉ ☎ m.l. ▆

The expectant executive can put her tailor on a retainer as her waistline expands, or she can look here for suitable maternity wear. For $3, Mothers Work mails the catalog with a set of fabric swatches for the different business separates. (The catalog fee is deductible from your order.)

The Mothers Work concept is winningly simple: Take a business jacket that you leave unbuttoned in late pregnancy and pair it with a maternity skirt and blouse in the early months, and with a jumper as size increases. The jacket can be worn after birth, and the jumpers are a handsome solution to the problem of how to achieve a polished, tailored look in late pregnancy without sacrificing comfort.

Mothers Work also sells charming print dresses in a variety of styles, coatdresses, and even lingerie and panty hose. The dresses and suit coordinates are offered in sizes 4 to 14.

Special Factors: Satisfaction is guaranteed; returns are accepted within 10 days for exchange, refund, or credit.

HOLLY NICOLAS NURSING COLLECTION

DEPT. W
P.O. BOX 7121
ORANGE, CA 92613-7121
714/639-5933

Brochure: free with double-
  stamped, self-addressed envelope
Save: up to 30%
Pay: check, MO, AE
Sells: nursing clothing
Store: mail order only

$$ ✉ ☎ 🍁 ▆

This business was founded in 1983 by a former fashion model, who began by creating nursing dresses for the mothers of her grandchildren, Holly and Nicolas. The clothes she produces are well designed, incorporating concealed openings for nursing into the lines of the garments.

The brochure we received from Holly Nicolas showed pretty, feminine blouses, dresses, and nightgowns designed for the nursing mother. The styles are classic: A sailor dress in dark blue Oxford cloth, square-neck blouse in pink or blue shirting stripe, and nightdress with robe in light-weight, coral poly/cotton are among the clothes offered. Prices are very reasonable, ranging from $20 for the nightgown with hidden openings for nursing, to $49 for a dress style. Samples of the actual fabrics are included in the brochure.

Holly Nicolas is offering readers of this book a 20% discount on the Transition Dress, a flattering style that will see you through the nine months and nursing afterward, thanks to concealed openings. It's self-belted and comes in a wool or cotton/poly blend. Identify yourself as a reader when you order. This WBMC reader discount expires February 1, 1992.

Special Factors: Returns are accepted within 30 days for exchange or refund; orders are shipped worldwide.

RUBENS & MARBLE, INC.

**P.O. BOX 14900-A
CHICAGO, IL 60614-0900
312/348-6200**

Brochure: free with SASE
Save: up to 60%
Pay: check or MO
Sells: infants' clothing and bedding
Store: 2340 N. Racine Ave.; Monday through Friday 9–3

Rubens & Marble has been supplying hospitals with infants' clothing since 1890 and offers the same goods to you at up to 60% below comparable list prices. This is an excellent source for babywear basics.

The flyer lists baby undershirts in sizes from newborn to 36 months, with short, long, and mitten-cuff sleeves; they're offered in snap, tie, plain, and double-breasted slipover styles (many are seconds, with small knitting flaws). First-quality cotton/wool blend and preemie-sized cotton under-shirts are available as well. Rubens & Marble also offers fitted bassinet and crib sheets, training and waterproof pants, kimonos, drawstring-bottom baby gowns, and terry bibs.

Special Factors: Send a self-addressed, stamped envelope for the price list; seconds are clearly marked; minimum order is 1 package (varying number depending on type of item).

SEE ALSO

CRAFTS AND HOBBIES

Materials, supplies, tools, and equipment for every sort of craft and hobby

If the high price of crafts supplies is blocking your creative urges, you'll find this chapter positively inspiring. There are suppliers here that can supply virtually every craft, including the needle arts, marquetry, miniatures, quilting, stenciling, basketry, clock making, wheat weaving, quilling, wood carving, spinning and weaving, batiking, decoy painting, jewelry making, and many more—and all of them sell at a discount. Some of these companies have been in business for generations and specialize in avocations that your local crafts shop may not even know exist. If you have a problem with a material or technique, most can help you solve it by phone or letter. And if your interests run to model trains, cars, planes, and boats, look here for savings of up to 40%.

Placing an order from these firms usually guarantees you a spot on the mailing list, which means you'll receive the sales flyers with savings of up to 70%. Do save your catalogs—they're invaluable for comparison-shopping and also may be necessary if the company runs promotions or clearances and sends you a leaflet instructing you to "deduct 50% from winter catalog prices on items FA 1001 through FX 5934," as some do.

If you do needlework and use DMC floss, be sure you have the DMC Embroidery Floss Card in your files. This reference includes samples of each DMC floss color and a guide to which colors are available in pearl cotton in sizes 3, 5, and 8. (Most discount sources carry DMC floss, but few include color guides.) The American Needlewoman sells the DMC Floss Card; request the free catalog from The American Needlewoman, P.O. Box 6472-WBMC, Fort Worth, TX 76115.

Since crafts and hobbies may involve the use of potentially dangerous materials, taking precautions while working is essential. For more information on hazards and how to protect yourself, see the introduction to "Art Materials." For related products that may be of interest, see the listings in that chapter, "Surplus," and "Tools." For lapidary equipment and findings, see the firms listed in "Jewelry."

AMERICA'S HOBBY CENTER, INC.

146-K W. 22ND ST.
NEW YORK, NY 10011
212/675-8922
FAX: 212/633-2754

Brochure: $1 each (see text)
Save: up to 40%
Pay: check or MO
Sells: radio-controlled planes, boats, helicopters, cars, and trains
Store: same address; Monday through Friday 9–5, Saturday 9–3:30

America's Hobby Center has been in business since 1931 and is staffed by avid hobbyists who can offer advice and assistance in the selection of a wide range of models. This source stocks "every known vehicular hobby item by every brand name."

The firm sells radio-controlled airplanes, cars, trains, helicopters, and boats, as well as the tools, materials, and supplies needed to build and run them. An extensive selection of books and manuals is available, and discounts run up to 40%, and even higher on specials. America's Hobby Center publishes two brochures, "Model Airplanes, Boats, and Cars" and "Model Railroad—HO and H-Gauge." Sample copies of the brochures cost $1 each, or both for $2; a subscription for 12 issues of both costs $10.

Special Factors: Price quote by phone or letter with SASE on items not listed in the catalog; C.O.D. orders (minimum $15) are accepted.

BUFFALO BATT & FELT CORP.

████████████

3307 WALDEN AVE.,
DEPT. WBMC
DEPEW, NY 14043
716/683-4100
FAX: 716/683-8928

Brochure and Samples: $1, refundable
Save: 40% plus
Pay: check, MO, MC, V
Sells: quilt and craft batting
Store: mail order only

$$ ✉ ☎

Buffalo Batt's "Super Fluff" polyester stuffing is so springy and resilient, the snowy-white samples nearly bounced out of the brochure we received. Buffalo Batt has been in business since 1913, and sells this crafts and upholstery stuffing by the case at savings of 40% or more on regular retail prices.

Super Fluff, which is manufactured in rolls 27″ wide by 20 yards long, is ideal for upholstery and crafts in which support and a downlike feel are desired. In addition to high loft and nonallergenic properties, Super Fluff is machine washable and dryable, mildew resistant, easy to sew, and can be obtained in fire-retardant form (upon request). Buffalo Batt also sells Super Fluff by the one-pound craft bag, pillow inserts in sizes from 12″ square to 18″ square, and "traditional" and two-inch-thick "comforter-style" quilt batts. The only negative is the minimum order of two cases, which translates into four rolls of Super Fluff stuffing, or a total of 50 pillows in the 14″ size, for example—more than most single projects require, but manageable for a home-based crafts business, quilting circle, or cooperative.

Special Factors: Price quote by phone or letter with SASE; quantity discounts are available; minimum order is 2 cases.

THE BUTTON SHOP

P.O. BOX 1065-HM
OAK PARK, IL 60304
708/795-1234

Catalog: free
Save: up to 50%
Pay: check, MO, MC, V
Sells: buttons and sewing supplies
Store: 7023 Roosevelt Rd., Berwyn, IL;
Monday through Friday 9–4, Saturday
10–2

$$ ✉ ☎ 🍁 ▬

The Button Shop may have stocked only buttons when it was founded in 1900, but it now sells closures of all types, as well as trims, sewing machine parts, scissors, and other sewing tools and notions.

To be fair, a fourth of the 18-page catalog is devoted to buttons—anonymous white shirt buttons, clear waistband buttons, tiny buttons for doll clothes, classic four-hole coat and suit buttons, gilt heraldic buttons for blazers, designs for dressy clothing, Navy pea coat buttons, braided leather buttons for tweeds, and dozens of others, including novelty designs for children's wear. Prices on the types we spot-checked were 40% to 50% below comparable retail.

If you want to custom-cover buttons with your own fabric, you'll find the Maxant and Prym kits; there are make-your-own fabric belt and buckle materials, gripper snaps and grommet sets, a huge variety of hooks and eyes, zippers (including odd sizes to 108″), and Velcro by the inch and yard. You'll find all kinds of ricrac, bias tape, cording, white and black elastic (from ⅛″ to 3″), replacement jacket cuffs, elbow patches, trouser pockets, pressing cloth, tailor's chalk, fusible backing, garment shoulder pads, and pins and needles for hand and machine sewing. All-cotton, cotton-covered polyester, and all-polyester thread are offered. The brands represented include Dritz, Fiskars, Gingher, Oncore, Prym, Singer, Suisse, Talon, Wiss, and Wrights.

The Button Shop has a comparatively deep inventory of sewing machine supplies and parts, including bobbins, bobbin cases, needle plates, button-holers, motors, foot controls, light bulbs, and belts. Please note that the catalog descriptions are brief and that line drawings are the only illustrations. If you're not sure an item is the right one and need more information, call or write before you order. You may also send a fabric swatch for the best color match if you're ordering trim, thread, or buttons.

Special Factors: Price quote by phone or letter with SASE; minimum order is $3, $10 with credit cards; orders are shipped worldwide.

THE CANING SHOP

926 GILMAN ST., DEPT.
WBM
BERKELEY, CA 94710
415/527-5010

Catalog: $1, refundable
Save: up to 30%
Pay: check, MO, MC, V
Sells: seat-reweaving and basketry supplies
Store: same address; Tuesday through
  Friday 10–6, Saturday 10–2

The Caning Shop stocks the materials, tools, and instructive materials you'll need to restore your woven-seat chairs. The owner of this business, who coauthored *The Caner's Handbook,* prides himself on offering the "highest quality materials that can be found in the jungles of Malaysia and Indonesia." Prices are lower here than those charged at some specialty shops, and somewhat higher than those charged by a discount source we used for comparison. But the selection is excellent, and it's worth paying more if you get materials that last longer.

The Caning Shop carries a variety of prewoven cane webbing, which is used in modern and mass-produced seating. Older chairs, which have holes in the frame around the seat opening, must be rewoven by hand. Hanks of cane in several sizes are available, as is binder cane. The Caning Shop also sells Danish seat cord, rawhide lacing, fiber rush, Hong Kong grass (seagrass), ash splint, Shaker tape, whole reed (for wicker), wicker braid, rattan, pressed fiber (imitation leather) seats, and tools to aid in installation. Basketry buffs should look here for kits, materials, hoops, and handles.

The Caning Shop bookshelf is a wonderful source for volumes on caning and seat reweaving, general furniture restoration, and basketry. If you live in or near Berkeley, you can get help with your project at the shop, which also gives classes in a variety of crafts.

Canadian readers, please note: Payment for the catalog and goods orders must be in U.S. funds.

Special Factor: Inquire for information on the workshops.

CIRCLE CRAFT SUPPLY

**P.O. BOX 3000-C
DOVER, FL 33527-3000
813/659-0992**

Catalog: $1, refundable
Save: up to 30%
Pay: check or MO
Sells: general crafts supplies
Store: mail order only

$$ ✉ 🍁 ▰

The 144-page catalog from Circle Craft Supply lists everything, from adhesives to yarn, you'll need for scores of arts, crafts, and hobbies. Circle Craft was founded in 1982, and sells at discounts that average 10% to 25%, though savings of 30% are possible on some items.

There are tools and materials here for a wide range of crafts and pastimes — jewelry making, basketry, flower making, drawing and painting, quick-count plastic canvas crafts, doll making, lamp making, decoupage, clock making, Christmas ornaments, clay crafts, macrame, art foam, calligraphy, chenille crafts, crocheting, and much more. In addition to the supplies, Circle Crafts has an extensive bookself with guides on a wide range of arts and crafts.

Special Factors: Authorized returns are accepted within 10 days; C.O.D. orders are accepted; orders are shipped worldwide.

CRAFT KING, INC.

**P.O. BOX 90637, DEPT. W
LAKELAND, FL 33804
813/686-9600**

Catalog: $2
Save: up to 60%
Pay: check, MO, MC, V
Sells: general project and crafts supplies
Store: 5675 New Tampa Hwy., Lakeland, FL; Monday through Saturday 9–5

Craft King's 100-page catalog is packed with supplies and kits for crafts popular in schools and camps, which happen to make great after-school amusements. Craft King was established in 1979, and has no minimum order requirement.

The catalog lists tools and materials for every sort of pastime and craft, including painting, macrame, lamp-shade making, cross-stitch, beadwork,

Christmas ornaments, felt crafts, pom-poms, doll making, miniatures, plastic canvas crafts, "fashion art," wood burning and carving, punch embroidery, and more. Patterns for plastic canvas projects and instruction books for all types of crafts are also available. Prices average 30% to 60% off list.

Special Factors: Satisfaction is guaranteed; price quote by phone or letter with SASE; authorized returns are accepted for exchange, refund, or credit.

CRAFT RESOURCES, INC.

**BOX 828
FAIRFIELD, CT 06430
800-243-2874**

Catalog: $1
Save: up to 50%
Pay: check, MO, MC, V
Sells: adult-oriented crafts kits
Store: mail order only

$ ✉ ☎

Craft Resources, formerly listed in this book as Curriculum Resources, special-izes in needlework projects in kit form. This firm, which was founded in 1976, offers "the largest selection of adult-oriented crafts available."

"Adult" connotes nothing naughty here; in fact, juvenile themes abound. Craft Resources sells kits for projects in latch hooking, needlepoint, long stitch, crewel, stamped and counted cross-stitch, string art, basketry, copper punch-ing, wood crafts, and "stained glass" (sun catchers). The kits range from very basic designs for the beginner to more complex patterns, but a patient novice should be able to tackle any of these projects, with reasonable to impressive results. Most yield purely decorative items, such as the latch-hook blocks, but there are kits to help you create small rugs, afghans, picture frames, baby bibs, pillows, and baskets.

Craft Resources also sells yarn, embroidery floss, needlestitch canvas, knitting needles and crochet hooks, embroidery hoops, pillow forms, fiberfill batts, stencils, picture mats, and frames. The best prices are on the kits sold by the dozen—the per-kit price can drop from $3 to $1.25. Therapists and instructors will find these bargains invaluable, but individuals should see the catalog if considering taking up any of the crafts mentioned. It's cheaper to buy a kit than it is to assemble the materials à la carte, and if you don't like the craft, you won't have made an investment that will be wasted.

Special Factors: Satisfaction is guaranteed; unused returns are accepted within 60 days; minimum order is $10 with credit cards.

CRAFTSMAN WOOD SERVICE CO.

1735 W. CORTLAND CT.,
DEPT. 1A
ADDISON, IL 60101
708/629-3100

Catalog: $1
Save: up to 50%
Pay: check, MO, MC, V
Sells: woodworking tools and supplies
Store: same address; Monday through
Friday 8:30–4:45, Saturday 8:30–12:30

$$$

The Craftsman 144-page catalog is jammed with the kinds of specialty tools and hardware, lumber, veneers, finishes, books, plans, and related products that inspire long workshop retreats. This firm has been serving woodworkers since 1930, and offers products for beginners as well as experienced hobbyists.

Craftsman is well-known for its exhaustive selection of veneers, cabinetry-grade lumber, stains, and finishes, and offers materials and equipment for picture framing, decoys, clock making, wood burning, upholstery, lamp refurbishing, toy making, and other pursuits. The catalog also shows routers, table saws, lathes, honers and sharpeners, clamps, jointers and planers, engravers, and other tools by American Machine & Tool, Arco, Dremel, Porter-Cable, Rockwell, Stanley, and Wen. Don't overlook the "Craftsman Library" of books on wood carving, finishing, cabinetry, toy making, veneering, and other topics, as well as the furniture-building plans.

Special Factors: Satisfaction is guaranteed; returns are accepted within 30 days; minimum order is $10, $15 with credit cards.

DHARMA TRADING CO.

P.O. BOX 150916
SAN RAFAEL, CA
94915-0916
800-542-5227
415/456-7657

Catalog: free
Save: up to 50%
Pay: check, MO, MC, V
Sells: textile art supplies
Store: 1604 Fourth St., San Rafael, CA;
Monday through Saturday 10–6

$$

The "whole earth" movement may have peaked in 1969, the year this firm was founded, but Dharma Trading has survived even the pinstripes of the 1980s. The firm sells tools and materials for the textile arts—dyes, paints, resists, and fabrics. The informative, 30-page catalog provides helpful information on the features of the dyes and paints, including suitable application techniques and fabrics.

Coloring agents by Deka, Delta/Shiva, DyeHouse, Jacquard, Pabeo (Orient Express), Peintex, Procion, Sennelier (Tinfix), Setacolor, Versatex, and other firms are offered, as well as color remover, soda ash, urea, Synthrapol, gutta serti, and other resists. The tools include bottles and droppers for dye mixing and application, textile pens, tjantings, brushes (flat, foam, sumi), and steamers for setting dyes. Dharma Trading also stocks an extensive collection of all-cotton T-shirts, vests, skirts, and pants in sizes for adults and children, oversized shirts that can double as minidresses, and Habotai silk scarves. A dozen cotton, rayon, and silk fabrics that have yielded good results with dyeing and painting are listed; a set of samples is available for $1.50. Selected books dealing with fabric design, painting, screening, direct dyeing, batiking, tie-dyeing, and other techniques are sold as well. Prices are good, running up to 50% off list or comparable retail.

Special Factors: Price quote by phone or letter with SASE; quantity discounts are available; orders are shipped worldwide.

FASHION TOUCHES

P.O. BOX 804
BRIDGEPORT, CT 06601
203/333-7738

Catalog: free
Save: up to 30%
Pay: check or MO
Sells: custom-covered buttons and belts
Store: mail order only

$$ ✉

Fashion Touches has been supplying home sewers with garment and upholstery buttons, belts, and buckles since 1947, at prices up to 30% less than those charged by other firms for similar services. You send the firm your fabric, specify the size and style from the many available, and Fashion Touches does the rest. Custom-covered buttons add a polished touch to home-sewn clothing, especially dressy and formal wear.

The wide range of buttons that may be covered runs from 1/3" balls to 2-1/8" half-ball styles, and includes upholstery buttons in a variety of backing styles—an open nylon hook, standard wire eye shank, nail, prong, threaded nail with washer, and pivot back with tack types. Clothing buttons in rectangular and squared shapes are also offered. Belts from 1/2″ to 4″ wide may be covered, and there are dozens of buckles in coordinating sizes. Covered screw-back earrings and French cuff links are also offered. Use your fabric or the stock synthetic leather, which is available in seven colors. Fashion Touches guarantees the buttons for the life of the garment, and buttons covered with washable fabric may be laundered.

Special Factors: Include a return-address label or facsimile with your catalog request; minimum order is $5.

A. FEIBUSCH
CORPORATION

33 ALLEN ST.
NEW YORK, NY 10002
212/226-3964

Information: price quote
Save: up to 50%
Pay: check or MO
Sells: zippers, thread, and notions
Store: same address; Monday through
Friday 9:30–5, Sunday 10–3:30

Feibusch has been helping New Yorkers zip up since 1941, handling requests from the mundane to the exotic. Unlike most specialty stores, Feibusch prices its enormous inventory at up to 50% below the going rate.

Zippers of every conceivable size, color, and type are sold here—from minuscule dolls' zippers to heavy-duty closures for tents, luggage, and similar applications. The zippers are offered in scores of colors, and if your requirements aren't met by the existing stock, Feibusch can have your zipper made to order. Talon and YKK zippers are available, and Feibusch also carries all-cotton thread in a full range of colors. Feibusch does not have a catalog, so *write* with your requirements. Describe what you're looking for or send a sample, specifying length desired, nylon or metal teeth, open or closed end, and other details. Enclose a scrap of fabric, if possible, to ensure a good color match. Be sure to include a self-addressed, stamped envelope with your correspondence if you wish to receive a reply.

Special Factor: Price quote by letter with SASE.

THE FIBER STUDIO

**P.O. BOX 637, DEPT.
  WBMC
HENNIKER, NH 03242**
603/428-7830

Catalog: $1 (see text)
Save: up to 40%
Pay: check, MO, MC, V
Sells: knitting, spinning, and weaving
  equipment and supplies
Store: 9 Foster Hill Rd., Henniker, NH;
  Tuesday through Saturday 10–4

$$$ ✉   ☎   🍁   ▬

The Fiber Studio has been serving the needs of knitters, spinners, and weavers since 1975 with a well-chosen line of tools and supplies, and yarn closeouts at great prices.

The catalog lists looms, knitting machines, and spinning equipment and accessories by Ashford, Glimraka, Harrisville Design, Kyra, Leclerc, Louet, and Schacht. The prices are not discounted, but shipping is included on some models (see "Special Factors," below). Natural dyes, mordants, and a good selection of spinning fibers—from Merino tops to silk roving—are offered at competitive prices. The sample card of current spinning fibers costs $3.50. The bookshelf offers scores of texts on knitting, spinning, and weaving.

The bargains here are on yarns, which are sold in two ways: through the stock shown in the sample set, which costs $3.50, and through the yarn closeouts. The stock yarns include rug wools, natural yarns, Superwash wool, Irish linen, cotton, silk, Shetland wool, and others, priced up to 35% less at The Fiber Studio than at other sources we spot-checked. Quantity discounts on these yarns run from 10% on orders over $100 to 20% on orders over $200. *After* you order the yarn card from The Fiber Studio, you can send $1 and four #10 double-stamped, self-addressed envelopes and ask to be put on the mailing list for the quarterly closeouts. There are outstanding values here, and our mailing included dozens of types of yarns—cotton flake, 8/4 cotton, chenille yarn, silk and blends, bouclé, alpaca, Shetland, and many others. Color selection was good even among the closeout offerings, and excellent on the stock yarn.

Canadian readers, please note: Only U.S. funds are accepted.

Special Factors: Specify the *spinning fibers* or *yarns* sample set ($3.50 each); price quote by phone or letter with SASE; shipping is included on Harrisville Design, Leclerc, and Schacht looms; quantity discounts are available; minimum order is $15 with credit cards; C.O.D. orders are accepted.

FORT CRAILO YARNS COMPANY

P.O. BOX G
NEWBURGH, NY 12550
914/562-2698

Brochure and Samples: $2.80
Save: up to 35%
Pay: check, MO, MC, V, Discover
Sells: yarn for handweaving
Store: Broadway and Wisher Ave.,
    Newburgh, NY; Monday through
    Saturday 9:30–5:30

Fort Crailo Yarns, in business since 1963, sells five types of yarn especially suited for handweaving. Prices run up to 35% below those of comparable yarns sold elsewhere.

Four lines of mothproofed, virgin wool yarns are available: Crailo Rya (570 yards/pound, 33 colors), Crailo-Spun (700 yards/pound, 30 colors), Crailo Lite-Spun (1,700 yards/pound, 28 colors), and the very fine Crailo Worsted (4,900 yards/pound, 27 colors). Fort Crailo's cotton yarn is sold in 8/2, 3, 4, 5, and 6 ply, in 17 colors, and is suitable for warp or weft. All of the yarns are sold on half-pound cones. The colors are clear and true, and the range of weights makes Fort Crailo an important source for weavers of anything from fine fabrics to rugs.

Special Factors: Price quote by phone or letter with SASE; quantity discounts are available.

GETTINGER FEATHER CORP.

16 W. 36TH ST.
NEW YORK, NY 10018
212/695-9470
FAX: 212/695-9471

Price List and Samples: $2
Save: up to 75%
Pay: MO or certified check
Sells: feathers
Store: same address (8th floor); Monday
    through Friday 9–4:30

Gettinger has been serving New York City's milliners and craftspersons since 1915 with a marvelous stock of exotic and common feathers. Write for the price list even if you're not a "creative" type—you can add cachet to a tired hat with a few ostrich plumes, and Gettinger's feather boas are a dashing alternative to furs for gala occasions.

Raw or dyed pheasant, guinea hen, turkey, duck, goose, rooster, and peacock feathers are available here loose or sewn (lined up in continuous rows of even length), by the ounce or the pound, beginning at $5 (loose) and $7 (sewn) per ounce. Pheasant tail feathers, six to eight inches long, cost $13 per hundred; yard-long peacock feathers are priced at $25 per hundred; and pheasant hides are offered at $9 per skin and up. Feather boas are available, sold in two-yard pieces, as well as ostrich and marabou fans. And if you're reviving old feather pillows, you may be interested in the bedding feathers, which are sold by the pound at $18 to $36 per pound, depending on the quality.

Special Factors: Price quote by phone or letter with SASE; minimum order is $20; orders are shipped worldwide.

GLOBAL VILLAGE IMPORTS

**1101 SW WASHINGTON
#140W
PORTLAND, OR 97205**

Brochure and Swatches: $3.50, refundable
Save: up to 70%
Pay: check or MO
Sells: Guatemalan ikat fabrics
Store: mail order only

$$$ ✉ ☎ 🍁 🇺🇸

Ikat is a type of weaving that uses tie-dyed warp threads to create striated designs that blend into overall patterns, which may be as subtle as Zen or as colorfully riotous as a Mardi Gras parade. (Double ikats, in which both warp and weft threads are so dyed, are a further refinement of the art.)

Global Village has been selling handwoven Guatemalan ikats since 1988, and donates a portion of its proceeds to groups working for "peace and justice in Central America" (including Amnesty International and MADRE). The refundable, $3.50 sample fee brings you an information packet and swatches of currently available single and double ikats. The fabric is 36" wide, 100% cotton, and is woven by hand on large looms. We received stacks of over 30 stunning single ikats and seven double ikats, as well as a strip of white stickers. Global Village makes it easy to buy: Just cut the swatch of the desired fabric in half, put a sticker on that piece, and write on it the number of yards you're ordering. Prices for single ikats range from $8.99 for up to five yards, down to $5.99 for 31 yards or more. Double ikats run from $10.99 to $7.99. (Double ikats, hard to find at any price, are woven by the roll especially for Global Village.)

The fabrics were priced an average of 50% below the rates prevailing in New York City specialty shops we checked. Global Village hopes to offer ikats from India soon, and eventually handwoven fabrics from around the world. Fabric designers should take note of the company's custom weaving services. Wholesale inquiries are invited.

Special Factors: Minimum order is 1 yard; C.O.D. orders are accepted; orders are shipped worldwide.

GREAT NORTHERN WEAVING

**P.O. BOX 361-D
AUGUSTA, MI 49012
616/731-4487**

Catalog and Samples: $1
Save: up to 50%
Pay: check or MO
Sells: rug-weaving supplies and tools
Store: mail order only

$$ ✉ 🍁 🇺🇸

The homey crafts of braiding and weaving rugs are served here at Great Northern Weaving. You can save up to 50% on supplies from this firm, which was established in 1984.

The 12-page catalog lists tools and materials for rug weaving, rug braiding, and shirret—Braid-Aids, Braidkins, Braid-Klamps, Fraser rag cutters, reed and heddle hooks, shuttles, and warping boards are all available. The materials include coned cotton warp (8/4 ply) in over two dozen colors, all-cotton rug filler in 15 shades, 16-ply rug roping, new cotton "rags" on rolls, and loopers in bulk (offered in white and grey). Reference books are also available. Prices we checked were 10% to 20% below competitors' on some items, and up to 50% less on rags and filler.

Canadian readers, please note: Shipping charges on orders sent to Canada are paid C.O.D., and order payment must be made in U.S. funds.

Special Factors: Shipping is included on orders over $20; C.O.D. orders are accepted.

HOBBY SURPLUS SALES

287 MAIN ST.
P.O. BOX 2170W
NEW BRITAIN, CT 06050
203/223-0600

Catalog: $3 (see text)
Save: up to 40%
Pay: check, MO, MC, V
Sells: trains, model planes, boats, and radio-controlled models
Store: Amato's, 283 Main St., New Britain, CT; Monday through Saturday 9:30–5:30; also Amato's, 418 Main St., Middletown, CT; Monday through Saturday 9:30–5:30

$$$ ✉   ☎   🍁   ▦

Hobby Surplus Sales involves the efforts of three generations of the Amato family and boasts some customers who have been doing business with them for decades. The Amatos publish a 128-page catalog of trains, models, and supplies for the hobbyist, at savings of up to 40%.

You'll find radio-controlled planes, cars, boats, and other vehicles, and a complete model train department that stocks American Flyer, Lionel, Mamod, and other HO and N gauge trains, as well as repair parts, power packs, tracks, and accessories. Hobby Surplus Sales also carries scale reproductions of vintage vehicles, working steam engines by Wilesco, and even folders and other supplies for collectors of stamps, coins, and base-ball cards. Hobby Surplus Sales sells kits for dollhouse furniture, wooden ship models, and model rockets, as well as paints, glues, finishing supplies, model airplanes, model cars, and X-Acto tools. Dozens of books and manuals on model building and radio control are offered, and prices are all reasonable.

This firm is giving readers a break on the cost of the catalog. If you identify yourself as a reader of this book, you pay just $2 for the catalog, instead of the regular price of $3. Remember to identify yourself as a WBMC reader when you order.

Special Factors: Satisfaction is guaranteed; returns are accepted for exchange, refund, or credit.

HOME-SEW

DEPT. WBI
BETHLEHEM, PA 18018
215/867-3833

Catalog: 50¢
Save: up to 65%
Pay: check, MO, MC, V
Sells: sewing supplies and notions
Store: mail order only

$$ ✉ ☎ 🍁 (see text) 🇺🇸

Home-Sew, which has been in business since 1960, offers savings of up to 65% on assorted laces and trims. The firm's 28-page catalog is well-organized and easy to use, with clear photographs of the laces, braids, ribbons, and decorator fringes.

Dozens of lace styles were offered in the catalog we reviewed, as well as elastics, satin and velvet ribbon, ricrac, tape, and appliqués. Thread for general sewing, overlock machines, carpets, and quilting is available on cones and spools. There are zippers, snaps, hooks and eyes, buttons, Velcro dots, belt and buckles, and other fasteners. Home-Sew also sells crafts supplies, such as floss, adhesives, Styrofoam wreaths, spangles, beads, animal eyes, interfacings, and related items, as well as pins, needles, scissors, and notions. If you're making your own curtains or slipcovers, check the prices on shirring and pleater tape, tasseled and moss fringe, cord filler, and related goods. Home-Sew's isn't the biggest catalog of its kind, but the products are very well chosen—just the things that can make your sewing and crafts projects easier, at the right price.

Canadian readers, please note: Send $1 (in Canadian funds) to Home-Sew Canada Inc., B.P. Box 1100, Dept. WBMC, Postal Station "E," Montreal, Quebec H2T 3B1, for the bilingual catalog.

Special Factors: Satisfaction is guaranteed; returns are accepted for exchange, refund, or credit; shipping is included on orders over $35; minimum order is $5.

J & J PRODUCTS LTD.

**117 W. 9TH ST., SUITE 111
LOS ANGELES, CA 90015
213/624-1840**

Swatch Cards: $3 each, refundable (see text)

Save: up to 40%

Pay: check, MO, MC, V

Sells: fine woolen fabrics

Store: mail order only

$$$ ✉   ☎   🍁   ▬

Here are quality yard goods in beautiful colors, at reasonable prices—gabardines, suitings, flannels, and other fine woolens. These are J & J's specialty, and each type of fabric is showcased in a swatch booklet that costs $3, refundable with a purchase from that line.

The swatch booklets include a 2-1/2″ by 4″ piece of fabric, with smaller snippets to show the choice of colors. "Gabardine," $18 per yard, is offered in 48 colors; the mid-weight "Flannel" is shown in 17 shades; "Lightweight Wool Suiting" is a wool broadcloth offered in 32 colors, including turquoise and fuchsia; "Cashmere" includes a number of herringbones and tweeds, in beautiful shadings; "Crepe" features a fine-quality wool crepe in red and several neutrals; and the "Linings" swatch booklet shows 16 fashion colors and neutrals of the acetate material, at $2.59 per yard (prices and colors all subject to change). You can order the swatch booklets by name for $3 each; each is refundable with a purchase from that particular booklet, and ordering information is included. The fabric is not inexpensive, but it has the luster and hand of fine-quality goods that wear well.

Special Factors: Satisfaction is guaranteed; price quote by phone or letter with SASE.

LEATHER UNLIMITED CORP.

███████████

7155 CTY. HWY. B, DEPT. WBMC
BELGIUM, WI 53004-9990
414/994-9464
FAX: 414/994-4099

Catalog: $2, refundable

Save: up to 50%

Pay: check, MO, MC, V

Sells: leathercraft supplies and equipment and finished products

Store: same address; Monday through Friday 7–3:30

$$$

Here's a catalog for the beginner, the seasoned leather worker, and the rest of us: It offers all sorts of leathercrafting supplies, from kits to raw materials, as well as leather cleaners and conditioners, a line of bags, attaché cases, and small leather goods, and even black powder supplies. Leather Unlimited has been in business since 1971.

Save substantial sums here on crafts supplies, beginning with leather—sold by the hide or in pieces. The weights run from fine lining grade to heavy belting leather, in a variety of finishes and colors. There are laces, belt blanks, shoe-repair pieces and soles, key tabs, and dozens of undyed embossed belt strips; these are matched by hundreds of belt buckles, which run from beautiful abalone inlays to a line with organization logos and sporting themes. The 64-page catalog features dozens of kits for making all sorts of finished goods, plus stamping tools, punches, carvers, rivets, screws, snaps, zippers, mallets, lacing needles, sundry findings, leather-care products and dyes by Fiebing's, and Missouri River patterns for making authentic frontier-style clothing.

Among the finished products available here are sheepskin rugs, slippers, mittens, hats, and purses made of sheepskin and deerskin, suede duffel and sports bags, leather totes, log carriers, and wineskins. Leather Unlimited is an authorized dealer for Harley-Davidson accessories—truckers' wallets, belts, keyrings, etc.—which are available. You'll also find top-grain belt leather attaché cases, briefcases, doctors' bags, portfolios, wallets, and other small leather goods listed in the catalog. The prices are outstandingly low—up to 50% below comparable retail on some items—and extra discounts are given on quantity or volume purchases.

Special Factors: Satisfaction is guaranteed; price quote by phone or letter with SASE; authorized returns are accepted within 10 days; minimum order is $30.

MONTEREY MILLS OUTLET STORE

P.O. BOX 271
JANESVILLE, WI 53547
800-438-6387

Price List: free with SASE (see text)
Save: up to 60%
Pay: check, MO, MC, V
Sells: fake-fur fabric
Store: same address; Monday through
  Friday 8–4:30, Saturday 8–12 noon

Monterey Mills has been manufacturing deep-pile fabrics for a quarter of a century, and it opened the Outlet Store in 1972. Deep-pile fabrics, popularly known as "fun fur," are used in clothing, toys, furnishings, and other industries.

The literature from Monterey Mills describes the fiber content of the different fur styles and lists the available colors, pile height, and ounces per yard. In addition to plain plush and shag, you'll find patterns and colors simulating the pelts of bears, foxes, seals, tigers, and Dalmatians. Prices are given per cut yard, per yard on the roll (there are 12 to 15 yards per roll), and for quantity orders. Cut yards run from $6.75 to $11.95 per yard, and prices drop from there. You may purchase the fabric in remnants (the Mill's choice), by the pound, or in cartons, at under $3 per pound. Stuffing for crafts projects is available as well, at 49¢ a pound and up.

Please note: A set of samples is offered for $4, a worthwhile investment unless you're buying only remnants.

Special Factor: Minimum order is $25.

BOB MORGAN WOODWORKING SUPPLIES

1123 BARDSTOWN RD.
LOUISVILLE, KY 40204
502/456-2545

Catalog: $1
Save: up to 30%
Pay: check, MO, MC, V
Sells: woodworking supplies
Store: same address; Monday through
  Friday 8–4:30, Saturday 9–1

Woodworking, marquetry, and cabinetry aficionados know Morgan for its select veneers, fine inlays, cabinet-grade plywood, and tools and supplies for woodworking. Morgan, "home of 1,037 hand tools," also stocks hardwood, thin lumber, edgings, and turning and carving stock.

The 64-page catalog features hardwood in bundles, scores of veneers of varying dimensions, inlay strips, hardwood plywood, thin lumber, hardwood spindles and pegs, walnut bowl blanks, and mill ends. You'll find hot glue and contact cement for the veneer work, as well as veneer saws, chisels, gouges, and other wood-carving tools. Dowel jigs, router accessories and bits, dovetailing jigs, planes, and hardwood bundles are sold. Freud and Footprint tools are discounted 20%, and raised-panel oak cabinet doors (manufacturer's seconds) are sold at about 75% below list. Reproduction finishing hardware, drawer slides, woven cane seating and spline, and hundreds of plans, patterns, manuals, and videotapes are offered. Some of the veneer prices are 25% to 30% less than those of other firms selling similar supplies, and all of the items are selected by experienced woodworkers.

Special Factor: Quantity discounts are available.

NATURAL FIBER FABRIC CLUB

521 FIFTH AVE., DEPT. NWM3
NEW YORK, NY 10175

Membership Fee: $10 (see text)
Save: 20% guaranteed (see text)
Pay: check, MO, MC, V
Sells: fabric and notions
Store: mail order only

$$$ ✉ ☎ ♦ (see text) ▀

Natural Fiber Fabric Club will send you swatched catalogs for a year for your $10 membership fee. The fabrics are guaranteed to be at least 20% below list price (although savings can be higher), and natural fibers are featured. The Club has been in business since 1975.

Ten dollars brings you four seasonal swatched catalogs and at least two additional swatched sale offers. The Club culls its selections from hundreds of fabrics produced each season, and you get the best of silk crepe de chine, broadcloth, and China silk; imported cotton lawn, broadcloth, poplin, and shirting; Irish linen, cotton-and-linen blends, and other imported linen suitings; wool flannel, worsted, wool crepe and gabardine, wool jersey, and much more. Please note that the swatches are sent with a booklet, but *you* put them in (everything is neatly ordered). It took us about five minutes to attach our swatches, and we examined the fabric more closely in the process, which we felt was a benefit.

Club members receive the "Basics Handbook" in addition to the seasonal swatch mailings. The Handbook includes swatches of the 24 "basic" natural-fiber fabrics that are kept in stock on a constant basis. Most of the basics are offered in a range of colors, and the Club sells them at a 20% discount. The firm's "Sewing Aids Catalog" is another membership benefit; it lists linings, thread, buttons of natural materials, books, Wiss scissors, notions, tailoring hams, and other sewing supplies—all at a minimum 20% discount. Patterns from Butterick, McCalls, Simplicity, and Vogue are offered as well. The Club is ideal for serious home sewers who want to keep up with fashion trends—at a discount—and an ideal gift for creative friends.

Canadian readers, please note: Club membership to Canadian addresses costs $20 (U.S. funds).

Special Factor: Satisfaction is guaranteed.

NEWARK DRESSMAKER SUPPLY, INC.

6473 RUCH RD.
P.O. BOX 2448, DEPT.
* WMC*
LEHIGH VALLEY, PA
* 18001*

Catalog: free
Save: up to 50%
Pay: check, MO, MC, V, Discover
Sells: sewing notions
Store: mail order only

$$$$ ✉   ☎   🍁   ▀

Newark Dressmaker has been in business since 1950 and is one of the best mail-order sources for home sewers, since it carries a huge array of notions and other supplies, from glass-headed pins to the material itself. The 56-page catalog features many hard-to-find goods, and the prices are excellent.

Searching for specialty patterns, smocking guides, bear joints, alphabet beads, silk thread, or toy squeakers? Such requests are routine at Newark, which boasts an exhaustive inventory of materials and equipment for a range of crafts. If your local shop doesn't have what you're looking for, or if you'd like to save money, see this catalog for its pages of trims, appliqués, scissors, piping, ribbon, lace, braid, twill, zippers, sewing gadgets, knitting supplies, name tapes and woven labels, interfacing, buttons, thread, floss, bias tape, rhinestones, supplies for making dolls and stuffed bears, fabric, upholstery materials, books and manuals, and much more. Among the brands of goods stocked here, you'll find Boye, Coats & Clark's, Deka, Dritz, Lily, Prym, Sta-Flex, and Talon. "Sew Little" patterns for infants' and children's clothing are stocked, as well as "Great Fit" patterns for women's styles in sizes 38 to 60, and doll patterns from Putnam Pattern and other firms.

Canadian readers, please note: Only U.S. funds are accepted.

Special Factors: Satisfaction is guaranteed; minimum order is $20 with credit cards.

SEVENTH AVENUE DESIGNER FABRIC CLUB

DEPT. SWM3
701 SEVENTH AVE.,
SUITE 900
NEW YORK, NY 10036

Membership Fee: $10 (see text)
Save: up to 50%
Pay: check, MO, MC, V
Sells: designer fabric
Store: mail order only

$$$ ✉ 🍁 (see text) ▥

The Seventh Avenue Designer Fabric Club sends you swatched catalogs for a year for your $10 membership fee. The yard goods are priced 20% to 50% below list, and designer fabrics are featured. The Club was founded in 1981.

Ten dollars will bring you four seasonal swatched catalogs and at least two additional swatched sale offers. The Club culls its selections from hundreds of fabrics produced each season, and you get the best of lines by Anglo, Jhane Barnes, Cantoni, Liz Claiborne, Christian Dior, J.G. Hook, Jones New York, Calvin Klein, Karl Lagerfeld, Ralph Lauren, Moygashel, Oscar de la Renta, Villager, and other firms and designers. Patterns from Butterick, McCalls, Simplicity, and Vogue are offered as well. The Club is ideal for serious home sewers who want to keep up with fashion trends—at a discount—and membership makes a perfect gift for creative friends.

Canadian readers, please note: Membership to Canadian addresses costs $20 (U.S. funds).

Special Factor: Satisfaction is guaranteed.

SMILEY'S YARNS

92-06 JAMAICA AVE.
WOODHAVEN, NY 11421
718/847-5038
718/849-9873 (STORE)

Brochure: free with self-addressed, stamped envelope
Save: up to 50% (see text)
Pay: check or MO
Sells: knitting and crocheting yarn, tools, etc.
Store: same address; Monday through Saturday 10–5:30

$$$ ✉ ▬

Smiley's, where "Yarn Bargains Are Our Business," has been selling first-quality yarns at a discount since 1935. The firm holds week-long "Yarn Riot" sales five times a year, which bring prices down by as much as 90%. The Yarn Riots are announced by flyer prior to the event; if you wish to be added to the mailing list, send your name and address.

Smiley's sells yarn, instruction books, needles, hooks, and other tools and supplies at everyday discounts of 20% to 50%. Among the manufacturers represented are Susan Bates, Bernat, Bouquet, Brunswick, Bucilla, Caron, Coats & Clark's, Leisure Arts, Lion Brand, Neveda, Patons, Pingouin, Red Heart, and Scheepjeswool. You can call or write for a price quote on goods by these firms, or inquire about knitting and crocheting yarns by other manufacturers—they may be available.

Special Factors: Price quote by phone or letter with SASE; quantity discounts are available.

SOLO SLIDE FASTENERS, INC.

P.O. BOX 528
STOUGHTON, MA 02072
800-343-9670
FAX: 617/341-4705

Catalog: free
Save: up to 50%
Pay: check, MO, MC, V
Sells: dressmaking and dry-cleaning equipment and sewing supplies
Store: 166 Tosca Dr., Stoughton, MA; Monday through Friday 9–5

$$ ✉ ☎ 🍁 ▬

This family-run business has been supplying dressmakers, cleaners, tailors, and other professionals with tools and equipment since 1953. Among the offerings in the 30-page catalog are many items we've seen in the "hard-to-find" sections of notions catalogs, but at prices as much as 50% less.

Solo offers an extensive selection of zippers by Talon and YKK, zipper parts (slides and stops), straight pins in several sizes, snaps, hooks and eyes, machine and hand needles, buttons (dress, suit, metal, leather, etc.), thread on cones and spools, knit collars and cuffs for jackets, shoulder pads, elbow patches, belting, elastic, and other notions. There are scissors in the most useful models from Gingher, Marks, and Wiss, and pressing boards for sleeves and hollow pressing, the Qualitex pressing pads and other hams and rolls, and professional irons and steamers by Cissell, Hi-Steam/Namoto, and Sussman. The catalog also shows commercial/industrial sewing machines (blindstitch and lockstitch) and overlock machines by Babylock, Consew, Juki, Singer, and Tacsew.

Special Factors: Price quote by phone or letter with SASE; authorized, unused returns (except custom-ordered or cut goods) are accepted within 30 days for credit; minimum order is $25; C.O.D. orders are accepted.

STRAW INTO GOLD, INC.

**3006 SAN PABLO AVE.,
DEPT. W2
BERKELEY, CA 94702
415/548-5241**

Catalog: free with double-
stamped, self-addressed envelope
Save: up to 30%
Pay: check, MO, MC, V
Sells: textile crafts supplies
Store: same address; Tuesday through
Saturday 10:30–5:30

Straw Into Gold, established in 1971, is a highly regarded mail-order source for textile crafts supplies and equipment, especially exotic and hard-to-find materials. Specials on fibers, yarns, books, and other goods appear regularly in flyers, at savings of up to 70%. The staff is helpful and informed, and classes are given at the shop.

Spinners, weavers, and hand and machine knitters will appreciate the selection of materials and equipment. The spinning fibers include silk of different types and silk blends, cotton, flax, ramie, wool, alpaca, mohair, camel's hair, and goat's hair. Ashford spinning equipment and looms (not discounted), bamboo and steel knitting needles, wool winders, umbrella swifts, and other helpful tools are offered as well. Straw Into Gold sells

Kaffe Fassett kits and yarns by Crystal Palace, Rowan Yarns, and Villawool, and a wide selection of other yarns and spun fibers. If you're a serious textile artist, investing in the sample books and cards is recommended. Straw Into Gold's bookshelf includes publications from Interweave Press, Bette Hochberg, and Shire (British), as well as videos and patterns by Rowan, Villawool, and Zimmerman.

Straw Into Gold is offering readers a discount of 10% on their first order. Be sure to identify yourself as a WBMC reader when you order, and deduct the discount from the cost of the goods only. This WBMC reader discount expires February 1, 1992.

Please note: The store is too busy to accept calls on Saturdays, so please phone during the week, Tuesday through Friday.

Special Factors: Send 4 double-stamped, self-addressed envelopes for catalog updates and flyers; quantity discounts are offered; orders are shipped worldwide.

SUNCOAST DISCOUNT ARTS & CRAFTS

**9015 U.S. RTE. 19
NORTH, BOX W-91
PINELLAS PARK, FL
34666**
813/577-6331
FAX: 813/576-0835

Catalog: $2
Save: 40% average
Pay: check, MO, MC, V
Sells: arts, crafts, and floral supplies
Store: same address; Monday through
Saturday 9–5:30

Suncoast, established in 1979, offers solid savings on a complete selection of crafts materials. The catalog offers over 300 pages of supplies for glass staining, fabric painting, "fashion crafts," wood crafts, basketry, beading, stenciling, calligraphy, oil and acrylic painting, sketching, chenille craft, crocheting, doll and toy making, doll houses, macrame, rug making, quilting, scherenschnitte, wood burning, and many other crafts. Among the products of interest are silk flowers and floral arrangement supplies, felt by the yard, cross-stitch fabric, quilting frames, music box movements, miniatures, beads, jewelry findings, grapevine wreaths, and calligraphy pens. The prices average 40% off suggested list, and savings run as high as 90% in the closeout flyers, which are sent out several times a year.

Canadian readers, please note: The catalog costs $3 (U.S. funds) if sent to Canada; shipping charges are 20% of the merchandise total.

Special Factors: Authorized returns are accepted; shipping is included on orders of $50 or more; minimum order is $25 with credit cards; C.O.D. orders are accepted.

SUSAN OF NEWPORT

P.O. BOX 3107-WM
NEWPORT BEACH, CA
92663
714/673-5445

Catalog: $5, deductible
Save: up to 70%
Pay: check or MO
Sells: lace
Store: mail order only

$$ ✉ ☎ 🍁 🇺🇸

Bartles & Jaymes, Betty Crocker, and even Aunt Jemima of pancake fame may be Madison Avenue fictions, but there is a Susan of Newport, and she sells lace by mail.

Susan's customers tend to be bullish on trim: the minimum order is $50, and the laces are sold chiefly in "loose packs" of 50, 100, and 250 yards. The $5 catalog fee brings you a folder of samples, clearly laid out with prices. Most of the laces in the folder we received were polyester or blends; several eyelet and Cluny lace styles were included. All of the lace samples are ruffled (gathered and stitched on one side), but the same laces are sold flat on full bolts at a much lower price per yard. And Wrights and Offray ribbon, strung pearls, and other crafts supplies are stocked as well. Prices we checked were as much as 75% less than those at other *discount* sources, but compare carefully—some samples were close to the same.

Remember to deduct the cost of the sample folio from your order. If you identify yourself as a WBMC reader when you order, you may deduct 10% from the goods total of your first order only. This WBMC reader discount expires February 1, 1992.

Special Factor: Minimum order is $35 prepaid, or $50 C.O.D.

TAYLOR'S CUTAWAYS AND STUFF

**2802 E. WASHINGTON,
DEPT. WBMC-91
URBANA, IL 61801-4699**

Catalog: $1 (see text)
Save: up to 75%
Pay: check, MO, MC, V
Sells: cutaways and patterns
Store: mail order only

$$ ✉

"Cutaways" are what's left when the pieces of a garment are cut from material. These scraps, sometimes running to a yard long, are perfect for doll clothing, piecework, quilting, and other crafts.

Taylor's Cutaways offers bundles of polyesters, cottons, blends, calicos, and other assortments, as well as silk, satin, velvet, felt, and fake fur cutaways. The 24-page catalog lists a wide variety of patterns and project designs for such items as draft stoppers, puppets, dolls, Teddy bears, pigs, ducks, and other animals. Crocheting patterns for toys and novelties, iron-on transfer patterns, button and trim assortments, and toy eyes, joints, and squeakers are available. Quilting templates and patterns, woven labels, and books on a variety of crafts are also sold. The complete catalog costs $1, but you can see a sample of the firm's selection in its four-page brochure, sent free on request.

The completely unskilled will appreciate Taylor's for its line of potpourris, already blended and scented, and the unscented dried flowers and plants, ground orris fixative, essential oils, and satin squares for making sachets. On the practical side, Taylor's sells "tea baglets," little fiber bags you fill with the tea of your choice and heat-seal with a household iron. (This is a great way to take a favorite loose tea with you when you travel.) Prices of these and most of the other goods average 50% below comparable retail, and savings can reach as high as 75%. This seems an especially good source for anyone who makes sachets and potpourris, dolls, toys, pieced quilts, and bazaar items.

Canadian readers, please note: The shipping surcharge for orders sent to Canada is 25%.

Special Factor: Quantity discounts are available.

THAI SILKS

252-W STATE ST.
LOS ALTOS, CA 94022
800-722-7455
IN CA 800-221-7455
415/948-8611

Brochure: free
Save: up to 50%
Pay: check, MO, MC, V, AE
Sells: imported silk fabric, scarves, and
lingerie
Store: same address; Monday through
Saturday 9–5:30

$$ ✉ ☎ 🍁 ▬

Beautiful, comfortable silk is quite affordable at Thai Silks, where the home sewer, decorator, and artist can save 30% to 50% on yardage and piece goods (compared to typical retail prices). Curiously, just 2% of the stock comes from Thailand. Thai Silks was established in 1964.

China, India, and Korea have contributed to this company's large selection of silks, which include sueded silk, jacquard weaves, crepe de chine, bouclé, pongee, China silk, silk satin, raw silk, silk velvet, tapestry weaves, silk taffeta, woven plaids, Dupioni silk, upholstery weights, and much more. Hemmed white silk scarves and neckties for painting and batiking, Chinese embroidered handkerchiefs, silk lingerie, and blouses are also available.

Special Factors: Satisfaction is guaranteed; price quote by phone or letter; quantity discounts are offered to firms and professionals; samples are available (details are given in the brochure); authorized returns are accepted; C.O.D. orders are accepted; minimum order is one-half yard of fabric; orders are shipped worldwide.

THREAD DISCOUNT SALES

P.O. BOX 2277
BELL GARDENS, CA
90201
213/562-3438
213/560-8177

Catalog: free
Save: up to 50%
Pay: check, MO, MC, V, AE, Discover
Sells: coned thread, sewing machines
Store: 5960 East Florence, Bell Gardens,
CA; Monday through Saturday 10–5

$$ ✉ ☎ 🍁 ▬

This firm sells machines and supplies for the serious sewer—sergers, overlock machines, and "coned" thread—at savings of up to 50% on list prices. Thread Discount, in business since 1962, sent us a sheaf of photocopied sheets featuring White and Singer sewing and overlock machines at an average 50% discount on list or original prices. (The machines were all "special purchase" items; see the current catalog for available brands and models.)

Among the coned thread offered in the list we received were rayon embroidery thread, 6,000 yards of overlock at under $3 a cone, and "woolly nylon" thread. J. & P. Coats general-purpose thread was offered at $1.99 for a 3,000-yard cone, which compares very favorably to the spool of just 325 yards selling for $1.29 in fabric shops. Most of the thread is offered in a full range of colors, which are listed by name and number (there are no samples or color guides). In addition, Thread Discount carries novelty metallics in a variety of colors and two sizes of nylon filament thread for "invisible" work.

Please note: A shipping surcharge is imposed on orders sent to Alaska, Hawaii, Puerto Rico, and Canada.

Special Factor: Minimum order is 6 cones of thread (on thread orders).

TOWER HOBBIES

DEPT. WBMC
P.O. BOX 778
CHAMPAIGN, IL 61820
800/637-4989

Catalog: $3
Save: up to 60%
Pay: check, MO, MC, V
Sells: radio-controlled vehicles
Store: mail order only

Tower Hobbies publishes a 300-page catalog of radio-controlled ships, planes, and other vehicles. Tower has been recommended highly by more than one reader, citing the firm's discounts—up to 60%—and good service.

Radio-controlled vehicles offer the pleasures of model building, electronics, piloting and driving, and tinkering. Tower Hobbies sells the newest releases from model manufacturers, and state-of-the-art electronics. There are kits for pickups, 4WDs, off-road cars, tractors, race cars, jeeps, and other vehicles by Kyosho, MRC/Tamiya, and other firms. The marine models include tugboats, yachts, hydroplanes, "swamp buggies," sailboats, cabin cruisers, and other ships, by Dumas, Kyosho, MRC, MRP, and other firms.

There are model planes from Ace, Airtronics, Cox, Flitecraft, Great Planes, Guillows, Kyosho, Lanier, Mark's, MRC, Royal, Scorpio, and Sureflite, among others.

Tower doesn't let you down when it comes to getting things up and running: Every tool and material you need to build the models is available, as well as engine radios, batteries, chargers, fuel, and related products. These goods are all sold at a discount. Tower's "combos," combinations of a model with appropriate charger or engine or other necessary components, afford even more savings. The catalog itself is a value, with over 16 "information-only" pages full of tips and instructions.

Special Factors: Satisfaction is guaranteed; returns of new, unused goods are accepted within 10 days.

UTEX TRADING ENTERPRISES

710 NINTH ST.
NIAGARA FALLS, NY
   14301
716/282-8211

Price List: free with SASE
Save: up to 50%
Pay: check or MO
Sells: imported silk fabric
Store: mail order only

 $$ ✉ ☎ 🍁 (see text) 🇺🇸

Utex trades in silk yard goods and sewing supplies, which are imported directly from China. This firm, established in 1980, is of special interest to textile artists, decorators, designers, and home sewers—Utex stocks over 100 weights, weaves, and widths of silk.

The enormous inventory includes silk shantung, pongee, taffeta, twill, habotai, peau de soie, lamé, and suiting. Most of the fabrics are 100% silk, and a guide that recommends appropriate fabrics for specific purposes is included in the price list. Unprinted scarves and ties, silk thread, floss, yarns, and fine brushes and dyes for fabric painting are also stocked.

Canadian readers, please note: Utex's Canadian address is 111 Peter St., #212, Toronto, Ontario, M5V 2H1; the phone number is 416/596-7565.

Special Factor: Volume discounts are available.

VANGUARD CRAFTS, INC.

**P.O. BOX 340170, DEPT.
WMC
BROOKLYN, NY
11234-9007
718/377-5188
FAX: 718/692-0056**

Catalog: $1, refundable
Save: up to 40%
Pay: check, MO, MC, V
Sells: crafts materials
Store: 1081 E. 48th St., Brooklyn, NY;
Monday through Friday 10–6, Saturday
10–5

$$$ 🍁 🇺🇸

Vanguard sells fun, in the form of crafts kits and projects. The 68-page catalog is geared to educators and others buying for classroom use, but it's a great source for rainy-day project materials at home.

The catalog we reviewed showed kits and supplies for hundreds of crafts, including shrink art, foil pictures, grapevine wreaths, mosaic tiling, basic woodworking crafts, suncatchers, Styrofoam crafts, leatherworking, decoupage, copper enameling, needlepunch, pom-pom crafts, stenciling, string art, crafts sticks projects, Indian crafts, basic weaving (looper looms), calligraphy, and other diversions. Basic art supplies—adhesives, scissors, paper, paint, pastels, etc.—are also available. The prices are *very* reasonable, and the large selection makes it easy to meet the $25 minimum order.

Special Factors: Price quote by phone or letter with SASE; minimum order is $25.

VETERAN LEATHER COMPANY, INC.

**204 25TH ST., DEPT. WBM
BROOKLYN, NY 11232
800-221-7565
IN NY 718/768-0300
FAX: 718/768-8361**

Catalog: $2, refundable
Save: up to 50%
Pay: check, MO, MC, V
Sells: leatherworking supplies
Store: same address; Monday through
Friday 8–5

$$

Veteran Leather's 48-page catalog offers a wide range of kits, tools, and materials for novice and experienced leatherworkers. Prices are up to 50% below those we found charged by crafts supply houses for similar products.

The kits include classic Western-style billfolds, keycases, belts, wrist-bands, coasters, handbags, and even moccasins. There are scores of belt buckles, including solid brass styles cast with relief images of deer, flying geese, trains, ships, trout, and similar themes. A full range of findings and hardware, including keyrings, key plates, conchos, money clips, bag locks, rivets, snap fasteners, and rings is available. Leather shears, bevelers, knives, pliers, chisels, punches, mallets, and stamps are sold, as well as Fiebing's dyes and leather finishes. Veteran offers the leather itself: oak, cowhide, cabretta, deerskin, suede (lamb, pig, and cow), skivers, cowhide embossed to resemble ostrich and alligator, and other types of splits and sides. Bundles of leather remnants, leather thread, and lacing are also sold. Books on a range of leather crafts are available.

Veteran Leather is offering readers of this book a 5% discount on their first order. Identify yourself as a WBMC reader when you order. This WBMC reader discount expires February 1, 1992.

Special Factors: Quantity discounts are available; minimum order is $25.

WEBBS

**P.O. BOX 349
18 KELLOGG AVE.
AMHERST, MA 01004
413/253-2580**

Price Lists and Samples: $2
Save: up to 80%
Pay: check, MO, MC, V
Sells: yarns and spinning and weaving equipment and books
Store: same address; Monday through Saturday 9:30–5:30

Knitters and weavers of all types—production, hand, and machine—will find inspiration in the sets of samples from Webbs. This firm has been doing business since 1980, selling yarns of all types at up to 80% below original prices. Each mailing from Webbs offers conventional and novelty yarns of cotton, wool, silk, rayon, and blends, sold in bags, coned, wound off, sometimes in balls, and in packs, unwound. (The packs come in assortments of 10, 25, and 100 pounds, at outstandingly low prices.)

Each set of samples is folded into a descriptive price sheet, which notes special considerations concerning supply, suitability for knitting or weaving, gauge, length per unit (e.g., yards per ball, cone, or pound), and prices and minimums. We found some great buys among the samples we received, including a gorgeous mohair in choice colors, a lovely ribbon yarn in several hues, fine-quality cotton yarns in different weights and fashion colors, and all-wool rug yarn. The stock includes yarns exclusive to Webbs, mill-ends, discontinued lines, and overstock. Savings can be boosted with an extra 20% discount if your yarn order totals $60 or more, or 25% on orders over $120. (Take note of the exceptions, marked "no further discount" or "NFD" in the price sheets.) Don't overlook the "Naturals Collection," listed separately, which includes cotton, linen, wool, and blended yarns for warping and other purposes—also well priced.

Looms, spinning wheels, drum carders, and knitting machines are available at nondiscounted prices, although shipping is free on these items (which can be worth $25 to even $100, depending on where you live and the weight of the article).

Special Factors: Shipping is included on looms, spinning wheels, drum carders, and knitting machines; quantity discounts are available; authorized returns are accepted within 30 days (a 15% restocking fee may be charged).

COMPANIES OUTSIDE THE U.S.A.

The following firms are experienced in dealing with customers in the U.S. and Canada. We've included them because they offer goods not widely available at a discount in the U.S., because they have a better selection, or because they may offer the same goods at great savings.

Before ordering from a non-U.S. firm, please read through the applicable sections of "The Complete Guide to Buying by Mail" at the back of this book. We recommend paying for your catalog with a camouflaged enclosure of cash. (Sending cash saves the company the bank charge of converting your check to different currency.) We further advise you to pay for your merchandise by credit card whenever possible, so that your transaction will be protected by the part of the Fair Credit Billing Act that allows you to dispute charges for goods not received. See page 545 for a complete discussion of the Act. Please note that only this portion of the Act applies, and the FTC's Mail Order Rule governing delivery time *does not.*

BABOURIS HANDICRAFTS

56 ADRIANOU ST.
105 55 ATHENS
GREECE
011-30-1-3247561

Price List and Samples: $4, deductible
Save: up to 50%
Pay: check, IMO, AE
Sells: handspun yarn and handknitted
sweaters
Store: same address; Monday through
Friday 10–4

Babouris Handicrafts, which has been doing business since 1959, sells yarn spun by hand from native wool, at up to 50% below the prices charged in the U.S. for the same kinds of yarn. More than three dozen natural shades and brilliant fast-dyed colors are available, and airmail postage is included in the prices. There's a minimum order of 5kg (about 11 pounds) of yarn, but colors may be mixed to meet this requirement. Hand-knitted woolen pullovers and cardigans are also available; inquire for information.

Special Factors: Price quote by phone or letter with SASE; shipping is included; minimum order is 5kg of yarn; orders are shipped worldwide.

MAURICE BRASSARD & FILS INC.

C.P. 4
PLESSISVILLE, QUEBEC
G6L 2Y6
CANADA
819/362-2408

Catalog: $9.95 (see text)
Save: 35% average
Pay: check or IMO
Sells: weaving yarns, looms, etc.
Store: 1972 Simoneau, Plessisville,
Quebec; Monday through Friday 9–5

Maurice Brassard's catalog is a looseleaf binder with two dozen pages of yarn samples, all neatly tied and labeled. Many of the descriptions are in French as well as English, and measurements are mixed—some are in grams, others ounces, some meters, others feet. The prices (calculated on a Canadian dollar worth U.S. 84¢) translated into savings of 30% and more, on average.

The yarns include cotton warp in 2/8, 2/16, 4/8, and bouclé, pearl cotton, polyester 2/8 and 2/16, Orlon, linen (natural, bleached, and dyed), silk noil, cotton slub, Merino and Superwash wools, and a variety of novelty yarns. The color selection is superb, and the quality of the goods first-rate. Brassard also sells cloth strips for weaving, braiding, and other crafts, in cotton, nylon, acetate, and acrylic. In addition to yarn, Brassard sells tools and equipment: cloth-cutting machines (to make strips), wool winders, a twisting device (for plying threads together), and looms and accessories by Leclerc.

The catalog and ordering instructions have been written for Canadian orders, so if you're buying from the U.S., we strongly suggest calling or writing to get exact shipping costs *before* ordering. If you wish to review Brassard's prices before purchasing the catalog, you may request the price list, which is free.

Canadian readers, please note: The catalog costs $7.95 within Canada.

Special Factor: Quantity discounts are available.

CAMBRIDGE WOOLS, LTD.

BOX 2572
AUCKLAND
NEW ZEALAND
011-64-9-390-769

Brochure and Samples: $2, refundable
Save: up to 66%
Pay: IMO
Sells: wools and knitwear
Store: 40 Anzac Ave., Auckland; Monday through Friday 9–5

We priced several samples of two-ply wool knitting yarn locally at $2.50 to $3 an ounce and found Cambridge selling virtually identical yarn for just $1 an ounce, or up to 66% less. This is native New Zealand wool, scoured and spun to the specifications of Cambridge Wools. Brightly colored two-ply (medium-weight) yarn costs $16 a pound in both all-wool and a mohair/wool blend, and a two-ply unscoured (greasy) yarn in natural colors is also priced at $16 a pound. These yarns serve the most popular applications: machine knitting, hand knitting, and weaving. Greasy and scoured spinning wools are sold uncarded in natural shades ($3.50 to $4 per pound), and carded in natural and six rich colors for $5 per pound.

The price list cites the availability of Aran handknitted pullovers and cardigans ($90), in sizes to fit up to 42". Sheepskins are also on offer, from "single" size (34" by 21", $40) to "quarto" size (66" by 40", $178). Car seat covers to fit seats in small and mid-sized cars cost $175 per pair. The good values here are not impaired by postage surcharges—shipping is included in the prices, and goods are sent by sea mail.

Cambridge Wools is offering readers of this book a 5% discount on their orders. Identify yourself as a WBMC reader when you order. This WBMC reader discount expires February 1, 1992.

Special Factors: Satisfaction is guaranteed; returns are accepted for exchange or refund; shipping (by sea mail) is included.

STAVROS KOUYOUMOUTZAKIS

WORKSHOP SPUN WOOLS
166 KALOKERINOU AVE.
712-02 IRAKLION, CRETE
GREECE
011-30-81-284-466

$$ ✉

Price List and Samples: $1, cash, deductible
Save: up to 65%
Pay: check
Sells: Cretan and Australian yarn
Store: same address

Mr. Kouyoumoutzakis sends out a price list bulging with lush, bundled snippets of yarns spun from the wools of Crete and Australia. The yarns are suitable for knitting, weaving, and crafts. The Cretan yarns, in natural (undyed) shades of cream, grey, and dark brown, cost $5.20 per pound in "thick" and "medium" weights, $5.80 for "thin," and $6.20 for two-ply. The same wools, dyed in brilliant purples, golds, reds, blues, and greens, cost $6.20 per pound, in either thick or medium weights. Creamy-colored Australian natural wool, thick or medium, costs $6.50 per pound, $7 in two-ply.

Prices are 10% higher if you order under 20 pounds, which is still a bargain. Airmail postage is included, and Mr. Kouyoumoutzakis believes that you should have your yarn within 20 to 30 days after your order is received in Greece. Remember to order enough of each color for your intended project, since dye lots are sure to differ. Please consult your customs office before ordering to get the current rates of duty.

Special Factor: Minimum order is 10 pounds (total).

D. MACGILLIVRAY & COY.

BALIVANICH
BENBECULA
WESTERN ISLES PA88
   5LA
SCOTLAND
011-44-870-2525

Price Lists and Catalog: $4
Save: up to 50%
Pay: check, IMO, MC, V, AE, Access, EC
Sells: Scottish fabrics, knitwear, and handcrafts
Store: Balivanich, Benbecula

Four dollars brings you MacGillivray's assortment of price lists and the catalog. MacGillivray offers everything from Hebridean perfumes to Highland dress accessories, but is best known for its bargains on woven goods.

The cream of the crop is the selection of authentic clan tartans. Three types of wools and weights are offered, from acrylic/wool blends at about $17 a yard to the all-wool, heavyweight worsted for about $29 a yard, in standard, ancient, and reproduction tartan colors. Also sold are many types of Harris tweeds, Scottish tweeds, suitings, coatings, linings, and dress fabrics, all preshrunk, from about $8 a yard. The muted tweeds are lovely, and the samples give an idea of the range of colors and textures available. (Samples of the tartans and other fabrics may be ordered from the catalog.)

Once made into garments, you can pair your tweeds with fine sweaters of lambswool, Shetland, or camel's hair, which are available in a palette of colors. The Fair Isle Aran sweaters are offered in jumper (pullover) and lumber jacket (high-necked cardigan) styles and as jerseys for children. Hand-knitted Harris wool sweaters for men and women begin at $48.

There are also shooting stockings, mohair stoles (about $27 here, $75 in the U.S.), heraldic wall shields, Harris tweed caps and ties, and hand-tailored kilts. Highland dress accessories, from bagpipes and skean dhus to waistcoats and bonnets, can be special ordered. On top of this, Mac-Gillivray will tailor clothing or make copies from illustrations, at prices at least 40% less than those charged by most dressmakers. MacGillivray is "always eager to adjust and exchange without any bother," and has been mailing orders to customers worldwide since 1942.

Special Factors: Satisfaction is guaranteed; returns (except made-to-measure and custom orders) are accepted within 14 days for exchange, refund, or credit.

RAMMAGERDIN H.F.

**P.O. BOX 7510
121 REYKJAVIK,
 ICELAND
011-354-1-11122**

Catalog: $2, deductible
Save: 30% plus
Pay: check, IMO, MC, V, AE, DC, EC,
 Access
Sells: Icelandic knitwear and yarns
Store: Hafnarstraeti 19, Reykjavik, Iceland;
 Monday through Friday 9–6, Saturday 9–
 12; also Hotel Loftleidir and Hotel Esja,
 Reykjavik; Monday through Sunday 8–8,
 both locations

The wool used to create the soft, soft Icelandic sweaters and accessories available in many catalogs can be bought here by the skein at prices much lower than those charged in specialty yarn stores in the U.S. Rammagerdin sells medium-weight, natural-colored and dyed yarn for $3.80 per 3-1/2-ounce skein, shipped by airmail. All of the yarn is washed and moth-proofed. The natural colors combine beautifully in the traditional sweater designs, and the dyed shades are poetic—heathery rose, moss, slate blue, and vibrant shades of purple, forest green, and cadet blue are examples. They could serve as accent color to the Icelandic designs or stand alone beautifully.

Most of Rammagerdin's 24-page color catalog is devoted to clothing. There are cardigans, pullovers, skirts, vests, and zippered jackets for men and women, coats and delicate shawls, cardigans for children, and socks, slippers, caps, scarves, mittens, and blankets made of Icelandic wool. Some of the garments incorporate the snowflakes and geometrics of classic Icelandic patterns, but most of the women's designs are very stylish and up-to-date. You'll also find Viking figures and sheep statuettes in the catalog, as well as Icelandic dolls. Prices are routinely 30% less than those charged for the same goods in the U.S.

Special Factors: Shipping and insurance are included; orders are shipped worldwide.

ROMNI WOOLS AND FIBRES LTD.

5345 WEST BLVD.
VANCOUVER, B.C. V6M
3W4
CANADA
604/263-0070
FAX: 604/875-9887

Catalog: $3
Save: up to 50%
Pay: check, IMO, V
Sells: yarns, tops, and spinning, weaving, and knitting equipment
Store: same address; Monday through Saturday 10–5:30

$$$ ✉

Romni is one source no spinner, weaver, or knitter should overlook. The 12-page catalog lists one of the best selections of unspun tops and fibers and yarns you'll find around, and the prices are 20% to 50% below comparable retail.

New Zealand fleece is sold here in natural colors, carded and uncarded, greasy and scoured; and acrylic, nylon, cotton, flax, ramie, jute, a variety of silks, alpaca, angora, cashmere, muskox, mohair, camel's hair, goat's hair, and karakul tops are available for spinning. The yarns and cords, suitable for weaving, embroidery, knitting, tapestry weaving, crocheting, and rug making, include single- through four-ply standard yarns as well as bouclés, tweeds, loops, slubs, hand-spuns, metallics, and other textures in a comparable range of fibers. Romni also stocks canvas in many gauges, and a full range of DMC tapestry wools and cotton embroidery floss. Quantity discounts are offered on certain yarns and fibers. Samples are available at prices listed in the catalog; we recommend ordering "The Works" ($17), samples of all of the yarns and fibers stocked. And Romni offers a broad range of dyes, mordants, and chemicals, including natural dyes (annato seed, cochineal, indigo, madder), and Deka and Dylon products.

You won't have to look elsewhere for equipment, either. Several Louet spinning wheels are listed, including castle, traditional, and folding models, and spinning chairs, drum and hand carders, card cloth, and pickers are offered as well. Romni sells frame and floor looms by Beka, Louet, Leclerc, and other firms, and warping boards, umbrella swifts, ball winders, reeds, shuttles, shed sticks, crochet hooks, and tapestry beaters and needles are available. Romni also sells buttons carved of abalone, yew, rosewood, bubinga, tulip wood, and zebra wood.

The catalog prices are given in Canadian dollars, and you should be sure to check the conversion rate before ordering. (At this writing, the Canadian dollar is worth about 84¢ in U.S. funds.) Customs charges and higher shipping costs will offset some of these savings for U.S. customers.

Special Factor: Authorized returns of most goods are accepted.

SEE ALSO

Astronomical Society of the Pacific ● charts, computer programs, tapes, slides, etc. on astronomy topics ● *BOOKS*

Baron Bridge Supplies ● teaching and playing supplies for bridge ● *TOYS*

The Bevers ● wooden toy wheels, balls, etc. ● *TOOLS*

Dick Blick Co. ● crafts supplies ● *ART MATERIALS*

BRE Lumber ● cabinet-grade lumber ● *HOME: MAINTENANCE*

Campmor ● tent zippers, Eureka yard goods, grommet kits, etc. ● *SPORTS*

Caprilands Herb Farm ● potpourri ingredients, pomanders, essential oils, etc. ● *FARM*

Ceramic Supply of New York & New Jersey, Inc. ● ceramics and sculpting materials, music box parts ● *ART MATERIALS*

Cherry Tree Toys, Inc. ● wooden toy kits, parts, and plans ● *TOYS*

Cleo (Ireland) Ltd. ● Irish yarns and fabrics ● *CLOTHING*

Crown Art Products Co., Inc. ● supplies and equipment for silk screening, stained glass, etc. ● *ART MATERIALS*

Custom Golf Clubs, Inc. ● supplies for making golf clubs, including stains, finishes, etc. ● *SPORTS*

Derry's Sewing Center ● name-brand sewing machines ● *APPLIANCES*

Discount Appliance Centers ● name-brand sewing machines and attachments ● *APPLIANCES*

Economy Enterprises ● plans for building toys, furniture, tools, etc. ● *TOOLS*

Eloxite Corporation ● jewelry findings, lapidary equipment, and clock-making supplies ● *JEWELRY*

Fabrics by Design ● name-brand decorator fabrics ● *HOME: DECOR*

Gohn Bros. ● sewing notions, quilting batts, scissors, thread, yard goods, etc. ● *CLOTHING*

Hong Kong Lapidaries, Inc. ● scarabs, inlaid intaglios, beads, and other crafts materials ● *JEWELRY*

House of Onyx ● semiprecious and precious gems, cabochons ● *JEWELRY*

International Import Co. ● cut precious and semiprecious gemstones ● *JEWELRY*

Jerryco, Inc. ● surplus material suitable for various crafts ● *SURPLUS*

Kicking Mule Records, Inc. ● "Lark in the Morning" video music lessons ● *BOOKS*

Meisel Hardware Specialties ● wooden craft parts and brass hardware, woodworking plans ● *TOOLS*

Metropolitan Music Co. ● violin wood, stain, varnish, tools, etc. ● *MUSIC*

Original Paper Collectibles ● vintage fruit-crate and other product labels for crafts use ● *ART, ANTIQUES*

Plastic BagMart ● zip-top plastic bags ● *HOME: MAINTENANCE*

The Potters Shop Inc. ● books on pottery and ceramics ● *BOOKS*

Protecto-Pak ● zip-top plastic bags ● *HOME: MAINTENANCE*

Arthur M. Rein ● fur tails and pelts ● *CLOTHING*

San Francisco Herb Co. ● dried flowers, other potpourri ingredients, potpourri recipes, etc. ● *FOOD*

Ginger Schlote ● economy jewelry findings ● *JEWELRY*

Sewin' in Vermont ● name-brand sewing machines and accessories ● *APPLIANCES*

Shama Imports, Inc. ● crewel-embroidered fabric ● *HOME: DECOR*

Singer Sewing Center of College Station ● sewing machines and sergers ● *APPLIANCES*

R.C. Steele Co. ● canine portrait needlework kits ● *ANIMAL*

Suburban Sew 'N Sweep, Inc. ● sewing and overlock machines ● *APPLIANCES*

That Fish Place ● aquarium supplies and equipment ● *ANIMAL*

Triner Scale ● pocket scale ● *OFFICE*

University Products, Inc. ● archival-quality collection storage, mounting, and display materials ● *GENERAL MERCHANDISE*

Weston Bowl Mill ● unfinished wooden boxes, spool holders, etc. ● *GENERAL MERCHANDISE*

Wood's Cider Mill ● natural (undyed) yarns ● *FOOD*

Woodworker's Supply of New Mexico ● woodworking tools and equipment ● *TOOLS*

FARM AND GARDEN

Seeds, bulbs, live plants, supplies, tools, and equipment

If you buy your plants at the local florist or nursery, you're probably going to find the selection somewhat limited, and the prices will be noncompetitive. But if you go the mail-order route, you'll have your choice of rare species of bulbs, plants, flowers, herbs, and other growing things—at considerable savings. Before ordering, however, make sure that the plants will survive in your climate or home environment—a delicate woods flower specimen will not last long in an eastern exposure or an overheated house.

Although our interest is saving you money, improvements in your landscaping can also *make* money. Investing $50 to $100 in "environmental improvement" may increase the value of your property by as much as $500. But the same cautions about plant survival inside your house apply outdoors, perhaps more strongly. For example, "hostile" soil often leads to repeated planting failures, until the gardener finally gets wise and has the soil tested—commonly finding that it can support only certain types of growth. Soil test kits are offered by many mail-order garden suppliers, and among them the LaMotte kits are highly regarded. LaMotte has been manufacturing test kits, reagents, and apparatus for analyzing water, air, and soil for over 65 years. The best kit for the home gardener costs about $35 (although a simplified version that tests just pH levels is available for about $9). The deluxe kit comes with all the reagents and charts you'll need to perform about 30 pH tests and 15 tests for nitrogen, phosphorus, and potassium. The "LaMotte Soil Handbook" that comes with the kit is a fascinating guide to the elements of soil, including a definition of soil nutrients and a "pH preference guide" for over 600 plants, shrubs, and trees. The LaMotte kits can be found in the spring and summer catalogs from Gardener's Supply, 128 Intervale Rd., Burlington, VT 05401. Gardener's Supply is *not* a discount source, but has a wealth of good and useful garden equipment and tools. The catalog is free.

The business of preserving old plant varieties is the concern of The Heirloom Gardener (Sierra Club Books, 1984), by Carolyn Jabs. This is a marvelous introductory book on "living heirlooms"—endangered, rare, and nearly extinct fruit and vegetable varieties. (By some estimates, only a fraction of the varieties that existed at the turn of the century can be found today.) The book includes a brief history of the business of seeds, information on seed "savers" and seed exchanges, finding "lost" varieties, capsule histories of some select heirloom varieties, seed research resources, tips on harvesting seeds, and much other useful information. The book may be purchased from Sierra Club Books through Sierra Club Mail-Order Service, 730 Polk St., San Francisco, CA 94109. Request the free catalog of publications.

Kent Whealy's *Garden Seed Inventory* is something of a bible for vegetable seed savers. This 422-page book, which bears accolades from Carolyn Jabs, Robert Rodale, and Wendell Berry, lists varieties alphabetically, describes each (height, appearance, variations, days to maturity), indicates which seed companies offer it, and also shows *how many* firms have offered that variety over the past few years. For example, the "Green Prolific" pickling cucumber was available from 23 firms in 1987, down from 34 who stocked the seed in 1981. There are many varieties offered by just one source of the 215 Mr. Whealy has included in this survey. The mandate is clear to seed savers: Buy, cultivate, and save those varieties! For price and ordering information on the current edition of the *Garden Seed Inventory,* send a request for the publication list with a long, self-addressed, stamped envelope to Seed Savers Exchange, RR 3, Box 239, Decorah, IA 52101.

If you're purchasing farm machinery, see the the listing of Central Michigan Tractor & Parts in "Auto." In addition to the publications of the Department of Agriculture, university cooperative extensions also disseminate technical information of use to farmers and production growers. Among those in the "Small Farms Series," published by the Northeast Regional Agricultural Engineering Service, we found the 34-page *Used Farm Equipment: Assessing Quality, Safety, and Economics* a clear and well-illustrated overview of points to consider before making such a purchase. Write to Northeast Regional Agricultural Engineering Service, Cornell University, 152 Riley-Robb Hall, Ithaca, NY 14853 for a list of current publications and prices.

The U.S. government operates an information clearinghouse staffed by agricultural pros who can advise you to on technical matters, including how to go organic ("sustainable agriculture" is part of the agency's mandate). Please note that you should turn here after consulting other sources, including your local extension agent; if you can't get help there, call ATTRA (Appropriate Technology Transfer for Rural Areas), at 800-346-9140, Monday through Friday, 8–5 CST.

If you're building your own greenhouse or cold frames, see the "Maintenance" section of "Home" for thermopane panels. Other garden-related products are sold by some of the firms listed in "Tools."

BOB'S SUPERSTRONG GREENHOUSE PLASTIC

BOX 42-WM91
NECHE, ND 58265
204/327-5540 (see text)

Brochure: $1 or 2 first-class stamps
Save: 33% average
Pay: check or MO
Sells: greenhouse plastic and fastening
    systems
Store: same address; by appointment

 $$ ✉ ☎ 🍁 (see text) 🇺🇸

Bob Davis and his wife, Margaret Smith-Davis, live on the Manitoba/North Dakota border. Resourceful gardeners, they experimented with different materials while trying to create an inexpensive greenhouse and discovered that woven polyethylene makes an ideal greenhouse skin, even in harsh climes. Their experiences with the material were so successful that they decided to market it themselves.

Their 11-year-old business, Bob's Superstrong Greenhouse Plastic (also known as Northern Greenhouse Sales), is a great source for other innovative gardeners who want to design their own greenhouses. The firm offers the "superstrong" woven poly and two anchoring systems. One is "Cinchstrap," a bright-white, flat, flexible poly strapping material that can be used for permanent anchoring, abrasion reduction in installation, and as a replacement for wood lathing in greenhouse assembly. The other, "Poly-Fastener," is a channel-system anchor that uses a flat spline to secure the poly. Prices for the woven poly run from 15¢ to 23¢ per square foot, depending on the quantity ordered; the standard width is ten feet, but Bob can heat-seal additional widths together to create a wider swath. The Poly-Fastener runs between 53¢ and 58¢ a linear foot in 300' and 100' rolls (or $1 per foot for cut pieces), and the Cinchstrap costs 10¢ a linear foot on 100' rolls.

The literature from this firm details the couple's experiences with these materials, and it discusses money-saving ideas. One is the use of "rebars," ("those long, rusty-colored iron rods placed in concrete to strengthen it") to create the greenhouse frame. There are many other tips, all of which are based on the experiences of the proprietors or those of their customers. Not the least of these is the fact that the applications of the poly are not limited to greenhouses and cold frames; woven poly has been used in solar collectors, vapor barriers, storm windows, pool covers, tent floors, and many other situations. Send $1 or two first-class stamps—or phone—for the charming and amazingly informative brochure. You may also speak to the proprietors by phone if you have questions; please note the phone hours, below.

Canadian readers, please note: Call or write to Box 1450WM, Altona, Manitoba R0G 0B0, for literature.

Special Factors: Price quote by phone or letter with SASE; calls are taken daily between 6 A.M. and 8 P.M., CST; C.O.D. orders are accepted.

BRECK'S

**6523 N. GALENA RD.
PEORIA, IL 61632
309/691-4616**

Catalog: free
Save: up to 50%
Pay: check, MO, MC, V, AE
Sells: Dutch flower bulbs
Store: mail order only

$$$ ✉

Breck's has been "serving American gardeners since 1818" with a fine selection of flower bulbs, imported directly from Holland. Discounts of up to 50% are offered on orders placed by July 31 for fall delivery and planting.

The 52-page, color catalog shows many varieties of tulips, as well as a selection of crocuses, daffodils, hyacinths, irises, jonquils, anemones, delphiniums, and wind flowers. Blooming period, height, color and markings, petal formation, and scent are all described in the text. Each order is shipped with the Breck's Dutch Bulb Handbook, which covers naturalizing, planting, indoor growing, bulb care, and related topics.

Special Factors: Satisfaction is guaranteed; early-order discounts are available; returns are accepted for exchange, replacement, or refund.

BUTTERBROOKE FARM SEED CO-OP

78 BARRY RD.
OXFORD, CT 06483
203/888-2000

Price List: free with #10 self-addressed, stamped envelope
Save: up to 75%
Pay: check or MO
Sells: seeds
Store: mail order only

$$$ ✉ 🍁 ▣

"Only pure, open-pollinated seeds will produce plants from which you can save seeds for planting another year." So says the straightforward price list from Butterbrooke Farm Seed Co-Op, where becoming "seed self-reliant" is one of several gardening objectives.

Butterbrooke, established in 1978, is a seed cooperative whose members include organic farmers and seed savers. For just $7.50 per year, members receive a 15% order discount, the Farm newsletter, advisory services, the opportunity to buy rare or heirloom seeds, and other benefits. This is no-frills gardening at its sensible best, from the selection of scores of seeds (a well-rounded kitchen-garden full) to the Farm's own collection for first-time planters—a group of vegetable favorites.

The packets are measured to reduce waste: the small size (45¢) will plant one to two 20-foot rows, and the large size (95¢), three to four times that. All of the seeds are fresh, and they've been selected for short growing seasons. Butterbrooke also offers booklets on related topics—composting, making mulch, saving seeds—at nominal sums. You don't have to be a co-op member to buy from Butterbrooke, but the price of membership is low and the advice service alone should justify the expense.

Special Factor: C.O.D. orders are accepted.

CAPRILANDS HERB FARM

**534 SILVER ST.
COVENTRY, CT 06238
203/742-7244**

Brochure: free with SASE
Save: up to 30%
Pay: check, MO, certified check
Sells: live herbs and country gifts
Store: same address; daily 9–5 except
  holidays

$$ ✉   🍁   ▦

Caprilands offers live and dried culinary and medicinal herbs and a pot-pourri of herbaceous gifts, seasonings, and rite materials. The Farm is run by Mrs. Simmons, a herbalist of fifty years' standing, who provides a legendary luncheon program for visitors to the 18th-century farmhouse. (Reservations are essential; details on the program are given in the brochure.)

Mrs. Simmons began her business in the 1930s, and today it is a respected source among collectors of hard-to-find herbs and those who dabble in the art of necromancy. Over 300 kinds of standard culinary herbs and less common plants can be bought here, including Egyptian onions, rue, wormwood, mugwort, monardas, artemisia, santolinas, germander, lamb's ears, nepetas, ajuga, chamomile, woodruff, and thyme, at $2 to $3 per plant. (The plants are available at the Farm only, not by mail.) Scented geraniums, roses, and flowers are also offered. Packets of seeds for herbs and herbal flowers are available by mail for 60¢ each. Mrs. Simmons' own guides to the cultivation and use of herbs are sold through the brochure, including one of the bibles of herbal horticulture—*Herb Gardening in Five Seasons*.

Caprilands offers a marvelous array of related goods: bronze sundials, wooden "good luck crows" for the garden, kitchen witches and costumed collectors' dolls, pomanders and sachet pillows, spice necklaces, wreaths, herbal hot pads, note paper and calendars, and much more. Amid this olfactory plenty is another great buy—rose buds and lavender flowers for $12 per pound, compared to $15 and $22 in other catalogs; essential oils are also sold.

Special Factor: Certain goods listed in the catalog are available only at the Farm.

CARINO NURSERIES

BOX 538
INDIANA, PA 15701
800-223-7075
412/463-3350
412/463-7480

Catalog: free
Save: up to 65%
Pay: check, MO, MC, V
Sells: evergreen seedlings and transplants
Store: mail order only

$$$ ✉

Carino Nurseries has been supplying Christmas tree farmers, nursery owners, and others with evergreen seedlings for more than 35 years. Prices and selection are better than those we've seen elsewhere—savings of 60% are routine.

The 32-page catalog lists varieties of pine (Scotch, white, Mugho, Ponderosa, Japanese black, American red, and Austrian), fir (Douglas, Balsam, Grand, Fraser, and Concolor), spruce (Colorado blue, white, Englemann, Black Hills, Norway, and Serbian), and birch, dogwood, olive, Canadian hemlock, arborvitae, and other deciduous shrubs and trees.

Each catalog entry includes a description of the variety, age, and approximate height of the plants and the number of years spent in original and transplant beds. The seedlings are sold in lots of 100 at prices up to 65% below those of other nurseries. If you're buying 500 or more, Carino's prices drop 50%. Recommendations on selecting, planting, and shearing (for later harvest as Christmas trees) are given, and the shipping methods and schedule policies are detailed in the catalog as well.

Special Factor: Shipments are made by bus or UPS.

CENTRAL TRACTOR FARM & FAMILY CENTER

3915 DELAWARE AVE.
P.O. BOX 3330
DES MOINES, IA 50316
800-247-7508
FAX: 515/266-4229

Catalog: free
Save: 30% average
Pay: check, MO, MC, V, Discover
Sells: new, used, and rebuilt tractor parts and farm equipment
Store: 45 stores nationwide (locations are given in the catalog)

$$

The oversized, 152-page catalog from this firm begins with livestock supplies and ends with shop manuals for hundreds of farm machines. Central Tractor Farm & Family Center has been in business since 1935 and has 170 outlets in the U.S. and Canada.

You'll find products for livestock and dairy farmers, accessories for pickup trucks, trailer hookups and parts, air compressors, welding equipment, shop tools, and Homelite chain saws. We've listed Central Tractor for its extensive inventory of used parts for tractors made by Allis Chalmers, David Brown, Case, John Deere, Ferguson, Ford, International Harvester, Massey Ferguson, Minneapolis Moline, Oliver, and White. (Details of the warranty terms are given in the catalog.) New replacement parts are available, and there are illustrated shop manuals for these and other makes.

Canadian readers, please note: Inquire for shipping rates.

Special Factor: Quantity discounts are available.

PETER DE JAGER BULB CO.

P.O. BOX 2010, DEPT. WBM
SOUTH HAMILTON, MA
01982
508/468-4707

Catalog: $1
Save: up to 50%
Pay: check, MO, MC, V
Sells: Dutch flower bulbs, seeds, and tubers
Store: same address; Monday through Friday 9–5, Saturday 9–12 noon

$$ ✉

Mr. de Jager imports his bulbs directly from nurseries in Holland, so he's able to offer them at excellent prices—at least 44% less than garden center rates, and even less if ordered in bulk.

Mr. de Jager has been selling flower bulbs since 1950 and offers hundreds of varieties of tulip, narcissus, hyacinth, daffodil, amaryllis, crocus, and other flower bulbs in every possible color and petal formation. The 32-page color catalog describes the color, scent, blooming period, and approximate height of the mature plant. Tubers and seeds for begonias, dahlias, ground cover, and peonies are sold as well. Collections for forcing and rock gardening are offered, and gift certificates are available.

Special Factors: Satisfaction is guaranteed on the bulbs; minimum order is $10.

DUTCH GARDENS INC.

DEPT. WBI
P.O. BOX 200
ADELPHIA, NJ 07710
201/780-2713
FAX: 908/919-0865

Catalog and Price List: free
Save: up to 50%
Pay: check, MO, MC, V, AE
Sells: Dutch flower bulbs
Store: mail order only

$$$$ ✉ ☎

Dutch Gardens publishes one of the most beautiful bulb catalogs around—over 160 color pages of breathtaking flower "head shots" that approximate perfection. Dutch Gardens has been in business since 1961, and prices its bulbs well below other mail-order firms and garden supply houses.

The fall planting catalog offers tulip, hyacinth, daffodil, narcissus, crocus, anemone, iris, snowdrop, allium, amaryllis, and other flower bulbs. The tulip selection alone includes single, double, fringed, parrot, lily, and peony types. The spring planting catalog we reviewed showed a dazzling array of lilies, begonias, dahlias, gladioli, peonies, anemones, freesia, and other flowers. Onions and shallots (for planting) were also available. Each Dutch Gardens catalog lists the size of the bulbs and the common and botanical names, height, planting zones, blooming period, and appropriate growing situations of each variety. A zone chart, guide to planting depth, hints on naturalizing, rock gardening, terrace planting, indoor growing, and forcing are included.

Special Factors: Bulbs are guaranteed to bloom (conditions are stated in the catalog); bulb bonuses or discounts are available on quantity orders; shipping is included; minimum order is $20.

FLORIST PRODUCTS, INC.

2242 NORTH PALMER DR.
SCHAUMBURG, IL 60173
800/828-2242

Catalog: free
Save: up to 50%
Pay: check, MO, MC, V, AE
Sells: greenhouse and gardening supplies
Store: same address

$$$ ✉ ☎ 🍁

The 92-page catalog of "hobby growing supplies" from Florist Products should answer the needs of gardeners of all varieties, from the desultory to the dedicated. Florist Products has been in business since 1952, and sells at savings of up to 50% on list or regular retail prices.

Serious horticultural pursuits are served here with greenhouses and greenhouse equipment (fans, heaters, watering and irrigation systems). Compression and hand sprayers, insecticides and fumigants, growth stimulators and hormones, plant food and fertilizers, soil testers, plant stands, propagation equipment, plastic pots and flats, hanging baskets, redwood planters, pruning shears and other garden tools, and weed barrier matting are also available. The brands are old favorites—Corona, Felco, Jiffy, Peters, Safer, and Sudbury are among them. If you have a greenhouse or are an active grower, see this catalog before you buy your next round of supplies elsewhere.

Special Factors: Satisfaction is guaranteed; price quote by phone or letter with SASE; unused returns are accepted for exchange, refund, or credit.

KRIDER NURSERIES, INC.

P.O. BOX 29
MIDDLEBURY, IN 46540
219/825-5714

Catalog: free
Save: up to 40%
Pay: check, MO, MC, V
Sells: bulbs, roses, shrubs, and trees
Store: 303 W. Bristol, Middlebury, IN;
Monday through Friday 8–5, Saturday 8–4 (closed Saturdays in January and February)

Krider Nurseries has been in business since 1896 and sells ornamental shrubs, shade trees, bulbs, berries, ground cover, and roses at savings of up to 45% on prices charged by the big mail-order nurseries for the same varieties. Krider is well known for its rose collection, which includes hybrid tea roses, mini varieties, floribunda, shrub roses, and climbers. The general nursery catalog is published in January, and a supplementary price list of roses is also available. The rose catalog includes planting instructions and details on the availability of stock throughout the year, and terms of Krider's guarantee that the roses will grow. If you're near Middlebury around the holidays, stop by the nursery to see the Christmas trees (growing and cut), garlands, and handmade wreaths.

Special Factors: Early-order discounts are available; returns are accepted.

MELLINGER'S INC.

**DEPT. WBMC, W. SOUTH
RANGE RD.
NORTH LIMA, OH
44452-9731
216/549-9861**

Catalog: free
Save: up to 45%
Pay: check, MO, MC, V
Sells: seeds, bulbs, and garden equipment
Store: same address; Monday through Saturday 8:30–5 (July through March); 8–6 (April through June)

Mellinger's publishes "the garden catalog for year-round country living," 112 pages of seeds, bulbs, live plants, reference books, greenhouses, garden equipment, and tools. Mellinger's, in business since 1927, offers many hard-to-find goods at savings of up to 45%. Like most of the firms listed in this chapter, Mellinger's has outstandingly low prices on some items, and offers nominal savings on others. (For example, we found no better prices anywhere on Blue Lake bush beans and Black-Seeded Simpson lettuce seeds, but no notable savings on the California Wonder pepper seeds.)

Mellinger's sells flower seeds and bulbs, potted trees and shrubs, shade tree and evergreen seedlings, herb plants, fruit trees, vegetable seeds and vines, tropical plants, and seeds for rare and unusual plants. Everything you'll need for successful cultivation is available, from seed flats to greenhouses. You'll find insect and animal repellants, plant fertilizers, soil additives, pruning and grafting tools, spades, cultivators, hoes, seeders, watering systems, cold frames, starter pots, planters and flower boxes, and related goods. In addition to chemical fumigants and insecticides, Mellinger's sells ladybugs, praying mantis egg cases, and other "natural" predators and beneficial parasites. Bird feeders and seed are also stocked.

Mellinger's also offers a wide variety of goods for hydroponic gardening, and poly-skin greenhouses in small and commercial sizes. Polyethylene is sold by the foot, and ventilation equipment, soil sterilizers, heaters, and thermostats are also available. Books on topics from plant propagation and insect control to flower pressing and food drying are offered, including the Brooklyn Botanic Garden Handbook manuals.

The catalog includes a guide to hardiness zones to help you make selections appropriate to your area and a statement of the terms of the warranty covering plant orders.

Special Factors: Authorized returns are accepted (a restocking fee of 10% may be charged); minimum order is $10 with credit cards.

J.E. MILLER NURSERIES, INC.

**5060 WEST LAKE RD.
CANANDAIGUA, NY
14424
716/396-2647**

Catalog: free
Save: up to 50%
Pay: check, MO, MC, V, AE
Sells: plants, shrubs, trees, and nursery stock
Store: same address; Monday through Friday 8–4:20 (seven days during the spring)

 $$$ ✉ ☎

A full range of plants, seeds, bulbs, shrubs, and trees is offered in Miller's spring and fall color catalogs. Savings run up to 50% here, compared to prices charged by nurseries and garden supply centers. Miller Nurseries has been in business for generations, and publishes a sale catalog each fall that features real bargains.

The comprehensive selection includes russet apple, golden plum, black grape, red raspberry, blueberry, cherry, strawberry, and dozens of other fruit and nut trees, plants, and vines. Shade trees are offered, including poplar, locust, maple, and ash; and there are plants for the vegetable garden and some common flower bulbs as well. Garden equipment (pruners, animal repellent, soil additives, mulch sheeting, etc.) is also offered. The catalog includes horticultural tips, and each order is sent with Miller's 32-page planting guide. This firm has gotten rave reviews from several readers of this book, who praise Miller's service and prices.

Special Factors: Trees and shrubs are sent as plants, guaranteed to grow; minimum order is $10 with credit cards.

NATIONAL ARBOR DAY FOUNDATION

100 ARBOR AVE.
NEBRASKA CITY, NE
68410

Information: inquire
Save: 33% plus
Pay: check, MO, MC, V, AE
Sells: trees, plants, bulbs, etc.
Store: mail order only

$$$ ✉

The first Arbor Day was marked in Nebraska in 1872, when a newspaper editor petitioned the Board of Agriculture to designate a day for planting trees. Arbor Day is now celebrated in every state in the Union, and in over a dozen other nations. The Arbor Day Foundation exists to encourage tree planting and tree care, which it does in the most direct way: by selling trees (bare-root stock) at prices that are at least one-third lower than those charged by many nurseries. A membership costs $10, at this writing.

Among its other benefits, membership in the Foundation entitles you to the bimonthly publication, *Arbor Day,* and a copy of "The Tree Book," a catalog/guide to plant identification and cultivation. "The Tree Book" shows scores of shade and ornamental trees, flowering shrubs and trees, hedges, fruit trees, nut trees, evergreens, and evergreen windbreaks. All of these may be ordered from the Foundation, and bulbs and other goods are also available.

Please note: Fall plant shipments are made between October 15 and December 10, and spring shipments are made between February 1 and May 31. Plants are *not* shipped to Alaska, Hawaii, California, or Arizona.

Special Factor: All horticultural products are guaranteed to grow.

NOR'EAST MINIATURE ROSES, INC.

58 HAMMOND ST.
ROWLEY, MA 01969
800-426-6485

Catalog: free
Save: up to 30%
Pay: check, MO, MC, V
Sells: miniature roses
Store: same address; also 955 West Phillips St., Ontario, CA; Monday through Friday 8-4, both locations

$$ ✉

Nor'East publishes a 16-page catalog of its specialty, miniature roses, which are priced at $4.95 each, compared to over $7 for the same varieties sold elsewhere. (Nor'East does not tack on a per-plant handling fee, as do some of its competitors.)

The firm sells dozens of types of miniature bush roses, including micro-minis (4" to 8" tall at maturity), climbers, and tree roses (miniatures budded to understocks). The varieties are grouped by colors, which include reds, pinks, yellows, oranges, apricots, whites, mauves, and blends. Among the fancifully named specimens are old favorites and new entries: Happy Go Lucky, Jim Dandy, Cupcake, Party Girl, Holy Toledo, Puppy Love, and Sunny Day, to name a few. The catalog descriptions include height of the mature plant, blooming pattern and coloring, scent, suitable growth situations, and other information.

Nor'East offers quantity discounts and specially priced bonuses for large orders. "We pick 'em" collections are also offered—prices drop to $3.79 per plant if you let the firm make the selection. Nor'East offers other collections, including easy-to-cultivate choices, fragrant types, and a begin-ners' kit that includes pots and potting mix. Planting and care directions are sent with each order. A selection of small vases and Sean McCann's book on miniature roses are also sold.

Special Factors: Returns of plants that fail to perform are accepted within 90 days for replacement; minimum order is $20 with credit cards.

PARK SEED CO.

**COKESBURY RD.
GREENWOOD, SC
29647-0001
803/223-7333**

Catalog: free
Save: up to 50%
Pay: check, MO, MC, V, AE
Sells: seeds, bulbs, garden equipment, etc.
Store: mail order only

$$$$ ✉   ☎

We took an informal survey among our gardening friends, and discovered that several of them relied upon Park for all their growables. As one woman put it, the quality and reliability of Park's stock makes it a best buy among the big mail-order seed and bulb companies.

This venerable firm (established in 1868) has a broad range of flower and vegetable seeds—new varieties and old favorites—chosen for perfor-mance in the U.S. Herbs are another strong suit, and house plants and perennials are well represented. The thorough catalog descriptions include germination and cultivation information, and a 16-page gardening guide accompanies every order. Basic gardening tools and propagating devices are offered in every catalog. In addition to pricing its seeds and plants up to 20% below other firms offering the same quality, Park offers quantity discounts, early-order discounts, and bonuses.

Special Factors: Satisfaction is guaranteed; quantity discounts are available; returns are accepted within 1 year; minimum order is $20 with credit cards.

PINETREE GARDEN SEEDS

**NEW GLOUCESTER, ME
04260
207/926-3400**

Catalog: free
Save: up to 30%
Pay: check, MO, MC, V
Sells: seeds, bulbs, and garden equipment
Store: same address; see catalog for map and current hours

Pinetree Gardens was established in 1979 to provide home gardeners with the seeds they wanted in small packets suitable for kitchen gardens. The firm has exceeded its goal, offering kitchen gadgets, gardening tools and supplies, books and other useful goods.

Pinetree's strength is the seeds that built the business—over 600 varieties of vegetable and flower seeds, of which just a handful are treated. Of special interest are the "vegetable favorites from around the world," including radicchio, fava beans, snow peas, entsai, burdock, flageolet, cardoons, epazotes, and chiles. You'll also find plants and tubers for shallots, asparagus, berries, and potatoes. The flower section features seeds, tubers, and bulbs for annuals, perennials, everlastings, and wildflowers.

The tools and equipment run from kitchen and canning helps to hand tools to the well-priced "Easylink" watering system from Suncast. Fertilizers, small greenhouses, Havahart traps, netting, and related goods are offered. Over 30 pages of the catalog are devoted to books, including some of the classics of gardening literature, cookbooks, garden planners, the Garden Way Country Wisdom bulletins, and handbooks published by the Brooklyn Botanic Garden. Prices are quite competitive, and even the 25¢ seed packets are backed by Pinetree's ironclad guarantee of satisfaction.

Canadian and non-U.S. readers, please note: The catalog costs U.S.$1.50 if sent to a non-U.S. address.

Special Factors: Satisfaction is guaranteed; returns are accepted for exchange, refund, or credit; orders are shipped worldwide.

PRENTISS COURT GROUND COVERS

P.O. BOX 8662
GREENVILLE, SC
  29604-8662
803/277-4037

Brochure: 50¢
Save: up to 50%
Pay: check, MO, MC, V
Sells: live ground-cover plants
Store: mail order only

$$$ ✉ ☎

Here's an attractive, labor-efficient alternative to a conventional lawn—ground cover. Prentiss Court, established in 1978, offers a wide range of plants at up to 50% below nursery prices. Spacing and planting guides are included in the brochure; the illustrations are minimal.

The broad selection of plants here includes ajuga, crown vetch, daylilies, Boston ivy, Euonymus fortunei, fig vine, English ivy and other Hedera helix, Japanese honeysuckle, St. Johnswort, jasmine, phlox, liriope and sedum, and Vinca major. The plants are sold bare-root and/or potted, at an average price of 50¢ each. The brochure includes tips on planting and caring for ground covers.

Special Factors: Shipping is included; minimum order is 50 plants of the same variety.

ROSEHILL FARM

GREGG NECK RD.
GALENA, MD 21635
301/648-5538

Catalog: free
Save: 30% average (see text)
Pay: check, MO, MC, V
Sells: miniature roses
Store: same address; Monday through
  Saturday 9–4

$$$ ✉ ☎

Rosehill Farm has been selling miniature roses since 1979 and brings out new varieties each year. The color catalog shows the standard-size minis, sweetheart sizes, micro-minis, climbers, and hanging basket types, including white, blush, yellow, gold, apricot, mauve, pink, orange, and red varieties. The catalog descriptions note special characteristics of each plant, height of the mature plant, suitable growing situations, color, and other useful information.

Rosehill's prices average about 30% below those of miniature roses we priced in local nurseries and other garden catalogs. Quantity discounts of 10% are given on orders of ten or more plants (15% on 15 or more). Real wholesale prices are available to not-for-profit organizations, nurseries, and garden centers. (Request the wholesale price list on your company letterhead.)

Special Factors: Quantity discounts are available; returns with tags are accepted within 60 days for replacement; minimum order is $20 with credit cards.

TURNER GREENHOUSES

P.O. BOX 1260
GOLDSBORO, NC 27530
919/734-8345

Catalog: free
Save: up to 35%
Pay: check, MO, MC, V
Sells: greenhouses and accessories
Store: mail order only

Turner has been making greenhouses since 1957 and offers three basic models with a choice of options. Turner's prices average 25% less than the competition, although we found two very similar greenhouses in other catalogs selling for 35% more.

Turner's greenhouses include a 7'-wide lean-to, and two freestanding models, 8' and 14' wide. The greenhouses come equipped with a ventilating system and aluminum screen door, and each can be expanded in length in 4' increments. You can choose from a polyethylene cover (6 mil), or fiberglass (warrantied for 20 years). Turner also sells electric and gas heaters, exhaust fans and air circulators, cooling units, greenhouse benches, thermometers, misters, sprayers, and insecticides. Don't miss the well-chosen books on composting, organic gardening, greenhouse growing, herb cultivation, and similar topics.

Special Factors: Satisfaction is guaranteed; authorized returns in original condition are accepted within 30 days for refund or credit (less freight); minimum order is $10.

K. VAN BOURGONDIEN & SONS, INC.

P.O. BOX A
BABYLON, NY 11702
516/669-3523

Catalog: free
Save: up to 40%
Pay: check, MO, MC, V, AE, DC
Sells: Dutch and domestic flower bulbs and plants
Store: mail order only

$$$ ✉   ☎

The spring and fall catalogs from Van Bourgondien offer a wealth of vegetation for home, lawn, and garden at up to 40% less than other suppliers. Both 64-page editions include hosta and hybrid lilies, ground covers, a wide range of flowers, and supplies and tools. This well-respected firm was founded in 1919.

Past fall catalogs have shown tulip, daffodil, hyacinth, iris, crocus, narcissus, anemone, allium, fritillaria, and other bulbs. Geraniums, delphiniums, shasta daisies, tiger lilies, lavender, flowering house plants, foxtails, black-eyed Susans, wildflowers, native ferns, and other greenery and flowers are usually offered. And if you can't wait for the thaw, you can buy prepotted lilies of the valley, Aztec lily, paperwhites, amaryllis varieties, and crocus bulbs, which can be forced. The spring catalog features house plants, herbs, carnivorous plants, begonias, dwarf fruit trees, shade trees and shrubbery, berries, grape vines, ground cover, nut trees, rhubarb, shallots, artichokes, and similar goods. Bulb planters, plant supplements, grow pots, potting benches, gardening gloves, and other accessories are offered as well.

Special Factors: Goods are guaranteed to be "as described" and to be delivered in perfect condition; early-order and quantity discounts are available; bonuses are offered with large orders.

SEE ALSO

Arctic Glass & Window Outlet • glass panels for cold frames, greenhouses • *HOME: MAINTENANCE*
Central Michigan Tractor & Parts • used and reconditioned parts for tractors and combines • *AUTO*
Clothcrafters, Inc. • knee pads, gardening aprons, and porous plastic sheeting • *GENERAL MERCHANDISE*

Dairy Association Co., Inc. • liniment for livestock • *ANIMAL*
Daleco Master Breeder Products • kits for yard ponds • *ANIMAL*
Manufacturer's Supply • replacement parts for lawnmowers, rototillers, trimmers, tractors, etc. • *TOOLS*
Northern Hydraulics, Inc. • trimmers, NorTrac tractors, lawnmower parts, etc. • *TOOLS*
A.W.G. Otten and Son • wooden shoes and clogs for gardening • *CLOTHING: FOOTWEAR*
Fred Stoker and Sons, Inc. • sweet potato plants and tobacco seeds • *CIGARS*
That Fish Place • live aquarium plants • *ANIMAL*
WearGuard Corp. • chore coats, overalls, work clothes, shoes, etc. • *CLOTHING*
Zip Power Parts, Inc. • lawnmower parts • *TOOLS*

FOOD AND DRINK

━━━━━━

Foods, beverages, and condiments

Herbs, spices, coffee, and tea are mail-order naturals, and all are available through the firms listed here. But these sources also offer you caviar and Italian truffles, Mexican and Lebanese foods, giant pistachio nuts, Vermont maple syrup at below-supermarket prices, and much more—at savings that run to 80%.

Most of the mail-order food purveyors listed here cater to gourmet and exotic tastes, but one cannot live by lotus-flavored tea alone. We found *The Goldbecks' Guide to Good Food* (New American Library, 1987) to be a fascinating and useful guide to everyday food shopping—from supermarkets to mail-order sources. Written by Nikki and David Goldbeck (authors of *The Supermarket Handbook*), it covers nutrition bugaboos and the vocabulary of labeling and mislabeling and includes extensive information on the organic market and additives and a wealth of other enlightening information on food. It's not a cookbook, though; for the best, all-purpose cookery manual, we still turn to *The Joy of Cooking* (Bobbs-Merrill Company, 1975), by Irma S. Rombauer and Marion Rombauer Becker. It's valuable for the comprehensive hows and whys of cooking, and the sensible recipes, but it's also the book you'll turn to time and again to find out how to handle "new" foods, such as millet, loquats, cardoons, and pigeon. The book's "Know Your Ingredients" sections are a home-ec course in themselves. And another cookbook caught our attention for its ferocious commitment to thrift without sparing pleasure: *Cooking for All It's Worth* (McGraw-Hill Book Company, 1983), by Jay Jacobs, who's written for *Gourmet* magazine for many years. Mr. Jacobs takes the kitchen and its contents in hand, wresting everything possible from every bit of food, albeit with style. Even if you're not up to following his lead and making stock and soups from scratch, the approach—and the recipes—may be inspiring.

Getting the most nutrition from your food dollars isn't easy, but *Nutrition Action Healthletter* can help. This 16-page newsletter is published ten times a year by the Center for Science in the Public Interest (CSPI), which takes a consumerist/advocacy position on matters of nutrition and food safety/ A recent issue covers second thoughts on oat bran, heat-released carcinogens in microwave food packages, the cholesterol controversy, using vitamins to prevent birth defects, and the pros and cons of shelf-stablemeals. A subscription to the newsletter is a benefit of membership in CSPI, which also publishes nutrition-related posters, books, pamphlets, software, and videotapes. For information, write to Center for Science in the Public Interest, 1501 16th St., NW, Washington, DC 20036-1499.

Most of us do our food shopping in the supermarket, with an envelope of cents-off coupons in hand. If you redeem coupons frequently, you may be interested in the "Thrift Coupon Exchange" program, one of the benefits of membership in the *Consumer Thrift Club*. You select your favorites from a listing of over 1,000 name-brand products, pay a fee, and the Thrift Club sends you coupons with a face value over three times the fee. (Complimentary order sheets worth up to $50 in coupons are included with your membership.) For more on Consumer Thrift Club, see the listing in "General."

If, like millions of Americans, you begin your day with a steaming cup of java or enjoy a tall glass of iced tea on a hot summer afternoon, don't miss *The Book of Coffee and Tea,* by Joel, David, and Karl Schapira (St. Martin's Press, 1982). The Schapiras started their coffee and tea business in 1903 and are experts on both beverages. In addition to a stimulating account of the history, cultivation, and processing of each, the book includes a guide to the common and exotic varieties available, brewing and serving tips, and recipes. The book is listed in the firm's brochure, along with a superb selection of coffee and tea. For a copy of the brochure, send a long, self-addressed, stamped envelope to Schapira Coffee Company, 117 W. 10th St., New York, NY 10011.

When ordering foods, be mindful of the weather. Don't purchase such highly perishable or temperature-sensitive items as chocolate, soft cheese, fruits, vegetables, or uncured meats during the summer unless you have them shipped by an express service and plan to eat them immediately. (Most catalogs include caveats to this effect, and some firms will not ship certain goods during warm weather under any circumstances.)

Consider the firms listed here when making out gift lists—whether you choose a packet of rare herbs or a year of gustatory delights provided by an "of-the-month" program, your presents will be remembered long after they're consumed, and many of these companies offer the convenience of direct shipment to the fortunate friend or relative. If you want to maximize your savings, choose a popular food gift such as pecans or dried fruit, buy it in bulk, and package it yourself!

WINE STORAGE AND SERVING EQUIPMENT

It's expeditious to stock your wine cellar or bar by going to local sources, rather than buying by mail, and adventurous oenophiles will enjoy the extensive sampling required to find good wine buys. It's helpful to patronize a local wine merchant, who can help you to choose wines to suit your palate as well as your pocket. (If you're interested in concocting your own liqueurs or becoming a small-scale vintner, see the listing for *E.C. Kraus* in this chapter. The firm sells supplies and equipment for making beer and wine, as well as extracts that can be mixed with vodka to create cordials.)

Storing and serving wine properly require some basic equipment and tools. The storage area should be dark, cool (45 to 60 degrees F), and clean. The typical kitchen is the *worst* place for your wine rack. If you're unable to find a good spot in your house, you might consider purchasing a minicellar. *The Wine Enthusiast,* listed in this chapter, sells a variety of wine storage units and refrigerators, as well as wine-related accessories. *Bennett Brothers* (in the "General" chapter) sells a temperature-controlled unit, the "Wine Steward," for under $500; it holds up to 19 bottles and can be installed under a kitchen counter. Both *Renovator's Supply* (in the "Maintenance" section of "Home"), and *Plexi-Craft Quality Products* (in the "Furnishings" section) sell conventional wine racks.

Serving equipment is available from a number of firms. Corkscrews are sold by *E.C. Kraus* and *Mr. Spiceman* (in this chapter), which also sells whisks and other bar tools. Ice and champagne buckets are sold by both *Bennett Brothers* and *Plexi-Craft,* and we've never seen a catalog from *Grand Finale* (in this chapter) that *didn't* have cocktail napkins, glass coasters, and wine coasters. The "Table Settings" section of "Home" includes a number of firms that can supply the perfect wine glass (uncolored, uncut crystal), but if you're throwing a party, try these sources for napkins and disposable stemware: *The Paper Wholesaler,* in "General," and *Paradise Products,* in "Toys."

BATES BROS. NUT FARM, INC.

15954 WOODS VALLEY RD.
VALLEY CENTER, CA 92082
619/749-3333

Price List: free with self-addressed, stamped envelope
Save: up to 40%
Pay: check, MO, MC, V
Sells: nuts and dried fruits
Store: same address; Monday through Sunday 8–5

$$

"Nuts from all over the world meet here" proclaims the brochure from the Bateses, who grow some of what they sell. The nuts and other treats are generally priced below those of a number of Bates' competitors; our price checks showed possible savings of almost 50% on selected items.

Nuts are featured here—raw, roasted and salted, smoked, and saltless nuts of all types. You'll find the standard almonds, walnuts, peanuts, cashews, pecans, and mixes, as well as macadamia nuts, filberts, pignolias, sunflower seeds, and pistachios. The dried fruits include apricots, raisins, dates, papaya, figs, banana chips, pineapple, and other sweets, as well as coconut. These are the ingredients for trail mix, which the Bateses also sell ready-made, as well as granola, wheat germ snacks, popcorn, and old-fashioned candy—malted milk balls, English toffee, nut brittle, taffy, candy corn, and licorice ropes, among others. Glacé fruit is a new addition to the catalog: fruitcake mix, cherries, colored pineapple wedges, orange and lemon peel, and citron. Gift packs are available year-round.

Special Factor: C.O.D. orders are accepted.

CAVIARTERIA INC.

29 E. 60TH ST.
NEW YORK, NY 10022
800-4-CAVIAR
IN NY 212/759-7410
IN CA 213/285-9773
FAX: 718/482-8985

Catalog: free
Save: up to 65%
Pay: check, MO, MC, V, AE
Sells: caviar and gourmet foods
Store: same address; Monday through Saturday 9–6; also 247 N. Beverly Dr., Beverly Hills, CA

$$$

Caviarteria, established in 1950, is the largest distributor of caviar in the U.S. Take advantage of the super prices on all grades, as well as a great lineup of other gourmet fare, through the descriptive 16-page catalog (updated quarterly with newsletters). This family-run business is known for its prompt, friendly service.

Caviarteria stocks every grade of Caspian Beluga and Sevruga caviar (fresh and vacuum-packed), plus American sturgeon, whitefish, and salmon caviar, at prices that begin at about $15 per ounce for Kamchatka bottom-of-the-barrel vacuum-packed and run up to about $185 for 3-1/2 ounces of Imperial Beluga. We compared prices of Caviarteria's Beluga Malassol with those of another caviar-by-mail firm and found savings of 40% here. Even Caviarteria's unparalleled collection of caviar servers is offered for at least 20% off list.

The catalog lists other gourmet treats: whole sides of smoked Scottish salmon, salmon steaks, Norwegian gravlax, fresh pâtés, foie gras from Israel and France, tinned white and black Italian truffles, as well as candied chestnuts and many other delicacies. The Beverly Hills branch features chestnuts and many other delicacies. The Beverly Hills branch features sturgeon (delivered locally and shipped nationwide) and other food specialties and desserts prepared in the firm's commissary. Caviarteria also sponsors annual "caviar cruises" on luxury liners, and it has a corporate gift program.

Special Factors: Satisfaction is guaranteed; minimum order is $25 with credit cards; orders are shipped worldwide.

DEER VALLEY FARM

R.D. 1
GUILFORD, NY 13780
607/764-8556

Catalog: 50¢
Save: up to 40% (see text)
Pay: check or MO
Sells: organic and natural foods
Store: Rte. 37, Guilford, NY; Monday through Friday 8–5; 19B Ford Ave., Oneonta, NY; Monday through Friday 9:30–5:30, Thursday 9:30–8:30; and 64 Main St., Cortland, NY; Monday through Friday 9:30–5:30, Thursday 9:30–8:30

Deer Valley Farm is a respected name in organic and whole foods and has been in business since 1947. The firm sells whole grains, flours, cereals, baked goods, and nut butters. You can buy "organically grown" meats here at substantial savings: Hamburger, typically priced at $4.50 to $6 per pound in health food stores, costs $3.05 per pound here. Deer Valley also sells raw milk cheese, and the cheddar is only $3.40 to $4.79 per pound, less than some of the supermarket varieties. The only drawback here is the minimum order, $150, necessary to reap savings of 25% to 40% over regular retail prices. But if you get your friends together, you can meet that amount easily with a combined order—just be prepared for an impromptu feast when the cartons arrive!

Special Factors: Price quote by phone or letter with SASE; deliveries are made by Deer Valley truck in the New York City area (elsewhere by UPS); minimum order is $10, $150 for wholesale prices.

DUREY-LIBBY EDIBLE NUTS, INC.

P.O. BOX 345
CARLSTADT, NJ 07072
201/939-2775
FAX: 201/939-0386

Flyer: free
Save: up to 50%
Pay: check or MO
Sells: nuts
Store: mail order only

Durey-Libby, established in 1950, picks and processes "delicious fresh nuts you don't have to shell out a fortune for." You can't eat fancy tins, stoneware crocks, and rattan baskets, so if you're buying nuts, make sure you're paying for nuts.

Durey-Libby sells walnuts, pecans, cashews, almonds, macadamia nuts, pistachios, and cocktail mixes, packed in bags and vacuum tins. The prices are up to 50% less than those charged by gourmet shops and many food catalogs. The smallest units are three-pound cans, which will give you enough for cooking and snacking.

If you identify yourself as a reader of this book when you order, you may deduct 10% from your order total (computed on the cost of the goods only). This WBMC reader discount expires February 1, 1992.

Special Factors: Satisfaction is guaranteed; price quote by phone or letter with SASE on quantity orders; shipping is included on orders within the contiguous U.S.

GIBBSVILLE CHEESE SALES

W-2663 CTH-00
SHEBOYGAN FALLS, WI
53085
414/454-3242
414/564-2731
FAX: 414/564-6129

Price List: free
Save: up to 30%
Pay: check or MO
Sells: Wisconsin cheese, summer sausage, and T-shirts
Store: same address; Monday through Saturday 7:30–5 (7:30–6 in December)

$$$ ✚   (see text)

We happened to mention our plans to list Gibbsville Cheese Sales in this book to another Wisconsin food retailer, and were treated to a fusillade of praise for Gibbsville's high standards and superior products. (This is in Wisconsin, the Dairy State, where *everyone* produces cheese.) Moreover, the prices are appetizingly low—as little as $2.20 a pound for mild cheddar in five-pound bulk packaging.

Gibbsville makes the most popular kinds of cheese, including cheddar (mild, medium, aged, super-sharp white, garlic, and caraway), Colby (including salt-free), Swiss (baby, medium, aged, and lace), provolone, Muenster, Romano, mozzarella, Monterey Jack (including Jacks flavored with salami, hot pepper, dill, and vegetables), Gouda, Parmesan, flavored cheese spreads (including onion, salami, hot pepper, bacon, smoke, etc.), and blue, Limburger, and string cheeses. You can buy in "economy" boxes of two or ten pounds, or in bulk with as little as a pound. Five pounds of rindless Colby cost just $2.25 a pound at this writing, and other prices are comparable. The price list indicates which cheeses are "lower in fat," and includes several "lite" versions of favorites.

Gibbsville also offers several types of summer sausage and beef sticks, and has assembled nine well-priced gift packages for a variety of budgets and tastes.

Please note: Shipments are not made during summer months (approximately June through September).

Canadian readers, please note: Deliveries to Canada are made by UPS.

Special Factor: Price quote by phone or letter with SASE.

GRANDMA'S SPICE SHOP

P.O. BOX 901, DEPT. B
ELON COLLEGE, NC
27244
919/584-3616

Catalog: free
Save: up to 60%
Pay: check, MO, MC, V
Sells: herbs, spices, coffee, tea, etc.
Store: mail order only

$$$

There *is* a Grandma behind this shop; the catalog shows her, sitting in a rocking chair, in front of a display of cookie cutters. Frankly, it's hard to believe that this woman has assembled the contents of this catalog, one of the most sophisticated stock lists we've seen.

To wit: *Danish* breakfast coffee, Nougatine coffee (flavored with hazelnut oil), Jasmine tea from Fukien province, candied angelica, raspberry leaves, and peach butter are but a few of the uncommon brews and foodstuffs listed in the 16 pages. The inventory includes coffees (regular, flavored, and decaffeinated), loose teas (green, black, flavored, decaffeinated) and rare estate teas, Benchley teabags, a large herb and spice selection, potpourri blends and essential oils, cocoa, popcorn seasonings, McCutcheon preserves, and fruit-sweetened preserves. Spice racks, teapots, mortar and pestle sets, Belgian waffle irons, Rema bakeware, and Melitta travel sets are all available. The herbs and spices afford the best savings, up to 60% if bought in bulk (half or full pounds). Coffee and tea connoisseurs should see the catalog for the unusual and rare varieties (not sold at a discount).

Special Factors: Price quote by phone or letter with SASE; quantity discounts are available.

JAFFE BROS., INC.

P.O. BOX 636-W
VALLEY CENTER, CA
92082-0636
619/749-1133
FAX: 619/749-1282

Catalog: free
Save: up to 50%
Pay: check, MO, MC, V
Sells: organically grown food
Store: (warehouse) 28560 Lilac Rd., Valley Center, CA; Sunday through Thursday 8–5, Friday 8–3

$$$

Jaffe Bros., established in 1948, sells organically and naturally grown nuts, seeds, beans, butters, fruit, and honey through its 20-page catalog. The prices average 30% below comparable retail, but there are greater savings on certain items, and quantity discounts are offered on many goods.

Jaffe's foods and goods are marketed under the Jaybee label, and virtually all of the products are grown "organically" (without fumigants or poisonous sprays but with "nonchemical" fertilizers) or "naturally" (similarly treated but not fertilized). You'll save on wholesome foods here—dried peaches, Black Mission figs, Monukka raisins, papaya, dates of several types, almonds, pine nuts, macadamias, nut butters, brown rice, whole-wheat pasta, flours and grains, seeds for eating and sprouting, peas and beans, unheated honey, coconut, jams, juices, carob powder, salad oil, olives, mushrooms, herb teas, and much more. (Most of the produce is packed in five-pound units or larger.) The current catalog also lists natural and dehydrated mushrooms, sun-dried tomatoes, canned organically grown olives, organic spaghetti sauce, low-salt dill pickles and sauerkraut, organic whole wheat pasta, kosher maple syrup, salt-free organic tortilla chips, organic applesauce, and even a biodegradable peppermint-and-castile soap/shampoo. Jaffe also sells organic baby food, including several fruits and vegetables for infants and toddlers. If you'd like to bestow goodness upon a friend, be sure to see the group of gift assortments—nicely packaged selections of favorites, at reasonable prices.

Special Factors: Quantity discounts are available; authorized returns are accepted within 10 days; store is closed Saturdays; C.O.D. orders are accepted.

E.C. KRAUS WINE & BEERMAKING SUPPLIES

P.O. BOX 7850-WC
INDEPENDENCE, MO
  64053
816/254-7448

Catalog: free
Save: up to 50%
Pay: check, MO, MC, V
Sells: wine- and beer-making supplies
Store: 9001 E. 24 Hwy., Independence, MO; Monday through Friday 8–5:30, Saturday 9–1

$$$ ✉   ☎   ▀

E.C. Kraus, founded in 1967, can help you save up to half of the cost of wine and even more on liqueurs by producing them yourself. The firm's 16-page catalog features supplies and equipment for making your own beer, wine, and liqueurs, and even includes several beer recipes.

Kraus sells everything you'll need to produce your own beverages: malt and hops, fruit and grape concentrates, yeasts, additives, clarifiers, purifiers and preservatives, fruit acids, acidity indicators, hydrometers, bottle caps, rubber stoppers, corks and corkscrews, barrel spigots and liners, oak kegs, tubing and siphons, Mehu-Maya steam juicers, fermenters, fruit presses, dried botanicals, and much more. The T. Noirot extracts can be used to create low-priced liqueurs, and there are books and manuals to provide help if you want to learn more. If you're just getting started, you may find the Kraus "Necessities Box"—equipment and supplies for making five gallons of wine or four gallons of beer—just what you need.

Special Factors: Local ordinances may regulate production of alcoholic beverages; minimum order is $5 with credit cards.

THE MAPLES FRUIT FARM, INC.

**P.O. BOX 167
CHEWSVILLE, MD 21721
301/733-0777**

Catalog: free
Save: up to 50%
Pay: check, MO, MC, V
Sells: dried fruit, nuts, etc.
Store: 1875 Pennsylvania Ave.,
Hagerstown, MD; Monday through
Thursday 9–6, Friday 8–8, Saturday 8–5

$$$ ✉   ☎   🍁   ▀

The 16-page catalog of dried fruits, raw and roasted nuts, and sweets from Maples Fruit Farm may have few pictures, but the prices are mouthwatering—we found savings of 25% to 54% on the items we spot-checked.

The dried fruits include apricots, dates, pears, peaches, currants, and pineapple. (Fruits prepared with sulphur dioxide are clearly indicated in the catalog.) Raw and roasted (salted and unsalted) nuts are offered, including cashews, almonds, peanuts, pecans, macadamia nuts, filberts, black walnuts, and a number of others. We compared several food catalogs and found that two pounds of raw pecans from Maples were 50% less expensive than those from a specialty pecan source, roasted macadamia nuts were 25% cheaper at Maples than in another catalog, honey-roasted peanuts 54% less, and cashews, 30% less. Among sweets, maple-sugar leaves and Maryland grade-A amber syrup both cost about 40% less than those offered by competitors (who sold Canadian and New York state products). Maples Fruit Farm also offers reasonably priced trail mixes, gift baskets, tins of nuts, and 38 varieties of gourmet coffees.

Special Factor: Satisfaction is guaranteed.

MR. SPICEMAN

615 PALMER RD., DEPT. W-6
YONKERS, NY 10701-5769
914/961-7776

Catalog: $1, deductible
Save: up to 94%
Pay: check, MO, MC, V
Sells: herbs, spices, seasonings, and candy
Store: 227 Union Ave., New Rochelle, NY; Wednesday 1–5, Friday 8:30–5

$$$ ✉   ☎   🍁   ▬

Mr. Spiceman publishes a catalog that runs from soup to nuts, but is best known for great buys on herbs, spices, and other seasonings. Founded in 1965, this firm supplies restaurants, delis, and fine food outlets, as well as consumers, at savings that average from 40% to 60%.

The catalog lists over 130 herbs and spices, available in small and bulk packaging, including ground allspice, cayenne pepper, ground cumin, curry powder, paprika, and other basics. Mr. Spiceman sells such unusual and hard-to-find seasonings as achiote and juniper berries, as well as Perugina and Mon Cheri chocolates, Ferrero Rocher confections, Tic Tac mints, crystallized ginger, Haribo gummi bears, hard candies, Knorr soup and sauce mixes, Gravy Master flavoring, 4C products, Virginia Dare extracts and flavorings, and herb teas.

The prices are excellent, and Mr. Spiceman is bettering them for new customers. As a reader of this book, you may deduct 10% from your first order (computed on the goods total only). This WBMC reader discount expires February 1, 1992.

Special Factors: Call before visiting the retail location; minimum order is $25 with credit cards.

NORTHWESTERN COFFEE MILLS

**217 N. BROADWAY
MILWAUKEE, WI 53202
800-243-5283
414/276-1031**

Catalog: 50¢
Save: up to 40% (see text)
Pay: check, MO, MC, V
Sells: coffee, tea, herbs, and spices
Store: same address

$$$

If coffee is America's drink, Wisconsin may be harboring a national treasure. It's the home of Northwestern Coffee Mills, which set up shop in 1875 in a town better known for a different sort of brew. The people who run Northwestern know their beans and don't cut corners. They begin with top-quality Arabica, and roast each type of bean separately, to develop its optimum flavor. In the illuminating, 12-page catalog, the owners state that "we take good coffee seriously, yet we know that the purpose of our coffee is to help our customers enjoy themselves." (What a refreshing change from the usual dictates of connoisseurship that take all the *fun* out of the object of desire!) The catalog describes each of the blends, straights, dark roasts, and decaffeinated coffees, noting relative strength, body, aroma, and flavor. Among the blends are American Breakfast, Fancy Dinner Blend (a strong, after-dinner coffee), Mocha Java, a New Orleans chicory blend, and "Stapleton's 1875 Blend," a favorite of local restaurateurs that "stands up well when heated for hours on end." There are fancy straights, including Brazil Santos (when available), Costa Rica Jarrazu, Kenya AA, Colombia Excelso, and Sumatra Lintong, which we tried and preferred to a locally obtained Sumatra Mandheling for the dimension of the flavor and absence of a "twang." If you've been disappointed by rare coffees from other sources, consider sampling Northwestern's stock. Fully certified Jamaican Blue Mountain coffee from the Mavis Bank Estate is available, as well as estate-grown Java and Hawaiian Kona. Northwestern sells Colombian coffee that's been aged under its supervision for five years, and Yemen Mocha Mattari (the *real* mocha from Yemen), Celebes Kalosi, and other rare straight coffees. Decaf drinkers can choose from solvent-processed or water-processed blends and straights. Coffee filters for all types of drip and percolator systems are sold, including Chemex, Filtropa, and the Wisconsin-made "Natural Brew" unbleached filters. Braun and Krups grinders and coffee makers are also available.

Although known for its coffee, Northwestern maintains a premium tea department. The catalog describes how tea is grown and processed, tea grading, and the types of teas Northwestern sells: flavored, black, green, oolong, and decaffeinated. The varieties include Ceylon, Indian Assam, Indian Darjeeling, Irish Breakfast, Russian Caravan, Japan Sencha, "China Dragon Well Panfired Leaf," and Orange Spiced tea, among others. Last but not least, Northwestern sells herbs, spices, and other flavorings in supermarket sizes and in bulk. Several capsicums (peppers) are offered, and dried vegetables (garlic granules, horseradish powder, mushrooms, etc.), blended salt-free and salted seasonings, and natural extracts (vanilla, almond, cocoa, cinnamon, orange, etc.) are also listed. You can use these extracts, says Northwestern, to create flavored coffees (which it does not sell).

Northwestern's prices on single pounds of coffee or four-ounce packages of tea are market-rate, but the firm will sell to consumers at bulk rates—something other distributors of premium coffees are reluctant to do. A pound of Baker's Blend (a coffee made to complement the French pastries of a local bakery) costs $5.95; if you buy six one-pound packages, the price drops to $5.45; if you buy 24, each costs $4.70. You can save more by buying in bulk: A ten-pound bag runs $4.90 a pound, and the per-pound cost drops to $3.65 for 25 pounds. Since coffee in whole-bean form will keep well for several months in the freezer, it makes sense to order as much as you can store. Do sample before buying, though—order half a pound of the intended brew to make sure it's what you want. Don't overlook the bulk prices on tea, and the quantity discounts on paper filters.

Special Factors: Satisfaction is guaranteed; quantity discounts are available; returns are accepted within 1 year for exchange, refund, or credit; orders are shipped worldwide.

PENDERY'S INC.

**304 E. BELKNAP ST.,
DEPT. W
FT. WORTH, TX
76102-2296
800/533-1870
817/332-3871
FAX: 817/332-7236**

Catalog: $2
Save: up to 75%
Pay: check, MO, MC, V, AE
Sells: herbs, spices, and Mexican seasonings
Store: same address; Monday through Friday 8:30–5:30, Saturday 9–5

Pendery's, formerly known as Mexican Chile Supply, has been spicing up drab dishes since 1870, and can add the authentic touch of real, full-strength chiles to your Tex-Mex cuisine for a fraction of the prices charged by gourmet shops.

The firm's 32-page catalog describes the origins of the company and its contributions to the development of Tex-Mex chile seasonings. It's not a coincidence that "those captivating capsicums" occupy three catalog pages and include pods, ground peppers, and blends. Scores of general and specialty seasonings and flavorings are offered, including fajita seasoning, jalapeño peppers, and spice-rack standards from allspice to white pepper. Among the unusual or hard-to-find ingredients available here are masa harina, Mexican chocolate, annatto, horseradish powder, Worchestershire powder, dehydrated cilantro, corn shucks for tamales and cornhusk dolls, and dried diced tomatoes. Prices of the spices are far lower than those charged by gourmet stores and supermarkets—up to 75% less on some of the specialty seasonings.

The catalog also offers handsome, handblown Mexican glassware, dried flowers and other potpourri ingredients, and related gifts.

Special Factor: Price quote by phone or letter with SASE.

SAN FRANCISCO HERB CO.

**250 14TH ST., DEPT. W
SAN FRANCISCO, CA
94103
800-227-4530
IN CA 800-622-0768
415/861-7174**

Catalog: free
Save: 50% plus
Pay: check, MO, MC, V
Sells: culinary herbs and spices and potpourri ingredients
Store: (wholesale outlet) same address; Monday through Friday 10–4

Reader-recommended San Francisco Herb is known for its excellent prices and selections of herbs, spices, potpourri ingredients, botanicals, and teas. This 18-year-old firm is primarily a wholesaler, but if you can meet the minimum order, you'll find San Francisco Herb a valuable source.

The culinary herbs and spices offered here range from the routine— allspice, cinnamon, marjoram, tarragon—to such uncommon seasonings as spice blends for Greek foods and cilantro leaf. The botanicals include alfalfa leaf, balsam fir needles, cornflowers, kelp powder, lavender, nettle leaf, orris root, pau d'arco, pennyroyal, spearmint leaf, and yerba maté, among dozens of others. (Some of the botanicals are suitable for consumption, while others are not; check with a reliable information source before ingesting botanicals in any form. The catalog notes which food items include sulfites.) Recipes for mulling spice blends, no-salt flavor enhancers, bouquet garni, and garam masala (a spice blend used in Indian cuisine) are given in the catalog.

The catalog also features dozens of recipes for different potpourris. San Francisco Herb has sent us recipe samples of "Hollyberry Christmas Jar Potpourri," which has a delectable scent and lovely combination of colors, and "Plantation Peach," which is delightfully fruity. If you're not experienced in making potpourri, we strongly recommend trying some of the recipes to become more familiar with blending colors and fragrances.

The spices and botanicals are sold by the pound (selected items are available in four-ounce units), with quantity discounts of about 10% on purchases of 25 pounds or more of the same item. San Francisco Herb also sells flavored teas in bulk, dehydrated vegetables, shelled nuts, sprouting seeds, and such miscellaneous food goods as arrowroot powder, bacon bits, and tapioca pearls. Prices of some of the items we checked were 70% below those of other sources, and satisfaction is guaranteed.

Special Factors: Satisfaction is guaranteed; quantity discounts are available; authorized returns are accepted within 15 days (a 15% restocking fee may be charged); minimum order is $30; C.O.D. orders are accepted.

SIMPSON & VAIL, INC.

P.O. BOX 309
38 CLINTON ST.
PLEASANTVILLE, NY
10570-0309
914/747-1336

Catalog: free
Save: up to 30%
Pay: check, MO, MC, V
Sells: coffees, teas, and brewing accessories
Store: same address; Monday through Saturday 9–5

$$ ✉   ☎   🍁   ▬

Simpson & Vail, established in 1929, sells gourmet coffees at prices up to 30% less than those charged by many New York City bean boutiques. Quarterly sales flyers are sent to current customers.

This firm offers over 50 coffees, including American (brown), French, Viennese, and Italian roasts, Kenya AA, Tanzanian Peaberry, Hawaiian Kona,

Sumatra Mandehling Kasho, and other straight coffees and blends. The water-process decaffeinated line includes American-style roast, espresso, mocha java, Tip of the Andes, and others. Coffee-making gear and supplies by Krups and Melitta are available.

The tea department features over 80 types, among them the classics of England and the East, blends, naturally flavored connoisseur teas (choco-late mint, almond, watermelon, coconut, etc.), and selected decaffeinated teas. You'll also find tea accessories—infusers and balls, strainers, and filters—as well as kettles, bone china mugs, tea cozies, warmers, canisters, tea bricks, and tea towels. The teapots are well chosen: the Jena glass teapot and matching warming stand, Rockingham and Stanley White pots in 2- to 16-cup sizes, a variety of pretty English pots with flowers and gold accents, and the 2-1/2-gallon Ming Tree teapot, for state occasions.

Simpson & Vail also stocks such temptations as butter cakes from Vermont, Scottish shortbread, fudge sauces, soups by Abbott's and Grant's, Canadian preserves, Indian chutneys, pickled Vidalia onions, and the delectable Dean & Deluca line of Italian foodstuffs and condiments.

Readers of this book may deduct 10% of the goods total from their first order only. Remember to identify yourself as a WBMC reader when you order. This WBMC reader discount expires February 1, 1992.

Special Factors: All beans are ground to order; gift packages are available; orders are shipped worldwide.

THE SPICE HOUSE

P.O. BOX 1633-W
MILWAUKEE, WI 53201
414/768-8799

Catalog: $1
Save: 35% average (see text)
Pay: check, MO, MC, V
Sells: seasonings
Store: 1048 N. Old World 3rd St., Milwaukee, WI; Monday through Saturday 10–5

The Spice House isn't just another seasonings emporium that offers bulk savings on herbs, spices, and blends. This family-run firm "grinds and blends our spices weekly to insure freshness," something no one else in the business seems to be doing. Moreover, The Spice House offers an extraordinary selection of items within categories—11 forms and types of cinnamon, for example. The firm, which was started in 1957, prices even one-ounce sizes of seasonings at below-supermarket rates, and offers savings of up to 40% on full pounds.

The informative, 24-page catalog begins with sweet California basil and ends with Tahiti vanilla beans. In between, you'll find Brady Street Cheese Sprinkle, Bicentennial "Rub" Seasoning (an early American blend), cassia buds from China, cardamom, chili peppers (rated for heat in Skoval units), tandoori chicken seasoning, fenugreek seeds, mulled wine spices, "Old World Seasoning," pot herbs for soups and stews, Spanish saffron, seasonings for salad dressings and homemade sausages, star anise, taco seasoning, French tarragon, and many other straight seasonings and blends. (Nearly three dozen are offered in salt-free versions, and there are is also a line of soup bases.) The descriptions include provenance, ingredients in the blends, and suggested uses.

Zassenhaus pepper mills and inexpensive jars for herb and spice storage are also available. The Spice House has also assembled some intriguing gift packages, including "Spicy Wedding," "Great Baker's Assortment," "Indian Curries," and a "Spice Replacement" set (when "the love of your life has left you taking all of your spices, maybe your house burned down or was just swept away by a tornado/hurricane"). If you can think of seasonings at times like these, you probably have the presence of mind to think of The Spice House.

Special Factors: Satisfaction is guaranteed; price quote by phone or letter with SASE; returns are accepted for exchange, refund, or credit; orders are shipped worldwide.

SULTAN'S DELIGHT, INC.

P.O. BOX 140253
STATEN ISLAND, NY
10314-0014
718/720-1557

Catalog: free with a stamped, self-addressed envelope
Save: up to 50%
Pay: check, MO, MC, V
Sells: Middle Eastern foods and gifts
Store: mail order only

$$ ✉ ☎ 🍁 🇺🇸

Authentic Middle Eastern food specialties are sold here at excellent prices—up to 50% below comparable goods in gourmet shops. Sultan's Delight was established in 1980.

Both raw ingredients and prepared specialties are offered, including the Near East and Sahadi lines of foods. See the catalog if you're looking for canned tahini, couscous, tabouleh, fig and quince jams, stuffed grapevine leaves, bulghur, green wheat, orzo, fava beans, Turkish figs, or pickled okra. Olives, herbs and spices, jumbo pistachios and other nuts, roasted chick peas, halvah, Turkish delight, marzipan paste, olive oil, Turkish coffee, fruit leather, filo, feta cheese, and other specialties are offered as well. Cookbooks for Greek, Lebanese, and Middle Eastern cuisine are available, as are gifts, belly-dancing clothing and accessories, musical instruments, cookware, and related items.

Sultan's Delight is offering readers of this book a 10% discount on their first order (computed on the goods total only). Identify yourself as a reader when you order. This WBMC reader discount expires February 1, 1992.

Special Factors: Price quote by phone or letter with SASE; minimum order is $15; orders are shipped worldwide.

ELBRIDGE C. THOMAS & SONS

RTE. 4, BOX 336
CHESTER, VT 05143
802/263-5680

Brochure: $1
Save: up to 50% (see text)
Pay: check or MO
Sells: Vermont grade-A maple syrup
Store: mail order only

$$ ✉ ☎ 🍁 🇺🇸

Mr. Thomas makes and sells the nectar of New England—pure, grade-A Vermont maple syrup. He's been in business since 1938, and his prices on large sizes are as much as 50% lower than those of his competitors—and even better than those charged for lesser grades of non-Vermont syrup.

The stock is pure and simple: Vermont maple syrup, grade A, available in half-pint, pint, quart, half-gallon, and gallon tins. Maple sugar cakes, which make irresistible gifts, are also offered (by special order only). The brochure includes a number of suggestions for using maple syrup in your favorite foods—maple milk shakes, maple ham, frosting, and baked beans are just a few examples.

Special Factors: Quantity discounts are available; prices are subject to change without notice; orders are shipped worldwide.

WALNUT ACRES

PENNS CREEK, PA 17862
717/837-0601

Catalog: free
Save: up to 40%
Pay: check, MO, MC, V
Sells: organically grown foods, natural
toiletries, cookware, etc.
Store: Penns Creek, PA; Monday through
Saturday 8–5

$$$ ✉ ☎ 🍁 ▬

Walnut Acres, in business since 1946, sells organically grown foods, nutritional supplements, cookbooks, and related items. Most of the goods are produced at the Farm, grown on "500 acres of chemical-free soil."

The Walnut Acres catalog has evolved from a closely printed stock list to a 48-page catalog that presents the bounty in full, appetizing color. In addition to canned fruits, vegetables, and beans, Walnut Acres offers grains, cereals, granola, bread and pancake mixes, flours, seeds and nuts, nut butters, soups, salad dressings, sauces, pasta, dried fruits, juices, honeys, and other goods. Herbs and spices, relishes, dehydrated vegetables, powdered milk, crackers, jams and preserves, cheeses, and baked goods are also offered.

The Farm sells nutritional supplements and some natural toiletries and unguents as well, and a lovely selection of cookware, bakeware, food preparation and storage equipment, and serving pieces.

Prices are not uniformly low, but most of those we spot-checked against two local health-food stores were at least 10% below the going rate for comparable items. We did find savings of 30% to 40%, however, on the Farm's dried fruits and nuts (compared to other mail-order sources). These were pound-for-pound comparisons; Walnut Acres sells its nuts, seeds, grains, cereals, and dried fruits in bulk packages (three and five pounds) at additional savings. We know of a couple with a standing order for the Farm's Black Mission figs and walnuts; in over a decade of doing business, they say they've never had a problem.

Special Factor: Products are guaranteed to be as represented.

THE WINE ENTHUSIAST

404 IRVINGTON ST.
P.O. BOX 39
PLEASANTVILLE, NY
  10570
800-356-8466
FAX: 914/747-0618

Catalog: free
Save: up to 40%
Pay: check, MO, MC, V, AE, Optima
Sells: wine storage units and accessories
Store: same address; Monday through
  Friday 9–5:30, Saturday 10–5

The Wine Enthusiast publishes a 40-page, color catalog of products to please the budget-conscious oenophile, from corkscrews and stemware to refrigeration units. The firm has been in business since 1980, and sells at discounts of up to 40% on list prices.

Wine storage units are the featured line here, including stained oak modular racks, brass and black enameled steel wall grids, cypress wall systems, and several lines of refrigerated cellars—Eurovare, Sommelier, and Vinotheque, among others. Carafes, stemware, corkscrews, ice buckets and coolers, and even books and videotapes on wine connoisseurship and history are available.

Special Factors: Satisfaction is guaranteed; returns (except food items, videotapes, and software) are accepted within 30 days for exchange, refund, or credit; orders are shipped worldwide.

WOOD'S CIDER MILL

RD #2, BOX 477
SPRINGFIELD, VT 05156
802/263-5547

Brochure: free with SASE
Save: up to 50% (see text)
Pay: check or MO
Sells: cider jelly and syrup
Store: mail order only

The Wood family has maintained a farm in Vermont since 1798 and today produces several wonderful treats for mail-order customers. The prices are better than reasonable—in fact, we found Wood's cider jelly selling in a well-known Vermont catalog at prices nearly twice as high as those charged by the Woods themselves! Put another way, the Woods charge about 50%

less than does the other firm, and buying from them directly gives you the chance to order other wonderful things.

The Cider Mill is best known for its jelly, which is made of evaporated cider. From 30 to 50 apples are needed to make the cider that is concentrated in just one pound of jelly, but you'll understand why when you taste it on toast or muffins or try it with pork and other meats as a condiment. Boiled cider is also available; it's a less-concentrated essence that is recommended as a base for a hot drink, as a ham glaze, and as a topping for ice cream and pancakes. For pancakes, however, our personal preference is the cider syrup, a blend of boiled cider and maple syrup. (We've also had outstanding success basting Thanksgiving turkeys, and even roast chicken, with it.) Straight maple syrup, also produced on the farm, is available in limited quantities. Even the farm's sheep contribute to the offerings: natural and black two-ply yarns are sold through the brochure as well.

Special Factors: Satisfaction is guaranteed; returns are accepted for exchange or refund; quantity discounts are available; orders are shipped worldwide.

SEE ALSO

Cabela's Inc. • freeze-dried foods, trail packs • *SPORTS*

Campmor • dehydrated camping food, beef jerky, etc. • *SPORTS*

Caprilands Herb Farm • live and dried herbs, herbal vinegars, and teas • *FARM*

A Cook's Wares • gourmet vinegars, mustards, and other foods and condiments • *HOME: KITCHEN*

New England Cheesemaking Supply Co. • cheese-making supplies and equipment • *HOME: KITCHEN*

The Paper Wholesaler • catering supplies, restaurant paper goods, disposable tableware • *GENERAL MERCHANDISE*

Plastic BagMart • plastic food storage bags • *HOME: MAINTENANCE*

Protecto-Pak • zip-top plastic bags • *HOME: MAINTENANCE*

Fred Stoker and Sons, Inc. • popcorn and table syrup • *CIGARS*

Triner Scale • pocket scale • *OFFICE*

Weston Bowl Mill • sugar buckets and butter churns • *GENERAL MERCHANDISE*

Zabar's & Co., Inc. • gourmet foods and condiments • *HOME: KITCHEN*

GENERAL MERCHANDISE, GIFTS, AND BUYING CLUBS

Buying clubs and firms offering a wide range of goods and services

Most firms listed in this chapter offer such a wide range of products that it might be confusing to put them elsewhere. So you'll find a potpourri of companies here, selling everything from mosquito netting to archival-quality document boxes. All of them offer good savings, including the mail-order giants, Bennett Brothers, Spiegel, and Sears. Bennett and Sears can be considered discount houses, and if you place regular orders with Spiegel, you'll receive sale catalogs with savings of up to 60% on many of the goods. Their service departments are first-rate, so buying and delivery—and returns, if needed—should be hassle-free. Go through the other listings carefully; there are some real finds here and countless answers to the question of what to give for Christmas, birthdays, anniversaries, and other occasions.

Shopping is much more convenient through 800 lines, but there's a lot more available through toll-free numbers than merchandise, including travel and lodging reservations, banking and investment assistance, product information and advice, and a wide range of services. We find the *AT&T Toll-Free 800 Consumer Directory* a big help in finding 800 numbers quickly; it has over 50,000 listings, in categories ranging from accountants to yarn. The current edition costs $9.95 (plus sales tax and handling), and can be ordered by calling 800-451-2100.

AMERICAN ASSOCIATION OF RETIRED PERSONS

1909 K ST., N.W.
WASHINGTON, DC 20049
202/872-4700

Information: inquire
Save: up to 40% (see text)
Pay: check, MO, MC, V
Sells: membership (see text)
Store: mail order only

$$$

You've probably seen the TV ads for the American Association of Retired Persons, a not-for-profit, nonpartisan organization dedicated to improving the lives of older Americans, especially in the realm of good health care. Membership is open to anyone aged 50 or older, retired or not, at a cost of just $5 a year. Among the benefits of membership are subscriptions to the bimonthly *Modern Maturity* and the monthly *AARP News Bulletin,* the opportunity to buy low-cost supplemental health insurance, participation in AARP Federal Credit Union, the AARP Motoring Plan (affiliated with Amoco Motor Club), publications on health topics, discounts on hotels and car rentals, and access to a pharmacy-by-mail. (See the listing for Retired Persons Services in "Medicine" for more details.)

When you write to the AARP for membership information, you may wish to request the group's publication, "Prescription for Action." This is a 68-page guide to approaching health care issues on a collective, community level. It gives guidelines and ideas for conducting price-comparison surveys of prescription drugs, compiling directories of physicians in your area who accept Medicare/Medicaid, cataloguing services for older persons, having a voice in government, and promoting proven alternative-care options and long-term home care. The book is a compendium of ideas, resources, and references—a must for all health-care activists.

Special Factor: Inquire for information.

BENNETT BROTHERS, INC.

30 E. ADAMS ST.
CHICAGO, IL 60603
312/263-4800
FAX: 312/621-1669
AND
211 ISLAND RD.
MAHWAH, NJ 07430
201/529-1900
FAX: 201/529-7855

Catalog: $5, redeemable
Save: up to 40%
Pay: check, MO, MC, V
Sells: jewelry, appliances, electronics,
luggage, furnishings, etc.
Store: in Chicago: Monday through Friday
8:15–5 (see the catalog for holiday
shopping hours); in New Jersey: Monday
through Saturday 9–5:30

Bennett Brothers has been doing business since the turn of the century, at which time a good deal of its trade was in jewelry, gems, and watches. Bennett's current offerings, shown in the annual "Blue Book," include giftware, leather goods, electronics, cameras, sporting goods, and toys.

The Blue Book is 450 color pages of name-brand goods, most of which make ideal gifts. In fact, the firm's "Choose-Your-Gift" program can be one of the easiest ways to deliver presents to employees and business associates. Two hundred pages of the catalog are devoted to jewelry—wedding and engagement bands, pearls, pins and bracelets, necklaces, and other pieces featuring all kinds of precious and semiprecious gems, as well as charms, lockets, medallions, anniversary jewelry, Masonic rings, and crosses and religious jewelry. Traditional and contemporary looks are both featured, in prices that start in the moderate range. The watch department offers models from Armitron, Benrus, Citizen, Jules Jurgensen, Pulsar, Seiko, and Timex.

Bennett Brothers offers a fine selection of clocks, timepieces, and weather instrument stations. Silverware and chests, a beautiful collection of silver-plated and sterling silver giftware, tea sets, pewterware, and fine china are also sold. The catalog shows kitchen cutlery sets, cookware sets, small kitchen appliances, microwave ovens, barbecue grills, vacuum cleaners, air machines, exercise equipment, sewing machines, personal-care appliances, bed linens, towels, tablecloths, and luggage. The leather goods department is especially good, including briefcases and attaché cases and luggage from American Tourister, Elco, Monarch, Samsonite, and Winn.

The Blue Book also features a large group of personal electronics and office supplies—clock radios, portable cassette players, stereo systems and components, TVs and video equipment, phones and answering machines,

CB equipment, home security systems, Casio keyboards, cameras, projectors, telescopes, binoculars, microscopes, pens, globes, cash registers, calculators, typewriters, safes, files, and office furnishings. Bennett also sells home furnishings, including reproduction Victorian pieces, Couristan rugs, Douglas dinette sets, Lane chests, patio furniture, Stakmore and Kestell folding bridge tables and chairs, and other goods. Playskool toys are offered, as well as Bachman collectors' trains, Cox radio-controlled cars and planes, playing cards, and board games. There are also golf clubs, basketballs, volleyballs and nets, gun cabinets, hunting knives, fishing rods, bocce ball and croquet game sets, dart boards, and sleeping bags. Metal detectors, flashlights and emergency beams, weathervanes, lawn-mowers, chain saws, and other power and hand tools are offered.

Bennett's prices are listed next to "suggested retail" prices throughout the book. After comparing prices of several types of goods, we concluded that Bennett's guideline prices (suggested retail) are fair and reliable. On that basis, we found that you can save between 30% and 40% here.

Special Factor: Authorized returns are accepted within 10 days for exchange or credit.

CHISWICK TRADING, INC.

33 UNION AVE.
SUDBURY, MA 01776-0907
800-322-7772
FAX: 508/443-8091

Catalog: free
Save: up to 35%
Pay: check, MO, MC, V, AE
Sells: resale packaging
Store: mail order only

Chiswick, "America's Leading Supplier of Poly Bags," boasts an inventory of 750 million of them. They come in sizes from 2-1/2" by 3" to 60" by 60", in zip-top styles and plain, for home and business packaging. Chiswick also sells paper and plastic shopping bags, gift boxes, bubble packaging and other shipping room supplies and equipment, poly film, antistatic packaging, labels, warehouse equipment, and related products. The prices on bulk orders drop by over 50%, and the selection of bag sizes and styles is hard to beat.

Chiswick is offering readers of this book a 15% discount on the *second* order placed with the firm. The discount applies to the cost of the goods only. This WBMC reader discount expires February 1, 1992.

Special Factors: Satisfaction is guaranteed; minimum order is $50.

CLOTHCRAFTERS, INC.

P.O. BOX 176, DEPT.
 WM91
ELKHART LAKE, WI
 53020
414/876-2112

Catalog: free
Save: up to 40%
Pay: check, MO, MC, V
Sells: home textiles
Store: mail order only

$$$

This firm, established in 1936, sells "plain vanilla" textile goods of every sort, from cheesecloth by the yard to flannel patches for cleaning guns. You'll find no logos or mottos anywhere, and there are many inexpensive, useful items.

The 16-page catalog offers a host of practical household goods: pot holders, red and white dish towels, chefs' hats, bouquet garni bags (12 for $3), salad greens bags, fabric coffee filters, striped denim place mats, cotton napkins ($9 per dozen), hot pads, and aprons. Clothcrafters has expanded its selection of well-priced kitchen tools, which include copper bowls, parchment paper, rubber spatulas, oven gloves, nut choppers, vegetable peelers, and other handy utensils.

You'll also find laundry bags, tote bags, flannel shoe bags, woodpile covers and firewood carriers, garment bags, cider-press liners, flannel polishing squares, and mosquito netting. The bed and bath department offers cotton duck shower curtains, lightweight cotton terry towels and bath wraps, terry tunics, beach mats, barbers' capes, cotton flannel sheets, pillowcases, sleeping bag liners, and crib sheets. Cloth diapers are also available. Textile artists should appreciate this source, since many of these items can be painted, embroidered, dyed, and otherwise embellished.

Gardeners will find the "PlyBan" porous plastic sheeting ideal for protecting newly planted rows from frost and insects ($8 for 4' by 50'). If you garden during the high insect season, you might want to add the mosquito-netting helmet to your order. While you're at it, consider the multipocketed apron—it has places for the trowel, seed packets, string, and all those stones that turn up. And don't overlook the denim knee pads—they fasten with Velcro, and are machine washable.

Canadian readers, please note: Only U.S. funds are accepted.

Special Factors: Satisfaction is guaranteed; shipping and insurance are included on orders over $15; returns are accepted for exchange, refund, or credit.

CONSUMER THRIFT CLUB

P.O. BOX 9394
MINNEAPOLIS, MN 55440
800-562-8888

Information: inquire
Save: up to 50%
Pay: check, MO, MC, V
Sells: memberships in buying club
Store: mail order only

$$$ ✉ ☎

The Consumer Thrift Club can help you save on everything from dog food to your next car through its various programs. Membership costs $49.95 per year, which can be recouped almost immediately through the "Coupon Exchange." (Membership comes with vouchers that allow you to request $50 in face-value coupons for name-brand foods, cleaning products, and health and beauty aids. After claiming your free allotment, you can order new supplies at a cost under one third the face value.)

Couponing is a great way to save nickels and dimes, but CTC membership gives you much more: prescription-filling services at a discount, savings on general merchandise (appliances, electronics, home furnishings, computers, jewelry, musical instruments, and even tapes and CDs), savings on United Van Lines services and Ryder truck rentals, real estate broker referrals, a 15% discount at Pearle Vision Centers, car pricing and dealer referral services, and travel planning services. Discounts on car rentals from several agencies are possible, as well as savings on hotel accommodations (through the Quest program), and even a 5% rebate on travel booked through the CTC travel agency. Membership includes the quarterly, *Thrift,* which features an updated list of coupons, specials on household appliances and gifts available through CTC, and articles on saving time and money.

CTC does not warehouse products itself, but has arrangements with different vendors to provide goods and services. (Please note that CTC derives no financial benefit from the sale of products or services—except memberships—and has no commission arrangements with the vendors.) We feel it only fair to mention the fact that the mail-order drugstore used is America's Pharmacy, the car pricing and dealer referral service is Car/Puter, and the vendor for pianos and organs is Altenburg Piano House. These firms are listed in this book, but your savings may be improved by buying from them as a CTC member. (For example, your first Car/Puter printout is free as a CTC member, and subsequent printouts cost $18 instead of the usual $20.) The CTC staff can answer any questions you may have about services and membership.

Special Factor: Inquire for information.

DAMARK INTERNATIONAL, INC.

7101 WINNETKA AVE. N.
BROOKLYN PARK, MN
55428
800-729-9000
FAX: 612/531-0380

Catalog: free
Save: 50% average
Pay: check, MO, MC, V, Discover
Sells: name-brand closeouts
Store: mail order only

$$$ ✉ ☎ ▬ (see text)

The monthly "Great Deal" catalog from Damark is packed with liquidation merchandise and manufacturers' overstock, which it sells at an average of 50% off original prices. We've ordered several items for the office from Damark since it began doing business in 1986, and have never had a problem with delivery or returns.

The current Damark catalog shows a Zenith 386 laptop computer that was originally tagged at $8,499 for $2,999, a Singer upright vacuum cleaner at half price, Sharp camcorders and Akai VCRs, Purofied goose-down comforters at fiberfill prices, roll-top teak cassette storage units for $19 each, Nautilus home exercise equipment, halogen lights, luggage, calculators, binoculars, and a variety of other goods. Detailed product information is included in the catalog descriptions, and Damark backs all sales with a guarantee of satisfaction.

Please note: Damark does not ship to P.O. Boxes, FPO addresses, or Canada.

Special Factors: Satisfaction is guaranteed; returns are accepted within 14 days for exchange, refund, or credit.

WALTER DRAKE & SONS, INC.

DRAKE BUILDING
COLORADO SPRINGS,
CO 80940
719/596-3854

Catalog: 25¢
Save: up to 40%
Pay: check, MO, MC, V, AE
Sells: stationery, notions, and household gadgets
Store: 4510 Edison Ave., Colorado Springs, CO; Monday through Friday 9–5

$$$

Walter Drake, established in 1947, publishes a 96-page catalog that offers a wide variety of useful items at very low prices. The quality is usually better than that of comparable items sold by other firms, and delivery and service are reliable as well.

Drake's return-address labels are one of the all-time bargains—$1.49 for 1,000. (Our local stationer was selling virtually identical gummed labels for $9.95 per box of 700.) The stationery line includes other moderately priced labels, notepads, business cards, correspondence paper and envelopes, and related goods. Drake's office items are especially useful for those who need small amounts, but who want to get "volume" prices. Our order of package mailing labels—a "generous 50"—numbered 56, and the per-label cost was about the same as the rate charged by a discount office supply firm for orders of 1,000 labels. (Please note: printed items are shipped individually, even if they're part of the same order.)

Kitchen gadgets, Christmas decorations, personalized accessories, grooming tools, toys, party goods and novelties, pet products, household organizers, energy savers, and other items are also offered regularly.

Special Factors: Satisfaction is guaranteed; do not request discounts on catalog prices.

GRAND FINALE

DEPT. NS 208
P.O. BOX 620049
DALLAS, TX 75262-0049

Catalog: $3, year's subscription, refundable
Save: up to 70%
Pay: check, MO, MC, V, AE, Discover
Sells: upmarket and name-brand goods
Store: mail order only

Your catalog fee brings you a year of "luxury for less," 48 pages (more in the holiday issues) of special purchases, clearances, and closeouts from gift houses and manufacturers. It's possible to save up to 70% on the original selling or list prices through Grand Finale.

Past catalogs have featured pearl earrings, hand-embroidered table linens, leather desk sets, cashmere mufflers, majolica teapots, needlepoint pillows, and Christmas decorations. Antique chinoiserie is shown in almost every catalog, as well as side tables, toys, Limoges bibelots, luggage, designer bed linens, cookware, and clothing for men and women. There's usually a sale section in the catalog featuring exceptional bargains; quantities of these items are limited, so order promptly. The quality is consistently high, and Grand Finale provides a gift boxing service ($1.75) and can forward presents to recipients directly.

Special Factors: Satisfaction is guaranteed; quantities may be limited, so order promptly; returns (except personalized and custom-ordered items) are accepted for exchange, refund, or credit.

LINCOLN HOUSE, INC.

**300 GREENBRIER RD.-
WBM91
SUMMERSVILLE, WV
26651
304/872-3000**

Catalog: free
Save: up to 40%
Pay: check, MO, MC, V
Sells: stationery, gifts, decorations, etc.
Store: mail order only

$$$

Lincoln House publishes a 48-page catalog of gifts, home accents, and stationery items that are offered at savings of up to 40% compared to goods of equal quality sold by other firms.

A recent catalog showed coordinated mug and place mat sets, brass candlesticks, scented candles, cloisonné jewelry, memo boards, ceramic picture frames, kitchen gadgets, and recipe files. Stationery, gift wrappings, paperweights, and similar goods are always available, and the themes are cute and whimsical. The fall catalog includes a good selection of holiday items: Christmas ornaments, decorations, candles, decorated cookie tins, gift bags, and cards.

Lincoln House rewards dedicated shoppers with discounts of about 20% on purchases of 6 to 15 items, and up to 40% if the purchase numbers 16 or more items. Most of the goods are made by the firm's parent company, Bright of America, which has been in business since 1964.

Special Factors: Satisfaction is guaranteed; shipping and insurance are included; returns are accepted.

NEW ENGLAND BASKET CO.

P.O. BOX 1335
N. FALMOUTH, MA 02556
508/759-2000

Brochure and Price List: free
Save: up to 50%
Pay: check, MO, MC, V
Sells: baskets
Store: mail order only

$$ ✉ ☎ 🍁

We've collected a small clutch of letters over the years from readers looking for good buys on baskets. New England Basket Co. sells a variety of baskets at prices up to 50% below those being charged by some national housewares chains.

The firm's four-page, color brochure shows the kinds of baskets that are stocked at our local import shop: Tightly woven willow baskets in round, oval, and square shapes; bamboo trays, picnic hampers, rustic rattan baskets, and "country" baskets with a wash of white or soldier blue were among over 100 shown. Dimensions are given, and there are three prices—for one set or piece, one case, and five cases. In addition to the obvious uses for baskets as decorative accents and a place for chips or rolls, don't overlook their possibilities as great gift containers, closet organizers, pet beds—the list is endless!

Special Factors: Price quote by phone or letter with SASE; quantity discounts are available; minimum order is $26.

THE PAPER WHOLESALER

795 N.W. 72ND ST.
MIAMI, FL 33150
305/285-9229

Catalog: $3
Save: up to 30%
Pay: check, MO, MC, V
Sells: party supplies, restaurant
disposables
Store: (cash and carry warehouse) 2638
S.W. 28th Lane, Coconut Grove, FL

$$ ✉ ☎

The Paper Wholesaler gives discounts of 30% on case lots of all kinds of party and entertaining supplies and related goods. The firm is affiliated with Graco Paper Co., in business since 1945.

The 32-page color catalog is chock-full of table goods, decorations, and the little things that add fun to festive occasions: paper plates and napkins in vibrant colors and snappy designs, including ensembles for children's birthdays, wedding parties, and showers; plastic cutlery and cups, tablecloths, doilies, balloons, crepe paper, party hats, streamers and pennants, favors, and other novelties. You'll find guest towels and toilet paper for the powder room, a good selection of candles, hors d'oeuvre picks and drink stirrers, cocktail napkins with amusing slogans, wrapping paper, gift bags, bows and ribbon, and invitations in upbeat designs and colors.

The Paper Wholesaler has a "serious" section for restaurateurs and caterers, which includes a selection of cake-decorating supplies, cake pans, deli and bakery containers, commercial-sized rolls of foil and poly film, ice scoops and bar tools, carafes, syrup pitchers, ash trays, and even the brooms, mops, and buckets you'll need when the guests are gone. Don't miss the selection of food—restaurant-sized containers of Pepperidge Farm Goldfish, Hellmann's mayonnaise, Orville Redenbacher popcorn, Planter's peanuts, and other condiments and snacks. The catalog includes tips on party planning, and the order form even features shopping lists so you don't overlook anything.

Special Factors: Satisfaction is guaranteed; returns of unopened, unused goods are accepted within 30 days for exchange, refund, or credit.

PUEBLO TO PEOPLE

1616 MONTROSE BLVD.,
  #5735
HOUSTON, TX 77006
713/523-1197

Catalog: free
Save: up to 40%
Pay: check, MO, MC, V, AE
Sells: handcrafts of Central and South America
Store: 1985 West Gray, Houston, TX; Monday through Thursday 10–6, Friday 10–7, Saturday 10–6, Sunday 12–5

Pueblo to People publishes a beautiful and fascinating catalog that is actually a mail-order cooperative, nearly half of whose proceeds go back to the people who produced its goods. Contrary to expectation, the prices here are quite low: We compared scarves, fabric, toys, jewelry, and other items to similar goods available in import shops in New York City, and found the Pueblo to People prices up to 40% less.

The catalogs feature handsome handcrafts and goods native to South and Central America—organic Peruvian coffee, Huichol beaded earrings, and a jointed mahogany bear are a few of the goods shown in one catalog we reviewed. Pueblo to People sells dozens of books and tapes on the culture and problems of these countries, and the catalogs include extensive discussions of farming, nutrition, health, food aid, and the economic realities of life. If you're interested in the issues, you'll find names and addresses of other not-for-profit assistance groups peppered throughout the catalog, which may be helpful in getting involved. But even if you go no farther than ordering a scarf or tote bag from Pueblo to People, it's nice to know that a good portion of the price goes to help those in need.

Special Factors: Satisfaction is guaranteed; returns are accepted for exchange, refund, or credit; C.O.D. orders are accepted.

ROCKY MOUNTAIN STATIONERY

**11725 CO. RD. 27.3
DOLORES, CO 81323
303/565-8230**

Samples and Price List: $1 with double-stamped, self-addressed envelope
Save: up to 50%
Pay: check or MO
Sells: handmade note cards
Store: Greenery, Durango, CO; daily 8 A.M.–9 P.M.

$$ ✉

This business is run by Rose Ruland, an artist who presses flowers and leaves from her garden and the surrounding wilds of the Rockies and uses them to create note cards. These are small and quite lovely, the flowers artfully arranged on pastel parchment card stock. Ms. Ruland also creates unusual oil "paintings" on cards; the sample we received was done with a good eye for color and design.

Rocky Mountain's "Nature" and "Just a Note" series are sold in collections of 12 in assorted colors, with envelopes. Each card collection costs $8.95, compared to $2 and up for *individual* cards of the same type sold in gift shops. Please note: Send $1 and a #10 double-stamped, self-addressed envelope for the samples and price list.

Special Factors: Satisfaction is guaranteed; returns are accepted.

SEARS, ROEBUCK AND CO.

233 S. WACKER DR.
CHICAGO, IL 60684
OR
4640 ROOSEVELT BLVD.
PHILADELPHIA, PA 19132
800-366-3000

General Catalog: $6, refundable
Save: up to 60%
Pay: check, MO, Discover
Sells: clothing, furnishings, appliances, etc.
Store: 800 stores and 2,300 order desks nationwide

$$$ ■

Does a direct-mail legend that at one time accounted for over 1% of the GNP really *need* an introduction? Six dollars brings you the latest Big Book from Sears (with a voucher for $5 off your next order), an inches-thick inventory of clothing, furnishings, maintenance equipment, and other home needs. Those looking for more extensive selections of uniforms, crafts supplies, cameras, toys, maternity and infant wear, home health-care equipment and supplies, power and hand tools, and appliances will find them in one of the "Specialogs" devoted to specialty merchandise. (Specialogs may be ordered through the Big Book.)

Sears' move into "everyday low pricing" has played to mixed reviews, but the values are good and the brands well represented. Black & Decker drills sit next to the Craftsman (Sears' brand) models, Whirlpool appliances alongside the Kenmores, and goods by Amana, AT&T, Bush, Casio, Levi, Pioneer, Pirelli, Samsonite, Sealy, Seiko, Spalding, Weber, Zenith, and other well-known manufacturers are featured in the Sears stores. Prices *are* low, often beating those of local discounters, and it's great to know you don't have to wait for a sale to save.

Special Factor: Specialogs are available free of charge in Sears stores.

SGF

SAVINGS ON GIFTS
** AND FURNISHINGS**
DEPT. DS 208
P.O. BOX 620047
DALLAS, TX 75262-0047

Catalog: $3, year's subscription, refundable
Save: up to 70%
Pay: check, MO, MC, V, AE, Discover
Sells: upmarket and name-brand goods
Store: mail order only

$$$ ♦

SGF, "Savings on Gifts and Furnishings," allows you to dress up your home and person and shower your friends with the finer things—indulgence costs you up to 70% less here. The $3 catalog fee buys a year of issues and is refundable with your first purchase.

SGF's 48-page color catalog, published seven times a year, is a treasury of gifts and home accents at real savings. A recent issue showed Karastan carpets, a Gucci shoulderbag and scarves, dressing table accessories, Limoges porcelain boxes, jade jewelry, a chinoiserie entertainment center, Wamsutta sheets, Italian earthenware, Russian lacquer boxes, antique Korean chests, a stunning wicker living room set, and leather attaché cases and luggage. The emphasis is on classical design and fine materials at the best prices.

Special Factors: Satisfaction is guaranteed; returns (except personalized goods) are accepted for exchange, refund, or credit.

SPIEGEL, INC.

**P.O. BOX 6340
OAK BROOK, IL
   60680-6340
800-345-4500**

Catalog: $3, refundable
Save: up to 50% (see text)
Pay: check, MO, MC, V, AE
Sells: clothing, home furnishings, electronics, etc.
Store: Chicago, Villa Park, Countryside, Arlington, and Downers Grove, IL; Monday through Saturday 8–4

$$$ ✉   ☎   ▬   (see text)

Spiegel sets the pace for fashion trends across the country and is the catalog of choice among a number of young mothers and businesswomen we know, who like it for after-work clothes and home accents. Spiegel runs sales frequently and sends sales catalogs to current customers. The firm was founded in 1865.

Spiegel's oversized catalogs offer stylish clothing and accessories for the whole family, distinctive home furnishings and decorative accents, and appliances and electronics. Laura Ashley sheets, jewelry, cashmere sweaters, Aigner shoes, French lingerie, leather jackets, custom window treatments, appliances designed for small spaces, and toys were among the offerings in a recent catalog. Savings can reach 50%, sometimes even more, in the regularly published sale catalogs. Good service and a hassle-free return policy have won Spiegel a loyal following.

APO/FPO readers, please note: Freight deliveries (affecting certain items) cannot be made to APO/FPO addresses.

Special Factors: Ordering from the "big book" usually guarantees later mailings of sale catalogs; returns are accepted for exchange, refund, or credit.

THAT'S A WRAP, INC.

1603 ORRINGTON AVE.,
  SUITE 1005
EVANSTON, IL 60201
708/475-0324
FAX: 708/475-0477

Brochure: free
Save: up to 30%
Pay: check, MO, MC, V
Sells: gift ribbon and stickers
Store: mail order only

$$ ✉ ☎ 🍁 ▆

That's a Wrap specializes in "Bow Magic" gift bows by 3M, and also sells stickers that are the perfect size for gift tags. The firm has been in business since 1983, and its prices are up to 30% below those of comparable goods sold in card shops.

That's a Wrap's big sellers are bows that are precut and looped, which you tweak into shape and affix to gifts with their own attached banding ribbons. There are several styles, in sizes from 2″ to 5″ across, for $2.50 and $3.50 for five. They're sold in a variety of colors, and special quantity packs are offered. The stickers have space for a written message, and can be used to label gifts, tins, jars, and other containers. They cost $2 for a set of ten, while stickers of the same size cost 35¢ to 50¢ each at our local gift shop. If you like the designs, these are good buys.

Special Factors: Minimum order is $10 with credit cards; orders are shipped worldwide.

UNIVERSITY PRODUCTS, INC.

517 MAIN ST.
P.O. BOX 101
HOLYOKE, MA 01041
413/532-9431
FAX: 413/532-9281

Catalog: free (see text)
Save: up to 40%
Pay: check, MO, MC, V, AE
Sells: archival-quality materials
Store: mail order only

$$$ ✉ ☎ 🍁 ▆

You may not know it, but anarchy reigns on your bookshelves, in the pages of your photo albums, and among the works of art on your walls. It's sad but true: Most of us store and display our precious belongings in materials and under conditions that damage them, sometimes irreparably.

Help is available from University Products, which publishes the comprehensive "Archival Quality Materials Catalog." University Products has been selling conservation and library supplies to institutions since 1968 and does business with preservation-minded individuals who want to protect their collectibles and other treasures. Unfortunately, the chemicals in wood-pulp paper cause it to yellow and become brittle and ultimately destroy books and documents. The gases emitted by conventional photo album pages can degrade the images of photographs and negatives. Both the materials used in display and storage and the conditions under which we keep them affect the long-term "health" of many collectibles. Problems with spotting, discoloration, and damage may also be seen in stamps, antique textiles, comic books, baseball trading cards, postcards, and even currency. To meet the need for safe storage of these goods, University Products makes acid-free manuscript boxes and interleaving pages, files, photo albums and Mylar page protectors, archival storage tubes, slide and microfiche storage materials, mounting materials and adhesives, an extensive selection of acid-free papers of all types, and related tools and supplies.

We found a number of products in the catalog that would be especially useful to us: the slipcased "Heritage Album" for old family photos, acid-free glassine envelopes for storage of negatives, interleaving (acid-free) sheets for an 1874 cookbook, Renaissance wax for cleaning a small collection of netsuke, and drop-front gallery boxes for a large collection of prints and memorabilia, among other items.

Most of the products are available in quantity, at prices up to 40% below those for single items. The catalog includes valuable information on conservation basics for a range of materials and collectibles. Since a "basic retouching" of an old photograph cost us $130, we are thoroughly convinced that each dollar spent in preservation can save a hundred in restoration—*if* restoration is possible.

Special Factors: Satisfaction is guaranteed; quantity discounts are available; institutional accounts are available; minimum order is $25.

U.S. BOX CORP.

1296 MCCARTER HWY.
NEWARK, NJ 07104
201/481-2000
718/387-1510
FAX: 718/384-3756

Catalog: $3
Save: up to 60%
Pay: check, MO, certified check
Sells: resale packaging
Store: mail order only

$$ ✉ ☎ 🍁 ▀

U.S. Box Corp. has been selling packaging—boxes, bags, canisters, and displays—since 1948. This is primarily a business-to-business firm, but it offers products that consumers use routinely: wrapping paper, tape, gift boxes, ribbon, tissue paper, and mailing bags, for example. Prices are as much as 60% less here than those charged for comparable items at variety and stationery stores. If you order thousands of units, savings per piece increase. Samples of the goods may be purchased at unit cost plus $2; this is highly recommended, since returns are not accepted.

U.S. Box's 100-page color catalog shows corrugated cardboard mailing boxes, packing and shipping tape and labels, shopping bags, gift and presentation boxes, poly bags, plastic display cases, showcase and window displays, and a full line of velvet boxes, inserts, and stands for jewelry sale and display. Both consumers and businesses should see the selection—and prices—of U.S. Box Corp.'s padded mailing envelopes, colored tissue paper, labels, candy boxes, gift totes, wooden "fruit" crates and baskets, ribbons, metallic stretch gift ties, bows, and cellophane and Mylar excelsior. If you're looking for a dramatic home accent, see the line of "classical displays." These cast stone figures are modeled after Michelangelo's David, Diana, Apollo, and even King Tut and the Sphinx. Prices are reasonable, beginning at under $25. Please note that the minimum order is $150, so get friends together if you can't meet it yourself. And do send for product samples if you're not completely familiar with what you plan to buy.

Special Factors: Returns are not accepted; minimum order is $150; orders are shipped worldwide.

LILLIAN VERNON CORPORATION

P.O. BOX 69-WBMC
MT. VERNON, NY 10551
914/699-0862
FAX: 914/699-7698

Catalog: free
Save: up to 50% (see text)
Pay: check, MO, MC, V, AE, Discover, DC
Sells: gifts, household accessories, personalized items, etc.
Store: 549 Main St., New Rochelle, NY; Monday through Saturday 10–6; also Loehmann's Plaza, 4000 Virginia Beach Blvd., Virginia Beach, VA; Monday through Friday 10–9, Saturday 10-6

What began with a $495 ad in *Seventeen Magazine* in 1951 has become a direct-mail fairy tale, with revenues of $140.6 million in 1989 and a name that's known to 29 million Americans: Lillian Vernon.

The business began with a personalized shoulder bag and belt, and the color catalogs still feature a number of items that can be engraved or printed with your initials. But Lillian Vernon's strength is in well-priced, well-designed gifts and home accessories. The typical catalog offers seasonal goods, bath accessories, closet organizers, toys and games, travel items, gardening gear, stationery, gift wrapping, and things for baby. Customers appreciate the basic good values they find here (the average item costs $15), but there's something better: *wholesale* pricing. If you're prepared to buy 15 or more of the same item, spending at least $250, you'll qualify for discounts of up to 50%. The number of items may seem daunting at first, but if you get together with friends, neighbors, and coworkers, you'll probably find more consensus than difference—especially when filling out gift lists at holiday time. There's no separate edition for the wholesale division; use the current Lillian Vernon catalog, and call or write for a quote. Businesses should note that Lillian Vernon offers a range of special services for corporate gift giving, including personalization.

Special Factors: Satisfaction is guaranteed; price quote by phone or letter with SASE; returns are accepted for exchange, refund, or credit; minimum order is $250, with a 15-piece minimum on each item.

WESTON BOWL MILL

P.O. BOX 218
WESTON, VT 05161
802/824-6219

Catalog: free
Save: up to 35%
Pay: check, MO, MC, V
Sells: woodenware and wooden household items
Store: Main St. (Rte. 100), Weston, VT; Monday through Saturday 9–5, Sunday 10–5

$$$

Weston is known for its bowls, but the Mill produces hundreds of other wooden items for use throughout the home. Prices of many of the goods in the catalog we reviewed were about 25% below comparable retail, and savings were even better on selected goods. Almost everything is available with and without finish (oil or lacquer).

The popular salad bowls, thick milled curves of wood, are offered in sizes from 6" to 20" across. You can save a good deal by buying the seconds (with small flaws that should not affect wear), which cost up to 20% less than the first-quality bowls. Weston sells much more for dining table and kitchen, including birch dinner plates and trays, maple and ash lazy Susans, salt-and-pepper shakers, cheese plates, knife racks, tongs, carving boards, cutting boards, and carbon steel knives.

The 16-page catalog offers a wide variety of other items for the home, including shelves with brackets, towel and tissue holders, spoon racks, pegged coat racks, door chimes, a large selection of wooden boxes, quilt racks, benches, stools, wooden fruits and vegetables, sugar buckets and churns, and baskets. Weston's bird feeders and whirligigs are well priced; likewise the delightful group of wooden toys—vehicles, tops, puzzles, game boards, cradles, and other classics—that are oil-finished. And the "country store" department includes "magic" massagers, lap boards, door stops and window props, outlet plates, spool holders, bells, yardsticks, and many other useful items.

Special Factor: Minimum order is $5, $20 with credit cards.

SEE ALSO

Acme Premium Supply Corp. • premium merchandise • *TOYS*

The American Stationery Co., Inc. • custom-printed stationery, wedding invitations • *BOOKS*

Atlantic Bridge Collection Corp. Ltd. • Irish handcrafts and gifts • *ART, ANTIQUES*

Baron Bridge Supplies • bridge-playing gifts • *TOYS*

Beauty by Spector, Inc. • wigs and hairpieces for men and women • *HEALTH*

Bruce Medical Supply • dining, dressing, bathing, and other aids for the disabled and motor-impaired • *MEDICINE*

Burden's Surplus Center • wide variety of tools, electrical components, security equipment • *SURPLUS*

Caprilands Herb Farm • herb charts, note cards, potpourri, pomanders, etc. • *FARM*

Caviarteria Inc. • gourmet gift assortments • *FOOD*

Current, Inc. • gifts, cards, stationery, etc. • *BOOKS*

The Dog's Outfitter • pet-related gifts • *ANIMAL*

Economy Enterprises • plans for building toys, furniture, tools, etc. • *TOOLS*

The Emerald Collection • Irish gifts, tableware, and apparel • *HOME: TABLE SETTINGS*

Fish'n Shack • gifts for hunters and fishers • *SPORTS*

Gohn Bros. • Amish "general store" goods • *CLOTHING*

H & R Corporation • general surplus goods of all sorts • *SURPLUS*

House of Onyx • imported soapstone, onyx, and other stone art carvings and gifts • *JEWELRY*

D. MacGillivray & Coy. • Scottish tartans, Highland dress accessories, etc. • *CRAFTS*

A.W.G. Otten and Son • carved wooden shoes and clogs • *CLOTHING: FOOTWEAR*

Paradise Products, Inc. • wide variety of party goods • *TOYS*

Pendery's Inc. • potpourri ingredients and gifts • *FOOD*

La Piñata • piñatas • *TOYS*

Plastic BagMart • plastic bags for every purpose • *HOME: MAINTENANCE*

Plexi-Craft Quality Products Corp. • Lucite and Plexiglas furniture, accessories, and gifts • *HOME: FURNISHINGS*

Rammagerdin • Icelandic yarns, knitwear, and souvenirs • *CRAFTS*

Rapidforms, Inc. • gift boxes and packing and shipping supplies • *OFFICE*

Nat Schwartz & Co., Inc. • bridal registry for gifts • *HOME: TABLE SETTINGS*

Shibui Wallcoverings • handmade wall coverings • *HOME: DECOR*

Albert S. Smyth Co., Inc. ● giftware, bridal and gift registry ● *HOME: TABLE SETTINGS*

Stecher's Limited ● clocks, watches, and giftware ● *HOME: TABLE SETTINGS*

R.C. Steele Co. ● gifts for pets and owners ● *ANIMAL*

TAI, Inc. ● variety of cloth goods with silk-screened military insignias ● *CLOTHING*

Thompson Cigar Company ● smoking-related gifts ● *CIGARS*

HEALTH AND BEAUTY

―――――――

Cosmetics, perfumes, and toiletries;

vitamins and dietary supplements; and

wigs and hairpieces

You can save up to 90% on your cosmetic and beauty needs and still get the same name brands featured in beauty emporiums and department stores by buying by mail. If your favorite perfume costs $160 an ounce, consider trying a "copycat" scent. Two of the firms listed here manufacture replicas of famous fragrances. Shop them both to see whose version comes closer to the real thing, and you may realize savings of up to 90% on the cost of the original. Please note that grey-market perfumes and toiletries are now commonly sold by mail, but we do not believe that any of the firms listed here sell such goods. For more information on this issue, see the introduction of "Cameras."

You can save more money on beauty products by using less of them. If you need reasons for cutting down other than your budgetary health, you'll find them in a fascinating book, *Being Beautiful,* published by the Center for the Study of Responsive Law. This compilation of essays and articles on a wide range of beauty topics includes a dictionary of ingredients that helps to explain the side panels of all those boxes, bottles, and jars. The book also gives the reader an appreciation of the FDA's role in the industry, and why it's so important to understand what's on—and omitted from—the labels and warnings of the products you use. Write to "Being Beautiful," P.O. Box 19367, Washington, DC 20036, for ordering information.

Beauty comes from within, which is why you'll find firms selling vitamins and dietary supplements listed here. What you take to augment your diet, if anything, is a question that you should take up with your physician.

If you're concerned about a specific issue, research it thoroughly in both consumer magazines and books and in scientific medical journals (bibliographies and abstracts of articles can be obtained through computer services). Don't overlook the government pamphlets available through local departments of health, and the commonsense health guides published by Consumers Union. The Public Citizen Health Research Group's *Health Letter* provides consumerist reporting on health issues in monthly, 12-page newsletters. For subscription information, write to Health Letter, Public Citizen Health Research Group, 2000 P St., N.W., Washington, DC 20036. Last but not least, consult a physician about specific health problems before embarking on a course of treatment for an existing condition.

For more firms selling related products, see the listings in "Medicine and Science."

BEAUTIFUL VISIONS

810 S. BROADWAY
HICKSVILLE, NY 11801
516/576-9000

Catalog: free
Save: up to 90%
Pay: check, MO, MC, V
Sells: cosmetics and toiletries
Store: same address; Monday through Friday 9:30–5:30

$$$ ✉

Imagine hundreds of name-brand beauty products at up to 90% off list prices! The Beautiful Visions catalog, published five times yearly, offers almost 50 pages of beauty essentials from top manufacturers. The firm was established in 1977.

Each issue of the catalog brings you cosmetics, skin-care products, and perfumes from Almay, Aziza, Biotherm, Charles of the Ritz, Coty, Diane Von Furstenberg, Jōvan, L'Oreal, Max Factor, Maybelline, Prince Matchabelli, Revlon, Vidal Sassoon, Vitabath, and other manufacturers. Current fashion shades, as well as the basics, are stocked. The catalog also features grooming tools, fashion jewelry, and gifts, all at very reasonable prices.

Special Factors: Satisfaction is guaranteed; returns are accepted.

BEAUTY BOUTIQUE

P.O. BOX 94520
CLEVELAND, OH
44101-4520
216/826-3008

Catalog: free
Save: up to 90%
Pay: check, MO, MC, V
Sells: cosmetics and toiletries
Store: mail order only

$$ ✚ ▬

Before paying top dollar for cosmetics and perfumes, see the 56-page catalog from Beauty Boutique—you can save up to 90% on the original prices. This firm's parent company has been in business since 1969.

The catalog shows page after page of name-brand cosmetics, toiletries, perfumes, and other goods by such firms as Elizabeth Arden, Elancyl, Giorgio, Jōvan, Estèe Lauder, Prince Matchabelli, Max Factor, Maybelline, Germaine Monteil, and Revlon. Cosmetic accessories, cases, makeup brushes, fashion jewelry, and even moderately priced clothing for women are usually available as well.

Special Factors: Satisfaction is guaranteed; minimum order is $10 with credit cards.

BEAUTY BY SPECTOR, INC.

DEPT. WBMC-91
MCKEESPORT, PA
15134-0502
412/673-3259

Catalog: free (see text)
Save: up to 50%
Pay: check, MO, MC, V
Sells: wigs and hairpieces
Store: mail order only

$$

Beauty by Spector, founded in 1958, offers the stylish Alan Thomas wigs and hairpieces at savings of up to 50% on salon prices, and the helpful sales staff can assist in making selections.

The 20-page "Hairgoods Portfolio" features a number of designer styles for women. The wigs range from neat, softly coiffed heads to "Ginger," a youthful head of curls falling past the shoulders. These are contemporary styles—pretty, relaxed, and well shaped. Included in the Portfolio are wiglets, cascades, and falls that are ideal for everyday wear as well as dressy or special occasions, and a special line of "ultra-lightweight" wigs for women. Men's hairpieces, made with thermal-conductive and mesh bases, are offered in 55 base styles. Both wigs and hairpieces are made of several types of synthetic fibers and human hair, and are offered in a choice of dozens of colors and textures. The firm will match your wig or piece to the closest shade if you provide a hair sample, or you may purchase the set of actual fiber samples.

Beauty by Spector offers readers of this book favorable prices (50% off suggested list), so be sure to identify yourself as a WBMC reader when you send for the catalog.

Special Factors: Specify men's or women's styles when requesting information; inquiries may be made by phone between 8 A.M. and 10 P.M., EST; orders are shipped worldwide.

ESSENTIAL PRODUCTS CO., INC.

90 WATER ST.
NEW YORK, NY
10005-3587
212/344-4288

Price List and Sample Cards: free with SASE (see text)
Save: up to 90% (see text)
Pay: check or MO
Sells: "copycat" fragrances
Store: same address; Monday through Friday 9–6

$$$$

"We offer our versions of the world's most treasured and expensive ladies' perfumes and men's colognes, selling them at a small fraction of the original prices." Essential was founded in 1895 and markets its interpretations of famous perfumes under the brand name of "Naudet."

Essential Products stocks 49 different copies of such costly perfumes as Beautiful, Coco, Eternity, Giorgio, Joy, L'Air du Temps, Obsession, Opium, Passion, Poison, White Linen, and Ysatis, as well as 19 "copycat" colognes for men, from Antaeus to Zizanie. A one-ounce bottle of perfume is $19 (1/2 ounce, $11), and four ounces of any men's cologne cost $10. When you write to Essential Products, please identify yourself as a WBMC reader, which entitles you to five free "scent cards" of Essential's best-selling fragrances. The sample cards give an idea of how closely the Naudet version replicates the original, but the product should be tried by the individual to evaluate it properly. You must also enclose a long, stamped, self-addressed envelope.

Special Factors: Satisfaction is guaranteed; returns are accepted within 30 days for refund; minimum order is $19.

FREEDA VITAMINS, INC.

36 E. 41ST ST.
NEW YORK, NY 10017
800-777-3737
IN NY 212/685-4980

Catalog: free
Save: up to 30%
Pay: check, MO, MC, V
Sells: dietary supplements
Store: Freeda Pharmacy, same address;
　　Monday through Thursday 8:30–6:00,
　　Friday 8:30–4

Freeda has been manufacturing vitamins and minerals in its own plant since 1928. This family-run operation is dedicated to providing the purest possible product; its formulations are free of coal tar dyes, sulfates, starch, animal stearates, pesticides, sugar, and artificial flavorings, and are suitable for even the strictest vegetarian diet. The Zimmermans, who run the firm, put an extra tablet in every bottle just to be nice. Comparing prices to those of similar products from other manufacturers, we found savings of up to 30% on some of Freeda's supplements—and the WBMC reader discount makes this the best buy around.

The catalog lists vitamins, minerals, multivitamins, and nutritional products, which are available in a dizzying choice of combinations and strengths. The vitamin "families" include A and D, B, C, and E; among the minerals are calcium, iron, magnesium, potassium, selenium, and zinc; amino acids, proteins, and other dietary extras are offered. We've listed Freeda not for its megadose formulations, but because of its emphasis on quality production and additive-free goods. It's great to find a source for children's (and adults') vitamins made without sugar, coal tar dyes, sulfiting agents, animal stearates, sulfates, or artificial flavorings. (Freeda's chewable vitamins are naturally flavored, and there is an unflavored version for children on restricted diets. All of the Freeda vitamins are approved by the Feingold Association.) Needless to say, the Freeda catalog is free of the preposterous claims and misleading information often given by supplement sellers. And as great as all of this sounds, it's still important to check with your health-care professional before taking supplements and to avoid megadoses unless they're specifically recommended.

Freeda is offering readers of this book a special discount of 20% on all orders. You must mention WBMC to take the discount, which should be computed on the cost of the goods only, and can't be combined with other discounts and specials. This WBMC reader discount expires February 1, 1992.

Special Factor: Courtesy discounts are given to health-care professionals.

HARVEST OF VALUES NUTRITIONAL PRODUCTS

**P.O. BOX 612167
SAN JOSE, CA 95161-2167
800-535-7742
IN CA 800-356-4190
408/947-7714**

Catalog: free
Save: up to 40%
Pay: check, MO, MC, V
Sells: nutritional supplements, toiletries, and cleaning products
Store: 1545 Berger Dr., San Jose, CA; Monday through Friday 8–5

$$

You can get "factory-direct" prices on vitamins, minerals, and other supplements by ordering from the manufacturer. The Harvest of Values products are made by its parent company, which was founded in 1959. Prices here are up to 40% less than those charged elsewhere for comparable goods.

A good selection of vitamins and nutritional supplements is offered here, listed in the comparatively hype-free, 32-page catalog. There are multivitamin and mineral formulations for adults, chewable versions for children, vitamins A, B-complex, C, and E; a "stress" formula; and chelated iron, bone meal, lecithin, alfalfa, amino acids, and protein powders. Complete label data on most products are given in the catalog.

Harvest of Values also sells vitamin E cream and aloe body lotion, a pH-balanced cream rinse, conditioning shampoo, liquid "soapless" soap, and a biodegradable, phosphate-free cleanser for dishes, hand-washables, and general cleaning.

Special Factors: Satisfaction is guaranteed; all goods are guaranteed against defects in manufacturing; shipping is included on orders over $25; returns are accepted within 30 days.

STAR PHARMACEUTICAL, INC.

DEPT. WBMC
1500 NEW HORIZONS BLVD.
AMITYVILLE, NY
11701-1130
800-274-6400

Catalog: free
Save: up to 40%
Pay: check, MO, MC, V
Sells: nutritional supplements, toiletries, and health-care products
Store: mail order only

$$ ✉ ☎

Star, started in 1954, sells its own line of nutritional supplements, including many formula-equivalents of name-brand goods. Over-the-counter health products are also offered.

Star is a mail-order pharmacy without the prescription department. The 32-page color catalog lists vitamins for athletes, women, children, and senior citizens; there are single vitamins and minerals, trace elements, and formula-equivalents of name-brand supplements. You'll find cosmetics, diet aids, remedies for colds, coughs, and allergies; laxatives, rubs and liniments, pill splitters, oral thermometers, sphygmomanometers, and books on health and nutrition.

Special Factors: Satisfaction is guaranteed; shipping is included on orders over $10; returns are accepted within 30 days; minimum order is $15 with credit cards.

TULI-LATUS PERFUMES LTD.

146-36 13TH AVE.
P.O. BOX 422
WHITESTONE, NY
  11357-0422
718/746-9337

Brochure: free
Save: up to 80% (see text)
Pay: check, MO, MC, V, AE, Optima
Sells: "copycat" fragrances
Store: mail order only

$$$ ✉ ☎ 🍁 ▤

Tuli-Latus, in business since 1970, sells its own versions of some of the world's finest, most expensive women's perfumes and men's scents, at up to 80% less than the cost of the originals.

Copies of 36 popular scents for women, including Chloé, Bal à Versailles, Joy, L'Air du Temps, Obsession, Patou's "1000," Opium, and Shocking are offered here. Men's scents, sold in perfume form, include a version of Russian Leather. Tuli-Latus also sells its own inspirations: "New Mown Hay" for men and "Jardin Exotique," a jasmine fragrance, and other florals for women. The brochure also shows necklaces of simulated pearls, and a line of facial creams, lotions, and cleansers.

Tuli-Latus is offering readers of this book $5 off their *first* order (of nonsale items only). Identify yourself as a WBMC reader when you order. This WBMC reader discount expires February 1, 1992.

Special Factors: Returns of unused perfume are accepted within 15 days for refund or credit; minimum order is $15 with credit cards.

SEE ALSO

D. MacGillivray & Coy. • Hebridean perfume • *CRAFTS*

Metacom, Inc. • motivational audio cassettes • *BOOKS*

Mother Hart's Natural Products, Inc. • Fuller Brush natural-bristle hairbrushes • *HOME: LINEN*

Retired Persons Services, Inc. • vitamins, beauty products, shampoo, etc. • *MEDICINE*

Royal Silk, Ltd. • "Royal Silk" perfume • *CLOTHING*

The Spice House • salt-free seasonings • *FOOD*

Walnut Acres • small selection of natural toiletries, additive-free nutritional supplements • *FOOD*

HOME

"**H**ome" is a potent complex of the symbolic and concrete, where physical shelter, the expression of personal aesthetics, the right to privacy, sensory pleasure, the ideology of family, and cultural dictums commingle. It's a fascinating merger of memory and expectation, circumstance and ingenuity. The right balance and proportion of these elements culminates in the wonderful sense of comfort that we think of as "home."

Since this place often comes attached to a 30-year mortgage, we may feel its fiscal importance outweighs the metaphysical. But the right decisions—from buying a new lamp to adding a wing—can bring pleasure to our lives while improving the equity in our homes, at the lowest possible cost. Veteran householders know that avoiding the infamous nightmares of redecorating and remodeling is a matter of good preparation, good budgeting, and good common sense.

DECOR

Floor coverings, wall and window treatments, lighting, upholstery materials, tools, and services

Do-it-yourself home decor has always been an important part of the market, but in the last few years the distinctions between D-I-Y and to-the-trade (i.e., professional decorators) have begun to blur. Lines once available to licensed designers only are now offered by discounters and full-price firms, and they're selling to consumers who've shopped the showrooms and read the shelter magazines, and are not going to settle for less than the best.

Unfortunately, success has a price—manufacturers are threatening to pull their product lines from discounters if their brand names appear in ads, or even in unpaid editorial mentions like the listings in this book. When alerted to this problem, we've deleted those particular brands from *all* listings. So even if you don't see the name, the firm may carry the line—call or write to find out.

Following are a few of the resources and tips we've picked up over the years during the course of our own decorating projects:

Wallpaper and painting: Painting is one of the cheapest and easiest ways to give your home or a room a quick face-lift. Choosing the right type of paint for the job is half the battle; the other is preparing the surfaces properly. Both topics are covered in depth in *Paint and Wallpaper,* one of the volumes in the Time-Life "Home Repair and Improvement" series of books, which should be available at your local library. The same book addresses the selection of wallpaper, application techniques, and troubleshooting problems that may arise. Another good guide to selecting wallpaper and estimating the amount needed, "The Wallcovering How-To Handbook," is published by The Wallcovering Information Bureau, 66 Morris Ave., Springfield, NJ 07081.

Upholstery and draperies: Pricing upholstery and drapery materials is sometimes tricky, since fabrics are commonly displayed on sample boards with the selvages—on which the manufacturer's name is usually printed—concealed. In fact, some mills print "pseudonyms" on the selvages, which also foils attempts at comparison shopping. (Decorators and stores have keys to these aliases, but unless you do, there is no way to know that the fabric that reads "House 'n Home Fabrics & Draperies, Inc." is really from John Wolf.) There are different ways you can undermine these schemes, but perhaps the easiest route to accurate price quotes is with the fabric itself: Buy a yard, and send large pieces of it out with your price quote requests. Remember to state how many yards you intend to order, since that may affect the cost per yard.

And while you're perusing the listings, please be aware of yet another bugbear in this market: At least one prominent manufacturer has threatened to stop supplying retailers whose ads don't conform to certain criteria. Although a listing in this book is not an ad—no firm ever pays to be mentioned—the manufacturers may not honor the distinction. Consequently, *some brand names have been omitted from listings, and you must call or write if you don't see what you're looking for.*

The price spread on fabrics can be considerable from store to store, so compare at least five sources before deciding on your supplier. Buying off the shelf is almost always cheaper than having a shop special order a fabric, and if you're buying 25 yards or more of the same fabric, you should expect an extra price break. Even if you're working with a full-service upholsterer or draper, you'll probably get better value overall if you supply your own fabric, since you can get exactly what you want, without paying an extra markup. (This is known as a COM— "customer's own material"—job.)

If you go the professional route and engage a decorator, consider working out a cost-plus or per-hour payment arrangement. This advice comes to us from the president of a thriving West Coast fabric store, where decorators buy at 50% off the tagged prices—and charge the client 100%.

Rugs and carpets: The Better Business Bureau publishes "Tips on Carpet and Rugs," a guide to selecting the best carpet for your needs. It's available from your local BBB office, or you can request the publications list and order form from: Council of Better Business Bureaus, Inc., 1515 Wilson Blvd., Arlington, VA 22209, Attn.: Publications Dept.

AMERICAN DISCOUNT WALLCOVERINGS

1411 FIFTH AVE.
PITTSBURGH, PA 15219
800-777-2737

Information: price quote
Save: up to 60%
Pay: check, MO, MC, V, Discover
Sells: wall coverings, related fabrics, and window treatments
Store: same address; Monday through Friday 8:30–5, Saturday 8:30–1

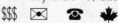

American Discount Wallcoverings, whose parent firm was founded in 1905, offers savings of up to 60% on the best in decorator wall and window treatments. Custom bedspreads and draperies by a prominent manufacturer are also discounted 20%.

Most of the wall coverings are discounted 30% to 50%; upholstery and decorator fabrics are priced 10% to 30% below regular retail here. All of the goods are name-brand: Among the firms and designers represented are Carey Lind, David & Dash, Decorator's Walk, Eisenhart, Essex, Ginger Tree, Greeff, Imperial, Jonap, Josephson, Judscott, Katzenbach and Warren,

Ralph Lauren, Quadrille, Sanitas, Van Luit, Walltex, Westgate, and Winfield. All of the custom window treatments made by Bali, Del Mar, Flexalum, Graber, HunterDouglas, Joanna, Kirsch, Levolor, LouverDrape, Nanik, and Verosol are discounted 25% to 60%.

American Discount is offering readers of this book a 65% discount on Bali mini blinds. (The discount is calculated on list price, and applies only to the Bali line.) This WBMC reader discount expires February 1, 1992.

Special Factors: Price quote by phone or letter with SASE; request order form when obtaining price quotes; all goods are first quality; returns (except cut rolls, borders, custom wall coverings, and custom window treatments) are accepted within 20 days (a 25% restocking fee is charged).

CUSTOM WINDOWS & WALLS

32525 STEPHENSON HWY., DEPT. WM MADISON HEIGHTS, MI 48071
800-772-1947
800-777-7747
FAX: 313/583-2863

Brochure: free
Save: up to 75%
Pay: check, MO, MC, V, Discover
Sells: wall coverings and window treatments
Store: mail order only

$$

After deliberating over window treatments and wallpaper patterns, make sure you go the final step and get the best price. Custom Windows & Walls, which has been in business since 1908 and selling by mail since 1982, should definitely be on your list of sources.

Our mailing from Custom contained a packet of manufacturers' brochures that described several currently popular lines, with price sheets and discount schedules. The firm offers window treatments by Bali, Del Mar, Kirsch, Levolor, and LouverDrape, as well as its own "Window Express" 1" mini and 1/2" micro blinds and vertical blinds in a choice of scores of colors and materials, at 50% to 75% below list prices. Measuring guides are included in the literature. Wall coverings and coordinating fabrics from "almost any book" are available, from Imperial, Marimekko, Walltex, and others, at 25% to 50% below list. A price-quote form is included in the information packet.

Please note that all of the window treatments are made to order and are *not* returnable. Measure and *remeasure* carefully before ordering.

Special Factor: Price quote by phone or letter.

THE FABRIC CENTER, INC.

P.O. BOX 8212
485 ELECTRIC AVE.
FITCHBURG, MA 01420
508/343-4402

Brochure: free
Save: up to 50%
Pay: check, MO, MC, V
Sells: decorator fabrics
Store: (showroom) same address; Monday through Saturday 9–5:30

$$$

The Fabric Center has been in business since 1932, selling fine fabrics for home decorating at savings of up to 50% on suggested list prices.

This firm offers decorator fabrics for upholstery and window treatments by Robert Allen, American Textile, Paul Barrow, Covington, George Harrington, Kravet, Thomas Strahan, and many others. The brochure includes a roster of selected manufacturers, and pictures representing just a sample of what is stocked.

Special Factor: Price quote by phone or letter.

FABRICS BY DESIGN

325 N.E. FIFTH AVE.
DELRAY BEACH, FL
33483
407/278-9700

Price List with Samples: $7.50
Save: 30% plus
Pay: check, MO, MC, V
Sells: decorator fabrics
Store: Woodland Fabrics (same address); Monday through Saturday 9:30–5:30

$$

Fabrics by Design, formerly listed here as Woodland Fabrics, sells its own collection of decorator fabrics as well as selected lines from well-known firms. You'll save a solid 30% or more by buying from this source, and the quality is excellent.

Your catalog fee brings you a thick swatch book featuring the firm's collection of charming country prints and solids. Some of the prints are reminiscent of the "traditional" lines in designer collections, but they cost a fraction as much as the name fabrics. All of the fabric is preshrunk cotton, treated with Scotchguard. Fabrics by Design also offers muslin, Osnaburg, and professional-quality drapery lining in white and ivory. Designer fabrics are offered as well, including lines from Robert Allen, Anju, Bloomcraft, Cohama, Covington, Cyrus Clark, Greeff, P. Kaufmann, Spectrum, Stroheim & Romann, John Wolf, and Jay Yang. Be sure to get the swatch collection or prices on these fabrics if you're upholstering furniture or making slip-covers, curtains, or draperies.

Special Factors: Satisfaction is guaranteed; price quote by phone or letter with SASE; returns (except lengths under 5 yards and worn or laundered fabric) are accepted within 2 weeks; minimum order is 1 yard; orders are shipped worldwide.

FABRICS BY PHONE

P.O. BOX 309
WALNUT BOTTOM, PA
17266
800-233-7012

Brochure and Samples: $3
Save: up to 50%
Pay: check, MO, MC, V
Sells: decorator fabrics
Store: Fabric Shop, 120 N. Seneca St., Shippensburg, PA

$$ ✉ ☎

If you're decorating, you should price several sources for fabric before buying. One of them should be Fabrics by Phone, which has been doing business since 1937.

Major lines and manufacturers are represented here, including Robert Allen, Artmark, Design Craft, Fabricut, Kinney, Michaels Textiles, Warner, and Westgate. Fabrics by Phone also makes draperies and accessories to order. For more information on the special services, send $3 for the literature, price list, and swatches.

Special Factors: Price quote by phone or letter with SASE; minimum order is 1 yard (on goods not in stock).

GOLDEN VALLEY LIGHTING

━━━━

**274 EASTCHESTER
  DRIVE, #117A
HIGH POINT, NC 27262
800-735-3377
919/882-7330**

Brochure: free (see text)
Save: up to 50%
Pay: check, MO, MC, V
Sells: floor, table, and wall lamps
Store: mail order only

$$ ✉

Golden Valley, a new firm founded and run by veterans of the lighting industry, offers savings of up to 50% on lamps and lighting fixtures from over 100 manufacturers.

   The firm's brochure urges you to shop around and call when you've determined what you want (have the manufacturer's name, model number, color, finish, and any other details at hand). You can also buy specific manufacturers' catalogs from Golden Valley Lighting for $5 each, and get the information that way. Please note that the firm's brochure lists some, but not all, of the manufacturers represented, so call and ask if you don't see what you're looking for. When you're ready to order, you can make a deposit of 50% of the lamp's cost and pay the balance before shipment, or prepay the entire amount (details are given in the brochure).

Special Factor: Price quote by phone or letter with SASE.

━━━━━━━━━━━━━━━━━━━━━━━━

HANG-IT-NOW WALLPAPER STORES

━━━━

**10517F N. MAIN ST.
ARCHDALE, NC 27263
800-325-9494
919/431-6341
FAX: 919/431-0449**

Information: price quote
Save: up to 65%
Pay: check, MO, MC, V, AE
Sells: wall coverings and decorator fabrics
Store: same address; also 4616 W. Market
   St., Greensboro, and 759 Silas Creek
   Pkwy., Winston-Salem, NC

$$ ✉   ☎

Hang-It-Now Wallpaper is run by a couple who set up shop in 1981, and now have three stores. They sell name-brand wall coverings at savings of 30% to 65% on list prices, and a limited selection of decorator fabrics at discounts of up to 40%.

All major brands of wall coverings (plus strings, grass cloth, and borders) are offered here, including Carefree, Carey, Color House, Eisenhart, Imperial, Katzenbach & Warren, Lind, Sanitas, Sunworthy, and York, among others. Hang-It-Now specializes in providing wall coverings to retail establishments, and has done numerous installations for furniture retailers and decorators. Regardless of the size of your order, the firm says that "service to the customer is still our number one aim."

Special Factor: Only first-class goods are sold.

HARMONY SUPPLY INC.

P.O. BOX 313
MEDFORD, MA 02155
617/395-2600
FAX: 617/396-8218

Information: price quote
Save: up to 60%
Pay: check, MO, MC, V
Sells: wallpaper and window treatments
Store: 18 High St., Medford, MA; Monday
to Saturday 8–5:30, Thursday 8 A.M.–9 P.M.

Harmony Supply, in business since 1949, can give your home a face-lift at a discount. Save up to 60% on wallpaper, coordinating fabrics, and window treatments.

Harmony carries over 2,500 wallpaper, grass cloth, and string cloth designs and patterns, including lines by Laura Ashley, and Walltex. You can also buy mini, micro, vertical, and pleated shades and blinds by Bali, Flexalum, HunterDouglas, Kirsch, Levolor, Louverdrape, and Verosol here. You'll save the most on goods that are currently in stock, but even special orders are discounted up to 50%. Call or write for a price quote—there is no catalog or price list.

Special Factors: Price quote by phone or letter with SASE; returns are accepted (a 25% restocking fee is charged on special-order goods).

HOME FABRIC MILLS, INC.

━━━━━━━━

882 SOUTH MAIN ST.
P.O. BOX 888
CHESHIRE, CT 06410
203/272-3529

Brochure: free
Save: up to 50%
Pay: check, MO, MC, V (see text)
Sells: decorator fabrics and custom services
Store: same address; also Rte. 202,
  Belchertown, MA; and 445 Saratoga Rd.,
  Rte. 50, Scotia, NY

We received a lovely color brochure from Home Fabric Mills, with samples of some of the firm's most popular upholstery and drapery materials. Home Fabric Mills has been in business since 1968 and is a good source for the home decorator who's unsure of what type of fabric is best for a particular project or is trying to match a color.

The three Home Fabric Mills stores are stocked with thousands of bolts of upholstery and drapery materials, lining, trims, and workroom supplies from Robert Allen, Covington, Graber, Kaufmann, Kirsch, Lanscot-Arlen, Rockland (Roclon lining material), Wolf, and other manufacturers. Only first-quality goods are sold, and Home Fabric Mills will sell in quarter-yard increments—great to know if you're still deciding on your fabrics.

Please note: Credit card payments are accepted on out-of-state mail orders only.

Special Factor: Price quote by phone or letter with SASE.

JOHNSON'S CARPETS, INC.

━━━━━━━━

3239 S. DIXIE HWY.
DALTON, GA 30720
800-235-1079
IN GA 404/277-2775
FAX: 404/277-9835

Information: inquire
Save: up to 80%
Pay: check, MO, MC, V, AE, Discover,
  Optima
Sells: name-brand floor treatments
Store: same address; Monday through
  Friday 8–5

Johnson's tells us that about 80% of the world's tufted carpeting is produced in the Dalton area. The firm's arrangements with the carpet mills permit it to offer lines from dozens of manufacturers at prices from 20% to 80% below those charged by department stores and other retail outlets.

Once you've determined what carpet or vinyl flooring you plan to buy, you can call or write with the name of the carpet manufacturer, the style name/number, and the square yardage required. Among the manufacturers represented at Johnson's are Armstrong, Bigelow, Cabin Craft, Collins & Aikman, Congoleum, Couristan, General Felt, Lees, Mannington, Tarkett, Salem, J.P. Stevens & Co., and Wunda Weave. Johnson's also sells padding, adhesives, and tack strip for installation.

A deposit is required when placing your order, and complete payment must be made before shipment (common carrier is used).

Special Factors: Price quote by phone or letter with SASE; orders are shipped worldwide.

KING'S CHANDELIER CO.

P.O. BOX 667, DEPT. WBM
EDEN, NC 27288
919/623-6188

Catalog: $3
Save: up to 50%
Pay: check, MO, MC, V
Sells: house-brand and Strass chandeliers
Store: Hwy. 14, Eden, NC; Monday through Saturday 10–4:30

The Kings have been designing and producing chandeliers since 1935 and offer much of their stock in the 100-page catalog. There are designs to suit every taste, at prices for all budgets.

The catalog shows page after page of chandeliers, candelabras, and wall sconces in a range of styles: Victorian, "Colonial," contemporary, and many variations on the classic lighting fixture dripping with prisms, pendalogues, faceted balls, and ropes of crystal buttons. Austere styles with brass arms and plain glass shades are also available, as well as the King's own magnificent designs made of Strass crystal. Options include different finishes on the metal parts, hurricane or candelabra tapers, and candelabra sockets or candle bases. Individual and replacement parts for these lighting fixtures are stocked as well.

Since the black and white catalog photos can't show the chandeliers to best advantage, King's has created a videotape that captures a number of their largest, most popular models. The VHS tape is available for a $25 deposit, refundable on its return.

Special Factors: Satisfaction is guaranteed; price quote by phone or letter with SASE; returns are accepted within 5 days for refund or credit; minimum order is $15 on chandelier parts, $100 with credit cards; orders are shipped worldwide.

LAMP WAREHOUSE/NEW YORK CEILING FAN CENTER

1073 39TH ST.
BROOKLYN, NY 11219
800-52-LITES
718/436-8500

Information: price quote
Save: up to 35%
Pay: check, MO, MC, V, AE
Sells: lamps and ceiling fans
Store: same address; Monday, Tuesday, and Friday 9–5:30, Thursday 9–9, Saturday and Sunday 10–5

$$

The Lamp Warehouse, established in 1954, is noted for its comprehensive inventory of lamps, lighting fixtures, and name-brand ceiling fans that are all sold at a discount.

Call or write for prices on lamps, lighting fixtures, and track lighting by American Lantern, Rembrandt, Stiffel, Thomas Industries, and most major manufacturers. Ceiling fans by Casablanca and Emerson are also stocked, and everything is sold at discounts of up to 35%.

Special Factors: Price quote by phone or letter with SASE; store is closed Wednesdays.

LUIGI CRYSTAL

7332 FRANKFORD AVE.
PHILADELPHIA, PA 19136
215/338-2978

Catalog: $1, refundable
Save: up to 50%
Pay: check, MO, MC, V, AE
Sells: crystal lighting fixtures
Store: same address; Monday to Saturday 9–5, Friday 9–8

$$$

Luigi Crystal may be located in the land of Main Liners, but its heart belongs to Tara. The firm has been creating crystal lighting fixtures since 1935, and the prices are surprisingly low—under $200 for a full-sized chandelier, for example.

The 44-page catalog has black-and-white photographs of each candelabra, chandelier, sconce, and hurricane lamp offered. Many of the styles are formal and ornate, heavily hung with prisms and pendalogues and set in marble or faceted crystal bases. Several lamps feature globe shades, gold cupid bases, "Aurora" crystal prism shades, and even stained glass. At the other end of the spectrum are simple "Williamsburg chimney lamps" for just $44.95 a pair, and several graceful five-arm chandeliers, at very low prices.

If you're searching for replacement parts for your own fixtures, see the catalog for glass chimneys, bobeches, strung button prisms, drop prisms in several styles (3″ to 8″ long), and pendalogues. In addition to the models shown in the catalog, Luigi's workshops can produce designs to your specifications; call or write to discuss details and prices.

Special Factors: Price quote by phone or letter with SASE; orders are shipped worldwide ($1,000 minimum order).

MUTUAL WALLPAPER & PAINT CO. INC.

812 W. MAIN ST.
LOUISVILLE, KY 40202
502/583-0525
502/583-8100

Catalog: see text
Save: 50% plus
Pay: check, MO, MC, V, Discover
Sells: wallpaper and window treatments
Store: same address; Monday through Friday 8:30–5, Saturday 9–4

Thrifty homeowners looking for traditional patterns in wallpaper will find "cottage" prints and subdued neutrals at Mutual Wallpaper & Paint, which has been in business since 1960. Prices are a fraction of those charged for designer papers, and less than the rates charged in many outlets for "no-name" paper and borders.

Mutual's catalog contains dozens of samples of unpasted wallpaper as well as a few patterns in vinyl, and color photos of other selections of vinyl wall coverings and borders. The designs are principally flower and stripe prints, cottage prints, and neutrals. Mutual's charming collection of borders may be used with coordinating wallpaper or alone, to finish a painted wall. The "folk art" sampler style would be perfect in an entryway or kitchen, and there are others for every room in the house. Mutual also offers Bali blinds and name-brand wall coverings and borders by such firms as Borden, Carefree, Color House, Imperial, Millbrook, Quality House, and Sunworthy. Details on getting price quotes are given in the catalog, which also features the tools necessary to do the job.

Special Factor: Returns of uncut double rolls are accepted within 30 days for credit or refund.

NATIONAL CARPET

1384 CONEY ISLAND
AVE.
BROOKLYN, NY 11230
718/253-5700

Catalog: $3 (see text)
Save: up to 40%
Pay: MO, MC, V
Sells: area carpets
Store: same address; Monday through Wednesday 9–6, Thursday 9–8, Friday 9–4, Sunday 10:30–5

National sells Karastan rugs, and will send you the Karastan catalog sampler featuring the different lines for your $2 catalog fee. The rugs include the Karastan Originals Collection—reproductions of Tabriz, Heriz, Bokhara, Kasham, and other classic designs; the Williamsburg Collection; and the Garden of Eden Collection, a line featuring floral motifs. National has over half a century of experience in selling rugs, and discounts up to 40% on suggested list prices.

Special Factor: Satisfaction is guaranteed.

PINTCHIK HOMEWORKS

2106 BATH AVE.
BROOKLYN, NY 11214
800-847-4199
IN NY 718/996-5580
FAX: 718/996-1966

Brochure: free
Save: up to 60%
Pay: check, MO, MC, V
Sells: wall, window, and floor finishes and treatments
Store: 278 and 1555 Third Ave. and 2475 Broadway, New York, NY

$$ ✉ ☎

This firm, founded by Nathan Pintchik in 1912, has become one of New York City's favorite sources for home-improvement items and decorative accessories. City agencies, decorators, and countless do-it-yourselfers are all customers. Pintchik is noted for carrying special finishes and colors not available elsewhere.

Pintchik stocks over 2,000 wallpaper patterns and window treatments; the brands include Bali, Del Mar, Duette, Graber, HunterDouglas, Joanna, Levolor, Louverdrape, and Verosol. The brochure includes a helpful guide to measuring your windows, as well as terms of Pintchik's lifetime warranty.

Paints by Pratt & Lambert, Benjamin Moore, Pittsburgh Paints, Luminall, Emalj, Red Devil, and other companies are also stocked. Paint color chips are available upon request. Custom wallpaper designs, including logos, can be produced, and vertical shades can be laminated with fabrics or wallpaper. In addition, Pintchik sells flooring by Armstrong, Hartco, Kentile, Lees, and other well-known companies. Store shoppers will find a complete selection of other home-improvement and hardware items.

Special Factors: Price quote by letter with SASE; institutional and commercial accounts are available; returns are accepted within 3 weeks (a 20% restocking fee is charged).

POST WALLCOVERING
DISTRIBUTORS, INC.

P.O. BOX 7026
BLOOMFIELD HILLS, MI
   48013
800-521-0650

Information: inquire

Save: up to 75%

Pay: check, MO, MC, V

Sells: wall coverings, blinds, and
   coordinating fabrics

Store: mail order only

$$ ☎

Post Wallcovering, in business since 1977, can save homeowners and decorators up to 75% on wall coverings and window treatments. The firm sells name-brand wallpaper, borders, murals, and blinds, and told us that "any wall covering in any wallpaper book can be ordered."

Before calling for a price quote on a wall covering, have the pattern number and book name at hand, and know the amount of paper needed. If calling for a price quote on a window blind, have the manufacturer's name, style name, color name and number, width, and height written down.

Special Factor: Price quote by phone.

ROBINSON'S
WALLCOVERINGS

DEPT. ILY
225 W. SPRING ST.
TITUSVILLE, PA 16354
800-458-2426
814/827-1893

Catalog and Samples: $2, refundable

Save: up to 50%

Pay: check, MO, MC, V, AE, Discover

Sells: wallpaper, decorator fabrics, and
   accessories

Store: 339 W. Spring St., Titusville; also
   3506 Liberty Plaza, Erie, and 2807
   Wilmington Rd., Rte. 18, New Castle, PA

$$$ ✉ ☎ ▥

Robinson's went into business in 1919, and its catalog prices look as if they haven't risen much in the intervening years. Wall coverings are the chief offerings, but coordinating borders, fabrics, and home accessories are also available.

Robinson's sells wall coverings in patterns suitable for bathrooms, dining rooms, dens, bedrooms, nurseries, and kitchens. The patterns range from the traditional to contemporary. Tools and supplies for hanging are also offered. Complementary fabrics and borders are available for many wallpaper patterns.

Robinson's also carries name-brand wall treatments, and can save you up to 50% on paper and fabric from popular manufacturers. Orders of the national brands are handled through the firm's Custom Order Sales Office; see the catalog for details.

Special Factors: Satisfaction is guaranteed; returns are accepted within 30 days for exchange or refund; minimum order is $10 with credit cards.

RUBIN & GREEN INC.

290 GRAND ST.
NEW YORK, NY 10002
212/226-0313
212/226-5015

Information: price quote
Save: 33% plus
Pay: check, MO, MC, V, AE
Sells: decorator fabrics
Store: same address; Sunday through
  Friday 9–5

$$$ ⊠ ✦ (see text)

Rubin & Green, established in 1945, offers savings of up to 40% on a wide selection of decorator fabrics. This firm formerly specialized in bed, bath, and table linens, which have been discontinued.

Decorator and upholstery fabrics from Robert Allen, David & Dash, Kravet, Stroheim & Romann, Jay Yang, and other firms and designers are sold by mail. You may consult the staff on your decorating needs by phone or when you stop by the store. Rubin & Green can also create custom-made comforters, bedspreads, draperies, and other decorative accessories. Inquire for information.

Canadian readers, please note: Deliveries to Canada are made by UPS only.

Special Factor: Price quote by phone or letter with SASE.

SANZ INTERNATIONAL, INC.

P.O. BOX 1794
HIGH POINT, NC 27261
919/886-7630
919/882-6212
919/883-4622

Brochure: free with self-addressed, stamped envelope
Save: up to 80%
Pay: check, MO, MC, V
Sells: wallpaper and decorator fabrics
Store: 1183 E. Lexington Ave., High Point, NC; and four other locations

Sanz, established in 1978, offers decorator discounts of up to 80% on wall coverings and upholstery and drapery fabrics from hundreds of manufacturers and designers, which are listed in the brochure. They include Robert Allen, Boussac of France, Brunschwig & Fils, Clarence House, Color House, Decorator's Walk, Ginger Tree, Greeff, Imperial, Lee Jofa, Katzenbach & Warren, Ralph Lauren, Milbrook, Quality House, Sanitas, Scalamandré, United, and York. Imported grass cloth is available (request information and samples). Volume discounts are offered.

Special Factors: Price quote by phone or letter with SASE; quantity discounts are available; shipping is included on most items; returns are accepted within 30 days.

SHAMA IMPORTS, INC.

P.O. BOX 2900, DEPT.
WBM-91
FARMINGTON HILLS, MI
48333
313/478-7740

Brochure: free
Save: up to 50%
Pay: check, MO, MC, V
Sells: crewel fabrics and home accessories
Store: mail order only

Shama offers excellent prices on Indian crewel fabrics and home accessories, featured in an eight-page brochure that also includes decorating suggestions.

Crewel fabrics, hand-embroidered on hand-loomed cotton, are offered here in traditional serpentine flower-and-vine motifs and other distinctive designs, in a range of colors. Background (unembroidered) fabric is available by the yard, and Shama stocks crewel chair and cushion covers, tote bags, bedspreads, and tablecloths as well. All of the fabric is 52" wide and can be washed by hand or dry cleaned. Samples are available for $1 each; those showing one-fourth of the complete pattern cost $5 (refundable). The brochure lists the pattern repeats for all of the designs.

Special Factors: Satisfaction is guaranteed; quantity discounts are available on purchases of full bolts; uncut, undamaged returns are accepted within 30 days for refund or credit; C.O.D. orders are accepted.

SHIBUI WALLCOVERINGS

P.O. BOX 1638, DEPT. WBM-91 ROHNERT PARK, CA 94928-9990 800-824-3030 IN CA 707/526-6170 FAX: 707/544-0719

Brochure and Samples: $4
Save: up to 50%
Pay: check, MO, MC, V
Sells: imported grass cloth and "natural" wall coverings
Store: mail order only

Shibui, which has been doing business since 1966, sells fine wall coverings made of natural materials—jute, grasses, strings, and textiles. Shibui stocks imported jute-fiber grass cloth, rush cloth, textile papers, textured weaves, and string wall coverings. The string wall coverings include several that look like silk but cost a fraction as much. Paper-hanging tool kits, adhesives, and lining paper are available.

Special Factors: Satisfaction is guaranteed; price quote by phone or letter; shipping is included on orders over $100; single and double rolls can be cut from regular bolts (not returnable); larger samples are available upon request; returns are accepted within 30 days; C.O.D. orders are accepted.

SILK SURPLUS

**235 EAST 58TH ST.
NEW YORK, NY 10022
212/753-6511**

Information: price quote
Save: up to 75% (see text)
Pay: check, MO, MC, V
Sells: discontinued decorator fabrics (see text)
Store: same address; Monday through Saturday 10–5:30, also 1147 Madison Ave., New York, 449 Old Country Rd., Westbury, 1210 Northern Blvd., Manhasset, and 281 Mamaroneck Ave., White Plains, NY

$

Silk Surplus is well-known to budget-minded New Yorkers who covet luxurious upholstery and drapery fabrics; here they can save up to 75% (and sometimes even more) on sumptuous Scalamandré closeouts and fabrics from other mills: silks, cottons, velvets, woolens, chintzes, brocades, damasks, and other weaves and finishes are usually available. Silk Surplus opened its doors in 1962.

Walk-in customers can select from among the bolts in any of the five Silk Surplus shops. But if you're buying by mail, you must know exactly which Scalamandré fabric you want, and in which color. If it's there, you're in luck. You may also send the store a fabric sample with a query. We emphasize that this is a great shopping stop on a trip to New York City, but only serious searchers for Scalamandré closeout fabrics should contact the store intending to buy by mail. If you're a design professional, you may ask for an additional trade discount.

Special Factors: Price quote by phone or letter with SASE; sample cuttings are free; all sales are final; orders are shipped worldwide.

SILVER WALLCOVERING, INC.

3001-15 KENSINGTON AVE.
PHILADELPHIA, PA 19134
800-426-6600

Brochure: $1
Save: up to 50%
Pay: check, MO, MC, V, AE, Discover
Sells: wall coverings
Store: mail order only

$$$ ✉ ☎

Silver is a well-known source for name-brand wall treatments, which it sells by phone and by mail at savings of up to 50%. You can call for quotes on any style you find in the current books of Imperial, Walltex, York, and *any other* wallpaper manufacturers. Borders and coordinating fabrics are also available. Silver has been in business since 1975 and may add window treatments to its product line in the future.

Special Factor: Price quote by phone or letter with SASE.

SLIPCOVERS OF AMERICA

E. BROAD AND WOOD STS.
P.O. BOX 590
BETHLEHEM, PA 18016-0590
215/868-7788

Catalog: free
Save: up to 30%
Pay: check, MO, MC, V
Sells: slipcovers, curtains, and furniture throws
Store: mail order only

$$ ✉

The cost of reupholstering a couch or chair often approaches the purchase price of the furniture itself. The least expensive way to improve the appearance of tired seating may be well-fitting slipcovers. Slipcovers of America sells "custom-look" slipcovers, looser "casually fitted" covers, and coordinating pillows, curtains, tablecloths, and other accessories.

Slipcovers that will stretch to fit dozens of couch and armchair styles are offered in velvet-look solids, bold florals, and country designs. There are throws and semifitted covers for nonstandard furniture, all at prices we found to be 25% and 30% lower than those charged by a major catalog company. Slipcovers of America gives step-by-step instructions for measuring your furniture so you can be sure to get the best fit. If you want to coordinate the rest of your room, see the complementing curtains, valances, pillows, tablecloths, and other accents. You can also make your own—the fabric is sold in three-yard packs.

Special Factors: Satisfaction is guaranteed; no phone orders are accepted; returns are accepted.

SOUTH BOUND MILLWORKS

P.O. BOX 349
SANDWICH, MA 02563
508/477-2638

Catalog: $1, refundable
Save: up to 50%
Pay: check, MO, MC, V
Sells: wooden and iron decorative
  hardware
Store: mail order only

$$ ✉ ☎ 🍁

Our local decorating supply sources seemed to have every size and style of curtain rod and bracket except what we needed: plain wooden closed-side curtain brackets to complement six-over-six windows in a Federal row house. We found them at South Bound Millworks, at very modest prices, along with all kinds of hardware and decorative things in wood and wrought iron.

South Bound's 26-page catalog shows line drawings of its birch curtain rod brackets, rod couplers for long rods, wooden finials, and wooden rings, all of which are carved in simple styles appropriate to many houses. Coordinating shelf supports, towel racks, and even shower curtain supports are offered in sanded hardwood. For an entirely different effect, see the wrought iron fixtures. The curtain cranes (pivoting half-rods) are an old alternative to stationary rods, and decorative hold-backs have been used for centuries. Iron pot racks and kitchen fixtures, fireplace tools, candle stands, lamps, bathroom fixtures, plant hooks and cranes, and even an iron dinner chime are offered. South Bound also sells small wooden boxes, painted animal silhouettes, jointed wooden bears, and colorful Cape Cod snakes (draft stoppers).

Special Factor: Returns are accepted within 14 days for exchange, refund, or credit.

TIOGA MILL OUTLET STORES, INC.

**200 S. HARTMAN ST.
YORK, PA 17403
717/843-5139**

Brochure: free (see text)
Save: up to 50%
Pay: check, MO, MC, V
Sells: decorator fabrics
Store: same address; Monday through
Thursday 9:30–6, Friday 9:30–8,
Saturday 9–5 (in July and August 9–3)

"When you think fabric, think Tioga!" urges the brochure from this source, which offers name-brand drapery and upholstery fabric at up to 50% off list prices. Tioga stocks material by Robert Allen, Bloomcraft, Covington, Imperial-Tex, John Wolf, and many other designers and manufacturers. If you've chosen your fabric, you can write or call Tioga for the price. If you're still shopping, you can avail yourself of the firm's decorating service by completing the "Special Project/Sample Request" portion of the order form and returning it with the $2 fee. Tioga will send you selected swatches, from which you may select your fabric. Drapery lining and upholstery materials are also available.

Tioga Mill Outlet has been in business since 1970, and it guarantees that all goods are first quality; flawed or damaged goods will be replaced or your money refunded. Returns due to customer error are not accepted, so *measure* and *remeasure* before you order.

Special Factor: Price quote by phone or letter with SASE.

WELLS INTERIORS INC.

▬▬▬▬▬

7171 AMADOR PLAZA
DR.
DUBLIN, CA 94568
800-547-8982

Catalog: free
Save: up to 75%
Pay: check, MO, MC, V
Sells: window treatments and accessories
Store: same address; Monday through
    Friday 10–6, Saturday 10–5, Sunday 12–
    4; 17 other locations in CA and OR

Wells Interiors guarantees "the lowest prices" on its goods, and will beat any other dealer's price down to cost on a wide range of top brands. Discounts run up to 75% on retail prices.

Wells carries Levolor's Riviera, Monaco, private-label blinds, and vertical lines (in all fabrics, materials, colors, and options offered by Levolor); HunterDouglas blinds; LouverDrape vertical blinds; and Del Mar woven woods, Duette blinds, Softlight shades, and metal blinds and verticals at up to 65% off. Kirsch woven woods, pleated shades, decorator roller shades, verticals, and miniblinds are also available, as well as new lines by the same firms.

The catalog includes a helpful guide to the current lines and instructions on measuring your windows and installing your blinds. Details of the Wells warranty are given in the catalog as well.

Special Factors: Price quote by phone or letter; written confirmation is required on phone orders.

SEE ALSO

Annex Furniture Galleries ● name-brand lamps, mirrors, etc. ● *HOME: FURNISHINGS*
Aristocast Originals Inc. ● reproduction cast moldings, fireplace surrounds, architectural details, etc. ● *HOME: MAINTENANCE*
Blackwelder's Industries, Inc. ● name-brand rugs, carpeting, clocks, lamps, etc. ● *HOME: FURNISHINGS*
BRE Lumber ● flooring, cabinet-grade lumber, and paneling ● *HOME: MAINTENANCE*
Buffalo Batt & Felt Corp. ● throw pillow inserts and upholstery stuffing ● *CRAFTS*

The Caning Shop • seat-weaving materials, replacement seats, upholstery supplies • *CRAFTS*

Cherry Hill Furniture, Carpet & Interiors • name-brand rugs, carpeting, and accessories • *HOME: FURNISHINGS*

CMC Music, Inc. • Howard Miller clocks • *MUSIC*

Craftsman Wood Service Co. • materials and tools for upholstery, clock making, lamp wiring • *CRAFTS*

Crawford's Old House Store • reproduction Victorian lighting, relief wall coverings, etc. • *HOME: MAINTENANCE*

The Deerskin Place • sheepskins • *CLOTHING*

Defender Industries, Inc. • teak kitchen and bath accessories • *AUTO*

Eldridge Textile Co. • name-brand window treatments • *HOME: LINEN*

Goldbergs' Marine Distributors • teak kitchen and bath accessories • *AUTO*

Home-Sew • upholstery supplies • *HOME: DECOR*

Leather Unlimited Corp. • sheepskin rugs • *CRAFTS*

Loftin-Black Furniture Company • name-brand lamps, mirrors, etc. • *HOME: FURNISHINGS*

D. MacGillivray & Coy. • sheepskin rugs • *CRAFTS*

Mallory's Fine Furniture • name-brand lamps, carpets, clocks, etc. • *HOME: FURNISHINGS*

Murrow Furniture Galleries, Inc. • name-brand lamps • *HOME: FURNISHINGS*

Newark Dressmaker Supply, Inc. • upholstery supplies • *CRAFTS*

Quality Furniture Market of Lenoir, Inc. • name-brand lamps, decorator fabrics, etc. • *HOME: FURNISHINGS*

Arthur M. Rein • custom-made fur throws and pillows • *CLOTHING*

The Renovator's Supply, Inc. • period lighting fixtures, hardware, tin ceilings, etc. • *HOME: MAINTENANCE*

James Roy Furniture Co., Inc. • name-brand lamps, clocks, carpeting, etc. • *HOME: FURNISHINGS*

Shuttercraft • interior and exterior wooden window shutters • *HOME: MAINTENANCE*

Stuckey Brothers Furniture Co., Inc. • clocks, mirrors, etc. • *HOME: FURNISHINGS*

Sultan's Delight, Inc. • leather "camel" saddlebag hassocks • *FOOD*

Thai Silks • upholstery-weight silk fabrics • *CRAFTS*

Utex Trading Enterprises • upholstery-weight silk fabrics • *CRAFTS*

FURNISHINGS

Household furnishings of all types, including outdoor furniture, office furnishings

It's possible to save as much as 50% by ordering your furniture from North Carolina, the manufacturing center of this industry. The North Carolina discounters don't take the staggering markups that make name-brand furnishings and accessories prohibitively expensive in department and furniture stores around the nation. That doesn't endear discounters to the furniture manufacturers, though; in fact, a number of manufacturers do their best to make it difficult for discounters to sell by mail, forbidding them to trade outside designated "selling areas" and sometimes even prohibiting the firms from having 800 lines. (Manufacturers elicit compliance by threatening to refuse to fill the discounters' orders.) This practice has the effect of limiting trade, and we find it reprehensible. To avoid creating problems for the discounters, we've *omitted brand names in their listings.* Most of them can take orders for goods from hundreds of manufacturers, can supply catalogs, brochures, and swatches, and give decorating advice over the phone. Call for details and price quotes.

We strongly recommend using "in-home delivery service" when a firm offers it, since the furniture will be uncrated exactly where you want it. If there are any damages, you'll see them immediately and can contact the company while the shipper is there to find out what you should do.

If you need help in selecting furniture, see the tips in "What to Look for in Wood and Upholstered Furniture," a booklet published by the National Home Fashions League. For a copy, send 50¢ to Consumer Furniture Booklet, National Home Fashions League, Inc., 107 World Trade Center, P.O. Box 58045, Dallas, TX 75258.

For listings of other firms that sell furnishings and decorative pieces for the home, see the "Decor" section of "Home," and "General."

ANNEX FURNITURE GALLERIES

**616 GREENSBORO RD.
HIGH POINT, NC 27260
919/884-8088**

Brochure: free
Save: up to 45%
Pay: check or MO
Sells: furnishings and decorative accessories
Store: same address; Monday through Saturday 9:30–5:30

Annex Furniture Galleries has nearly 45 years of experience selling North Carolina's finest furnishings and home accessories. If you can't visit the 45,000-square-foot showroom, you can order by mail. The brochure lists brand names and describes the sales policy, including deposit requirements, delivery estimates, and shipping method (van line and common carrier). Annex makes the observation here that "furniture is made from trees" in an effort to remind customers that no two pieces are identical. The point is well taken: You should always allow for natural variations in grain and tone when ordering furniture, from any source.

Special Factor: Price quote by phone or letter.

BLACKWELDER'S INDUSTRIES, INC.

**U.S. HWY. 21 N., RR12-390
STATESVILLE, NC 28677
800-438-0201
IN NC 704/872-8922
FAX: 704/872-4491**

Catalog and Brochures: $7.50, refundable (see text)
Save: up to 50%
Pay: check, MO, MC, V
Sells: home and office furniture and accessories
Store: mail order only

This firm, founded in 1938 with the aim of giving the consumer access to fine furniture at fair prices, delivers value, selection, and service. Blackwelder's is well regarded among consumers and offers extra savings through a discount program that is detailed in the brochure. An "information/work sheet" is available upon request.

Home and office furnishings, grandfather clocks, pianos, Oriental rugs and carpeting, lamps, and other goods from scores of manufacturers are showcased in the master catalog, which costs $7.50 (refundable, sent by first-class mail). Blackwelder's also has a well-priced line of classic and contemporary leather-upholstered furniture, manufactured under its own name, and the Windsor R. Martinsville collection of solid-wood furniture in pine, oak, and cherry. If you're shopping for traditional furniture, invest $2 in the brochure of this collection. The designs are classic, and the prices are *less* than those being charged for veneered particle board. You may inquire about the contract services Blackwelder's offers and quantity prices on large runs, and the firm's international sales department is equipped to handle export orders.

Special Factors: Satisfaction is guaranteed; price quote by phone or letter with SASE; shipments are made by van or common carrier; returns are accepted within 30 days (a 20% restocking fee is charged, applicable to a subsequent purchase made within 90 days), orders are shipped worldwide.

CHERRY HILL FURNITURE, CARPET & INTERIORS

P.O. BOX 7405,
FURNITURELAND
STATION
HIGH POINT, NC 27264
800-328-0933
800-888-0933
IN NC 919/882-0933

Brochure: free
Save: up to 50%
Pay: check or MO
Sells: home and office furniture and accessories
Store: mail order only

$$$

Cherry Hill, in business since 1933, offers a wide range of home and office furnishings, accessories, and rugs and carpeting at prices that average 45% off list. The Contract Division serves the needs of developers, purchasing directors, architects, and others who are doing residential or commercial installations. Cherry Hill can supply office furnishings, floor coverings, home furnishings, and accessories from over 500 manufacturers. A listing of brands and ordering information is free upon request, and a video catalog profiling popular lines is available—call for information.

Special Factors: Price quote by phone or letter with SASE; inquiries are accepted over the 800 line; shipment is made by common carrier or van line.

FACTORY DIRECT TABLE PAD CO.

1036 N. CAPITOL AVE.,
   SUITE C-210
INDIANAPOLIS, IN 46204
800-428-4567

Prices and Samples: $1
Save: up to 50%
Pay: check, MO, MC, V, Discover
Sells: custom-made table pads
Store: mail order only

Factory Direct tells us that about half of the cost of a custom-made table pad is the fee paid to the person who measures the table. If you send for information, you'll receive a guide to doing this yourself, as well as a discount coupon for $50 off Factory Direct's retail prices. Our mailing included several sample chips of the table pad top, which can be made in pebble-grain or smooth finish, in plain colors or in wood grain, in different thicknesses. The pads are warrantied for 5, 10, 15, or 20 years, and complete details are given in the literature.

Special Factors: Price quote by phone or letter; authorized returns are accepted within 15 days.

THE FURNITURE BARN

**1190 HWY. 74 BYPASS
SPINDALE, NC 28160
704/287-7106
FAX: 704/287-8785**

Brochure: free
Save: up to 50%
Pay: check, MO, MC, V, Discover
Sells: home furnishings, bedding, and
accessories
Store: same address; Monday through
Saturday 9–5

$$$$ ✉ ☎ 🍁 🇺🇸

The Furniture Barn has been providing fine furnishings at great prices since 1970 and is known for its prompt handling of orders and excellent delivery service.

Furniture, bedding, and decorative accents may be bought here at savings of up to 50%. The brands include the best-known names in furnishings; a complete list is given in the brochure, which includes details on the terms of sale.

Special Factors: Price quote by phone or letter with SASE; shipment is made by "a professional delivery specialist"; a 33% deposit is required.

GENADA IMPORTS

**P.O. BOX 204, DEPT. W-91
TEANECK, NJ 07666
201/790-7522**

Catalog: $1
Save: up to 40%
Pay: check, MO, MC, V
Sells: Danish and modern furniture
Store: mail order only

 $$ ✉ 🍁

Danish modern furniture has been revived at Genada in its most American incarnation: low-slung, teak-finished chairs and couches, with loose-cushion backs and seats of tweed-covered foam. Actually, the style has weathered fad and fatigue quite well, and the furniture's basic appeal is only enhanced by its low prices. Armchairs begin at under $90, and couches start at under $150. Genada also carries reproductions of the Barcelona chair and other modern classics, folding chairs with woven rope seats and backs, knock-down bookcases and cabinets, butcher block table tops and bases, gateleg tables with chairs that store in the base, and bentwood chairs. If you're shopping for a bridge table with folding hardwood chairs, you'll find several styles here at reasonable prices.

Special Factor: Specify upholstery and finish materials when ordering.

HARVEST HOUSE FURNITURE

**P.O. BOX 1440
DENTON, NC 27239
704/869-5181**

Information: inquire (see text)
Save: 45% to 50% average
Pay: check, MO, MC, V
Sells: home and office furnishings
Store: Hwy. 109 S., Denton, NC; Monday
through Friday 9–5, Saturday 9–1

Harvest House has been doing business since 1977, selling name-brand home and office furnishings at savings that average 45% to 50% off list. During the periodic "sales," prices are a flat 50% off manufacturers' suggested retail (with a minimum order of $400).

If you're still deciding which furniture to buy, you can send for the Harvest House brochure that includes a brands list and a questionnaire, which you may complete and return with $5 (refundable with purchase). Harvest House will send you an information packet, with manufacturers' brochures selected to suit your tastes and needs. If you've selected your furniture and are price shopping, you can call or write for a quote. Be sure to ask for the "Sales and Delivery Policy" sheet before you order, since it describes the delivery terms and procedures in detail.

Special Factor: Price quote by phone or letter with SASE.

INTERIOR FURNISHINGS LTD.

P.O. BOX 1644
HICKORY, NC 28603
704/328-5683

Brands List and Brochures: $3
Save: up to 50%
Pay: check, MO, certified check
Sells: home furnishings and accessories
Store: mail order only

$ ✉ 🍁

The brands list from Interior Furnishings includes the names of some of North Carolina's best-known manufacturers, who produce home furnishings, bedding, lamps, mirrors, table pads, and other accessories. Only first-quality goods are sold, and Interior offers both common carrier and van line deliveries.

Special Factor: Price quote by phone or letter with SASE.

LIBERTY GREEN

P.O. BOX 5035, STATION I
WILMINGTON, NC 28403
800-255-9704
919/395-1440

Catalog: $3, refundable
Save: up to 60%
Pay: check, MO, MC, V, AE, Discover, Access
Sells: country furnishings
Store: mail order only

$$$ ✉ ☎ 🍁 ▬

Liberty Green is nestled deep in the land of furniture discounters, but takes a different approach from most: Instead of offering every line from every manufacturer in North Carolina, Liberty Green sells only the work of its own craftsmen, at prices as much as 60% less than those of comparable goods bought from other furniture retailers. The firm has been doing business since 1984.

Liberty's 12-page, color catalog features "Plantation-style" furniture, which may be best described as simple country pine with a nod to the Shakers. Among its offerings are raised-panel entertainment centers, rush-seat ladderback chairs, a hutch in Welsh dresser style, pencil-post bed and coordinating bureaus and nightstands, wardrobes, lingerie chests, corner and jelly cupboards, and related pieces. The furniture is offered in a choice of stains with a satin lacquer finish, or painted in any of three colors. A modified camel-back sofa and wing chair are also available, in a range of fabrics. As a finishing touch, Liberty Green will even affix a small brass plaque declaring your selection "custom crafted" for you if the piece costs over $200. If you like the country look but have been shocked at the prices in the catalogs catering to this style, you'll find this firm a pleasant relief.

Special Factors: Satisfaction is guaranteed; returns are accepted within 90 days for exchange, refund, or credit; orders are shipped worldwide.

LOFTIN-BLACK FURNITURE COMPANY

111 SEDGEHILL DR.
THOMASVILLE, NC 27360
800-334-7398
IN NC 919/472-6117
FAX: 919/472-2052

Brochure: free
Save: up to 50%
Pay: check, MO, MC, V
Sells: furnishings, bedding, and accessories
Store: same address; Monday through Saturday 8:30–5:30

$$$$

Loftin-Black, founded in 1948, delivers selection, service, and savings. The firm offers fine home, office, and patio furniture and bedding, and accessories from hundreds of firms, including the top names in furnishings. Check with Loftin-Black before ordering mirrors, table pads, and bedding—they're available here, at sizable savings. The brochure includes a brands listing and general sales information. In-home delivery and setup is provided by the firm, although you can engage a common carrier if you prefer. A 50% deposit is required when ordering, and the balance is due upon delivery.

Special Factors: Price quote by phone or letter; delivery (in-home) is made by Loftin-Black's van service.

MALLORY'S FINE FURNITURE

P.O. BOX 1150-WM
JACKSONVILLE, NC
28540
919/353-1828
919/447-2136

Brochure: free
Save: up to 45%
Pay: check or MO
Sells: furnishings, carpets, lamps, etc.
Store: 2153 Lejune Blvd., Jacksonville, and Hwy. 70 W., Havelock, NC; Monday through Saturday 9–6, both locations

$$ ✉ 🍁

Mallory's has been serving price-conscious furniture buyers since 1947, offering name-brand furnishings and accessories at up to 45% off list or fully marked-up retail prices. The company has two large showrooms, in Jacksonville and Havelock, where samples are displayed.

In addition to furnishings, Mallory's offers name-brand carpets, bedding, bedspreads, clocks, lamps, and other decorative accessories. Brochures featuring individual brands and lines may be ordered through Mallory's as well. The sales policy is detailed in the literature Mallory's sends upon request, including delivery schedule estimate, cancellation policy, and shipping choices (common carrier, private carrier, and North American Van Lines).

Special Factors: Price quote by phone or letter with SASE; minimum order is $150.

MURROW FURNITURE GALLERIES, INC.

P.O. BOX 4337, DEPT.
WBMC
WILMINGTON, NC 28406
919/799-4010
FAX: 919/791-2791

Brochure: free
Save: up to 50%
Pay: check or MO
Sells: home furnishings, bedding, and accessories
Store: 3514 S. College Rd., Wilmington, NC; Monday through Friday 8:30–5:30, Saturday 9–5:30

 $$$$ ✉ ☎ 🍁

Murrow, founded in 1979, represents over 500 furnishings manufacturers (listed in the brochure). Furnishings, bedding, and accessories are available. The extensive selection of brands and consistently good savings make this one of the best furniture discounters around. If you're able to visit the store in Wilmington, you'll find five huge gallery showrooms of 45,000 square feet with fine furnishings and accessories on display. Delivery options and terms of sale are detailed in the brochure.

Special Factors: Price quote by phone or letter with SASE; deposit by check or money order is required; orders are shipped worldwide.

PLEXI-CRAFT QUALITY PRODUCTS CORP.

**514 W. 24TH ST.
NEW YORK, NY
10011-1179
800-24-PLEXI
212/924-3244**

Catalog: $2
Save: up to 50%
Pay: check, MO, MC, V
Sells: acrylic furnishings and accessories
Store: same address; Monday through Friday 9:30–5, Saturday 11–4

Plexi-Craft manufactures its own line of Lucite® and Plexiglas® goods, and its prices are up to 50% less than those charged for comparable products by department and specialty stores. New items are added regularly, and the firm handles custom work. Plexi-Craft was founded in 1972.

Acrylic furnishings and accessories of all kinds are shown in the 16-page catalog. There are a number of tables—dining, cocktail, Parsons, TV, snack, and side—and those with separate bases may be ordered with glass instead of acrylic tops. There are several rolling bar models, chairs, pedestals, computer stands, vanities and stools, luggage racks, magazine units, and telephone tables. Desk sets, kitchen organizers and paper towel holders, and bathroom fixtures round out the selection. Antistatic cleaner and a polish formulated for acrylic are also available.

Special Factor: Price quote by phone or letter on custom work.

QUALITY FURNITURE MARKET OF LENOIR, INC.

2034 HICKORY BLVD.
S.W.
LENOIR, NC 28645
704/728-2946
FAX: 704/726-0226

Information: price quote
Save: up to 47%
Pay: check, MO, MC, V
Sells: furnishings, bedding, and accessories
Store: same address; Monday through
  Saturday 8:30–5

$$$$

Quality Furniture Market, in business since 1953, takes its name seriously; you're invited to check the firm's ratings with Dun and Bradstreet, the Lyons listing, and the Lenoir Chamber of Commerce. The excellent selection is offered at prices that are 15% to 20% over cost, compared to the usual 110% to 125%.

Quality Furniture sells indoor and outdoor furniture, bedding, and home accessories by literally hundreds of firms. The terms of sale and other conditions are stated clearly in the brochure, as well as a list of available brands. We've received long letters from readers who were very pleased with Quality's prices and the firm's in-home delivery service. If you're traveling through Lenoir, drop by and get lost in the 48,000 square feet of display.

Special Factors: Price quote by phone or letter with SASE; all orders must be prepaid before shipment; shipment is made by common carrier or in-home delivery service.

QUEEN ANNE FURNITURE COMPANY, INC.

RTE. 2, BOX 427
TRINITY, NC 27370
919/431-2562
919/434-4990

Brochure with Swatches: $3 (see text)
Save: 45% average
Pay: check, MO, MC, V
Sells: home furnishings
Store: mail order only

$$

Queen Anne Furniture Company has found its inspiration as well as its name in "the Gallant Era of the 18th Century Splendor." The firm has been producing Queen Anne sofas, wing chairs, and other classics since 1983, at prices that average 45% below retail.

The six-page brochure shows clear, black-and-white photographs of the firm's sofas, loveseats, wing chairs, swivel rockers, Martha Washington chairs, slipper chairs, upholstered ottomans, and other seating. Dimensions of each piece are stated, and you may select from three leg styles (cabriole with pad feet, Chippendale, or ball and claw), which may be finished in cherry or oak stain and lacquer. Swatches of the firm's fabric come with the brochure as part of the $3 fee; you can use the firm's material or provide your own, in which case Queen Anne Furniture drops the price of the piece.

In addition to its own line, Queen Anne represents a number of well-known manufacturers of furniture and home accessories, which it also sells at a discount. See the brochure for a list of the available brands, or call for information and a price quote.

Special Factors: Price quote by phone or letter with SASE. Pay the brochure/swatch fee by check or money order—not credit card.

JAMES ROY FURNITURE CO., INC.

15 E. 32ND ST.
NEW YORK, NY 10016
212/679-2565

Brands List: free
Save: 33% plus
Pay: check, MO, MC, V (see text)
Sells: home and office furnishings, bedding, and carpeting
Store: same address; Monday to Saturday 9:30–5:00, Sunday 12–5

James Roy offers you *guaranteed* discounts of 33% and more on the suggested list prices of furnishings and bedding from over 400 manufacturers. Roy has been in business for over 25 years and provides professional service. Furnishings, accessories, and bedding are offered, and the brochure includes a complete roster of brands represented, as well as terms and conditions of sale.

Special Factors: Price quote by phone or letter with SASE; credit cards are accepted for payment of deposit only; final payments must be paid by check, money order, or certified check.

SHAW FURNITURE GALLERIES, INC.

P.O. BOX 576
RANDLEMAN, NC 27317
919/498-2628

Brochure: free
Save: up to 45%
Pay: check, MO, MC, V
Sells: furnishings
Store: 131 W. Academy St., Randleman, NC; Monday through Friday 9–5:30, Saturday 9–5

$$$

The Shaw family has been selling furniture at a discount since 1940 and offers more than 300 brands from which to choose. The brochure lists about half of the manufacturers represented; inquire if you're pricing an item by a firm not mentioned, since it may be carried.

Shaw boasts a $2-million-plus inventory of furnishings by top furnishings manufacturers. Sales terms are detailed in the brochure. Please note: Final payments must be made by certified check or money order.

Special Factors: Price quote by phone or letter with SASE; shipments are made by van line or common carrier.

STUCKEY BROTHERS FURNITURE CO., INC.

RTE. 1, P.O. BOX 527
STUCKEY, SC 29554
803/558-2591

Information: price quote
Save: up to 50%
Pay: check, MO, certified check
Sells: indoor and outdoor furnishings and accessories
Store: same address; Monday through Friday 9–6, Saturday 9–5

$$

Stuckey is South Carolina's answer to High Point—it sells a full line of furniture and accessories at North Carolina prices, and has been doing business by mail since 1946.

Stuckey carries furnishings and accessories, including patio and nursery furnishings, from over 300 manufacturers. Clocks, lamps, mirrors, and bedding are available as well. Request the brochure that details the sales terms and shipping options (van line or common carrier).

Special Factors: Price quote by phone or letter with SASE; orders are shipped worldwide.

MARION TRAVIS

P.O. BOX 292
STATESVILLE, NC 28677
704/528-4424

Catalog: $1
Save: up to 50%
Pay: check, MO, MC, V
Sells: country chairs, benches, and tables
Store: 354 South Eastway Dr., Troutman, NC; Monday through Thursday 8–3:30, Friday 8–12 noon

$$$ ✉

You can pay hundreds of dollars for an oak pedestal table at your local antique shop, and search every tag sale in the state for a matched set of ladder-back chairs. Or you can send Marion Travis $1 for a catalog, which shows these and other furnishings.

The ten-page catalog shows black-and-white photographs of country furniture, including a large selection of ladder-back chairs with woven cord seats. There are armchair and rocker styles and children's models, beginning at under $25. Plain, slat-seat kitchen chairs and a classic oak kitchen table with utility drawer are shown, as well as a deacon's bench, porch swing, and Kennedy-style rockers with cane backs and seats. The prices cited are for unfinished furniture, but Marion Travis will stain and finish your selection in natural, oak, or walnut.

Special Factor: Authorized returns of defective goods are accepted within 30 days.

TURNER TOLSON, INC.

P.O. DRAWER 1507
NEW BERN, NC 28560
800-334-6616
IN NC 919/638-2121

Brochure: free
Save: up to 50%
Pay: check, MO, MC, V
Sells: home and office furnishings
Store: Hwy. 17 South, New Bern, NC;
Monday through Saturday 10–6

$$$ ✉ ☎ 🍁

Turner Tolson, in business since 1887, is an authorized dealer for prominent names in home and office furnishings. The firm's brochure includes a partial list of brands, and inquiries are invited on names not mentioned. Manufacturers' catalogs are available for a fee; write with the name of the line in which you're interested. Turner's prices are 40% to 50% lower than list, and shipping charges include in-home delivery and setup. You are invited to check the company's references with the New Bern Chamber of Commerce and the local bank. And if you make your purchase in person from the 36,000-square-foot showroom, Turner Tolson may pick up the check for your lodgings in New Bern—inquire for details.

Special Factors: Price quote by phone or letter with SASE; a 25% deposit is required when ordering.

ZARBIN & ASSOCIATES, INC.

401 N. FRANKLIN ST.,
4TH FLOOR
CHICAGO, IL 60610
312/527-1570

Information: price quote
Save: up to 40%
Pay: check, MO, certified check
Sells: furniture, bedding, and carpeting
Store: mail order only (see text)

$$$ ✉

The Zarbin family has been selling furniture, bedding, and carpeting since 1963, and its reliable mail-order department offers you a hassle-free way to save 40% on the best in home decor. Professional designers on staff can assist you in your selections and guide you through the showroom of the Merchandise Mart in Chicago, where samples are displayed.

Full lines of furnishings and accessories are available from scores of well-known manufacturers. Most of the goods are shipped from manufacturers' warehouses to the trucker; delivery charges and services include uncrating and setup.

Special Factor: Price quote by letter with SASE (include manufacturer's name, item stock number, and fabric and grade numbers, if applicable).

SEE ALSO

Alfax Wholesale Furniture • office and institutional furnishings • OFFICE

American Discount Wallcoverings • upholstery and decorator fabrics • HOME: DECOR

Barnes & Noble Bookstores, Inc. • folding beechwood bookshelves • BOOKS

Bennett Brothers, Inc. • small selection of home furnishings • GENERAL MERCHANDISE

Ben's Babyland • name-brand juvenile furniture • CLOTHING: MOTHER AND CHILD

Business & Institutional Furniture Company • office and institutional furniture • OFFICE

Buy Direct, Inc. • computer furniture • OFFICE: COMPUTING

Cole's Appliance & Furniture Co. • name-brand home furnishings • APPLIANCES

Frank Eastern Co. • office furniture • OFFICE

The Fabric Center, Inc. • upholstery and decorator fabrics • HOME: DECOR

Fabrics by Design • name-brand upholstery and decorator fabrics • HOME: DECOR

Fashion Touches • custom-covered upholstery buttons • CRAFTS

Grayarc • small selection of office chairs and work stations • OFFICE

Harmony Supply Inc. • decorator fabrics • HOME: DECOR

Monarch • radiator enclosures • HOME: MAINTENANCE

SGF • selected name-brand furnishings and home accents • GENERAL MERCHANDISE

Shama Imports, Inc. • crewel upholstery fabric and cushion covers • HOME: DECOR

Slipcovers of America • slipcovers • HOME: DECOR

Irv Wolfson Company • small selection of name-brand bedding, recliners, and dinette sets • APPLIANCES

KITCHEN

Cookware, bakeware, restaurant equipment, and food storage

E valuating kitchen equipment is a difficult business, and the book that handled it best is now out of print: *The Cooks' Catalogue* (Avon Books, 1975), edited by a consortium that included the late James Beard, Barbara Kafka, and Milton Glaser. Although it predates Calphalon and some other important additions to the *batterie de cuisine,* it's a standard that has yet to be equalled or updated. *The International Cooks' Catalogue* (Random House, 1977), another valuable reference compiled by the same team, compares specialty cookware used around the world for different ethnic cuisines. Both of these books may be available in your local library or from out-of-print booksellers.

THE CHEF'S PANTRY

P.O. BOX 3
POST MILLS, VT 05058
800-TRY-CHEF
802/333-4141

Catalog: free
Save: up to 50%
Pay: check, MO, MC, V
Sells: gourmet and specialty foods
Store: mail order only

$$$ ✉   ☎

Unless you're a food professional or live in a large city, you're not likely to know where to find a good selection of the kinds of foodstuffs popular among gourmet cooks, caterers, and serious home bakers. The Chef's Pantry, just two years old, remedies this problem with a 12-page catalog of condiments and delicacies, which it sells at prices as much as 50% less than those charged by its competitors. (Further discounts are available on quantity purchases.)

The catalog we reviewed featured the 11-pound bar of Callebaut bittersweet chocolate for $47.50 ($65 in other catalogs), Nielsen Massey vanilla extract at 25% below the competition, two grams of Mancha saffron for $9.50 ($16 elsewhere), and shallots from Brittany for just $2.45 per pound. Other baking supplies, such as candied fruits, flowers, and extracts, as well as vinegars, mustards, oils, preserved nuts and fruits, and other condiments and ingredients, are also stocked. The Chef's Pantry selects preferred brands and varieties—Dauphi Noix nut oils, Italian porcini and German chanterelles, and Menetrel Helix escargot are a few examples. If you've got a gourmet cook on your gift list, check the roster of gift assortments available, which run from "Bakers Treat" to "Risotto Makings". If you don't see what you're looking for in the catalog, call or write—we were told that Dutch cocoa, almond paste, and sliced almonds were among what's available, but they weren't listed. (A minimum order quantity may be imposed on such special orders.)

Special Factors: Satisfaction is guaranteed; price quote by phone or letter with SASE; returns are accepted for exchange, refund, or credit.

COLONIAL GARDEN KITCHENS

HANOVER, PA 17333-0066
717/633-3333

Catalog: free
Save: up to 40%
Pay: check, MO, MC, V, CB, DC, Discover
Sells: kitchen equipment and household helps
Store: mail order only

$$ ✉ ☎

Colonial Garden Kitchens is a Hanover House company that's been going strong since 1956. Several readers have recommended CGK, and we compared prices and found savings of up to 40% on selected items.

A third or more of the goods in the color catalog are usually on "sale," or priced 20% to 40% below their regular prices (and the "regular" prices did not appear to be inflated). Each catalog features kitchen appliances, specialty cookware and utensils, work units and food storage containers, serving and entertaining equipment, and lots of handy things to have around the house. The issue we saw offered the KitchenAid food processor, commercial oven mitts, asparagus steamers, cast iron woks, a dinosaur muffin tin, insulated bakeware, microwave steamers, inexpensive bath towels, sock organizers, and the economy size of Simple Green cleaner. Everything is backed by the firm's no-questions-asked guarantee of satisfaction.

Special Factors: Satisfaction is guaranteed; returns are accepted for exchange, refund, or credit; minimum order is $15 with credit cards.

A COOK'S WARES

WEST MAYFIELD BORO
211 37TH ST.
BEAVER FALLS, PA
   15010-2103
412/846-9490

Catalog: $2
Save: up to 50%
Pay: check, MO, MC, V, AE
Sells: cookware and kitchen utensils
Store: mail order only

This firm, established in 1981, is run by two devoted cooks who choose the best in cookware and food preparation equipment and sell it at savings of up to 50%. The informative, 46-page catalog features many hard-to-find items.

The stock includes cookware lines by All-Clad (the Cop-R Chef, anodized aluminum, and Master Chef lines), Chantal, Le Creuset, Cuisinart, Leyse, Spring Copper, and Vollrath, and Mauviel's hotel-weight copper pots and pans. New to us is the Jacques Pepin Collection from Bourgeat, featuring heavy copper pans with stainless steel linings and cast iron handles. Alessi's "Orion's Belt" cookware collection (of which the Michael Graves teakettle is best known) is offered as well. A Cook's Wares also carries bakeware by Apilco, Pillivuyt, Isabelle Marique Blue Steel, Kaiser, and Chicago Metallic (Village Baker and Silverstone-on-Steel). All sorts of cookie cutters from Ateco are listed in the current catalog, and you'll find molds for ladyfingers, petit fours, madeleines, macaroons, and other sweets as well. The finest in cutlery and food preparation and serving equipment is stocked: KitchenAid mixers and accessories, Bron and Moha mandolines, Melior infusion coffee makers, Gaggia espresso makers, Krups equipment (coffee grinders, coffee makers, scales, and timers), Vitantonio and Mouli appliances, J.K. Adams wooden knife blocks, Rosti utensils and storage containers, and Cuisinart food processors. The complete Henckels cutlery and kitchen gadget lines are available. Also offered are goods by Atlas, William Bounds, Copco, F. Dick, DMT, Lola, Sparta, Victorinox, Westmark, Wusthof-Trident, and other firms.

A Cook's Wares has brought the same standards to its line of foodstuffs, primarily condiments: Paul Corcellet vinegars and mustards, Classic American mustards, Blanchard & Blanchard condiments, Select Origins herbs and spices, pumate (sun-dried tomatoes), olive spread, and other goods are available. Cooking and eating chocolate from Callebaut, Ghirardelli, and Lindt is offered, as well as Clearbrook Farms' dessert sauces, Tiptree preserves, and Vermont maple syrup.

Special Factors: Satisfaction is guaranteed; price quote by phone or letter with SASE on items not listed in the catalog; returns are accepted within 30 days.

FIVENSON FOOD EQUIPMENT, INC.

324 S. UNION ST.
TRAVERSE CITY, MI
49684-2586
616/946-7760
IN MI 800-632-7342

Catalog: $2, refundable
Save: up to 50%
Pay: check, MO, MC, V, AE, Discover
Sells: commercial restaurant, bar, and concession equipment
Store: mail order only

Fivenson has been selling restaurant equipment to the food-service industry since 1937 and offers consumers the same products at prices up to 50% below list.

The catalogs we reviewed showed pizza ovens, convection ovens, popcorn machines, Gold Medal equipment, and commercial refrigerators. Fivenson sells ranges from Garland, South Bend, Vulcan, and Wolf. Also available are Hobart (commercial) mixers and equipment, meat grinders, ice machines, stainless sinks, steam tables, griddles, fryers, Belgian waffle makers, ice cream makers, food storage units, and restaurant furnishings, including stacking chairs, bar stools, and even booths. Hamilton Beach bar mixers, Univex deli slicers and mixers, coffee brewers, Libbey glassware, and Pyrex and Corning china are especially popular among consumers. (The china and glassware are sold by the case only.) You can call or write for a price quote on specific models, or send $2 for the 16-page catalog.

Special Factors: Price quote by phone or letter with SASE; kitchen layout and design services are available; minimum order is $25; orders are shipped worldwide.

H AND M COMMERCIAL SERVICES

**1100 KENTUCKY
QUINCY, IL 62301
217/224-6372**

Manufacturers' Brochures: $3, refundable
Save: up to 50%
Pay: check or MO
Sells: commercial ice machines
Store: mail order only

$$ ✉

H and M Commercial Services sells commercial (restaurant) ice cube machines, flakers, storage bins, and drink dispensers. The two brands available are Manitowoc and Ross-Temp, and your $3 catalog fee brings you the manufacturers' brochures on both companies' lines. While these machines exceed the needs of most householders, anyone who entertains frequently or is running a food service or catering business may find such equipment helpful.

H and M discounts the machines 40% or 50% from list prices, depending on the line. If you know which model you want, you can call or write for a specific price quote and shipping estimate.

Special Factor: Price quote by letter only with SASE.

KAPLAN BROS. BLUE FLAME CORP.

**523 W. 125TH ST.
NEW YORK, NY
10027-3498
212/662-6990**

Brochure: free with SASE
Save: up to 50%
Pay: check, MO, certified check
Sells: commercial restaurant equipment
Store: same address; Monday through Friday 8–5

$$$ ✉

Kaplan Bros., established in 1953, sells commercial restaurant equipment at discounts of up to 50% on list prices. Manufacturers' brochures are sent on request if you supply a self-addressed, stamped envelope; inquire for Kaplan's prices. The service is prompt and the discounts are hard to match.

Kaplan is known best as a source for Garland commercial stoves, including the popular six-burner model that costs over $1,900 at list price, but $950 here. (Garland's Residential Range model is available.) Garland fryers, ovens, griddles, and salamanders are stocked, as well as Frymaster and Pitco fryers, and equipment by Blickman, Blodgett, and Vulcan.

Please note: Goods are shipped to "mainland U.S.A." only—no orders to Alaska, Hawaii, Canada, or APO/FPO addresses.

Special Factors: Price quote by phone or letter with SASE; request brochures by name of manufacturer; if purchasing a stove for residential installation, have kitchen flooring, wall insulation, and exhaust system evaluated before ordering and upgrade if necessary.

NEW ENGLAND CHEESEMAKING SUPPLY CO.

BOX 85
ASHFIELD, MA 01330
413/628-3808

Catalog: $1
Save: up to 80% (see text)
Pay: check, MO, MC, V
Sells: cheese-making supplies and equipment
Store: Ashfield, MA; Monday through Friday 8–4 (call first)

Making cheese at home is one of the few do-it-yourself endeavors with a nominal price tag that *doesn't* require a significant time or skills investment. New England Cheesemaking Supply, in business since 1978, can provide you with all the tools and materials you'll need to produce hard, soft, and semi-soft cheeses, at savings of up to 80% on the prices charged in stores for the same kinds of cheeses.

Soft cheese is the easiest to make, and may be the cheapest, since you can get as much as two pounds from a gallon of milk. Milk is selling for $1.10 a half gallon in some parts of the country, while flavored soft cheeses often cost $4.50 to $7.00 per pound, or as much as $2.60 for packaged, four-ounce varieties. Using the "Gourmet Soft Cheese Kit," you can recoup the $15.95 cost, plus the price of the milk, after making as little as two pounds of soft cheese. This kit is designed for the beginner, and comes with cheese starter, cheesecloth, a dairy thermometer, and recipes. It can be used to make *crème fraiche* as well as *fromage blanc*—generic soft cheese, in as little as ten minutes. (If you use skim milk, you can produce low-calorie, low-cholesterol cheese, and omit the salt for sodium-restricted diets.)

New England Cheesemaking Supply also sells a "basic" cheese kit (for ricotta, Gouda, Monterey Jack, cheddar, etc.), and others for making mozzarella and goat cheese, as well as rennet (animal and vegetable), a large selection of starter and direct-set cultures, lipase powder, mold powder, annato color tablets, cheese wax, cheesecloth, thermometers, French cheese mats for draining and drying cheese, molds for shaping hard and soft cheese, and several books on cheese production. Experienced cheese producers should see the 14-page catalog for the machinery as well: a home milk pasteurizer, Wheeler hard cheese press, Deva nonelectric devices for making yogurt and soft cheese, and the White Mountain electric and hand-cranked ice cream machines are all available. The couple who run this firm are experienced cheese producers, and can answer your questions by phone or letter.

Special Factors: Price quote by phone or letter with SASE; minimum order is $20 with credit cards; C.O.D. orders are accepted; orders are shipped worldwide.

PARIS INTERNATIONAL INC.

■■■■■■■■■

PARIS BREAD PANS
500 INDEPENDENCE
  AVE., S.E.
WASHINGTON, DC 20003
202/544-6858

Price List: free with SASE
Save: up to 50%
Pay: check or MO
Sells: bakeware
Store: mail order only

$$$

When Clyde Brooks returned from a stay of several years in Paris, he found himself longing for French bread and could find no substitutes here. After experimentation, he developed recipes that captured the flavor but couldn't find a pan that would give the bread its characteristic shape and texture. So he designed one himself, and Paris International was born. The pans compare to others sold for twice as much and have been recommended in *The Cook's Catalogue*. Other useful, well-priced baking equipment is available as well.

The Paris International French bread pans are made of nonstick quilted aluminum (two 18″ double-trough pans, $12, or a set of four for $18) for French baguettes and breads. Mr. Brooks has experimented with other breads since getting into the pan business in 1973, and offers a larger-trough pan for Italian loaves and San Francisco sourdough bread for $8. Recipes are included with all of the pans. Paris also sells the "Whole Oven Baking Sheet" in two sizes, for standard and wall ovens, which is useful for large batches of cookies, sweet rolls, and other baked goods. It costs $8 and comes with recipes for cookies and meringues. Mr. Brooks will forward any of these items to your favorite cook, enclosing your note or card if you so desire.

Canadian readers, please note: Only U.S. funds are accepted.

Special Factors: Price quote by phone or letter with SASE; orders are shipped worldwide.

ZABAR'S & CO., INC.

2245 BROADWAY
NEW YORK, NY 10024
800-221-3347
IN NY 212/787-2000

Catalog: free
Save: up to 50%
Pay: check, MO, MC, V, AE, DC
Sells: gourmet food, cookware, and housewares
Store: same address; Monday through Friday 8–7:30, Saturday 8 A.M.–midnight, Sunday 9–6; housewares mezzanine 9–6 daily

Zabar's, characterized as New York City's ultimate deli, offers the whole nation a sumptuous sampling from its famed counters and housewares mezzanine via a 62-page catalog. Zabar's has been around since 1934 and prices its goods up to 50% below the going rate.

Past catalogs have shown smoked Scottish, Norwegian, and Irish salmon, plum pudding, peppercorns, Brie, Bahlsen cookies and confections, pâtés, mustards, crackers, escargot, Lindt and Droste chocolate, Tiptree preserves, Dresden stollen, olive oil, prosciutto and other deli meats, and similar gourmet fare. The cookware selections include Mauviel hotel-weight copper pots and pans; Calphalon, Cuisinart, Farberware, Le Creuset, Magnalite, and Revere Ware equipment; Krups and Simac ma-

chines, Braun coffee makers, Robot Coupe food processors, Sharp microwave ovens, Mouli kitchen tools, and products by Melitta, Henckels,
Toshiba, and other firms.

Zabar's distinguishes itself among kitchenware vendors for the enormous selection of goods and the substantial discounts. The catalog features
a representative selection from the store, but if you don't see it—call.
Zabar's probably has what you need right on the shelves.

Special Factors: Price quote by phone or letter with SASE on cookware
not shown in the catalog; minimum order is $10.

SEE ALSO

Bernie's Discount Center, Inc. ● microwave ovens and large and small
kitchen appliances ● *APPLIANCES*

Bruce Medical Supply ● food preparation equipment for those with
limited strength and mobility ● *MEDICINE*

Cabela's Inc. ● camping cookware, stoves, etc. ● *SPORTS*

CISCO ● Insinkerator garbage disposers ● *HOME: MAINTENANCE*

Clothcrafters, Inc. ● pot holders, chefs' hats, coffee filters, greens bags,
kitchen gadgets, etc. ● *GENERAL MERCHANDISE*

Current, Inc. ● canning labels, recipe boxes, etc. ● *BOOKS*

Fish'n Shack ● camping kitchenware, cookstoves, etc. ● *SPORTS*

Grandma's Spice Shop ● spice racks, wine racks, mortar and pestle sets,
teapots, etc. ● *FOOD*

Jessica's Biscuit ● cookbooks ● *BOOKS*

E.C. Kraus Wine & Beermaking Supplies ● bottle washers, cherry
pitters, funnels, corkscrews ● *FOOD*

LVT Price Quote Hotline, Inc. ● microwave ovens, major appliances,
etc. ● *APPLIANCES*

The New England Slate Company ● salvaged slate for countertops,
etc. ● *HOME: MAINTENANCE*

The Paper Wholesaler ● disposable bakeware and cake-decorating
supplies ● *GENERAL MERCHANDISE*

Percy's Inc. ● major appliances ● *APPLIANCES*

Plastic BagMart ● garbage can liners ● *HOME: MAINTENANCE*

The Renovator's Supply, Inc. ● iron pot racks, hooks, and towel
holders ● *HOME: MAINTENANCE*

Robin Importers, Inc. ● name-brand kitchen cutlery, knife blocks,
pepper mills, etc. ● *HOME: TABLE SETTINGS*

S & S Sound City ● microwave ovens ● *APPLIANCES*

Simpson & Vail, Inc. ● teapots, coffee makers, grinders, filters, etc. ●
   FOOD
The Spice House ● pepper mills and spice jars ● *FOOD*
Spiegel, Inc. ● name-brand cookware ● *GENERAL MERCHANDISE*
Sultan's Delight, Inc. ● Turkish coffee pots and cups, mamoul and falafel
   molds, mortars and pestles ● *FOOD*
Suncoast Discount Arts & Crafts ● cookie cutters ● *CRAFTS*
Walnut Acres ● cookware, bakeware, serving pieces, etc. ● *FOOD*
Weston Bowl Mill ● woodenware, knives, and kitchen helpers ●
   GENERAL
The Wine Enthusiast ● wine cellars, storage units, corkscrews, etc. ●
   FOOD

LINEN

Bed, bath, and table textiles, accessories, and services

There's never a reason to wait for a white sale when you can buy your sheets, towels, pillows, and table linens from discounters who sell at savings of up to 60% every day, year-round. Some of the firms sell both first-quality and irregular goods, and some sell only first-quality—ask before placing your order to be sure you're getting what you want. In addition to offerings from the major mills, several of these firms provide custom services, such as sheets to fit waterbeds and oddly shaped mattresses, rejuvenation of down pillows and comforters, and bed ruffles and coordinating lamp shades made to order.

Your bed, bath, and table textiles will last longer if you follow the manufacturers' care instructions explicitly. Although we've never seen it on a label, we've read that down-filled goods should never be stored in cedar or camphor, since they'll pick up those odors permanently. Some experts also advise against storing down-filled products in plastic—use a cloth bag or pillowcase instead. And if you keep your down-filled comforter slipcased in a duvet, you'll cut down on the cleaning frequency, and extend the comforter's useful life.

EZRA COHEN CORP.

307 GRAND ST.
NEW YORK, NY 10002
212/925-7800
FAX: 212/925-9767

Information: price quote
Save: up to 60%
Pay: check, MO, MC, V, AE, Optima
Sells: bed and bath linens
Store: same address; Sunday through
   Thursday 9–5, Friday 9–4

$$$ ✉   ☎

Cohen has been selling bed and bath linens since 1903 and stocks full lines from the major mills, as well as a wide range of accessories. Bed linens from Cannon (including the Versailles Collection), Fieldcrest, Martex (including Atelier), Revman, J.P. Stevens, and Wamsutta are available, including Laura Ashley, Katja, Adrienne Vittadini, Eileen West, and other designer lines. There are bath linens by Avanti, Fieldcrest's Royal Velvet and Charisma lines, and the lush Patrician towels by Martex. Comforters and bedspreads by Croscill, Crown Crafts, Dakotah, Dyne (down comforters), Nettlecreek, and Northern Feather are available. Call or write for prices on Fieldcrest bath carpeting, Regel scatter rugs, polyester and down bedding, and Ferncraft daybed covers. Cohen's custom department can produce shams, bed ruffles, and sheets for nonstandard mattresses.

Special Factors: Price quote by phone or letter with SASE; there is no catalog.

THE COMPANY STORE INC.

DEPT. PR001
500 COMPANY STORE
   RD.
LA CROSSE, WI 54601
800-356-9367
608/785-1400
FAX: 608/785-7037

Catalog: free
Save: up to 50%
Pay: check, MO, MC, V, AE, Discover
Sells: down-filled bedding and outerwear
Store: outlets in IL, MN, and WI (locations
   are given in the catalog)

The Company Store publishes a 56-page color catalog of well-priced down bedding and a range of linen. The Company Store is known for its excellent selection of top-quality goods and prompt service. The parent firm was established in 1911.

Comforters of all weights, sizes, and types are offered here, including box, channel, and ring-stitched down-filled comforters, summer-weight down comforters, and all-cotton comforters. High fill power, down-proof materials, and hand-guided quilting are among the product features. Complementing pillows in baby/boudoir, neckroll, European, standard, queen, and king sizes and shapes are also available. The Company Store has an appealing selection of all-cotton linens—sheets, bed ruffles, duvets (comforter slipcases), pillowcases, shams, and more, priced well below comparable sheets from the major mills. The catalog we reviewed also showed a lap throw, travel afghan, and even a feather-stuffed "dog bed" for small human beings. The Company Store's nursery department features bedding in pastel solids, and crib comforters, bumpers, pillows, and shams are offered. The "Custom Shop" can take your ideas for comforters, covers, pillows, and bed ruffles, and create them in your fabric or theirs. Comforter refurbishing and monogramming services are also available.

A portion of the catalog is devoted to The Company Store's extensive line of down-filled outerwear and accessories for men, women, and children. The offerings run from baby buntings to goose down jumpsuits for women, and prices are competitive.

Special Factors: Satisfaction is guaranteed; returns are accepted for exchange, refund, or credit.

DOMESTICATIONS

HANOVER, PA 17333-0040
717/633-3313

Catalog: $2
Save: up to 35%
Pay: check, MO, MC, V, CB, DC, Discover
Sells: bed and bath linens
Store: mail order only

$$ ✉ ☎

Domestications, a Hanover House Industries catalog, offers a colorful selection of linens for bed, bath, and table. Mickey Mouse, cabbage roses, Memphis design elements, and baseball players are among the many sheet motifs we've seen in past Domestications catalogs. Bold designs and romantic floral patterns figure prominently in the selections from Bibb, Cannon, Fieldcrest, Martex, Dan River, J.P. Stevens, Utica, Wamsutta, and other firms. All-cotton and blends are offered, in sheets sets and individually. Traditional and novelty blankets and bedspreads from Barclay, Crown Crafts, Georgia Tufted, and Countess York have been featured, and pillows, mattress pads, tablecloths, curtains, and even lamps and decorative accents are carried as well. We found prices especially low on sheet sets, but even single pieces were usually discounted 20% and more.

Special Factors: Satisfaction is guaranteed; returns are accepted; minimum order is $20 with credit cards.

ELDRIDGE TEXTILE CO.

**277 GRAND ST.
NEW YORK, NY 10002
212/925-1523
FAX: 212/219-9542**

Brochure: free (see text)
Save: up to 40%
Pay: check, MO, MC, V
Sells: bed, bath, and table linens
Store: same address; Sunday through
Friday 9–5:30

Eldridge has been selling soft goods and housewares since 1940 and offers mail-order customers savings of up to 40% on top brands. Other home decor lines are sold in the store.

Eldridge stocks bed, bath, and table linens by Laura Ashley, Beau Ideal, Cameo, Cannon, Croscill, Crown Crafts, Dakotah, Faribo, Fieldcrest, Fashion Home, India Ink, Jackson, Kosan (down quilts), Martex, Nettlecreek, Newmark (bath rugs), Northern Feather, Pacific Designs, André Richard, Dan River, Saturday Knight, Springmaid, Utica, Wamsutta, and other firms. Some of the best-selling sheet and towel lines are listed in the brochure, but if you're shopping for bedspreads, shower curtains, or comforters, call or write for a price quote. Window treatments, tablecloths, and rugs are available to in-store shoppers at savings of up to 40%.

Please note: The brochure is free upon request if you mention WBMC, or $3 if you don't.

Special Factors: Price quote by phone or letter with SASE; returns of unused goods are accepted for refund or credit; minimum order is $25.

HARRIS LEVY, INC.

**278 GRAND ST., DEPT.
WBM
NEW YORK, NY 10002
800-221-7750
IN NY 212/226-3102
FAX: 212/334-9360**

Information: price quote
Save: up to 50%
Pay: check, MO, MC, V, AE, Optima
Sells: bed, bath, and table linens
Store: same address; Monday through
  Thursday 9–5:30, Friday and Sunday
  9–4:30

$$$$ ✉ ☎

Levy, established in 1894, is one of the plums of New York City's Lower East Side—a firm that sells the crème de la crème of bed, bath, and table linens at savings of up to 50%. One-of-a-kind and imported items are available in the store, and *none* of the stock is seconds or discontinued.

Levy's imports include Egyptian percale and linen sheets, Belgian kitchen towels, Irish damask tablecloths, and bedding from Switzerland, England, France, and Italy—all worth a trip to the store. Mail-order shoppers can call or write for price quotes on bed and bath linens from the major mills: Cannon, Fieldcrest, Martex, Revman, Dan River, Springmaid, J.P. Stevens, and Wamsutta. A large selection of bath accessories, shower curtains, rugs, and towels is also available. Levy's is known for its custom services and can provide monogramming and sheets in special sizes and shapes, tablecloths, dust ruffles, curtains, pillowcases, and other products from stock sheets or your own fabric.

Please note: Phone orders are accepted Monday through Friday 10–4 only.

Special Factors: Price quote by phone or letter with SASE; minimum order is $15 with credit cards.

MOTHER HART'S NATURAL PRODUCTS, INC.

P.O. BOX 4229
BOYNTON BEACH, FL
  33424-4229
  407/738-5866
  407/734-5942

Catalog: free
Save: up to 70%
Pay: check, MO, MC, V
Sells: natural-fiber bed and bath linens and clothing
Store: 3300 S. Congress Ave., Suite 3, Boynton Beach, FL; Monday through Friday 9–5

Mother Hart is just the sort of firm we're always looking for, a small company run by decent people who sell worthwhile goods at very considerate prices. It's not uncommon to find savings of 50% to 70% on the products sold here, which are chiefly textiles for bed and bath, activewear, and underthings.

We found stunning buys on flannel sheets and sheet blankets in all sizes in the catalog we reviewed, as well as down pillows, fleece mattress pads, cotton duvet covers in solids and prints, box spring covers and pads, and quilted cotton comforters. Among the other goods shown were were canvas luggage, natural-bristle hairbrushes, laundry bags, handkerchiefs, cotton throws, and aprons. Danskin leotards, tights, leg warmers, camisoles, sweaters, nightshirts, and other clothing were also available at great savings. Note that some items may be available in limited quantities, so order promptly. All irregular goods are clearly indicated as such.

Special Factors: Satisfaction is guaranteed; unused returns are accepted within 30 days.

J. SCHACHTER CORP.

85 LUDLOW ST.
NEW YORK, NY 10002
800-INTO-BED
212/533-1150
FAX: 718/384-7634

Catalog: $1
Save: up to 40%
Pay: check, MO, MC, V, Discover
Sells: linens and down-filled bedding
Store: same address; Monday through Thursday 9–5, Friday 9–2, Sunday 9–4:30

$$ ✉ ☎ 🍁 (see text) ▀▀

Schachter has been making comforters and pillows for the bedding industry and recovering old comforters for private customers since 1919. Custom work is featured in the 16-page catalog, but stock goods are also available.

Schachter specializes in custom jobs: Comforters, coverlets, bed ruffles, pillow shams, duvets, and shower curtains are popular requests. Filling choices for the comforters include lambswool, polyester, white goose down, and a nonallergenic synthetic down alternative. Schachter carries bed and bath linens by the major mills—Cannon, Croscill, Fieldcrest, Martex, Springs Industries, and Wamsutta—and labels from France, Germany, England, Switzerland, Italy, and Belgium—Bruna, Palais Royal, Peter Reed, Sferra, and Sufolla. Carter cotton bath rugs, Northern Feather pillows, Dyne comforters, and blankets by Chatham, Faribo, Hudson Bay, and Northern are offered. Schachter's own stock comforters and accessories are all available, and the firm can recover and sterilize old down pillows and comforters.

Canadian readers, please note: Orders are delivered by UPS only.

Special Factors: Price quote by phone or letter with SASE; minimum order is $35 with credit cards.

SPRINGMAID/WAMSUTTA MILL STORE

36 GROCE RD.
LYMAN, SC 29365
803/433-4645
OR
II GATEWAY BLVD.
  SOUTH
SAVANNAH, GA 31419
912/921-0790
OR
1340 TUNNEL RD.
ASHEVILLE, NC 28805
704/298-3393
OR
3700 AVENUE OF THE
  CAROLINAS
FORT MILL, SC 29715
803/548-7444
OR
1110 MARKET ST.
CHATTANOOGA, TN
  37402
615/756-0805
OR
HIGHWAY 9
LANCASTER, SC 29720
803/286-2491

Information: price quote
Save: up to 50%
Pay: check, MO, MC, V
Sells: Springmaid and Wamsutta bed and
  bath linens and accessories
Store: same addresses; call for hours

$$$ ✉ ☎

Springmaid and Wamsutta, two respected home-textiles brands now owned by Spring Industries, run six mill stores that offer their products at prices up to 50% below suggested retail. Current first-quality, discontinued, and irregular bed and bath linens are available.

Discontinued, first-quality sheets and towels are sold at a discount at the mill stores, and prices on irregulars are substantially reduced. (Since we usually miss the yearly "irregulars" sales on Wamsutta sheets at our local department store, we found this source quite handy.) The mill stores also carry complementing window treatments and a range of bath accessories.

There is no catalog, and we recommend calling to see if what you want is in stock. Be sure you know the exact name of the style or pattern, the size needed, and the color (and an alternative, if possible), and specify whether you want irregular or first-quality goods. (We were told that the Lyman store tends to get more irregulars than the others, but all of them are worth trying if one is out of the desired item.)

Special Factor: Price quote by phone.

SEE ALSO

Atlantic Bridge Collection Corp. Ltd. ● Irish double-damask table linens ● *ART, ANTIQUES*

Ben's Babyland ● nursery linen and bedding ● *CLOTHING: MOTHER AND CHILD*

Campmor ● sleeping bags, sleeping bag liners ● *SPORTS*

Capital Cycle Corporation ● goose-down comforters ● *AUTO*

Clothcrafters, Inc. ● plain cotton sheets, towels, table linens, etc. ● *GENERAL MERCHANDISE*

Gettinger Feather Corp. ● pillow feathers ● *CRAFTS*

Gohn Bros. ● flannel sheets, wool blankets ● *CLOTHING*

D. MacGillivray & Coy. ● woven blankets and tartan bedspreads ● *CRAFTS*

Mallory's Fine Furniture ● Nettlecreek bedspreads ● *HOME: FURNISHINGS*

Plexi-Craft Quality Products Corp. ● acrylic bathroom accessories ● *HOME: FURNISHINGS*

Quilts Unlimited ● antique and new quilts ● *ART, ANTIQUES*

Retired Persons Services, Inc. ● waffle-type foam bed pads ● *MEDICINE*

Robin Importers, Inc. ● Carefree table linens ● *HOME: TABLE SETTINGS*

Rubens & Marble, Inc. ● bassinet and crib sheets ● *CLOTHING*

Rubin & Green, Inc. ● custom-made comforters, bedspreads, etc. ● *HOME: DECOR*

Shama Imports, Inc. ● crewel-embroidered bedspreads ● *HOME: DECOR*

Shannon Duty Free Mail Order ● linen damask and lace tablecloths ● *HOME: TABLE SETTINGS*

Thai Silks ● embroidered Chinese table linens ● *CRAFTS*

Irv Wolfson Company ● foreign-current electric blankets ● *APPLIANCES*

MAINTENANCE AND BUILDING

Hardware, tools, equipment, supplies, and materials

Maintaining your home—keeping it clean and in good repair—can involve an enormous amount of time and energy, often unnecessarily. *Make Your House Do the Housework* (Writer's Digest Books, 1986) can help you create the closest thing to a maintenance-free house, from selecting easy-care furniture and carpeting to eliminating gutters. You probably won't use every idea proposed by Don Aslett and Laura Aslett Simons, but their book has many timesaving tips and pointers we haven't seen elsewhere.

Consumers Union publishes a number of books to help you with everything from buying your next home to cleaning the windows. *Home Improvement Cost Guide, How to Buy a House, Condo, or Co-op, Home Security* (on locks, alarms, etc.), and *How to Clean Practically Everything* are among the titles available at this writing. See the current issue of *Consumer Reports* to order, or check your local bookstore.

Antiquities and precious objects require special care. If you have old or antique furniture or rugs, art, a book collection, or fine old porcelain and glass, you may find *The National Trust Manual of Housekeeping* (Penguin Books, 1984) quite helpful. Compiled by Hermione Sandwich and Sheila Stainton (former head housekeeper and deputy conservator of the British National Trust), it's a small treasury of "dos, don'ts, and nevers" on the care and handling of ceramics, furniture, textiles, pictures, floors, glass, metals, and much more. You'll learn *why* bookcases should be ventilated from the back, and that sloppy washing of stone floors can cause a white dust to appear on furniture legs. Unfortunately, the suppliers it recommends for various products are located in the U.K.

For sources closer to home, as well as advice ranging from reviving linoleum to reshingling the roof, we turn to *The Old House Journal. OHJ* was founded in 1973 as a forum about rehabbing and restoring old (pre-1930) houses. The bimonthly magazine can be bought by subscription, single back issue, or in bound yearbooks. *OHJ* books on plastering, Victorian decor, and the useful *Old House Journal Catalog* are also available. Write to The Old House Journal Corporation, 69A Seventh Ave., Brooklyn, NY 11217, for subscription rates and book information.

We've cited a few of our favorite cleaning agents in the introduction to the "Clothing" chapter. And we recommend the sulfur-free Pylox gloves from Direct Safety (in the "Tools" chapter) for all types of chores; they're ideal for anyone who's allergic to rubber or sensitive to materials in conventional rubber gloves.

ARCTIC GLASS & WINDOW OUTLET

RTE. I-W
HAMMOND, WI 54015
715/796-2292
800-657-4656

Catalog: $2, refundable
Save: up to 70%
Pay: MO, certified check, MC, V, Discover
Sells: exterior doors, windows, skylights, glass panels
Store: I-94 at Hammond Exit, 16 miles east of Minnesota/Wisconsin border; Monday 9–8, Tuesday through Saturday 9–5, Sunday 12–4

When Joseph Bacon found that second-quality patio door panes doubled perfectly as passive solar panels in the greenhouse he was building and cost up to 70% less, he turned the solution into a business venture. He founded his firm in 1979, and has watched it outgrow several facilities and triple its revenues over the past five years.

Arctic Glass sells surplus and second-quality patio door panels from two of the best-known manufacturers in the business. Different types of double and triple panes are available (some with "low-e" coating) and, except for the middle panes of triple-pane panels, most of the glass is 3/16″ thick; all of the panes are double-sealed. The flaws of the seconds should not affect the performance of the panes, and suitable applications and uses are listed in the literature. Arctic also stocks Velux skylights and the complete line of Weather Shield skylights, doors, and windows—wood-framed casements, tilts, slider, direct-set, eyebrow, and fanlight windows and a variety of doors. Kolbe & Kolbe windows and doors are available as well. Prices run from

40% to 70% below list, and all of the panels are guaranteed against leakage or failure for ten years. The warranty terms and installation instructions, including retrofitting, are detailed in the literature. And if you have any questions, you can talk them over with Mr. Bacon himself.

Special Factors: Price quote by phone or letter with SASE; quantity discounts are available; minimum crating charge is $50 for mail orders; returns are accepted within 30 days for exchange, refund, or credit.

ARISTOCAST ORIGINALS INC.

6200 HIGHLAND PKWY.,
DEPT. 20
SMYRNA, GA 30082
404/333-9934

Catalog: $3
Save: up to 50%
Pay: check, MO, MC, V, AE
Sells: architectural ornamentation
Store: same address; Monday through Friday 9–5

$$ ♦

Aristocast Originals has been selling architectural ornamentation and details since 1971. The line of niches, ceiling medallions, moldings and cornices, fireplace surrounds, archways, corbels, and exterior details — porticoes, balustrades, canopies, corbels, columns, and door surrounds — is manufactured in England and sold here at prices up to 50% lower than those charged by other firms for goods of comparable quality.

What we found notable about Aristocast was the variety of styles and the superior quality of the design, something in lamentably short supply among other firms serving the do-it-yourself market. Aristocast's products are made of reinforced plaster, fiberglass, Herculite, and polyurethane (interior beans), and are easy to handle and install. Complete specifications and dimensions are listed for each item in the 28-page color catalog, and adhesives and other "fixing materials" are also available.

Special Factor: Authorized returns are accepted (a 20% restocking fee is charged).

BRE LUMBER

10741 CARTER RD.
TRAVERSE CITY, MI
  49684
616/946-0043
FAX: 616/946-6221

Information: price quote
Save: up to 30%
Pay: check, MO, MC, V
Sells: lumber and flooring
Store: same address; Monday through
  Friday 8–5:30, Saturday 10–2

Home remodeling involves endless dilemmas, like realizing that pre-finished parquet floor tiles have their merits, but you want a *real* floor. Unfortunately, it's usually out of line with the budget.

BRE Lumber may be able to help you put down the genuine article, at a price better than those of other specialty dealers (though you won't beat the floor-in-a-box prices). BRE sells cabinet-grade lumber flooring, wide-plank flooring, paneling, molding, and "dimensional lumber." The woods available in flooring include maple, padauk, bubinga, Brazilian cherry, and teak, among others, and the stock is "long and clear." You can save up to 30% on the delivered cost of the flooring (sometimes more depending on prices prevailing in your area). If you're planning to build or remodel, get BRE's current price list and consider all the options before buying veneer-faced particle board.

Special Factors: Price quote by phone, fax, or letter with SASE; orders are shipped worldwide.

CISCO

1502 WEST CHERRY
CHANUTE, KS 66720
316/431-9290
316/431-9289
FAX: 316/431-7354

Information: price quote
Save: up to 40%
Pay: check, MO, certified check
Sells: plumbing supplies and fixtures
Store: same address; Monday through
  Friday 8–5, Saturday 8–12 noon

CISCO, formerly listed here as Chanute Iron & Supply Co., stocks a full range of fixtures and equipment for plumbing, heating, and air conditioning. A portion of the inventory is available by mail, at savings that should inspire do-it-yourself remodeling efforts. The firm has been in business since 1941.

CISCO stocks plumbing supplies, fixtures, and tools of all sorts: Delta and Moen faucets, Insinkerator garbage disposers, Wayne pumps, Burnham boilers, Miami Carey medicine chests and accessories, whirlpools and fixtures by Aqua Glass, Benjamin, Owens-Corning, and Passport, Elkay and Polar sinks, Crane fixtures, swimming pool supplies, tools by Rigid, and the professional line of tools by Makita are available. Replacement parts for all types of faucets are also stocked.

Please note: No catalog is available.

Special Factors: Price quote by phone or letter with SASE; minimum order is $10.

CRAWFORD'S OLD HOUSE STORE

■■■■■■■■

550 ELIZABETH ST.,
ROOM 103
WAUKESHA, WI 53186
800-556-7878

Catalog: free
Save: up to 30%
Pay: check, MO, MC, V, AE
Sells: reproduction hardware, lighting, plumbing fixtures, etc.
Store: mail order only

$$

The Crawford's catalog consists of a number of brochures and flyers on the firm's best sellers. The firm's oak and beech corner beads are quite popular, a welcome alternative to clear plastic corner protectors, and they're priced from under $11. Bullseye-design corner blocks, used at the top corners of door and window frames, cost $3 or less, depending on the quantity ordered. Oak newel post caps and other large finials are available as well.

Crawford's also sells a full range of "old house" building hardware, as well as Anaglypta and Supaglypta wall coverings, cast moldings and ceiling medallions, Victorian-style light fixtures and replacement shades, Chicago faucets, bath fixtures, and plumbing hardware, and period cabinet hardware and decorative accents in porcelain, brass, and wrought iron.

Special Factors: Quantity discounts are available; minimum order is $5, $15 with credit cards.

MONARCH

2744 ARKANSAS DR.
BROOKLYN, NY 11234
201/796-4117

Brochure: $1
Save: up to 35%
Pay: check, MO, MC, V
Sells: all-steel radiator enclosures
Store: mail order only

$$ ✉

Radiators are not, for the most part, enchanting objects. If you've tired of looking at the exposed ribs of those in your home, consider enclosures. They not only render the unsightly more decorative, but also help to direct the heat into the room.

Monarch sells enclosures in two dozen styles, ranging from simple models with plain grilles to designs that incorporate built-in cabinets and bookshelves. Unlike cheaper enclosures, these are constructed of heavy steel and come with closed backs. The tops of some of Monarch's enclosures are insulated, the joints are welded, and the finishes include four stock enamel colors. Custom sizes and other colors, including woodgrain finishes, are available as well.

Monarch's literature includes a guide to measuring your radiator prior to ordering. (Please note that, like window treatments and other goods ordered to your own measurements, the enclosures are not returnable.) We called local sources for prices on two enclosure sizes in a plain, round-corner style, and found that Monarch's models were up to 35% less expensive.

Special Factor: Inquiries from contractors and institutions are welcomed.

THE NEW ENGLAND SLATE COMPANY

R.D. #1, BURR POND RD.
SUDBURY, VT 05733
802/247-8809

Brochure: free
Save: up to 50%
Pay: check, MO, teller's check
Sells: new and recycled roofing and
    flooring slate
Store: same address

$$$ ✉ 🍁

There's an area running across New York State and Vermont called the Taconic Overthrust, which holds this country's only deposits of colored slate. Chuck Smid, also known as "Mr. Slate," set up his business here in 1975 selling both the characteristic slate of the area and recycled slate that had been reclaimed from buildings all over the Eastern seaboard.

The firm is now known as The New England Slate Company, and sells grey, green, purple, brown, and the highly coveted red slate, as well as black slate from Maine and Pennsylvania. (The Maine slate, known as "monson" slate, is no longer actively quarried and can be obtained only through recyclers.) Slate is pricier than more commonly used roofing materials such as asphalt and fiberglass tile, but its 30-year-plus lifespan makes it much more cost effective. It's also the only appropriate choice for many historic properties, as well as universities and other public buildings. New England Slate's rooming line features new and salvaged slate in random widths and standard 3/16" to 1/4" thicknesses, in 12" to 24" lengths. Prices at this writing run from $195 for a square (100 square feet) of "semi-weathering green" in 12" lengths to $1,300 for a square of new, "unfading red" in 24" lengths. (Salvaged slate, when available, costs 20% to 25% less than newly quarried material.) Slate hammers, cutters, and rippers are available, as well as copper roofing nails, snow guards, roofing gloves, and even "The Slater's Bible." Custom cutting and color matching services can be provided.

The New England Slate Company also runs Vermont Cobble Slate, which offers salvaged slate for use in flooring, hearths, kitchen counters, bathrooms, and as veneer on vertical surfaces. This firm's brochure shows several installations in which the rich texture of the material and the interplay of colors are used to maximum effect, and the literature includes guidelines for setting and grouting the flooring and veneer. Boxes of ten square feet of random-size pieces cost $34, and are offered in black, purple, and mixed colors. The prices for salvaged materials are the best, but New England Slate is very competitive on newly quarried slate as well.

Special Factors: Satisfaction is guaranteed; price quote by phone or letter with SASE.

PLASTIC BAGMART

**904 OLD COUNTRY RD.
WESTBURY, NY 11590
516/997-3355**

Price List: free with SASE
Save: up to 60%
Pay: check, MO, certified check
Sells: plastic bags
Store: same address; Monday through
Friday 9–5, Saturday 9–3

$$$ ✉ ☎ 🍁

Plastic BagMart, established in 1980, offers plastic bags in sizes most frequently used in homes, offices, and industry. Prices are up to 60% less than those charged by supermarkets and variety stores for smaller lots.

The BagMart stocks plastic bags in sizes from 6″ by 8″ to 50″ by 48″, one to four mils thick. Garbage and trash cleanup bags, kitchen and office waste-can bags, food-storage bags, large industrial-type bags, zip-top styles, plastic shopping bags, and other types are available. The bags are sold in case lots only (100 to 1,000 bags per case, depending on size). The price list features the most popular lines, but if you don't see what you need, write with particulars.

The BagMart is offering readers of this book a 5% discount on their *first* order (computed on the goods total only). This WBMC reader discount expires February 1, 1992.

Canadian readers, please note: Orders are shipped by UPS only.

Special Factors: Satisfaction is guaranteed; price quote by letter with SASE; returns are accepted within 10 days.

PROTECTO-PAK

**P.O. BOX 5096, DEPT. A
LONGVIEW, TX 75608
214/757-6092
214/297-3985**

Price List and Samples: $2, refundable
Save: up to 50%
Pay: check or MO
Sells: zip-top plastic bags
Store: mail order only

$$$ ✉ 🍁 🇺🇸

Protecto-Pak, established in 1983, offers plastic zip-top bags at savings that average 35% below comparable retail. Their uses are almost endless, and they're great space-savers if storage is limited.

Protecto-Pak's all-purpose zip-top, heavy-duty plastic bags run from 2″ by

2″ to 13″ by 15″; their seals make them relatively watertight. The suggested uses include storage of crafts supplies, spare parts from kits, polished silverware (wrapped in treated cloth), buttons and surplus trim for different garments, tobacco, daily doses of medications and dietary supplements, office supplies, photographs, hosiery and clothing in luggage and drawers, hardware, jewelry, and other items. Special sizes and thicknesses are available, and printing services are offered (minimum order 10,000). All of the bags are approved for food storage.

Special Factors: Price quote by phone or letter with SASE; quantity discounts are available; minimum order is $10.

THE RENOVATOR'S SUPPLY, INC.

6794 OLD MILL
MILLERS FALLS, MA
01349
413/659-2211

Catalog: $5
Save: up to 50%
Pay: check, MO, MC, V
Sells: reproduction hardware and fixtures
Store: same address; also Canton, CT; Brookline and Sturbridge, MA; Parkville, MD; Flemington and Cherry Hill, NJ; Albany and Wappingers Falls, NY; Camp Hill, PA; and Providence, RI (locations are listed in the catalog)

Three dollars will bring you six issues of "America's most irresistible home decorator discount catalog," 48 color pages of hardware, fixtures, and accessories for period homes. Renovator's Supply, founded in 1978, is known for its selection of hard-to-find reproduction hardware.

Renovator's has answered the prayers of rehabbers and do-it-yourselfers with a full complement of home necessities: iron, brass, and porcelain bath hardware and plumbing fixtures; oak bathroom accessories; and drawer, window, and door hardware of every era in brass, porcelain, and iron. There are lighting fixtures of all types, glass lamp shades, wall plates, copper lanterns and weathervanes, wrought-iron door knockers and latches, hinges, screws, sash hardware, brass mailboxes, bolts, fireplace tools and firebacks, register grills, candle holders, tin and copper matchboxes, pierced tin lamp shades, brass candlesticks, replacement fiber chair seats, tin ceilings, wall coverings, and much more. The catalog carries advertising from other firms that offer a wide variety of renovation materials for older houses.

Special Factors: Satisfaction is guaranteed; shipping is included on orders over $20; quantity discounts are available; returns are accepted within 30 days.

SACO MANUFACTURING & WOODWORKING

39 LINCOLN ST.
SACO, ME 04072
207/284-6613

Flyers: free with SASE (see text)
Save: up to 30%
Pay: check or MO
Sells: hand-turned newel posts, lampposts, and pine canisters
Store: same address; Monday through Friday 7:30–3:30

Saco Manufacturing has been doing business since 1872, and although the firm has changed hands over the years, it still sells some of the same things it offered at the turn of the century.

One of these items is turned lampposts. These are center-bored, unfinished pine or poplar posts that are ready to be finished, wired, fitted with a lighting fixture, and installed outside your home. The posts are available in heights from 8' to 12', and are priced from $75 for the 8' posts. Saco sells newel, porch, and mailbox posts in pine and other woods, in a choice of several finial styles. "Colonial Columns" and pilasters are also available; these custom-made supports can be created in Doric or Tuscan styles, or to the specifications of your contractor or architect.

Saco recently added large pine canisters to the offerings; they're 12" across, come with fitted lids, and are made in 12", 20", and 30" heights. They're handy as general-purpose storage containers, but can also be used as stools.

Please specify the literature you want when you send your self-addressed, stamped envelope: the flyer on lampposts, Colonial Columns, newel posts and finials, or canisters.

Special Factor: Price quote by letter with SASE on nonstandard sizes.

SHUTTERCRAFT

282 STEPSTONE HILL RD.
GUILFORD, CT 06437
203/453-1973

Brochure: free with SASE
Save: up to 30%
Pay: check, MO, MC, V
Sells: exterior house shutters and hardware
Store: same address; Monday through Friday 9–5

$$ ✉ ☎ 🍁 ▤

Authentic, "historic" exterior wood shutters with movable louvers are sold here at prices often charged for flimsier models available at do-it-yourself centers. The white pine shutters can be bought in widths up to two feet, and in lengths to 96″. Also available are fixed-louver and raised-panel shutters, interior styles, S-shaped holdbacks, and shutter hinges. Shuttercraft will prime, paint, trim, and rabbet your shutters for a fee; details are given in the brochure.

Special Factor: Shipping is included on shutters up to 60″ long and on orders totaling $400 or more.

VINTAGE WOOD WORKS

513 S. ADAMS
FREDERICKSBURG, TX 78624
512/997-9513

Catalog: $2
Save: up to 30%
Pay: check, MO, MC, V
Sells: "Victorian gingerbread" architectural details
Store: same address; also Hwy. 34, Quinlan, TX

$$$ ✉ ☎ 🍁

Vintage Wood Works publishes a 40-page catalog of "Victorian and country gingerbread ... for Romantic Rooms & Pleasant Porches." The firm has been producing Victorian-style millwork since 1979, and charges up to 30% less than other firms do for the same kinds of goods.

The offerings include spandrels, cutwork grills and running trim, fan brackets and regular (support) brackets for shelves, decorative pieces to place over doors and windows, shelves, corbels, window cornices, gallery rails, porch posts, balusters, newel posts, finials, shingles, gable (roof-end) decorations, and individual components—spindles, balls, knobs, dowels, and even wooden toy parts. The catalog describes each piece, includes its dimensions, and suggests a variety of uses and applications.

Special Factors: Satisfaction is guaranteed; quantity discounts are available; returns are accepted.

SEE ALSO

AAA-All Factory, Inc. • floor-care machines and supplies • *APPLIANCES*
ABC Vacuum Cleaner Warehouse • floor-care machines and supplies • *APPLIANCES*
Bob's Superstrong Greenhouse Plastic • super-strong woven polyethylene and anchoring straps • *FARM*
Discount Appliance Centers • floor-care machines and supplies • *APPLIANCES*
Clothcrafters, Inc. • mosquito netting and flannel polishing cloths • *GENERAL MERCHANDISE*
Grayarc • trash bags, wipes, door mats, etc. • *OFFICE*
Harry's Discounts & Appliances Corp. • vacuum cleaners • *APPLIANCES*
King's Chandelier Co. • replacement parts for chandeliers • *HOME: DECOR*
Manufacturer's Supply • woodburning furnaces and heaters • *TOOLS*
Midamerica Vacuum Cleaner Supply Co. • floor-care machines and janitorial supplies • *APPLIANCES*
Northern Wholesale Veterinary Supply, Inc. • Orvus WA Paste cleaner • *ANIMAL*
Oreck Corporation • Oreck vacuum cleaners and floor machines • *APPLIANCES*
Percy's Inc. • garbage disposals • *APPLIANCES*
Pintchik Homeworks • name-brand house paint • *HOME: DECOR*
Sewin' in Vermont • vacuum cleaners • *APPLIANCES*
South Bound Millworks • wrought iron decorative hooks and bath fixtures • *HOME: DECOR*
Staples, Inc. • cleaning products, janitorial supplies, paper towels, brooms, trash bags, etc. • *OFFICE*
Value-tique, Inc. • safes for home, office, and business • *OFFICE*
Wholesale Veterinary Supply, Inc. • disinfectants and cleaning products • *ANIMAL*

TABLE SETTINGS

China, crystal, glass, flatware, woodenware, and related goods

Purchasing tableware that's currently in production is as easy as picking up the phone and calling nearly any of the firms listed here. But if your pattern—in china, crystal, or silver—is discontinued, you'll have to turn to a specialist. Three of these firms—Beverly Bremer, Buschemeyer, and Midas—sell discontinued silver flatware (also called "estate" silver). Walter Drake's Silver Exchange (see the listing in "General") may be able to help as well. If you're missing pieces of a china or crystal pattern, write to Replacements, Ltd., 302 Gallimore Dairy Rd., Greensboro, NC 27400-9723, or call 919/275-7224. This firm has over 250,000 pieces in stock, and can help you identify your pattern if you're not sure of the name.

BARRONS

**22790 HESLIP DR.
NOVI, MI 48050
800-538-6340
313/348-0816
FAX: 313/344-4342**

Catalog: free
Save: up to 40%
Pay: check, MO, MC, V, Discover
Sells: tableware and giftware
Store: mail order only

$$$ ✉ ☎ 🍁 ▬

Barrons has been selling fine tableware since 1975, and while it doesn't have a store, it does offer savings of up to 40% on the list prices of china, crystal, flatware, and gifts.

The 24-page, color catalog we received from Barrons showcased popular lines of china from Bernardaud Limoges, Block, Dansk, Fitz & Floyd,

Franciscan, Gorham, Johnson Brothers, Lenox, Mikasa, Noritake, Royal Doulton, Royal Worcester, Spode, Villeroy & Boch, and Wedgwood. Crystal from Atlantis, Baccarat, Gorham, Lenox, Mikasa, Noritake, Sasaki, and Wedgwood is offered, and you can save on stainless steel, silver plate, and sterling flatware from Dansk, Gorham, International, Kirk-Stieff, Lunt, Mikasa, Oneida, Reed & Barton, Towle, Wallace, and Yamazaki. Goebel and Royal Doulton figurines, Gorham crystal gifts, Towle silver serving pieces, and other collectibles and accessories are also sold at a discount.

Special Factors: Satisfaction is guaranteed; price quote by phone or letter with SASE; returns are accepted within 30 days for exchange, refund, or credit; orders are shipped worldwide.

BEVERLY BREMER SILVER SHOP

DEPT. WBMC
3164 PEACHTREE RD.,
N.E.
ATLANTA, GA 30305
404/261-4009

Information: inquire
Save: up to 75%
Pay: check, MO, MC, V, AE
Sells: new and estate silver flatware, gifts, etc.
Store: same address; Monday through Saturday 10–5

$$

The engaging Beverly Bremer presides over an astounding inventory of things silver—from new flatware to old loving cups. "The store with the silver lining," which opened in 1975, is worth a detour if you're traveling anywhere around Atlanta.

The briskest mail trade here is done in supplying missing pieces of silverware, in new, discontinued, and hard-to-find patterns. If you know your pattern name, you can call to see whether the desired piece is in stock; you can also send a photocopy of both sides of a sample piece if you're unsure of the name.

Although the shop's specialty is silver flatware, the shelves and cases sparkle with vases, epergnes, picture frames, candlesticks, jewelry, christening cups, thimbles, and other treasures. This is a source silver collectors should note: over 1,000 patterns are carried in stock, "beautiful as new," and Ms. Bremer notes that there are no monograms on the old silver. (She doesn't sell silver on which monograms have been *removed* either.) Request a current inventory list of your favorite flatware pattern.

Special Factors: Price quote by phone or letter with SASE; sterling silver pieces are bought; appraisals are performed.

BUSCHEMEYER & COMPANY

515 S. FOURTH AVE.
LOUISVILLE, KY 40202
800-626-4555

Information: price quote
Save: up to 40%
Pay: check, MO, MC, V, AE, DC, Discover
Sells: new and discontinued flatware
Store: mail order only

Buschemeyer can help you save on purchases of new flatware (sterling, silverplate, and holloware), and if you're looking for a discontinued pattern, may have what you need. The firm stocks "all active and inactive sterling and silverplate flatware," and will place your name on a want list if your pattern is not available. You can call or write for a price quote on current silver lines, and call (if you know the pattern name) about discontinued pieces, or send a photocopy of the front and back of a teaspoon or fork if you're not sure of the name.

Buschemeyer is offering readers of this book a 10% discount on top of the discounted prices of new silverware. This applies to your *first* order only, and you must identify yourself as a reader when you order to qualify. This WBMC reader discount expires February 1, 1992.

Special Factor: Price quote by phone or letter with SASE.

CHINA CABINET, INC.

24 WASHINGTON ST.
TENAFLY, NJ 07670
800-545-5353
201/567-2711

Information: price quote
Save: up to 30%
Pay: check, MO, MC, V, AE, Optima
Sells: tableware
Store: same address; Monday to Saturday 10–6, Thursday 10–8

China Cabinet, in business since 1988, represents scores of manufacturers of fine china, crystal, and flatware. In addition to such widely available brands as Dansk, Gorham, Orrefors, and Wedgwood, China Closet offers goods from Avitra, Colle, Godinger, Jacques Jugeat, Ranmaru, Silvestri, and Wilton, among others. Savings run up to 30%, and giftware from selected manufacturers is offered as well as place settings and serving pieces.

Special Factors: Price quote by phone or letter with SASE; minimum order is $25 with credit cards.

THE CHINA WAREHOUSE

P.O. BOX 21797
CLEVELAND, OH 44121
800-321-3212
216/831-2557

Catalog: free
Save: up to 40%
Pay: check, MO, MC, V
Sells: tableware and gifts
Store: mail order only

The China Warehouse, in business since 1983, offers "all major china and crystal lines," as well as flatware, decorative accessories, and collectible figurines. The brands include Franciscan, Hutschenreuther, Lenox, Lladró, Minton, Orrefors, Reed & Barton, Riedel, Royal Doulton, Sasaki, Spode, Towle, Wallace, Waterford, Wedgwood, and dozens of others in china, crystal, and stainless and sterling flatware. A catalog is available, but you can call or write for a price quote.

Special Factors: Price quote by phone or letter with SASE; orders are shipped worldwide.

THE EMERALD COLLECTION

280 SUMMER ST., DEPT.
  DCCR
BOSTON, MA 02210
617/423-7685

Catalog: $2
Save: up to 35%
Pay: check, MO, MC, V, AE, Access
Sells: Irish collectibles and handcrafts
Store: Ballingeary, County Cork, Ireland

This well-known Irish firm, which is actually located in County Cork, has order-processing arrangements with an agent in the U.S. Catalog prices are lower than those charged by U.S. firms for the same goods.

Emerald, established in 1962, offers substantial savings on an extensive selection of Waterford crystal stemware and giftware. The color catalog shows tableware and gifts by Waterford and Belleek, Coalport, Royal Doulton, Royal Worcester, Spode, Villeroy & Boch, and Wedgwood. The complete lines of Beatrix Potter figurines, Bunnykins, and Peter Rabbit lamps and table settings are offered. Irish Dresden figurines are carried, as well as others by Belleek, Border Fine Arts, Goebel, Hummel, Irish Dresden, Lladró, and Royal Doulton. Caithness paperweights and other authentic Irish handcrafts round out this lovely catalog.

If you collect figurines or buy gifts frequently, you may find membership in Emerald's "Collector's Club" worthwhile. It includes newsletters with special offers, advance catalog mailings, and discount coupons—all for a $15 fee.

Special Factors: Satisfaction is guaranteed; authorized returns are accepted.

FORTUNOFF FINE JEWELRY & SILVERWARE, INC.

P.O. BOX 1550
WESTBURY, NY 11590
800-223-2326
516/294-3300
212/671-9300

Catalog: $2
Save: up to 50%
Pay: check, MO, MC, V, AE, DC
Sells: jewelry, tableware, and giftware
Store: 681 Fifth Ave., New York, and 1300 Old Country Rd., Westbury, NY; also Paramus Park Mall, Paramus, West Belt Mall, Wayne, and 441 Woodbridge Center Dr., Woodbridge, NJ

Fortunoff, while known for its stupendous selection of estate and contemporary jewelry, features fine tableware, giftware, and housewares at sale prices all year. The prices of the sterling flatware in particular are very good.

In addition to spectacular buys on fine jewelry and watches, Fortunoff is a top source for name-brand place settings in stainless, silverplate, and sterling silver. Attractive groups of silver giftware—chafing dishes, tea and coffee services, candlesticks, ice buckets, picture frames, and antique vanity accessories—appear frequently in the catalogs. The flatware brands list includes Empire Silver, International, Kirk-Stieff, Lauffer, Mikasa,

Oneida, Reed & Barton, Retroneau, Roberts & Belk, Supreme, Towle, C.J. Vander, and Yamazaki. Some of the Fortunoff stores carry a broader variety of products, including outdoor furniture, leather goods, decorative accents for the home, linens for bed and bath, organizers, and similar items.

Special Factors: Price quote on flatware by letter with self-addressed, stamped envelope; minimum order is $25; orders are not shipped outside the U.S.

THE JOMPOLE COMPANY, INC.

**330 SEVENTH AVE.
NEW YORK, NY 10001
212/594-0442**

Information: price quote
Save: up to 50%
Pay: check or MO
Sells: table settings, figurines, watches, and pens
Store: same address; Monday through Friday 9–5

Jompole, which has been in business since 1913, offers a fine selection of table settings, giftware, and writing instruments.

Jompole can help you save up to 50% on china, flatware, crystal, and other tableware. The china lines include Bernardaud Limoges, Coalport, Denby, Franciscan, Hutschenreuther, Lenox, Mikasa, Minton, Pickard, Royal Copenhagen, Spode, and Wedgwood, among others. Crystal stemware is available from Baccarat, Fostoria, Gorham, Kosta Boda, Orrefors, Rosenthal, Val St. Lambert, and Waterford, as well as flatware from Alvin, Community, Fraser, International, Georg Jensen, Kirk-Stieff, Lauffer, Lunt, Oneida, Reed & Barton, Supreme Cutlery, Towle, Tuttle, Wallace, and other firms. Figurines and collectibles by some of the same firms, as well as Hummel, Lladró, Norman Rockwell, Swarovski, and others, are also stocked.

You can call or write for prices on pens and pencils from Cross, Mont Blanc, Parker, and Waterman, or watches by Borel, Cartier, Heuer, Patek-Philippe, Rolex, or Seiko. Jompole also carries premium items for businesses—"from balloons and lollipops to diamonds and furs"—and invites inquiries from interested firms.

Special Factors: Price quote by phone or letter with SASE; institutional accounts are available.

MAREL COMPANY

6 BOND ST.
GREAT NECK, NY 11021
516/466-3188

Information: price quote
Save: up to 50%
Pay: check or MO
Sells: tableware and giftware
Store: same address; Monday through
   Friday 9–5:30, Saturday 9–5

$$

Marel Company has taken over the mail-order operations of A. Benjamin & Co., a New York City merchant formerly listed in this book. Like Benjamin, Marel Company sells top brands in china, stemware, flatware, and giftware since 1944, at savings of up to 50%.

Marel carries stainless, plated, and sterling silverware, holloware, and giftware by Gorham, Heirloom, International, Kirk-Stieff, Lunt, Oneida, Reed & Barton, Supreme, Towle, and Wallace. China, stemware, and crystal by Coalport, Franciscan, Haviland Limoges, Hutschenreuther, Lenox, Mikasa, Minton, Noritake, Rosenthal, Royal Doulton, Spode, Val St. Lambert, and Wedgwood is also offered. The stock includes current lines and discontinued patterns and styles, and you can write or call for current prices.

Special Factor: Price quote by phone or letter with SASE.

MIDAS CHINA & SILVER

4315 WALNEY RD.
CHANTILLY, VA 22021
800-368-3153

Catalog: free
Save: up to 60%
Pay: check, MO, MC, V, AE, Discover
Sells: china, crystal, and silver tableware
Store: same address; Monday through
   Friday 10–6, Saturday 10–4; also 7223
   Commerce St., Springfield, VA, and
   1346-48 Gaskins Rd., Richmond, VA

$$$

Midas has been doing business for 25 years, selling fine crystal, china, and silver giftware and table settings. The prices here are up to 60% below full retail, and estate silver (including discontinued patterns) is also sold.

Midas sells china place settings and gifts by Aynsley, Coalport, Fitz and Floyd, Gorham, Hummel, Lenox, Lladró, Minton, Noritake, Orrefors, Rosenthal, Royal Crown Derby, Royal Doulton, Royal Worcester, Spode, and Wedgwood. Crystal gifts, barware, and stemware by Baccarat, Gorham, Orrefors, and Waterford are available at overseas prices. Sterling candelabra from Gorham, and stainless, plate, and sterling place settings by Alvin, Durgin, Easterling, Gorham, International Silver, Kirk-Stieff, Lunt, Manchester, National, Oneida, Reed & Barton, Royal Crest, Statehouse, Towle, Wallace, Westmoreland, Whiting, and Wiedlich are available. Midas also sells silver chests and silver bags. The catalog lists patterns and prices, but you can call or write for a quote.

Special Factors: Price quote by phone or letter; returns (except special orders) are accepted within 30 days for exchange, refund, or credit.

ROBIN IMPORTERS, INC.

510 MADISON AVE.,
DEPT. WBM
NEW YORK, NY 10022
800-223-3373
IN NY 212/753-6475

Brands List: free with SASE
Save: up to 50%
Pay: check, MO, MC, V, AE, DC, Optima
Sells: tableware, giftware, and kitchenware
Store: same address; Monday through Friday 9:30–5:30, Saturday 10–5

Robin carries an exhaustive stock of tableware, kitchenware, and table and kitchen linens at prices up to 50% below list. The brochure lists the available brands, but no prices are given—call or write for a quote. The firm was established in 1957.

Robin carries china place settings and serving pieces by Adams, Arabia, Arzberg, Bernardaud Limoges, Block, Cartier, Coalport, Denby, Fitz and Floyd, Franciscan, Heinrich, Hutschenreuther, Meissen, Mikasa, Rosenthal, Spode, Villeroy & Boch, and other firms. Crystal stemware and gifts from Atlantis, Baccarat, Daum, Gorham, Iittala, Kosta Boda, Lalique, Orrefors, Riedel, Sasaki, Val St. Lambert, and Waterford are available. And the flatware and cutlery lines include Christofle, Dansk, W.M.F. Fraser, Georgian House, Gorham, Henckels, Lauffer, Lunt, Oneida, Retroneau, Ricci, Stanley Roberts, Supreme, Towle, Wallace, and Yamazaki.

Robin completes the table with linens—Carefree cloths and napkins, in all sizes and colors, at 50% off list. Knives by Gorham, Henckels, and

Wusthof-Trident are sold at savings, as well as knife blocks, salt-and-pepper mills, and other useful kitchen items.

Special Factor: Price quote by phone or letter with SASE.

ROGERS & ROSENTHAL

22 W. 48TH ST., ROOM 1102
NEW YORK, NY 10036
212/827-0115

Information: price quote
Save: up to 50%
Pay: check or MO
Sells: tableware
Store: mail order only

$$$ ✉ ▆

Rogers and Rosenthal, two old names in the silver and china business, represent the business of this firm: the best in table settings at up to 60% below list prices.

The firm has been in business since 1960, selling flatware (stainless, plate, and sterling) by top manufacturers. The brands include 1847 Rogers, 1881 Rogers, Fraser, Gerber, Gorham, International, Jensen, Kirk-Stieff, Lauffer, Lunt, Oneida, Reed & Barton, Sasaki, Frank Smith, Supreme, Towle, Tuttle, Wallace, and Yamazaki. There are china and crystal lines by Arabia, Aynsley, Bernardaud Limoges, Block, Coalport, Fitz and Floyd, Franciscan, Gorham, Haviland Limoges, Hornsea, Hutschenreuther, Lauffer, Lenox, Mikasa, Noritake, Pickard, Portmeirion, Rosenthal, Royal Copenhagen, Royal Doulton, Royal Worcester, Spode, and Wedgwood. Also stocked are silver baby gifts, Lladró and Norman Rockwell figurines, and pewter holloware. Please write or call for a price quote—*there is no catalog.*

Special Factors: Price quote by phone or letter with SASE; returns are accepted for exchange.

RUDI'S POTTERY, SILVER & CHINA

176 STATE HWY. 17
PARAMUS, NJ 07652
201/265-6096

Information: price quote
Save: up to 60%
Pay: check, MO, MC, V
Sells: tableware
Store: same address; Monday through
Saturday 10–5:30, Tuesday and Thursday
10–9

$$$ ✉ ☎

Rudi's has been in business for 20 years, and in that time has expanded its stock to include some of the finest goods available, at savings of up to 60% on list prices.

China, crystal, and flatware are stocked here; the silverware brands include Buccellati, Gorham, International, Kirk-Stieff, Lunt, Reed & Barton, Towle, Tuttle, and Wallace. Rudi's china dinnerware and crystal stemware lines include Arzberg, Baccarat, Belleek, Bernardaud Limoges, Coalport, Fitz and Floyd, Galway, Kosta Boda, Lalique, Lenox, Mikasa, Minton, Noritake, Orrefors, Rosenthal, Royal Copenhagen, Royal Doulton, Royal Worcester, Sevres, Spode, Stuart, Tiffin, Val St. Lambert, and Wedgwood. Call or write for a price quote on your pattern or suite.

Special Factor: Price quote by phone or letter with SASE.

NAT SCHWARTZ & CO., INC.

549 BROADWAY
BAYONNE, NJ 07002
800-526-1440

Information: inquire
Save: up to 50%
Pay: check, MO, MC, V
Sells: tableware and giftware
Store: same address; Monday, Thursday,
Friday 11–8, Tuesday and Saturday 11–5
(closed Wednesday and Sunday)

$$$ ✉ ☎

Schwartz, established in 1967, publishes a 48-page color catalog filled with fine china, crystal, flatware, and gifts that represent just a fraction of the firm's inventory. The customer service department is top-notch.

Schwartz's china and giftware department stocks Belleek, Edward Marshall Boehm, Coalport, Fitz and Floyd, Lenox, Lladró, Minton, Noritake, Royal Crown Derby, Royal Doulton, Royal Worcester, Spode, Villeroy & Boch, and Wedgwood. Crystal suites and gifts by Galway, Gorham, Lenox, Stuart, Val St. Lambert, Waterford, and Wedgwood are available. Also featured are flatware and holloware by Gorham, International, Kirk-Stieff, Lunt, Oneida, Reed & Barton, Retroneau, Ricci, Towle, Tuttle, Wallace. and Yamazaki.

Schwartz offers a number of valuable services, including coordination of silver, crystal, and china patterns; gift and bridal registry; and a corporate gift program.

Special Factors: Satisfaction is guaranteed; price quote by phone; special orders are accepted with a nonrefundable 20% deposit (unless the order is canceled while still on back order); undamaged returns are accepted within 30 days (a restocking fee may be charged).

ALBERT S. SMYTH CO., INC.

**29 GREENMEADOW DR.,
DEPT. WM91
TIMONIUM, MD 21093
800-638-3333
IN MD 301/252-6666**

Catalog: free
Save: up to 50%
Pay: check, MO, MC, V, AE
Sells: tableware, giftware, and jewelry
Store: same address; Monday to Saturday 9–5, Thursday 9–9

$$$ ✉ ☎ ▆

All that gleams and glitters can be found at Smyth, at savings of up to 50% on comparable retail and list prices. Smyth has been doing business since 1914, and has an excellent customer service department.

The catalog features a wide range of jewelry, including diamonds, strands of semiprecious beads, colored stone jewelry, and pearls. Watches by Citizen, Pulsar, and Seiko have been offered in the past, as well as Mont Blanc pens, mahogany jewelry chests, Royal Doulton figurines, Virginia Metalcrafters gifts, and Kirk-Stieff pewter and silver gifts.

Tableware and home decorative accents are sold here at impressive savings, including such items as British carriage clocks, Baldwin brass gifts, and fine picture frames. You'll find pewter candlesticks, coffee sets, punch bowls, and place settings by Aynsley, Gorham, Kirk-Stieff, Lenox, Noritake,

Reed & Barton, Royal Doulton, Spode, Towle, Villeroy & Boch, Wallace, Waterford, and Wedgwood among the offerings.

Smyth provides a bridal registry, gift consultations, and a gift-forwarding service. The catalog shows a fraction of the inventory, so write or call for a price quote if you don't see what you're looking for.

Special Factors: Satisfaction is guaranteed; price quote by phone or letter with SASE; returns (except personalized and custom-ordered goods) are accepted within 30 days.

THE YANKEE MERCHANT GROUP, LTD.

15 COURT SQUARE
BOSTON, MA 02108
617/742-0470

Information: price quote
Save: up to 50%
Pay: check, MO, MC, V
Sells: table settings and jewelry
Store: same address; Monday through
Friday 9–5, Saturday 10–4

$$ ✉ ☎

The Yankee Merchant Group, in business since 1979, sells fine flatware at savings of up to 50% on list prices. If you know what you're looking for, you may find it easiest to write or phone for a price quote.

Yankee sells silver holloware and flatware by Buccellati, Fraser, Gorham, International Silver, Georg Jensen, Kirk-Stieff, Lunt, Oneida, Reed & Barton, Ricci, Towle, Wallace, and Yamazaki. Call or write for prices on any patterns from these firms.

Special Factors: Satisfaction is guaranteed; price quote by phone or letter with SASE; authorized returns (except special orders and personalized goods) are accepted within 14 days.

COMPANIES OUTSIDE THE U.S.A.

The following firms are experienced in dealing with customers in the U.S. and Canada. We've included them because they offer goods not widely available at a discount in the U.S., because they have a better selection, or because they may offer the same goods at great savings.

Before ordering from a non-U.S. firm, please read through the applicable sections of "The Complete Guide to Buying by Mail" at the back of this book. We recommend paying for your catalog with a camouflaged enclosure of cash. (Sending cash saves the company the bank charge of converting your check to different currency.) We further advise you to pay for your merchandise by credit card whenever possible, so that your transaction will be protected by the part of the Fair Credit Billing Act that allows you to dispute charges for goods not received. See page 545 for a complete discussion of the Act. Please note that only this portion of the Act applies, and the FTC's Mail Order Rule governing delivery time *does not*.

SHANNON DUTY FREE MAIL ORDER

SHANNON FREE
 AIRPORT, DEPT. WM91
IRELAND
011-353-61-62610

Catalog: $2
Save: up to 40%
Pay: check, IMO, MC, V, AE, Access
Sells: tableware, Irish knits, and giftware
Store: same address

$$$

Shannon has been doing business by mail since 1954, and its catalog features china and crystal, with clothing, table linens, and gifts and collectibles rounding out the 54 color pages. The china firms represented in the current catalog include Adams, Aynsley, Belleek, Beswick, Coalport, Limoges, Masons, Midwinter, Royal Doulton, Royal Tara, Royal Worcester, Spode, and Wedgwood. The emphasis is on giftware—vases, candy dishes, ring stands, cachepots—but select place settings and serving pieces are also offered. Savings, without the shipping charges, are usually more than 30% on the U.S. retail prices, and are often more substantial.

The flash and fire of 24% lead crystal by Galway and Waterford can be had at Shannon at savings of up to 40% off list prices. Several suites are available, as well as serving and decorative pieces. In addition, Shannon carries Anri figurines, Royal Doulton character mugs, Royal Doulton's Bunnykins figures, Wedgwood's Beatrix Potter nursery accoutrements, Goebel collectibles, and lovely Claddagh jewelry. Aran sweaters, tartan skirts, tweed capes, Jimmy Hourihan capes and jackets, and stylish accessories from Iceland, England, and Germany are available as well. Genuine bargains can be found among the Irish linen handkerchiefs, Nottingham lace tablecloths, and double-damask table linens.

Please note: Shannon now ships orders from New York City to addresses in the continental U.S.—guaranteed free of duty charges. Orders sent to

Alaska, Hawaii, and Puerto Rico may be assessed duty, which Shannon will refund or credit to a future order. See the catalog for details.

Canadian readers, please note: Shipping charges listed in the catalog are valid on orders sent to Canada. Prices are given in U.S. dollars, but Canadian funds are accepted. Use the rate of exchange in force on the day you order.

Special Factors: Satisfaction is guaranteed; returns are accepted within 30 days for exchange, refund, or credit; minimum order is $25 with credit cards; orders are shipped worldwide.

SKANDINAVISK GLAS

4 NY ØSTERGADE
1101 COPENHAGEN K
DENMARK
011-45-3313-8095
FAX: 011-45-3332-3335

Brochure and Price Lists: $3, refundable

Save: up to 50%

Pay: check, MO, MC, V

Sells: crystal and china table settings and giftware

Store: same address; Monday through Friday 9:30–6, Saturday 9:30–2

Skandinavisk Glas, previously listed here as A.B. Schou, was founded in 1920 and sells the finest European crystal and porcelain. The firms represented include Aynsley, Bing & Grøndahl, Goebel, Herend, Hummel, Lladró, NAO, Royal Copenhagen, Royal Doulton, Wedgwood, and David Winter. The prices at Skandinavisk Glas, which *include* postage (surface), are superb: place settings are priced 25% to 50% below New York City rates, and Lladró figurines cost about 30% below retail.

The crystal collection is comparable; in addition to a comprehensive listing of Waterford stemware, vases, and giftware, Skandinavisk Glas sells decorative and service pieces by Baccarat, Daum, Galway, Hadeland, Iittala, Mats Jonassen, Kosta Boda, Lalique, Marcolin, Nachtmann, Orrefors, and Swarovski.

Canadian readers, please note: A 25% surcharge is imposed on payments made in Canadian funds.

Special Factors: Shipping and insurance are included; orders are shipped worldwide.

STECHER'S LIMITED

27 FREDERICK ST.
PORT-OF-SPAIN
TRINIDAD, WEST INDIES
809/62-35912, 32586

Brands List: free
Save: up to 40%
Pay: check or IMO
Sells: tableware, watches, jewelry, and giftware
Store: same address; Piarco International Airport; also Hilton Hotel, Long Circular Mall, and Westmall in Port-of-Spain; Gulf City Mall, San Fernando; Main Street, Scarborough; Crown Reef Hotel, Tobago; and Arnos Vale Airport and Cobblestone Inn, Bay Street, Kingston in St. Vincent

$$ ✉ ☎ 🍁

Here in Trinidad is one of the world's best sources of luxury goods, which are sold at impressive discounts. Stecher's carries the best of the best in tableware, watches, clocks, pens, and lighters, at savings of up to 40%.

The stock includes crystal by Baccarat, Dartington, Daum, Hoya, Iittala, Kosta Boda, Lalique, Nybro, Orrefors, Riedel, Rosenthal, St. Louis, Schott-Zwiesel, Sevres, Swarovski, Val St. Lambert, Vannes Le Chatel, and Waterford. Place settings, gifts, and figurines from Aynsley, Belleek, Bing & Grøndahl, Capodimonte, Coalport, Haviland Limoges, Hutschenreuther, Kaiser, Lladró, Minton, Noritake, Paragon, Rosenthal, Royal Albert, Royal Copenhagen, Royal Crown Derby, Royal Doulton, Royal Worcester, Spode, Villeroy & Boch, and Wedgwood are available. The flatware lines include Georg Jensen and Wallace, among others.

This is an impressive list, but Stecher's is more frequently cited for its bargains on watches, clocks, jewelry, pens, and lighters. Again, the goods are first-rate: timepieces by Audemars Piguet, Borel, Cartier, Consul, Girard-Perregaux, Heuer (chronographs), Movado, Patek-Philippe, Seiko, and similar firms are offered, in addition to pens and lighters from Pierre Cardin, Cartier, Cross, Dunhill, Dupont, Lamy, Mont Blanc, Parker, Sheaffer, and Waterman, as well as a wide variety of fine jewelry (including cultured pearls) and leather goods, pipes, Swiss Army knives, Ray-Ban sunglasses, and other gifts.

Stecher's has no catalog, but will send a list of brands and lines of merchandise currently available. The firm invites written inquiries concerning specific goods and manufacturers, and will send specific brochures and prices upon request. Stecher's has been doing business since 1946 and has satisfied the whims of such shoppers as Tony Curtis and Robert Mitchum.

Special Factor: Price quote by letter.

SEE ALSO

Atlantic Bridge Collection Corp. Ltd. • china and crystal tableware • ART, ANTIQUES

Bruce Medical Supply • dining aids and cutlery for those with limited strength or muscle control • MEDICINE

A Cook's Wares • cutlery and serving pieces • HOME: KITCHEN

Fivenson Food Equipment, Inc. • restaurant appliances, tableware, and serving pieces • HOME: KITCHEN

The Friar's House • china and crystal • ART, ANTIQUES

Harris Levy, Inc. • table linens • HOME: LINEN

Pendery's Inc. • Mexican glassware • FOOD

Saxkjaers • Bing & Grøndahl and Royal Copenhagen place settings • ART, ANTIQUES

Weston Bowl Mill • wooden plates, trays, and tableware • GENERAL MERCHANDISE

The Wine Enthusiast • stemware and decanters • FOOD

JEWELRY, GEMS, AND WATCHES

Fine, fashion, and costume jewelry; loose stones, watches, and services

This chapter gives you access to firms that offer everything from flea-market neck chains for pennies to diamond and emerald collars costing close to $200,000. Before you buy in the "high end," you must know and understand terms and industry standards so you can determine what offer represents the best value. And that means becoming an educated consumer.

There are many worthwhile publications on gems and jewelry; one that you may find useful is *All About Jewelry: The One Indispensable Guide for Buyers, Wearers, Lovers, Investors,* by Rose Leiman Goldenberg (Arbor House Publishing Co., 1983). The book covers precious and semiprecious stones, pearls, metals, and other materials used in jewelry. It may be available in your local library. We've been greatly entertained by an inside look at the business, *Modern Jeweler's Consumer Guide to Colored Gemstones,* by David Federman (Modern Jeweler Magazine, 1990) (with dazzling color photographs by Tino Hammid). A gemlike production in its own right, it reveals the intrigue and chicanery that shape each stone's market, and discusses such problems as irradiation and heat treatment of gems. Write to Modern Jeweler, Vance Publishing Corporation, P.O. Box 1416, Lincolnshire, IL 60069-9958 for the current price and ordering information.

The FTC has established guidelines for the jewelry trade and publishes pamphlets for consumers that discuss the meanings of terms, stamps and quality marks, and related matters. Request "Gold Jewelry," "Bargain Jewelry," and "Guidelines for the Jewelry Industry" from the Federal Trade Commission, Public Reference Office, Washington, DC 20580.

The Gemological Institute of America can tell you what should appear on a GIA report and confirm whether an appraiser has been trained by the organization. For more information, write to the Gemological Institute of America, Inc., 1180 Avenue of the Americas, New York, NY 10036. There is also a GIA office in California (P.O. Box 2110, 1660 Stewart St., Santa Monica, CA 90406).

If you're interested in diamonds, request the consumer information package on diamonds from American Gem Society, 5901 W. Third St., Los Angeles, CA 90036. It provides a bounty of tips on selecting and buying diamonds.

The Jewelers' Vigilance Committee can tell you whether your dealer is among the good, the bad, or the ugly. This trade association monitors the industry and promotes ethical business practices. For more information, write to the Jewelers' Vigilance Committee, 1180 Avenue of the Americas, 8th Fl., New York, NY 10036.

Lastly, you cannot be too careful when buying gems, pearls, and precious metals as investments. Approaching the field with few facts, a lot of money, and high hopes is a recipe for financial disaster. Treat undocumented appreciation figures with a large grain of salt. Don't ever believe that you can better dealers who've been in the business for 20 years and who know exactly what they're selling. And don't mistake an appraisal value for the amount of money you could get for your gems or jewelry. It's a measure of the *market* value of the stones, which may be as high as three to four times the resale value. Since inflated appraisals may cost you extra insurance premium dollars, make sure your valuations are realistic. Protect yourself by getting at least two, preferably by GIA-trained jewelers or dealers, before making any large investment. Since investment-grade stones are usually sold on an approval basis, you should be able to arrange inspections before you complete the purchase.

If you need help in finding an appraiser, contact the American Society of Appraisers at 212/687-6305. The Society will locate an appraiser in your area and have that person contact you, at no charge. (The Society's senior members have at least five years of experience and are required to pass an exam; they handle all "appraisables," not just jewelry.)

DIAMONDS BY RENNIE ELLEN

15 W. 47TH ST., RM. 401
NEW YORK, NY 10036
212/869-5525

Catalog: $2
Save: up to 75%
Pay: check, MO, teller's check, bank draft
Sells: stock and custom-made jewelry
Store: by appointment only

$$$ ✉

It's hard to believe that you can buy diamond engagement rings wholesale, but that's Rennie Ellen's business. You can save up to 75% on the price of similar jewelry sold elsewhere by buying here. Rennie Ellen is honest, reputable, and personable, and she's been cutting gems since 1960.

Rennie Ellen sells custom-cut diamonds of all shapes, sizes, and qualities, set to order in platinum or gold. The color catalog shows samples of Ms. Ellen's design work, including rings, pendants, and earrings set with diamonds, rubies, sapphires, emeralds, amethysts, tourmalines, pearls, and opals. The factory is open to customers by appointment only.

Please note that the catalog, which is $2, has information for both Diamonds by Rennie Ellen and her other concern, R/E Kane Enterprises (see that listing in this chapter).

Special Factors: Price quote by phone or letter with SASE; a detailed bill of sale is included with each purchase; returns are accepted within 5 working days; minimum shipping, handling, and insurance charge is $10.

ELOXITE CORPORATION

806 TENTH ST., DEPT. 4
WHEATLAND, WY 82201
307/322-3050

Catalog: 25¢
Save: up to 75%
Pay: check, MO, MC, V
Sells: jewelry findings
Store: same address; Monday through Friday 8:30–4, Saturday 8:30–3

$$$ ✉ ☎ 🍁 ▭

Eloxite has been selling jewelry findings, cabochons, beads, and other lapidary supplies since 1955. The prices here are up to 75% less than those charged by other crafts sources for findings and jewelry components.

Jewelry findings with a Western flair are featured here: bola ties and slide medallions, belt buckles and inserts, and coin jewelry are prominent offerings. Also shown are pendants, rings, earrings, lockets, tie tacks, and pins made to be set with cabochons or cut stones, as well as jump rings, chains, pillboxes, screw eyes, and ear wires. The stones themselves are sold—cut cubic zirconia and synthetic gemstones and oval cabochons of abalone, agate, black onyx, garnet, opal, obsidian, jasper, and malachite. The catalog we reviewed included mother-of-pearl cameos and necklaces, loosely strung gemstone bead necklaces, and jewelers' tools and supplies.

Sandwiched between the pages of jewelry components are quartz clock movements and blanks for clock faces, clock hands, oil paints and palettes, and ballpoint pens and letter openers for desk sets. Quantity discounts are available on most items, and specials are usually offered with orders of specified amounts; orders are shipped worldwide.

Special Factors: Undamaged returns are accepted within 15 days for exchange or refund (a $2 restocking fee may be charged); C.O.D. orders are accepted.

HONG KONG LAPIDARIES, INC.

2801 UNIVERSITY DR.
CORAL SPRINGS, FL
33065
305/755-8777
FAX: 305/755-8780

Catalog: $3
Save: up to 50%
Pay: check, MO, certified check
Sells: jewelry supplies and finished jewelry
Store: mail order only

Hong Kong Lapidaries, established in 1978, sells a wide range of precious and semiprecious stones in a variety of forms. The 32-page catalog shows items of interest to hobbyists as well, and the prices run as much as 50% below comparable retail. The catalog shows hundreds of cabochons, beads, loose faceted and cut stones, and strung chips of pearl, garnet, amethyst, onyx, abalone, and many other types of semiprecious stones. Egyptian clay scarabs, coral, cameos, cubic zirconia, yellow jade, cloisonné jewelry and objets d'art, 14K gold-filled beads, and ball earrings are available. Craftspersons should note the square and disc inlays in intaglios (suitable for decorating jewelry boxes or game boards), as well as the tiger's eye and onyx belt buckles, stone buttons, and similar goods.

Special Factors: Satisfaction is guaranteed; quantity discounts are available; returns are accepted within 12 days; minimum order is $25; orders are shipped worldwide.

HOUSE OF ONYX

THE AARON BUILDING
GREENVILLE, KY 42345
800-626-8352
IN KY 800-992-3260
502/338-2363
FAX: 502/338-9605

Catalog: free
Save: up to 60%
Pay: check, MO, MC, V
Sells: investment-grade stones, jewelry, and gifts
Store: same address; by appointment

$$$ ✉ ☎ 🍁 ▥

The House of Onyx publishes a 56-page tabloid catalog filled with reports on the gem industry and listings of diamonds and other precious stones, as well as specials on gifts and jewelry. The House of Onyx, which has gained over 50,000 clients worldwide since it opened its doors in 1967, enjoys a reputation for good service and prices.

Imported goods from Mexico, China, and India have been offered in the past, including Aztec onyx chess sets, ashtrays, bookends, vases, statuettes, candlesticks, and jewelry. There are cloisonné and vermeil beads, jewelry, and artware, and carvings of soapstone, rose quartz, tiger's eye, Burmese jadeite, lapis lazuli, carnelian, turquoise, and agate. The jewelry includes semiprecious bead necklaces, freshwater and cultured pearls, diamond rings, earrings, and pendants, from department-store grade to fine one-of-a-kind pieces. Collectors of crystals and mineral specimens should check here for amethyst, fluorite, quartz, pyrite, and others, and spheres of several minerals.

Vast quantities of choice, heavy, solid gold chains are stocked, and fine handmade jewelry can be produced to your specifications. The House also offers a wide range of investment-quality stones, with discounts of 50% and 60% offered on parcels of $2,000 to $12,500. The investment stones account for much of the business here, and the catalog is packed with useful information and commentary on the field.

Special Factors: Satisfaction is guaranteed; shipping is included on orders over $100; investment gemstones are sold with an unlimited time return guarantee and "100% purchase price refund" pledge; other returns are accepted within 30 days; minimum order is $25.

INTERNATIONAL GEM CORPORATION

3601 HEMPSTEAD TPK.
LEVITTOWN, NY 11756
516/796-0200

Catalog: $2
Save: up to 40%
Pay: check, MO, certified check
Sells: semiprecious stone jewelry
Store: mail order only

$$ ✉ 🍁 ▆

International Gem Corporation, which has been selling to the trade since 1950, offers consumers the opportunity to buy at wholesale prices—up to 40% below comparable retail. Semiprecious stone necklaces, earrings, and bracelets are featured.

The 12-page, color IGC catalog lists the different jewelry collections and describes available options. Hand-knotted strands of 8mm balls of a variety of gemstones are offered, in everything from aventurine to unikite. There are strands of beads and freshwater pearls, with gold bead and cloisonné spacers, in a choice of sizes and arrangements; drop and stud earrings to match both collections are also pictured. And black onyx jewelry, beggars' beads, sumptuous ropes made of several strands of 4mm balls and pearls twisted together, and cloisonné jewelry and accessories are also offered. Options include the addition of gold spacer beads to some strands, custom lengths, and hand-knotting of loose strands.

Special Factors: Price quote by phone or letter with SASE on quantity orders; minimum order is $25.

INTERNATIONAL IMPORT CO.

3340 PEACHTREE RD.
ATLANTA, GA 30326

Catalog: $2, refundable
Save: see text
Pay: check, MO, certified check
Sells: cut and polished stones
Store: mail order only

$$$ ✉

International lists about 3,000 different cut precious and semiprecious stones in its catalog, a fraction of the firm's inventory of 100,000 stones. This firm, established in 1949, is highly respected in the gem trade and deals extensively with professionals.

The firm's catalog lists cut gems, from actinolite to zircon, with weight, size, shape, and color specifications. Many investment-grade stones are listed. Prices run from a few dollars to several thousand, and average about a third less than retail for comparable stones. All purchases are made on an approval basis, and a 50% deposit is required. The catalog details the sales terms and ordering information.

Special Factors: Returns are accepted within 5 days; minimum order is $15.

R/E KANE ENTERPRISES

P.O. BOX 1745,
   ROCKEFELLER PLAZA
NEW YORK, NY 10185
212/869-5525

$$$$ ✉

Catalog: see text
Save: up to 75%
Pay: check, MO, teller's check
Sells: stock and custom-made cubic zirconia jewelry
Store: mail order only

If you have diamond tastes but a rhinestone budget, consider the best alternative to the natural stone—cubic zirconia (C.Z.). This division of "Diamonds by Rennie Ellen" sells stock and custom-made C.Z. jewelry at just $10 a carat, including rings, earrings, bracelets, and necklaces, in both stock and custom designs. C.Z., a synthetic stone, is harder than glass or zircons and the best impostor on the market. C.Z. weighs 80% more than diamonds; a 1.8-carat C.Z. stone is about the same size as a one-carat diamond.

Please note that the catalog for R/E Kane is combined with the "Diamonds by Rennie Ellen" catalog. See the listing for that firm in this chapter for more information.

Special Factors: Price quote by phone or letter with SASE; minimum shipping, handling, and insurance charge is $10.

GINGER SCHLOTE

BOX 19523BB
DENVER, CO 80219

Catalog: $1, refundable
Save: up to 60%
Pay: check, MO, certified check
Sells: economy jewelry, mountings, and findings
Store: mail order only

Mrs. Schlote started her business in 1981, bringing to it years of experience in her family's jewelry/mounting-parts business. She offers many bargains for the craftsperson on a budget, and runs specials regularly.

Mrs. Schlote's 36-page catalog is crammed with economy chains, findings, and finished jewelry. Some of the items are gold-filled or sterling silver, but most are made of base metal with a white or yellow (golden) "lifetime" finish. Over three dozen chain styles are shown, starting at under 60¢ each, as well as novel pendants, rings, keyrings, bolas, cord tips, and tack pins. The jewelry and lapidary supplies include earring wires and clips, pendant mountings, bell caps, jump rings, clutchbacks, and push-nuts. Each catalog includes a number of bonus offers—freebies and extra discounts—and a coupon with which you can redeem the cost of the catalog. Be sure to mention this book to qualify for extra savings.

Special Factors: Satisfaction is guaranteed; shipping and insurance are included; returns are accepted within 10 days.

SEE ALSO

Central Skindivers ● underwater timepieces ● *SPORTS*

Circle Craft Supplies ● economy jewelry findings, boxes, etc. ● *CRAFTS*

Defender Industries, Inc. ● waterproof watches ● *AUTO*

Elderly Instruments ● cloisonné pins of musical instruments ● *MUSIC*

Fortunoff Fine Jewelry & Silverware, Inc. ● fine jewelry and watches ● *HOME: TABLE SETTINGS*

The Jompole Company, Inc. ● fine watches ● *HOME: TABLE SETTINGS*

Royal Silk, Ltd. ● small group of fashion jewelry ● *CLOTHING*

Saxkjaers ● Bing & Grøndahl pendants ● *ART, ANTIQUES*

Nat Schwartz & Co., Inc. ● fine jewelry ● *HOME: TABLE SETTINGS*

Shannon Duty Free Mail Order ● Claddagh and Irish jewelry ● *HOME: TABLE SETTINGS*

Albert S. Smyth Co., Inc. ● fine jewelry and watches ● *HOME: TABLE SETTINGS*

Stecher's Limited ● fine watches and clocks ● *HOME: TABLE SETTINGS*

The Yankee Merchant Group, Ltd. ● fine jewelry ● *HOME: TABLE SETTINGS*

LEATHER GOODS

Small leather goods, handbags, briefcases,

attaché cases, luggage, trunks,

and services

The firms listed here stock everything you should need to tote your effects around town, to the office, and around the world. In addition to handbags, briefcases, suitcases, steamer and camp trunks, and small leather goods, some companies also stock cases for musical instruments and portfolios for models and artists.

If you're buying luggage, consider the different luggage materials available and the pros and cons of each before making your purchase. Molded plastic is almost indestructible, but it's heavy and scuffs easily. Rip-stop nylon is the lightest material that's widely available, but it's easily punctured and affords the contents little protection against hard knocks or even rain. Soft-sided vinyl and reinforced fabric luggage can be punctured and torn, but it isn't as heavy as the molded type. Leather is luxurious and can be quite durable, but it usually shows scuffs and makes a great target for thieves working baggage areas at airports. You can add to this list on your own: Consider your own needs and buy accordingly.

Other tips: Don't buy luggage with attached wheels if you're doing any flying. Baggage handlers say the wheels often jam in conveyor systems and are usually ripped off by the time you've taken a few trips. Collapsible luggage carriers, which can be taken with you as hand baggage, solve the problem of getting bags around in huge, porterless terminals. And buy luggage that can be locked, since an unsecured bag is an invitation to pilferage.

Additional listings of firms selling small leather goods and handbags can be found in "Clothing," portfolios and display cases and binders are available from a number of the companies listed in "Art Materials," and companies selling travel accessories are listed in "Travel."

ACE LEATHER PRODUCTS, INC.

▬▬▬▬▬▬

2211 AVE. U
BROOKLYN, NY 11229
800-DIAL ACE
IN NY 718/891-9713

Catalog: $1, refundable
Save: up to 40%
Pay: check, MO, MC, V, AE, Optima
Sells: luggage and leather goods
Store: 2211 and 2122 Ave. U, Brooklyn, NY; Monday to Saturday 10–6, Thursday 10–8

$$$ ✉ ☎ 🍁 (see text)

Top brands in luggage and leather goods are available here, at savings of up to 40% on manufacturers' suggested list prices. The 36-page color catalog (published in the holiday season) features gift merchandise, but price quotes are given throughout the year.

Ace, which was established in 1960, sells luggage by American Tourister, Andiamo, Boyt, Amelia Earhart, French, Hartmann, Lark, Lucas, Members Only, Pegasus, Samsonite, Scully, Skyway, LeSport Sac, Tumi, and Ventura at a discount. Briefcases and attaché cases by Atlas, Bond Street, Boyt, Lodis, Renwick, Schlesinger, Scully, Tumi, and Yamani are available. Also offered are handbags and small leather goods by Etienne Aigner, Le Baron, Bond Street, Bosca, Garys, and Anne Klein. You'll find travel alarms, lighters, pens, and other small luxuries by Bulova, Colibri, Cross, Mont Blanc, Seiko, and Waterman in the store. The catalog shows a fine selection of goods for personal and business gift-giving.

Canadian readers, please note: Orders to Canada are shipped via UPS.

Special Factor: Price quote by phone or letter with SASE.

AL'S LUGGAGE

2134 LARIMER ST.
DENVER, CO 80205
303/295-9009
303/294-9045

Catalog: $2
Save: up to 50%
Pay: check, MO, MC, V, AE, Discover
Sells: leather goods and luggage
Store: same address; Monday through
Saturday 8:30–5:30

$$$ ✉ ☎ 🍁 (see text)

The two dollars you send to this luggage discounter brings you a sheaf of photocopied materials, including manufacturers' price lists, ordering instructions, and shipping rate charts. Al's Luggage has been selling name-brand leather goods and luggage since 1965.

All of the popular brands are carried: Diane Von Furstenberg, Jordache, Lion Leather, London Fog Luggage, Members Only, Platt, Samsonite, Stebco, Winn, and WK. In addition to current lines of suitcases, overnight bags, cosmetics cases, totes, wardrobes, duffels, and garment bags, Al's offers attaché cases, portfolios, and even Samsonite's camcorder carrying case. The price sheets (for Samsonite) show the suggested list prices and the prices at Al's Luggage—30% to 50% less. If you're shopping for an item by a manufacturer *other* than Samsonite, you'll be better served by calling or writing for a price quote.

Canadian readers, please note: A minimum-order requirement may be imposed on orders to Canada; write for a shipping quote before sending order payment.

Special Factors: Price quote by phone or letter with SASE; C.O.D. orders are accepted.

A TO Z LUGGAGE CO., INC.

4627 NEW UTRECHT AVE.
BROOKLYN, NY 11219
800-342-5011
IN NY 718/435-2880

Catalog: free
Save: up to 50%
Pay: check, MO, MC, V, AE, CB, DC
Sells: luggage and leather goods
Store: same address; Sunday through Friday 9–6; also 425 Fifth Ave., New York, NY; Sunday through Friday 9–6; and 790 Seventh Ave., New York, NY; Sunday through Friday 9–8

$$$ ✉ ☎ 🍁

A to Z has been supplying New Yorkers with luggage and leather goods since 1945, discounting prices up to 50%. The catalog is published for the holiday season; calling or writing for price quotes is recommended.

A to Z sells luggage, briefcases and attaché cases, and other leather goods by Adolfo, American Tourister, Andiamo, Boyt, Amelia Earhart, Hartmann, Lark, Lucas, Members Only, Samsonite, Verdi, Wings, Zero Halliburton, and other designers and manufacturers. Artists' portfolios, steamer trunks, and related gifts are also available. And A to Z discounts pens by Cross and Mont Blanc. The 28-page catalog has dozens of gift ideas—desk and travel accessories, executive novelties, etc.—in addition to leather goods.

Special Factors: Price quote by phone or letter with SASE; service and repairs are available; orders are shipped worldwide.

CLASSIC DESIGNS

P.O. BOX 994
MARION, MA 02738
508/748-2425

Catalog: $1, refundable
Save: up to 40%
Pay: check, MO, MC, V
Sells: leather business and personal accessories
Store: mail order only

$$$ ✉ ☎ 🍁 (see text)

Classic Designs, which was founded in the late 1970s, sells handcrafted leather goods at prices up to 40% less than those charged elsewhere for the same items. The briefcases, note pads, portfolios, planners, and other accessories are made of full-grain cowhide in "elegant, yet functional" styles with what the firm characterizes as a "down east" look, and are very well priced: A six-ring personal planner with snap closure costs about $50, briefcases and portfolios begin at under $100, and note pad covers cost $15 to $47. Everything is covered by Classic Designs' guarantee of satisfaction.

Canadian readers, please note: Request a shipping estimate before ordering.

Special Factors: Satisfaction is guaranteed; price quote by phone or letter with SASE.

INNOVATION LUGGAGE

**487 HACKENSACK AVE.
RIVER EDGE, NJ 07661
800-722-1800**

Information: price quote
Save: up to 50%
Pay: check, MO, MC, V, AE, DC
Sells: leather goods and luggage
Store: 14 locations in CT, NJ, and NY

$$$ ✉ ☎

Innovation, the "largest independent Samsonite dealer in the U.S.," has an excellent selection of luggage, briefcases, and other leather goods from a range of manufacturers. Innovation used to publish a brochure during the holiday season but has discontinued it; inquire for a price quote.

Innovation carries luggage, portfolios, briefcases and attaché cases, handbags, and small leather goods by American Tourister, Amelia Earhart, Hartmann, Invicta, Land, Lark, Samsonite, Skyway, Tumi, Ventura, and many other firms. Excellent savings can be found on one-of-a-kind items and closeouts that are sold in the stores only—Bally briefcases have appeared at 50% off list. The holiday brochure, which is free, includes a selection of gift items as well as stock leather goods.

Special Factors: Price quote by phone or letter with SASE; minimum order is $15.

THE LUGGAGE CENTER

960 REMILLARD CT.
SAN JOSE, CA 95122
408/288-5363

Information: price quote
Save: up to 50%
Pay: MO, MC, V, AE
Sells: luggage, business cases, and travel accessories
Store: locations in Bakersfield, Berkeley, Burlingame, Fresno, Los Gatos, Mountain View, Pleasant Hill, Redwood City, San Francisco, San Jose, San Lorenzo, San Rafael, Visalia, and Walnut Creek, CA

$$ ✉   ☎   🍁   (see text)

The Luggage Center, which bills itself as "California's #1 Discounter of First Quality Luggage," can save you up to 50% on the top names in luggage, and more when the firm is running a sale.

The Luggage Center stocks the latest lines from well-known firms, which include Atlantic, Atlas, Caribou, Halliburton, High Sierra, Lark, London Fog, Members Only, Pegasus, Ricardo, Samsonite, Skyway, and Ventura. Attaché cases, garment bags, and travel accessories are carried as well. Call or write for a price quote.

Canadian readers, please note: Orders to Canada are shipped via UPS.

Special Factors: Price quote by phone or letter with SASE; returns are accepted within 15 days.

NEW ENGLAND LEATHER ACCESSORIES, INC.

P.O. BOX 127
ROCHESTER, NH 03867
603/332-0707

Brochure and Samples: $2, refundable
Save: up to 50%
Pay: check, MO, MC, V, AE
Sells: leather handbags
Store: 11 Portland St., Rochester, NH; Monday through Saturday 9–5; also Rte. 1, Tidewater Mall, Kittery, and 2 Depot St., Freeport, ME; Monday through Saturday 10–6, both locations

The eight-page brochure published by New England Leather is illustrated with line drawings of its sturdy leather bags, which are priced up to 50% below comparable leather goods. New England Leather was founded in 1976.

The brochure shows drawings of dozens of handbags and small leather items, mainly classic envelopes, hobo bags, and variations on simple pouch designs. Samples of the richly colored, semimatte cowhide are included with the brochure; the leather is supple and sturdy enough to last for years and withstand a lot of abuse before showing it. (A very well-known maker of plain, sturdy leather bags produces "lite" leather models, similar to those from New England Leather's, at up to twice the price.) The bags are constructed with solid brass hardware, which won't silver with age, and they're lined with cotton twill. Prices run from $2.50 for a snap change purse to $72 for a tailored town shoulder bag.

New England Leather also carries a line of leather business accessories, including card cases, agendas, diary covers, portfolios, briefcases, and related goods. Savings on these items are not significant, however, unless the goods are bought in quantity.

Special Factor: Returns are accepted.

SEE ALSO

Bennett Brothers, Inc. • small leather goods, luggage, and luggage carts • *GENERAL MERCHANDISE*

Custom Coat Company, Inc. • deerskin handbags, gloves, billfolds, etc.
• *CLOTHING*
Dairy Association Co., Inc. • Tackmaster leather balm • *ANIMAL*
The Deerskin Place • deerskin leather goods • *CLOTHING*
A. Feibusch Corporation • replacement luggage-weight zippers •
CRAFTS
Gander Mountain, Inc. • backpacks and lightweight luggage • *SPORTS*
Holabird Sports Discounters • racquet-sports bags • *SPORTS*
IMPCO, Inc. • Lexol leather conditioner • *AUTO*
Justin Discount Boots & Cowboy Outfitters • leather-care
preparations • *CLOTHING: FOOTWEAR*
Lands' End, Inc. • canvas luggage and attaché cases • *CLOTHING*
Leather Unlimited Corp. • leatherworking hardware, leather finishes,
small leather goods • *CRAFTS*
Mother Hart's Natural Products, Inc. • cotton canvas luggage •
HOME: LINEN
Pagano Gloves, Inc. • deerskin handbags, gloves, slippers, etc. •
CLOTHING
The Renovator's Supply, Inc. • trunk hardware • *HOME:
MAINTENANCE*
Shannon Duty Free Mail Order • leather handbags • *HOME: TABLE
SETTINGS*
United Pharmacal Company, Inc. • leather conditioner • *ANIMAL*
Veteran Leather Company, Inc. • leather-care products • *CRAFTS*
Western Suppliers • saddles and tack • *ANIMAL*
Wholesale Veterinary Supply, Inc. • leather-care products • *ANIMAL*

MEDICINE AND SCIENCE

Prescription and over-the-counter drugs,
hearing aids, contact lenses and
eyeglasses, and post-surgery supplies and
equipment

Buying your medications by mail is convenient and can be less expensive than having prescriptions filled at the local drugstore. Even the prices of generic drugs may be lower by mail, affording you savings of up to 60% on some commonly prescribed remedies. You can also save up to half on the usual cost of hearing aids, contact lenses, breast forms, and products for ostomates, diabetics, and convalescent patients by buying them from the firms listed here.

Be sure to consult your doctor before ordering, though, especially if the mail-order product is different from your usual prescription or corrective aid. Always see a doctor about a hearing loss, and do not buy contact lenses from a firm that does not require an actual prescription. Exercise care with medications: Don't use another person's prescription even if your problem seems to be identical. Take medications as prescribed, and discard leftovers. Maintaining a "fresh" medicine chest militates against the problems that may develop with aging products. It also prevents the use of a product that has since been reformulated or withdrawn from the market. Check the expiration dates of the OTC (over-the-counter) products in your medicine chest, and discard any medications or other items that are beyond their "best" use dates.

Do you hang on to your old eyeglasses after your prescription has changed? You can put them to good use by sending them to New Eyes for the Needy, P.O. Box 332, Short Hills, NJ 07078. Your castoff specs will go to buy new glasses for others who can't afford them, even at a discount.

Want to keep up with government news on medicine and regulatory matters? Subscribe to *FDA Consumer,* published ten times yearly. You can order a subscription through the Consumer Information Catalog, which is available free upon request from the Consumer Information Center, Pueblo, CO 81002.

For related products, see the listings in "Health and Beauty."

AMERICA'S PHARMACY

P.O. BOX 10490
DES MOINES, IA
   50306-0490
   515/287-6872

Catalog: free
Save: up to 50%
Pay: check, MO, MC, V
Sells: OTC and prescription drugs and health aids
Store: mail order only

$

America's Pharmacy provides prescription-filling services by mail, including generic equivalents of name-brand drugs for up to 50% less. The firm also sells vitamins and dietary supplements, OTC remedies, beauty aids, and other drugstore goods at a discount.

Generic prescription drugs, which are formula equivalents of name-brand products, are sold at prices considerably lower than the branded versions. The drugs are listed with trade names, chemical names, list prices, and the lower generic prices; service is prompt. If you order from America's Pharmacy, you may request a printout of all of your prescriptions at the end of the year—a great help when you're doing your taxes.

The 52-page catalog also lists goods for diabetics, copycat fragrances, skin-care products, dietary supplements, pain relievers, cold and allergy remedies, nonprescription reading glasses, weight-control products, hearing aid batteries, Attends, condoms, and Spenco wraps.

Special Factors: Satisfaction is guaranteed; returns are accepted within 30 days; shipping and insurance are included; minimum order is $15.

B & B COMPANY, INC.

**2417 BANK DR., SUITE
  201
P.O. BOX 5731, DEPT.
  WC01
BOISE, ID 83705
208/343-9696**

Brochure: free
Save: up to 50% (see text)
Pay: check, MO, MC, V
Sells: breast forms
Store: mail order only

$$

After recovering from her mastectomy in 1965, the founder of this firm began searching for a comfortable, reasonably priced breast form. Dissatisfied with what was then available, she tried making one herself. The first seed-filled form she stitched together over 20 years ago became the prototype for the Bosom Buddy. This unique prosthesis is weighted and shaped to ideal dimensions with cushioned pillows, each of which contains 1-1/2 ounces of tiny glass beads. The weight may be adjusted by adding or removing pillows. The form itself is all-fabric (no silicone is used), made of nylon softened with fiberfill, with an all-cotton backing that rests next to your skin. Bosom Buddy is listed in sizes from 32AA to 46DDD, and it costs $55 ($60 for sizes DD and DDD). These prices are about 50% below those of other silicone models. The brochure gives complete details, and B & B's staff can answer any questions you may have by phone.

Special Factors: Satisfaction is guaranteed; returns are accepted; C.O.D. orders are accepted; orders are shipped worldwide.

BRUCE MEDICAL SUPPLY

**411 WAVERLY OAKS RD.,
  DEPT. 10736
WALTHAM, MA 02154
800-225-8446
FAX: 617/894-9519**

Catalog: free
Save: up to 60%
Pay: check, MO, MC, V
Sells: ostomate and general medical
  products
Store: mail order only

$$$$

The Bruce Medical Supply catalog is a valuable aid to persons who have had tracheostomies, colostomies, ileostomies, or urostomies, as well as diabetics and anyone who needs general nonprescription medical supplies and equipment. Bruce also stocks products designed to make all sorts of routine tasks easier.

The 56-page catalog offers a comprehensive range of ostomy supplies, including collection pouches, dressings, adhesives and removers, disks and seal rings, irrigators, lubricants, cleansing products, and disinfectants. Diabetes monitoring supplies and equipment, bathtub safety benches, tub grips, decubitus (bedsore) protection, wheelchairs, walkers, canes, crutches, magnifying glasses, sphygmomanometers, stethoscopes, compresses, and similar products are also stocked. Most of the goods are from well-known firms, including Ames, Hollister, Johnson & Johnson, Squibb, 3M, and United.

Books on related topics and sundry nursing and medical-care supplies are available. The catalog also features a good selection of dining, food preparation, dressing, grooming, and bathing aids for persons whose range of movement or strength is limited.

Special Factors: Satisfaction is guaranteed; goods are shipped in unmarked boxes; overnight delivery is available; C.O.D. orders are accepted.

RIC CLARK COMPANY

36658 APACHE PLUME DR.
PALMDALE, CA 93550
805/947-8598

Catalog: free
Save: 50% plus
Pay: check or MO
Sells: hearing aids
Store: mail order only

$$$ ✉ 🍁 ▤

The Ric Clark Company publishes a catalog featuring six hearing aid models, designed for varying degrees of hearing loss. Please note that the firm recommends that you see a physician before buying an aid; you must sign a waiver if you don't provide a physician's note stating that you need an aid.

Clark's aids are suitable for losses from mild to severe and include in-the-ear models, "compression" aids said to "cushion" sudden loud noises, and standard models. Prices are about half those charged by hearing-aid dealers. A $10 deposit entitles you to a month's free trial, after which you may return the aid for a complete refund or keep it and pay the balance. Batteries and repairs are also available.

Special Factors: Satisfaction is guaranteed; all aids are warrantied; a budget payment plan is available.

CONTACT LENS REPLACEMENT CENTER

P.O. BOX 1489
MELVILLE, NY 11747
516/491-7763

Price List: free with SASE
Save: up to 70%
Pay: check or MO
Sells: contact lenses
Store: mail order only

$$

The Contact Lens Replacement Center can sell you lenses of every type at savings of up to 70%. The firm has been in business since 1986 and deals by mail only.

The replacement lenses offered by the Center include hard, soft, extended-wear, disposable, and gas-permeable types, and toric and bifocal prescriptions are filled. Every major brand is available: American Hydron, American Optical, Bausch & Lomb, Boston, Ciba, Cooper Vision, Hydro-curve, Johnson & Johnson (Acuvue), and Wesley-Jessen (brown to blue). Please note: This is a *replacement* service—not for first-time lens wearers—and you must supply a current prescription. The prices are so low that it may make sense to discontinue your lens insurance and rely on this service if you lose or damage your contacts. All lenses are shipped in factory-sealed vials.

Special Factors: Price quote by phone or letter with SASE; orders are shipped worldwide.

THE EYE SOLUTION, INC.

P.O. BOX 262-H
GALION, OH 44833
419/683-1608

Catalog: free
Save: up to 70%
Pay: check, MO, MC, V
Sells: contact lens solutions, accessories
Store: mail order only

$$$

If you wear contact lenses, we don't have to tell you about the high cost of care products. The Eye Solution remedies the problem by saving you up to

70% on the cost of cleaning, disinfecting, and lubricating preparations and equipment.

We went into a *discount* drugstore with the four-page catalog and made a few comparisons: Alcon Opticlean II, 12 ml size, cost $2.39 from The Eye Solution, and $4.19 at the drugstore; Bausch & Lomb Sensitive Eyes Daily Cleaner was $2.99 in the catalog, compared to $4.49; the Alcon Opti-Zyme enzyme kit with 8 tablets and vials costs $2.29 from The Eye Solution, and $4.49 in the drugstore. The catalog lists saline and rinsing solutions, daily and weekly cleaners, rewetting drops, and disinfection units (heat) and chemicals (cold) for soft lenses, and similar products for hard and gas-permeable lenses. The brands include Alcon, Allergan, Barnes-Hind, Bausch & Lomb, Blairex, Boston, Ciba Vision (AOSept), Cooper Vision, and Wesley-Jessen. A number of "introductory" and travel kits were shown in the catalog we reviewed, as well as Easy Eyes tinted cases. And sunglasses by Bausch & Lomb, Ray-Ban, and Vuarnet are available—inquire for information.

Special Factor: Minimum order is $20 with credit cards.

HIDALGO

45 LA BUENA VISTA
WIMBERLEY, TX 78676
800-950-8086
FAX: 512/847-2393

Catalog: free
Save: up to 50%
Pay: check, MO, MC, V, AE, CB, DC, Discover, Optima
Sells: prescription eyeglasses, sunglasses, etc.
Store: Wimberley North Too Shopping Center, Wimberley, TX; Tuesday through Friday 10–5, Saturday 10–2

Hidalgo's 48-page catalog makes ordering your eyeglasses by mail seem so easy you'll wonder why you haven't tried it before. The firm has been in business since 1967 and appreciates the concerns of the mail-order shopper. The catalog includes detailed descriptions of the frames, lenses, and special coatings, and includes a "Consumers' Guide to Sunglasses" that answers every question we'd ever thought of. There are instructions on taking your "pupil distance" measurements, and a chart that shows the light transmission data on the lenses sold by Hidalgo. We really appreciate the "try-on program" that allows you to order up to three frames and try them out *before* ordering your glasses—a great feature for people who have a hard time finding frames that fit or flatter.

Hidalgo's own frames dominate the selection, and there are sunglasses by Bausch & Lomb, Ray-Ban, and Vuarnet. Replacement parts for Ray-Ban sunglasses are also available. The lens options include a choice of materials (glass, plastic, etc.), colors, coatings, and UV protection. Terms of Hidalgo's warranty are stated clearly in the catalog, as well as details on the "try-on" program. The prices run up to 40% below regular retail on the non-prescription eyewear, and 50% or more on prescription glasses.

Special Factor: Returns in new, unused condition are accepted within 30 days for exchange, refund, or credit.

LINGERIE FOR LESS

C & H SALES, INC.
11411 E. NORTHWEST
HWY.
DALLAS, TX 75218
214/341-9575

Leaflet: free with SASE
Save: up to 50%
Pay: check or MO
Sells: mastectomy breast forms
Store: same address; Monday through
Friday 10–6, Sunday 1–4

$$$ ✉

Lingerie for Less sells a mastectomy form that's won praise from many women for its comfort as well as its price. The shop also offers discounted underthings for women.

The best buy here is the "Soft Touch Breast Form" (under $75), Spenco's molded gel breast form that has been compared favorably to others selling for more than three times as much. It's available in seven sizes and is designed to fit all types of brassieres. Name-brand lingerie is also available *(to in-store customers only)* at savings of up to 60%.

Special Factors: Breast forms are warrantied for 1 year (see the brochure for details); price quote by phone or letter with SASE (include size); returns are accepted.

MASUEN FIRST AID & SAFETY

**P.O. BOX 901
TONAWANDA, NY 14151
800-831-0894
FAX: 800-222-1934**

Catalog: free
Save: up to 30%
Pay: check, MO, MC, V, AE
Sells: first-aid kits, medical supplies
Store: mail order only

$$ ✉ ☎ 🍁 ▦

Masuen, "Your Source for First Aid & Safety," publishes a 48-page catalog that's full of stock items for the medicine chest. Masuen's specialty is first-aid kits, and over a dozen are shown in the catalog, from small kits for the glove compartment to the "Masuen Portable First Aid Cabinet," which provides treatment for up to 120 persons. Masuen also sells resuscitators, sphygmomanometers, thermometers, all kinds of adhesive bandages and dressings, swabs, cotton rolls, splints, braces, antibiotic creams, soaps, analgesics, and protective clothing, eyewear, and gloves. Some of the prices are higher than those charged in local drugstores, but with quantity discounts you can realize savings of up to 30% on some items.

Special Factors: Price quote by phone or letter; quantity discounts are available; minimum order is $25.

MEDICAL SUPPLY CO., INC.

**P.O. BOX 609
HEWITT, NJ 07421-0609
201/728-7204**

Price List: free with SASE
Save: 30% average
Pay: check or MO
Sells: incontinence products
Store: mail order only

$

Coping with incontinence is easier with the products that have come onto the market in recent years, especially briefs for adults. Unfortunately, alleviating anxiety can become expensive over time, so it's great to find a source for incontinence products at a discount.

Medical Supply Co., formerly listed here as Disposable Supply, has been in business since 1977 selling Depends briefs and Chux underpads at savings of up to 50%. For example, Depends selling for 90¢ each in a local drugstore are sold here as "Incontinence Pants" at 50¢ each (in cases of 50).

The Chux underpads run from 13¢ to 41¢ each (sold in cases), depending on the size. Medical Supply accepts Medicaid (in New Jersey only) and does not charge shipping on orders delivered in Connecticut, New Jersey, New York, and Pennsylvania. (Customers in other states pay UPS charges collect.)

As a reader of this book, you may deduct 10% of the goods total from your *first* order. This WBMC reader discount expires February 1, 1992.

Special Factors: Shipping is included on deliveries to CT, NJ, NY, and PA; minimum order is 1 case.

MEDI-MAIL, INC.

P.O. BOX 98520
LAS VEGAS, NV
89193-8520
800-331-1458

Brochure: free
Save: up to 80%
Pay: check, MO, MC, V
Sells: prescription drugs and health-care products
Store: mail order only

$$ ✉ ☎ (see text) ▬

Medi-Mail is a national membership pharmacy-by-mail that offers name-brand prescription drugs at competitive prices, and an additional 20% off the prices of *generic* drugs if you're a member of American Federation of Police, End Notch Discrimination, Hadassah, Pace Membership Warehouse, Seniors' Program for Lower Medical Costs, and other organizations—call to see if any of your affiliations may qualify. Medi-Mail also honors membership in the American Association of Retired Persons (AARP).

The firm's brochure answers general questions on buying prescription drugs by mail, and lists scores of generic over-the-counter remedies, nutritional supplements, and beauty preparations. Among other services, Medi-Mail provides a refill slip (when appropriate) and itemized receipt with each prescription, and will send you a printout of your past orders on request.

Medi-Mail is offering you a gift of any nonprescription item (health or beauty product) costing up to $5 with your first *prescription* order. Identify yourself as a reader when you order. This WBMC reader offer expires February 1, 1992.

Special Factors: Price quote by phone or letter with SASE; shipping is included; minimum order is $2.50, $10 with credit cards.

NATIONAL CONTACT LENS CENTER

1188 MONTGOMERY DR.
SANTA ROSA, CA
95405-4802
707/542-3407

Brochure: free
Save: up to 75%
Pay: check, MO, MC, V
Sells: soft contact lenses
Store: same address (Santa Rosa
Optometry Center); Monday through
Friday 9–1, 2:30–5

$$$ ✉ ☎ 🍁 🇺🇸

The Santa Rosa Optometry Center runs this lens-by-mail service, which can save you up to 75% on your next pair. You must already be a lens-wearer to buy here, since the Center can't provide through the mail the fitting and monitoring services needed by first-time wearers. The Center was established in 1974 and also carries Bausch & Lomb sunglasses at a discount.

National sells all the major soft contact lens brands, including lines by American Hydron, Aquaflex, Bausch & Lomb, Ciba, Cooper Vision, Hydrocurve, Johnson & Johnson (Acuvue), Wesley-Jessen (brown to blue), and Syntex. Colored, standard, and extended-wear lenses are available, as well as toric (for astigmatism), bifocal, and aphakic (for cataracts) lenses. Hard and gas-permeable lenses are also available. The prices are based on a cost-plus-$15 markup. National Contact Lens Center must have a copy of your lens prescription, or the original vials from your current lenses, to process your order.

Special Factors: Satisfaction is guaranteed; price quote by phone or letter with SASE; prescription is required for filling order; returns are accepted within 30 days for replacement, exchange, refund, or credit; orders are shipped worldwide.

PHARMAIL CORPORATION

**P.O. BOX 1466
CHAMPLAIN, NY
12919-1466
800-237-8927
518/298-4922**

Catalog: free
Save: up to 50%
Pay: check, MO, MC, V
Sells: prescription drugs, vitamins, and health-care products
Store: 87 Main St., Champlain, NY; Monday through Thursday 10–3
$$ ✉ ☎

Pharmail wants you to be able to "pay 'insurance plan prices' for prescription drugs and enjoy benefits of scale on quantity purchases." This pharmacy has been dispensing prescription drugs, both name-brand and generic, since 1988.

You can request Pharmail's eight-page catalog, which is a partial list of the available drugs, or call for prices. The firm must have your physician's signed prescription to fill orders (authorized refills may be requested by phone), and birth date information is also required. There are no membership requirements, and Pharmail accepts EPIC, GHI, NPA, PAID, and PCS (attach a photocopy of your drug plan card to your order). Quantity prices are excellent, and if you're on a maintenance medication and can order a six-month supply, you'll save on the per-dose cost and spare yourself price increases. Pharmail can also provide a list of your purchases for the year, which is helpful at tax time. Request the catalog and literature for complete details and prices of commonly used name-brand and generic medications.

Pharmail is offering readers of this a special savings: If you're ordering *three* new prescriptions (not refills), you may deduct one-half the cover price of this book; if you're ordering *five* new prescriptions, you may deduct the entire cover price. Identify yourself as a WBMC reader when ordering. This WBMC reader offer expires February 1, 1992.

Special Factors: Price quote by phone or letter with SASE; shipping is included; quantity discounts are available; minimum order is $10.

PRISM OPTICAL, INC.

**10992 N.W. 7TH AVE.,
  DEPT. WC91
NORTH MIAMI, FL 33168**
305/754-5894

Catalog: $2, refundable
Save: up to 50%
Pay: check, MO, MC, V, AE
Sells: prescription eyeglasses
Store: same address; Monday through
Friday 9–5

$$ ⊠ ☎ 🍁 ▆

Prism Optical has been selling prescription eyeglasses by mail since 1959, and also carries sunglasses by Boeing Carrera and Bolle, and Rec Spec eye protectors. The 16-page catalog shows dozens of eyeglass frames for men, women, and children, including designer styles, metal frames, half-eye frames, and a few nerd models as well. The frames are discounted an average of 30% to 50%.

One of the benefits of ordering from Prism is being able to choose from a number of lens options. These include photochromic lenses, polycarbonate (ultra-thin) lenses, permanently tinted lenses, lenses with grey mirror-finish, and UV-filtering coating and scratch-resistant coating. The lens styles include single-vision and bifocal lenses, trifocals, and "invisible" bifocals, among others. Prism guarantees that the glasses will fit correctly, and the catalog provides guides to gauging the correct size of the temple and bridge pieces.

Prism is offering readers of this book a discount of 10% on their *first* order only. Identify yourself as a WBMC reader when you order. This WBMC reader discount expires February 1, 1992.

Special Factors: Satisfaction is guaranteed; price quote by phone or letter with SASE; returns are accepted within 30 days for refund or credit; C.O.D. orders are accepted.

RETIRED PERSONS SERVICES, INC.

**500 MONTGOMERY ST.
ALEXANDRIA, VA
22314-1563
703/684-0244**

Catalog: free
Save: up to 80%
Pay: check or MO
Sells: prescription drugs, health and beauty aids, etc.
Store: stores in CA, CT, DC, FL, IN, MO, NV, NY, OR, PA, TX, and VA; locations are listed in the catalog

$$$ ✉

Retired Persons Services is the mail-order arm of the American Association of Retired Persons (AARP). Ordering from this pharmacy-by-mail is a benefit of membership in the AARP, which may be the smartest $5 you ever spend. (See the listing for the AARP in "General.")

The 64-page catalog lists nutritional supplements, over-the-counter remedies, analgesics, supplies for diabetics, nail clippers and scissors, magnifying glasses, perfumes and products for skin and hair, sun blockers, liniments, razor blades, sphygmomanometers, support hosiery and foot-care products, dental-care items, hearing aid batteries, and much more.

Prices for the generic and branded versions of about 75 prescription drugs are listed in the catalog, and you can fill in a form enclosed in the catalog to request a price quote on your maintenance drugs if they're not listed, or call. (Have prescriptions for antibiotics, pain killers, and other drugs that should be taken promptly filled locally. And note that certain drugs are not available from this source.) Orders are filled on an invoice basis. The catalog features dozens of coupons worth 25¢ to 75¢ on selected items, and numerous articles on medical and general health topics.

Special Factors: Satisfaction is guaranteed; returns (except prescription drugs) are accepted for exchange, refund, or credit.

RITEWAY HEARING AID CO.

**P.O. BOX 597635
CHICAGO, IL 60659
312/539-6620**

Brochure: free
Save: up to 50%
Pay: check or MO
Sells: hearing aids
Store: mail order only

$ ✉

The brochure features eight hearing aids for a range of hearing losses, sold at up to 50% less than dealer prices. Riteway was founded in 1959.

Riteway stocks Royaltone and Danavox aids, including in-the-ear, over-the-ear, power (body), and other models. The brochure includes specifications on frequency, range, and battery type and life for each aid. Riteway's 30-day trial policy allows you to try the aid for 30 days before paying for it. Mercury, silver oxide, and zinc aid batteries are also sold at 25% below list.

Special Factors: Satisfaction is guaranteed; warranty terms are stated in the literature.

SURGICAL PRODUCTS, INC.

99 WEST ST.
P.O. BOX 500
MEDFIELD, MA 02052
508/359-2910

Catalog: $1
Save: up to 30%
Pay: check, MO, MC, V, AE
Sells: support hosiery and therapeutic apparel
Store: same address

$$ ✉ ☎ 🍁 ▀

Surgical Products, Inc., may be known better under its catalog name, "Support Plus." Supportive hosiery and underwear for men and women are the catalog's chief focus, and although discounts average about 15%, we found some items sold at 30% off typical retail.

If your physician recommends or prescribes support (elastic) hosiery, you'll find this catalog a helpful guide to what's available. Support Plus offers panty hose, stockings, knee-highs, and men's dress socks in different support strengths. (The compression rating for each style is given in the catalog descriptions.) Among the brands sold here are Bauer & Black, Berkshire, Futuro, Hanes, T.E.D., and Support Plus' own line. Maternity, cotton-soled, control-top, open-toe, and irregular styles are available.

Support Plus also sells posture pads for chairs and beds, joint "wraps" for applications of heat and cold, Curity sphygmomanometers, Dale abdominal and lumbrosacral supports, Futuro braces and joint supports, and personal-care products and bathing aids—bedding, underpads and disposable pants, bath seats and rails, and toilet guard rails. Women's foundation garments, Daniel Green shoes and slippers, Isotoner gloves and slippers, and Enna Jettick shoes have been offered in past catalogs.

Special Factors: Unworn returns are accepted; minimum order is $20 with credit cards.

SEE ALSO

Astronomical Society of the Pacific • publications on astronomy topics • BOOKS

Astronomics/Christophers, Ltd. • name-brand telescopes • CAMERAS

Allyn Air Seat Co. • air-filled seats for wheelchairs • SPORTS

American Association of Retired Persons • pharmacy-by-mail services • GENERAL MERCHANDISE

Bailey's, Inc. • selection of first-aid kits • TOOLS

Bennett Brothers, Inc. • microscopes and telescopes • GENERAL MERCHANDISE

Campmor • snake bite kits, variety of first-aid kits • SPORTS

Clover Nursing Shoe Company • Nurse Mates nurses' shoes • CLOTHING: FOOTWEAR

Daleco Master Breeder Products • medicines for tropical fish • ANIMAL

Danley's • name-brand telescopes • CAMERAS

Defender Industries, Inc. • marine binoculars, first-aid kits, etc. • AUTO

Direct Safety Company • earplugs, safety goggles, stretchers, first-aid kits, etc. • TOOLS

Exceptionally Yours, Inc. • coordinated separates for adults and children with limited mobility • CLOTHING

Kansas City Vaccine Company • livestock and pet biologicals and medications • ANIMAL

Leather Unlimited Corp. • leather doctors' bags • CRAFTS

Mardiron Optics • name-brand telescopes • CAMERAS

Northern Wholesale Veterinary Supply, Inc. • animal biologicals and dietary supplements • ANIMAL

Okun Bros. Shoes • nurses' shoes • CLOTHING: FOOTWEAR

Omaha Vaccine Company, Inc. • biologicals and pharmaceuticals for livestock • ANIMAL

Orion Telescope Center • name-brand telescopes • CAMERAS

PBS Livestock Drugs • livestock biologicals and instruments • ANIMAL

Plastic BagMart • zip-top plastic bags • HOME: MAINTENANCE

Scope City • telescopes • CAMERAS

Star Pharmaceutical, Inc. • nutritional supplements, OTC remedies, and sphygmomanometers • HEALTH

Todd Work Clothing • lab coats • CLOTHING

United Pharmacal Company, Inc. • biologicals and instruments for animal care and treatment • *ANIMAL*
WearGuard Corp. • lab coats • *CLOTHING*
Wholesale Veterinary Supply, Inc. • biologicals and veterinary surgical supplies • *ANIMAL*

MUSIC

Instruments, supplies, and services

Professional musicians don't pay full price for their instruments. Chances are good that, if they're based in New York City, they buy from one of the sources we've included here. Our listees sell top-quality instruments, electronics, and supplies, and while they usually serve the knowledgeable, they can assist you even if you're a rank neophyte. One afternoon spent hanging around the counters at Sam Ash or Manny's can teach you more about what to look for in a quality instrument than a month of culling magazine articles for tips and advice. If you catch the clerks during a lull in store trade, you can usually get the same kind of help over the phone—but be warned: These stores are usually very busy. Some of the stores take trade-ins, some rent instruments, and most sell used equipment.

By purchasing from these sources, you can save hundreds of dollars on top-rate equipment, and if you're equipping a band, you might save enough money to buy the van and pay the roadies. Buy the best that you can—instruments can last a lifetime, or even several, and the resale market for quality pieces is good. Buy wisely today and you may be selling your "vintage" ax to Guitar Trader or Mandolin Brothers 20 years down the road for several times what you paid!

A.L.A.S. ACCORDION-O-RAMA

**16 W. 19TH ST.
NEW YORK, NY 10011**
212/675-9089
212/206-8344

Catalog: free (see text)
Save: up to 40%
Pay: check, MO, MC, V
Sells: accordions, accessories, and services
Store: same address (11th Floor); Tuesday through Friday 9–4, Saturday 11–3

$$$

A.L.A.S., in business since 1950, has an extensive inventory of new and rebuilt accordions and concertinas that are all sold at a discount. A.L.A.S. is an authorized dealer and factory-service center for several leading brands, and can customize your instrument to meet your requirements (including MIDI). In addition to price sheets and brochures, A.L.A.S. can send you a demonstration video for $25 (refundable deposit).

Concertinas and electronic, chromatic, diatonic, and piano accordions are offered here at considerable savings. A.L.A.S. carries its own line, as well as instruments by Arpeggio, Avanti, Cordovox, Crumar, Dellape, Elka, Excelsior, Farfisa, Ferrari, Gabbanelli, Galanti, Guerrinni, Hohner, Polytone, Sano, Scandalli, Solton, Sonola, Paolo Soprani, Vox, and other firms. The catalog features color photos of individual models with specifications. New and reconditioned models are stocked, and accordion synthesizers, amps, speakers, generators, organ-accordions, and accordion stands are available. When you write for information, be sure to describe the type of accordion that interests you.

A.L.A.S. is offering readers of this book an extra 2% discount on purchases of new, full-size models. This WBMC reader discount expires February 1, 1992.

Special Factors: Price quote by letter with SASE; trade-ins are welcomed; orders are shipped worldwide.

ALTENBURG PIANO HOUSE, INC.

1150 EAST JERSEY ST.
ELIZABETH, NJ 07201
800-526-6979
IN NJ 800-492-4040

Brochure: free
Save: 35% minimum
Pay: check, MO, MC, V, AE
Sells: pianos and organs
Store: same address; Monday through
  Friday 9–9, Saturday 9–6, Sunday 12–5

$$$

The Altenburg Piano House has been doing business since 1847, and it's run even today by a descendant of the founder. Altenburg sells pianos and organs by "almost all" manufacturers, including lines by Baldwin, Hammond, Kawai, Kimball, Mason, and Yamaha. Prices are at least 35% below list or suggested retail.

If you write to Altenburg for literature, you'll receive information on its own line of pianos—upright, grand, and console models. Complete specifications are listed for each piano, including details on the encasing, keys, pinblock, bridges, soundboard, action, strings, hammer felt, and warranty. If you're pricing a name-brand model, call or write with the name of the piano or organ for price and shipping details.

Special Factor: Price quote by phone or letter with SASE.

SAM ASH MUSIC CORP.

**401 OLD COUNTRY RD.
CARLE PLACE, NY 11514
800-4-SAM ASH
516/333-8700
718/347-7757**

Information: inquire
Save: up to 50%
Pay: check, MO, MC, V, AE, CB, DC, Discover, Optima
Sells: instruments and electronics
Store: same address; Monday and Friday 10–9, Tuesday through Thursday, and Saturday 10–6; also Forest Hills, Huntington Station, White Plains, Brooklyn, and New York, NY; and Edison and Paramus, NJ

In 1924 a violinist and bandleader named Sam Ash opened a musical-instruments shop in Brooklyn. It's still family-run, but now boasts eight stores and patronage by superstars, schools and institutions, and the military, in addition to individuals. Regular half-off specials are a feature here, so don't buy elsewhere until you've given Ash a call.

Ash carries musical instruments, musical electronics, software, sound systems, recording equipment, digital home pianos, specialized lighting, and accessories by hundreds of manufacturers, including Akai, AKG, Alembic, Armstrong, Atari, Audio-Technica, Bach, Bose, Buffet, Bundy, Casio, Cerwin-Vega, Charvel, Conn, dbx, DeltaLab, Electro-Voice, Ensoniq, Fender, Gemeinhardt, Gibson, Guild, Hartke, Ibanez, Jackson, JBL, Karaoke (sing-along machines), Kawai, Kenwood, KLH, King, Kramer, Kurzweil, Leblanc, Ludwig, Marshall, Martin, Ovation, Pearl, Rickenbacker, Roland, Samson, Selmer, Sennheiser, Paul Reed Smith, Suzuki, Tama, Tascam, Technics, Toa, Washburn, Yamaha, and Zildjian. Sheet music is stocked, repairs and service are performed, and trade-ins are accepted at the stores.

Special Factors: Price quote by phone or letter with SASE; minimum order is $25; orders are shipped worldwide.

FRED BERNARDO'S MUSIC

**212 W. LANCASTER,
   DEPT. WM
SHILLINGTON, PA 19607**
215/777-3733

Catalog: $1
Save: up to 40%
Pay: check, MO, MC, V
Sells: replacement strings for fretted
   instruments
Store: same address; Monday through
   Saturday 11–7

$$$ ✉ ☎ 🍁

This firm, also known as Fred's String Warehouse, offers strings for almost every sort of fretted instrument at savings of up to 40% off list or comparable retail. Electronics are also stocked.

The catalog lists steel, brass, and bright-bronze and phosphor-bronze strings for all guitars, as well as a selection for pedal steel, mandolin, bass, banjo, violin, sitar, autoharp, and bouzouki. The brands include Aranjuez, Ernie Ball, Black Diamond, D'Addario, Darco, Fender, GHS, Gibson, Guild, Martin, John Pearse, Savarez, Dr. Thomastick-Infeld, and Vega. Picks, cables, harmonicas, DiMarzio pickups, Ibanez effects boxes, the Crybaby, mikes, and capos are also available at a discount.

Special Factor: Authorized returns are accepted within 14 days.

CARVIN

**1155 INDUSTRIAL AVE.
ESCONDIDO, CA 92025**
800-854-2235

Catalog: free
Save: up to 40%
Pay: check or MO
Sells: Carvin instruments and accessories
Store: 7414 Sunset Blvd., Hollywood, CA;
   Monday through Friday 11–8, Saturday
   11–6

$$ ✉ 🍁

Carvin manufactures its own line of instruments and equipment, made to exacting standards. The color catalog lists the specifications, features, and individual guarantees of each instrument; prices are up to 40% less than those of comparable models.

Mixers, amps, mikes, monitor systems, and electric guitars are offered here. The guitars are professional-quality instruments, designed for contemporary music needs. All of the products are sold under a ten-day free trial arrangement; servicing and performance testing is done free of charge during the warranty period; and warranties range from one to five years, depending on the item.

Special Factors: Satisfaction is guaranteed; returns are accepted for refund.

CMC MUSIC, INC.

**1385 DEERFIELD RD.
HIGHLAND PARK, IL
60035
708/831-3252**

Information: price quote
Save: up to 50%
Pay: check, MO, MC, V, Discover
Sells: pianos, organs, keyboards, and clocks
Store: same address; Monday through Friday 10–6, Saturday 10–5:30

$$$

CMC Music, which is also known as Conn Music, sells pianos, organs, and other keyboard instruments at discounts of up to 50% on list prices. Howard Miller clocks are also available.

CMC has no catalog, but you can write for prices on pianos by Young Chang, Kimball, and Wyckoff, organs by Galanti, Kawai, and Technics, and keyboards by Bontempi, Kawai, Kurzweil, and Technics. Digital pianos and related electronics are also available. Write for a price quote and shipping estimate.

Special Factors: Price quote by letter with SASE.

DISCOUNT REED COMPANY

**SUITE 496; P.O. BOX 6010
SHERMAN OAKS, CA
91403
818/990-7962**

Price List: free with SASE
Save: up to 45%
Pay: check or MO
Sells: reeds for musical instruments
Store: mail order only

$$$

You'll find "mail order reeds at fantastic savings" here—buy by the box and save up to 45%. Discount Reed, which began business in 1980, also sells related goods.

Don't scrimp on reeds or push them beyond their natural life spans—your music will suffer. If you buy them by the box from Discount Reed, you'll always have spares, and you'll save in the bargain. This firm stocks reeds for all types of clarinets and saxophones, as well as oboes and bassoons, in strengths from 1 to 5-1/2 (soft to hard). The brands include Fred Hemke, Java, Jones (double reeds), Mitchell Lurie, La Mode, Olivieri, Queen, Rico, V-12, Vandoren, and La Voz. (If you're looking for a reed not listed in the flyer, call or write, since it may be available.) In addition to reeds, the firm sells Harrison and Vandoren reed cases, trimmers, La Voz reed guards, sax straps, swabs, and related accessories.

Special Factors: Satisfaction is guaranteed; price quote by phone or letter with SASE.

ELDERLY INSTRUMENTS

P.O. BOX 14210-WM91
LANSING, MI 48901
517/372-7890
FAX: 517/372-5155

Catalog: free (see text)
Save: 33% average
Pay: check, MO, MC, V, Discover
Sells: new and vintage musical instruments, books, and recordings
Store: 1100 North Washington, Lansing, MI; Monday through Wednesday 11–7, Thursday 11–9, Friday and Saturday 10–6

This wonderful company has an extraordinary selection of in-print, hard-to-find recordings of all types of music, from folk and bluegrass to jazz and classical. The closely printed 96-page catalog we received included releases from B.B. King, contemporary Celtic music, American Indian war dances, rockabilly albums, and a wide variety of bluegrass. (For a sample of Elderly's picks, call "Dial-a-Ditty-a-Day," several minutes of an Elderly selection: call 517-372-1212.) Elderly Instruments also sells books on dance, repair and construction of instruments, music history, folklore, and even songbooks and videotapes.

Despite the impressive publication department, this firm made its name on its vintage instruments. Fenders, Martins, Dobros, Gibsons, and other electric and acoustic guitars have been offered in the past, as well as violins, mandolins, and other fretted instruments. And there are two additional catalogs—one for electric guitars and effects, and another for acoustic guitars and accessories. Elderly Instruments also sells new instruments and lays claim to the title of the world's largest dealer of new Martin guitars and is among the top 20 Gibson dealers. You'll find a good selection of equipment here by Alvarez-Yairi, Boss, Crate, DiMarzio, Dobro, DOD, E.S.P., Gibson, Guild, Kahler, Kramer, Martin, Roland, Sigma, Stelling, Taylor, and Yamaha, among other firms. The monthly "used instruments list" is sent free with catalog orders, or you may subscribe for $4. Prices are as low as 50% off list, and everything is covered by the Elderly guarantee of satisfaction (see the catalog for details).

Please note: Mail-order hours are Monday through Saturday, 9–5.

Special Factors: Satisfaction is guaranteed; price quote by phone or letter with SASE; unused, authorized returns are accepted within 5 days for exchange, refund, or credit.

FREEPORT MUSIC, INC.

**41 SHORE DR.
HUNTINGTON BAY, NY
11743
516/549-4108**

Catalog: $1, refundable
Save: up to 60%
Pay: check, MO, MC, V
Sells: instruments and accessories
Store: mail order only

Freeport, established in 1921, endears itself to musicians with a "we-will-not-be-undersold" discount policy and a good selection.

Freeport offers it all: Ludwig drums at 40% off, drums and sets by Pearl, Slingerland, and Tama, and guitars by Dobro, Gibson, Guild, Ibanez, Martin, Rickenbacker, and Yamaha. MIDI equipment and software are available, as are amps and electronics by Ampeg, Boss, Fender, Korg, Marshall, Morley, Roland, Ross, and Simmons. DiMarzio pickups, Shure mikes, Franz metronomes, and other accessories are all available.

Freeport also sells woodwind instruments by Buffet, King, Leblanc, and Selmer; and Selmer brasses, Leigh woodwind accessories, and Armstrong flutes. Simmons electronics and Casio keyboards are listed in the 24-page catalog, and Hohner harmonicas, strings, reeds, stands, valve oil and cleaning supplies, cases, disco lighting and special effects, and FM wireless transmitters are all sold here. The firm specializes in hard-to-find items and can supply musical saws, pipes of Pan, piano-tuning kits, and bubble machines, among other items. Freeport also buys and sells used instruments.

Special Factors: Price quote by phone or letter with SASE; minimum order is $10, $25 with credit cards.

GIARDINELLI BAND INSTRUMENT CO., INC.

7845 MALTLAGE DR.
LIVERPOOL, NY 13090
800-288-2334
IN NY 212/575-5959
FAX: 315/652-4355

Catalog: free
Save: up to 50%
Pay: check, MO, MC, V, AE, Discover
Sells: brasses, woodwinds, and accessories
Store: same address; Monday through
Friday 8:30–5:00, Saturday 9–1

 $$$

Giardinelli has been selling fine brasses and woodwinds since 1948. Giardinelli's own line is sold in the store and through the catalog, as are fine instruments by other manufacturers.

The 24-page catalog is an exhaustive listing of brass instruments, woodwinds, and accessories for both. Trumpets, flugelhorns, trombones, French horns, euphoniums, tubas, clarinets, flutes, piccolos, saxophones, oboes, and bassoons are all available. The brands include Amati, Bach, Besson, Buffet, Bundy, Cimbasso, Couesnon, Courtois, DEG, Emerson, Farkas, Gemeinhardt, Getzen, Haynes, Holton, Humes & Berg, Leblanc, Martin, Mercedes, Mirafone, Schilke, Schreiber, Selmer, Signet, Meinl Weston, Denis Wick, Yamaha, Yanigasawa, and others. Mouthpieces, mutes, reeds, metronomes, tuners, cases, stands, cleaning supplies, and books are also available. Giardinelli features its line of fine stock and custom mouthpieces for brasses; request the separate "Mouthpieces Brochure" for a complete listing. Savings run up to 50%, and the service department can assist you if you have questions or need advice.

Special Factors: Satisfaction is guaranteed; price quote by phone or letter with SASE; returns are accepted for exchange, refund, or credit; institutional accounts are available.

GUITAR TRADER

**561 U.S. HWY. I
EDISON, NJ 08817
201/985-3939**

Catalog: $1 (see text)
Save: up to 40%
Pay: check, MO, MC, V, AE
Sells: electronics and used and vintage
 instruments
Store: same address; Monday through
 Friday 10–6, Saturday 10–5

The catalog from Guitar Trader, *Vintage Guitar Bulletin*, costs $10 for a year's subscription (12 issues; two years for $17). The price is refundable with a purchase, and single copies are offered at $1 each. Want lists for vintage instruments are accepted. This firm is run by experts who can handle any request you might have about the instruments listed in the *Bulletin*.

Used and vintage guitars, violins, banjos, mandolins, ukeleles, and amps and other electronics are stocked here. Guitar Trader also sells new acoustic and electric guitars on a limited basis—inquire for a price quote. The *Bulletin* will keep you posted on recent arrivals of vintage stock. A subscription would make a super gift for your favorite musician/collector.

Special Factors: Price quote by phone or letter with SASE; layaways are available; orders are shipped worldwide.

INTERSTATE MUSIC SUPPLY

**P.O. BOX 315
NEW BERLIN, WI 53151
414/786-6210
FAX: 414/786-6840**

Catalog: free
Save: up to 60%
Pay: check, MO, MC, V
Sells: instruments, electronics, and
 accessories
Store: Cascio Music Co., 13819 W.
 National Ave., New Berlin, WI; Monday
 through Thursday 10–8, Friday 10–5,
 Saturday 10–2

Interstate Music Supply is a division of Cascio Music Company, which has been in business since 1949. IMS serves the needs of schools and music teachers with a wide range of equipment, which is listed in the 164-page catalog. You'll find savings of up to 60% here on instruments, electronics, and accessories from major manufacturers.

IMS stocks everything from woodwind reeds and corks to full lines of brass, woodwind, percussion, and stringed instruments, including repair kits and parts, cleaning supplies, neckstraps, cases, storage units, music stands, stage lighting, sound systems, piano labs, and even riser setups for bands and orchestras. There are great buys on the house brand, IMS, as well as goods from Anvil, Bach, Blessing, Buffet, Bundy, Dynamic, Emerson, Engelhardt, Fender, Fostex, Franz, Gemeinhardt, Gibson, Holton, Korg, Kramer, Leblanc, Ludwig, Mesa-Boogie, Orff, Ovation, Pearl, Peavey, Roland, Sansui, Schilke, Seiko, Selmer, Trace-Elliot, Vandoren, Vito, Yamaha, and Zildjian. The catalog shows a fraction of the extensive inventory, so call or write if you don't see what you're looking for.

Special Factors: Satisfaction is guaranteed; price quote by phone or letter with SASE; returns are accepted within 10 days for exchange, refund, or credit; institutional accounts are available; minimum order is $25.

KENNELLY KEYS MUSIC, INC.

5030 208TH ST., S.W.
LYNNWOOD, WA 98036
800-426-6409
IN WA 800-562-6558

Catalog: free
Save: up to 50%
Pay: check, MO, MC, V, AE, Discover
Sells: musical instruments and accessories
Store: same address; Monday through Friday 8–5; also Bellevue, Everett, Redmond, and Seattle, WA

Marching bands, student musicians, guitarists—take note: Kennelly has an excellent selection of instruments and equipment for all of you, at savings of up to 50% on suggested list prices. Kennelly has been in business since 1960 and runs a repair department that offers its services to mail-order customers.

Kennelly carries woodwind, brass, and percussion instruments, as well as guitars, speakers, amps, tuners, effects boxes, autoharps, mikes, stage lighting, mike cords, snakes, and more. The brands include AKG, Armstrong, Artley, Atlas, Bach, Blessing, Brilhart, Bose, Buffet, Bundy,

Conn, DEG, Emerson, Fender, Gemeinhardt, Getzen, Gibson, Haynes, Holton, King, Korg, Larilee, Latin Percussion, Leblanc, Ludwig, Mitchell Lurie, Manhasset, McCormicks, Meyer, Mirafone, Muramatsu, Musser, Paiste, Pearl, Polytone, Remo, Rico, Rogers, Roland, Roth, Selmer, Shure, Studio 49, Vandoren, Vito, and Zildjian.

Special Factors: Price quote by phone or letter with SASE; institutional accounts are available; authorized returns are accepted; minimum order is $25.

LONE STAR PERCUSSION

10611 CONTROL PL.
DALLAS, TX 75238
214/340-0835
FAX: 214/340-0861

Catalog: free with a long, self-addressed, stamped envelope
Save: 40% average
Pay: check, MO, MC, V
Sells: percussion instruments
Store: same address; Tuesday through Friday 9:30–5:30, Saturday 9:30–2

Concert, marching, jazz, and rock percussion: Lone Star stocks it all. This firm has been doing business with individuals and institutions worldwide since 1978.

The 52-page catalog lists drums and heads, drumsticks, keyboard mallets, cymbals, castanets, gongs, tambourines, triangles, wood blocks, bells, percussion for Latin music, and much more. The brands represented include American Drum, Balter, Bruno, Deschler, Feldman, Vic Firth, Tom Gauger, Grover, Hinger, Holt, Hyer, Latin Percussion, Linwood, Malletech, Musser (Ludwig), Payson, Pearl, Premier, Promark, Regal Tip, Remo, Ross, Sabian, Silverfox, Tama, Yamaha, and Zildjian. In the unlikely event you don't see what you're looking for among the thousands of items listed, call or write—it's probably available.

Special Factors: Satisfaction is guaranteed; price quote by phone or letter with SASE; authorized returns are accepted within 2 weeks (a restocking fee of up to 20% may be charged); institutional accounts are available; orders are shipped worldwide.

MANDOLIN BROTHERS, LTD.

**629 FOREST AVE.
STATEN ISLAND, NY
10310-2576
718/981-3226
FAX: 718/816-4416**

Catalog: free
Save: up to 35%
Pay: check, MO, MC, V, AE, Discover, Optima
Sells: new and vintage fretted instruments, electronics, and accessories
Store: same address; Monday through Saturday 10–6

$$$ ✉ ☎ 🍁 ▬

Mandolin Brothers has been selling vintage fretted instruments at good prices since 1971 and offers select new instruments at a standard discount of 35% from list prices. If you're in the Staten Island area, you can visit the showroom and try out any of the instruments.

Mandolin Brothers' 48-page catalog is packed with listings of vintage guitars, mandolins, mandolas, banjos, electric basses, and other stringed instruments. A recent issue showed a number of early Martin and Gibson guitars, which were competitively priced. Part of the catalog is devoted to new equipment—guitars, mandolins, banjos, electronics, and accessories. The instrument lines include Alvarez-Yairi, Deering, Dobro, Epiphone, Flatiron, Gibson, Guild, Kentucky, Lowden, Martin, OME, Ovation, M.V. Pedulla, Jose Ramirez, Rickenbacker, Santa Cruz, Sierra, Sigma, Steinberger, Stelling, Taylor, Washburn, Wildwood, and Yamaha. There are amps, tuners, effects boxes, and other electronics by Boss, Crate (amps), DOD, Seymour Duncan, Fostex, Korg, Gallien Kreuger (amps), Marshall (amps), Ovation, Roland, and other firms; pickups by DeArmond, DiMarzio, and Seymour Duncan; and cables, strings, straps, frets, mutes, capos, books, videos, and more. Written instrument appraisals and repairs are available, and Mandolin Brothers ships in-stock instruments and amps on a three-day approval basis—and that includes vintage equipment.

Special Factors: Satisfaction is guaranteed; price quote by phone or letter with SASE; returns are accepted within 3 days; minimum order is $50 with credit cards; orders are shipped worldwide.

MANNY'S MUSICAL INSTRUMENTS & ACCESSORIES, INC.

156 W. 48TH ST.
NEW YORK, NY 10036
212/819-0577

Information: price quote
Save: up to 50%
Pay: check, MO, MC, V, AE, Discover
Sells: instruments, electronics, and accessories
Store: same address; Monday through Saturday 9–6

Manny's has been selling musical instruments since 1935, and it's rare that this store on New York City's "Music Row" doesn't have a rock luminary or two checking out the equipment. Sales are run on a regular basis, bringing the standard 30% discounts up to 50%.

Manny's carries instruments, electronics, and accessories of every type, from amps and mixers to fine woodwinds and brass instruments. The roster of brands includes Acoustic Research, Alembic, Bach, Bose, Buffet, Bundy, Casio, Cerwin-Vega, DeltaLab, Electro-Voice, Fender, King, Gibson, Guild, Hohner, Ibanez, Leblanc, Ludwig, Marshall, Martin, Moog, Multivox, Ovation, Pearl, Peavey, Polytone, Wurlitzer, and Yamaha. You'll find just about anything you need here, and if an item isn't stocked, Manny's can probably get it for you.

Special Factor: Price quote by phone or letter with SASE.

METROPOLITAN MUSIC CO.

P.O. BOX 1415
STOWE, VT 05672
802/253-4814
FAX: 802/253-9834

Catalog: free
Save: up to 50%
Pay: check or MO
Sells: stringed instruments and accessories
Store: mail order only

Metropolitan, in business since 1925, sells stringed instruments and accessories and maintains a workshop for repairs and adjustments. There are some "student" quality instruments here, but most of the models are chosen for professional musicians.

Metropolitan carries John Juzek violins, violas, cellos, and basses, and bows by F.N. Voirin, Glasser, and Emile Dupree. Bridges, Taperfit and other pegs, bow hair and parts, fingerboards, necks, chin rests, Resonans shoulder rests, Ibex tools, strings, cases, and bags are all stocked. This is an excellent source for the experienced musician who is familiar with the instruments and accessories. Books on instrument repair and construction are available, as well as a fine selection of wood, parts, and tools. The prices listed in the catalog are subject to discounts of 30% to 50%.

Special Factors: Price quote by phone or letter with SASE; minimum order is $15.

NATIONAL EDUCATIONAL MUSIC CO., LTD.

1181 RTE. 22
P.O. BOX 1130, DEPT.
W-91
MOUNTAINSIDE, NJ
07092
800-526-4593
IN NJ, AK, HI
201/232-6700
FAX: 201/789-3025

Catalog: free
Save: up to 50%
Pay: check, MO, MC, V, AE
Sells: instruments and accessories
Store: mail order only

NEMC has been supplying school bands with instruments since 1959 and offers you the same equipment at savings of up to 50% on list prices.

Brass, woodwind, and percussion instruments by Alpine, Amati, Bach, Blessing, Bundy, Decatur, DEG, Fox, Gemeinhardt, Getzen, Holton, John Juzek, Korg, Larilee, Leblanc, Ludwig, Meisel, Mirafone, Olds, Pearl, Schreiber, Selmer, Signet, Vito, and other firms are listed in the 32-page catalog. Imported master violins and violas are offered, as well as cases, stands, strings, bows, and other accessories. Music software by Passport is also carried. NEMC provides "the longest warranty in the industry" on woodwinds, drums, and brass and stringed (except fretted) instruments.

Special Factors: Price quote by phone or letter with SASE; returns (of instruments) are accepted within 7 days (a restocking fee may be charged); minimum order is $100 on accessories.

PATTI MUSIC CORP.

414 STATE ST., DEPT. WC
MADISON, WI 53703
608/257-8829
FAX: 608/257-5847

Catalog: free
Save: 20% average
Pay: check, MO, MC, V
Sells: sheet music and metronomes
Store: same address

One of the hardest items to find at a discount is sheet music, but that's the raison d'être of Patti Music Corp.'s mail-order department. The firm has been in business since 1936, and publishes a 60-page catalog of sheet music, for piano and organ, and a selection of metronomes and tuners. Savings on the sheet music run around 15%, and the metronomes are discounted up to 33%.

Piano methods, ensembles, and solos are featured, from scores of music publishers. The catalog lists organ music for religious holidays, Christmas music and Broadway shoes, and flashcards, manuscript paper, theory books, and other teaching aids. The proficiency levels of the music and instructional material run from beginner to advanced. In addition to sheet music, there are key-wound, quartz, and electronic metronomes from Franz, Matrix, Seiko, and Wittner, and chromatic tuners by Seiko.

Special Factor: Discounts are available through the catalog only, not in the store.

RAINBOW MUSIC

RTE. 9, POUGHKEEPSIE
PLAZA MALL
POUGHKEEPSIE, NY
12601
914/452-1900

Catalog: free
Save: up to 50%
Pay: check, MO, MC, V, AE, Discover
Sells: electronics and new and used
vintage instruments
Store: same address; Monday through
Saturday 11–6

Rainbow's choice group of stringed instruments, electronics, MIDI, and percussion is featured in the catalog, which also shows a good selection of used and vintage equipment. Rainbow, which began business in 1976, invites inquiries about new equipment from Alembic, Crown, dbx, Fender, Fostex, Gibson, Guild, Ibanez, JBL, Kramer, Marshall, Martin, Ovation, Pearl, B.C. Rich, Rickenbacker, Roland, Steinberger, Subian, Tama, Tascam, Zildjian, and other manufacturers. Effects boxes, pickups, strings, keyboards, speakers, equipment cases, mixers, tape decks, and other goods are stocked, available at savings of up to 50%. Rainbow buys used guitars and amps, and accepts trade-ins.

Special Factors: Price quote by phone or letter with SASE; orders are shipped worldwide.

SHAR PRODUCTS COMPANY

P.O. BOX 1411
ANN ARBOR, MI 48106
313/665-7711

Catalog: free
Save: up to 50%
Pay: check, MO, MC, V
Sells: sheet music, stringed instruments, accessories
Store: 2465 S. Industrial Hwy., Ann Arbor, MI; Tuesday through Saturday 9–5

$$$ ✉ ☎ 🍁 (see text) ▬

"Shar is managed by knowledgeable string players and teachers, who are sympathetic to the needs of the string community." Shar, in business since 1962, prices its goods up to 50% below list or full retail prices.

The 64-page catalog gives equal time to stringed instruments and to the firm's extensive collection of classical music recordings and sheet music. If you play violin, viola, cello, or bass, see the catalog for the cases, bows, chin and shoulder rests, strings, bridges, tailpieces, pegs, music stands, humidifying tubes, endpipes, and other supplies and equipment. Student violins by Glaesel, Schroetter, and Suzuki are available, as well as fine violins by master violin makers.

The accessories catalog features hundreds of books of sheet music, manuals, videotapes, and audio cassettes. (The separate sheet music catalog, with thousands of titles, is available for $3.) Shar sells the Suzuki books and records line, videotapes of master artists (Casals, Segovia, Pavarotti, Heifetz, and others) in performance, classical recordings on cassette, and sheet music for a wide range of instruments. Not all goods are discounted, but savings overall average 30%, and selected lines are offered at further savings periodically.

Canadian readers, please note: Personal checks are not accepted.

Special Factors: Satisfaction is guaranteed; price quote by phone or letter with SASE; C.O.D. orders are accepted.

WEINKRANTZ MUSICAL SUPPLY CO., INC.

870 MARKET ST. SUITE 1265
SAN FRANCISCO, CA 94102
415/399-1201
FAX: 415/399-1705

Catalog: free
Save: up to 50%
Pay: check, MO, MC, V
Sells: stringed instruments, parts, and supplies
Store: same address; Monday through Friday 9–5

$$$ ✉ ☎ 🍁

Stringed instruments are the whole of Weinkrantz's business—violins, violas, cellos, and basses. Weinkrantz, founded in 1975, prices the instruments and parts 30% to 50% below suggested retail.

The 40-page catalog lists the available instruments and outfits, cases, music stands, metronomes, bows, strings, and other supplies. There are several pages of strings alone, principally German lines (Jargar Kaplan, Pirastro, Prim, and Thomastik). Weinkrantz carries violins and violas by Helmut Mayer, T.G. Pfretzschner, Roth, and Nagoya Suzuki, and Roman Teller. Cellos by these firms and Karl Hauser, Wenzel Kohler, and Anton Stohr are cataloged, as well as basses from Enesco, and Emanual Wilfer. If you don't wish to purchase an outfit, you can order the bow, case or bag, rosin, string adjusters, and other equipment à la carte. Strings, bow hair, chin rests, bridges, metronomes, and tuners are all sold at a discount. Instrument cases by Gewa, Jaeger, and Winter are also available.

Canadian readers, please note: Orders must be paid in U.S. funds.

Special Factors: Satisfaction guaranteed (see the catalog for the policy on strings); price quote by phone or letter with SASE; minimum order is $10 with credit cards; orders are shipped worldwide.

WEST MANOR MUSIC

831 EAST GUN HILL RD.
BRONX, NY 10467
212/655-5400

Price List: free
Save: 40% average
Pay: check, MO, MC, V
Sells: musical instruments
Store: same address; Monday through
Friday 9–4, Saturday 10–3

West Manor Music has been supplying schools and institutions with musical instruments since 1959 and offers a wide range of instruments at an average discount of 40%.

The 12-page catalog lists clarinets, flutes, piccolos, saxophones, oboes, trumpets, trombones, French horns, cornets, flugelhorns, euphoniums, Sousaphones, violas, violins, cellos, guitars, pianos, drums, cymbals, xylophones, glockenspiels, and other instruments. Drum stands and heads, strings, reeds, cases, music stands, metronomes, mouthpieces, and other accessories are sold.

The brands represented here include Alpine, Amati, Armstrong, Artley, Benge, Besson, Blessing, Buffet, Bundy, Conn, DEG, Fender, Fox, Gemeinhardt, Holton, King, Leblanc, Ludwig, Meisel, Noblet, Olds, Premier, Sabian, Selmer, Signet, Vito, and Zildjian, among others. West Manor also offers an "overhaul" service for popular woodwinds and brasses, and repairs can be performed. All of the instruments sold are new, guaranteed for one year.

Special Factors: Price quote by phone or letter with SASE; quantity discounts are available; minimum order is $50; orders are shipped worldwide.

SEE ALSO

Barnes & Noble Bookstores, Inc. ● audio cassette cases and accessories ● BOOKS
Bennett Brothers, Inc. ● Casio musical keyboards, small selection of other instruments ● GENERAL MERCHANDISE
Berkshire Record Outlet, Inc. ● classical recordings on records, tapes, and CDs ● BOOKS

Blackwelder's Industries, Inc. ● name-brand pianos ● *HOME: FURNISHINGS*

Forty-Fives ● original 45's from 1950 to the current year ● *BOOKS*

Front Row Photos ● photos of rock stars and groups ● *BOOKS*

Kicking Mule Records, Inc. ● "Lark in the Morning" video music lessons ● *BOOKS*

Metacom, Inc. ● audio cassettes ● *BOOKS*

Publishers Central Bureau ● audio cassette and CD storage units ● *BOOKS*

Sultan's Delight, Inc. ● Syrian derbakkehs, cymbals, tambourines, ouds, etc. ● *FOOD*

Wholesale Tape and Supply Company ● tape duplicating machines and equipment ● *APPLIANCES*

OFFICE

Office machines, furniture, and supplies; printing and related services

If you're using a single source for your office supplies, chances are good you're not getting the best prices on supplies, printing, furnishings, and the countless items needed to keep the workplace running. You can begin a cost-control program by having the person you delegate as purchaser send for the catalogs listed here, so you can build a file of discount sources for all of your needs. And to avoid problems with questionable firms, consider making one simple rule: Don't buy from suppliers who solicit your firm by phone or fax.

If you're the head of a small business, you may find that your best buy on printed envelopes is the U.S. Postal Service. The USPS and the Stamped Envelope Agency, a private concern, offer envelopes with embossed stamps (postage) in windowed or plain styles, size 6-3/4 or 10, with up to seven lines of printing (maximum of 47 characters per line). The prices are excellent: A box of 500 plain #10 envelopes costs $136.90 at this writing. That's $125 for first-class postage and $11.90 for the envelopes *and* printing. Considering the fact that a box of plain envelopes alone often costs that much, it's like getting the printing free. (Our local printer charges $30 for unfranked envelopes of comparable quality printed in the same fashion, so the USPS prices can represent savings of up to 60%). Ask for PS Form 3203 from your local post office. You can also order stamps by mail or phone, from books of 20 to coils of 500. Ask for PS Form 3227 at your local post office, or call 800-STAMP-24 to order by phone.

Several of the firms listed here sell computers and supplies, but hardware and software specialists are listed in the subsection of this chapter, "Computing." Look there for vendors of computers, peripherals, programs, furniture, paper goods, supplies, and services.

ALFAX WHOLESALE FURNITURE

**370 SEVENTH AVE.,
  SUITE 1101
NEW YORK, NY
  10001-3900
800-221-5710
212/947-9560**

Catalog: free
Save: up to 50%
Pay: check, MO, MC, V
Sells: office and institutional furniture
Store: mail order only

$$ ☎

Alfax has been selling office furnishings since 1946 and does a brisk business with institutional and commercial buyers, especially schools and churches. The best discounts are given on quantity purchases, but even individual items are reasonably priced.

The 64-page color catalog shows furnishings for offices, nurseries (institutional), cafeterias, libraries, and conference rooms. Stackable chairs are offered in several styles, as well as a range of files and literature storage systems. P.A. systems, trophy cases, carpet mats, lockers, hat racks, park benches, heavy steel shelving, prefabricated office and computer stations and work stations are just a few of the institutional furnishings and fixtures available. Many products have home applications, and all of the equipment is designed for years of heavy use.

Special Factors: Satisfaction is guaranteed; institutional accounts are available.

BROWN PRINT & CO.

**P.O. BOX 935
TEMPLE CITY, CA 91780
818/286-2106**

Price List and Samples: $1
Save: up to 40%
Pay: check or MO
Sells: custom-designed business cards
Store: mail order only

$$ ✉

Brown Print & Co. has been designing and printing business cards and stationery since 1966 and offers the person looking for something different just that. Mr. Brown, the proprietor, sent us a sample packet of dozens of cards, ranging from a photo backdrop of the Statue of Liberty at sunset to standard black and white cards with raised printing. Foils, embossed design, foldovers, and other options are available. Mr. Brown's talents would be wasted on someone who wanted a conventional card; his specialty is unusual design, and he enjoys working with his customers to create "the amusing, the novel, and other effective visual concepts."

Special Factors: Quantity discounts are available; minimum order is 500 cards.

BUSINESS ENVELOPE MANUFACTURERS, INC.

900 GRAND BLVD.
DEER PARK, NY 11729
516/667-8500
FAX: 516/586-5988

Catalog: free
Save: up to 75%
Pay: check, MO, MC, V
Sells: imprinted envelopes, stationery, forms, and office supplies
Store: mail order only

Business Envelope has been manufacturing envelopes and other office stationery for over 60 years and can save you up to 75% on the usual prices on a wide range of supplies.

The 48-page catalog shows a full line of envelopes and letterhead, plain and imprinted, as well as commonly used business forms, copier paper, computer paper, labels, pens, pencils, literature organizers, bulletin boards, cash registers, mailing room supplies, rubber stamps, and much more. The prices on the printed stationery are at least 50% below the going rate among local stationers we checked, and the choice of typefaces is better than what's usually offered by discounters.

Special Factors: Satisfaction is guaranteed; quantity discounts are available; minimum order is $20 with credit cards.

BUSINESS & INSTITUTIONAL FURNITURE COMPANY

611 N. BROADWAY
MILWAUKEE, WI 53202
800-558-8662
414/272-6080
FAX: 414/272-0248

Catalog: free
Save: up to 50%
Pay: check, MO, MC, V
Sells: office and institutional furnishings
Store: mail order only

$$$ ✉ ☎

Although the best prices at B & I are found on quantity purchases, even individual pieces are competitively priced. The catalog is geared for those who are furnishing offices, but many items are appropriate for home use as well. B & I, in business since 1966, has a "will not be undersold" pricing policy.

B & I stocks office furniture and machines, including desks, chairs, files, bookcases, credenzas, panels and panel systems (for office partitioning), phones, and coin sorters. There are data and literature storage units, computer work stations, waste cans, mats, announcement boards, outdoor furniture, energy-saving devices, and much more. Over 250 brands are available, and orders are processed promptly.

Special Factors: "15-year, no-risk guarantee"; price quote by phone or letter; quantity discounts are available.

COPEN PRESS, INC.

100 BERRIMAN ST.
BROOKLYN, NY 11208
718/235-4270
FAX: 718/235-4290

Catalog: free
Save: 20% plus
Pay: check or MO
Sells: printing services
Store: mail order only

$$ ✉

Copen, in business since 1950, handles everything from short runs of business-reply mailers to books, and the prices better those of typical web-offset presses by 20% and more.

Booklets, catalogs, and self-mailing order forms are priced in detail in the 16-page catalog. The minimum catalog run is 1,000, and stock choices are listed. Covers can be printed in different inks on Bristol stock or Kromcote. Folding, stitching, perforating, and three-hole drilling price schedules are given, and rates are listed for printing in one or two colors on plain or coated stock of different weights, in sizes running from 8-1/2″ by 11″ to 20″ by 22″. Reductions, halftones, blue-line proofs, numbering, and screens can all be produced, and Copen can even handle your catalog mailings. Inquire for more information on services not listed.

Special Factor: Price quote by phone or letter with SASE.

FAX CITY, INC.

2711-B PINEDALE RD.
GREENSBORO, NC 27408
919/288-2454
FAX: 919/288-1735

Brochure: free
Save: up to 50%
Pay: check, MO, MC, V, AE
Sells: fax machines and supplies
Store: same address; Monday through
    Friday 8:30–5

Fax City, in business since 1986, sells facsimile machines, supplies, and related goods at savings of up to 50% on list or full retail prices.

You can call or write for a quote, or see the price list for models by Avatek, Brother, Canon, Minolta, Murata, Nissei, Omnifax, Panafax, Panasonic, Ricoh, Sanyo, Sharp, or Toshiba. Fax paper, line switches, surge suppressors, and laser printer peripheral interfaces are also available.

Fax City is offering readers of this book a discount of 20% on their first order of *fax paper only.* Identify yourself as a reader when you order. This WBMC reader discount expires February 1, 1992.

Special Factors: Price quote by phone or letter with SASE; orders are shipped worldwide.

FRANK EASTERN CO.

599 BROADWAY
NEW YORK, NY 10012
212/219-0007

Catalog: $1
Save: up to 50%
Pay: check, MO, MC, V
Sells: office, institutional, and computer furniture
Store: same address; Monday through Friday 9–5

$$$ ✉ ☎

Frank Eastern, in business since 1946, offers furnishings and equipment for business and home offices at discounts of up to 50% on list and comparable retail. Specials are run in every catalog.

The 72-page color catalog from Frank Eastern features desks, chairs, filing cabinets, bookcases, storage units, computer work stations, and wall systems and panels. Seating is especially well represented: ergonomic, executive, clerical, drafting, waiting room, conference, folding, and stacking models in wood, leather, chrome, and plastic, were all shown in the catalog we reviewed. Ergonomic seating is a Frank Eastern specialty, and the prices here are a good 25% less than those listed in two other office-supply catalogs we checked. Don't overlook good buys on solid oak bookcases, wall organizers, lateral filing cabinets, and mobile computer work stations.

Special Factors: Satisfaction is guaranteed; price quote by letter; quantity discounts are available; returns are accepted; minimum order is $75 with credit cards.

GRAYARC

GREENWOODS
INDUSTRIAL PARK
P.O. BOX 2944
HARTFORD, CT 06104
203/379-9941

Catalog: free (see text)
Save: up to 50%
Pay: check, MO, MC, V
Sells: business forms, office supplies, and equipment
Store: mail order only

$$$ ✉ ☎

Grayarc's business forms, machines, and office supplies are priced to save your company money and designed to expedite all kinds of business procedures. The 60-page catalog is packed with good values, and you can save up to 50% on some items.

Business forms are featured here: Reply messages, purchase orders, work proposals, invoices, statements, sales slips, insurance memos, bills of lading, receiving reports, and credit memos in carbon and carbonless sets are among the most popular types. Many are offered in designs and formats to suit different business situations. There are plain and windowed envelopes in several sizes and colors; inter-office envelopes; Tyvek, brown kraft, and white paper mailers; business letterhead, cards, and memos; and other necessities. Custom designs and printing services are available. Grayarc's equipment lines include printing calculators from Royal, Seiko, and Unitrex; Brother electronic typewriters; 3M compact copiers; cash registers, time clocks, literature racks, shelving, office chairs, and much more. The computer supplies are featured in a separate catalog, and include a wide range of forms and paper goods.

Special Factors: Satisfaction is guaranteed; specify "general supplies" or "computer forms" catalog (include make and model of your computer or word processor with the computer catalog request); returns are accepted within 30 days.

ROBERT JAMES CO., INC.

P.O. BOX 2726, DEPT. W-91
BIRMINGHAM, AL 35202
800-633-8296
IN AL 205/251-5154

Catalog: free
Save: up to 60%
Pay: check, MO, MC, V, AE, Optima
Sells: office supplies
Store: 3600 Seventh Ct. South, Birmingham, AL

$$$ ✉ ☎ ▤

Robert James, in business since 1939, offers first-quality office supplies at job-lot prices through its 40-page Office Supply catalog. Robert James also sells hotel goods through a 32-page Hospitality Supply catalog, making this an excellent source for office and institutional needs.

Printed and plain business envelopes, kraft envelopes, mailers, copier paper, labels, and forms are all available through the Office Supply catalog. There are typing and word-processing ribbons, tapes, wheels, and elements; binders and binding machines; phones, answering machines, autodialers, desk organizers, literature racks, files and filing cabinets, shipping supplies, computer work stations, time clocks, paper shredders, chairs of all types, desks, and many other items. Savings are especially good on large quantities.

The Hospitality Supply catalog features hotel/motel supplies, including cotton towels, paper goods by the case, disposable razors, light bulbs, coat hangers, travel sizes of toothpaste, shampoo, and other toiletries. Stainless steel grab bars, rollaway beds, large-volume trash receptacles, park benches, vinyl-strap outdoor furniture, hand dryers, cribs, TV mounts, lamps, laundry and cleaning carts, and door viewers are among the other items available.

Robert James is offering readers of this book a 10% discount on their *first* orders. Identify yourself as a reader when you order. This WBMC reader discount expires February 1, 1992.

Special Factors: Satisfaction is guaranteed; specify catalog desired by name; price quote by phone or letter with SASE; quantity discounts are available; returns are accepted within 30 days.

L & D PRESS

78 RANDALL ST., BOX 641
ROCKVILLE CENTRE, NY 11570
516/593-5058

Price List: free
Save: up to 50%
Pay: check or MO
Sells: custom-printed stationery
Store: mail order only

L & D, founded in 1959, sells printed business cards, envelopes, and stationery. Prices on small orders of stationery are much better than those charged by similar firms.

L & D has a good selection of business card styles in flat and raised thermographic print; colored stock and inks and 118 typefaces are available. Business letterheads, envelopes in a variety of styles and sizes, pressure-sensitive labels, and imprinted reply messages are offered at savings of up to 40%. Engraved business letterheads, envelopes, and cards can be provided, and dies may be made to order. Personal stationery is offered in Princess and Monarch sizes in ivory, white, and pale blue, and there are Embassy informals and notepads with self-sealing envelopes. L & D also sells the Boston personal paper shredder.

Special Factor: Inquire for information about custom services.

LINCOLN TYPEWRITERS AND MICRO MACHINES

100 W. 67TH ST.
NEW YORK, NY 10023
212/769-0606

Information: price quote
Save: up to 40%
Pay: check, MO, AE
Sells: office machines
Store: same address; Monday through
Friday 9–6, Saturday 11–4

Lincoln specializes in typewriters and calculators, runs a busy repair and service department, and accepts corporate accounts. Savings run up to 40% on many items; identify yourself as a reader of this book when requesting price quotes to get the best discounts. Lincoln stocks computer peripherals, typewriters, calculators, and other office machines by Brother, Hermès, IBM, Minolta, Olivetti, Olympia, Royal, SCM, Silver Reed, and other manufacturers. Ribbons, cartridges, cables, and other supplies are available in the store.

Special Factors: Price quote by phone or letter with SASE; manufacturers' warranties on some items will be extended by Lincoln.

MAIL CENTER USA

ONE DE ZAVALA
* CENTER*
12734 CIMARRON PATH,
* SUITE 104*
SAN ANTONIO, TX
* 78249*
512/699-0311
FAX: 512/699-3419

Catalog: $5 (see text)
Save: up to 40% (see text)
Pay: check, MO, MC, V
Sells: office supplies and equipment
Store: mail order only

Mail Center USA runs a fleet of mailing centers in San Antonio and Austin, but is listed here for its mail-order office-supply business. You'll save 30% to 40% on *everything* in the big catalog ($5), and up to 70% on products featured in the quarterly sales catalogs, which are free.

The big catalog runs to 328 pages in the current edition and offers everything in office needs from accordion files to ZIP-code directories. The manufacturers represented include AccuFax, Bates, Canon, Curtis, Day Runner, Fellowes, G.E., Hewlett Packard, ITT, Ledu, Maxell, Mont Blanc, Panasonic, Pollenex, Qume, Rolodex, Stabilo, and Verbatim, among others. Mail Center USA offers great discounts: 30% on goods totals of $15 to $50, 35% on $50.01 to $100, and 40% on orders over $100. These discounts are computed on the catalog prices, which are not inflated, and cover printing services as well (greeting cards, order forms, checks, labels, business stationery, etc.).

Mail Center USA also publishes 78-page sale catalogs, which offer close-outs of seasonal goods and office supplies at savings of up to 75%. You can request the current sale catalog, which is free; if you order from it, you'll receive the large office-supply catalog at no cost.

Special Factors: Satisfaction is guaranteed; authorized returns are accepted for exchange, refund, or credit; institutional accounts are available; minimum order is $15.

NATIONAL BUSINESS FURNITURE, INC.

222 E. MICHIGAN ST.
MILWAUKEE, WI 53202
800-558-1010

Catalog: free
Save: up to 40%
Pay: check, MO, MC, V
Sells: office and computer furnishings
Store: mail order only

$$$ ✉ ☎

Furnish your office for less through the 72-page NBF catalog, which offers everything from announcement boards to portable offices. Savings run up to 40% from this firm, which was established in 1976.

Whether you're shopping for a new chair or desk or planning a complete office installation, get the NBF catalog before you buy. The firm sells office systems, desks and tables for every purpose, credenzas, bookcases, shelving, computer work stations, desk organizers, literature racks, service carts, lockers, floor mats, coffee centers, silk (fabric) plants, and much more. The selection is super: There's a range of filing cabinets, and the seating includes executive, clerical, luxury, ergonomic, conference, folding, stacking, and reception chairs, and a range of filing cabinets. The manufacturers include Belcino, Cole, Fire King, Globe, Haskell, High Point Furniture, Indiana Desk, Jansko, Jefsteel, La-Z-Boy Chair, Meilink Safe,

National Office Furniture, Paymaster, O'Sullivan, Rubbermaid, Safco, Samsonite, Sauder, Stylex, and Tennsco, among others.

Special Factors: Price quote by phone or letter with SASE; quantity discounts are available.

QUILL CORPORATION

100 SCHELTER RD.
P.O. BOX 4700
LINCOLNSHIRE, IL
  60197-4700
708/634-4800
FAX: 708/634-5708

Catalog: free (see text)
Save: up to 70%
Pay: check, MO, MC, V
Sells: office supplies and equipment
Store: mail order only

$$$ ✉ ☎

Quill, founded in 1956, offers businesses, institutions, and professionals savings of up to 70% on a wide range of office supplies and equipment. There are real buys on Quill's house brand of typing and computer supplies, which are comparable in performance and quality to name brands costing much more.

Quill's monthly 64-page catalogs feature general office supplies and equipment, including files, envelopes, mailers, and ribbons and elements for typewriters, word processors, and computer printers. There are labels, scissors, paper trimmers, pens and pencils, copiers and supplies, word processors, telephones, fax machines, binders and machines, dictating machines, accounting supplies, chairs, and much more. Quill also gives excellent discounts on custom-imprinted business stationery, labels, and forms. The computer lines include paper products and business programs, surge suppressors, disks, storage units, and related goods. The values are excellent, and delivery is prompt.

Please note: Quill does business with companies and professionals. In order to receive the catalog, *you must send your request on business letterhead*.

Special Factors: Satisfaction is guaranteed; request the catalog on business letterhead; institutional accounts are available; returns are accepted.

RAPIDFORMS, INC.

301 GROVE RD.
THOROFARE, NJ 08086
800-257-8354

Catalog: free (see text)
Save: up to 40%
Pay: check or MO
Sells: business forms and products
Store: mail order only

$$

Rapidforms offers a range of over 3,500 business forms designed for every commercial purpose, which are formatted to expedite routine transactions. The firm has been doing business since 1939, and emphasizes prompt shipment as one of its strengths.

Five different catalogs are available from Rapidforms: The Manufacturing and Wholesale catalog features invoices, bills of lading, delivery receipts, shipping products, purchase orders, work orders, checks, estimate and price quote forms, labels (in virtually every size, shape, design, and style), memos, stationery, and personnel forms. The Retail catalog offers a complete line of sales slips, labels guns, gift certificates, shopping bags, service and repair forms, tags, and many other merchandising items and related goods. The Condensed catalog features forms for contractors and a varied selection of other forms and products. The Property Management catalog includes the line of rental, real estate, and maintenance forms, and a special Holiday Card catalog (available in late summer) offers a range of corporate greeting cards. Each forms catalog includes a line of continuous computer forms, with a compatibility index for numerous software packages.

Special Factors: Request the catalog desired *by title;* shipping is included on prepaid orders; quantity discounts are available; C.O.D. orders are accepted.

THE RELIABLE CORPORATION

1001 W. VAN BUREN
CHICAGO, IL 60607
800-869-6000
FAX: 800-326-3233

Catalog: free
Save: up to 50%
Pay: check, MO, MC, V, AE, Discover
Sells: home office equipment and supplies
Store: mail order only

$$$

We seldom see catalogs as glossy as Reliable's "Home Office" from discount suppliers, and rarely from a company that's been in business since 1917. One of our readers recommended Reliable for its good prices, which are up to 50% below retail, and attention to service.

The 40-page color catalog focuses on the home office, featuring products that have been chosen for their design quality as well as function and price. The edition we reviewed showed ergonomic chairs, compact file/desk units, halogen and fluorescent desk and floor lamps, oak computer carts, copiers, filing cabinets, "barrister" bookcases, drafting tables, wire grid organizers and wall units, telephones, travel accessories, room intercoms, fax supplies, and even luggage and briefcases. There were quite a few fun items—colored staples, transparent phones, lead crystal globes, and a portable exercise kit—making this a great source for gifts and indulgences, at good prices.

Special Factors: Satisfaction is guaranteed; minimum order is $15 with credit cards.

STAPLES, INC.

**P.O. BOX 160, DEPT. C
NEWTON, MA 02195
617/965-7030**

Catalog: free
Save: 50% average
Pay: check, MO, MC, V, Staples Charge
Sells: office and computing supplies
Store: 24 stores in CT, DC, MA, NJ, NY, PA, and RI (locations are listed in the catalog)

Staples brings us "The Price Revolution in Office Products" in the form of a superstore concept with deep discounts on every item. Staples has been in existence since 1986, and has earned a loyal following among buyers for small and home offices, as well as larger firms.

Staples publishes a 106-page catalog of products with the "catalog list" prices and the Staples price. These are not closeouts, seconds, or unbranded goods, but first-quality products from Acco, Alvin, Bates, Canon, Cross, Curtis, Dennison Carter's, Eldon, Esselte, Faber Castell, Globe-Weis, Hammermill, Hewlett Packard, Maxell, Mont Blanc, Panasonic, Parker, Rolodex, Rubbermaid, SCM, Sentry (safes), Sony, Southworth (paper), Texas Instruments, 3M, Tops (forms), Vanguard, Velobind, Verbatim, and

Wilson Jones, among others. You can order office furniture, computer supplies and programs, paper and forms, filing supplies, attaché cases, calendars, pens and pencils, adhesives, drafting equipment and tools, mailing room supplies, janitorial products, fax machines, copiers, phones and phone machines, and much more.

If there's a tradeoff for the savings and product choice, it's in *options*, like color or odd sizes. But we've been shopping at our local Staples for many years, and came away empty-handed only once: We had gone there to buy a Norton's "Utilities" program and learned that only those stores with Egghead Discount Software departments sell software (they're listed in the catalog).

We urge you to sign up for the free, no-obligation membership card, since it entitles you to extra savings on selected items. A separate Staples charge card is also available. Please note that delivery charges are 5% of your order, with a minimum charge of $15.

Special Factors: Returns in original packaging are accepted within 30 days for exchange, refund, or credit; minimum order is $15 with credit cards.

TRINER SCALE

**2842 SANDERWOOD
MEMPHIS, TN 38118
901/795-0746**

Flyer: free
Save: 30% (see text)
Pay: check or MO
Sells: pocket scale
Store: same address; Monday through
Friday 8–4:30

$ ✉

Triner Scale, which may be known as "AAA Scale" to readers of previous editions of this book, sells a pocket scale with all sorts of uses.

The precision scale measures up to four ounces, and it comes packed in a pocket-sized case with a list of current postal rates tucked inside. A finger ring allows the scale to hang while measurements are taken. Suggested uses include postage determination, food measurement, lab use, craft and hobby use, and weighing herbs. It's a useful item to have on hand, and it can give you pretty close approximations of postage costs. Triner also sells a full line of mechanical and electronic postal scales that are competitively priced; inquire for information.

Special Factor: Shipping is included.

TURNBAUGH PRINTERS SUPPLY CO.

104 S. SPORTING HILL RD.
MECHANICSBURG, PA
17055-3057
717/737-5637

Catalog: $1
Save: see text
Pay: check or MO
Sells: printing supplies and new and used equipment
Store: same address; Monday through Friday 8:30–4

$$$ ✉ ☎ 🍁

Turnbaugh offers the printer working in the manner of Gutenberg new and used presses, type, and related equipment and supplies. Savings on used equipment are as much as 70% compared to the price of new goods. The stock is listed in *Printer's Bargain News,* a broadside that is published every two years. This firm has been in business since 1931.

Turnbaugh sells printing presses of every vintage, including hand, antique, treadle, and power (but not computerized) presses; offset machines, paper trimmers, stapling machines, folders, booklet stitchers, punching machines, numbering machines, and related equipment. Goods by Baltimore, Chandler & Price, Gordon, and Kelsey show up frequently. The catalog descriptions include the general condition and bed dimensions of the presses. Type, leads, rules, leaders, quoins, keys, spacers, gauge pins, printers' saws, composing sticks, cold padding cement, ink, type cleaner, rollers, type cabinets and cases, engraving tools, bone paper folders, embossing powder, paper stock, shipping tags, and other goods are offered as well.

Special Factors: Price quote by letter with SASE; *no printing services are available;* minimum order is $10; orders are shipped worldwide.

20TH CENTURY PLASTICS, INC.

3628 CRENSHAW BLVD.
LOS ANGELES, CA 90016
800-421-4662

Catalog: free
Save: up to 35%
Pay: check, MO, MC, V, AE
Sells: custom-imprinted binders and office products
Store: mail order only

$$ ✉ ☎ 🍁

We found 20th Century while pricing vinyl sheets that have pockets for slides for presentation and storage of a large project. After hearing figures approaching $1 a sheet, it was gratifying to find them here for only 40¢ each (in quantity). And two free loose-leaf binders were included in our order as a bonus!

20th Century Plastics sells more than two dozen types of slide and transparency storage sheets, as well as video and audio cassette portfolios, magazine binders, static-proof computer disk storage, and portable key and business-card files. The firm carries a variety of binders that can be imprinted with your message or logo. Tab sets, file folders, report covers, presentation materials, time-management systems, records storage, and many other related products are shown in the catalog.

Special Factors: Satisfaction is guaranteed; returns are accepted within 30 days for exchange, refund, or credit.

TYPEX BUSINESS MACHINES, INC.

23 W. 23RD ST.
NEW YORK, NY 10010
800-221-9332
212/243-2500

Information: price quote with SASE
Save: up to 50%
Pay: check, MO, MC, V, Discover
Sells: typewriters, fax machines, copiers, etc.
Store: same address; Monday through Thursday 9:30–6, Friday 9:30–2

$$$ ✉ ☎

Typex, in business since 1979, offers the latest in office machines and supplies. Service and repairs are available in the store and to local customers. Specialty typewriters are featured, and savings average 30%. Call or write for prices on typewriters, calculators, answering machines, copiers, cash registers, fax machines, and supplies by and for Brother, Canon, IBM, Murata, Panasonic, Olympia, Ricoh, Royal, Sharp, and Silver Reed. Smith Corona typewriters and word processors are a house specialty, with savings that average 35% to 50%. Foreign language typewriters are also available.

Special Factors: Price quote by phone or letter with SASE; SASE is required with all correspondence if a reply is desired; minimum order is $50 with credit cards.

VALUE-TIQUE, INC.

**P.O. BOX 67, DEPT. WBM
LEONIA, NJ 07605
201/461-6500**

Catalog: $1 (see text)
Save: 20% plus
Pay: check, MO, MC, V, AE, DC, Discover, Optima
Sells: Sentry safes
Store: 117 Grand Ave., Palisades Park, NJ; Monday through Friday 9–5, Saturday 9–1

Value-tique has been selling home and office safes since 1968 and offers a range of well-known brands at discounts of 20% and more. Your savings are actually greater, because Value-tique also pays for shipping. And the $1 catalog fee buys a $5 credit certificate, good on any purchase.

Value-tique sells different Sentry Safe models—a fireproof model camouflaged as a cabinet, the Media-Safe for computer disk storage, a standard office safe, and different wall safes. Centurion, Elsafe, Fichet-Bauche, Gardall, and Star safes are available, as well as Pro-Steel gun safes. Models include wall and in-floor safes, cash-drop safes, and many others for home and business use. If you're not sure of the best type for your security purposes, call Value-tique to discuss your needs. And before you order, *measure* to be sure the safe will fit into its intended location.

Special Factors: Price quote by phone or letter with SASE; shipping is included.

VIKING OFFICE PRODUCTS

13809 SO. FIGUEROA ST.
LOS ANGELES, CA 90061
800-421-1222
FAX: 800-SNAPFAX

Catalog: free (see text)
Save: up to 67%
Pay: check, MO, MC, V
Sells: office supplies and furniture
Store: mail order only

$$ ✉ ☎

Viking Office Products began business in 1986 selling office supplies, furnishings, and computer products at discounts of up to 67%. The company publishes a general, 208-page discount catalog full of daily office needs, from pens and markers to ergonomic seating and filing cabinets. Specials on selected goods are offered in the monthly sale catalogs, and separate editions featuring office furniture and computer supplies are also available. Both name brands and Viking's own label are on hand, and the firm promises prompt delivery and free shipping on orders of $25 or more (in the continental U.S. only).

Special Factors: Satisfaction is guaranteed; price quote by phone or letter with SASE; shipping is included on orders over $25 (to the continental U.S. only).

VULCAN BINDER & COVER

BOX 29
VINCENT, AL 35178
800-633-4526
205/672-2241
FAX: 205/672-7159

Catalog: free
Save: up to 40%
Pay: check, MO, MC, V, AE
Sells: binders and supplies
Store: mail order only

$$$ ✉ ☎ 🍁

Three-ring binders can be quite pricey at stationery stores, which is why you should buy from the manufacturer. Vulcan can save you up to 40% on all of your binder needs, from light-duty binders with flexible covers to heavy-duty binders with 3″ D-rings. Vulcan's 48-page catalog also shows magazine files and binders, zippered binders, catalog binders, 19-ring binders, pocket sizes, tabbed inserts, notepad holders, report covers, page protectors, cassette cases, and even attaché cases and leather luggage. Custom imprinting is available on the binders and tabbed dividers.

Special Factors: Satisfaction is guaranteed; price quote by phone or letter with SASE; quantity discounts are available; returns are accepted within 15 days for exchange, refund, or credit; minimum order is $25.

WOLFF OFFICE EQUIPMENT CORP.

23 W. 18TH ST.
NEW YORK, NY 10011
212/633-2233

Information: price quote
Save: up to 40%
Pay: check, MO, MC, V
Sells: office machines, computers, and furnishings
Store: same address; Monday through Friday 8:30–5

Wolff has an extensive inventory of office machines and furniture, as well as a full range of computers and supplies. It's known to local businesses for its well-staffed service and repair department. Savings run up to 40%.

Wolff stocks typewriters, calculators, check writers, dictation machines, and phone machines by SCM, Olivetti, IBM, Sharp, Sanyo, Olympia, Kaypro, Hewlett Packard, Texas Instruments, Smith-Victor, and other well-known firms. Computers and peripherals, word processors, and software by a range of manufacturers, including IBM and Wang, are also featured.

Special Factors: Price quote by phone or letter with SASE; authorized returns are accepted (a 15% restocking fee is charged); minimum order is $100.

SEE ALSO

Ace Leather Products, Inc. ● attaché cases and briefcases ● *LEATHER*
The American Stationery Co., Inc. ● custom-printed stationery, notepads, and envelopes ● *BOOKS*
A to Z Luggage Co., Inc. ● attaché cases and briefcases ● *LEATHER*
Bennett Brothers, Inc. ● corporate gift program ● *GENERAL MERCHANDISE*
Bernie's Discount Center, Inc. ● name-brand phones and phone machines ● *APPLIANCES*

Blackwelder's Industries, Inc. • name-brand office furnishing • *HOME: FURNISHINGS*

Dick Blick Co. • flat files and display equipment • *ART MATERIALS*

Caviarteria Inc. • corporate gift program • *FOOD*

Cherry Hill Furniture, Carpet & Interiors • name-brand office furnishings • *HOME: FURNISHINGS*

Crutchfield Corporation • copiers, phone machines, fax machines, etc. • *APPLIANCES*

Walter Drake & Sons, Inc. • labels, notepads, stationery • *GENERAL MERCHANDISE*

Flax Artist's Materials • drafting furniture, supplies, and equipment • *ART MATERIALS*

Innovation Luggage • attaché cases and briefcases • *LEATHER*

Jerry's Artarama, Inc. • ergonomic chairs and flat files • *ART MATERIALS*

The Jompole Company, Inc. • name-brand pen and pencil sets, premiums, etc. • *HOME: TABLE SETTINGS*

Leather Unlimited Corp. • leather attaché cases, card cases, portfolios, etc. • *CRAFTS*

Loftin-Black Furniture Company • name-brand office furnishings • *HOME: FURNISHINGS*

The Luggage Center • attaché cases • *LEATHER*

LVT Price Quote Hotline, Inc. • calculators, typewriters, phones, fax machines, pens, etc. • *APPLIANCES*

New York Central Art Supply Co. • Alvin drafting furniture, taborets, stools and chairs, lighting, etc. • *ART MATERIALS*

Plastic BagMart • trash can liners • *HOME: MAINTENANCE*

Plexi-Craft Quality Products Corp. • acrylic racks, desk accessories, etc. • *HOME: FURNISHINGS*

Protecto-Pak • zip-top plastic bags • *HOME: MAINTENANCE*

James Roy Furniture Co., Inc. • name-brand office furnishings • *HOME: FURNISHINGS*

S & S Sound City • phones and phone machines • *APPLIANCES*

Turner Tolson, Inc. • name-brand office furnishings • *HOME: FURNISHINGS*

Turnkey Material Handling, Inc. • parts bins, office and institutional furnishings, and fixtures • *TOOLS*

University Products, Inc. • archival-quality storage supplies for microfiche and microfilm; library supplies and equipment • *GENERAL MERCHANDISE*

U.S. Box Corp. • product packaging for resale • *GENERAL MERCHANDISE*

Wholesale Tape and Supply Company • labels, shipping envelopes • *APPLIANCES*

COMPUTING

Computers, peripherals, software, supplies, furniture, and accessories

If you're a first-time buyer or want to upgrade your current system, learn as much as you can from as many sources as possible. Attend demonstrations of new products, watch colleagues at work with different systems and programs, and ask questions. Don't assume that any software will perform as promised, no matter who's vouching for it. (Beware especially of enthusiastic friends, whose needs may differ radically from yours.) Check for software support—price (if any) for access to a tech, hours, and ease in getting through. Evaluate your current and anticipated requirements as carefully as possible, since buying the right equipment the first time is the best money spent. Do you *need* 100 megabytes, a laser printer, or EGA monitor? What will you do with the computer? How much RAM will your software require? Is portability sufficiently important to make a laptop a good buy? Consult the repair shop of a large computer outlet to get an idea of how much repairs run on different types of equipment. Can you get by with a good 9-pin NLQ printer, and buy an ink-jet or 24-pin when the prices come down?

The absolute neophyte can consult the Peter A. McWilliams books, which many find helpful in demystifying the entire subject. More experienced users, and those looking for sources, should consult the quarterly *Whole Earth Software Review,* as well as *How to Buy Software: The Master Guide to Picking the Right Program,* by Alfred Glossbrenner (St. Martin's Press, 1984). The quarterly costs $18 per year (four issues) from Whole Earth Software Review, P.O. Box 27956, San Diego, CA 92128. We've cited these texts because they're accessible and their authors are honest. Furthermore, their reviews of products we've used coincided with our own evaluations. There are hundreds of publications on the market to guide you through the purchase of hardware and software and the use of specific systems, and many of them merit your attention. (There are many that *don't,* though, like the $30 rehashes of the enigmatic DOS manual that defies translation. Do not surrender to their glossy covers in confidence: Pick a thorny problem you solved yourself, and see whether the book covers it. This may entail thumbing through dozens of volumes at the local computer store or bookseller, but it's worth the time.) In addition to books, there are hundreds of magazines and newsletters covering every niche in computing and, perhaps most valuable, user networks or groups (modem-accessed). Once you're beyond the rank beginner stage of computer literacy, you may find some of these helpful in getting the most from your system. The books previously mentioned include reviews of a number of prominent and obscure periodicals and can serve as a guide to what you may find worthwhile.

In previous editions we listed computer software and programs in the "Books" chapter, because they're publications. But books can be stacked on the floor if they don't fit the shelves, and putting a telephone directory next to *War and Peace* shouldn't cause problems to either. The world of software is not that simple, and we find that programs behave less like publications than carnival sideshows: thrills, chills, and two-headed calves. In addition, software has to "fit" the hardware (the amount of RAM, the presence of color monitors, modems, graphics cards, etc.), or it may not run or perform properly. To make more sense of the choices you face when you're buying both, we've consolidated the software sellers with the computer suppliers in this section.

There are tens of thousands of programs now in the public domain, which means they can be copied without infringement of copyright (hence the term "free programs"). They're sold at very low prices — often $10 and under — and can be as valuable as protected programs that cost $300 to $900 each. The definitive reference to locating sources and evaluating what's available is Alfred Glossbrenner's *How to Get Free Software,* which may be found in bookstores and libraries nationwide. One word of caution, however: Viruses, which can damage your data, do crop up in the world of "shareware." If you want to protect yourself completely, don't use shareware or download programs from bulletin boards. And do remember to use a surge suppressor, and back up your disks!

BUY DIRECT

216 W. 18TH ST.
NEW YORK, NY 10011
800-742-6377
IN NY 212/255-4424

Catalog: $2, refundable
Save: up to 40%
Pay: check, MO, certified check
Sells: computer supplies and office
   machines
Store: mail order only

$$$ ✉

Buy Direct, once known for its great deals on stationery, typewriter ribbons, and other materials for the world of "paper," has developed a complete computer supplies department. You'll save up to 40% on purchases from this firm, which was established in 1954.

Buy Direct has a comprehensive selection of products for computers, word processors, copiers, microfiche systems, and other office machines, including disks, ribbons, daisy wheels, typing elements, correction film, disk storage units, copier supplies, cleaning kits, labels, envelopes, forms, and many other goods. The brands include Burroughs, Camwil, Diablo, GP Technologies, IBM, Maxell, Nashua, NEC, Qume, 3M, Verbatim, and Wilson Jones. Office furniture, including computer stands and ergonomic seating, is offered as well, in addition to name-brand office machines of all types. Buy Direct also carries the complete line of Bush stands for TVs and stereos.

Special Factors: Price quote by phone or letter with SASE; authorized returns are accepted (a restocking fee may be charged); minimum order is $25.

COMPUTER MAIL ORDER

101 REIGHARD AVE.
WILLIAMSPORT, PA 17701
800-233-8950
717/327-9575
FAX: 717/327-1217

Information: price quote
Save: up to 40%
Pay: check, MO, certified check, MC, V
Sells: computer peripherals
Store: same address

$ ✉ ☎

Computer Mail Order sells computer systems, disk drives, boards, monitors, printers, modems, software, and accessories by a number of firms, at savings of up to 40%. CMO also sells its own computers (XT, 286, and 386 models) under the "Access" label. Save on goods by Amdek, AST, Bernoulli, C. Itoh, CMS, Curtis, Epson, Hewlett Packard, IBM, Juki, Kensington, Leading Edge, Lotus, Magnavox, NEC, Okidata, Panasonic, Seagate, Star Micronics, Xerox, and Zenith. You can check CMO's ad in *PC Magazine* for current specials.

Special Factors: Price quote by phone or letter with SASE; authorized returns are accepted (a restocking fee may be charged).

DAYTON COMPUTER SUPPLY

**1220 WAYNE AVE.
DAYTON, OH 45410
800-331-6841
IN OH 513/252-1247**

Price List: free
Save: up to 60%
Pay: check, MO, MC, V, Discover
Sells: computer printer ribbons
Store: mail order only

$$

Dayton Computer publishes a six-page brochure listing over 300 types of printer ribbons (proprietary and branded), diskettes, tape, and paper for fax machines and printers. We found Dayton's prices on diskettes and tapes by 3M and Verbatim competitive, and the firm offers a good selection of continuous paper and labels. If you're buying your ribbons from your local stationer, or even a discounter, you're in for a shock. We compared prices and found that Dayton was charging up to 60% less than the going rate for unbranded ribbons for printers by Apple, Brother, Commodore, Diablo, Epson, Hewlett Packard, IBM, Mannesman Tally, NEC, Okidata, Panasonic, Qume, Star Micronics, and other prominent manufacturers. (A small selection of "genuine" ribbons is offered, at prices higher than the generic ribbons but discounted from list.) You can write for the brochure, or call with the model number of your printer for current prices.

Special Factors: Satisfaction is guaranteed; price quote by phone; quantity discounts are available; minimum order is 6 ribbons; C.O.D. orders are accepted.

DISK WORLD, INC.

2200 W. GREENLEAF ST.,
#WBMI
EVANSTON, IL 60202
800-255-5874
FAX: 708/492-5067

Catalog: free
Save: up to 50%
Pay: check, MO, MC, V, Discover
Sells: disks, cartridge tapes, storage
   equipment, etc.
Store: mail order only

Getting caught short of disks and having to buy from a computer boutique at near-list price is an entirely preventable travesty, if you buy in bulk from Disk World. This firm, in business since 1983, sells disks, data cartridges (tape), storage units, printer ribbon, fax paper, and computer paper.

Disk World stocks 3-1/2″, 5-1/4″, and 8″ disks (as available) from Athana, BASF, Dysan, Fuji, Maxell, Nashua, and Verbatim, data cartridges from BASF and Nashua, and 5-1/4″ and 8″ Iomega Bernoulli cartridges (at savings of up to 38% off list). Prices average 45% to 55% off list, and Disk World's selection is excellent. In addition to name brands, the firm offers Super Star disks, which are made to its specifications and sold in standard tens, and at a lower price in bulk. Scores of unbranded printer ribbons are available, at prices among the lowest we could find *anywhere*. Disk sleeves, labels, and mailers are also available, as well as cleaning kits for laser printers, fax machines, dot-matrix printers, disk drives, surge suppressors, cables, an inexpensive monitor stand, keyboard templates, a mini-vacuum cleaner, and a good selection of disk storage units. There are great buys on fax paper, green bar, plain white computer paper, and laser printer supplies. Warranty terms and return policies are stated clearly in the catalog.

Disk World is offering readers of WBMC a 4% discount on *first orders only*, so remember to mention this book when you place your first order. This WBMC reader discount expires February 1, 1992.

Special Factors: Satisfaction is guaranteed; price quote by phone or letter; returns are accepted within 30 days for exchange, refund, or credit; minimum order is $25; orders are shipped worldwide.

EASTCOAST SOFTWARE

48 DERRYTOWN MALL
HERSHEY, PA 17033
800-877-1327

Catalog: free
Save: up to 35%
Pay: check, MO, MC, V
Sells: computer systems, software, disks, and peripherals
Store: same address; Monday through Friday 10–8, Saturday 10–4

$$

Eastcoast's 24-page tabloid catalog lists thousands of educational, business, and recreational programs for Apple, Macintosh, Commodore 64, Amiga, and IBM-compatible computers. Blank disks, paper, peripheral covers, cables, printer stands, and some peripherals are also cataloged, at savings of up to 35%. Both list and discount prices are given, and the terms of Eastcoast's "30-day replacement policy" are stated in the catalog.

Special Factors: Institutional accounts are available; returns are accepted within 30 days for exchange, refund, or credit.

EDUCALC CORPORATION

27953 CABOT RD.
LAGUNA NIGUEL, CA
92677
714/582-2637
FAX: 714/582-1445

Catalog: free
Save: up to 40%
Pay: check, MO, MC, V, AE, Discover, Optima
Sells: calculators, computer peripherals, and software
Store: same address; Monday through Friday 8–5

$$$

EduCALC specializes in portable computation, specifically peripherals that maximize the functions of the Hewlett Packard IL, 28S, 41, and 48SX series of hand-held computer/calculators. Canon, Casio, Franklin, Sharp, and Texas Instruments calculators are also carried, and used calculators are available. The savings average 25%, but some items are discounted up to 40%.

The HP calculators, when linked with available peripherals, can be linked to PCs, edit programs, save data on mag cards, develop programs, and analyze mathematical, scientific, engineering, and business data with the aid of HP modules. The equipment currently available includes printer/plotters, optical wands, modules, interface units, cassette drives, couplers, disk drives, video monitors, and adapters. EduCALC also sells personal (portable) dialers and diaries. Stands, covers, keyboard overlay systems, ribbons, printing paper, disks, plotter pens, and other supplies are offered as well. The 68-page catalog should be noted for its comprehensive bookshelf—both general and calculator-related reference texts on astronomy, navigation, engineering, higher mathematics and statistics, programming, and computer systems and languages are listed. The catalog descriptions are comprehensive, easy to understand, and include product specifications.

Canadian readers, please note: A $10 *per-item surcharge* is levied on orders shipped to Canada.

Special Factors: Satisfaction is guaranteed; price quote by phone or letter with SASE; returns are accepted within 15 days; orders are shipped worldwide.

800-SOFTWARE, INC.

918 PARKER ST.
BERKELEY, CA 94710
800-888-4880
FAX: 415/644-8226

Catalog: free
Save: up to 50%
Pay: check, MO, MC, V, AE
Sells: computer software
Store: same address; Monday through Friday 9–5, Saturday 10–2

800-Software has won recommendations from computer users who have access to discount sources in New York City but prefer 800's prices, selection, and technical support.

The well-designed, 72-page catalog lists programs for PCs, Macintosh computers, and some UNIX products, including databases, graphics, utilities, operating systems, personal finance programs, spreadsheets, desktop publishing programs, and word processing software. There are lines and products by Alpha, Amdek, Apple, Ashton-Tate, AST Research, Central Point Software, Computer Associates, Digital Research, Fox & Geller, Funk Software, Hayes, IMSI, Intel, Lotus, Micropro, Microsoft, Oasis Systems, Paperback Software, Quadram, Revelation Technology, Software Solutions, Toshiba, Word Perfect, XyQuest, and many others. You'll also find boards, buffers, graphics cards, keyboards, mice, monitors, printers, surge suppressors, and other peripherals and accessories for PCs. Specials are run on a frequent basis, and the catalog is a great source for information on what's new in word processing, spreadsheet, data management, educational, and other types of programs.

Special Factors: Products are guaranteed against manufacturing defects; price quote by phone or letter with SASE on items not listed in the catalog; institutional accounts are available; quantity discounts are available.

LYBEN COMPUTER SYSTEMS

1050 EAST MAPLE RD.
TROY, MI 48083
313/589-3440

Catalog: free
Save: up to 50%
Pay: check, MO, MC, V
Sells: computer supplies
Store: same address; Monday through
 Thursday 8:30–6, Friday 8:30–5,
 Saturday 9:30–2:30

Lyben offers a full range of computer supplies, but has especially good prices on software and diskettes—up to 50% off suggested list. The best prices here are on software, disks, ribbons, printer paper, and other computer supplies by BASF, Dysan, Maxell, Memorex, Sony, 3M, Verbatim, and other top manufacturers. All of the goods are sold by the box or carton. The 148-page catalog also shows daisy wheels, dust covers for peripherals, data storage units, maintenance products, strip outlets, surge suppressors, cables, data switches, buffers, modems, joysticks, ergonomic seating, power backup units, mice, forms feeders, fax paper, copier cartridges, mini-vacuum cleaners, and hundreds of other items.

Special Factors: Price quote by phone or letter with SASE; minimum order is $15; C.O.D. orders are accepted.

MACCONNECTION

14 MILL ST.
MARLOW, NH 03456
800-622-5472
FAX: 603/446-7791

Price List: free
Save: 25% to 40% average
Pay: check, MO, MC, V
Sells: Macintosh computer hardware,
  software, and accessories
Store: same address (pickup center for
  orders)

$$$$ ✉ ☎ 🍁 ▀

This source has received resounding praise from readers and friends, whose comments include "There is no better source than MacConnection," and "price, service, stock, courtesy—unparalleled!" (These are taken verbatim from our reader mail.) MacConnection was founded in 1984 by the same people who established PC Connection two years earlier. (See that firm's listing in this section for IBM-compatible products.)

MacConnection stocks the latest program versions of business and entertainment software by scores of publishers, from Aatrix Software to Zedcor. Most of the listings indicate whether the software is copy-protected or not. MacConnection also sells modems, mice, keyboards, work stations, printers, monitors, maintenance and cleaning products, disks by Fuji, Maxell, Sony, and Verbatim, and subscription kits to on-line services from CompuServe and Dow Jones. Savings average 25% to 40%, and MacConnection is praised for its commitment to service—it provides warranty backup and support for all the products it sells.

Special Factors: Price quote by letter; minimum order is $250 on "international" orders; orders are shipped worldwide.

NEBS, INC.

500 MAIN ST.
GROTON, MA 01470
508/448-6111

Catalog: free (see text)
Save: up to 35%
Pay: check or MO
Sells: forms and supplies
Store: mail order only

$$ ✉ ☎

NEBS, or New England Business Service, publishes two catalogs: "Business Forms and Supplies" and "Computer Forms." Prices at NEBS are often up to

35% less than those charged by other office supply firms for the same or comparable items.

The general business forms catalog has 88 pages of invoices, receipts, purchase orders, bookkeeping forms, and scores of other forms for small businesses. Labels, rubber stamps, shipping supplies, shopping bags, memos, business cards, stationery, and other office and business necessities are available.

The 54-page "Computer Forms" catalog offers continuous-form stationery in several paper types, with raised or flat printing, and coordinating envelopes. Postcards, dozens of types of mailing labels, and all kinds of printout paper are stocked. NEBS has designed forms to work with business software from Radio Shack, CYMA, Great Plains, BPI Systems, DAC Software, Star Software, and many other publishers. These products, including invoices, statements, payroll checks, job proposals, and like forms, are offered in multipart designs, some with coordinating envelopes.

Although business applications are this firm's specialty, even computer-based poets should appreciate NEBS for its good prices on ribbons and disks (in proprietary and name brands), disk storage units, and computer maintenance tools and dust covers. We found one item here that's helpful to anyone trying to use up old stocks of cut-sheet stationery—a "print pouch" that loops through your printer so that you can set it on the continuous print mode. Prices are competitive, and most of the stock is available in small lots, as well as larger amounts at quantity discounts.

Special Factors: Satisfaction is guaranteed; specify "Business Forms" or "Computer Forms" catalog.

PC CONNECTION

6 MILL ST.
MARLOW, NH 03456
800-243-8088
FAX: 603/446-7791

Price List: free
Save: 25% to 40% average
Pay: check, MO, MC, V
Sells: IBM-compatible hardware, software, and supplies
Store: same address (pickup center for orders)

Several of our friends who use Macintosh computers, as well as readers of this book, have commended MacConnection (listed earlier in this section)

for superior pricing, stock, and service. The same people who operate MacConnection actually began with IBM-compatible systems in 1982 when they founded PC Connection—which they run with the same commitment to selection and service.

You can write to the firm for its current price list, see the ad in the current issue of *PC World,* or send for a price quote. The latest versions of software are carried by publishers that include Aldus, Ashton-Tate, Borland International, Broderbund, Electronic Arts, 5th Generation, Fox Software, Funk Software, Lotus, Microlytics, MicroPro, Microrim, Microsoft, Peter Norton, Sierra On-Line, Softlogic Solutions, Spinnaker, Springboard, Sublogic, Symantec, Word Perfect, Xerox, and XyQuest, among others. Most of the listings indicate whether the software is copy-protected or not. Hardware and accessories—computers, disk drives, emulation boards, printers, modems, monitors, joysticks, etc.—are also available; the brands represented at this writing include AST Research, Amdek, Curtis, DCA, Epson, Everex, Hayes, Intel, IOMEGA, Logitech, Magnavox, Mountain Computer, Practical Peripherals, Princeton Graphics, Seagate, Teac, Toshiba, and others. Disks by Fuji, Maxell, Sony, and Verbatim are offered, and you can also save on the CompuServe Subscription Kit and Grollier's OnLine Encyclopedia.

PC Connection provides warranty backup and support for all the products it sells, and is a factory-authorized repair center for Epson and Iomega products.

Special Factors: Price quote by letter with SASE; minimum order is $250 on "international" orders; orders are shipped worldwide.

VISIBLE COMPUTER SUPPLY CORP.

3626 STERN AVE.
ST. CHARLES, IL
60174-9987
800-323-0628

Catalog: free
Save: up to 60%
Pay: check, MO, MC, V, AE, CB, DC
Sells: office and computer supplies
Store: mail order only

$$$ ✉ ☎

The 270-page color catalog from this firm is packed with great buys on office essentials. A monthly, 32-page catalog features special promotions and sale items. Visible Computer, a subsidiary of Wallace Computer Services, has been doing business since 1942.

The focus here is on computer support products, but there are scores of general office items shown in the catalog. You'll want to see the latest issue if you're shopping for phone message books, binding supplies, loose-leaf notebooks, pens and highlighters, labels, tape, Post-It notes, wastebaskets, files, records storage, telephones, phone machines, and shredders. The computer department stocks forms bursters, computer work stations, printer stands, continuous form paper, disks and disk storage, monitor screen filters, cables, outlet strips, and maintenance supplies and equipment. There are bonuses with minimum orders, and quantity discounts are available as well.

Special Factors: Satisfaction is guaranteed; returns are accepted within 30 days for exchange, refund, or credit; quantity discounts are available.

WESTERN S & G

P.O. BOX 12345
SAN LUIS OBISPO, CA
    93406-2345
800-233-9750
IN CA 800-843-8181

Price List: free
Save: up to 45%
Pay: check, MO, MC, V
Sells: computer software and disks
Store: mail order only

Western S & G offers great buys on IBM computer software, disks, and storage units. Specials are run on a regular basis.

See the price list or call for the latest rates on disks and diskettes by Dysan, Fuji, Maxell, Memorex, 3M, and Verbatim. Western S & G also carries floppy-disk storage units, disk-saver kits, and head-cleaning diskette kits. The software packages—business, entertainment, and word-processing programs—are listed in the catalog.

Special Factors: Price quote by phone; shipping is included; minimum order is 10 disks.

SEE ALSO

Astronomical Society of the Pacific • astronomy-related computer programs • *BOOKS*

Dick Blick Co. • computer work stations • *ART MATERIALS*

Business & Institutional Furniture Company • computer work stations • *OFFICE*

Crutchfield Corporation • PCs, word processors, software, and supplies • *APPLIANCES*

Frank Eastern Co. • computer work stations • *OFFICE*

Marv Golden Discount Sales, Inc. • aviation computers • *AUTO*

Grayarc • computer forms and paper goods • *OFFICE*

Robert James Co., Inc. • computer work stations • *OFFICE*

Jerry's Artarama, Inc. • computer work stations • *ART MATERIALS*

Lincoln Typewriters and Micro Machines • computer peripherals • *OFFICE*

Mail Center USA • name-brand computer peripherals, disks, and accessories • *OFFICE*

National Business Furniture, Inc. • computer work stations • *OFFICE*

Plexi-Craft Quality Products Corp. • acrylic computer stands • *HOME: FURNISHINGS*

Quill Corporation • computers, word processors, programs, work stations, paper products, disks, etc. • *OFFICE*

Rapidforms, Inc. • continuous forms • *OFFICE*

The Reliable Corporation • computer accessories, work stations, etc. • *OFFICE*

Staples, Inc. • computer disks, data binders, work stations, programs, etc. • *OFFICE*

20th Century Plastics, Inc. • static-proof disk storage • *OFFICE*

Viking Office Products • computer supplies, peripherals, and furniture • *OFFICE*

Wolff Office Equipment Corp. • computers and peripherals • *OFFICE*

SPORTS AND RECREATION

Equipment, clothing, supplies,
and services for all kinds of sports
and recreational activities

If the high price of recreation equipment seems unsporting to you, you've turned to the right place. Discounts of 30% are standard among many of the suppliers listed here, who sell clothing and equipment for cycling, running, golfing, skiing, aerobics, tennis and other racquet sports, skin and scuba diving, camping, hunting, hiking, basketball, triathloning, soccer, and other pleasures. Racquet stringing, club repairs, and other services are usually priced competitively as well. Buying your gear by mail may be the only sport that repays a nominal expenditure of energy with such an enhanced sense of well-being.

Before investing in a new athletic pursuit, be sure it's right for you. Joining a local team or group gives you a taste of the sport at minimal expense. If you've been sedentary for some time, you should have a complete physical before beginning any workout program or sport. Stop and cool down if you're in pain, but don't give up. You can make running, aerobics, and racquet sports easier on your joints by wearing properly fitted shoes, learning correct foot placement, and working out on a resilient surface. Low-impact aerobics, fast-paced walking, and swimming are usually less stressful than running, calisthenics, and traditional sports. Getting fit should be a pleasure, and if you take the time to find an enjoyable, challenging sport or workout routine, cardiovascular health and vigor will be more easily won.

ALLYN AIR SEAT CO.

18 MILLSTREAM RD.,
  DEPT. WBMC
WOODSTOCK, NY 12498
914/679-2051

Flyer: free with SASE
Save: up to 50%
Pay: check or MO
Sells: air-filled vehicle seat cushions
Store: mail order only

$$$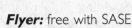

Allyn Air Seat sells air-filled cushions that should help you go the distance, whether you're traveling by bike, car, plane, truck, or wheelchair. Allyn Air, which was established in 1979, keeps its prices a good 30% below its competitors.

The stock includes heavy-duty, air-filled seats for bicycles ($13), motorcycles ($35), standard and bucket auto seats, aircraft seats, wheelchairs, and trucks ($35). The cushions help absorb road vibration and bumps, making travel easier and less wearying. Allyn Air Seat also sells covers for lawn and garden tractors, ATVs, snowmobiles, and motorcycles. The firm's newest offering for cars and motorcycles is vinyl "pockettes," which hold maps and other items.

Allyn is giving readers of this book special 10% to 60% discounts, depending on the quantity of goods ordered. Identify yourself as a reader when you order to qualify. This WBMC reader discount expires February 1, 1992.

Special Factors: Price quote by phone or letter with SASE; C.O.D. orders are accepted; orders are shipped worldwide.

AUSTAD'S

DEPT. 00102
P.O. BOX 1428
SIOUX FALLS, SD
  57196-1428
800-759-4653 EXT. 00102

Catalog: free
Save: up to 40%
Pay: check, MO, MC, V, AE, CB, DC
Sells: golf equipment and apparel
Store: Tenth and Cleveland, Sioux Falls, SD; Monday through Friday 9–8, Saturday 9–5, Sunday 12–5

$$

Austad's, established in 1963, devotes all 48 pages of its color catalog to the needs of the golfer. You can choose from clubs for men, women, and junior players by Dunlop, Spalding, Wilson, and Yamaha, as well as the firm's private-label clubs. The catalog also shows bags, carts, footwear, accessories, practice equipment, golfing videotapes, and gifts for golfers. Audstad's features its own line of clothing, "designed for golfers, by golfers."

Special Factors: All goods are unconditionally guaranteed against defects for 1 year; returns are accepted within 30 days for exchange, refund, or credit; orders are shipped worldwide.

BART'S WATER SKI CENTER, INC.

P.O. BOX 294-WBM
NORTH WEBSTER, IN
   46555
800-348-5016
IN IN 800-552-2336
FAX: 219/834-4246

Catalog: free
Save: up to 40%
Pay: check, MO, MC, V, AE, Discover, Optima
Sells: water-skiing gear and equipment
Store: same address; Monday through Saturday 9–6

$$$ ✉   ☎   🍁   🇺🇸

The thrills of water skiing are cheaper at Bart's, where wet suits and skis cost up to 40% below list, and clearance items are offered at even greater savings. Bart's has been in business since 1971, and it backs every sale with a guarantee of satisfaction.

The 48-page color catalog features water skis that range from beginners' to tournament models by Connelly, EP Skis, Jobe, Kidder, and O'Brien. Kneeboarders can choose from two pages of boards and accessories, and there is a large selection of floats, tubes, and other inflatables (called "toys" in the catalog). Ski vests and wet suits for men, women, and children are offered, in addition to wet suit accessories, swim trunks, T-shirts, and sunglasses. Gloves, slalom (tow) lines, boat hardware, and manuals and videotapes on water skiing are shown in the catalog.

Special Factors: Satisfaction is guaranteed; price quote by phone or letter; quantity discounts are available; returns are accepted within 60 days.

BASS PRO SHOPS

**1935 S. CAMPBELL
SPRINGFIELD, MO 65898
800-227-7776
FAX: 417/887-2531**

Catalog: $2, refundable (see text)
Save: up to 40%
Pay: check, MO, MC, V, AE
Sells: fishing tackle and boating equipment
Store: same address; Monday through
  Saturday 7A.M.–10P.M., Sunday 9–6

The Bass Pro Shops catalog is something of an epic: On page one is a photo of President Bush with the company's founder. A sweepstakes offer follows, then dozens of boats, and on page 43, an application for a Bass Pro Shops VISA card. Following that are over 400 full-color pages of rods, reels, lures, bait, hooks, books and videotapes, camping gear, clothing, boating equipment and electronics, and much more—all at discounts of up to 40%. Bass Pro Shops, which has been doing business since 1971, stocks the most popular brands and models. The big catalog costs $2, but comes with a $3 merchandise certificate. The 195-page sale catalogs are free, and focus on fishing goods. If your interests include a range of water sports, the $2 you spend for the big catalog is a worthwhile investment.

Please note: Orders must be paid in U.S. funds.

Special Factors: Satisfaction is guaranteed; price quote by phone or letter with SASE; returns are accepted; orders are shipped worldwide.

BERRY SCUBA CO.

**DEPT. WBMC
6674 N. NORTHWEST
  HWY.
CHICAGO, IL 60631
800-621-6019
IN IL 312/763-1626
FAX: 312/775-1815**

Catalog: free
Save: up to 40%
Pay: check, MO, MC, V, AE, Discover,
  Optima
Sells: scuba-diving gear
Store: same address; Monday, Thursday,
  Friday 10–9, Tuesday and Saturday
  10–5; also Lombard and Palatine, IL, and
  Atlanta, GA

Berry, "the oldest, largest, and best-known direct-mail scuba firm in the country," carries a wide range of equipment and accessories for diving and related activities. The brands list is enormous, and specials are run frequently.

Shop here for regulators, masks, wet suits, fins, tanks, diving lights, strobes, underwater cameras and housing, Seiko diving watches, pole spears, and other gear and accessories for underwater use. The brands include Arena, Aquacraft, Chronosport, Cyalume, Dacor, Deep Sea, Desco, E.B.S., Eska, Fuji, Gerber, Global, Henderson, Heuer, I.D.I., Ikelite, Mako, Metzeler, Nikon, Ocean Apparel, Parkway, Pennform, Scuba Sextant, Scuba Systems, Sea Suits, Seatec, Sherwood, Tabata, Undersea Guns, Underwater Kinetics, U.S. Divers, U.S. Tech, Viking, Voit, Waterlung, and Wenoka. Metzeler inflatable boats are also stocked. Berry does business on a price-quote basis, but also offers a complete 64-page catalog, free of charge.

Special Factors: Price quote by phone or letter with SASE; minimum order is $25 with credit cards.

BETTER HEALTH FITNESS

5201 NEW UTRECHT AVE.
BROOKLYN, NY 11219
718/436-4693
FAX: 718/854-3381

Catalog: free
Save: up to 50%
Pay: check, MO, MC, V, AE, Optima
Sells: exercise equipment
Store: same address; Monday through Wednesday 10–6, Thursday 10–8, Sunday 12–5 (closed Friday and Saturday)

Whether you're buying a stationary bicycle for rainy-day workouts or outfitting an entire gym, you can get equipment for less at Better Health. The firm has been selling top-of-the-line models since 1978, and can provide design and layout services to local customers.

We were sent a lengthy list of *some* of the manufacturers Better Health represents, which include Altero Technologies, Alva (barres), Avita, Barracuda, Bodyguard by Oegland, Cal-Gym, Cat-Eye, Coffey, Everlast, Exercycle, Fitness Master, Healthometer, H.W.E. Massage, Life Fitness, Marcy Fitness, Monark (cycles), Pacemaster (treadmills), Penco (lockers), Precor, Pro-Tec, Titan, Trotter (treadmills), Tunturi, and Vectra. You can save up to 40% on the regular prices of equipment by these and other manufacturers. Call or write for quotes on multi-station units, free-weight benches, mats, dance studio equipment, hot tubs, locker room equipment, and related goods, or see the catalog for a partial listing. Better Health also carries Danskin and Everlast sportswear.

Better Health is offering readers of this book a discount of 5% on all orders. Identify yourself as a reader when you order. This WBMC reader discount expires February 1, 1992.

Special Factors: Satisfaction is guaranteed; price quote by phone or letter with SASE; authorized returns are accepted within 15 days for exchange, refund, or credit.

BIKE NASHBAR

P.O. BOX 3449, DEPT. WBM9
YOUNGSTON, OH
44513-3449
800-NASHBAR

Catalog: free
Save: up to 40%
Pay: check, MO, MC, V, Discover
Sells: bicycles, accessories, apparel, and equipment
Store: 4111 Simon Rd., Youngston, OH; also 4 other locations (listed in the catalog)

Bike Nashbar, one of the country's top sources for the serious cyclist, publishes a 64-page catalog of everything from water bottles to top-of-the-line frames, sold at "guaranteed lowest prices."

Bike Nashbar sells its own line of road, touring, dirt, and racing bikes, which have features usually found on more expensive models. There are full lines of parts and accessories, including frames by Gios and Vitus; saddles from Avocet, Brooks, Sella Italia, and Vetta; gears, brakes, chain wheels, hubs, pedals, derailleurs, handlebars, and other parts by Biopace, Campagnolo, Dia-Compe, Dura-Ace, Shimano, SR, Suntour, and other firms. Top-quality panniers and bags, racks, helmets, protective eyewear, gloves, tires and tubes, wheels, toe clips, locks (Citadel and Kryptonite), handlebar tape, grips, tire pumps, lights, and other accessories are offered. Bikers' skin shorts and jerseys, which have enjoyed a vogue among non-cyclists, are available here in a wide range of vivid colors and designs. Shoes by Duegi, Look, and Sidi are carried as well. The catalog includes helpful information on the different bike models available, and a listing of "qualified installers" across the country who can help you to assemble and maintain your bike is available upon request.

Special Factors: Satisfaction is guaranteed; returns (except used items, specials, and closeouts) are accepted within 10 days for refund or credit.

BOWHUNTERS WAREHOUSE, INC.

1045 ZIEGLER RD., BOX 158
WELLSVILLE, PA 17365
717/432-8611

Catalog: free
Save: up to 40%
Pay: check, MO, MC, V
Sells: equipment for bow hunting, hunting, and archery
Store: same address; Monday to Friday 9–5, Wednesday 9–9, Saturday 9–1

Save up to 40% on a complete range of supplies for bow hunting, bow fishing, archery, and hunting through the 100-page catalog from this firm. Bowhunters Warehouse was established in 1978.

Bowhunters Warehouse features a large selection of bows and arrows, and also carries points, feathers, bow sights, rests, quivers, targets, bowhunting books and videotapes, optics, game calls, camouflage clothing and supplies, shooting equipment, and other gear for outdoor sports. Bear, Browning, Bushnell, Darton, Easton, Golden Eagle, Indian, Jennings, Martin, Quillian, PSE, and other manufacturers are represented. Specifications are included with the information on the hunting equipment, making this a good reference catalog as well as a source for real savings.

Special Factors: Authorized returns are accepted (a restocking fee may be charged); minimum order is $10.

CABELA'S INC.

812 13TH AVE.
SIDNEY, NE 69160
308/254-5505

Catalog: free
Save: up to 40%
Pay: check, MO, MC, V, AE, Discover
Sells: hunting, fishing, and camping gear
Store: same address; Monday through Saturday 8–5:30

Cabela's, the "world's foremost outfitter" of fishing, hunting, and outdoor enthusiasts, has been praised by several readers who are involved in outdoor sports. Savings run up to 40% on some goods, and the firm is committed to its customers' satisfaction.

Cabela's sells rods, reels, and tackle from well-known manufacturers, including Berkley, Daiwa, Fenwick, Garcia, Mitchell, Shakespeare, and Shimano. Lures, line, tackle boxes, hooks, nets, and other fishing gear are stocked. The catalog shows pages of Minn Kota electric boat motors, boat covers, boat seats, dinghies, downriggers, winches, batteries, and trailer parts. Fishing is the strong suit in the spring and summer catalogs, but a comparable range of hunting equipment is offered in other issues.

General outdoor needs are served by the camping department: tents, sleeping bags and mats, gear bags, backpacks, cookware and kitchen equipment, heavy-duty flashlights, binoculars, sunglasses, knives, and related products are offered. And a good selection of outdoor clothing is sold, including waders, camouflage wear, fishing vests and hunting jackets, snakeproof boots, moccasins, bush jackets, parkas, jeans, and even stylish weekend wear for men and women.

Special Factors: Satisfaction is guaranteed; returns are accepted for exchange, refund, or credit.

CAMPMOR

P.O. BOX 997
PARAMUS, NJ 07653-0997
201/445-5000

Catalog: free
Save: up to 50%
Pay: check, MO, MC, V, AE, Discover
Sells: camping gear and supplies
Store: Rte. 17 N., Paramus, NJ; Monday, Wednesday, Saturday 9:30–6; Tuesday, Thursday, Friday 9:30–9

Campmor's 120-page catalog is full of great buys on all sorts of name-brand camping goods, bike touring accessories, and clothing. Campmor, established in 1946, offers savings of up to 50% on list prices.

Campmor's catalog features clothing by Borglite Pile, Columbia Interchange System, Sierra Designs, Thinsulate, and Woolrich, and as well as duofold and Polypro underwear, Sorel and Timberland boots, and other outerwear. Swiss Victorinox knives are sold here at 30% off list, and there are Buck knives, Coleman cooking equipment, Sherpa snowshoes, Silva compasses, Edelrid climbing ropes, Eureka tents, and books and manuals on camping and survival. You'll also find sleeping bags by Coleman, The North Face, Slumberjack, and Wenzel, and backpacks by JanSport, Kelly Camp Trails, and Peak.

Special Factors: Returns are accepted for exchange, refund, or credit; minimum order is $20 on phone orders.

CENTRAL SKINDIVERS

160-09 JAMAICA AVE.
JAMAICA, NY 11432-6111
718/739-5772

Information: price quote
Save: up to 40%
Pay: check, MO, MC, V, AE, Discover
Sells: scuba-diving gear
Store: same address; Monday through Saturday 10–6:30

$

Central Skindivers, in business since 1952, sells name-brand diving gear at savings of up to 40%. The firm no longer publishes a catalog, so call for a price quote.

The extensive inventory includes tanks from Dacor, Sherwood, and U.S. Divers, and a full range of regulators, masks, fins, gauges, computers, suits, and other gear. There are bouyancy jackets from Beuchat, Dacor, Seaquest, Seatec, Sherwood, Tabata, and U.S. Divers, and watches and timers from Chronosport, Citizen, Heuer, and Tekna.

Special Factors: Price quote by phone; shipping is included; minimum order is $50, $75 with credit cards.

CHEAP SHOT INC.

294 RTE. 980
CANONSBURG, PA 15317
412/745-2658
FAX: 412/745-4265

Catalog: free
Save: 33% plus
Pay: check or MO
Sells: ammunition
Store: mail order only

$$

Cheap Shot is "shooters serving shooters since 1976," at savings of 33% and more on the usual prices of ammo. No reloads, second, old stock, or "low quality imported ammo" is sold, just cartridges, buckshot, shotshells, rimfire ammo, centerfire rifle ammo, magnum loads, and supplies for reloaders. The brands include Federal, Remington, Targ-Dot, and Winchester. The 16-page catalog also offers a "reloading library," with several manuals on the subject.

Please note: Federal regulations on age and identification requirements are stated in the catalog, and you must provide signature and driver's license number in order to purchase ammunition.

Special Factors: Price quote by phone or letter with SASE; authorized returns are accepted (a 20% restocking fee may be charged); C.O.D. orders are accepted.

CREATIVE HEALTH PRODUCTS

50 SADDLE RIDGE RD.
PLYMOUTH, MI 48170
800-742-4478
IN MI 313/996-5900
FAX: 313/996-4650

Catalog: free
Save: 30% average
Pay: check, MO, MC, V, AE
Sells: fitness equipment, related medical devices
Store: mail order only (see text)

Creative Health Products has been selling health, fitness, and exercise equipment since 1976 and carries some of the best product lines available. Savings vary from item to item, but average 30% on list or regular retail prices.

The 12-page catalog lists current models of stationary bicycles, ergometers, rowers, treadmills, stair climbers, and accessories by Avita, Cateye, Coursetter, Marathon, Monark, Oglend-Bodyguard, Trackmaster, and Tunturi. There are pulse monitors from Accusplit, Biosig Instruments, CIC, Nike, Nissei, and Tunturi, and skin-fold testers, body-fat analyzers, strength and flexibility testers, Chatillon scales for underwater weighing, and professional scales by Detecto, Health-O-Meter, and Seca. Stethoscopes, sphygmomanometers, otoscopes, and ophthalmoscopes are also sold, and the catalog includes guides on buying different types of devices. Please note that this is professional equipment and, even with discounts, the prices are not low. Creative Health welcomes questions about any of the products it sells, and can help you find the best equipment for your needs. Although primarily a mail-order firm, Creative Health welcomes visitors, so drop by if you're in the area.

Special Factors: Price quote by phone or letter with SASE; quantity discounts are available; institutional accounts are available; C.O.D. orders are accepted; orders are shipped worldwide.

CUSTOM GOLF CLUBS, INC.

10206 N.
INTERREGIONAL HWY.
35
AUSTIN, TX 78753
512/837-4810

Catalog: $1
Save: up to 50%
Pay: check, MO, MC, V
Sells: customized golf clubs, accessories, and repair equipment
Store: same address; Monday through Friday 7–7, Saturday 8–4

$$$ ✉ ☎ 🍁 🇺🇸

The "Accessories" catalog from Custom Golf Clubs features its special line of "Golfsmith" clubs, made to order, and a full line of golfing accessories. The "Repairs" catalog shows over 160 pages of replacement parts and repair supplies. Custom Golf, which opened its doors in 1966, offers savings of up to 50% on the cost of comparable name-brand products.

The custom department can make golfing woods and irons in a choice of left- or right-handed models, men's or women's styles, in five degrees of flexibility and any length, weight, color, or grip size. All professional-quality, name-brand golf club lines are available as well, from such names as Dunlop, Hogan, MacGregor, Ping, PowerBilt, Spalding, Titleist, and Wilson. The Accessories catalog also features name-brand clothing, footwear, bags, carts, gloves, manuals, balls, club covers, and other golfing essentials, plus instructional videotapes and books. The Repairs catalog offers a line of replacement club heads, grips, refinishing supplies, and tools, as well as instruction manuals. Service and repairs are also available to mail-order customers, and if you'd like to learn how to become a professional club maker, check into the Custom Golf Training Program.

Canadian readers, please note: Orders must be paid in U.S. funds.

Special Factors: Request catalog desired by name ($1 each); orders are shipped worldwide.

CYCLE GOODS CORP.

**2801 HENNEPIN AVE. SO.
MINNEAPOLIS, MN 55408
800-328-5213
612/872-7600**

Catalog: $1
Save: up to 40%
Pay: check, MO, MC, V, AE, DC, Optima
Sells: cycling gear and equipment
Store: 2801 Hennepin Ave., Minneapolis,
   MN; Monday through Thursday 10–8,
   Friday 10–6, Saturday 10–5, Sunday 12–4

$$$ ✉   ☎   🍁   ▧

Cycle Goods (also known as Cycl-Ology) publishes a 106-page catalog of cycling gear and supplies that includes valuable tips for improved performance and routine maintenance, along with detailed product information. The firm has been doing business since 1979.

Cycle Goods stocks a wide selection of racing and touring equipment, plus parts, tools, and clothing. Among the manufacturers represented here are Araya, Atom, Avocet, Bendix, Berec, Bollé, Brooks, Campagnolo, Cinelli, Citadel, Columbus, Cycle Pro, Descente, Guerciotti, Kingsbridge, Kirtland, Kryptonite, Lemond, Maillard, Mavic, Messinger, Michelin, Nike, Oakley, Omas, Reynolds, Rhode Gear, Rigida, Rossin, Sergal, Shimano, Sidi, and Weinmann. Save up to 40% on equipment and accessories, and more on specials.

Special Factors: Price quote by phone or letter with SASE; orders are shipped worldwide.

FISH'N SHACK

**P.O. BOX 1080-W
CAMDENTON, MO 65020
314/346-4044**

Catalog: free
Save: up to 50%
Pay: check, MO, MC, V
Sells: fishing and hunting gear, boat
   equipment
Store: Hwy. 54 W., Camdenton, MO;
   Monday through Friday 8–8

$$$ ✉   ☎   🍁

Fish'n Shack has been selling freshwater fishing tackle and boating gear since 1978—everything from Eagle Claw fish hooks to Lake Raider fishing boats is available here.

The 132-page color catalog shows reels, rods, tackle boxes, fishing line, bait, hooks, marlins, downriggers, and books and videotapes on fishing, fly tying, cleaning and cooking the catch, and related topics. Goods by Angler's Pride, Arbogast, Arkie, Bagleys, Berkley, Daiwa, Eagle Claw, Heddon, Johnson Reels, Kangaroo, Lunker Lure, Martin, Bill Norman (lures), Penn Reels, Plano, Rapala, Rebel, Ryobi, Shakespeare, Shimano, Storm, and Zebco are stocked. You'll also find boat equipment: Cruise 'n Carry and Minn Kota motors, Apelco (Raytheon) electronics, depth gauges and sounders, B & M boat seats, trailer kits, winches, Coleman dinghies, and much more.

Despite the name of this firm, almost half of the catalog is devoted to outdoor wear, camping gear, and hunting equipment. The catalog we reviewed showed Buck and Fiskars knives, Seaway camouflage waders, Celestron binoculars and spotting scopes, Gore-Tex camouflage rainwear, Sperry shoes, Camel tents, smokers and cookstoves, Coleman lanterns and kitchen equipment, a wide selection of high-beam flashlights, Barnett crossbows, Daisy pellet rifles, and other hunting and outdoor goods.

Prices run up to 50% below list or comparable retail, and extra savings can be realized on the house-label goods.

Special Factor: Returns are accepted within 10 days.

GANDER MOUNTAIN, INC.

P.O. BOX 6
WILMOT, WI 53192
800-554-9410

Catalog: free
Save: up to 35%
Pay: check, MO, MC, V, Discover
Sells: hunting, fishing, camping, reloading, and boating gear
Store: Wilmot/Johnsburg Rd., Wilmot, and 19555 West Bluemound Rd., Brookfield, WI; Monday through Friday 9–9, Saturday 9–6, Sunday 10–5

Gander Mountain has been recommended by several readers as a great source for outdoor sports gear and clothing, getting high marks for selection and service. Prices are also reliably low—savings of up to 35% were found on several items we checked.

Fishing and hunting needs are served here through a 172-page color catalog of equipment and clothing. The rod and reel department offers gear by Berkley, Browning, Daiwa, Eagle Claw, Fenwick, Garcia, Johnson, Liberty, Mitchell, Quantum, Ryobi, Shakespeare, Shimano, Sigma, and Zebco. There are lures by Bagley's, Mepps, Normark, and many other firms, and fishing line, nets, tackle boxes, rod cases, and other gear. Boat seats, covers, winches, bilge pumps, Minn Kota and other motors, Cannon downriggers, depth meters, recorders, radios, sonar devices, and Humminbird electronics are all offered as well.

Hunters will find a similar range of products for their sport: CVA blackpowder rifles, Lyman and MEC reloaders, Ram-line magazines and autoloaders, Hastings replacement parts for shotguns, Gun Guard gun cases, Treadlok gun safes, Michaels holsters, practice equipment, shell boxes, and related goods. Spotting scopes, hunting binoculars, mounts, and tripods by Bushnell, Leupold, and Tasco are also available.

Gander's video department sells Warburton and other tapes on big game hunting, shooting and handling guns, game calls and hunting techniques, training hunting dogs, hunting wild birds, and fishing for bass, walleye, and trout. Specialty clothing for both hunting and fishing — waders, hunting and shooting jackets, camouflage wear — is carried, as well as rugged clothing suitable for outdoor wear. The catalog we reviewed offered chamois cloth shirts, rain suits, leather jackets, and footwear from American Eagle, Browning, Coleman, Danner, Hi-Tec, Long Haul, Tony Lama, Maine Classic, Minnetonka, Rocky, Sorel, and other firms. Bushnell sunglasses, backpacks and luggage, camp cookware, sleeping bags, tents, Buck knives, and other generally useful outdoor gear are available.

Special Factors: Satisfaction is guaranteed; returns are accepted; orders are shipped worldwide.

GOLF HAUS

**700 N. PENNSYLVANIA
LANSING, MI 48906
517/482-8842**

Price List: free
Save: up to 60%
Pay: check, MO, MC, V
Sells: golf clubs, apparel, and accessories
Store: same address; Monday through Saturday 9–5:30

Golf Haus has "the absolute lowest prices on pro golf clubs" anywhere — up to 60% below list — and stocks goods by every possible manufacturer. All of the models sold here are available nationwide, which means that, unlike the "exclusive models" offered by a number of discounters, the goods at Golf Haus can be price-shopped fairly.

Golf Haus carries clubs, bags, putters, balls, and other golf equipment and supplies by Dunlop, Hogan, Lynx, MacGregor, Ping, PowerBilt, Ram, Spalding, Tiger Shark, Titleist, Wilson, and other firms. There are Bag Boy carts, Etonic shoes, gloves, umbrellas, spikes, scorekeepers, visors, rainsuits, tote bags, socks, and much more.

Special Factors: Price quote by phone or letter with SASE; shipping and insurance are included on orders shipped within the continental U.S.; minimum order is $50; orders are shipped worldwide.

HOLABIRD SPORTS DISCOUNTERS

9008 YELLOW BRICK RD.
BALTIMORE, MD 21237
301/687-6400
FAX: 301/687-7311

Brochure: free
Save: up to 40%
Pay: check, MO, MC, V, CHOICE
Sells: tennis, racquetball, and squash equipment and court shoes
Store: mail order only

$$$$ ✉ ☎ 🍁 ▬

Buy here and get the "Holabird Advantage": equipment for racquet sports at up to 40% below list prices, service on manufacturers' warranties, and free stringing with tournament nylon on all racquets.

Holabird carries tennis racquets by scores of firms, including Bard, Donnay, Dunlop, Estusa, Fin, Fox, Head, Kneissl, Match Mate, Prince, Pro-Kennex, Puma, Rossignol, Slazenger, Snauwaert, Spalding, Wilson, Wimbledon, Yamaha, and Yonex. There are tennis balls by Dunlop, Penn, Tretorn, and Wilson and ball machines by Lobster and Prince. The footwear department offers the newest styles from Adidas, Asahi, Asics Tiger, Avia, Brooks, Converse, Diadora, Ellesse, Etonic, Foot-Joy, Head, K-Swiss, Kaepa, Keds, L.A. Gear, Le Coq Sportif, New Balance, Nike, Pony, Prince, Pro-Kennex, Puma, Reebok, Saucony, Sergio Tacchini, Tretorn, Turntec, and Wilson.

Racquetball players should check the prices on racquets by Ektelon, Leach, Pro-Kennex, Voit, and Wilson. The squash department features racquets by Black Knight, Donnay, Dunlop, Ektelon, Estusa, Head, Pro-Kennex, Prince, Rossignol, Slazenger, Snauwaert, Spalding, Unsquashable, and Wilson, and eye guards by Bausch & Lomb, Ektelon, Leader, and Pro-Kennex. Pros can save their clubs sizable sums on court equipment and maintenance supplies, such as court dryers, tennis nets, ball hoppers, and stringing machines.

Holabird also stocks a full line of basketball, cross-training, aerobic, workout, running, walking, and golf shoes, along with a complete line of name-brand T-shirts, socks, and caps. See the monthly 8-page catalog for specials, or call or write for a price quote.

Special Factors: Price quote by phone or letter with SASE; authorized returns (except used items) are accepted within 7 days; orders are shipped worldwide.

LAS VEGAS DISCOUNT GOLF & TENNIS

**5325 S. VALLEY VIEW BLVD., SUITE 10
LAS VEGAS, NV 89118
702/798-7777
FAX: 702/798-6847**

Catalog: free
Save: up to 40%
Pay: check, MO, MC, V, AE, CB, DC
Sells: tennis, golf, and racquetball gear
Store: 4813 Paradise Rd., Las Vegas, NV; also stores in AL, AZ, CA, CO, FL, GA, HI, IL, LA, MA, MD, NE, NV, NY, OK, OR, PA, TN, VA, Canada, France, Japan, and Spain (locations are listed in the catalog)

Las Vegas sells name-brand gear and equipment for tennis, golf, racquetball, and jogging at savings of up to 40%. The latest styles and models are featured. The 48-page, color catalog shows golf clubs (drivers, putters, wedges, chippers), bags, and balls by Dunlop, Ben Hogan, Lynx, MacGregor, Mizuno, PGA, Powerbilt, Ram, Spalding, Taylormade, Stan Thompson, Tiger Shark, Titleist, Wilson, and Yamaha. The latest clothing from Foot-Joy, Izod, Lamode, and other firms is available, as well as instructional books and videotapes.

Las Vegas Discount also carries tennis racquets by Bancroft, Davis, Donnay, Dunlop, Head, Prince, Pro-Kennex, Spalding, Wilson, and Yamaha, as well as racquet strings and balls by Dunlop, Penn, Tretorn, and Wilson. There are lines of tennis shoes and apparel from several manufacturers, plus racquetball racquets from Ektelon, Head, and Wilson. Check the catalog for eye guards, Voit jump ropes, and miscellaneous sports accessories.

Special Factors: Price quote by phone or letter with SASE; orders are shipped worldwide.

OVERTON'S SPORTS CENTER, INC.
━━━━━━━━━━━━━━

P.O. BOX 8228, DEP. 21022
GREENVILLE, NC 27835
800-334-6541
IN NC 800-682-8263

Catalog: free
Save: up to 40%
Pay: check, MO, MC, V, AE, Discover
Sells: water sports equipment
Store: 111 Red Banks Rd., Greenville, and 1331 Buck Jones Rd., Raleigh, NC

$$$ ✉ ☎ 🍁 🇺🇸

Overton's lays claim to title of "world's largest water sports dealer," selling equipment for boating, water skiing, snorkeling, and other avocations. Overton's was established in 1975, and sells at discounts of 40% and more.

The firm's 32-page, color Water Sports catalog features skis and accessories ranging from junior trainers to experts' tricks, jumpers and slaloms by such companies as Connelly, EP, Jobe, Kidder, and O'Brien. Wetsuits, kneeboards, water toys, inflatables, snorkeling accessories, boating accessories, books, videotapes, and other goods are also offered.

The Overton's 104-page, color Discount Marine Catalog answers your boating needs with a wide range of products: boat seats and covers, safety equipment, instruments, electronics, hardware, cleaners, fishing equipment, clothing, fuel tanks, and performance equipment. The brands include Apelco, Aqua Meter, Brinkman, Eagle, Humminbird, Interphase, Ray Jefferson, Maxxima, Newmar, PowerWinch, Shakespeare, and Si-Tex, among others. The catalogs give the both the list or comparable retail prices, and Overton's.

Canadian readers, please note: Only U.S. funds are accepted.

Special Factors: Satisfaction is guaranteed; quantity discounts are available; unused returns are accepted within 30 days for exchange, refund, or credit; C.O.D. orders are accepted; orders are shipped worldwide.

PERFORMANCE BICYCLE SHOP

P.O. BOX 2741
CHAPEL HILL, NC 27514
919/933-9113

Catalog: free
Save: up to 40%
Pay: check, MO, MC, V
Sells: bicycle parts and cycling apparel
Store: mail order only

$$ ☎ ♥

Serious cyclists may know Performance for its own line of high-end road bikes, which run from under $500 to about $1,000. The firm's parts department is well-stocked, and it carries components for maintenance and improvement by Campagnolo, Cinelli, Nitto, Shimano, Sugino, and Suntour. There are cycling jerseys and shorts by Cannondale, Northface, and Sunbuster, as well as riding helmets, cycling shoes, gloves, panniers, and hundreds of products to enhance cycling performance.

If you find identical equipment advertised at a lower price elsewhere, you can send Performance a copy of the ad (or tell the phone operator where you saw it) and pay the lower price. Details on the "Price Protection Guarantee" are given in the catalog.

Special Factor: Satisfaction is guaranteed.

PROFESSIONAL GOLF & TENNIS SUPPLIERS, INC.

7825 HOLLYWOOD
BLVD.
PEMBROKE PINES, FL
33024
305/981-7283
FAX: 305/983-7033

Brochure: free with SASE
Save: 30% plus
Pay: check, MO, MC, V, AE
Sells: gear and apparel for golf and racquet sports
Store: same address; Monday through Sunday 9–6:30; other locations in AL and FL

$$$ ♥

This firm represents several divisions, which together offer an impressive array of equipment for golf, tennis, racquetball, and squash at savings of up to 40% on list prices.

The quarterly catalog shows pro golf clubs by Acushnet, Jerry Barber, Browning, Dunlop, First Flight, Hagen, Ben Hogan, Lynx, MacGregor, Tony

Penna, PGA, Ping, Pinseeker, PowerBilt, Ram, Rawlings, Sounder, Spalding, Stan Thompson, Taylor Made, Tiger Shark, Titleist, and Wilson. There are gloves, bags, shoes, balls, carts, and other golfing supplies as well.

Check here for buys on tennis racquets from Bancroft, Davis, Donnay, Dunlop, Durbin, Fila, Fischer, Head, Kneissl, Le Coq Sportif, Match Mate, P.D.P., Prince, Pro Group, Pro-Kennex, Rossignol, Scepter, Slazenger, Snauwaert, Spalding, Volkl, Wilson, Yamaha, and Yonex. Name-brand running and tennis shoes and balls, nets, ball machines, hoppers, stringing machines, bags, and other tennis goods are carried. The squash department offers racquets by Donnay, Dunlop, and Head; there are racquetball racquets by Ektelon, Head, Leach, Voit, and Wilson as well, plus name-brand shoes, bags, balls, and gloves.

Special Factors: Price quote by phone or letter with SASE; a 3% surcharge is levied on MasterCard and VISA orders; shipping and insurance are included on most items; orders are shipped worldwide.

ROAD RUNNER SPORTS

**6310 NANCY RIDGE RD.,
SUITE 101
SAN DIEGO, CA
92121-3209
800-551-5558**

Catalog: free
Save: up to 35%
Pay: check, MO, MC, V, AE
Sells: running shoes and apparel
Store: same address; Monday through Friday 9–5, Saturday 9–3

Road Runner Sports boasts "the absolute lowest running shoe prices," selling at a 10% markup on the wholesale cost, or up to 35% below list prices. The company has been in business for over 30 years and has thousands of pairs of shoes in stock.

Running shoes by Adidas, Avia, Brooks, Etonic, Foot-Joy, Hind, New Balance, Nike, Reebok, Saucony, Sub 4, Tiger, Scott Tinley, and Turntec are stocked here, as well as running shorts, socks, T-shirts, Gore-Tex running suits, duffel bags, and other accessories. The 80-page color catalog features current best-sellers, and you can call or write for prices on styles not shown.

Special Factors: Price quote by phone or letter with SASE; orders are shipped worldwide.

SAILBOARD WAREHOUSE, INC.

300 S. OWASSO BLVD.
ST. PAUL, MN 55117
800-992-SAIL

Catalog: free
Save: 35% average
Pay: check, MO, MC, V, AE
Sells: windsurfing equipment
Store: same address

$$$ ✉ ☎

Put wind and water together, and you have the prime ingredients for the nearly addictive sport of windsurfing, or sailboarding. The right equipment helps, which is what you'll find at Sailboard Warehouse—at discounts that average 35%, but run much deeper on sale items.

Sailboard Warehouse, in business since 1982, sells light to heavy wind sailboards, sails, masts, harnesses, fins, and a broad selection of windsurfing apparel. You'll find equipment by Aero, Bic, Boardworks, Calvert, DaKine, F2, HiFly, Kerma, Klepper, Maui Magic, Naish, Neilpryde, O'Brien, RAF, Sailboard, Sea Trend, Tiga, Topsails, Weichart, West Wind, Windcatcher, Windsurfing Hawaii, and other manufacturers represented in the color catalog. The boards run from entry-level to custom models for pros, and the catalog we reviewed included several pages of helpful information on choosing equipment and evaluating construction and materials. Automaxi car racks, Bollé sunglasses, windsurfing books and videos, and wetsuits, drysuits, harnesses and other accessories by O'Neill and Ronny are also available.

Special Factors: Satisfaction is guaranteed; price quote by phone or letter with SASE; shipping is included on orders of 2 or more boards; authorized returns are accepted within 20 days for exchange, refund, or credit.

SAMUELS TENNISPORT

7796 MONTGOMERY RD.
CINCINNATI, OH 45236
800-543-1153
IN OH 800-543-1152
513/791-4636

Brochure: free
Save: up to 35%
Pay: check, MO, MC, V, AE, Discover
Sells: racquets and court clothing
Store: same address; Monday through
   Friday 9–6, Saturday 10–5, Sunday 12–4

$$$ ✉ ☎ 🍁

Despite the firm's name, Samuels Tennisport offers equipment for racquetball and squash as well as court and platform tennis and badminton. Prices on the equipment are discounted up to 35%, but note that most of the clothing and accessories are sold at full retail.

The racquet department offers current tennis racquet models by Donnay, Dunlop, Fox, Head, Kneissl, MacGregor, Prince, Pro-Kennex, Puma, Rossignol, Wilson, Wimbledon, Yamaha, and Yonex. There are racquetball racquets by Ektelon, Head, and Pro-Kennex, and squash racquets by Donnay, Dunlop, Head, and Pro-Kennex. The badminton department has racquets by Black Knight, Carlton, HL, Victor, and Yonex, and string sets, shuttlecocks, and accessories. Custom stringing in nylon or gut is available at a surcharge. Ball machines, nets, court sweepers, Weathashade windscreens, and other court equipment is stocked.

The clothing and accessories department offers shoes and separates for on and off the court (including running shoes) by a number of prominent firms: Adidas, Asics, Avia, Brooks, Cerrutti, Diadora, Donnay, Ellesse, Fila, Foot-Joy, Head, K-Swiss, Le Coq Sportif, Nike, Fred Perry, Prince, Puma, Reebok, Rossignol, Saucony, Sergio Tacchini, Tretorn, Wilson, and Yonex. Bags from many of these firms are offered, and visors, wristbands, shoe repair products, insoles, eye guards, and gloves are available as well.

Special Factors: Satisfaction is guaranteed; price quote by phone or letter with SASE; C.O.D. orders are accepted; orders are shipped worldwide.

SKIN DIVER WETSUITS

1632 S. 250TH ST., DEPT. HR
KENT, WA 98032
206/878-1613

Brochure: free with SASE
Save: up to 60%
Pay: check, MO, MC, V
Sells: skin-diver wet suits
Store: mail order only

$$$  (see text)

Skin Diver Wet Suits has been selling custom-fitted wet suits since 1957. The firm maintains that "you're not comfortable unless you have a perfect-fitting suit," which it aims to provide at prices up to 60% less than those charged elsewhere for similar goods and features.

Skin Diver will make your wet suit to specification, in a choice of nylon fabrics. The standard model has a nylon lining, triple-sewn and glued seams, high collar, high-waisted pants, and a noncorrosive zipper with twist locks. Custom design features—knee and spine pads, arm and leg zippers, large sizes, etc.—are available for a surcharge. Send a self-addressed, stamped envelope for information and the measurement sheet/order form.

Canadian readers, please note: Payment is required in U.S. funds, by certified check or money order.

Special Factor: Satisfaction is guaranteed.

SPORT SHOP

P.O. BOX 340
GRIFTON, NC 28530
919/524-4571

Catalog: free
Save: up to 50%
Pay: check, MO, MC, V, CHOICE
Sells: hunting gear
Store: 110 Gordon St., Grifton, NC;
Monday through Saturday 8–5

The sport served here is bowhunting, for which Sport Shop offers a 64-page, color catalog of bows and hunting gear, at discounts of up to 50%. Sport Shop has been in business since 1955.

Bows by Holt, Jennings, Oneida, Pearson, and PSE are featured, as well as Neet belt quivers, Easton arrows and shafts, vanes, straighteners, points, broadheads, sights, rests, releasers, strings, and targets. Bowfishing equipment and even some hunting items are sold—RWS and Thompson/Center blackpowder guns and blackpowder supplies, among other goods. Camouflage clothing and maintenance products are available, as are lures, game calls, and footwear by Rocky and Topline.

Special Factors: Price quote by phone or letter with SASE on goods not shown in the catalog; returns are accepted for exchange, refund, or credit; minimum order is $15 with credit cards; orders are shipped worldwide.

SQUASH SERVICES, INC.

P.O. BOX 491
RICHBORO, PA 18954
215/364-4999

Information: price quote
Save: up to 35%
Pay: check, MO, MC, V
Sells: tennis and squash racquets and
  equipment
Store: mail order only

$$$ ✉ ☎

Squash Services ranks among the best discounters of racquet sports gear and equipment. The service is good, and you'll save up to 35% on top lines.

Tennis racquets are available here from Dunlop, Head, Prince, Pro-Kennex, Slazenger, and Wilson, as well as shoes by Adidas, Converse, Foot-Joy, Nike, and Pro-Kennex. Also available are squash racquets and equipment by AMF Head, Century Sports, Donnay, Dunlop, Goudie, Gray's, Manta, Pro-Kennex, Slazenger, and Spalding, and court shoes by Adidas, Foot-Joy, Nike, Pro-Kennex, and Tretorn. Accessories—Tourna Grip, eye guards, gloves, bags, etc.—are also carried.

Special Factor: Price quote by phone or letter with SASE.

STUYVESANT BICYCLE, INC.

349 W. 14TH ST.
NEW YORK, NY 10014
212/254-5200
212/675-2160

Information: price quote
Save: up to 30%
Pay: check, MO, certified check
Sells: bicycles and cycling equipment
Store: same address; Monday through
  Saturday 9:30–6, Sunday (in summer)
  12–5

$$ ✉ 🍁

Stuyvesant has been selling bicycles, cycling equipment, and supplies since 1939, and mailing them since 1946. The staff is helpful and experienced.

Stuyvesant stocks cycles ranging from children's bicycles to top-notch track and racing bikes (a specialty), including tandems, city bikes, used bikes, touring bikes, specials, and closeouts. Parts, helmets, jerseys, shoes, toe clips, pumps, locks, water bottles, and other accessories are also available. The brands include Atala, Bianchi, BMX, Bottechia, Campagnolo, Cinelli, Corso, Gipiemme, Huffy, Raleigh, Regina, Ross, and Suntour, and the top-of-the-line Simoncini frame sets and Sergal clothing are featured.

Special Factor: Price quote by phone or letter with SASE.

TELEPRO GOLF SHOP

17622 ARMSTRONG AVE.
IRVINE, CA 92714-5791
800-333-9903

Brochure: free
Save: up to 40%
Pay: check, MO, MC, V, Discover
Sells: golf clubs
Store: same address

$$$ ✉ ☎ 🍁 ▦

Telepro, a division of Shamrock Golf Shops and an affiliate of Teletire (see "Auto"), sells first-quality golf clubs and accessories at savings of up to 40%.

Telepro's informative brochure shows pro lines of clubs by Hogan, Lynx, MacGregor, PowerBilt, Quantum, Ram, Shamrock, Spalding, Wilson, and other manufacturers. There are golf shoes, Wilson golf gloves, bags, Bag Boy carts, and other equipment, which are sold at various discounts. The brochure includes a questionnaire on your golfing style, which will help Telepro to determine the best clubs for your game.

Special Factors: Satisfaction is guaranteed; price quote by phone or letter with SASE; returns (except special orders) are accepted within 30 days (a 10% restocking fee may be charged).

THE TENNIS CO.

30610 SOUTHFIELD RD.
SOUTHFIELD, MI
48076-1220
313/258-9366

Information: price quote
Save: up to 35%
Pay: check, MO, MC, V
Sells: squash and tennis equipment
Store: mail order only

$$$ ✉ ☎

The Tennis Co. sells tennis and squash equipment at savings of up to 35% on list prices. Custom stringing services are also available.

Call or write for prices on tennis racquets by Head, Prince, Pro-Kennex, and Wilson, and squash racquets by AMF Head, Donnay, Dunlop, Manta, Pro-Kennex, Slazenger, and Spalding. Merco squash balls and other supplies are stocked as well.

Special Factor: Price quote by phone or letter with SASE.

WIDE WORLD OF SPORTING GOODS

220 SOUTH UNIVERSITY DR.
PLANTATION, FL 33324
305/475-9800

Price List: free
Save: up to 30%
Pay: check or MO
Sells: racquets and shoes
Store: same address; Monday through Friday 9–6

$$ ✉ ☎

This firm, formerly known as Athlete's Corner, offers winning savings on name-brand racquets as well as court and running shoes.

Tennis racquets by Donnay, Dunlop, Head, Prince, Pro-Kennex, Wilson, Yamaha, and other firms are stocked, as well as shoes by Adidas, Asahi, K-Swiss, New Balance, Nike, Reebok, and other firms. Wide World carries racquetball and squash racquets by well-known firms, and racquet-stringing services are offered.

Special Factors: Price quote by phone or letter with SASE; returns of unused goods are accepted for exchange.

WILEY OUTDOOR SPORTS, INC.

DEPT. WBMC 1991
P.O. BOX 5307
HUNTSVILLE, AL 35814
205/837-3931
FAX: 205/837-4017

Catalog: $3, refundable
Save: 30% average
Pay: check, MO, MC, V
Sells: hunting gear and equipment
Store: 1808 Sportsman Lane, Huntsville, AL

$$$ ✉ ☎

This family-run business has been outfitting hunters since 1953 with a full range of equipment and gear. Savings at Wiley average 30%, but can run as high as 50% on certain items and lines.

Hunters will find everything from boots to blackpowder supplies in the 168-page catalog, including scopes, binoculars, and other optics from Aimpoint, Burris, J.B. Holden, Leupold, Nikon, Redfield, Simmons, Tasco, and Zeiss. Blackpowder rifles by Lyman and Thompson/Center are available, as well as reloading and bullet-casting equipment by Forster Products, Hornady, Lee, Lyman, and MEC. Holster, gun maintenance products, gun slings, tree stands, and related hunting accessories are stocked. There are game calls of all types, game scents, compasses, airguns for adults, and camping accessories. Clothing by Browning, Carhartt, Columbia, Hodgman, Mossy Oak, Remington, and Walls is sold, as well as duofold thermal underwear, footwear from Rocky Boots, and Serengeti sunglasses.

For a different type of hunting needs, Wiley carries crossbows by Barnett, bowhunting gear, and an excellent selection of hunting and specialty knives by Al Mar, Browning, Buck, Case Cold Steel, Gerber, Remington, Victorinox, and Wyoming Knife.

Special Factors: Satisfaction is guaranteed; unused returns are accepted within 10 days; minimum order is $25; C.O.D. orders (via UPS only) are accepted; orders are shipped worldwide.

SEE ALSO

Astronomics/Christophers, Ltd. • spotting scopes for bird watching • CAMERAS
Bruce Medical Supply • small selection of fitness equipment • MEDICINE
CISCO • swimming pool chemicals and supplies • HOME: MAINTENANCE
Clothcrafters, Inc. • flannel gun-cleaning patches, mosquito netting, and sleeping bag liners • GENERAL MERCHANDISE
Custom Coat Company, Inc. • custom tanning, dyeing, and tailoring of green hides • CLOTHING
Danley's • sports binoculars, rifle scopes, etc. • CAMERAS
E & B Marine Supply, Inc. • water skis • AUTO
Exceptionally Yours, Inc. • coordinated separates with Velcro closings • CLOTHING
A. Feibusch Corporation • replacement tent zippers • CRAFTS
The Finals, Ltd. • swimwear, athletic wear, and accessories • CLOTHING

Iron Works Cycle • street bike accessories • *AUTO*

Leather Unlimited • black powder supplies, suede duffel bags • *CRAFTS*

Mardiron Optics • name-brand binoculars and telescopes for hunting, bird watching, etc. • *CAMERAS*

Mass. Army & Navy Store • government surplus camping and survival gear • *SURPLUS*

Mr. Spiceman • beef jerky and other camp foods • *FOOD*

Newark Dressmaker Supply, Inc. • replacement zippers for sleeping bags and tents • *CRAFTS*

Okun Bros. Shoes • name-brand sports shoes • *CLOTHING: FOOTWEAR*

Orion Telescope Center • name-brand binoculars • *CAMERAS*

Pagano Gloves, Inc. • deerskin archers', hunters', and bowhunters' gloves • *CLOTHING*

Racer Wholesale • auto racing safety equipment and accessories • *AUTO*

Roby's Intimates • running bras • *CLOTHING*

Ruvel & Co., Inc. • government surplus camping supplies and survival goods • *SURPLUS*

Scope City • field binoculars, spotting scopes • *CAMERAS*

SURPLUS

Surplus and used goods of every sort

Surplus was probably the original generic type of "bargain" merchandise, and there are still enough surplus goods around to make bargain hunters happy. This is the world of military overstock, obsolete electronics, and the 90% discount.

Many of the surplus dealers accept inquiries for goods not listed in their catalogs, but most of us don't know what's available. *The Army/Navy Store Catalog* (Penguin Books, 1982), by Andrew I. Adler, Roger Adler, and William G. Thompson, provides a good guide to a wide range of popular items. It's illustrated with line drawings and features extensive listings of surplus suppliers in the U.S. and abroad. If you've just gotten the deal of the century on ammo boxes and hatch covers but aren't quite sure what to do with them, see Leslie Linsley's *Army/Navy Surplus: A Unique Source of Decorating Ideas* (A Delta Special/Dell Publishing Co., 1979). She's taken surplus goods and throwaways and given them useful new lives with the aid of paint and imagination. The book is illustrated with photographs and includes listings of surplus and salvage sources. If all else fails, you can stow your finds in the attic — twenty years down the road, they'll probably be valuable heirlooms.

BURDEN'S SURPLUS CENTER

P.O. BOX 82209-WMC91
LINCOLN, NE 68501
800-228-3407
FAX: 402/474-5198

Catalog: free
Save: up to 85%
Pay: check, MO, MC, V, AE, Discover
Sells: surplus tools and hardware
Store: 1015 West O St., Lincoln, NE;
Monday through Saturday 9–6, Sunday
12–5

Burden's, established in 1933, offers great buys on tools and hardware of all sorts. Blowers, compressors, pressure washers, hand tools, electrical equipment and supplies, surveying equipment, plumbing equipment and tools, grinders, and other goods for commercial and industrial use are stocked here, by Briggs & Stratton, Cessna, G.E., Gresen, Hypro, Kawasaki, and other manufacturers. The Burdex line of security and surveillance equipment is also carried, as well as other brands. The 120-page catalog is dominated by industrial products—hydraulic equipment, AC and DC electric motors, gas engines, compressors, air tools, winches, generators, transformers, etc.—but well-priced consumer items are usually offered. The catalog we reviewed showed a variety of casters, automotive products, Dremel and other hand tools, phones and accessories, halogen spotlights, Mag-Lite flashlights, and Redington measuring wheels, among other goods.

Special Factors: Returns are accepted (a restocking fee may be charged); C.O.D. orders are accepted.

E.T. SUPPLY

P.O. BOX 78190
LOS ANGELES, CA
90016-8190
213/734-2430
FAX: 213/734-1511

Catalog: free
Save: up to 90%
Pay: check, MO, MC, V
Sells: industrial surplus goods
Store: mail order only

Despite the name, this is not an outlet for extraterrestrial necessities. E.T. Supply is a six-year-old company that sells military and commercial surplus, with an emphasis on electrical components. The bulk of the 64-page catalog is devoted to accumulators, actuators, blowers, circuit breakers, generators, hydraulic cylinders, pumps, relays, rheostats, solenoids, switches, and similar items.

The catalog we reviewed also showed several pages of tools, hardware, and parts that would be useful in vehicle repairs—wrench and socket sets, pliers, casters, tachometers, and aircraft instruments. Many of the items were made by prominent manufacturers—Bendix, G.E., Kidde, Lear, Motorola, Raytheon, Weston, and others. The concise catalog descriptions include functions, specifications, and prices—up to 90% below original selling cost.

Special Factor: Authorized returns are accepted (a 15% restocking fee may be charged).

H & R CORPORATION

**401 E. ERIE AVE.
PHILADELPHIA, PA
19134-1187**
215/426-1708
FAX: 215/425-8870

Catalog: free
Save: up to 60%
Pay: check, MO, MC, V
Sells: surplus electronics, computer
components, etc.
Store: same address; Monday through
Friday 8:30–4:45, Saturday 9:30–2

H & R (Herbach & Rademan), established in 1934, publishes a catalog of surplus bargains, chiefly electronics and computing equipment.

The 40-page H & R catalog is dominated by such items as adapters, capacitors, oscillators, potentiometers, solenoids, transformers, keyboards, monitors, video and audio cables, circuit breakers, electric meters, disk drives, printers, modems, mag card readers, power line filters, and joysticks. There are many items attractive to less skilled hobbyists, do-it-yourselfers, and the rest of us: telephones, handsets, cords, and other phone accessories; heavy-duty outlet strips and surge suppressors; hygrometers, thermometers, and other weather instruments; mini-vacuum cleaners for computers; security devices, robotics components, compasses, binoculars, cabinet slides, tool cases and cabinets, luggage carriers, Luxo lamps, magnets, poly cutting slabs, baseboard heaters, flashlights, and reference books on computing and technical topics.

Product specifications are given in the catalog, and item order numbers are coded to indicate whether a product is in limited supply.

Special Factors: Satisfaction is guaranteed; price quote by phone or letter; returns with original packing materials are accepted within 30 days; minimum order is $15 (U.S.$20 on orders shipped to Canada).

HARBOR FREIGHT SALVAGE CO.

3491 MISSION OAKS BLVD.
CAMARILLO, CA 93010
800-423-2567
805/388-3000

Catalog: free
Save: up to 50%
Pay: check, MO, MC, V, AE, Optima
Sells: tools, hardware, and surplus goods
Store: same address; also Bakersfield, Fresno, Herperia, Lancaster, Santa Maria, and Visalia, CA, and Lexington, KY

$$$ ✉ ☎ ▬

Great prices can be found in this firm's "riot of hardware" mailings, which offer toolbox necessities at savings of up to 50% on list and comparable retail. Specials are run frequently; this is a valuable source for the hobbyist and do-it-yourselfer.

Past catalogs have offered drill and auger bits, Stanley measuring tapes, Pittsburgh Forge socket wrenches, mildew-proof tarps, Black & Decker power tools, pipe-sealing tape, camp knives, work benches, saw blades, wood lathes, heavy-duty bench grinders, disk sanders, drill presses, and similar goods.

Special Factor: Shipping is included on orders over $50.

JERRYCO, INC.

**601 LINDEN PL., DEPT.
WBM
EVANSTON, IL 60202
708/475-8440**

Catalog: 50¢
Save: up to 95%
Pay: check, MO, MC, V
Sells: industrial and military surplus goods
Store: 5696 Northwest Hwy., Chicago, IL;
also 5430 W. Layton Ave., Milwaukee,
WI; Monday to Friday 10–6, Thursday
10–9, Saturday 9–5, Sunday 11–5, both
locations

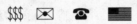

Jerryco, an affiliate of American Science Center, offers its surplus wares through amusing catalogs that are published about six times yearly. Just fifty cents brings you four issues.

American Science Center has been selling surplus since 1946, and Jerryco has sold by mail since 1976. The catalogs proffer that blend of the strange and useful that is peculiar to fans of surplus, who claim "teachers, labs, tinkerers, small manufacturers, collectors of the bizarre, artists," and the curious among their members.

Past Jerryco catalogs have shown small DC motors, staplers, heat guns, microscopes, magnets, odd bottles, drill bits, O-rings, dozens of types of tape, surgical scissors, silk thread, Spanish spats, telescoping antennas, oil changer pumps, casters, rubber body-organ replicas, piano hinges, drawer slides, and magnifying lenses. (Please *don't* expect to find these particular items in the catalogs you receive—these are surplus goods, and stock is limited.) The descriptions, which are witty and explicit, note the original and possible uses for the products, as well as technical data, when available. Savings on original and if-new prices can reach 95%.

Special Factors: Satisfaction is guaranteed; returns are accepted within 15 days; minimum order is $12.50.

MASS. ARMY & NAVY STORE

15 FORDHAM RD., DEPT. WBM91
BOSTON, MA 02134
617/783-1250
FAX: 617/254-6607

Catalog: free
Save: up to 40%
Pay: check, MO, MC, V, AE
Sells: government surplus apparel and accessories
Store: 895 Boylston St., Boston, and 1436 Massachusetts Ave., Cambridge, MA; also Central War Surplus, Inc., 433 Massachusetts Ave., Cambridge, MA

Mass. Army & Navy is among the new breed of surplus centers: its 52-page color catalog offers both reproduction and genuine government surplus, presented as a fashion statement. The firm has a "will not be undersold" pricing policy.

Past catalogs have featured camouflage clothing, French Foreign Legion caps, pith helmets, leather pilots' caps, U.S. Air Force sunglasses, Canadian battle pants, Vietnam jungle boots, survival manuals, and similar surplus. Casual footwear, knapsacks, bandannas, sleeping bags, air mattresses, backpacks, duffel bags, camping equipment, gloves, mess kits, night sticks, handcuffs, insignias and patches, Lee and Levi's jeans, bomber jackets, pea coats, and other useful miscellany are offered on a regular basis.

Special Factors: Returns are accepted for exchange, refund, or credit; orders are shipped worldwide.

RUVEL & CO., INC.

4128-30 W. BELMONT AVE.
CHICAGO, IL 60641
312/286-9494

Catalog: $2
Save: up to 70%
Pay: check, MO, MC, V
Sells: government surplus
Store: same address; Monday through Friday 10–4:30, Saturday 10–2

Ruvel, established in 1965, is the source to check for good buys on government-surplus camping and field goods—it has a large stock and some of the best prices around on this kind of gear.

U.S. Army and Navy surplus goods are featured in the 64-page catalog, including G.I. duffel bags, high-powered binoculars, leather flying jackets, mosquito netting, rations, carbine stocks, dummy grenades, U.S. Army technical manuals, and similar goods. Past catalogs have offered Justrite carbide and electric lamps, Kevlar helmets, hammocks, snowshoes, strobe lights, mess kits, dinghies, night sticks, snowshoes, Primus camp stoves, parade gloves, first-aid kits, and toxicological aprons.

Ruvel is noteworthy because of its low prices and extensive stock of real surplus—there are hundreds of "genuine" government-issue items available here, and many intriguing, useful surplus things that are increasingly hard to find these days.

Special Factors: Price quote by phone or letter with SASE; order promptly, since stock moves quickly.

SEE ALSO

All Electronics Corp. • surplus electrical components • *TOOLS*

TOOLS, HARDWARE, ELECTRONICS, ENERGY, SAFETY, SECURITY, AND INDUSTRIAL GOODS

_____

Materials, supplies, equipment, and services

This section offers the do-it-yourselfer, hobbyist, logger, and small-time mechanic a wealth of tools and hardware, some of it at rock-bottom prices. Repair and replacement parts for lawnmowers, trimmers, garden tractors, snowmobiles, snow throwers, blowers, go-carts, mini-bikes, and even plumbing and electrical systems are available from these companies. The tools run from pocket screwdrivers and fine wood chisels to complete work benches and professional machinery, and the hardware includes hard-to-find specialty items as well as stock nuts, bolts, nails, etc.

When you're working, be sure to observe safety precautions and use goggles, dust masks, respirators, earplugs, gloves, and other protective gear as indicated. Make sure blades are sharp and electrical cords are in good repair. Keep tools, hardware, and chemicals out of the reach of children and pets. If you're using a chain saw, you may want to make sure that it's fitted with an approved antikickback device. Contact the manufacturer for recommendations.

For more tools and related products, see "Crafts and Hobbies," "General," the "Maintenance" section of "Home," and "Surplus."

ALL ELECTRONICS CORP.

P.O. BOX 567
VAN NUYS, CA 91408
800-826-5432
818/904-0524
FAX: 818/781-2653

Catalog: free
Save: up to 60%
Pay: check, MO, MC, V, Discover
Sells: surplus electronics and tools
Store: 905 S. Vermont Ave., Los Angeles,
CA; Monday through Friday 9–5,
Saturday 9–4; also 6228 Sepulveda Blvd.,
Van Nuys, CA; Monday through Friday
9–5:30, Saturday 9–4

$$$ ✉ ☎ 🍁 ▆

Electronics hobbyists should see All Electronics', 60-page catalog, published five times a year, for the huge number of surplus parts, hardware items, and tools. The firm, established in 1967, maintains a large inventory of stock items.

A recent All Electronics catalog offered semiconductors, transducers, heat sinks, sockets, cables and adapters, fans, collectors, plugs, switches, solenoids, relays, capacitors, piezoelectric elements, fuses, resistors, transformers, potentiometers, keyboards, computer fans, and P.C. boards. While much of the stock is for electronics hobbyists, the catalogs usually offer such items as telephone cords and jacks, TV and video accessories, screwdrivers, socket wrenches, hemostats, solar cells, magnets, and rechargable batteries.

Special Factors: All parts are guaranteed to be in working order; price quote by phone or letter with SASE; authorized returns are accepted within 15 days; minimum order is $10; orders are shipped worldwide.

BAILEY'S, INC.

WESTERN DIVISION
44650, HWY. 101
P.O. BOX 550
LAYTONVILLE, CA 95454
707/984-6133
FAX: 707/984-8115
OR
SOUTHERN DIVISION
1520 S. HIGHLAND AVE.
P.O. BOX 9088
JACKSON, TN 38314
901/422-1300
FAX: 901/422-6118
OR
EASTERN DIVISION
3 SELINA DR.
P.O. BOX 14020
ALBANY, NY 12212
518/869-2131
FAX: 518/869-0725

Catalog: $2, year's subscription
Save: up to 70%
Pay: check, MO, MC, V
Sells: logging, woodcutting, and reforestation supplies and equipment
Store: same addresses; Monday through Friday 6 A.M.–9 P.M., Saturday 8–5 (CA); Monday through Friday 6–6, Saturday 8–5 (TN); and Monday through Friday 6–6, Saturday 8–5 (NY)

Bailey's, one of the country's best sources for chain-saw parts and other logging gear, stocks a large number of goods everyone will find useful—boot dryers, leather conditioners, outdoor clothing, and safety gear. Savings run as high as 60% on goods in the general catalog, and even more on items offered in the biannual sales flyers.

The 84-page catalog lists all kinds of Oregon chain reels and bars for Homelite, Husqvarna, McCulloch, Pioneer, and Stihl saws. Silvey chain grinders, spark plugs, tape, guide bars, bar and chain oil, bar wrenches and files, and other tools are available. Calked and heavy-duty boots by Chippewa, Currin, and Wesco are stocked, as well as climbing equipment, Duerr log splitters, Alaskan saw mills, winches, and other equipment. Campers and even urbanites will appreciate the well-priced outerwear (Filson jackets and pants, Five Brothers flannel shirts, rain slickers, etc.), and the first-aid kits and portable fire extinguishers. In addition, there are boot dryers, E.A.R. plugs and headset noise mufflers, and work gloves.

Bailey's is the place to call if you have questions about your chain saw. (Check for details on the firm's "Chain Saw Safety Awareness Program.") Orders are shipped promptly, the staff is quite helpful, and the toll-free order number if featured prominently in the catalog.

Special Factors: Quantity discounts are available; C.O.D. orders are accepted; orders are shipped worldwide.

THE BEVERS

P.O. BOX 12
WILLS POINT, TX
75169-0012
214/272-8370

Catalog: $2, refundable
Save: up to 50%
Pay: check, MO, MC, V
Sells: hardware and woodworking parts
Store: mail order only

The Bevers began doing business in 1977, selling a variety of hardware and parts for routine and special needs. This is an excellent source for the hobbyist and do-it-yourselfer, and the Bevers are honest and committed to offering the best possible values.

The 44-page catalog lists a plethora of hardware and equipment for woodworking, construction, and household repairs. There are steel and brass wood screws with round and flat heads, lock and flat washers, a full range of eye bolts and squared screw hooks, Tap-Lok threads, machine screws with a choice of head styles, hex heads and carriage bolts, cotter pins, brass-plated hinges, picture hangers, lag screws, countersinks, doweling drill bits, clamps, and rotary and sandpaper drums for drills. A good selection of wooden parts for making toys and repairing furniture is available, including wood balls, toy wheels, Shaker pegs, peg boards, game pieces, golf tees, screw-hole buttons, knobs and pulls, and turned finials and spindles. A number of the items sold here are almost impossible to find in the average hardware store, so consult the catalog if you're having trouble locating a special screw or bolt.

Special Factor: Price quote by letter with SASE on quantity orders.

CAMELOT ENTERPRISES

P.O. BOX 65, DEPT. W91
BRISTOL, WI 53104-0065
414/857-2695

Catalog: $1, refundable
Save: up to 50%
Pay: check, MO, MC, V
Sells: fasteners, tools, and hardware
Store: 8234 199 Ave., Bristol, WI; hours
by appointment

$$$ ✉ ☎ ▆

Camelot, founded in 1983, sells "quality fasteners, hardware, and tools direct to the craftsman" at savings of 30% to 60%, compared to similar goods available elsewhere.

The quarterly, 14-page catalog offers a full range of nuts (hex, K-lock, wing, stop, etc.), bolts (hex-head, machine, carriage), screws (wood, lag, drywall, machine), washers, thread fittings, cotter pins, anchors, and other hardware. The tools include screwdrivers, punches, and other hand and power tools by Astro, Camelot, Chicago Tool, Continental, Ingersoll Rand, Lisle, Makita, Milton, Milwaukee, Rockford, and Truecraft, among others. We found well-priced shop welders, Excalibur fastener sets, Gesipa pop rivets, and Camelot's own twist drills and fasteners in the catalog we received.

Camelot is offering readers of this book a 5% discount on orders of $50 or more (excluding shipping and sales tax). Please identify yourself as a reader when you order. This WBMC reader discount expires February 1, 1992.

Special Factors: Satisfaction is guaranteed; returns are accepted within 10 days for replacement, refund, or credit; no collect calls are accepted.

DIRECT SAFETY COMPANY

7815 S. 46TH ST.
PHOENIX, AZ 85044-9990
602/968-7009

Catalog: free
Save: up to 30%
Pay: check, MO, MC, V, AE
Sells: industrial safety equipment
Store: mail order only

$$$ ✉ ☎

Direct Safety, recommended by a reader of this book, sells products that are used routinely by hobbyists and in all types of industries. In pricing different items, we found gloves costing 25% less here than comparable styles sold by another industrial products firm, and quantity discounts of about 10% are available.

No workshop should be without a good pair of safety glasses, for example, and it's smart to use a respirator if you're working with paint or dusty materials, and especially if you're rehabbing an old building. Direct Safety offers protective gloves designed to resist solvents, acids, oils, knife cuts, heat, and PCBs. There are sulfur-free gloves, ideal for those who are allergic to natural rubber, and PVC gloves treated with a bacteria-controlling agent that helps to prevent the development of contact dermatitis in the wearer. At least a dozen first-aid kits are available, as well as emergency showers and eyewash stations, fire extinguishers, flammable-materials containers and cabinets, security and emergency lights, voltage testers and electrical safety equipment, smoke detectors, hand-held metal detectors, emergency pilons and other vehicle safety equipment, antislip floor strips and coatings, and hazardous materials management gear. Monitors that measure the level of carbon monoxide in your home and car and devices that detect microwave leakage, radiation, pH levels, and blood alcohol levels (breath analyzers) are all available.

Special Factors: Satisfaction is guaranteed; quantity discounts are available; price quote by phone or letter with SASE; returns are accepted (a 15% restocking fee may be charged).

ECONOMY ENTERPRISES

POOR MAN'S CATALOG
P.O. BOX 23-W
HIGHLAND, MD 20777
301/776-3792

Catalog: $2
Save: up to 80% (see text)
Pay: check or MO
Sells: plans
Store: mail order only

If Johnny Blackwell had been able to afford the engraving machine he wanted 20 years ago, we might not have the Poor Man's Catalog today. The enterprising Mr. Blackwell spent a winter with his son working on an engraver of his own design—and perfected one for less than $25 in materials.

Having saved himself nearly $1,000, he turned his attention to other tools and equipment he needed, developing plans and designs. He began selling the plans, and he's now published six compilations of these ideas in the "Poor Man's Catalog," 24 pages describing plans of "u-build-it" power tools, energy-saving projects, toys, furniture, and woodworking ideas, as well as the engraving machine that started it all. (The next edition of the catalog is in the works and should be available in 1991.) The plans run from the obvious to the arcane, including instructions for a metal-turning lathe, heavy-duty belt sander, jigsaw, mini-cement mixer, Aeolian harp, kangaroo pull-toy, shop vacuum cleaner, smelting furnace, and "razor-blade radio," among others. The plans cost $2 to $4 each, and qualify for quantity discounts.

Mr. Blackwell has applied his talents to problems even the most impecunious of us never experiences. When we spoke with him, he'd just finished developing a low-cost limekiln, which will be used by volunteers in New Guinea for farming. He's worked up plans for housing that's been built in Africa with found and recycled materials. And he combined forces with a principal at Edmund Scientific to come up with a battery that could be powered with the heat from a candle, so that a group of missionaries on a remote island would not be without vital weather information. That's Yankee ingenuity at its best!

Canadian readers, please note: Orders must be paid in U.S. funds.

Special Factors: Satisfaction is guaranteed; quantity discounts are available; orders are shipped worldwide.

H & H MANUFACTURING & SUPPLY CO.

**P.O. BOX 692
SELMA, AL 36701
205/872-6067**

Price List: free
Save: up to 50%
Pay: check, MO, certified check
Sells: chain-saw parts and logging equipment
Store: 111 Hwy. 80 E., Selma, AL; Monday to Friday 7–5, Wednesday 8–12 noon

$$$ ✉   🍁

H & H Manufacturing, whose mail-order division is known as "Saw Chain," has been offering savings of up to 50% on saw chain and other logging needs since 1965.

Saw chain, guide bars, and sprockets are offered here for chain saws by Craftsman, John Deere, Echo, Homelite, Husqvarna, Jonsered, Lombard, McCulloch, Olympic, Pioneer, Poulan, Remington, Stihl, and other firms. The chain, which is distributed by H & H, is sold in a range of pitches and gauges, and both gear-drive and direct-drive sprockets are stocked to fit all models. Swedish double-cut files, Esco rigging products, Windsor and Tilton saw chain and bars, wire rope, logging chokers, slings, and other logging equipment is also available. Remember to give all requested information when ordering chain and sprockets—make and model, chain pitch, gauge, number of drive links, type of bar, and length.

Special Factors: Price quote by phone or letter with SASE; chains, bars, files, and sprockets are guaranteed to last as long as or longer than any other make; returns are accepted for replacement.

MANUFACTURER'S SUPPLY

**P.O. BOX 167-WBMC-91
DORCHESTER, WI
54425-0167
800-826-8563**

Catalog: free
Save: up to 50%
Pay: check, MO, MC, V
Sells: replacement parts for lawnmowers, snowmobiles, chain saws, etc.
Store: mail order only

$$$ ✉ ☎ 🍁 🇺🇸

All machines, from lawnmowers to snowmobiles, give out eventually. If you're handy, you can save a tidy sum on the cost of professional repairs by doing them yourself. Manufacturer's Supply is your source for all the parts you'll need to get things functioning again, and the prices are up to 50% below list or comparable retail, saving you more money.

Consult the 144-page bible from Manufacturer's for parts for chain saws, lawnmowers, motorcycles, snowmobiles, three-wheel vehicles, snow throwers, trimmers, trailers, and rototillers: sprockets and nose assemblies, chains, grinders, files, air filters, T-wrenches, starter springs, carburetor parts, and guide bars (stocked for dozens of saw brands). Parts for standard and riding lawnmowers are stocked, as well as semipneumatic tires for mowers and shopping carts, wheelbarrows, and hand trucks.

There are wheels, hubs, bearing kits, roller chains, sprockets, clutches, belts, and other goods for trailers, minibikes, go-carts, riding mowers, snow throwers, rototillers, garden tractors, and three-wheelers. The snowmobile parts include everything from lubricants to windshields—carburetors, fuel filters, cleats, tracks, pistons, gaskets, fan belts, suspension springs, and engines, among other items. Also available are wood-chopping tools and Woodchuck wood-burning furnaces, as well as Magic Heat air circulators and chimney cleaning brushes.

Special Factors: Price quote by phone or letter with SASE; authorized, unused returns are accepted within 30 days (a 20% restocking fee may be charged); minimum order is $10.

MEISEL HARDWARE SPECIALTIES

**P.O. BOX 70WM
SPRING PARK, MN 55384
800-441-9870**

Catalog: $1
Save: up to 40%
Pay: check, MO, MC, V
Sells: hardware, wood crafts parts and plans
Store: 4310 Shoreline Dr., Spring Park, MN; Monday through Friday 9–6, Saturday 9–5

Woodworkers, toy makers, and the creatively handy should appreciate this catalog of plans and ingredients for all kinds of projects. Meisel offers a number of items we haven't seen in other catalogs, and our price comparisons of such commonly available items as lamp harps, wood screws, and foam brushes indicated that savings of up to 40% are possible here.

The 80-page catalog shows woodworking plans for toys, vehicles, lamps, games, playground equipment, useful things for the home, kitchen projects, dollhouses, and gifts. Parts and supplies for many projects are stocked, including wooden wheels in ten sizes, pegs and dowels, moving eyes for dolls, folk-motif stencils, turned spindles and posts, finials, wooden furniture knobs, cork sheets, box hinges, clock movements and parts, and picture-hanging hardware. Meisel specializes in door harps, and sells harp plans, harp wire, clapper balls, and tuning pins. We found a number of items needed for projects languishing on our workshop shelves: small brass escutcheons and box corners, miniature box hasps, hardware for knock-down furniture, bread box tambour, and brass candle cups.

The catalog is also a good source for fix-up materials—turned spindles and legs for chairs and small tables, screw-hole buttons and furniture knobs, casters, magnetic cabinet catches, furniture glides, and picture frame wire are all available.

Special Factors: Satisfaction is guaranteed; returns are accepted for exchange, refund, or credit; minimum order is $25.

NORTHERN HYDRAULICS, INC.

**P.O. BOX 1499, DEPT. 68075
BURNSVILLE, MN 55337
800-533-5545
IN MN 612/894-8310
FAX: 612/894-0083**

Catalog: free
Save: up to 50%
Pay: check, MO, MC, V, Discover
Sells: hydraulics, logging equipment, and machine parts
Store: Atlanta, GA; Burnsville, Fridley, Rochester, and Rogers, MN; Charlotte, Greensboro, Matthew, and Raleigh, NC; and Richmond, VA

Northern Hydraulics makes it easy to save up to 50% on hydraulics, gas and electric engines, logging equipment, trailer parts, air tools and compressors, winches, hand tools, farm and garden equipment, and much more.

The 136-page catalog offers an enormous selection of log splitters, wedges, Homelite and McCulloch chain saws, Oregon chain and bars, files, and other logging gear. The hydraulic pumps include lines by J.S. Barnes and Parker, and there are Orbmark motors, motor valves, hydraulic tanks, strainers, hoses, and other parts and equipment. Gas engines for use with log splitters, lawn and riding mowers, rototillers, and other machines are stocked, including vertical- and horizontal-shaft models by Briggs & Stratton, Kohler, Onan, and Tecumseh. Air compressors and related equipment by American IMC and Campbell Hausfeld are offered, as well as air tools from Chicago Pneumatic, Ingersoll-Rand, and other firms. The catalog has a section devoted to go-cart parts and accessories, minibike parts, ATV tires and wheels, halogen tractor lamps, sandblasting equipment, pressure washers, air compressors, Aqua Siphon water heaters, propane tanks, and small hand tools. The farm and garden equipment includes filament trimmers, cultivators, NorTrac tractors, garden carts, agricultural pumps, mower tires, blowers, sprayers, tillers, and much more. You'll also find

Dickies overalls, Northlake boots, and purely recreational items—Toshiba personal stereos, giant inflatable tubes, and tiny Casio TVs, to mention a few.

Special Factors: Price quote by phone or letter with SASE; minimum order is $10.

TOOLS ON SALE

SEVEN CORNERS ACE HARDWARE, INC.
216 W. SEVENTH ST.
ST. PAUL, MN 55102
800-328-0457
612/224-4859
FAX: 612/224-8263

Catalog: free
Save: up to 40%
Pay: check, MO, MC, V, Discover
Sells: tools for contractors, masons, and woodworkers
Store: same address; Monday through Friday 7–5:30, Saturday 7–1

$$$ ✉ ☎ ▆

If you can't get to St. Paul to visit Seven Corners Ace Hardware, where there are "over 35,000 items on the floor," you can do business with the firm's mail-order division, Tools on Sale. The parent company was founded in 1933, and specializes in tools for contractors and masons.

The Tools on Sale catalog is one of the last great freebies in America—767 pages of name-brand tools, at discounts of up to 40%. You'll find everything from air compressors to work benches here, from manufacturers that include Black & Decker (Elu), Bosch, Delta, Dremel, Freud, Hitachi, Jet, Jorgensen, Leigh, Makita, Milwaukee, Porter-Cable, Ryobi, Senco, and Skil, among others. If you're looking for stair templets, demolition hammers, moisture meters, water stones, mechanics' cabinets, or just want to *see* 29 pages of construction aprons and nail bags, look no farther. Free freight on orders shipped to the U.S. (except Alaska and Hawaii) is an added bonus.

Special Factors: Price quote by phone or letter with SASE; shipping is included on orders shipped within the contiguous U.S.; authorized returns are accepted for exchange, refund, or credit (a 15% restocking fee may be charged).

TREND-LINES, INC.

WOODWORKERS
  WAREHOUSE OUTLET
375 BEACHAM ST.
CHELSEA, MA 02150
617/884-8951

Catalog: $1
Save: up to 50%
Pay: check, MO, MC, V, AE, Discover
Sells: tools and hardware
Store: same address; call for hours

$$ ✉ ☎ 🍁 ▦

Trend-lines markets complete lines of tools and a selection of hardware for the professional woodworker. Savings run up to 50% on some items, especially abrasives and hardware. Trend-lines has been doing business since 1981.

The 72-page, color catalog features a solid selection of woodworking tools, including saws (jig, miter, band, reciprocating, scroll, radial-arm, and chain); drills, routers, trimmers, planers, jointers, sanders, nibblers, polishers, grinders, bits, blades, and other accessories. AEG, Black & Decker, Delta, Freud, Hitachi, Makita, Milwaukee, Porter-Cable, Ryobi, Shopcraft, Skil, and other popular names are represented. The catalog also shows full lines of parts and supplies, such as abrasives (sheets, belts, and disks), lubricants, adhesives, paste stains and varnishes, milk-based paint, wood plugs and buttons, Shaker pegs, dowels, toy wheels, and a number of dollhouse kits, as well as hand tools and cabinetry hardware. Woodworking manuals, plans, and instructive manuals are also offered.

We found a number of helpful and unusual items in the catalog we reviewed, including basswood shelf brackets in several styles, lint-free polishing cloth by the 90' roll, wood moisture meters, neckties with woodworking motifs, ponyband clamps, corner chisels, oak bath fixtures, and even wooden fruit. (Gift shops are selling boxes of perfumed acorns for $10; a set of six similar unfinished acorns costs $1.95 here—rub in the potpourri oil of your choice and you have a far less expensive sachet!)

Special Factors: Satisfaction is guaranteed; returns (except custom-made or cut-to-size items) are accepted within 30 days for exchange, refund, or credit; minimum order is $20 with credit cards.

TURNKEY MATERIAL HANDLING CO.

**P.O. BOX 1050
TONAWANDA, NY
14151-1050
800-828-7540**

Catalog: free
Save: up to 50%
Pay: check, MO, MC, V, AE
Sells: commercial and industrial furnishings, storage units, etc.
Store: mail order only

$$$ ✉ ☎ 🍁 ▓

This firm's products are geared for industrial and commercial applications, but there are many home uses for the sturdy "high-tech" storage units and other equipment sold here. Turnkey has been doing business since 1946.

The 116-page catalog features commercial shelving and metal storage bins in a huge selection of sizes and styles, from small parts bins ideal for hardware storage to 108-drawer steel wall cabinets, plus plastic bin-and-frame arrangements—all of which are appropriate for home use. The catalog also shows a good selection of mats and runners, work benches, storage cabinets, stainless-steel rolling carts, office and folding chairs, suspension files, lockers, flat and roll files, moving pads, canvas tarps, security gates, hoists, ceiling fans, hand trucks, rolling ladders, trash cans, hydraulic lifts, first-aid kits and protective gear, power-failure lights, pumps, and many other product lines.

Special Factors: Satisfaction is guaranteed; price quote by phone or letter with SASE; authorized returns (except custom-made items) are accepted (a 20% restocking fee may be charged); minimum order is $25.

WHOLE EARTH ACCESS

**2950 7TH ST.
BERKELEY, CA 94710
415/845-3000**

Catalog: free
Save: up to 40%
Pay: check, MO, MC, V
Sells: power tools and equipment
Store: same address; also 401 Bayshore, San Francisco, and 863 E. Francisco Blvd., San Rafael, CA

$$ ✉ ☎

Whole Earth Access, established in 1969, offers name-brand woodworking tools and equipment at savings of up to 40% on list prices.

The 48-page catalog offers a wide range of hand and power tools for woodworking—saws and sanders of all types, drills, routers, planers, and related machines. The brands include Black & Decker, Bosch, Delta, Freud, Hitachi, Makita, Milwaukee, Porter-Cable, Ryobi, and Skil, among others. Whole Earth Access sells Emglo air compressors, equipment by David White Instruments, Leigh dovetailing jigs, Bostich finish nailers, and Lamello hand joining machines, among other specialty items. You can order from the catalog, or call or write for price quotes on particular models.

Special Factors: Price quote by phone or letter with SASE; authorized returns are accepted.

WOODWORKER'S SUPPLY OF NEW MEXICO

5604 ALAMEDA PL. N.E.
ALBUQUERQUE, NM
87113
505/821-0500

Catalog: free
Save: up to 30%
Pay: check, MO, MC, V
Sells: woodworking tools and equipment
Store: same address; Monday through Friday 8–5:30, Saturday 9–1

$$$

Woodworker's Supply publishes a 96-page, full-color catalog of woodworking tools and hardware, priced up to 30% below comparable goods sold elsewhere.

The catalog we reviewed offered basics from abrasives to work benches, as well as a number of hard-to-find items. We found drills (including cordless models), power screwdrivers, routers, saws (circular, jig, orbital, contractor's, band, etc.), sanders (finish, belt, orbital, etc.), laminate trimmers, heat guns, biscuit joiners, power planes, grinders, power staplers, jointers, drill presses, shapers, and other tools. The manufacturers represented include Black & Decker, Bosch, Delta, Freud, Gerstner, Glit, Jorgensen, Porter-Cable, Sioux, Skil, Top Gun, and Woodtek, among others. Drawer slides by Alfit, Delta, and Knape & Vogt are carried, as well as Mepla hinges for pie-cut doors, coated-wire fittings for custom kitchen cabinets, furniture and cabinet levelers, oak chair and table bases, cassette storage tracks, halogen canister lights, wood project parts, veneers, butcher block, locks and latches, glue scrapers and injectors, steel wool-backed sheets for finish sanders, Preserve nontoxic wood finish, plans for rocking pigs and goats, Haas knock-down joint fasteners, and a Japanese miter square. Like the best of such sources, Woodworker's Supply can give you as many ideas for new projects as it provides solutions to old woodworking problems.

Special Factors: Satisfaction is guaranteed; returns are accepted within 90 days; minimum order is $5 ($25 to Canada); orders are shipped worldwide.

WORLD ABRASIVES CO., INC.

**1866 EASTERN PARKWAY
BROOKLYN, NY
11233-4398
718/495-4301**

Catalog: $1.25, refundable
Save: up to 60%
Pay: check or MO
Sells: abrasives and sanding materials
Store: same address; Monday through Friday 8:30–4:45

$$$ ✉ ☎ 🍁

World Abrasives sells all kinds of sanding products and related goods, including hard-to-find sizes and types of abrasives. The firm, which has been in business since 1972, does extensive business with industrial customers and can answer just about any question you may have on abrasives.

Sanding belts for wood, metal, and plastic are stocked, as well as waterproof belts for wet grinding of glass and ceramics. The grits run from 16 to 1000, and all sizes are available. There are sanding discs, sheets, rolls of sanding materials, grinding wheels and points, wire wheels, and buffing wheels. The belts are sold in lots of ten, discs in lots of 25, and sheets in packages of 25, but there are small assortments for single jobs. Polishing compounds, oil and honing stones, 3M dust masks, goggles, disc adhesives, and belt cleaners are stocked. World Abrasives also sells Cryocut, a dry chemical coolant that is applied to sanding belts or discs to reduce the heat buildup caused by friction, making the abrasive last longer. Prices here are low, even in small quantities, and custom abrasives can be produced (at no surcharge) for special applications.

Special Factors: Satisfaction is guaranteed; price quote by phone or letter with SASE.

ZIP POWER PARTS, INC.

P.O. BOX 10308
ERIE, PA 16514-0308
800-824-8521

Catalog: free
Save: up to 45%
Pay: check, MO, MC, V
Sells: parts for chain saws, lawnmowers, snowmobiles, etc.
Store: 2008 E. 33rd St., Erie, PA; Monday through Friday 8–5, Saturday 9–4

$$$ ✉   ☎

If you own a chain saw, you may already know about Zip Power Parts (formerly known as Zip-Penn) which is one of the country's best sources for chain-saw parts. In business since 1962, the firm also sells other machinery components and outdoor power equipment.

Zip Power Parts sells chain saws by Homelite, Poulan, and Pro-Kut, as well as saw chain, bars, bar guards, and sprockets to fit all makes and models of chain saws. Saw chain grinders and chain saw repair parts, and small engine parts are all available. Brush cutters, chain saws, table saws, and band saws are also stocked. There are shop tools for filing and grinding, wedges, lubricants, "mini-mills," hand tools, manuals, safety clothing and equipment, and woodcutting accessories. Additional parts for lawnmowers—mufflers, air filters, blades, starter rope and handles, fuel lines and filters, points, condensers, electronic ignitions, etc.—are listed in the 32-page, tabloid catalog.

Special Factors: All products are guaranteed against defects in materials and workmanship; returns are accepted.

SEE ALSO

Alfax Wholesale Furniture ● institutional furnishings and fixtures ● OFFICE

America's Hobby Center, Inc. ● tools, hardware, and accessories for model assembly ● CRAFTS

Arctic Glass & Window Outlet ● replacement patio door panes and passive solar panels ● HOME: MAINTENANCE

Bennett Brothers, Inc. ● home-security equipment ● GENERAL MERCHANDISE

Business & Institutional Furniture Company • institutional furnishings and fixtures • *OFFICE*

Cahall's Department Store • name-brand work clothing and rugged footwear • *CLOTHING*

Central Tractor Farm & Family Center • shop and power tools, chain saws, welding equipment • *FARM*

Cherry Tree Toys, Inc. • wooden toy parts, hardware, etc. • *TOYS*

CISCO • professional power tools • *HOME: MAINTENANCE*

Clothcrafters, Inc. • shop aprons, woodpile covers, and tool holders • *GENERAL MERCHANDISE*

A Cook's Wares • Taylor Woodcraft work tables • *HOME: KITCHEN*

Craftsman Wood Service Co. • veneers, lumber, stains, finishes, and tools for marquetry and cabinetry • *CRAFTS*

Crutchfield Corporation • security systems for car and home • *APPLIANCES*

Cycle Goods Corp. • bicycle repair tools • *SPORTS*

Defender Industries, Inc. • wood treatment products (marine), hardware • *AUTO*

E.T. Supply • wrenches, socket sets, pliers, etc. • *SURPLUS*

Frank Eastern Co. • industrial and institutional supplies and furnishings • *OFFICE*

Goldbergs' Marine Distributors • wood treatment products (marine), hardware • *AUTO*

H & R Corporation • electrical and electronic components • *SURPLUS*

Harbor Freight Salvage Co. • hardware and tools • *SURPLUS*

Jerryco, Inc. • surplus tools, electronics, etc. • *SURPLUS*

Metropolitan Music Co. • tools and supplies for making musical instruments • *MUSIC*

Bob Morgan Woodworking Supplies • woodworking tools • *CRAFTS*

Okun Bros. Shoes • work and safety footwear • *CLOTHING: FOOTWEAR*

Oreck Corp. • beam flashlights and power-failure lights • *APPLIANCES*

The Renovator's Supply, Inc. • fireplace and stove accessories, ironware, brassware, reproduction house hardware • *HOME: MAINTENANCE*

S & S Sound City • surveillance equipment • *APPLIANCES*

Sears, Roebuck and Co. • Craftsman tools • *GENERAL MERCHANDISE*

Shuttercraft • shutter-hanging hardware • *HOME: MAINTENANCE*

Staples, Inc. • Falcon fire extinguishers • *OFFICE*

Todd Work Clothing • work clothing and footwear for men and women • *CLOTHING*

WearGuard Corp. • protective gloves, tool kits, shop aprons, etc. • *CLOTHING*

Workmen's Garment Co. • work clothing and gloves • *CLOTHING*

TOYS AND GAMES

Juvenile and adult diversions

Unfortunately, this is not a large chapter. After years of research, we've concluded that the toy market is not conducive to discounting. Aside from the large off-price chains, there are very few firms selling toys at savings of 30% or more. Why?

It's a seller's market, and no one is forced to discount to remain competitive. We'll continue to search for firms that sell playthings at a discount, but at the same time we urge parents to sit down with their children and talk about what's on their gift lists. All too often they seem to be rosters of what's been run on TV commercials aired on weekend mornings. (This includes the shows themselves, which are often half-hour "stories" that are simply ads for the featured characters.) You might consider asking your child to take time out from "Smurfs," "Kissyfur," and "Muppet Babies" one Saturday morning and have a consumer awareness lesson. There are ways of discussing the manipulative effects of advertising without turning your children into cynics, crushing the holiday spirit, or jeopardizing the myth of Santa Claus. You might be aided by *Penny Power,* published by Consumers Union. It's written for those who are 8 to 13 years old and includes product reports, articles on money management for juveniles, and tips on wise shopping. A year's subscription (six issues) costs $11.95 and can be ordered from Penny Power, Subscription Dept., Box 54841, Boulder, CO 80321. Good luck!

ACME PREMIUM SUPPLY CORP.

4100 FOREST PARK BLVD.
ST. LOUIS, MO 63108-2899
800-325-7888, EXT. 23
FAX: 314/531-2106

Catalog: free
Save: up to 50%
Pay: check, MO, MC, V
Sells: toys, novelties, and premium goods
Store: same address

$$

We've listed Acme Premium in this chapter because so much of its stock is toys, games, and novelties. The 136-page color catalog is bursting with stuffed animals, balloons, games, and other diversions. But please note that Acme's targeted customers are businesses, clubs, churches, and carnivals; hence, the $50 minimum order. Acme also states that its merchandise "is not intended for use by children under 5 years of age."

We found a number of items everyone can use, at very good prices — glass and plastic tumblers, can openers, flashlights, and pens and pencils, for example. If you're throwing a party or organizing a bazaar, see the catalog for the wide selection of dart games, ball toss and hoop game equipment, bingo supplies and equipment, and similar goods. Imprinting is offered on T-shirts and windbreakers, visors, balloons, buttons, key rings, mugs, pens, and pencils. Complete details on the sales policy are given in the catalog.

Special Factors: Authorized returns are accepted (a restocking fee may be charged); minimum order is $50.

BARON BRIDGE SUPPLIES

3800 CHAMBERLAIN LANE, 230
LOUISVILLE, KY 40241-1989
502/426-0410

Catalog: free
Save: up to 40% (see text)
Pay: check, MO, MC, V
Sells: playing and teaching materials for bridge
Store: mail order only

$$

Baron Bridge Supplies carries all sorts of materials and equipment for bridge players, but is listed here because it stocks hundreds of books on the game, and sells them at quantity discounts of up to 25%. (Sale items are marked up to 40% below original selling prices.) Baron has been in business since 1973, and specializes in teachers' materials.

Baron's book department offers a wide range of teaching manuals and texts, books on strategy and bidding, bridge history and reference texts, and complete courses in bridge. Videotapes and instructional software are also available, as well as playing cards, scoring cards and club forms, recap sheets, and a variety of gifts and equipment—bridge-motif china, magnetic card sets, timers, bumper stickers, pens and pencils, polo shirts, and even an electric card shuffler. You can also order subscriptions to *Bridge World* and other bridge-related magazines through Baron's catalog.

Special Factors: Satisfaction is guaranteed; quantity discounts are available; returns are accepted within 10 days for exchange, refund, or credit (videotapes and software for exchange only); C.O.D. orders are accepted; orders are shipped worldwide.

CHERRY TREE TOYS, INC.

**408 S. JEFFERSON
P.O. BOX 369-140
BELMONT, OH 43718
614/484-4363
FAX: 614/484-4388**

Catalog: $1
Save: up to 50%
Pay: check, MO, MC, V
Sells: wooden toy kits and parts
Store: I-70, Belmont, OH; Monday
through Saturday 9–5, Sunday 11–5

Cherry Tree Toys sells kits for delightful playthings, as well as scores of wooden parts for your own designs. The company was founded in 1981, and the prices are as much as 50% less than those charged for similar goods in toy and gift shops.

The 64-page color catalog shows kits for dozens of whirligigs, decorative clocks depicting motifs ranging from trains to football helmets, door harps, wooden wagons and sleds, pull toys, miniatures, dollhouses, "Wild West" wagons, and vintage cars. Clock movements and markers, music boxes, and hundreds of wooden parts—wheels, spindles, smokestacks, beads, knobs, pulls, pegs, etc.—are offered as well. Cherry Tree sells plans, kits, and books on making toys, dollhouses, whirligigs, clocks, and door harps, in addition to the supplies you'll need to finish the projects. If you're able to visit the factory outlet store in Belmont, you'll find discontinued catalog items and seconds at up to 75% off regular prices.

Special Factors: Satisfaction is guaranteed; returns are accepted within 10 days for exchange, refund, or credit; C.O.D. orders are accepted.

PARADISE PRODUCTS, INC.

**P.O. BOX 568
EL CERRITO, CA
94530-0568
415/524-8300**

Catalog: $2
Save: up to 50%
Pay: check, MO, MC, V
Sells: party paraphernalia
Store: mail order only

Paradise Products has been sponsoring bashes, wingdings, and festive events since 1953, when it began selling party products by mail. The 88-page catalog is a must-see for anyone throwing a theme event.

Paradise sells materials and supplies for over 120 different kinds of events, including Oktoberfest, the 50s, Roaring 20s, St. Patrick's Day, fiestas, "Las Vegas Night," Hawaiian luaus, pirate parties, Super Bowl celebrations, and July Fourth parties. Balloons, streamers, tissue balls and bells, party hats, banquet table coverings, crepe paper by the roll, pennants, garlands, and novelties are among the items available. Paradise's prices are as much as 50% below those charged by other party-supply stores.

Special Factors: Goods are guaranteed to be as represented in the catalog; shipments are guaranteed to arrive in time for the party date specified (terms are stated in catalog); minimum order is $30.

LA PIÑATA

**NO. 2 PATIO MARKET,
OLD TOWN N.W.
ALBUQUERQUE, NM
87104
505/242-2400**

Brochure and Price List: $1 or SASE
Save: up to 30%
Pay: check, MO, MC, V
Sells: piñatas and paper flowers
Store: same address; Monday through Saturday 10–5, Sunday 12–5

$$ ✉ ☎

La Piñata is a marvelous source for piñatas, the hollow papier-mâché animals and characters that are traditionally filled with candy and broken by a blindfolded party guest. Prices here are low; many items are under $10.

The stock includes piñatas in the shapes of superheroes like Batman and Superman, springing cats, pumpkins, Santa, snowmen, witches, stars, reindeer, and other seasonal characters. And there are all sorts of animals, including bears, burros, cats, elephants, frogs, pigs, kangaroos, and penguins. Most of the piñatas are offered in three sizes. La Piñata, which has been in business since 1961, also carries inexpensive, colorful paper flowers in several sizes.

Special Factor: Gift orders are filled.

SEE ALSO

America's Hobby Center, Inc. ● model cars, trains, planes, ships, etc. ● CRAFTS

Bart's Water Ski Center, Inc. ● water tubes and other inflatables ● SPORTS

Bennett Brothers, Inc. ● small selection of children's toys, board games, and cards ● GENERAL MERCHANDISE

The Bevers ● wooden wheels, balls, and other components for toy making ● TOOLS

Dover Publications, Inc. ● cut-and-assemble projects, stickers, dioramas, etc. ● BOOKS

A. Feibusch Corporation ● zippers for doll clothing ● CRAFTS

Gohn Bros. ● "Dutch blitz" card game ● CLOTHING

Home-Sew ● dolls' eyes ● CRAFTS

House of Onyx ● Mexican onyx chess sets and boards ● JEWELRY

Jerryco, Inc. ● educational materials for elementary-grade sciences ● SURPLUS

D. MacGillivray & Coy. ● woolen stuffed toys ● CRAFTS

Meisel Hardware Specialties ● wooden wheels and other toy parts, toy plans ● TOOLS

Newark Dressmaker Supply, Inc. ● supplies for making dolls and toys ● CRAFTS

The Paper Wholesaler ● party supplies ● GENERAL MERCHANDISE

Pueblo to People ● small selection toys and dolls from Central and South America ● GENERAL MERCHANDISE

Rammagerdin • Icelandic dolls • *CRAFTS*

Arthur M. Rein • mink Teddy bear • *CLOTHING*

South Bound Millworks • jointed wooden bears • *HOME: DECOR*

R.C. Steele Co. • trivia game for dog lovers, dog-breed playing cards, etc. • *ANIMAL*

Taylor's Cutaways and Stuff • kits and patterns for making dolls and toys • *CRAFTS*

Tower Hobbies • radio-controlled vehicles • *CRAFTS*

Woodworker's Supply of New Mexico • wooden toy parts, plans, and dollhouse plans • *TOOLS*

TRAVEL

The business of getting from point A to point B seems simple enough, until you try to do it cheaply. But travel savings can be realized in a number of ways, depending upon the nature of the traveler and the trip.

CONSOLIDATORS/BUCKET SHOPS

Consolidators are travel wholesalers. They buy cruise slots, blocks of rooms, and plane seats from the airlines, hotels, and charter agents. They resell these rooms and seats for less than the hotels, airlines, or often the charter operators themselves are willing to accept for individual tickets or rooms. Consolidators' customers are often travel agents, but individuals may buy from them too, often saving 20% to 30% on the APEX fares, and much more on full economy tickets.

Unitravel Corporation is one of the oldest consolidators in the business and sells directly to individuals. Contact Unitravel about a month before you anticipate traveling, and allow for some uncertainty, since tickets might not be available until shortly before the day of the flight. Unitravel books flights in the U.S. and Europe. Call 800-325-2222 or 314/727-8888 for more information.

Council Charter enjoys an excellent reputation; it's been in business for over 40 years, and is affiliated with the Council on International Educational Exchange, a not-for-profit travel concern. For information on what's currently available, call 800-223-7402 or 212/661-0311.

Nouvelle Frontiers is another off-price travel broker that sells to consumers, as well as to travel agencies. For information, call 212/764-6494, or 415/781-4480. You can also try *Destinations Unlimited,* at 212/980-8220, and *European-American Travel,* at 800-848-6789, or 202/789-2255.

DISCOUNT TRAVEL AGENTS

Simple common sense tells you that commissions pegged to the selling price of a ticket may be something of a disincentive to getting travel agents to find you the lowest fare. On top of this problem is the real difficulty in getting "hard" information in a market that literally changes overnight, every night. Inexperienced and undermotivated travel agents can be impaired on both counts, for which you pay the price.

These real difficulties make *Travel World* (also known as *Farefinders*) worth checking before your next trip. This agency is run by Annette Forest, who's been in the business for over a decade and uses a wide range of information sources to find the lowest fares. Travel World will search for the best rates on travel by air, train, or ship, as well as cruises and tours to any destination worldwide. You can buy your tickets and book reservations through Travel World, but it's optional—there's no obligation for the fare-finding services. Ms. Forest also mentioned that she teaches hands-on college classes for aspiring travel agents at Travel Smart, and invites inquiries. Write to Travel World, 8621 Wilshire Blvd., Beverly Hills, CA 90211, or call 213/652-6305 for information.

STANDBY TRAVEL

If your travel plans, including departure and return, are flexible, consider the world of standby travel. It really is a last-minute affair, but it can be the cheapest way to fly—under $200 each way to Europe, at this writing.

Airhitch is an old friend among travelers who favor this mode of travel. The firm has offices near campuses—Columbia, Yale, and UCLA—and in several large cities, but does most of its business by mail. You first phone for information, have a registration form sent to you, apply for the desired dates or range, send in a fee of $25, and then start calling for availability three days before your desired departure dates. The procedure is involved, but it works. The friendly phone system at Airhitch has been programmed to dispense all the details of the standby program. Make sure you have pen and paper at hand before calling 800-372-1234, or 212/864-2000.

Access International also books standby flights from New York to points in Europe. It works on a registration/fee basis, and publishes a brochure that describes the services. Call 212/333-7280 for information.

CONNECTIONS

Most of us insist on the lowest possible prices for airline tickets, but are willing to squander comparatively large sums on the last leg of the journey—the trip from the airport to the hotel. You can avoid this pitfall with the help of *Crampton's International Airport Transit Guide,* which lists schedules and rates of taxis, car services, trains, buses, car-rental agencies, and other connections from airports worldwide to nearby cities. The pocket-sized guide costs under $5, is updated yearly, and is sold by The Complete Traveller Bookstore (see "Resources," following). You may also contact the publisher, Salk International Travel Premiums, Inc., at P.O. Box 1388, Sunset Beach, CA 90742, or 213/592-3315, for more information.

EDUCATIONAL TRAVEL

Imagine taking up painting on the coast of Cornwall, or embarking on a safari by jeep in New Mexico. These are two of hundreds of educational opportunities we read of in *Learning Vacations* (Peterson's Guides, 1986), by Gerson G. Eisenberg. Although some of the programs are limited to enrolled students, most are extension courses taught on campuses in the U.S., Canada, Europe, and as far afield as Tanzania. Prices for the courses vary considerably from program to program, usually depending on the type of accommodations. *Learning Vacations* is available from The Complete Traveller Bookstore, listed in the "Resources" section at the end of this chapter.

Combining education with travel isn't a new concept, but *Elderhostel* brings it to a specific group—those 60 and over—and does it so successfully that it's created a loyal group of followers who plan their travel around Elderhostel programs. The organization was founded in 1981 and currently offers programs in hundreds of colleges in the U.S., Canada, and overseas—from Australia to West Germany. There are study cruises, "RV" programs for hostelers who are bringing their own accommodations (tent or RV), and "Intensive Studies" programs that offer more in-depth courses, as well as the popular courses held on campuses around the country. Previous catalogs have offered programs as diverse as "Sociology of the Family" at the University of Alabama, "Dog Mushing in Alaska" at the University of Alaska, "Drawing Basics" at Stetson University in Florida, and "King Arthur and His Knights" at the University of Reno, in Nevada. The price is right: Programs in the U.S. currently run about $235 to $285 each, and include everything except transportation—classes, meals, lodging, and even entertainment. (The overseas programs cost more, since they include round-trip airfare, sightseeing, transfers, and all other costs.) Even the RV hostelers are bussed to the campus or course site, where they receive all their meals.

We spoke with an Elderhostel staff member who's visited many programs and expressed some regret that there is no equivalent for younger people. (You, or your spouse, must be at least 60 to participate.) She said that all of the programs offered opportunities for socializing and meeting new people, but are structured to allow each participant to take things at his or her own pace. This is a wonderful way to develop new interests, make new friends, and see another part of the country—or another land, at a reasonable price. For information, write to Elderhostel, 80 Boylston St., Suite 400, Boston, MA 02116. Please note: There is no membership fee.

STUDENT TRAVEL

Like seniors, students can benefit from a variety of travel opportunities and savings. One of the best-known names in this field is *Council on International Educational Exchange (CIEE)*, which also runs Council Charter (see the previous section, "Consolidators/Bucket Shops"). CIEE can issue you an International Student Identity Card (ISIC) if you're a full-time high school or college student. You'll need this card to qualify for discounts on train and plane travel, admission to cultural and entertainment centers, and CIEE's own travel programs. The card costs $8, and comes with a brochure detailing available discounts. CIEE also publishes the "Student Work-Study-Travel" catalog and "Update," which describe work and study opportunities, and the highly recommended *Work, Study, Travel Abroad: The Whole World Handbook,* by Marjorie Cohen and Margaret Sherman. For information on the identity card and other publications, write to Council on International Educational Exchange, 205 E. 42nd St., New York, NY 10017, or call 212/661-1414.

CAMPUS ACCOMMODATIONS

Staying on campus *sans* academics is often the cheapest alternative to everything but no-frills of budget hotels. Rooms are usually available during college vacation periods, at prices as low as $19 per night. Amenities vary widely, but the rates are so good that it makes sense to explore this alternative when planning a trip.

One firm, *Campus Holidays USA, Inc.,* has been arranging campus accommodations and other travel services since 1975. You can call or write for a list of the U.S. and British accommodations currently on offer, and purchase a book of coupons that can be used to pay for your stay. Campus Holidays can provide "lower-cost youth/student and teacher airfares," and tours of Europe, Asia, Africa, South America, and Australia for travelers who are 18 to 35 years old. Among these trips, its "Top Deck" tours are quite popular: British double-decker buses that have been converted to hotels (sleeping quarters on top, dining and kitchen facilities below) take intrepid travelers on jaunts that last two to 20 weeks. (The overland trek from London to Katmandu is a standout.) For information, write to Campus Holidays USA, Inc., 242 Bellevue Ave., Upper Montclair, NJ 07043; you can also call 201/744-8724, or fax a letter to 201/744-0531. Please note that Campus Holidays is offering readers of this book a 5% discount on all purchases. Identify yourself as a WBMC reader when purchasing a voucher book or paying for travel.

If you're interested in exploring the university option, don't miss the directory published by *Campus Travel Service,* "U.S. and Worldwide Travel Accommodations Guide." This 76-page book lists 600 universities in the U.S., and others in Canada, Australia, Ireland, England, Wales, Scotland, Scandinavia, Europe, Israel, Japan, Mexico, New Zealand, Africa, Asia, and Yugoslavia. Name, address, and phone number of each institution are given, as well as rates for singles and doubles, open dates, food service availability, nearby cultural and entertainment opportunities, whether children may stay, etc. The guide features listings of YMCA residences (51 in the U.S., 67 in Canada, and 23 overseas), including prices, amenities, restrictions, and booking policies. There are also several pages of valuable tips and references—on travel overseas, information on youth hostels, bargains for those under 30, travel opportunities for educators, toll-free airline numbers, bed-and-breakfast reservation services worldwide, home-exchange services, addresses of U.S. and foreign tourist offices, and some excellent health advice for travelers. All of this costs $13.00 ($11.95 plus $1.05 shipping); send a check or money order for the "Travel Accommodations Guide" to Campus Travel Service, P.O. Box 5007, Laguna Beach, CA 92652.

HOME EXCHANGES

One of the cheapest ways to save on hotel bills, especially if you're quartering a family, is to billet in someone else's home. There are a number of organizations that can help you effect a trade, either by arranging it or by providing a directory of like-minded parties with whom you negotiate.

Home Exchange International arranges the trades of homes of persons in the U.S., France, Italy, England, and other locations. To register, you pay a $50 one-time fee and supply photos of your home. As soon as you've planned your vacation or narrowed your choices, you contact the agency with details. When a trade is arranged, you also pay a "closing fee" that runs from about $150 to $500, depending on the length of stay planned, type of home, etc. Request a brochure from the Home Exchange International office nearer you: 185 Park Row, P.O. Box 878, New York, NY 10038, or

212/349-5340; or 22458 Ventura Blvd., Suite E, Woodland Hills, CA 91364-1581, or 818/992-8990.

Do-it-yourselfers may prefer dealing with *International Home Exchange Service/Intervac,* an organization that compiles three directories a year that list more than 9,000 homes worldwide (most of which are outside the U.S.). A year's subscription costs $44 ($35 plus $9 for postage), and entitles you to one free listing. The apartments and houses in this directory are available for exchange *and* rent, so you don't necessarily have to exchange your own home to take advantage of a good deal. For more information, write to International Home Exchange Service/Intervac, P.O. Box 190070, San Francisco, CA 94119, or call 415/435-3497.

THE TRAVELER WITH DISABILITIES

Travel can be especially trying for persons with disabilities, which is why *Access to the World* (Henry Holt and Company, 1986), by Louise Weiss, is such an important book. It lists hotels with accommodations for the handicapped, covers all aspects of travel by plane, bus, train, ship, car, and RV, and gives hundreds of references to *other* access guides, travel services for the disabled, and travel tips. *Access to the World* is available from The Complete Traveller Bookstore, listed in the "Resources" section at the end of this chapter.

Whole Person Tours, an enterprise providing tours for the disabled in Europe and the U.S., also publishes *The Itinerary,* a bimonthly magazine for the disabled traveler. The cost is $10 for one year, or $18 for two, from The Itinerary, P.O. Box 1084, Bayonne, NJ 07002.

PROBLEMS ABROAD

No one plans to fall ill while traveling, but it happens. If you're planning a trip abroad, consider becoming a member of the *International Association for Medical Assistance to Travelers (IAMAT).* Your $10 contribution to this not-for-profit organization confers membership and brings you a roster of English-speaking doctors in hundreds of foreign cities, as well as tips on staying healthy during your trip. For more information, write to IAMAT, 736 Center St., Lewiston, NY 14092.

The State Department "assists Americans in distress abroad," and may be able to provide information about the arrest, welfare, or whereabouts of a traveler through its Overseas Citizens Emergency Center. The State Department issues travel advisories for countries afflicted by civil unrest, natural disasters, or outbreaks of serious illnesses. All of this information, as well as visa requirements for travel to specific countries, may be obtained by calling 202/647-5225.

Planning problems out of your trip is the best way to avoid them. These pamphlets may help: "Your Trip Abroad," "Travel Tips for Senior Citizens," "A Safe Trip Abroad," and "Tips for Americans Residing Abroad." Each booklet costs $1; request them by title from The Superintendent of Documents, U.S. Government Printing Office, Washington, DC 20402.

NEWSLETTERS

If you travel frequently, or would like to be able to afford to, you'll find the following newsletters of interest:

Consumer Reports Travel Letter, produced by Consumers Union, is widely regarded as the best "consumerist" publication of its kind. *CRTL* has conducted in-depth comparisons of accommodations and prices in the U.S. and abroad, scrutinized airline food, investigated travel scams, recommended methods of screening travel agents, and has probed the mare's nest of airline booking systems. Each monthly issue of *CRTL* runs around 12 pages; a year's subscription costs $37 at this writing. See the current *Consumer Reports* for an order form, or write to Consumer Reports Travel Letter, 256 Washington St., Mount Vernon, NY 10553, Attn.: Circulation Dept., for information. (Single copies of back issues are available for $5 each.)

Travel Smart is another newsletter that stays current with travel opportunities of all types, including discount fares and rates. Subscribers are offered special deals on car rentals, cruises, accommodations, and air travel. A year of monthly issues costs $37; for more information, write to Travel Smart, 40 Beechdale Rd., Dobbs Ferry, NY 10522.

RESOURCES

Whether your travels are confined to your armchair, or you actually get up and go, you'll find travel guides a great help in planning your trip. The best-known series are *Fodor's, Fielding's, Frommer's, Baedeker's,* and *Birnbaum's.* These are reliable, general-purpose guide books to whole countries and major cities. The Frommer "$-A-Day" series is especially helpful if you're budgeting the whole trip, but don't overlook the other books. If you're traveling abroad and want an informed guide to culturally and historically significant sites, see the *Blue Guide* series, which is highly recommended. The Zagats have entered the fray stateside with *Zagat's United States Hotel Survey,* a compilation on accommodations nationwide that have been rated by the Zagats' corps of paying guests and diners.

Many of the firms in "Books" sell travel guides and related literature, but specialty bookstores have far better stock and selection, and the staff can usually provide personal assistance in selecting the right book for your needs, even by mail.

The Complete Traveller Bookstore does a brisk mail-order trade through its 48-page catalog, which lists all the major guides, as well as *Insider's Guides*, the *Michelin* green and red guides, *Crown Insider's Guides* (written by expatriate Americans), the fascinating *Lonely Planet* books, which take you to the Cook Islands as well as Canada, and scores of specialty guides that cover everything from Alaskan hideaways to shopping in Seoul. Maps, foreign language tapes, and travel accessories are sold through the catalog as well. Store shoppers can peruse the collection of antiquarian travel books, including some early Baedekers, which are perched at the tops of the bookcases. For a copy of the catalog, send $1 to The Complete Traveller Bookstore, 199 Madison Ave., New York, NY 10016. Please note: This is *not* a discount bookseller.

The Forsyth Travel Library has an extensive selection of popular guides, road maps to cities and countries around the world, Berlitz phrase books, Audio-Forum language tapes, and Thomas Cook surface transit timetables. Through Forsyth, you can order rail passes to Europe and Britain (including "The Britainshrinkers" sightseeing tours), join American Youth Hostels (an application form is provided in Forsyth's brochure), and even subscribe to over a dozen travel publications, including *Consumer Reports Travel Letter.* Voltage converters and plug adapters, money belts, and other travel accessories are also available. Send 50¢ for the current brochure to Forsyth Travel Library, Inc., 9154 W. 57th St., Shawnee Mission, KS 66201-1375. Forsyth does *not* sell at a discount.

TravelBooks bills itself as "the compleat travel bookstore for domestic or international travel literature," and offers publications on adventure travel, trekking, hiking, student opportunities, and hundreds of maps. Write for the free catalog from TravelBooks, 113 Corporation Rd., Hyannis, MA 02601-2204, or call 800-869-3535.

Traveler's Checklist specializes in travel accessories, including money converters, adaptors and plugs, personal-care items, and related goods. Request a catalog from Traveler's Checklist, Cornwall Bridge Rd., Sharon, CT 06069. Please note that Traveler's Checklist does *not* sell at a discount.

SEE ALSO

Ace Leather Products, Inc. • travel clocks, gift items • *LEATHER*

Consumer Thrift Club • discounts on car rentals, air fares, tours, cruises, etc. • *GENERAL*

Grandma's Spice Shop • Melitta coffee travel kit • *FOOD*

The Luggage Center • travel accessories • *LEATHER*

The Reliable Corporation • pocket translators, leather luggage, travel plugs, etc. • *OFFICE*

The Lillian Vernon Corporation • travel accessories • *GENERAL*

THE COMPLETE GUIDE TO BUYING BY MAIL

For U.S. Deliveries

If you don't know UPS from PP, this section will prove helpful in untangling the web of confusion that can ensnare mail-order shoppers. Armed with knowledge and endowed with patience, you'll be prepared to conquer the world of mail-order bargains and emerge victorious—a satisfied customer reaping savings. Read this section before you order a catalog or call for a price quote. It will save you time, and may save you even more money.

If you're ordering from another country, having goods shipped abroad, or sent to an APO or FPO address, please see "Shipments Abroad," page 000–000, for special mail-order tips.

CATALOGS, PRICE QUOTES, AND INFORMATION

CATALOGS

Most mail-order firms publish price lists, leaflets, brochures, or catalogs. These can range in volume and sophistication from photocopied, one-sheet price lists to massive, four-color books. Some firms send just one issue of their catalogs; others add your name to their mailing lists for a number of issues; still others offer their catalogs on a subscription basis, like magazines.

A diminishing number of catalogs are sent free of charge. Most firms now request a fee, usually $1 to $5. Sometimes, instead of a charge, firms will request a business-sized (#10), self-addressed, stamped envelope (SASE). Some firms request *both* a SASE and a nominal fee. If a SASE is requested and you do not send one, do not expect a response.

If you're always running out of stamps, you'll be interested in a valuable service provided by the U.S. Postal Service—stamps and stamped envelopes by mail. These are the ordinary variety you'd get at the post office, not the philatelic line. Ask your postmaster or carrier for PS Form 3227, "Stamps by Mail," or request it from the Consumer Advocate, U.S. Postal Service, Washington, DC 20260. You can also call 800-STAMP-24 and charge your order to your MasterCard or VISA. (There is a $3 handling fee and a $12.50 minimum order requirement on phone orders.) Your stamps are usually delivered within a few days.

"Refundable" Catalogs: Some firms allow you to recoup the cost of the catalog when you order; this is indicated by the word "refundable" following the price of the catalogs listed in this book. Procedures for reimbursement vary: The catalog may come with a coupon tucked or printed inside with instructions to enclose it with your order and *deduct* the amount from the total (the same as *redeeming* a coupon). You may be asked to include the coupon with your order without deducting the amount, and wait for a *refund* check from the firm. Often there is no coupon in the catalog, in which case your best bet is to deduct the amount from the order total *after* adding tax, shipping, and other surcharges, writing an explanation for the deduction on the order form or in a separate letter. Be sure you meet minimum-order requirements when you make your purchase.

Please note that many of the coupons are dated, which means that you must order within a limited time period in order to recoup the fee.

Sending for Catalogs: When you send for a catalog, write a complete letter stating which catalog you want (some firms have several), and *always include your return address, printed clearly, in the letter.* Please refer to WBMC as your source, since it may qualify you for special discounts. Mention all enclosures so they're not overlooked. Keeping a separate mail-order log of dates on which catalog requests and orders are sent, inquiries made, and orders received is an excellent idea if you shop by mail frequently. Just remember that keeping complete records of all mail-order correspondence will prove very important if anything goes wrong.

If the catalog costs $1 or less, you can send a dollar bill or coins taped securely between thick pieces of cardboard. For catalogs costing $1 or more, send a check or money order. *Never* send stamps unless the firm specifies, and don't use a credit card to pay for a catalog or a subscription to a series of catalogs unless the listing states that this is permitted.

Catalogs from Foreign Firms: When sending for a catalog from a foreign firm, use an international money order (IMO) or personal check if the catalog costs $5 or more, and cash or International Reply Coupons (IRCs) if it costs less than that. Money orders can be purchased at a bank or post office. If you send a personal check, it's a good idea to add about $4 to the total. This will cover the currency-conversion charge the firm has to pay to change your dollars to pounds, francs, marks, or rupees. It's a considerate gesture, but not mandatory.

IRCs are certificates that can be exchanged for units of surface postage in foreign countries. They are available at the post office for 65¢ each. Use IRCs when they are requested or when the catalog costs 50¢ or less.

While you can use one of these conventional methods of payment, you can save handling charges if the catalog costs $5 or less by sending cash through the mail. (In fact, several firms have requested it.) Technically it's risky and should be used only when you're dealing with dollars, not change, but there's a foolproof way to conceal the money and enclosures completely, and remain within the half-ounce weight limit of a 45¢ stamp. Get a piece of black flint (illustration) paper from your local art-supply store, or lacquered wrapping paper. Cut the paper into pieces that just fit inside the envelope you're using. Place the money within the folded letter, and the letter and piece of opaque paper inside the envelope. *Voilà!* Complete privacy, even with lightweight stationery. Remember to mention enclosures of cash, coupons, money order, or check in the letter you send with your catalog request.

Receiving Catalogs: Catalog publication schedules vary widely. Some firms publish new price lists weekly, while others bring out massive catalogs every ten years. When firms run out of catalogs, are between printings, or issue catalogs seasonally, there can be a delay of months before you receive your copy. Some firms will notify you by letter or postcard when this occurs. Most will not. Compounding the problem is the fact that every time a firm is mentioned in an article or book such as this, it may receive hundreds or even thousands of catalog requests over the course of a few weeks. Small firms are often swamped with bags of mail, and the fulfillment process is further slowed. If the catalog supply is exhausted, it may take weeks to get a print order filled, labels prepared, and catalogs sent. The delays are troublesome not only for the firm, which may lose sales to other firms whose catalogs arrive quickly, but also for the potential customer who needs an item by a certain date. Unfortunately, many of the delays are also illegal.

Delayed Shipment of Catalogs: According to the FTC Mail Order Rule (also known as the "30-Day Rule"), a firm must ship goods ordered by mail within 30 days after receiving a properly completed order. The Rule doesn't apply to catalogs for which you send absolutely nothing except the request, or to subscriptions to catalogs (except the first issue of the subscription).

Catalog Shipments from WBMC Firms: Please allow six to eight weeks for shipment of any nonfree catalog or literature ordered from a firm listed in this book.

PRICE QUOTES

Some mail-order firms offer their goods on a price-quote basis. They almost invariably sell name-brand goods that can be identified by manufacturer's name, stock or model number, and color or pattern name or code. Cameras, appliances, audio and TV/video components, tableware, furniture, and sporting goods are commonly sold by discounters on a price-quote basis.

A price quote is simply the statement of the cost of that item from that firm. The company may guarantee that price for a limited period of time, or until stock is depleted. Some firms include tax, shipping charges, insurance, and handling in their price quotes, giving you one figure for the final cost. Don't accept such a price quote—make sure each fee or surcharge is itemized separately. The importance of this will become apparent if you have to return the item for a refund, in which case you probably won't be reimbursed for the shipping and handling charges.

Finding the Information: Before writing or calling for a price quote, you'll need to know the manufacturer's name, product code (model or style number or pattern name), and size and color information, if applicable. These data can be found on the factory cartons or tags of goods in stores and in manufacturers' brochures. (Obtain the latter by writing to the customer service department of the manufacturer and requesting a brochure or specification sheet on the product or line.) If you're pricing an item you found in a catalog, remember to look for the manufacturer's data, not the catalog code numbers that are usually listed next to the item price. If you're using a buying guide or magazine as a source for information, be cautioned that the material may be out of date and errors may occur in printing, so verify the information before requesting price quotes.

Price Quotes by Letter: Most of the firms listed in this book will give quotes over the phone, but a letter is usually cheaper, and it gives you a record of the quote. When you write requesting price quotes, include all of the available information about the item or items. Leave blanks next to each item so the person giving the quote can enter the price, shipping cost or estimate, and any related charges. Ask the firm to note how long it will honor the given prices, and request the signature of the store manager, and his or her name printed next to it, on the letter. *Request prices on no more than three items at a time.* (Retailers tell us that they relegate photocopied sheets requesting 20 price quotes to the wastebasket, since the sender appears to be doing a survey rather than serious shopping.) And you *must* include a SASE with your request. If you don't, do not expect a response.

Price Quotes by Phone: If you phone for a price quote, be sure to have all of the information in front of you when you call. *Don't* make collect calls, and don't use the "800" number for price quotes unless the listing states specifically that inquiries are permitted on those lines. To avoid problems later, ask to speak to the manager. Take down his or her complete name and tell the person that you're making a note of all the information given. Treat phone calls as seriously as letters; the notes you take may be the only tangible record you will have.

NOTE: If you make a purchase over the phone using a credit card, certain aspects of the transaction are not currently protected by the laws that regulate mail orders. For more information, see "The FTC Mail Order Rule," on page 000–000.

REQUESTING INFORMATION

A small percentage of mail-order firms offer services or custom-made products and conduct business on an *inquiry* basis. When you contact such a firm, your request for information must be specific. First, read the listing carefully. Send an article to be repaired, restored, or matched only when the listing so indicates—otherwise, write to the firm with a description of the article you're looking for or want matched (include rubbings, drawings, or photographs if appropriate) or describe the article and its condition, and what repairs, alterations, or service you need. When sending any item, include a cover letter describing what you want done (even if you've already stated this in a previous letter—correspondence is often mislaid). Insure the package, and send return postage and insurance by separate cover in case the firm can't do the work or you decide against having it done. (In such an event, be sure that your cover letter includes a request to the firm to insure the item, and before sending valuables or antiques check with your home-insurance carrier to see whether loss or damage to the item will be covered under your policy.) Allow at least a month for the firm to evaluate the job and send you an estimate—many specialty shops are run by just one or two people and tend to have backlogs.

COMPLAINTS

COMPLAINT PROCEDURES

You make a formal complaint to a firm after you've informed it of a problem and asked for resolution, following procedures outlined in the catalog, warranty, or this guide. Generally, you give the firm one last chance to remedy the situation, and then you ask for help from outside agencies. If, however, your problem concerns nondelivery of or dissatisfaction with goods and you paid with a credit card, you may be able to withhold payment under the Fair Credit Billing Act. See "The Federal Trade Commission," following, for more information.

The Complaint Letter: State your complaint clearly and concisely with a history of the problem and all the appropriate documentation: photocopies of previous letters, proof of payment, the warranty, repair receipts, etc. Do not send original documents—send photocopies and keep the originals in your file. Make sure your letter includes your name and address, the order or product number or code and descriptive information about the product, and the method of payment you used. Type or print the letter, and *do not* use abusive language or profanity. Tell the firm exactly what you want done. Give a deadline of 30 days for a reply or resolution of the problem, and state that if you don't receive a response by that time, you'll report the firm to the Better Business Bureau, Direct Marketing Association, Federal Trade Commission, or other appropriate agency. (See "Obtaining Help," following, for information on whom to contact.)

If the firm doesn't acknowledge the request or you're not satisfied by the response, take action.

OBTAINING HELP

There are several agencies and organizations that can help you with different types of problems. Some undertake investigations on a case-by-case basis, while others compile files on firms and act when the volume of complaints reaches a certain level.

When you seek help, provide a copy of your final complaint letter to the firm, as well as the documentation described in the preceding section, "Complaint Procedures."

Consumer Action Panels (CAPs): CAPs are third-party dispute resolution programs established by the industries they represent. They investigate consumer complaints, provide service information to consumers, and give their members suggestions on improving service to consumers.

MACAP helps with problems concerning major appliances. Write to Major Appliance Consumer Action Panel, 20 N. Wacker Dr., Chicago, IL 60606, or call 800-621-0477 for information.

Better Business Bureaus (BBBs): Better Business Bureaus are self-regulatory agencies, funded by businesses and professional firms, that monitor advertising and selling practices, maintain files on firms, help resolve consumer complaints, and disseminate service information to consumers. BBBs also perform the vital service of responding to inquiries about a firm's selling history, although they can't make recommendations. Most BBBs have mediation and arbitration programs, and are empowered to make awards (binding arbitration).

Whether you want to check a firm's record before ordering or file a complaint, you must contact the BBB nearest the *company,* not the office in your area. You can obtain a directory of BBB offices by requesting a copy from the Council of Better Business Bureaus, Inc., 1515 Wilson Blvd., Arlington, VA 22209. (Include a SASE with the request.) Write to the appropriate office, and ask for a "consumer complaint" or "consumer inquiry" form, depending on your purpose.

Direct Marketing Association (DMA): The DMA is the largest and oldest trade organization of direct marketers and mail-order companies in existence. Over half of its members are non-U.S. firms; this gives it some clout in dealing with problematical foreign orders placed with member firms.

The DMA's *Mail Order Action Line (MOAL),* established almost 20 years ago, helps resolve nondelivery problems with any direct-marketing firm. Upon receiving your *written* complaint, the DMA contacts the firm, attempts to resolve the problem, notifies you that it's involved, and asks you to allow 30 days for the firm to solve or act on the problem. To get help, send a copy of your complaint letter and documentation to Mail Order Action Line, DMA, 6 E. 43rd St., New York, NY 10017.

Consumers may also have their names added to or removed from mailing lists through the DMA's Mail Preference Service. Write to the DMA at the above address and ask for an "MPS" form.

The Federal Trade Commission (FTC): The FTC is a law-enforcement agency that protects the public against anticompetitive, unfair, and deceptive business practices. While it does not act upon individual complaints, it does use your complaint letters to build files on firms. When the volume or nature of problems indicates an investigation is warranted, the FTC will act.

Several levels of action are possible, including court injunctions and fines of up to $10,000 for each day the violation is occurring. Do report deviations from FTC regulations; your letter may be the one that prompts an investigation.

The Fair Credit Billing Act (FCBA), passed in 1975 under the FTC's Consumer Credit Protection Act, offers mail-order shoppers who use credit cards as payment some real leverage if they have a problem with nondelivery. The Act established a settlement procedure for *billing errors* that include, among other discrepancies, charges for goods or services not accepted or not delivered as agreed. The procedure works as follows:

- You must write to the creditor (phoning will not trigger FCBA protection) at the "billing error" address given on the bill.
- The letter must include your name and account number, the dollar amount of the error, and a statement of why you believe the error exists.
- The letter must be received by the creditor within 60 days after the first bill with the error was mailed to you. The FTC recommends sending it via certified mail, return receipt requested.
- The creditor has to acknowledge your letter, in writing, within 30 days of receipt, unless the problem is resolved within that time.
- You do not have to pay the disputed amount, the related portion of the minimum payment, or its finance charges while it's being disputed.
- If an error is found, the creditor must write to you, explaining the corrections—the amount must be credited to your account, late fees and finance charges removed. If the creditor finds that you owe part of the amount, it must be explained in writing.
- If the creditor finds that the bill is correct, the reasons must be explained in writing and the amount owed stated. You will be liable for finance charges accrued during the dispute and missed minimum payments.
- You may continue to dispute at this point, but only if your state's laws give you the right to take action against the *seller* rather than the creditor. Write to the creditor within ten days of receiving the justification of the charge and state that you still refuse to pay the disputed amount. If you continue to challenge, contact your local consumer protection agency, since the creditor can begin collection proceedings against you and the agency may be able to recommend other means of handling the problem that don't jeopardize your credit rating.

Disputes over the *quality* of goods or services are covered under the FCBA if state law permits you to withhold payment from a *seller*. This applies to credit-card purchases over $50 that are made in your home state or within 100 miles of your mailing address. (The limits do not apply if the seller is also the card issuer, as is often the case with department stores.) Contact your local consumer protection agency for advice before taking action.

The United States Postal Service (USPS): The USPS takes action on complaints and resolves about 85% of the problems. This may be because, under provisions of the U.S. Code, it can go to court, get a restraining order, and withhold mail delivery to a company. (This is a very serious action and is never undertaken simply at a private citizen's request.) More than one experienced consumer has told us that the USPS acts more swiftly, with better results, than do any of the other agencies we've cited here. You can send a copy of your final complaint letter and documentation to the Chief Postal Inspector, U.S. Postal Service, Washington, DC 20260—but readers have told us that writing directly to the Postmaster of the post office *nearest the firm* is what does the trick.

Form 2150, *Notice for Prohibitory Order Against Sender of Pandering Advertisement in the Mail,* should put a stop to the mailing of anything you consider erotic or sexually provocative. You can fill out this form at your local post office.

Bankruptcy Courts: Bankruptcy courts may offer information, if no actual compensation, on errant orders and refunds. If you've written to the company and received no response and its phones have been disconnected, you may want to contact the U.S. Bankruptcy Court nearest the firm. State the nature of your complaint and ask whether the company has filed for reorganization under Chapter 11. If it has filed, request the case number and information on filing a claim. Chapter 11 protects a business against the claims of its creditors; all you can do is file and hope. As a customer, your claim comes after those of the firm's suppliers, utilities, banks, etc. The "take a ticket" approach is no guarantee that you'll get anything back, but if it's your only shot, take the trouble to file.

COMPLAINTS ABOUT FOREIGN FIRMS

For general information on handling complaints about foreign firms, see "Delayed Shipments from Foreign Firms," page 567.

The DMA may be able to undertake an investigation on your behalf. See page 544 for more information on the organization and its address.

The Council of Better Business Bureaus has affiliates in Canada, Mexico, Israel, and Venezuela. If the firm is located in any of those countries, write to the Council for the address of the office nearest the company, and contact that office with the complaint. See page 544 for more information and the Council's address.

The foreign trade council representing the firm's country may be able to provide information that could prove helpful. Contact the council and briefly describe your problem. Ask whether the organization can supply the name of a regulatory agency or trade organization in that country that might be of help. The councils have offices in New York City, and directory assistance can provide you with their phone numbers. You may also contact us (see the following) for their names, numbers, and addresses.

We'll try to help you to resolve problems with all of the firms, domestic and foreign, listed in this book. See "Feedback," page 587, for more information and our mailing address.

SHIPMENTS ABROAD

Shipments to and from Canada: The U.S.–Canada Free Trade Agreement. The Free Trade Agreement (FTA) is a pact between the U.S. and Canada intended to promote trade and expand and enhance markets in both countries by removing some existing restrictions. The linchpin of the FTA is the mutual elimination of tariffs, or duties, by 1998. Duties are being reduced in three ways: Some were eliminated when the FTA went into effect January 1, 1989; others are being reduced 20% a year over five years; and all others are being phased out over ten years. This tripartite formula permits industries that are ready for the increased competition to benefit from the new policy immediately, while protecting others that might be destabilized by a rapid abatement of the tariffs.

The FTA affects an enormous range of raw materials and consumer goods—from fish and computers to ferrous alloys and plywood—but only those goods that are *produced* in the U.S. or Canada are entitled to free-trade treatment. (Tariffs on products of third countries are unaffected by the FTA, which is intended to benefit the U.S.–Canadian market.) The pact permits restrictions and quotas on products of certain industries and includes provisions dealing with "dumping" of goods at below-market prices and special considerations for government-subsidized products of both countries.

Despite the scope of the Free Trade Agreement, it's worth noting that *prior* to its enactment, more than 75% of the goods traded between the U.S. and Canada were exempted from tariffs. It may take a number of years for the effects of economies of scale and specialization to be discerned in the marketplace. And since only domestically produced goods are covered and phase-in periods may apply, mail-order shoppers must consult the nearest office of U.S. Customs or the Customs and Excise Office in Canada for rates and current information before buying. In other words, for the time being, it's business as usual for consumers.

SHIPMENTS TO APO/FPO ADDRESSES

Many of the firms listed in this book will send goods to APO and FPO addresses. Finding out which is easy: Look for the *stars and stripes* next to the maple leaf on the line with the dollar signs and phone and envelope symbols. (For more on the meanings of those symbols, turn to "The Listing Code," page viii.)

Mail-order firms generally ship orders via the USPS's PAL (parcel airlift) to the military mail dispatch center, where they are shipped overseas via SAM (space available mail). The size restrictions are 60″ in combined girth and length, and 30 pounds in weight. Firms sometimes charge additional handling fees for shipping to APO/FPO addresses, so read the catalog carefully and write for a shipping estimate *before* ordering if instructions are not clear. Please note that neither UPS nor Federal Express makes APO/FPO deliveries, and that the USPS does not offer C.O.D. service to such addresses.

SHIPMENTS WORLDWIDE

Many of the firms that ship to Canada and U.S. military personnel also ship orders worldwide. (This is noted in the "Special Factors" section at the end of each listing, if applicable.) If you're planning to have goods delivered to Japan, Israel, Europe, or any other non-U.S. or Canadian address, see the catalog (if available) for details on the firm's shipping policy. If it's not clear, or the firm sells on a price-quote basis, *write* to the company before sending any funds and request a shipping quote. Since most of the staff at firms listed in this book are not familiar with import restrictions and duty rates in other countries, please check these *before* placing your order to avoid unpleasant surprises. Most firms will request payment in U.S. funds; this may be most expeditiously handled by having your purchase charged to your credit card, but check with your issuing bank for rates and charges which may apply to converting funds before you order. And please note that the foregoing sections of "The Complete Guide to Buying by Mail," pages 538–587, are written for readers who are having goods delivered to U.S. addresses, and will not apply in all parts to non-U.S. deliveries.

HOW TO ORDER

Before you pick up the phone or pen to order, compare costs to make sure you're really getting the best deal.

COST COMPARISONS

Your chief consideration is the *delivered* price of the product. Gather all your price quotes and/or catalogs and compute this price. Then compare the figure to the *delivered* cost of the item if purchased from a local supplier. To be fair, you should place a monetary value on the time it takes to order versus the time involved in going to a retailer, purchasing the item, and bringing it home or having it sent to you. You must also consider, if applicable, such costs as mileage if you must drive to the local source, sales and use tax, shipping and trucking, installation, parking costs, etc. If you're purchasing a gift, you may also have to compare the costs of having the catalog house wrap and send the item to the costs of your own time, materials, and mailing. Finally, you must weigh the intangibles—the various return policies, the prospect of waiting for a mail delivery versus getting the item immediately, the guarantees offered by the retailer and mail-order firm, and so forth. After contemplating costs and variables, you'll have arrived at the bottom line and will be ready to order, if that's your choice.

ORDERING

Locate the order blank in the catalog and use it. If supplied, use the self-sticking address label on the catalog. If there's no order blank, use one from another catalog as a guide. Transcribe all pertinent information—code numbers, name of item, number of items ordered, units, prices, tax, shipping and handling charges—onto a separate piece of paper. Include your name, address, phone number, the firm's name and address, and appropriate information if you're having the order sent to another address. Observe minimum-order requirements. If the catalog is more than six months old, get a new edition and order from that (unless the listing indicates the catalog is published once a year)—prices can change without notice. Some firms can guarantee all prices in a catalog to a certain date, but the most all companies can do is to guarantee a price as of the order date. You may find yourself billed for the difference between the old price and the new if you order from an out-of-date catalog. Make a copy of the order, and file it with the catalog.

Second Choices and Substitutions: When the firm advises it and you're willing to accept them, give *second choices*. These usually refer to differences in color, not product. If you will accept *substitutions,* which may be different products that the firm considers comparable to what you ordered, you must give permission in writing on the order form. Making substitutions without written authorization from the buyer is unlawful. If you don't want to accept second choices in color and want to be sure the firm knows this, write "NO SECOND CHOICES OR SUBSTITUTIONS ACCEPTED" in red on the order form.

WBMC Reader Offers: If you wish to take advantage of a WBMC reader discount, rebate, bonus, or other special, be sure to comply with the conditions stated in the listing. Unless otherwise indicated, calculate discounts on the total cost of the *goods only,* not from the total that includes shipping, handling, insurance, and tax.

PHONE ORDERS

Many of the firms listed in this book take orders over the phone and have toll-free "800" numbers that enable you to order without incurring costs. Understanding what these numbers are and how they work is part of becoming an informed shopper.

WATS Lines: The phone numbers with "800" area codes are WATS (Wide Area Telecommunication Service) lines. When you call a firm on its 800 line, no charge is made to your phone bill, even though the call *originated* from your phone. Instead, the cost of the call is billed (in terms of prepriced minutes) to the 800 number, where the call *terminates*.

A firm wishing to offer WATS to its customers chooses the calling areas it wants to serve from seven bands that include the contiguous 48 states, Alaska, Hawaii, Puerto Rico, and the Virgin Islands. (There are three calling areas serving Canada as well.) Sometimes WATS includes all of the bands, but exempts from service the state in which the 800 number terminates. In order to offer in-state customers a toll-free order or response mechanism, a firm may have a separate 800 number to be used by callers in that state exclusively. It may also have a branch office in another state handle those calls, or ask in-state customers to use its toll lines. Some firms electing to use the last method accept collect calls from in-state callers on those non-800 lines as a compromise. Please note that there is no way to determine whether an 800 number serves your area—or country—other than attempting to place a call on it.

Another option available to the mail-order firm is the vendor. While operating "in-house" or "proprietary" lines works well for some companieers choose to have a specialist (also known as a "telemarketer") handle the orders, inquiries, and complaints. Telemarketers offer companies new to phone selling an opportunity to test the power of an 800 number without investing in line installation and operator training. Although telemarketing operators may not themselves be able to give you information on the products, they should be able to give you the order total, including the shipping and tax. A good telemarketing service will have a statement of the firm's return policy in its data bank. Do not order from a firm whose operator or service representative cannot describe the terms of the policy. And do not order when you're told that returns are not accepted under any circumstances, unless you're willing to take the gamble.

ORDERING

Before picking up the phone to place your order, follow this procedure:

1. Have your credit card ready.
2. Make sure the card is accepted by the firm, has not expired, and has a credit line sufficient for the purchase.
3. Have the delivery name, address, and ZIP code available.
4. Have the ordering information—catalog code numbers, units, colors, sizes, etc.—written down in front of you (using the order form is the easiest way to record the data).
5. Have the catalog from which you're ordering at hand—the operator may ask for encoded information on the address label.

When you place the call, ask the operator these questions:

1. What is your name or operator number? (Operators are not a subspecies; they do have last names, and you should make sure they tell you theirs. If the operator is reluctant to do so, ask why—and reconsider purchasing from the firm if there is hesitation on this point.)
2. Are any of the items out of stock?
3. When will the order be shipped?
4. Will any of the items be shipped separately?
5. What is the total, including shipping and tax, that will be charged to my account?
6. What are the terms of the return policy?
7. Every operator should answer questions 1, 5, and 6. Only those operators with stock information will be able to answer question 2, and, in all likelihood, only in-house operators can answer 3 and 4.

Please note that many operators are instructed to ask for your home phone number, and sometimes your office number as well. This is done for your protection, so they can verify that you are the person placing the order rather than a criminal who's obtained your card information from a carbon slip or stolen card. Since the firm may have to absorb the losses arising from fraud, it may choose to refuse an order from you if you won't divulge your phone number, especially if you're buying certain types of goods and your order total is high.

While you're on the phone, the operator may try to sell you more goods. This may be an "upsell," in which you're induced to buy tennis balls if you've purchased a racquet, a sweater if you've bought pants, etc. Beware of this technique if you're trying to stick to a budget. On the other hand, you may be offered a real bargain on goods the firm is clearing out: When a company has too few of an item to run it in a catalog, it's sometimes put "on sale" to phone customers. When this occurs, the company's loss is your gain. Just make sure you really want the item—a bargain you'll never use is no bargain at all.

Once the transaction is completed and you've noted the operator's name or number, checked off the items you ordered, struck off those you didn't, entered the billing amount, and noted the time and date of the call, put this record in your file. It may prove valuable later, if you have problems with your order. And save the catalog.

The Pros and Cons of Phone Orders: Phone orders have certain advantages over mail orders. They're usually processed more quickly and, when the phone operator has stock information, you can know immediately whether or not an item is available. There are disadvantages, however, which relate to regulations governing shipment of goods. For more information, see "The FTC Mail Order Rule" on page 563.

ORDERING FROM FOREIGN FIRMS

Despite the fact that the world was supposed to be switching to the metric scale, many of the catalogs from Europe and elsewhere use the U.S. system—inches and pounds—in measurements. Converting metric measurements to U.S. equivalents is easy, though. Use the chart on page 586.

There are fundamental and confusing differences in sizing systems, color descriptions, and generic terms in different countries. Sizes fall into three categories: U.S., British, and Continental. The sizing chart on page 586 can be used as a general guide to size equivalents. Always measure yourself before ordering clothing, and list the measurements on the order form if you're unsure of the proper size.

Color descriptions and terms can leave you with more questions than answers. Is "emerald" a deep or pale shade of green? Will the "Provençal pink" speak of shy blushes or apoplexy? Color charts can resolve these questions, but you must allow for variations between photographic reproductions and the product itself. When the descriptive terms in a noncolor catalog leave you in doubt as to the shade, write to the firm and ask for samples *before* you order. Never try to match the color of an item you already have without a sample of the actual material you intend to order (and even then, allow for subtle differences from one dye lot to another). These caveats apply to all orders, domestic and foreign.

There are some words used in Great Britain that have different meanings in the U.S. For example, the trunk of a car is called the "boot" in England; the hood is the "bonnet." A "jumper" is not a sleeveless dress worn over a blouse, it's a pullover sweater. Woven "rugs" are usually blankets sized to cover the top of a bed; a "torch" is a flashlight; a "spanner" is a wrench; a "beaker" is often a large cup, rather than a lab flask; a "cot" is a baby's crib. Note these differences, and write to the firm before ordering if you have questions about a term.

The majority of foreign firms listed in this book state prices in U.S. dollars. If they do not, you'll have to convert the firm's currency to dollars when you order. First, compute the total, including shipping, insurance, and other charges (but do not include duty). Next, convert this figure to dollars using the rate of exchange prevailing on the day you send the order. You can get the rate from most banks, business newspapers, or your nearest American Express office. You can get the most recent issue of the table by requesting the "Currency Guide" from Deak International, 41 E. 42nd St., New York, NY 10017.

Before you order, determine the rate of duty you'll be charged when the goods arrive and any shipping or transportation costs not included in your order total. See these sections for more information: "Paying for Goods from Foreign Firms," page 559; "Shipments from Foreign Countries," page 581; "Duty," page 584; and "Deliveries from Foreign Firms," page 566.

PAYMENT

There are many ways to pay for your order; at times the differences among them can be confusing. This section represents an effort to define terms, explain procedures, and correct some common misconceptions. For the purposes of this book, we've developed two classifications for payment methods: "prepaid" and "charge, credit, and debit cards." We've made this distinction based on the rules that apply to refunds under the FTC Mail Order Rule, but we stress that some methods have characteristics of both categories.

Prepaid Orders: These payment methods are sometimes defined as "cash" by catalog companies, since the firm receives dollars instead of extending credit on the basis of a promise to pay.

Personal checks, accepted by most firms, are inexpensive and can be sent without a visit to the bank or post office. Since some firms wait until your check has cleared before sending your order, shipment may be delayed by as much as two weeks when you pay by check. (The increasing implementation of electronic transmittal systems and centralized banking should reduce this lag in the future, but many firms will still hold the order until they know the check has cleared.) Paying by check has the added advantage of providing you with a receipt (the canceled check), which is returned to you with your monthly statement.

Certified checks are guaranteed personal checks. You bring your check to the bank on which it's drawn, and pay a fee of about $5 to $9. The bank marks the check "certified" and freezes that sum in your account. Every firm that accepts personal checks will accept a certified check, and the guarantee of funds should preclude the delay for clearance. The canceled certified check is returned with the other canceled checks in your statement. Firms that request certified checks for payment will usually accept a *bank check,* a *teller's check,* or a *cashier's check* instead.

Bank money orders can be obtained at any bank for a fee generally ranging from $1 to $3. You ask the teller for an order in the desired amount and fill in the firm's name and your name and address. If the order isn't dated mechanically, insert the date. Most come with a carbon receipt; some have stubs that should be filled in on the spot before you forget the information.

Bank money orders are generally treated as certified checks (i.e., no waiting for clearance). If necessary, you can have the order traced, payment stopped, and a refund issued. You'll find this vital if your order is lost in the mail, since there's always a chance it's been intercepted and an unauthorized party attempts to cash it.

Postal money orders, sold at the post office, are available in amounts up to $700 and cost from 75¢ to $1. They're self-receipting and dated, and can be replaced if the order is lost or stolen. Copies of the cashed money order can be obtained through the post office for up to two years after it's paid. This can prove quite helpful in settling disputes with firms that claim nonreceipt of payment. And, like stamped envelopes and stamps, money orders can be bought through postal carriers by customers on rural routes or those with limited access to the post office.

Bank international money orders, issued by banks, are used to pay foreign firms. You complete a form at the bank and, if the catalog prices are listed in foreign currency, the bank computes the amount in dollars based on the day's exchange rate. These orders cost a few dollars or more, and they are receipted. Like domestic money orders, you send them to the firm yourself with the order. They are usually treated as immediate payment.

Postal international money orders are used to pay foreign firms; their cost varies, depending on the amount of the order. (For example, the service charge on a $200 postal IMO sent to Britain is $3 at this writing.) The ceilings on amounts to different nations vary from $200 to $500, and postal IMOs cannot be sent to every country. Amounts of $400 or more must be registered. When you buy a postal IMO, you fill out a form stating your name and address and the name and address of the firm, and you pay the order amount and surcharge. The post office forwards the data to the International Exchange Office in St. Louis, Missouri, which sends a receipt to you and forwards the money order, in native currency, directly to the firm (or to the post office nearest it, which sends it on). We're told the entire procedure takes a few weeks; if you use postal IMOs you must allow for this delay.

Bank drafts, or transfer checks, are the closest you can come to sending cash to a foreign firm through the mail. You pay the order amount, a mailing fee, and a service charge to your bank, then send one copy of the draft form to the firm and another to the firm's bank. The name of the bank may be given in the catalog; if not, your teller will give you the name and address of one in the area. Upon receipt of the form, the firm takes it to the bank, matches it to the other copy, and collects the funds. It will take five to ten days for the forms to reach the foreign country, provided you send them by airmail. Most banks charge $5 and up for bank drafts, depending on the amount of the check. All foreign firms accept them.

Credit, Charge, and Debit Cards: Those wafers of plastic in your wallet have been important factors in the mail-order boom, and the pairing of WATS lines and credit cards has proven an irresistible combination for millions of consumers, creating phenomenal growth in the phone-order field.

Using plastic to pay for an order is simplicity itself—you make sure the firm accepts the card you're using, make out the order form, and provide your account number, card expiration date, phone number, and signature in the blanks. When you're ordering from a catalog without a form, supply the same data on the paper where you've written the item names, code numbers, prices, units, etc. Using the card is especially practical when shipping costs are omitted or difficult to calculate—they'll be added to the order total and will appear on your itemized statement, and the order won't be held up as it might be if you paid by check or with a money order. Always check the minimum-order requirements before ordering when using a card, since they're usually higher than those imposed on prepaid orders.

If you're low on cash but determined to order from a firm that doesn't accept cards, you can have Western Union send the company a money order and charge it to your MasterCard or VISA account. The surcharge is high—$14 to $37, and higher if you call in the order instead of placing it in person at a Western Union office. But it can be a worthwhile expense if you might otherwise miss out on the buy of a lifetime.

The fact that there are differences in payment structure, membership fees, and services has led some to believe that there are two categories of cards, "charge" and "credit." The distinction is based on the notion that one type of card permits you to borrow money and the other doesn't. In truth, you can borrow money—in the form of cold cash, traveler's checks, or money orders—on almost every card, provided you have the proper credit line and fulfill the conditions set by the card issuer. And, although some card firms request payment in full each month, they usually offer programs that permit you to spread payments over several billing periods on specific types of payments. These payments are assessed finance charges, further blurring the distinctions between the "charge" and "credit" cards.

"Debit" cards, however, are another category altogether; strictly speaking, they should be listed in the "prepaid" section. Debit cards *look* like regular credit cards, but when the issuing bank receives the invoices for purchases, it deducts those amounts from your depository account—checking, savings, or money management—instead of *charging* your account and billing you. As electronic transmittal networks develop and replace the paper system, the debiting process will occur in nanoseconds at the point of authorization, and the debit card will become electronic cash. At this writing, the problem of applying the existing terms of the FTC Mail Order Rule to a means of payment that appears to be a credit card but acts like a check is being discussed. It's important to know that the FTC views debit-card payments as cash payments. Since the card firms foresee extensive growth in their debit-card divisions, we hope that the FTC will be able to define its regulations further to include provisos for debit cards, or to promulgate new rules. Until then, we recommend that if you're using a debit card to pay for an order you write on the order form, under the account number: "THIS IS A DEBIT ACCOUNT. THIS PAYMENT MUST BE TREATED AS CASH." See the discussion of the FTC Mail Order Rule for more information on the debit-card issue.

The card companies, banks, and financial institutions that issue cards consider your past credit history, your current salary, and the length of time you've been at your current job when reviewing your application for a card. Minimums are raised when the interest rate climbs, but at this writing, a salary of about $20,000 and two years' employment with the same firm should net you a MasterCard or VISA account, provided you're credit-worthy in other respects. Getting an American Express, Diners Club, or debit card usually requires a higher salary and an excellent credit rating, and the issuers of "gold" accounts that offer larger credit lines and special programs geared for business and travel use usually look for an income of at least $40,000 and an excellent credit history.

Since there are about 2,000 card issuers and the market is considered saturated, the consumer is being wooed: yearly fees and annual percentage (interest) rates, or APRs, are being pared, and the cards are being sweetened with such benefits as extended warranties on products purchased with that card, tie-ins with frequent-flyer programs that earn the customer bonus miles for *all* purchases made on that card, personal and auto insurance while traveling "on" that card, discounts on lodging, and other goodies. If you need help comparing cards, Bankcard Holders of America, a not-for-profit consumer advocacy organization, may be able to help. This group publishes a list of banks with low APRs, and its bimonthly newsletters have useful information and updates on pending legislation that will affect bank card holders. For a copy of the publications list and information on membership ($18 per year), write to Bankcard Holders of America, 460 Spring Park Place, Suite 1000, Herndon, VA 22070.

MasterCard had 87 million cards in circulation in the U.S. and Canada in 1987, and over 30 million in other countries. MasterCards are issued by financial institutions—most large banks offer the card. If you get your MasterCard through your bank, you'll probably enjoy the convenience of one-stop banking—deposits, balance information, payments—on all of your accounts through automated teller machines. But consider shopping around. Some states have lower usury ceilings than others, which is why interest rates on these accounts can range from about 14% to 21% per annum. And fees for the cards themselves vary, although most banks charge $16 to $20 a year ($36 to $60 for gold cards). You don't have to be a resident of another state to get a card from a bank there, so if you're in a high-interest area, you'd be wise to check rates elsewhere before you apply at your home bank.

VISA, with about 120 million cards in circulation in the U.S. and Canada, is similar to MasterCard in its structure and services. You can apply for a VISA card at any issuing bank. The advice about shopping for a low annual percentage rate applies to VISA as well as MasterCard. The annual fee averages about $20, or $40 for the gold card.

American Express has about 22 million cards in circulation and issues them directly to consumers. Unlike MasterCard and VISA, this account must be paid in full when it's billed. The American Express Company does offer special services, such as its "Sign and Travel" program, that enable you to pay off travel and entertainment expenses over several billing periods. Finance charges are imposed on unpaid balances. The fee is $55 for the green card ($65 for the gold), and there's a $20 charge for each additional card issued on the same account.

Diners Club has just under 5 million cards in circulation worldwide. It's similar to American Express in its programs and billing structure, and in the fact that it issues cards directly to consumers. Diners Club International is part of Citicorp, whose aggressive marketing programs should make the Diners Club card serious competition for American Express, since they're both geared for "T&E" (travel and entertainment). Like American Express, Diners Club charges a yearly membership fee that's higher than Master-Card and VISA—$55 at this writing—and additional cards on the same account cost $20 each.

Carte Blanche, with over one million cards in use, is also owned by Citicorp. It's a T&E card that's accepted by most establishments that honor Diners Club, and the annual fee is $40 (additional cards cost $20 each).

CHOICE, a six-year-old entry in the credit-card market, is owned by Citibank (Maryland) N.A. The card is issued by that institution and other banks. CHOICE was introduced with some attractive features: no annual fee, a rebate of 0.5% of a customer's total annual billings if these exceed $600, and annual percentage rates comparable to those of other cards. The billing structure is similar to that of MasterCard or VISA, and cash advances and savings programs are part of its package of services. There is now an annual fee ($20), and the rebate has disappeared, but the APR is acceptable (16.8%; 13.8% on unpaid balances over $1,000).

Discover was launched by Sears (the Sears Financial Network) in 1985 with millions of dollars in promotion, advertising it as the card that "pays you back" every time you use it. Card holders are paid dividends each year at rates based on their total purchases: 0.25% for amounts up to $1,000, 0.5% for totals from $1,000 to $2,000, 0.75% from $2,000 to $3,000, and 1% for higher amounts. Sears has held to the no-annual-fee policy to date, and the APR ranges from 18% to 19.8%. The dividends can be applied to card balances, Sears gift certificates, or a depository account with one of the Sears financial-services affiliates. Discover began life with an ideal potential customer base—the pool of nearly 30 million SearsCharge card holders—and has flourished. It's widely accepted by retailers, and consumers appreciate the no-fee aspect. Whether it will push MasterCard or VISA down a rung remains to be seen.

Optima, the newest entrant in the field, is the long-awaited "blue" card from the American Express Company. It's a revolving-credit card like MasterCard or VISA, but with important differences: It's been offered only to select American Express card holders who've had good payment records, the APR is just 13.5%, and the annual fee is $15. Unfortunately, you must continue to hold at least one American Express card in addition to Optima, which means you'll be paying $70 in yearly fees *before* you pay a dollar in finance charges.

Access is MasterCard's United Kingdom card; see *MasterCard,* page 557, for more information.

Eurocard is a MasterCard affiliate used on the Continent; see *Master-Card,* page 557, for more information.

Paying for Goods from Foreign Firms: The most commonly used methods of paying for goods from foreign firms are personal checks, certified checks, bank drafts, and credit cards. These are described in detail on pages 554–559.

If you use a credit card, be aware that you'll be charged for the currency-conversion expense by the card issuer. When the card firm receives the receipt for your purchase from the store, it converts the foreign currency to dollars at a rate determined daily, and then adds a surcharge of anywhere from 0.25% to 1% to the total. Your statement should tell you the date the conversion was made and the surcharge. Some card firms also state the total in foreign currency that was converted. The methods used by card companies to determine the rate of exchange vary widely and are subject to the regulations existing in each foreign country. When you get your statement, check it carefully. The foreign currency total should be the same as your original order total, unless there was a price increase, short shipment, or shipping costs were higher than originally calculated. Check the *interbank* rate of exchange valid on the day the money was converted or the invoice was processed by the card company (your bank should be able to quote this). If there's a significant discrepancy between the inter-bank rate and the one the card firm used, write to the customer-service department and ask for an explanation.

Be sure to read "Ordering from Foreign Firms," page 552, *before* you order.

RETURN POLICIES

Approaches to returns vary from firm to firm, from "no returns accepted under any circumstances" to "no-questions-asked" policies honored years after the product has been purchased. Most catalog firms guarantee satisfaction and accept returns within 10, 14, or 30 days after you've received the order. Firms selling on a price-quote basis usually accept returns only if the product is defective.

Some goods—personalized or monogrammed, custom-made, surplus, and sale items—are routinely exempted from full return policies. (If a firm has to special order an item for you, it may refuse to accept returns on that item—and may require you to buy a minimum number.) Health regulations usually prohibit returns of intimate apparel and bathing suits, but some companies do accept them. (These items should not be returned to stock.)

Check the firm's return policy before you order. If you're shopping for a product that also carries a manufacturer's warranty, obtain a copy of that *before* you buy.

For more information, see "Returns," page 568.

CANCELING YOUR ORDER

Do you have the right to cancel your order once you've placed it? The answer is no.

When you order goods or services from a firm, whether by phone or mail, you enter into a contract of sale. You don't have the right to call the firm and rescind an order, nor do you have the right to stop payment on a check or money order on the basis of what an FTC staffer described as "buyer's remorse." (This term seems almost poetic in an industry that thrives on ill-considered impulse purchases.) Different states have different laws governing matters of contract, but your second thoughts could give the firm cause to bring legal action against you. This is especially true if the company has undertaken action on an order, in what is termed "constructive acceptance of payment."

If, however, you send an order to a firm on Monday and read on Tuesday that it's commencing bankruptcy proceedings or reorganization, stopping payment might be worth the possible risks. And a firm in such a position is probably too absorbed in its own problems to take action against you for reneging on your obligation. In any case, if you do decide to try to cancel, check the terms of the offer first. Magazine and book subscriptions are often sent on an approval basis, giving you a cancellation option. Goods offered with an unconditional guarantee of satisfaction can be sent back when they arrive. If these terms aren't offered and you're determined to cancel, write to the firm, request permission to cancel, and state your reasons. If you've stopped payment on a check or money order or taken any other action to default on payment, note that as well.

RECEIVING YOUR ORDER

What do you do when your order arrives? What steps do you take if it doesn't? You have certain rights and responsibilities in this respect, and as an informed consumer, it helps to understand both.

ACCEPTING DELIVERIES

When the postal clerk, UPS carrier, or trucker delivers your order, check the carton, bag, or crate before signing for it. If you're having someone else accept the package, instruct that person to do the same. If there is damage to the packaging extensive enough that the contents could be affected, you can refuse to sign for or accept the goods. This is not a procedure we wholly recommend, and the reasons are explained in "Returns," in this section.

If the box, bag, or carton is in good condition, accept it and open it as soon as possible. Unpack the goods carefully, putting aside the packing materials and any inserts until you've examined the contents. Most firms include a copy of your order form or a computerized invoice itemizing the order. If it's a printout or there's no invoice at all, get your file copy of the order you sent or phoned in and check to make sure you've received what you ordered. Remember to check the outside of the box, since some firms insert packing slips in adhesive plastic envelopes that are affixed to the top or side of the carton.

Check your order for the following: damaged goods, short shipment, unauthorized substitutions, wrong sizes, colors, styles, or models; warranty forms if the products carry manufacturers' warranties; missing parts; and instruction sheets if a product requires assembly. Since some firms return clothing modeled for catalog layouts to stock, examine the insides of collars for traces of makeup. Make sure ensembles are complete—that scarves, belts, hats, vests, ties, ascots, and other components have been included. Test electronic goods as soon as possible to make sure they function properly, and *do not* fill out the warranty card until you've tried the product and are satisfied that it is not defective. Try on clothing and shoes to make sure they fit. Check printed, engraved, or monogrammed goods for accuracy. If you decide to return a product, see "Returns" for more information.

If the goods are damaged, contact the seller immediately. Describe the condition of the goods and what you'd like done to correct the problem. If the firm instructs you to file a complaint with the delivery service, request shipping information from the seller (the seller's shipping address, day of shipment, seller's account number, applicable shipment codes, and other relevant data). File the complaint with the delivery service, documenting your claim with photographs, if possible, and send a copy of the complaint to the seller. If you charged the purchase and the card issuer offers an extended warranty program, contact the issuer about the matter. Be persistent and methodical in your pursuit of a remedy, and be prepared to accept some compromise. (We know of a couple who ordered $10,000 in furniture, two pieces of which arrived damaged. They waited months to put their complaints in writing, refused to comply with the seller's request to file a claim with the trucking company, and were not satisfied with the replacement of one piece and the offer of on-site repairs for the other—they wanted *all* of the furniture taken back, despite the fact that several pieces had arrived undamaged and they had used the furniture for over a year. Had they filed claims with the shipper immediately upon receipt and taken the seller's offer to have repairs done locally at the seller's expense, they might have spared themselves much unhappiness and resolved the problem.)

If you receive a short shipment (one or more items you ordered are not included in the package), the firm may have inserted a notice that the product is being shipped separately or an option notice if the product is out of stock. (See "The Option Notice," page 564, for information on the latter.) Some companies do not back order and include a refund check with the order or under separate cover when a product is out of stock or bill your account with the adjusted total if you used a credit card. If you receive a short shipment without an explanatory enclosure, first check the catalog from which you ordered to see whether that item is shipped from the manufacturer or shipped separately by the firm. If there's no mention of special shipping conditions or delays in shipment in the catalog, contact the customer service department of the firm immediately.

Don't let the moment of delivery become the moment you realize that doors are only three feet wide. *Prior* to ordering any large item, measure all of the doorways through which the article must pass, allowing for narrow hallways, stairs, and the like. Some savvy shoppers even construct a carton dummy of the item by taping boxes together, and maneuver that through a dry-run delivery before they place the order. Remember: Measure *before* you buy.

DELAYED SHIPMENTS

The editor of this book once received a letter from a lawyer representing a woman who'd purchased a refrigerator from a firm listed in another book. The customer had engaged the lawyer because, three weeks after phoning the order to the firm, the appliance had not arrived. Did the woman have a case against the company?

Absolutely not, and once you've read this section you should understand why.

The FTC Mail Order Rule: The Federal Trade Commission's "Mail Order Rule," promulgated in 1975, addresses the biggest problems in the mail-order industry: late delivery and nondelivery of goods. Every person buying goods from a U.S. firm should understand the principles of the Rule, know what types of transactions are exempt from its protection, and understand what actions a consumer is obliged to take to ensure protection under the regulations.

Please note: When a state or county has enacted laws similar in purpose to the functions of the FTC Mail Order Rule, the laws affording the consumer more protection take precedence.

General terms of the Rule: The Rule specifies that a firm, or "seller," must ship goods within 30 days of receipt of a *properly completed order,* unless the firm gives another date in its catalog, advertisement, or promotional literature. The operative term here is "ship"—the firm does not have to have *delivered* the goods within 30 days under the terms of the Rule. And it must have received a *properly completed order:* Your check or money order must be good, your credit must be good if you're charging the order, and the firm must have all the information necessary to process the order. The 30-day clock begins ticking when the firm gets your check or money order made out in the proper amount, but stops if it's dishonored. If you're paying with a credit card, it begins when the firm charges your account. (An amendment to the Rule has been proposed under which the clock would begin ticking when data sufficient to process the order—credit card number, expiration date, etc.—are received.)

If your check or money order is insufficient to cover the order total or is dishonored by the bank, if your credit card payment is refused authorization, or if you neglect to include data necessary to the processing of your order (which could include size or color information, your address, etc.), the 30-day clock will not start until the problems are remedied—the firm receives complete payment, payment is honored by the bank, the credit card purchase is authorized, or you supply the missing data.

Again, the 30-day limit applies only when a firm does not ask you to allow more time for shipment. (Most such qualifiers request extra time for *delivery,* which only confuses the issue. One luxury linens catalog requests an allowance of two years for delivery of some of its Madiera tablecloths; this is not only legal but intelligent, since it takes well over a year to have the cloths made by hand, and customers feel they're worth the wait.)

Certain types of goods and purchases are not protected by the Rule. These include: mail-order photo finishing; seeds and growing plants; C.O.D. orders; purchases made under negative-option plans (such as book and record clubs); magazine subscriptions and other "serial deliveries," except for the first issue; and orders placed by phone that are paid by credit card.

Catalogs for which payment or compensation is requested fall under the terms of the Rule. See "Delayed Shipment of Catalogs, " page 540, and "Catalog Shipments from WBMC Firms," page 541, for more information.

The typical phone order is not protected by the Rule. See "The Rule and Phone Orders," following, for more information.

Assuming your order is covered under the Rule, the firm from which you're ordering must follow a specific procedure if it's unable to ship your order within 30 days. You must respond under the terms of the Rule if you want to retain all of your rights. Read on.

The Option Notice: When a firm knows that it will be unable to ship within 30 days of receiving your properly completed order, or by the deadline it's given in its literature, it must send you an option notice. An option notice written in compliance with the Rule will inform you that there is a delay in shipping the item and may include a revised shipping date. If it does and that date is up to 30 days later than the original deadline (either 30 days or a date specified by the firm), it should offer you the option of consenting to the delay or canceling the order and receiving a refund. The option notice must also state that *lack of response* on your part is *implied consent* to the delay. If you decide to cancel the order, the firm must receive the cancellation *before* it ships the order.

If the new shipping deadline is over 30 days after the original date, or the firm can't provide a revised shipping date, the option notice must say so. The notice should also state that your order will be automatically canceled unless the firm receives consent to the delay from you within 30 days of the original shipping date, and unless it's able to ship the order *within* 30 days after the original deadline and has not received an order cancellation from you as of the time of shipping.

The firm is required to send notices by first-class mail and to provide you with a cost-free means of response—a prepaid business-reply envelope or postcard. Accepting collect calls or cancellations over WATS lines is acceptable as long as the operators are trained to take them. If you want to cancel an order, get the response back to the firm as quickly as possible after you receive the option notice. We recommend that you photocopy the card, form, or letter, and send it "return receipt requested" if you want absolute proof of the date of delivery. (Remember, if the firm ships your order the day after it received your cancellation, and you can prove it, you have the right to refuse delivery, have the order returned to the firm at its expense, and claim a prompt refund or credit.)

The renewed option notice: When a firm is unable to meet its revised shipping deadline, it must issue you a renewed option notice in advance of the revised deadline. Unlike the first notice, second and subsequent notices must state that if you don't agree *in writing* to a new shipping date or indefinite delay, the order will be canceled. And the consent to a second delay must be received before the first delay period ends, or the order must be canceled, according to the Rule.

If you consent to an indefinite delay, you retain the right to cancel the order at any time before the goods are shipped. And the firm itself may cancel the order if it's unable to ship the goods within the delay period, and *must* cancel the order under a variety of circumstances.

The Rule and refunds: Under the terms of the Rule, when you or the firm cancel the order, you're entitled to a prompt refund. "Prompt" means that, if your order was prepaid, the firm must send you a refund check or money order by first-class mail within seven working days after the cancellation is made. If you paid with a debit card, inform the firm when you cancel, or when it notifies you that it's canceling the order, that it must treat the payment as if it were cash, a check, or a money order, and reimburse your account within seven working days. If you used a credit card, the Rule states that refunds must be made within one billing cycle. (We assume that these "refunds" are credits to your account, which will void the charge made for the goods.) The firm is *not* permitted to substitute credit vouchers for its own goods instead of making a reimbursement.

The Rule and phone orders: As mentioned previously in "Phone Orders," orders placed by phone and paid by credit card are not protected by the Rule. When the Rule was promulgated 15 years ago, phone orders comprised a much smaller proportion of the direct-mail industry than they do today.

The FTC is aware of consumers' concern and in 1990 entered the hearings phase of the rulemaking process on the Telephone Marketing Amendment, which is the proposed change to the Mail Order Rule that would protect transactions taking place by phone and via such newly developed technologies as interactive cable. The rulemaking process is quite time consuming, but we hope to have new developments to report in our next edition.

Until changes are legislated, remember that, if your state has laws protecting phone orders, those regulations apply to your transactions. If you order goods by phone and charge a deposit or partial payment to your credit card, but finalize the sale (complete payment) by *mailing* a check, money order, or card data to the company, the purchase is protected. (This practice is common in the furniture industry.) But you cannot trigger protection by simply confirming a phone order in writing after you've called it in.

The Rule and the truth: What's the actual rate of compliance with the requirements of the FTC Mail Order Rule? In the industry parlance, the option notice is known as a "delay notice," and that's often what you receive: "The Wonder Duz-All you ordered is temporarily out of stock and will be sent as soon as it's available." How soon? As soon as the patent fight is over? As soon as the Hong Kong firm that makes the gadget rebuilds its factory after that devastating fire? As soon as the boat docks?

The wording on the "Duz-All" notice was lifted from an actual option notice, sent by one of the most prestigious mail-order houses in the country. Another notice, from a respected kitchenware catalog, was dated October 27th and was enclosed with a short shipment. It declared that the missing item was "temporarily out of stock" but was expected to arrive "shortly." The product arrived in mid-January, which is "shortly" only if you're thinking in terms of the following Christmas.

We had seen very few notices with an anticipated delivery date, or cost-free response mechanisms, before asking readers to provide sample notices they'd received. We appreciate the responses, which have shown that a good number of large firms are acting in compliance with the Rule. But our own recent experiences and reader mail tell us that many firms are simply telling customers, "It's on back order," and leaving them to wonder whether they'll get the item, and when. We'd like to know more about your experience with back orders; see "Feedback," page 587, for our address.

See "Complaint Procedures," page 543, for information on dealing with unresolved delivery problems.

DELIVERIES FROM FOREIGN FIRMS

The general guidelines outlined in "Accepting Deliveries," page 561, apply to deliveries from foreign firms. Please note, however, that *most* FTC regulations do not apply to shipments from non-U.S. firms.

The delivery procedure for foreign orders is determined by the shipping method the firm has used. For a complete discussion of carriers, see "Shipments from Foreign Countries," page 581.

You usually pay duty, or Customs charges, at the time you take possession of your order. The amount you pay is based on the value, type, and origin of the goods. See "Duty," page 584, for more information.

Most orders from foreign firms are mailable and are delivered by your postal carrier. Before your goods reach you, they're sent through Customs.

Orders processed with the least delay are those with goods designated as duty-free because they qualify under certain provisions of Customs laws, or those worth under $50 that are marked "unsolicited gift." Some firms mark mail-order packages as gifts to save you money; this is not in keeping with Customs regulations, unless the order originates outside the U.S. Do *not* ask a firm to send your order as an unsolicited gift—evasion of duty is a serious offense.

The clearance procedure on dutiable goods includes entry, inspection, valuation, appraisal, and "liquidation," another term for determination of duty. Provided the necessary permits and entry papers have been filed with U.S. Customs and shipment of the goods violates no regulations, the Customs department will attach an entry form listing a tariff item number, rate of duty, and the amount of duty owed on the goods to the package. It will be sent to the post office and delivered to you by your postal carrier. He or she will collect the amount of duty and a "Customs Clearance and Delivery Fee," currently $3.25, as "postage due." The use of this term annoys some foreign firms, since customers assume that the charge is for insufficient postage and complain to the company. Postal authorities have told us that the handling fee is not charged unless the order is assessed duty. But even if your order has dutiable goods, you may not have to pay any Customs charges—a high proportion of small orders are delivered fee-free.

If your parcel is held at the post office and you don't collect it within 30 days, it will be returned to the firm. Should you disagree with the duty charge, you can challenge it within 90 days of receiving the order by sending the yellow copy of the mail-entry form to the Customs office named on the form, along with a statement explaining your reasons for contesting the charge.

DELAYED SHIPMENTS FROM FOREIGN FIRMS

You can reasonably expect your goods to arrive within six to eight weeks, provided you sent the order by air, are having it shipped by airmail or air freight, didn't order custom-made goods, and paid the correct amount—as long as the country concerned is not at war. If you sent the order via surface mail and/or are having the goods shipped that way, are having any custom work done, or the country is in turmoil, don't hold your breath. We know of one shopkeeper who buys much of his stock from foreign firms. He usually places relatively small orders with many firms and says that, on the average, goods take three to six months to arrive when sent by surface mail. He never orders from a country afflicted by a major strike, since it can affect the entire economy and slow order processing further. In all cases, it is best to send credit card data as payment for the order.

Transactions with foreign firms generally come under the jurisdiction of international law. Before taking any formal action if an order does not arrive, give the firm every possible chance to inform you of the status of the order. Write to the company, including photocopies of your order and proof of payment, and send the letter by registered airmail. Allow at least one month for a response, then try again. If you still haven't heard from the firm and the check you sent hasn't been cashed, put a stop on it. Put a tracer and a stop on any money orders you used. If the check or money order has been cashed, proceed to the post office and fill out an "International Inquiry" form. It will be forwarded to the postal service in the country concerned, which should investigate the matter. Notify the firm of your actions. Where possible, retain copies of all correspondence related to the affair, since you may need them at a later date.

If you paid with a credit card and you have not received your order, follow the querying procedure outlined above. If you do not hear from the company, but find that your credit card has been charged for the order, dispute the charge immediately under the provisions of the Fair Credit Billing Act. You may do this only if you have not received the goods at all and if the bank issuing the credit card is a U.S. bank. See page 545 for a complete discussion of the Act.

For more information on resolving problems with foreign companies, see "Complaints About Foreign Firms," page 546.

RETURNS, GUARANTEES, AND WARRANTIES

Your right to return goods is determined by the policy of the firm, the problem with the order, the conditions under which you made the return, and state and federal laws. See "Return Policies" and "Accepting Deliveries" for general information. Product warranties, whether written or implied, apply to many goods bought by mail. "Guarantees and Warranties" provides a comprehensive discussion of all types of warranties.

RETURNS

Return policies are often extensions of a firm's pledge of satisfaction. The wording of the policy determines how quickly you must return the product after receipt (if there's a time limit), what are acceptable causes for return, and what the firm will do to remedy the problem. A few companies will take anything back, but most exclude custom-made goods, personalized items, special orders, intimate apparel, bathing suits, and hats. Some also exempt sale or reduced goods. The most bare-bones policy usually makes provisions for exchanges when the firm has erred or the product is defective. It's important to read "Implied Warranties" for information on laws concerning product performance and rights you may have that are not stated in the catalog.

Obtaining Authorization: Before returning a product for any reason, check the inserts that may have been packed with the order as well as the catalog for instructions on return procedures. If none is given, write to the firm for return authorization. State the reason you want to return the product, the item price and order number, date delivered, and the action you'd like taken. Depending on the firm's policy, you may request repairs or replacement of the item, an exchange, refund check, credit to your charge account, or scrip for future purchases from the firm. Keep a photocopy or carbon of the letter for your files.

Restocking Fees: Some firms impose a charge on returned goods to offset the labor and incidental costs of returning the item to inventory. Restocking fees are most commonly charged by firms selling furniture, appliances, and electronics.

Sending the Item: Follow the mailing procedure outlined in the catalog, order insert, or authorization notice from the firm. When you send the goods back, include a dated letter with your name and address, the order number, authorization number or name of the person approving the return (if applicable), and a statement of what you'd like done. Depending on the circumstances, you may have to enclose invoices, sales slips, and a check for a restocking fee as well. Keep photocopies of your letter and invoices for your files.

Pack the item in the original box and padding materials if requested, and be sure to insure it for the full value of its contents. Allow the firm at least 30 days to process the return or respond before writing again.

Refunds and Credits: If you want your charge account credited for the return, be sure to provide the relevant data. Not every firm will issue a refund check or credit your account; some will offer replacement or repair of the product, an exchange, or catalog credit only.

Exchanges: If you're exchanging the product for something entirely different, state the catalog code number, size, color, price, unit, etc. of the item you want in the letter you enclose with the return.

Postage Reimbursement: Some firms will permit you to return goods postage-collect, or will reimburse you for the shipping and insurance charges on a return. Most will not. Businesses are not required by federal law to refund the cost, even when you're returning goods as a result of the firm's error. State laws, however, may make provisions for this; check your state and local laws to see whether they do.

GUARANTEES AND WARRANTIES

Although the terms "guarantee" and "warranty" are virtually synonymous, this guide makes a distinction between the two for the purpose of clarity. Here, a "guarantee" is the general pledge of satisfaction or service a firm offers on sales. Guarantees and related matters are discussed in "Return Policies," "Returns," and "Implied Warranties." A "warranty" is, generally, the written policy covering the performance of a particular product. Both guarantees and warranties are free; a paid policy is a service contract.

Warranties are regulated by state and federal law. Understanding policy terms will help you shop for the best product/warranty value; knowing your rights may mean the difference between paying for repairs or a replacement product and having the firm or manufacturer do it.

The Magnuson-Moss Warranty — Federal Trade Commission Improvement Act: Also known as the Warranty Act, this law was enacted in 1975. It regulates warranties that are in print. And note well: A spoken warranty is worth the wind it's written on when it comes to getting service.

The Warranty Act requires that warranties be written in "simple and readily understood language" and that all terms and conditions be stated in the warranty. If the product costs more than $15, a copy of the warranty must be available *before* purchase. In a store, it should be posted on or near the product, or filed in a catalog of warranties kept on the premises with a notice posted concerning its location. Mail-order firms comply with the law by making copies of warranties available upon request. A survey of current catalogs indicates that many are diligent in this respect.

The Warranty Act requires the warrantor to use the term "full" or "limited" in describing the policy. A single product can have several warranties covering different parts, and each can be labeled separately as "full" or "limited." For example, a TV set may have a full one-year policy on the set and a limited 90-day policy on the picture tube. Generally speaking, the conditions stated here apply to warranties on goods costing over $15.

Full warranties provide for repair or replacement of the product at no cost to you, including the removal and reinstallation of the item, if necessary. The warranty may be limited to a certain length of time, and must state the period plainly. Full warranties can't be limited to the original purchaser — the warrantor must honor the policy for the full term even if the item has changed hands. Implied warranties may not be limited in duration by the terms of the full warranty, and in some states may last up to four years.

The item should be repaired within a "reasonable" length of time after you've notified the firm of the problem. If, after a "reasonable" number of attempts to repair, the product is still not functioning properly, you may invoke the "lemon provision." This entitles you to a replacement or refund for the product.

Registering your product with the warrantor under a full warranty is voluntary, and that fact must be stated clearly in the terms. You may return the card supplied with the policy to the firm, but this is at your discretion and not necessary to maintain the protection of the warranty.

Limited warranties provide less coverage than full warranties. Warrantors using the "limited" designation can require you to remove, transport, and reinstall a product; pay for labor on repairs; and return the warranty card to the firm in order to validate the policy. They can also limit the warranty to the original purchaser and give you prorated refunds or credits for the product. (The "lemon provision" is not included in a limited warranty.)

Warrantors may also limit implied warranties to the length of time their policies run, but no less. If they limit the implied-warranty time, they must also state: "Some states do not allow limitations on how long an implied warranty lasts, so the above limitation may not apply to you." The warrantor may not limit the extent of protection you have under implied warranties, however.

Other provisions of the Warranty Act include the following:

- As long as you've complained within the warranty period, the firm has to act to remedy the problem within the terms of the warranty.
- If a *written* warranty is provided with the product, the warrantor cannot exclude it from protection under implied warranties.
- A warrantor can exclude or limit consequential damages from coverage under both full and limited policies. If this is done, the warranty must also state: "Some states do not allow the exclusion or limitation of incidental or consequential damages, so the above limitation or exclusion may not apply to you."
- All warranties must include information on whom to contact, where to bring or mail the product, the name of the warrantor, and the address or toll-free number of same.
- All warranties, full and limited, must state: "This warranty gives you specific legal rights, and you may have other rights that vary from state to state."

Implied Warranties: Implied warranties are state laws that offer protection against major hidden defects in products. Every state has these laws, and they cover every sale unless the seller states that no warranties or guarantees are offered; that goods are sold "as is." But if a particular product sold by a firm with a no-guarantee policy carries a *written* warranty, the implied warranty is valid on that item. The terms of implied warranties differ from state to state, but many have similar sorts of provisions.

The warranty of merchantability is a common implied warranty. It means that the product must function properly for conventional use—a freezer must freeze, a knife must cut, etc. If the product does not function properly and your state has a warranty of merchantability, you're probably entitled to a refund for that item.

The warranty of fitness for a particular purpose covers cases in which the seller cites or recommends special uses for the product. For example, if a seller says that a coat is "all-weather," it should offer protection in rain and snow. If it claims that a glue will "bond any two materials together," the glue should be able to do just that. When a salesperson offers you these assurances orally, check the printed product information to verify the recommendation. If no such use is offered in print by the manufacturer, ask the salesperson to put the pledge *in writing*. And if the product information contradicts the clerk's suggestion, ask for another product—and a more ethical or better-informed salesperson.

Consequential Damages: Incidental or consequential damages occur when the malfunction of a product causes damage to or loss of other property. The FTC uses the example of an engine block cracking when the antifreeze is faulty. Less extreme is the food spoilage caused by a refrigerator breakdown or the damage resulting from a leaky waterbed mattress.

Written warranties usually entitle you to consequential damages, but warrantors may exempt this coverage under both full and limited warranties. If the warrantor excludes consequential damages from coverage, the warranty must state: "Some states do not allow exclusion or limitation of incidental or consequential damages, so the above limitation or exclusion may not apply to you."

Provisions for consequential damages entitle you to compensation for the property damage or loss, as well as repair or replacement of the defective product. In the engine block example, the exemption of damages must be considered as a definite disadvantage when evaluating the product/warranty value.

Evaluating Warranties: Develop the habit of appraising the written warranty as thoroughly as you do the product's other features *before* you buy.

In reading the warranty, keep in mind any past experiences with products and warranty service from that manufacturer or seller, experiences with similar products, and your actual needs. Know that the first few models of a new product, especially in electronics, are seldom as trouble-free or well-designed as subsequent models. New products usually carry higher price tags than their descendants—remember the first color TVs, pocket calculators, and computers?

In evaluating a warranty, ask yourself these questions:

- Is the warranty full or limited?
- Does it cover the whole product, or specific parts?
- How long is the warranty period?
- Do you contact the manufacturer, seller, or a service center for repairs?
- Will you have to remove, deliver, and reinstall the product yourself?
- Do you have to have repairs done by an authorized service center or representative? If so, how close is the nearest facility?
- Will the warrantor provide a temporary replacement for use while your product is being serviced?
- Are consequential damages excluded? If the product proved defective, would the consequential damages entail a significant loss?
- If reimbursement is offered on a pro-rata basis, is it computed on a time, use, or price schedule?
- Do you have the choice of a refund or replacement product if the item is not repairable?

Envision a worst-case scenario in which the product breaks down or malfunctions completely. What expenses might you incur in terms of consequential damages, supplying a substitute product or service, transporting the product to the service center or seller, and repair bills? Will returning the product be troublesome, and living without it while it's being repaired inconvenient? Your answers determine the value the warranty has for *you*. Consider that quotient along with the price and features of the product when comparison shopping, and you'll find your best buy.

Complying with Warranty Terms: Understanding and fulfilling the conditions of a warranty should be simple, but we've outlined a few tips that may make it easier:

- Keep the warranty and dated receipt or proof of payment in a readily accessible file.

- If the manufacturer offers a rebate on the product that requires sending the proof of payment, photocopy the receipt and keep the copy with the warranty.
- Read the warranty card as requested.
- Read the instructions or operations manual before using the product, and follow directions for use.
- Abuse, neglect, and mishandling usually void the warranty. Other practices that may invalidate the policy include improper installation, repair or service by an unauthorized person or agency, use of the product on the wrong voltage, and commercial use. If other people will be using the product, be sure they know how to operate it and understand what restrictions there may be on its functions or use.
- Perform routine maintenance (cleaning, oiling, dusting, replacement of worn components, etc.) as required by the manual, but attempt no repairs or maintenance that is not required or permitted in the warranty or guide.

If you have a question about maintenance or use, call the seller or manufacturer. If you void the warranty by violating its terms, you'll have to absorb the costs of repairs or replacement.

Obtaining Service: If your product breaks down or malfunctions, you'll find that you can resolve the problem faster and more easily if you follow these guidelines:

- Read the operating manual or instructions. The problem may be covered in a troubleshooting section, or you may find that you expected the product to do something for which it wasn't designed.
- Contact the warrantor, whose name, address, and/or phone number appear on the warranty, unless the seller offers service under warranty.
- Call, write, or visit as appropriate. State the nature of the problem, the date it occurred, and whether you want a repair, replacement, refund, and/or consequential damages. Bring a copy of the warranty and proof of payment when you visit, and include copies if you write. (Remember that your rights in respect to the nature and extent of compensation depend upon the terms of the warranty and your state's laws.)
- If you leave the product for repairs or have it picked up, get a signed receipt that includes the date on which it should be ready, an estimate of the bill if you have to pay for repairs, and the serial number of the product, if one is given.

- If you send the product, insure it for the full value. Include a letter stating the nature of the problem, the date on which it occurred, and how you'd like it resolved.
- After a call or visit, the FTC recommends sending a follow-up letter reiterating the conversation. Keep a photocopy, and send it by certified mail to the person or agency with which you spoke.
- Keep a log of all actions you take in having the warranty honored, the dates on which actions, visits, and calls were made, and a record of the expenses you incur in the process.
- If you've written to the seller or manufacturer concerning the problem and received no response after three to four weeks, write again. Include a photocopy of the first letter, ask for an answer within four weeks, and send the second letter by certified mail (keep a photocopy). Direct the letter to the head of customer relations or the warranty department, unless you've been dealing with an individual.
- If you've written to the manufacturer, it may help to contact the seller (or vice versa). A reputable firm doesn't want to merchandise through a seller who won't maintain good customer relations, and an intelligent seller knows that marketing shoddy goods is bad for business. Bilateral appeals should be made after you've given the responsible party an opportunity to resolve the problem.
- If you have repairs done, ask to see the product demonstrated *before* you accept it, especially if you're paying for repairs. If there are indications that the problem may recur (e.g., it exhibits the same "symptoms" it had before it broke or malfunctioned), tell the service representative—it may be due to something that wasn't noticed during the repair.
- If you're paying for repairs, ask for a guarantee on parts and/or labor so you won't face another bill if the product breaks down shortly after you begin using it again.
- If the product keeps malfunctioning after it's repaired and it's under full warranty, you can probably get a replacement or refund under the "lemon provision." Write to the manufacturer or seller, provide a history of the problems and repairs, plus a copy of the warranty, and ask for a replacement or refund. If the warranty is limited, the terms may entitle you to a replacement or refund. Write to the manufacturer or seller with the product history and a copy of the warranty, and ask for a new product or compensation if you're entitled to same.
- Don't neglect to investigate your rights under your state's implied-warranty and consequential-damages laws. They may offer you protections not given in the warranty.
- If you've been physically injured by a malfunctioning product, contact your lawyer.

- If, after acting in good faith and allowing the manufacturer or seller time to resolve the problem, you are still dissatisfied, contact your local consumer-protection agency for advice.

You may also report problems to other agencies and organizations. For more information, see "Obtaining Help," following.

SHIPPING, HANDLING, INSURANCE, SALES TAX, AND DUTY

When you compare prices on goods from firm to firm, consider the costs of shipping, insurance, tax, and handling as part of the total. (See "Cost Comparisons," page 549, for more information.)

SHIPPING

This section addresses the concerns of those buying from U.S. firms and having goods delivered to addresses in the U.S.

Shipping Computations: The largest ancillary cost of an order is usually shipping. Mail-order firms use a variety of methods in figuring shipping charges. It's helpful to know how each works, so you can shop intelligently.

Postpaid item prices, which appear to be "free" of shipping charges, are beloved by mail-order shoppers because they eliminate extra computation. The shipping and packing costs are, however, passed along in the item price, and if the order is taxed, consumers should remember that they're paying sales tax on the shipping fee as well as the item cost. (Although the majority of states and localities *require* payment of sales tax on delivery and handling, not all do. Very few firms collect the tax, even when they're required to do so by law. If the departments of revenue concerned begin cracking down, you may see more complicated order forms in the future and find yourself paying a bit more when you order from certain companies.)

Itemized shipping costs are often seen as amounts in parentheses following the price or code number of the product. If you compare the UPS or USPS tape on the delivered parcel, you'll often find that the price you paid the firm for shipping was higher. That's because it includes the costs of packing and materials. The price may also be prorated. For example, a California firm will compute all shipping charges based on the price of sending goods to Kansas, midway across the country. The profits made on local deliveries wind up subsidizing the losses on shipments to the East Coast. Some firms simply charge the maximum possible shipping cost. For example, we added up a few items from a holiday catalog—a pair of shearling slippers, a silk tie, a box of Christmas cards, a small brass stamp box, and a set of cocktail napkins—and found that the shipping costs came to $12.55, or 14% of the order total of $90. This order weighed no more than three pounds, did not involve breakables, and did not require extra insurance—and so represents a profit to the seller of several dollars on shipping alone. Some firms deal with consumers' outrage with this situation by limiting the maximum amount of shipping charges per order to $10 to $15. But remember—even if the price you pay the firm is much higher than the actual shipping cost, don't ask the firm for the difference. Instead, suggest that it change its method of computing the charges, or at least place a ceiling on the shipping costs.

Numeric charges are based on the number of items you're ordering, as in "$2.50 for the first item; 75¢ each additional item." Firms structuring charges in this way often limit shipping to $7 to $12, so additional purchases made after you reach that limit are exempted from shipping charges entirely.

Flat order fees are simple dollar amounts charged on all orders, usually regardless of the number of items or weight. (The firm often imposes an additional fee if part of the order is shipped to another address.) A flat fee represents a bargain if you're placing a large order, but resist the temptation to order extra products just to make the shipping charge proportionately lower. And note that some firms selling on this basis do charge extra for heavy, outsized, or fragile items. Check the catalog carefully *before* you order.

Free shipping is offered, often by smaller companies, on large orders. Customarily, orders under a certain dollar or item amount are charged shipping on some basis, but if your order exceeds a certain amount, you pay no shipping at all. The fact is often noted on the order blank—"on orders $100 and over, WE pay postage," or "free shipping on three dozen pairs or more same size, style, & color"—usually with the proviso that the order must be sent to one address.

Don't order more than you need just to meet the minimum, unless the extra item costs less than the postage and you're sure it can be used at a later date.

Sliding scales, tied to the cost of the order, are used by many firms. For example, if the goods total $15.00, you pay $2.75 for shipping; from $15.01 to $30.00, the charge is $3.50, etc. This is advantageous when you're ordering many inexpensive, heavy products, but seems inequitable when you're buying a single, costly item. Some firms remedy this by using itemized shipping charges for small, high-ticket goods. Most limit the shipping charges to a maximum dollar amount, usually $7 to $12. Again, avoid padding your order to get the "most" from your shipping charge—you'll spend many more dollars on dubious purchases than you "save" on postage.

Tables, based on the weight and sometimes delivery distance of the order, are used by a number of companies, including Spiegel and Sears. Tables entail the most work on your part, since you must tally the shipping weights given with the item prices separately, locate your zone or area on the chart, and then find the shipping charges. Large, nonmailable goods will have to be shipped by truck; their catalog code numbers often have a suffix letter indicating this.

The advantage to table computation is fairness of price. While you won't get the shipping "bargains" possible from firms using other methods to calculate those costs, neither will you find yourself paying exorbitant sums to ship small, light items.

Saving on Shipping Costs: When you have a chance to save on shipping by placing a large order, consult friends and neighbors to see if they want to combine orders with you. But unless you can view conferring, consolidating orders, and distributing the goods when they arrive as a "social activity," you'll have to count it as part of the cost of the order. Time is money, which is probably one of the reasons you shop by mail!

Carriers: No matter which method a firm uses to calculate shipping, it's going to send your goods by USPS, UPS, or truck. Many firms, especially those selling highly perishable goods, also use overnight delivery services. Goods are sent by truck when they exceed the size/weight restrictions of UPS and the USPS.

United Parcel Service (UPS): UPS is the delivery system businesses prefer for mail order. UPS is cheaper, all costs considered, than USPS; it automatically insures each package for up to $100; and it also picks up the packages at the firm's office or warehouse. (Although in the past UPS has seemed more reliable and prompt than USPS, we have heard challenges on that score by readers and found problems ourselves. One of the biggest is a certain insouciance on the part of delivery personnel, who do not seem concerned about dumping parcels on porches if no one's home to sign for them, or leaving them in vestibules in city buildings where theft is a predictable result. Our experience with having parcels traced showed poor documentation of the parcels from origination to destination. We'd like to hear your experiences with UPS; see "Feedback," page 587, for our address.)

Under its Common Carrier Service, UPS handles packages weighing up to 70 pounds that have a combined girth and length measurement of up to 108″ (with some qualifications). UPS offers overnight delivery to certain states and ZIP codes through its Next Day Air service, and 2nd Day Air delivery to the 48 contiguous states and some parts of Hawaii. Residents of

Alaska and Hawaii should note that UPS uses Next Day Air and 2nd Day Air services for deliveries to those states, not all parts of the states are served, and charges are higher than those for its standard Common Carrier Service. UPS cannot deliver your order without a street address.

The amount of postage charged by UPS is determined by the delivery address, the location of the firm shipping the goods, the service used, and the dimensions and weight of the package.

UPS has divided the country into 63 sections. Each section has a zoning chart that breaks the rest of the country into seven zones, which run from "Zone 2" through "Zone 8," according to distance, using the first three digits of the ZIP code. A firm located in Manhattan uses a zone chart that lists Manhattan ZIP codes (generally prefix 100) as 2, or the closest zone; and California ZIP codes (prefix 900) as 8, or the farthest zone. In California, 900 prefix ZIP codes are in zone 2, while Manhattan ZIP code prefixes are in zone 8.

To translate these zone numbers into shipping costs, consult a current Common Carrier Rate Chart. This chart lists rates for packages weighing up to 70 pounds to zone 8. The rate chart also lists surcharges for additional services, such as C.O.D. delivery, address correction, and acknowledgment of delivery. If your package exceeds the size/weight restrictions, it will be transported by a private trucking firm.

Some firms include in their catalogs all the rate charts you will ever need to figure exact costs; others state at the bottom of the order form, "Add enough for postage and insurance. We will refund overpayment." When faced with this, you can consult a catalog that lists the weight of a comparable item both before *and* after packing, add the difference to the weight of the item you're ordering, and then call your local UPS office for the rates. You can also call the firm itself and ask the shipping department to give you a quick calculation over the phone. You could send in the order without adding anything for shipping and ask the firm to bill you, but this may delay delivery. UPS rate charts are reproduced in the "Charts" section of this book, but be sure to check with your local UPS office for the most recent rates and regulations if you're doing calculations yourself.

United States Postal Service (USPS)—Parcel Post (PP): The costs for Parcel Post, or fourth-class mail, are somewhat higher than UPS charges, but PP offers one distinct advantage: *only packages sent by Parcel Post can be delivered to a post-office box.* (UPS must have a street address to deliver goods, although carriers will usually deliver to rural routes.) If you're having a package sent to a post-office box, you can avoid delays and the possibility that the package will be returned to the company if sent via UPS. Just write "DELIVERY BY PARCEL POST ONLY; UPS NOT ACCEPTABLE" in bold red letters on the order form, unless there's a box to check to indicate your preference. On the check, write "GOODS TO BE DELIVERED BY PARCEL POST ONLY." Once the firm endorses or cashes the check, it agrees implicitly to this arrangement and must send the goods by Parcel Post.

While postal rates have escalated by leaps and bounds, the size/weight restrictions remain relatively constant. USPS accepts parcels with a combined girth and length measurement of up to 84″ that weigh up to 70 pounds. Packages weighing under 15 pounds that have a combined girth/length measurement over 84″ are accepted at rates for 15-pound packages.

Private trucking firms: When the firm specifies that the goods must be sent by truck, or if you have ordered both mailable (could be sent by UPS or PP) and nonmailable goods, the entire order may be sent by truck. Firms indicate that goods are to be trucked with the term "FOB," followed by the word "warehouse," "manufacturer," or the name of the city from which the goods are trucked. "FOB" stands for "free on board," and it means that the trucking charges will be billed from that point. When the word "manufacturer" follows FOB in the catalog, it means that the firm is probably having that item "drop-shipped," or taking orders for the product and sending the orders to the manufacturer rather than maintaining warehouse inventories. If you want to order nonmailable goods that you have reason to believe will be drop-shipped, you should learn the location of the manufacturer's warehouse so you can estimate the trucking costs. If you want the item quickly, you should also ask the firm that takes the order to verify that the manufacturer has the product in stock.

Truck charges are usually collected upon delivery. Since these charges are based on weight and distance, the additional expense is a real factor to consider when ordering very heavy items from a firm that's located far from you. A typical minimum charge for a 100-pound order is $35. Truckers usually make "dump deliveries," which means they unload the goods on the sidewalk in front of your home. For an additional fee (usually $10 to $20), you can have the goods delivered inside your house or apartment. This charge may escalate if there are stairs—some firms charge $1 extra per step. Additional fees may be incurred if your order happens to be the only one the trucker is picking up from the firm that day or if the driver has to notify you of delivery. You can always arrange to pick up your order at the truck terminal and save some money. Before you decide to purchase anything you know will have to be trucked, get the final cost of the item *plus* trucking charges and compare it to the cost of the same item if bought locally and delivered.

Remember that when the carrier arrives, you must be able to pay the charges with cash or a certified check—personal checks and credit cards are seldom accepted.

SHIPMENTS FROM FOREIGN COUNTRIES

After your payment has been authorized or has cleared the bank, the firm should ship your order. Depending on the dimensions and weight of the package, it may be shipped by mail or sent by sea or air freight.

Mailable Orders: If the package weighs up to 20kg (about 44 pounds) and has a length of up to 1.5m (about 59″) and a length/girth measurement of up to 3m (about 118″) for surface mail or up to 2m (about 79″) for airmail, it can be mailed. Almost everything you buy from a foreign country will be mailable. Your decision when ordering will be choosing air, surface, or accelerated surface shipment (provided the firm offers all three). Mailed packages are delivered by your postal carrier, regardless of the service used by the company. Duty is collected by the carrier upon delivery.

Airmail is the most expensive service; airmailed packages generally take a week to ten days to arrive after they're posted, although some firms ask you to allow three weeks for delivery.

Surface mail, which includes both overland and boat shipment, is the cheapest service, but orders shipped by surface mail can take up to two months to reach you.

Accelerated surface mail is now available in some countries; it's priced between standard surface and airmail rates, and hastens delivery time to about three weeks. It's known as "Fastmail" in some British catalogs, and represents the best shipping buy if you're neither desperate for an item nor prepared to wait a season for it. Please note that some firms are offering only Fastmail and standard surface. These firms will usually arrange to ship via airmail, but if you're paying by anything other than a credit card, this doesn't make sense. It will take at least a week to request the added postage costs, at least a week for that information to reach you, another week for your order to get to the firm with correct payment, and at least a week for the goods to arrive. That's a total of four weeks, the same length of time you might expect to wait if you were ordering using Fastmail (a week for the order to reach the firm, and three weeks for the goods to be delivered). If you pay by credit card, however, you can send the order and ask the firm to ship by air and bill your account for the extra charges. Do this *only* when you're frantic to get something, since the shipping charges for airmail will be from 50% to 100% higher than those for surface mail.

Nonmailable Orders: If the package exceeds mail weight and/or size restrictions, it will have to be sent by an air or ship carrier.

Air freight is the best choice when the item or order just exceeds mail restrictions. Charges are based on the weight and size of the order, as well as the flight distance. The firm—via the U.S. Customs office that's closest to your delivery address—arranges to have the order sent to the airport. You pay the firm for air-freight charges, it sees the order to the airport, and sends you a Customs declaration form and invoice. When the airport apprises you of arrival, get right over with the forms, since most airports will charge a holding fee on goods still unclaimed five to ten days after delivery. In addition, you should make arrangements to have the package trucked to your home if it's too large to transport yourself. Once you clear Customs you can take the goods home or release them to the truckers you've hired and they'll make delivery.

Sea freight is much less expensive than air, but it can take months for an order to reach you. If you live near a port, you may want to handle Customs clearance yourself and engage a trucking firm to deliver the goods to your home. You may also hire an agent (customs broker) to clear Customs and arrange inland trucking. This service will cost from $75 to $125, but it's the only practical way to deal with the process if you live far from the docking site and the foreign firm that sent the goods doesn't have arrangements with a U.S. agent who could take care of these details for you.

The procedure is similar to that of clearing an air shipment: You present the forms the firm has provided to the shipper and Customs officer, pay duty charges, and transport the goods home or release them to the truckers you've hired.

For information on duty rates, trademark regulations, and shipment of problematical or prohibited goods, see "Duty," page 584. For information on payment of duty on mailed goods, see "Deliveries from Foreign Firms," page 566.

HANDLING

Some firms charge an extra fee for handling or packing your order. The fee, which is usually not more than one or two dollars, may be included in a flat shipping fee. Handling is often waived on orders over a certain dollar amount. The handling fee helps to cover the costs of labor and materials used in preparing your order for shipment. This surcharge, along with the shipping fee, may be taxed in certain states.

You can recoup part of the handling cost, whether paid as a fee or included in the item markup, by reusing the carton and plastic peanuts or excelsior when you send gifts or pack fragile things for storage. If you're remailing the box, be sure to black out any marks made by the carrier, remove postage tapes, and delete addresses printed on the sides or top. It won't be pretty, but resourcefulness has its own style.

INSURANCE

Most firms insure orders as a matter of course. Shipments worth up to $100 are automatically insured by UPS; you should not have to pay extra insurance on those orders. (If you're ordering from a firm that delivers via UPS but has a preprinted charge for insurance on the order form, don't pay it.) UPS charges 25¢ for each additional $100 in value on the same package—a fee usually covered in the shipping charge. The USPS does not insure automatically, so if you're having your package delivered by the USPS, be sure to request insurance. Charges for postal insurance range from 70¢ for goods worth up to $50, to $5.00 for package contents worth from $400.01 to $500.00. Goods valued at more than $500 but under $25,000 must be registered as well as insured. Some types of goods cannot be insured. If the product you're purchasing is not insurable by the USPS, have the firm arrange shipping with a carrier that will insure it.

Most insurance claims arise as a result of damage to or loss of goods. Procedures for claiming and reimbursement vary according to the carrier's rules and the firm's policy. Under any circumstances, you should contact the firm as soon as you discover any damage to your shipment and ask the customer service department what you should do. If there is documentation (signature of receipt on the UPS carrier's log or USPS insurance receipt), the claim can be verified and processed, and eventually you should be reimbursed or receive replacement goods. If there is no documentation and the worst happens—the goods never arrive—the firm may absorb the loss and send a replacement order. It may also refuse to do so, especially if its records indicate that the order was shipped. In such cases, it will be almost impossible to prove that you didn't receive the order. If repeated entreaties for a refund, credit, or duplicate order meet resistance, state your case to the agencies listed in "Obtaining Help" in this section. And be sure to tell us—see "Feedback" for more information.

If you have any doubts about whether the firm will have your goods insured, *ask before you order.* The small fee is a worthwhile expense, something you know if you've ever had an uninsured order go awry. See "Accepting Deliveries" for more information.

SALES TAX

You have to pay sales tax on an order if (1) you're having goods delivered to an address in the same state in which the mail-order firm, a branch office, or representative is located and (2) the laws governing the state or locality of the delivery address require payment of tax on the ordered goods. You pay the rate of sales tax prevailing in your area, whether it's none (in New

Hampshire) or 8.25% (in New York City), according to the laws of your area. As previously stated in this guide, most states require payment of sales tax on handling, packing, and shipping charges.

Those are the general rules. The right of a state to create its own definition of "doing business" in that state, or "establishing nexus," has raised the ire of both consumers who have to pay tax on what they perceive as out-of-state orders, and businesses that have the headaches of tax collection and accounting. The issue of nexus is no stranger to the Supreme Court; one energetic individual took on both Sears and Montgomery Ward over 40 years ago and lost, and other mail-order firms have done battle with state governments and lost as well.

The good news is that many firms neglect to collect all of the sales tax they're required to, and very few request tax on the shipping and handling charges as required by state laws. That's good for you. But some states may be losing hundreds of thousands of dollars yearly as a result; if they should undertake enforcement, more mail-order purchases will be taxed. While you may enjoy saving some money now, please add the sales tax you *know* you should pay even if the firm doesn't request it. And if the firm asks you to pay a rate lower than the one you should, pay at the proper rate.

Be aware that state governments are now trying to collect tax on *all* mail-order purchases delivered to residents of their states, calling such a tax a "use" tax (the actual sale takes place out of state, at the seller's place of business). The issue is being tested across the U.S. in a number of courts, with some of the biggest mail-order firms in the country. The companies balk at acting as tax collectors for all 50 states, and consumers realize that they stand to lose one of the benefits of shopping out-of-state: no sales tax on their purchases (unless the aforementioned state of nexus exists). Until the issue is resolved, keep paying sales taxes according to previously established guidelines.

DUTY

Orders from foreign firms are not charged state sales taxes, but make up for it with duty charges. You cannot prepay duty to foreign firms. Duty is paid to the postal carrier who delivers your package or the Customs agent if the order is delivered by air or sea freight.

Assessment of Duty: U.S. duty was once charged on the wholesale value of the goods (about a third less than the actual price), but the method of assessment has changed. The rate of duty is now calculated on the transaction value, or actual price, of the goods being imported, on an *ad valorem* (percentage) or *specific* (per-unit) basis, and sometimes a combination of the two. To add to the confusion, the U.S. Customs Service classifies foreign countries in three different categories, each of which has a different rate of duty. Goods made in Communist-bloc countries are charged the highest rate of duty, up to 110%—with the exceptions of Romania, Yugoslavia, Poland, and Hungary. These rates apply to any goods made in the bloc countries, even if they're not sold there. Customs designates other countries as "most favored," with much lower rates of duty. Note that there are some goods—such as certified antiques, postage stamps, truffles, and original paintings—that are imported duty-free from countries in both categories. The third rate of duty applies to what are known as "developing countries," none of which are represented in this book. Check your local U.S. Customs office for current regulations, since rates and classifications may change.

Prohibitions and Restrictions: Before you order from a foreign firm, you should know that there are some goods that can be imported only under certain conditions, and others that are prohibited altogether. You can't import narcotics, pornography, fireworks, switchblade knives, absinthe, poison, or dangerous toys—and to our knowledge, none of the firms listed in this book sells them. If ordered, these items will be confiscated by U.S. Customs. If you want to import animals, animal products, biologicals, petroleum products, plants, or seeds, you must make prior arrangements with certain agencies and obtain the necessary permits. And if you want to buy name-brand goods, you should be sure to check trademark restrictions. The manufacturers of certain goods register the trademarks with Customs, which limits the number of those items an individual may import. Sometimes the manufacturers allow importation of more than one of the item, as long as the trademarked symbols or names are removed. This is done by the firm selling the goods or by the Customs agent. If you want to exceed the limits the manufacturer has set, you may write to the firm and apply for consent. The letter of permission should be presented to the Customs agent or left on file at the Customs office. Types of goods that often fall under trademark restrictions include cameras, lenses, optics, tape recorders, perfumes, cosmetics, musical instruments, jewelry, flatware, and timepieces. Note that many foreign firms offer trademark-restricted goods in their catalogs, but don't inform you of conditions of importation of these products.

Obtaining Information: If you plan to order from a foreign firm and want to know more about duty rates and classifications, import restrictions, permits, and prohibitions, request the free booklet "Rates of Duty for Popular Tourist Items" from the Office of Information and Publications, Bureau of Customs, 1301 Constitution Ave., N.W., Rm. 6303, Washington, DC 20226.

Use it as a general guide only—contact your local Customs office for the latest rates. Be sure you are able to provide a description of the goods you're ordering, including materials, composition, decoration or ornamentation, etc., since the classification of goods is more specific than indicated by the brochure. For example, loose pearls and permanently strung pearls are assessed at different rates, and spoons have a rate different from that of knives and forks. In addition, rates may change in response to the protectionist/free-trade philosophy prevailing in the current administration. Let your Congressional representative know how you feel about the country's trade policy.

If you want to import fruits, vegetables, or plants from abroad, write to Quarantines, Department of Agriculture, Federal Center Building, Hyattsville, MD 20782, and ask for an import permit application.

For more information on related matters, see "Ordering from Foreign Firms," page 552; "Paying for Goods from Foreign Firms," page 559; "Shipments from Foreign Countries," page 581; and "Deliveries from Foreign Firms," page 566.

CHARTS

Clothing Sizes

Women's Garments

U.S.A.	6	8	10	12	14	16	18	20
Great Britain	8	10	12	14	16	18	20	22
Europe	36	38	40	42	44	46	48	50

Women's Sweaters

U.S.A	XS	S	M	M	L	L
Great Britain	34	36	38	40	42	44
Europe	40	42	44	46	48	50

Women's Shoes

U.S.A.	5	5½	6	6½	7	7½	8	8½	9	9½	10
Great Britain	3½	4	4½	5	5½	6	6½	7	7½	8	8½
Europe	36		37		38		39		40		41

Men's Suits

Sweaters	S	S	M	M	L	XL
U.S.A.	34	36	38	40	42	44
Great Britain	34	36	38	40	42	44
Europe	44	46	48	50	52	54

Men's Shirts

U.S.A./G. Britain	14	14½	15	15½	15¾	16	16½	17	17½	18
Europe	36	37	38	39	40	41	42	43	44	46

Men's Shoes

U.S.A	7½	8	8½	9	9½	10	10½	11	11½	12	12½
Great Britian	6	6½	7	7½	8	8½	9	9½	10	10½	11
Europe	39½	40	40½	41	42	42½	43	44	44½	45	45½

Metric Conversions

Length

1 inch	2.54 cm
1 foot	.30 m
1 yard	0.91 km
1 mile	1.61 km
1 millimeter (mm)	0.039 in.
1 centimeter (cm)	0.39 in.
1 meter (m)	3.28 feet
1 kilometer (k)	0.62 mile

Weight

1 gram	0.04 ounce
1 kilogram	2.2 pounds
1 ounce	28.35 grams
1 pound	0.45 kilograms
1 ton	0.91 metric tons

FEEDBACK

Consumers and businesses, *we want to hear from you!* Your suggestions, complaints, and comments have helped to shape this edition of *The Wholesale-by-Mail Catalog®*, and are valued highly. We thank every reader who's contacted us in the past and urge you to keep writing. You can help us by using the guidelines that follow.

Firms: If you'd like to have your company included in the next edition of WBMC, have your marketing director send us a copy of your current literature. Firms are listed at our discretion and must meet our basic criteria to qualify for inclusion.

Consumers: If you're writing a letter of complaint, please read the sections of "The Complete Guide to Buying by Mail" that may apply to your problem, and attempt to work it out yourself. If you can't remedy the situation on your own, write to us and include:

- a brief history of the transaction
- copies (not originals) of all letters and documents related to the problem
- a list of the dates on which events occurred, if applicable (the date a phone order was placed, goods were received, account charged, etc.)
- a description of what you want done (goods delivered, warranty honored, return accepted, money refunded or credited, etc.)

Be sure to include your name, address, and day phone number in your cover letter. We will look into the matter, and while we cannot guarantee resolution, we may be able to help you.

If you just want to sound off, we'd like to hear from you, too. If you're moved to sing the praises of any mail-order company, please do so—let us know what has impressed you. Suggestions for the next edition of WBMC are welcomed. Send your letter to:

WMBC 1991
P.O. Box 505, Village Station
New York, NY 10014-0505

COMPANY INDEX

PRODUCT INDEX

bucket shops, 529
by the disabled, 534
consolidators, 529
educational, for seniors, 531
guides, 535, 536
medical assistance abroad, 534
newsletters, 535
standby, 530
student discounts, 532
U.S. State Department information on, 534
treadmills, 476, 481
tree-climbing supplies and equipment, 508, 513
Trees
evergreen, 236, 242
fruit, 241, 242
shade, 239, 241, 242, 247
trims, 209, 214
Trucks, 68
accessories, 237
truffles, 253
trunks, 399
tuners, 434, 436
TV and video components, 16, 21–23, 25–29, 33, 272
Typewriters, 445, 447, 449, 457
foreign-language, 455
ukeleles, 428
upholstery buttons, custom-covered, 197
upholstery fabric, *see* fabric, decorator
upholstery tools and supplies, 191, 196, 204, 210
Vacuum cleaners, 19, 20, 24, 25, 29, 31, 34, 37, 272, 276

mini (for computers), 463, 466, 501
vans, 68
vegetables, dehydrated, 263
veneer, wood, 196, 208
vet supplies, 1, 5–10, 13, 14
Victorian architectural ornamentation, 369
Videotapes
animal, grooming and training, 6
blank, 26, 32, 35, 125
dog show, 11
educational, 98
horse-related, 9, 15
motivational, 107
movies, new and vintage , 92, 98, 107
music, 98, 105
instructional, 104
on astronomy, 91
on bow hunting, 478
on bridge, 525
on fishing, 475
on golfing, 474, 482
on hunting topics, 485
on textile arts, 212
on water sports, 488
on windsurfing, 491
on woodworking, 208
vintage cartoons, 105
violas, 433, 436
violins, 425, 428, 433, 435, 436
Vitamins, 296, 297
natural, 295
waffle irons, Belgian, 256
Walkers
adults, 407
infants, 183

wallpaper, 301–303, 306, 307, 311, 313, 314, 316, 317, 319
Watches, 372, 376, 385
diving, 476
water heaters, 515
water skiing supplies and equipment, 474, 488
weathervanes, 367
weaving supplies and equipment, 55, 199, 212, 220, 222, 227
wet suits, 474, 476, 491, 492
Wheelchairs, 407
cushions, 473
Wheels
auto, 77, 84
performance, 84
whirlpools, 363
white goods, 16, 21, 26
wigs and hairpieces for men and women, 293
window treatments, 302, 303, 307, 311, 313, 314, 322
windows, 360
windsurfing supplies and equipment, 491
Wine
do-it-yourself supplies, 258
serving equipment, 268
storage equipment, 268
wood-chopping tools, 514
woodburning supplies, 195, 213
woodworking tools and equipment, 196, 208, 509, 510, 514, 517, 519
yarn, 194, 195, 199, 200, 211, 212, 220, 222–224, 226, 227, 269
zippers, 192, 198, 209, 212